The Scope of
Psychoanalysis

The Scope of
PSYCHOANALYSIS

1921-1961

SELECTED PAPERS OF
FRANZ ALEXANDER

Basic Books Inc., New York

© 1961 by Basic Books Publishing Co., Inc.
Library of Congress Catalog Card Number: 62–11200
PRINTED IN THE UNITED STATES OF AMERICA

Designed by Joan Wall

Introduction

by Thomas M. French, M.D.

Franz Alexander is an investigator who has been extremely fertile both in ideas and in projects for testing them. He is ideally suited for the task which has been one of the main objectives of his scientific career—to bring psychoanalysis out of its early isolation. During the last fifty years, a gradual narrowing of the gap between psychoanalysis and other streams of scientific inquiry has occurred. Alexander has been one of those who have contributed most to this change.

Alexander is the author of many books in which he has outlined successively the main streams underlying his scientific thinking. A selection even from the best of his shorter writings must remain fragmentary for those who are not familiar with his longer works. In this introduction, accordingly, I shall try to survey the development of his ideas in historical perspective.

Psychoanalytic theory

One of Alexander's earliest papers, "The Castration Complex in the Formation of Character," published in 1923, ushered in a first phase in his scientific development. This phase was inspired by Freud's recently published observations on the role of an "unconscious sense of guilt" and "need for punishment" in the genesis both of neuroses and of certain character types.[1] In the paper mentioned above, Alexander reported a detailed analysis, illustrating the role of such a "need for punishment" in a patient with a "neurotic character." One of the most important symptoms of this patient was what Alexander calls a "passive

[1] See Sigmund Freud, "Some Character-Types Met With in Psycho-Analytic Work" (1915), in *Collected Papers*, New York: Basic Books, 1959, Vol. IV, 318-344; and *The Ego and the Id* (1927), New York: Norton, 1960.

kleptomania," a compulsion to maneuver his best friends into situations in which they were tempted to steal from him. This article was followed two years later by a book (*Psychoanalysis of the Total Personality*, 1925) in which Alexander spells out the part played by the need for punishment in a number of different neuroses, in melancholia, and in masochistic perversions. In this more comprehensive work, Alexander elaborates more fully a thesis which had already been sketched out in the earlier paper. This thesis is that in many neuroses there is a kind of collusion, comparable to that between the police and organized crime in a big city. In the neuroses, the bargain is that by accepting punishment, the patient's id buys indulgence for gratification or even for acting out of his criminal impulses. Alexander points out further that by closing its eyes to what is going on, the ego, too, is implicated in the corrupt bargain.

This thesis is further illustrated in four papers that have been included in this collection: "Dreams in Pairs or Series," "The Need for Punishment and the Death Instinct," "About Dreams with Unpleasant Content," and "The Neurotic Character."

Interest in the "criminal from a sense of guilt" (Freud's phrase) later led Alexander into psychoanalytic studies of criminals. The first of these studies were published together with Hugo Staub in 1931 [2] in *The Criminal, the Judge and the Public*.

Later, these studies were continued and extended, in collaboration with William Healy, at the Judge Baker Foundation in Boston. The extended studies were published, in 1935, in another book, *Roots of Crime*. This later work shows already the influence on the author of the American scene. In these studies Alexander is much impressed by a type of criminal whom he suspects is a social consequence of the blocking of opportunities for pioneering adventure by the closing of the frontiers in America. These are youthful criminals with "a hard shell but soft inside" whose need is to prove themselves tough in order to deny their babyish dependent needs.

A highly important theoretical product of these studies of American criminals is a short article entitled, "Remarks About the Relation of Inferiority Feelings to Guilt Feelings," which is included in this collection, as is "The Relation of Structural and Instinctual Conflicts."

The next and a centrally important phase in Alexander's interest is represented only sketchily in this collection. The reason is that his most important contributions to psychosomatic medicine have already been published in book form—in "The Influence of Psychologic Factors Upon Gastrointestinal Disturbances: A Symposium" (first published in the *Psychoanalytic Quarterly* in 1934, and then later in book form), and in *Psychosomatic Medicine,* a two-volume work published in 1950 and

[2] Date of first German edition.

1952. Of the papers included in the present book, the one in which Alexander calls attention to a relationship between "zest" and carbohydrate metabolism and the paper in which he outlines a psychosomatic theory of thyrotoxicosis are of particular theoretical interest.

The paper entitled, "The Logic of Emotions and Its Dynamic Background," is an important theoretical paper which also belongs to this phase. This paper was written in the course of Alexander's attempts to understand the psychodynamic backgrounds of patients with peptic ulcer, spastic colitis, and chronic constipation, respectively. In it he advances his "vector" theory of the personality, which generalizes and, to some extent, expands intuitive impressions which had previously been formulated in terms of the "oral erotic," "anal erotic," and "genital" character types. Oral eroticism, for example, he now suggested was one special case of a receptive vector; anal eroticism, of eliminatory and retentive vectors. In the paper just mentioned, Alexander elaborates a number of the implications of this concept, with especial application to the problems of understanding psychosomatic diseases of the gastrointestinal tract.

The vector theory elaborated in "The Logic of Emotions" soon afterward began to undergo revision, or rather expansion, in Alexander's thinking. The new theory is first spelled out clearly in "Psychoanalysis Revised," published in 1940 and included here.

The main phases of life are growth towards maturation, reproduction after having achieved maturation and, finally, decline towards death. The life process itself is based on incorporation of energy and substance from the environment, their retention and elimination. . . . In the young maturing individual, more energy and substance is retained than eliminated; hence it grows. The psychological expression of this phase of life appears in the form of so-called pregenital tendencies which all center around incorporation and retention. . . . Only after the child has reached or has approached the limit of individual growth, that is to say maturity, does a new physiological phenomenon appear: reproduction, together with a new psychological orientation, love of others in the mature sense. The surplus energies which can no longer be used for growth create a tension which the individual resolves in the form of reproduction. Reproduction in multicellular organisms follows the same principle as in primitive monocellular organisms: basically it is an asymmetric form of cell division. In the monocellular organism, after the limits of the individual growth are reached cell division takes place. The corresponding process in the complex polycellular beings is the elimination of the germ cells. . . . The important fact is that all these processes which are connected phenomenologically with sexual pleasure and which primarily are released through the genito-urinary tract are manifestations of surplus energy or surplus tension.

In a book, *Fundamentals of Psychoanalysis*, published in 1948, Alexander recapitulated and expanded this surplus energy theory of sexuality. He first postulates pleasure in stimulation or activity for its own sake as a criterion for distinguishing erotic behavior from other behavior. Then he follows out an early suggestion of Ferenczi's as the starting point for his own surplus energy theory.

Ferenczi maintained in his ingenious biopsychological speculations that the organism expresses sexually all tensions which it cannot or need not coordinate for useful purposes. This is essentially the equivalent of the view I later elaborated—that sexuality discharges any surplus excitation, regardless of its quality. . . . Propagation results from surplus energy generated by growth. The psychological equivalent of propagation is love.

To this surplus energy theory of sex Alexander added a closely related theory of play (a concept first proposed in simple and vivid terms by the poet Friedrich Schiller, and later elaborated by Herbert Spencer). The spontaneous play of children, too, Alexander regards as an overflow of surplus energy. By this he means that it is not subordinated to any utilitarian purpose. "The child plays and exercises its voluntary body functions merely for the sake of the pleasure derived from these activities." Alexander identifies such play with erotic behavior. "The Greek god, Eros," he reminds us, "was the god of both love and play and was represented appropriately by a child."

In a later paper, "Three Fundamental Principles of the Mental Apparatus and of the Behavior of Living Organisms," included in this collection, Alexander summarizes again his concept of "the principle of surplus energy," together with that of two other principles ("the principle of stability," and "the principle of economy or inertia") which had been basic to his concept of the dynamics of behavior ever since the publication of his very early paper, "A Metapsychological Description of the Process of Cure."

In a still more recent theoretical paper, "Unexplored Areas in Psychoanalytic Theory and Treatment," Alexander has attempted a more far-reaching generalization, bringing his theory of surplus energy into relation with the physical concept of entropy and with communication theory. "The erotic value of an action," he writes, "is inversely related to the degree to which it loses the freedom of choice and becomes . . . subordinated to other functions and . . . a part of an organized system, of a goal structure."

Psychoanalytic treatment

In a recent book entitled, *Psychoanalysis and Psychotherapy*, published in 1956, Alexander has reviewed the development of the theory of psychoanalytic treatment. The present collection includes a number of the stepping stones in the building up of his own concept of psychoanalytic therapy.

An early paper entitled "A Metapsychological Description of the Process of Cure" is of interest because it foreshadows a number of ideas which Alexander elaborated more extensively later. It is also notable as a first attempt to make use of Freud's recently published analysis of the structure of the personality for study of the therapeutic process. In the early paper just mentioned, Alexander pictures the psychoanalyst as first taking over the role of the patient's superego and then later giving back this role, not to the patient's superego, but to his conscious ego. The superego, Alexander compares to an ancient and rigid criminal code, based on the realities of the patient's relation to his parents in childhood. The role of the superego, which the patient transfers to the analyst, is really the role once played by the patient's parents. By reliving in the present his relation to the parents, the patient can secure the analyst's help in revising the ancient code. Instead of repressing and automatically rejecting or accepting punishment for his drives, the patient, with the help of the analyst's interpretations, becomes conscious of them and learns to accept or renounce them in accordance with his conscious judgment.

In a paper published 16 years later, Alexander returned to the problem of the role of the analyst's interpretations and of the patient's insight in psychoanalytic treatment. In this paper Alexander has taken as his text a quotation from Freud: "The voice of the intellect is soft but it does not rest until it has gained a hearing." Once a patient has reached a clear insight, Alexander paraphrases, it is impossible for him to get rid of it completely.

Alexander illustrates this thesis with the report of an analysis. In this case discussion he is particularly interested in the process of resolution of conflict that results from the patient's increasing insight and also in problems concerning termination of treatment.

In a book, *Psychoanalytic Therapy* (published in 1946 in collaboration with French and other members of the Staff of the Chicago Institute for Psychoanalysis), Alexander writes:

In all forms of etiological psychotherapy, the basic therapeutic principle is the same: to re-expose the patient, under more favorable circumstances, to emotional situations which he could not handle in the past. The patient, in order to be helped, must undergo a corrective emotional experience suitable to repair the traumatic influence of previous experiences.

This concept is Alexander's outstanding contribution to understanding of the therapeutic process in psychoanalytic treatment. He writes further:

In the formulation of the dynamics of treatment, the usual tendency is to stress the repetition of the old conflict in the transference relationship and to emphasize the similarity of the old conflict situation to the transference situation. The therapeutic significance of the *differences* between the original conflict situation and the present therapeutic situation is often overlooked. And in just this difference lies the secret of the therapeutic value of the analytic procedure. Because the therapist's attitude is different from that of the authoritative person of the past, he gives the patient an opportunity to face again and again, under more favorable circumstances, those emotional situations which were formerly unbearable and to deal with them in a manner different from the old.

In this collection there are two papers that are related to Alexander's development of this concept of a "corrective emotional experience." "The Problem of Psychoanalytic Technique" may be regarded as leading up to this concept. In this paper he points out that most of the suggested innovations in psychoanalytic technique involve a one-sided overemphasis on one or the other of two factors, both of which are essential for the curative effect of psychoanalytic therapy. These factors are emotional abreaction and intellectual insight. Emotional abreaction, he points out, leads only to temporary symptomatic relief (as in the early hysteria analyses of Freud). On the other hand, intellectual insight without emotional experience is of little value. Every correct interpretation, Alexander contended, "serves both purposes," integrating abreaction and insight into a single act. Later, as we have already indicated, Alexander succeeded in formulating the nature of such integration of abreaction and insight in his concept of a corrective emotional experience.

In a later paper, "Analysis of the Therapeutic Factors in Psychoanalytic Treatment," Alexander not only spelled out at greater length his concept of corrective emotional experience. He also made the suggestion that the analyst might speed up such a corrective experience by deliberately adopting an attitude exactly the opposite to that of the person who had played the most important role in the patient's past.

This last suggestion is one example of a new orientation toward psychoanalytic therapy with which he and his colleagues at the Chicago Institute for Psychoanalysis had begun to experiment.

Early in the development of psychoanalysis, Freud had suggested a number of detailed rules which many of his followers felt should be adhered to rigidly. The patient should lie on the couch and the analyst should sit behind him, out of his sight. The patient should free associate and the analyst's activity should be limited to making interpretations of his free associations with chief emphasis on his resistances. The analyst should particularly avoid giving any advice about decisions with which the patient was faced in real life. Moreover, the patient should be seen not less than five days a week as long as the analysis continued. While the analysis lasted, the analyst should also reveal to the patient as little as possible of the analyst's own life and personality patterns. In particular, he should avoid all social and other contacts with the patient outside of the analytic hours.

All of these rules Alexander felt were good as a standard to be followed whenever there were no contraindications. As soon as the analyst begins to get a better understanding of the patient's problems, however, his approach should be more flexible. There are times, for example, when it is better for the patient to sit up facing the analyst. When the patient is in danger of becoming too dependent on the analyst, it is often desirable to reduce the frequency of interviews. Sometimes it is indicated even to give the patient advice. For example, late in the treatment, if the patient is contemplating marriage, it may even be in the interests of the treatment for the analyst to encourage the patient to break away from his dependence on the analyst by taking such a step.

The desirability of all such deviations from the rules is limited by one condition, however. When the analyst has not yet thoroughly understood the patient's psychodynamic situation at the moment, it is much safer to follow the rules. The flexibility that Alexander and his colleagues advocate is indicated only when it is guided by real understanding of the patient, only when the analyst knows exactly what he is trying to accomplish.

This desired flexibility of therapeutic approach has been discussed in some of the papers in this collection, notably:

"Current Views on Psychotherapy," "Two Forms of Regression and Their Therapeutic Implications," "Current Problems in Dynamic Psychotherapy in Its Relationship to Psychoanalysis," and "Psychoanalysis and Psychotherapy."

Several years ago, Alexander briefly concentrated attention on another problem to which he had already briefly alluded in a number of his earlier writings.[3] Following Freud, he distinguishes between two different kinds of regression. In the one case, "when the Ego is confronted with a conflict that it cannot master," it "seeks security by returning to a phase in its development when it was still successful." Another type of regression and fixation is "fixation to an unresolved traumatic conflict." In this kind of regression, as in a traumatic neurosis, the ego "returns again and again to the traumatic event in order to achieve a mastery of it."

In a paper entitled, "Two Forms of Regression and Their Therapeutic Implications," Alexander tries to work out the implications of

[3] See, for example, his footnote 2, in "A Metapsychological Description of the Process of Cure."

this distinction for the handling of the transference in psychoanalytic therapy. He cites two cases to show, for example, that the development of an oral dependent transference to the analyst is often not a sign that the patient's chief fixation is on a pregenital phase in his development. Perhaps more frequently, the patient's dependent transference is an evasion of a later conflict—at the level of the Oedipal conflict. In such a case, the therapeutic indication is to induce the patient to give up his regressive flight and to return to his attempt to master the Oedipal conflict.

Social and political studies

Since very early in his scientific development, Alexander has been interested in extending his inquiries beyond the limits of individual psychology, and in applying psychoanalytic understanding to the elucidation of social, political, and cultural phenomena. In this extension of his interest, he was, of course, following the example of Freud and of a number of other pioneers in psychoanalysis.

Alexander's interest in the neurotic criminal was one of his first steps in this direction. In *The Criminal, the Judge and the Public* he and Staub do not confine themselves to study of individual criminals. They try to understand also the emotional sources and significance of the concept of justice in our community life, and the disruptive effects of miscarriages of justice on the community's legal institutions for dealing with criminals and for the prevention of crime. Of particular interest is the authors' concept of the sense of justice as based on a kind of bargain, established early in life, between the child and his parents. "I shall refrain from gratifying some of my desires, to which you object. I renounce the pleasure for your sake in order to keep your love." This bargain tends to lose its restraining power whenever justice miscarries. "If other people are punished unjustly, then my personal freedom is in danger, or if *another* escapes the punishment he deserves, why should *I* continue to conform?"

Aspects of the community's reaction to crime and criminals are spelled out here in greater detail in "Psychiatric Contributions to Crime Prevention."

We have already mentioned the fact that Alexander later found another criminal type more prevalent in the American scene. "Crimes committed for prestige in order to appear a 'tough guy,' an independent daring person, and crimes committed to avoid the necessity of . . . accepting charity," he says, "were more common here than in Europe." Later, in *Our Age of Unreason*, he brought this observation into relation with Turner's analysis of the effects on American culture of the closing of the frontier. In the days of an ever-expanding frontier, "the ideal of the successful, resourceful, brave, self-made man who owes everything to himself and nothing to anybody else is the traditional ideal." Then the conditions of the frontier were replaced by "an organized and standardized industrial structure." When this occurs, the traditional ideal of the frontier becomes for most men unattainable and must be replaced, for example, by the fantastic appeal "of those films in which the life of today is depicted as offering unlimited possibilities." In some individuals this "anachronistic" drive takes the form of criminal impulses to defy the fear of punishment by "independent, dangerous and courageous acts." In this collection, Alexander's analysis of these phenomena is spelled out in his article, "The Don Quixote of America."

Alexander was greatly stimulated by the contrast that he observed between the cultural climates in Europe and in America. In America, he says, "I sensed the freshness of a youthful world, deeply involved in the problems of adolescence, full of energy, as yet unsure of itself, hectically competitive, and always on trial, a dormant colossus unaware of his exceptional potentialities." This exuberance in the American scene he contrasts with "the regressive mentality of a disillusioned, tired old man, living on the forced vigor of second childhood."

Later, Alexander became interested in democracy as an evidence of maturity in a people, and the emergence of totalitarian states as a regression to more dependent patterns.

"Loosely organized groups," he points out, when "exposed to external danger increase in social cohesion. History is full of such examples. When war threatens, individuals submit more willingly to social discipline, accept greater restrictions on personal freedom, and suspend internal hostilities." Thus, "mutual dependence increases with insecurity and fear and is responsible for social cohesion." The "dependent tendency which contributes so largely to social cohesion shows that it is patterned after the child's attitude toward his parents. The relation of the subject to the ruler is an extension of the child-father, or in matriarchal societies, of the child-mother relationship. As Freud pointed out, "the leader or king plays the role of the father in the tribe, clan, or nation."

Such dependence of a people on a leader, Alexander contrasts with "the individualistic tendencies that oppose social cohesion." "Security and freedom," he says, "are to some extent mutually incompatible. What we have called progressive impulses are clearly those which spur individuals to take chances and prefer the expression of their own individuality to a passive security." As examples of such "centrifugal forces" in social life, he cites the developments in European culture since the Renaissance. At that time, he points out, "expansive forces roused by intellectual curiosity and released from tradition worship" resulted in vast social changes:

Change, adventure, and self-expression became the order of the day in art, science, and politics. The inventor, Leonardo da Vinci, the political opportunist, Cesare Borgia, and the great travellers, like Columbus and Marco Polo, became the heroes of the age. . . . Courage, self-assurance and enterprise are the valued qualities and are expressed in creative, overflowing activity . . . and abundant energy. Three centuries ago on the American continent this individualistic development received a new impetus, unhampered by the traditional restrictions of the Middle Ages. At present we are facing fateful questions: Have we arrived at the end of this era of expansive social change? Are we about to enter a new phase of totalitarian mediaevalism? . . . Is the opposite extreme of totalitarianism unavoidable?"

These few excerpts, of course, give only a much oversimplified sketch of Alexander's discussions of democracy and totalitarianism in *Our Age of Unreason*, published in 1941. In the present collection, the following papers deal with this and other closely related problems: "The Don Quixote of America," "Adventure and Security in a Changing World," and "Introduction to *Group Psychology and the Analysis of the Ego* by Sigmund Freud."

In conclusion, we shall call attention to an exceedingly valuable theoretical by-product of Alexander's interest in the evolution of democracies as well as in the dynamics of personality development. In the evolution of self-governing democracies, education has a crucial and central role to play, but in order to understand just what education can achieve, and how, one must have a good grasp of just how heredity and environment interact in the development of a child's personality. In his "Educative Influence of Personality Factors in the Environment," Alexander points out that this problem has been approached from a number of different one-sided points of view. In this paper the author has surveyed and attempted to integrate these several points of view. In the last half of the nineteenth century, European writers tended to stress heredity alone, reflecting a traditional aristocratic structure of society. At the other extreme, American political theorists, starting with the thesis "that all men are created equal," inclined toward the assumption that "man at birth is a *tabula rasa* and that all his later personality traits are molded by external circumstances." In partial support of this theoretical bias, American sociologists could contribute the "sound, well-founded, everyday observation that in this country people belonging to all the different races of Europe were, in a brief period, transformed into a new and different type of personality." "Second generation immigrants, under favorable conditions, lost all distinguishable racial or national characteristics and assumed features common to the inhabitants of this country." Finally, psychoanalytic observation could find a way of reconciling these two extreme views, by demonstrating the predominant influence of the intimate family environment in the child's early years, and by calling attention to the fact that the intimate early environment was sometimes highly specific for a particular child's family, and at other times reflected patterns that are common to a particular culture.

Preface

This volume represents contributions to psychoanalysis and its borderline fields over a span of forty years. The papers are arranged in chronological order. This allows the reader to follow the development of the author's views. Changes in his views reflect general developmental trends of psychoanalysis during these four decades, although some of these changes are still controversial. In all fields of scientific endeavor changes in theory are to be expected, since the development of science consists in new observations and in the progressive clarification of concepts which in turn requires reformulation of theory. Such changes, as a rule, meet with initial resistance because of the universal propensity of men to adhere to the arduously acquired notions of the past. Even the innovators and reformers have to overcome their own tendency to retain formulations which first seemed successful for the understanding of the complexities of apparently chaotic and disconnected phenomena.

Since the development of ideas is gradual, it is most instructive to compare the earliest contributions with the latest ones. The reader will notice if he compares the first article in the section on theory, The Castration Complex in the Formation of Character, with the last one in this section, Unexplored Areas in Psychoanalytic Theory, that in the former the author applies the generalizations of the libido theory and the structural theory of personality more naively than in the latter. The whole tenor of this last article is more critical.

Following step by step the sequence of articles, the author's increasing interest in the integrative functions of the ego becomes evident. There is also a growing tendency to view human behavior from three correlated parameters: the physiological, the psychological, and the sociological. The earlier trend to view the psychic apparatus as if it were suspended in a vacuum, disregarding its physiological substratum and the social field in which the individual moves, became less and less acceptable to the author.

The earliest of the theoretical articles were written under the influence of Freud's first attempts (after 1920) to view psychological processes comprehensively as processes within an organized system, the total personality (the psychic apparatus). This introduced what is usually referred to as "ego psychology."

The initial impact of Freud's structural abstractions, the ego, the id, and the superego, was enormous because of their ability to describe psychological processes in their mutual interrelationship within an organized system. Only gradually could the author substitute more concrete, more dynamic concepts for these structural abstractions—ego functions instead of more statically conceived structural compartments of the personality.

In the theory of instincts the author gradually moved away from the original libido theory. Instead of operating with two qualitatively different instincts—sexual and nonsexual—he found it more adequate to differentiate sexual from nonsexual impulses by the degree of their participation as organized components in the goals of the total organism. In formulating this concept the author was strongly influenced by the basic fact of psychopathology, that all such impulses—curiosity, pride, hostile aggression, and love itself—can be discharged in both sexual and nonsexual forms. An impulse discharge acquires its sexual quality when it does not participate in a goal structure in which it is subordinated to the interest of the total organism. In other words, isolated discharge of impulses for their own sake without their being subordinated to other goals acquire the quality of sexuality, independent of the quality of the impulse. Thomas French's lucid description of goal structures was of great help in formulating this view.

Another area in which the author's views underwent considerable changes is the field of psychoanalytic treatment. The main shift of emphasis was upon the overwhelming significance of the emotional experiences which the patient undergoes during psychoanalytic treatment, and which outweigh the effects of cognitive insight. With the concept of "corrective emotional experience" the author tried to do justice to both therapeutic factors: cognitive insight and emotional experience. Essentially this was an attempt to draw the ultimate therapeutic conclusions from the discovery of the transference phenomenon.

The significance of the influence of the therapist's personality upon the course of the treatment has been more and more recognized by psychoanalysts, and the author tried to include this factor in the therapeutic model which hitherto described the therapeutic process as if the therapist entered into it only as an abstract intellect and not as a definite unique personality. Above all, the author became more and more convinced that a more realistic theory of treatment can evolve only if the totality of the therapeutic process is viewed by nonparticipant observers who are in a position to evaluate not only the patient's reactions but also the therapist's participation in the process as an individual person.

The changes in the conceptualization of the therapeutic process necessarily require changes in teaching psychoanalysis to students. The author's dissatisfaction with the early standardization of teaching the treatment procedure is expressed in his latest publications. He regards this trend toward premature standardization as something which retards the development of psychoanalysis.

The author's interest in the integration of the sociological point of view with the individual psychodynamics is another growing trend clearly expressed in the articles included in Part Four, Sociology, Politics, Esthetics, Criminology.

Only four articles pertaining to psychosomatic medicine have been included in this volume because most of the author's contributions to this field have been published in other comprehensive publications— *Psychosomatic Medicine* and *Studies in Psychosomatic Medicine,* the latter written in collaboration with staff members of the Institute for Psychoanalysis in Chicago.

The steady flow of new ideas and trends both in his own as well as in his contemporaries' writings makes the author confident that psychoanalysis is neither—as some of his critics believe—a solidified creed, nor—as some of his adherents and organizers treat it—a more or less finished product, but a dynamic scientific movement bent on steadily improving its methods of observation, conceptualization, and treatment.

What the author considers the most consistent feature in his writings is the conviction that psychoanalysis is in dire need of critical reevaluation and further development of its theory and its method of treatment. Because psychoanalysis originally represented an extraordinary advancement in the understanding of personality functions and dysfunctions, and therefore revitalized an at that time primarily descriptive and custodial psychiatry, it developed an inordinately conservative tendency to preserve its original formulations and methods and to rest on the laurels of past accomplishments.

Franz Alexander

Contents

◄ *One* ►

Psychoanalytic
Theory

The Castration Complex in the Formation of Character

◄ 1923 ►

Preliminary remarks on the dynamics of symptom formation

A particularly favorable opportunity to gain some comprehension of the dynamics of symptom formation presents itself in the study of those so-called "transitory symptoms" which arise under our eyes in the course of analytic work—a sort of product of the laboratory. Ferenczi, who first described these manifestations, pointed out their theoretic importance in that they enable experimental observations to be made of the dynamics of falling ill. Ferenczi[1] explains these symptom formations arising during analytic work as manifestations of resistance against the process of making conscious certain unconscious tendencies which are displeasing to the ego and which have been brought near to the level of consciousness by analysis. Driven out of their old neurotic "positions" these tendencies are seeking an outlet in new symptoms and struggling to reach equilibrium afresh by this means. Truly a unique opportunity to study symptom formation!

These transitory artificial products of the neurosis make their appearance in an unusually pronounced form during the analysis of what are called "neurotic characters." These are types well known to the analyst, people who suffer from no very definite symptoms of illness but whose behavior in life is in the highest degree impulsive and frequently even compulsive; they are unusually subject to the domination of their unconscious instinctual tendencies. The lives of such people display some remarkably irrational features and their apparently senseless behavior—like the symptoms of neurotics—is comprehensible only to the trained eye of the analyst, able to perceive the unconscious mo-

This article, originally published in German in 1922, received the Freud Prize in that year. The English translation was not done by the author.

[1] Sandor Ferenczi, "Transitory Symptom-Construction during the Analysis," *Contributions to Psychoanalysis*, New York: Basic Books, 1950.

tives behind it. This irrational behavior is obviously equivalent to neurotic symptoms in others; these people form a transition-type between the neurotic and the healthy. Their neurotic way of living has also some resemblance to the blunders of everyday life, which also owe their origin to unconscious motives; only, these impulse-ridden characters gratify their repressed tendencies not in trivial everyday blunders but in irrational compulsive actions literally at the most important and decisive moments of their lives. Whereas in the neuroses the unconscious makes use of special mechanisms, such as hysterical conversion, symbolic obsessive acts, delusional ideas, all characteristically isolated as far as possible from the rest of the person's life, the neurotic character interweaves his life with his neurosis—his life constitutes his neurosis. Teleologically considered, the symptoms of illness serve the purpose of satisfying, in a relatively harmless manner, those wishes that are in conflict with the conscious ego, of *localizing* them to the symptoms, and thereby preventing them from injuring the rest of life. The best illustration of the self-healing function of symptoms is provided by the final state of the paranoiac, which corresponds to a recovery with disablement. His behavior in and capacity for the common activities of life is often perfectly normal, his delusional system alone excepted; it has absorbed the whole of the pathologic matter into itself, as it were. All feeling of illness is lacking too, and with some justification; the analyst will certainly reflect carefully before disturbing this equilibrium. Naturally in most types of neuroses the outcome is not so favorable, the tendencies that are incompatible with the ego cannot always be isolated in this way. As a contrast to this recovery with disablement we have many phobias—in which the anxiety encroaches even further and further into life, making it at last intolerable—or certain obsessional neuroses, inhibiting every activity. With neurotic characters, however, the morbid process has not yet reached the stage of symptom formation; the unconscious tendencies that would otherwise form symptoms can still find an outlet in certain irrational actions which are hardly influenced by consciousness and make no use of any particular mechanisms.

It is difficult to find an answer to the dynamic problem: whether the pressure of the factor leading to illness—the damming-up of the libido—is not great enough to open up new paths and form symptoms as an outlet, or whether the defense reaction of the organism—the repression—is not powerful enough altogether to exclude satisfaction in reality. In any case, the irrational neurotic behavior of the abnormal character entails more real satisfaction than a neurotic symptom does, and in its blind impulse-ridden way often creates more misery than a neurosis. Indeed, we know from Freud, especially from his recent work, that the repressing faculty (*Instanz*) is the conscience; that is, a social faculty, one that guards the individual from the satisfaction in reality of his asocial wishes and even punishes him for the satisfaction of them in fantasy. A section of the neurotic characters, certain impulse-ridden criminal types, plainly suffer from a deficiency of these defense reactions. And it is just as unquestionable that another section of these people, driven by their instinctual tendencies perpetually to injure themselves in life, do not fall ill of a neurosis simply *because,* by means of their apparently senseless self-injuries, they replace the symbolic overcompensations (self-punishments) of the obsessional neurotic by real ones, and in this way keep their oversensitive consciences clear. Should they be at any time deprived of the possibility of this real satisfaction, then, if these dynamic considerations are scientifically sound, we should expect them to fall ill of a neurosis. In actual fact, when such people come into the hands of an analyst, it is found that they already suffer from various neurotic symptoms. Yet as long as it is possible for the tendencies that are incompatible with the ego to be realized in behavior which eludes the vigilance of the censorship, all consciousness of illness is lacking; and this is the reason why, when such people are induced by those around them to undergo analysis, they are particularly difficult. Even when this impulse-ridden behavior leads to the greatest hardships it is still consistently maintained, while its calamitous consequences are ascribed to the cruelty of fate or to chance. The unconscious is always victorious and seizes its satisfaction at the expense of the most elementary interests of the ego, as is plainly shown by the not at all uncommon final fate of such people —death by suicide.

The conclusion to which we are led by these reflections is that every "neurotic character" contains in it the germ of a particular form of neurosis, which must then break out if any deprivation ensues of the satisfaction in reality of the neurotic tendency. Curtailment of the real satisfaction may occur in two ways: by external circumstances, or by internal ones—the interference of the conscious ego. This second way occurs in the course of the analytic work, when the meaning of the irrational impulse-ridden conduct is made conscious on the occasions of its repetition in transference; so that under the control of consciousness the previous satisfactions are renounced. According to the considerations adduced above, it would be in this stage of the analysis that the transitory symptoms would arise—more, that a transitory and hitherto latent neurosis would develop. The analytic work removes the previous possibilities of satisfaction, by bringing the tendencies incompatible with the ego more and more under the control of the conscious faculties; under the pressure of this artificially-induced damming of the libido these tendencies escape into those neurotic symptons which have hitherto been replaced by the actual neurotic satisfactions in life, and in which the tendencies find a fresh subterranean outlet. Neurosis is here also the obverse of neurotic behavior, just as it is of the perversions, with this difference, that the perverse satisfaction is accepted by the ego, whereas the neurotic behavior with its illogicality is unrecognized as a satisfaction.

The conditions under which "transitory symptoms" appear are in these cases unusually pronounced; the lines on which the interchangeable occurrence of neurosis or neurotic behavior may proceed are laid down by the patient's previous life. The circumstances are thus peculiarly favorable to comprehension of the origin and mechanism of development of a neurosis, because the disease is then a product of the laboratory and actually develops before our eyes out of apparent health. We can thus observe the universal mechanism by which the neuroses develop ordinarily, since it is even probable that an attempt at actual satisfaction *always* precedes the symbolic satisfaction of the incompatible tendencies in symptoms, and that symptoms only arise as substitutive satisfactions after this attempt is found to be impracticable or in consequence of an inner prohibition.[2]

It must not be forgotten that these transitory illnesses during the treatment are actually nothing but transference manifestations in the Freudian sense and consequently produced by resistance; they are the last attempts of the repressed tendencies to find a discharge in the form of action. Freud describes the transference as a "new edition" of an old disease.[3] The analysis of neurotic characters, in which the transitory symptoms and other transference manifestations arise not as substitutes for previous neurotic symptoms but as an apparently quite new neurosis, shows the transference in this character of a neurosis in a peculiarly convincing, perhaps even at first in a startling, manner. The predilection shown by such cases for forming transitory symptoms may also be explained by the fact that with them it is not a *symptom* that is being discharged into the transference, but a much more real sort of satisfaction; consequently more is expected in the transference. Dynamically considered, every "transitory symptom" is merely an expression of the fact that a neurotic attachment has been loosened so quickly that it is not possible for the cathexis which has been set free to work itself out in transference manifestations; that is, by resolving the symptoms one takes from the patient more satisfaction than can at the moment be made good to him in the transference or still less in reality. The block leads to new symptoms which nevertheless still retain a relation to the transference. In treating abnormal characters we destroy not symptoms, but real or almost real

---

[2] I would point to the development of children in this respect.

[3] S. Freud, *Introductory Lectures on Psycho-Analysis,* London: Allen & Unwin, 1922.

satisfactions; the tension caused by the difference between the real satisfaction and the transference satisfaction is too great, and so there arise transitory symptoms, or even a transitory neurosis, as by-products or also as transition stages.

After these dynamic considerations I will add some observations.

The castration complex in the formation of character

In his essay "Some Character Types Met With in Psycho-Analytic Work," [4] Freud gives us the prototype of an analytic understanding of neurotic characters. Our knowledge of certain more definite character traits begins with his treatment of the subject of anal erotism. A sharp line of demarcation between certain exaggerated character traits and neurotic characters could hardly be drawn. By a character trait we mean a certain stereotyped attitude in life; those people whom we call neurotic characters show this stereotyped attitude in the whole rhythm of their lives, at the most decisive moments and most important turning points. Whereas the hysteric makes his body and the obsessional neurotic makes the everyday performances of life the medium in which he expresses his neurotic wishes, for the neurotic character, ridden by his instinctual tendencies, this medium consists of the whole course of his life, his actual *destiny*.

Freud gives us in *Beyond the Pleasure Principle* [5] a profound insight into the essential unity of neurotic symptoms, transference, and human destiny, by his view of them as the expression of a compulsion toward the repetition of an attempt to solve an unresolved conflict, to master subsequently a real experience that had been insuperable.

In the analytic readjustment of a neurotic character, therefore, we pursue the same object as with the neuroses; namely, that of discovering the real experience which is forever being repeated in the impulse-ridden behavior, and in which the irrational actions would for once have been justified.

During the analysis of such a neurotic character I was able to observe with unusual clearness the impulse-ridden actions being successively replaced by conversion hysterical and paranoid symptoms. The dynamic processes described above came out with particular clearness in the course of the analysis. After the almost complete amnesia covering the first six to seven years of his life had been gradually dispersed, the patient's whole life lay before us as a series of situations and actions repeated again and again since his earliest childhood, under the weight of a truly demonic compulsion in the

[4] S. Freud, "Some Character-Types Met with in Psycho-Analytic Work," *Collected Papers of Sigmund Freud*, New York: Basic Books, 1959, Vol. IV, 318-344.

[5] S. Freud, *Beyond the Pleasure Principle*, New York: Liveright, 1961.

sense of an ever-recurring attempt to solve a primal conflict. His neurotic behavior in life took the place of the symptoms of this latent neurosis, so that, as the meaning of the actions replacing these symptoms was revealed and they were brought under the control of the judging, inhibiting faculty of consciousness and given up, this latent neurosis was bound to come to the fore. The dynamic process involved was similar to that in "active therapy," by which the patient is required to refrain from certain symptomatic acts, only that here the analyst's prohibition was replaced by the patient's conscious renunciation actuated by his new knowledge.[6] The life of this heavily impulse-ridden character contained nothing worthy of special mention; and yet the transparent way in which his life had formed itself under the pressure of the castration complex, and still more the paranoid symptoms which transiently appeared during the analysis—I might call it a paranoia in a nutshell, developing and dispersing before my eyes—offered an unusual opportunity for discovering much about the mechanism of this disease. The circumstances were also favorable in that the patient, though an intelligent man, was not of a complicated type; his youth had been spent in rough, uncivilized surroundings and his later life in a large metropolis, so that he had been forced to go through ontogenetically in a double manner the phylogenetic adaptation of humanity to the requirements of a civilized community. This adaptation he accomplished externally quite well; he rose high in the business world and acquired a large fortune.

He came for advice on account of difficulties in his married life. He was beginning to doubt his wife's love and yet he somehow felt as if he himself were also responsible for the unhappiness of his marriage. After many years of married life he was just beginning to realize that his wife had married him for his money. He treated his wife—unconsciously, it is true—like a prostitute, overwhelmed her with luxury and demanded nothing from her but intercourse. Their married life consisted of nothing but the man's struggles to be allowed intercourse, which was always paid for in the same material way. These payments were often grotesque; the wife wanted a hat, perhaps, and he would give her six hats at once. The woman, who was sexually frigid in any case, began to perceive in her unconscious the meaning of this strongly anal erotic tendency and reacted to it with a corresponding craving for presents. They were bound to each other, like the nut and the screw. His experience with women had always been the same; his first marriage and his earlier love affairs

---

[6] In another analysis of a neurotic character, the meaning of an attitude in life which was continually reproduced under compulsion was not discoverable until, after a prohibition in regard to it, it had taken the form of repetition in dreams and transitory symptoms.

were merely unfinished versions of the same drama. His type of love object was always the cold, calculating woman who if she possessed a remnant of capacity for love was always forced back into anal erotic regression by deliberate measures. One unconscious tendency in this was the well-known one described by Freud—the tendency to debase the love object—which played an important part.[7] The woman is paid and thereby becomes a prostitute, being thus detached from the mother *imago;* instead of tenderness she receives money. The repressed idea came back in another form, however. His wife was far superior to him in refinement, she corrects his speech, writes his letters, represents him in society; he feels inferior to her and thus reproduces the mother-son relationship. In his marriage therefore he made use of the well-known mechanism of a partial repression. The wife is made into a prostitute and the love regresses to an anal erotic form of satisfaction, but along with this the superiority of the woman in the mother *imago* is retained as an important factor.

The libido which was not attached anal erotically sought an outlet by many and devious paths in his social[8] activities, his relations with friends and other businessmen, in the form of disguised (sublimated) homosexuality. Affectionate love for any woman was completely unknown to him; the remnant of love which had not regressed and become fixed on the anal erotic level was fixed homosexually and sublimated. In the analysis the fate of this remnant came to be investigated first, and from it arose during the treatment the paranoid symptoms which will interest us principally.

The disatisfactions and difficulties in his marriage first arose when his social activities began to be destroyed by external catastrophes. Social upheaval made it necessary for him to leave his home and to give up his occupation. In a few months all that he had achieved was reduced to nothing; he saved a small part of his fortune, it is true, but was condemned to almost complete inactivity by the outer circumstances. The outlet that the libido had hitherto found in his work, which on account of its neurotic element must be discussed in more detail, was thus cut off, and the damned-up libido led to dissatisfaction in his married life. It appeared as a dim longing for love, which was unrealizable in the married life that had been formed on the anal erotic level and had satisfied the previous needs of the libido. Efforts to take up his former activities again also came to nothing, on account of both internal and external difficulties. And yet, since

[7] S. Freud, in "The Most Prevalent Form of Degradation in Erotic Life," *Collected Papers of Sigmund Freud*, N. Y.: Basic Books, 1955, Vol. IV, 203-216.

[8] [*Sozial*. This Latin word is confined to scientific usage in German and has not the wide and often tendentious implications that it has in English. It simply means "in the world," "among people."—Tr.]

it seemed that the capacity to absorb libido anal erotically had reached its height and no more libido could be dealt with in this manner, it was essential that the previous social activities, which as we shall see were already highly neurotic, should be replaced by new ones, in order to re-establish an equilibrium of the mental forces. There remained two possible alternatives: either the neurosis which was already latent in the neurotically-tinged sublimations must be replaced by a manifest neurosis, or the marriage must be dissolved and an attempt made to find an outlet for the libido dammed-up by the overthrow of the sublimations in a new love relationship on the genital level. At the beginning of the treatment the second alternative was much in the patient's mind; but the several attempts he had already made to leave his wife had come to nothing, which made him hesitate now. We know of course that this path was impassable and that every attempt to find a genital outlet would have come to grief. The Oedipus complex which had never been overcome stood in the way; even without a neurotic disposition, indeed, it stands as a formidable barrier against unlimited genital satisfaction and necessitates the formation of sublimations, that is, it forces a part of the sexual energy into social paths. In a neurotic character such as this, the capacity for love on the genital plane which is so narrowly restricted by the Oedipus complex must first be enlarged by analysis, in order to make satisfaction of a normal kind in the relation to the love object possible.

The external changes in his life were not of course alone responsible for the overthrow of the sublimations. The analysis showed that the social upheaval merely provided an occasion for the demonic feature in the neurosis of his life to appear in a more pronounced form and bring it about that the life's work of this man, who was in any case continually injuring himself in life from a neurotic sense of guilt, should be finally destroyed. He was forty years of age and it was indeed in reality no light matter for him to begin again; but the difficulty was materially increased by the neurotic tendency to self-injury which throughout his whole life had hindered the healthy tendencies toward sublimation and had rendered a great part of his energy sterile. The situation was similar to that of a professional violinist suffering from a neurotic cramp in his fingers, who then by chance or by some blunder injures his hand as well.

Attempts to take up his activities again under difficult external circumstances failed on account of neurotic behavior in the course of his work, which now evinced itself more and more. As a young man in favorable external conditions he had tolerated these neurotic inhibitions without serious disadvantage; but in the difficult conditions after the collapse of his business they made it impossible for him to succeed in obtaining a position in the world even approximating to what he had had before, and thus to obtain a similar field for his activities.

This was the situation when the analysis began. Without following the course of the analysis chronologically, I shall endeavor to describe the course taken by that part of the libido which had hitherto been attached to social activities (homosexual), and which by being blocked had led to the dissatisfactions in married life and to the slight hypochondriacal symptoms which brought him to the analyst.

As has been said, the patient had never in his best years succeeded in sublimating his homosexual libido without neurotic signs, especially as it was strongly reinforced from the heterosexual libido, which was driven into a narrow channel by the Oedipus complex and found no adequate outlet. Analysis soon revealed a remarkable attitude which had been repeated in a stereotyped manner throughout his whole business career, the first occurrence of which was traced back to early childhood. He showed an impulse to injure himself and, as it turned out, in a particular way—by being exploited or defrauded in some way. I should like to describe this impulse as *passive kleptomania*, kleptomania become narcissistic and turned against the self. With an instinctive knowledge of men he knew how to choose his friends in such a way and how to combine with friendship some material transaction or other, usually of a financial nature, that in the end he was invariably simply cheated and defrauded. He did business only with friends and made his friends his business clients. Friendship and business were intimately connected, and always so that in the end he come off badly. Or else he lent money, pressed it on the borrower, especially when he knew that he would never get it back. He applied the proverbial saying, "Opportunity makes the thief," with an amazing ingenuity so that he might be stolen from. It was astonishing to find, as the story of his friendships unrolled itself in the analysis, that he had not had a single friend with whom there had not been some monetary transaction and by whom he had not in the end been more or less seriously injured. It had not been difficult to gratify his peculiar need; he could reckon upon one of the strongest impulses in man, his avarice, and had been able to select the right objects for his purpose with sure intuition. Nor was it difficult for him to ascribe his misfortunes among his friends to the cruelty of fate; in any case he learned nothing from his experiences and would learn nothing, but always repeated the same trick.

His peculiarity also showed itself in a well-known and less pathological form, in meticulous overconscientiousness and honorableness, to which quality he owed in part his considerable success in his career. It would have been tempting to regard his peculiar passive kleptomania as an exaggerated, caricatured conscientiousness and thus as an anal erotic overcompensation; but the almost complete removal of the infantile amnesia showed that it represented first and foremost a persistent attempt to realize a castration wish, and that the equivalence of "money" and "penis," with a slighter emphasis on the connecting link "feces," formed the unconscious basis of his impulse-ridden behavior. Through his whole career his attitude to those in authority and to representatives of the father had been highly characteristic. His great conscientiousness and trustworthiness always won him their good opinion and he had often been entrusted with very responsible offices. He always formed his relation with those in authority more and more into that of a father and son; and then, urged on by a dim sense of guilt, he worked with tense energy and utter self-sacrifice for their business interests. Through these qualities he acquired a high position in a trade syndicate in his own country and great wealth. Yet every acquisition of money made him feel guilty, and he relieved his conscience partly by devotion to work and partly by losing a part of it again in the passive kleptomaniac manner described above.[9] This attitude is well known to us as an anal erotic overcompensation, but in this case its origin in the Oedipus complex was clearly betrayed by transference factors involved, and was only fully comprehensible after elucidation of his castration complex. By transference factors I mean that it was not a matter of indifference to him who caused him these material losses; but that he always selected as the objects of his passive kleptomania friends who were socially or intellectually superior to him, that is, who represented the father. He was inexorable against dishonesty in his subordinates; the unconscious basis of this attitude will be discussed later.

We know from Freud[10] that the loss of the feces is felt as one of the earliest narcissistic wounds, in that it constitutes the loss of a pleasure-giving part of the body, and that it can suitably represent castration. I should like here to emphasize that the principal factor in the equivalence of feces and penis seems to consist in their *affective association*, to which the similarity in shape of the two objects is merely secondary. The *tertium comparationis* of this affective association may be expressed more or less as follows: The loss of a pleasure-giving part of the body *as a result* of a previous pleasurable sensa-

[9] In this light his behavior looked like a caricature of charitableness and betrays the unconscious motives of this social expression of a sense of guilt. I found the anal erotic basis of this attitude in an unsublimated form in another patient; as a child he used to retain the feces as long as he could, then evacuate a small portion of them and let it dry on the orifice, then take it off with his hand and throw it away, retaining the remainder for a while longer.

[10] S. Freud, "On the Transformation of Instinct with Special Reference to Anal Eroticism," *Collected Papers*, N.Y.: Basic Books, 1959, Vol. II, 164-171; and "The History of an Infantile Neurosis," Vol. III, 473-605.

tion produced by it (stimulation of the mucous membrane). Every human being learns as he grows that every pleasure ends in "pain"; he learns it through the primal castration experiences—the loss of the pleasure-giving nipple after the pleasure of sucking (*oral* primal castration according to Stärcke[11]) and later the loss of the pleasure-giving stool after the anal pleasure of retention (*anal* primal castration according to Freud). An affective basis is therefore well prepared on which the fear or expectation of castration may arise. As the earliest affective basis of all for the expectation of castration we may regard the act of birth, which entails the loss of the mother's body, actually a part of the child's own body, and also the loss of the fetal membranes.[12] At the moment of birth a pleasurable condition (the pleasure of absence of stimuli) and a pleasure-giving organ (the uterus) are lost for the first time in life, and are replaced by a painful condition.

The growing human being learns that every pleasure is closely followed by the loss of the pleasure-giving bodily organ (uterus, nipple, stool); so that on reaching the pleasure of onanism he is already prepared affectively to lose the corresponding pleasure-giving organ, the penis, and easily accepts the threat of castration as an obvious conclusion. The temporal sequence of the unconscious affective impressions is elaborated into a causal one (rationalized) and castration is to follow as a result of onanism. This affective basis also explains how the castration complex can play such an important part without any threat having been given—and that without drawing upon any phylogenetic explanation.

Whereas the loss of the nipple is felt as an impersonal cosmic necessity, the first transference factors come into play during the training in cleanliness; and these the instinctive comprehension of the child's attendants recognizes, by endeavoring to soothe its narcissistic wound with praise and other signs of love. A sense of guilt, the conscience as an inhibitory faculty, plays no part so far. Feces are given up in return for a narcissistic equivalent, praise and tokens of love from those around. The Oedipus complex, the first social factor, first introduces an inhibitory faculty into the ego system in the shape of the conscience, and the first dim consciousness of guilt bears upon the incest committed in the fantasy accompanying onanism. The ideal set up within the ego (the conscience) coincides with the person of the father[13] (introjection of the father); the castration punishment is

11 A. Stärcke, "The Castration Complex," *Int. J. Psycho-Anal.*, II (1921), 179.

12 One is reminded of the penis significance of garments, cloaks, etc., in dreams!

13 S. Freud, "On Narcissism: an Introduction," *Collected Papers*, N.Y.: Basic Books, 1959, Vol. IV, 30-59. "The institution of the conscience was

usually expected at the hands of the father. This ideal, as Freud has shown in his *Group Psychology,* is later identified with the leader and finally with the community itself.[14] The incest wishes are renounced first of all for love of an ideal which is identical with the father, and then later for love of an ideal which becomes woven more and more into the ego itself.

With these considerations I hoped to make it clear that money as a narcissistically valuable substance is particularly well adapted, by the affective basis already established, to replace the penis in castration wishes. The same circumstance naturally brings about the other unconscious connection—money and feces—which is even earlier in time; and it is in accordance with the temporal sequence of things that the equivalence of money and penis should develop by way of anal erotism.

With his passive kleptomania our patient was first continually being castrated by those of his friends who were in some way superior to him; and then, when the social revolution brought in a new standard and private property was condemned, he rendered up his fortune to the community itself by a series of quite transparent blunders, and thus transferred to the community the role of the castrator. In order to make comprehensible the paranoid symptoms which appeared during the treatment I must trace back to his youth the history of his castration wishes—which so far have been mentioned only as an impulse-ridden tendency to self-injury.

At the time of the revolution he rescued the fortunes of certain of his friends and got them transferred abroad—and literally forgot to do the same for his own! It is true that he concealed a few articles of value, but later he allowed them to get into the hands of a friend who absconded with them. Before this he once performed a very great service for a business friend, for which he took nothing in return, and was later suspected of high treason for it. His whole life was a series of such incidents, which most frequently ended simply in money being stolen from him. In his youth he reacted with a quite special affectivity to detecting anyone, particularly a subordinate, in an attempt to defraud his chief. At the age of twenty he one day discovered a fellow employee in the act of embezzling a large sum; the man offered him a big price for his silence, but he denounced him nevertheless. After this affair, which agitated him exceedingly, he suffered for a year from a gastric neurosis. He could take no food but fluids,

---

originally an embodiment of parental criticisms, later that of social criticisms, a process which repeats itself—the origin of a repression-tendency was originally an external prohibition or hindrance."

[14] S. Freud, *Group Psychology and the Analysis of the Ego,* New York: Liveright, 1940.

and had a strong aversion to almost anything solid. After this recollection came up in the analysis there followed a transitory symptom in the form of an attack of diarrhea, which took the place of his habitual constipation. Hypochondriacal sensations of a globular nature in the larynx—he felt a stick in his throat—were repetitions of similar sensations which he had first had in youth at the same time as the gastric symptoms, after the affair of the embezzlement.

The analysis of these transitory bodily symptoms brought a mass of material into consciousness, of which one little kleptomanic incident in his childhood deserves special attention. It first gave me the assurance that I could justly regard his later tendency to self-injury, which I have called passive kleptomania, as a reversal of a primarily active tendency into a passive one. The mechanism of this reversal is that of a "turning of sadism upon the self," and here too the prominent part played by a sense of guilt in this reversal is evident.

As a schoolboy of nine or ten he stole obsessively from two of his schoolfellows—chiefly pencils, pens, money, etc. Pocketknives he would have liked to take, but did not "because they were too expensive." He most particularly wanted the schoolbag of one of these boys, but he could not take it; it would have been too noticeable. They were both unusually clever boys, much cleverer than he, the best in the class; and on this account he envied them, but at the same time he liked them very much. After he had stolen anything he had an intense feeling of guilt, and very often put back the stolen article. He struggled with this compulsion and begged God to free him from this vice. It is to be noted that he stole only from these two friends.

Although the unconscious determination of this "relative kleptomania"—by which I would describe its restriction to particular persons —is transparent enough, I asked him to associate to the stolen articles, but without success. Nothing came to his mind. Only in regard to the schoolbag which he so much wanted to steal did the censorship permit a gleam of light to fall on to the unconscious; probably because the chain of associations connecting this object to the repressed idea was longer than that connecting pens, pencils, etc, to it.

ASSOCIATIONS TO SCHOOLBAG

"The schoolbag had fur; it was made of hide . . . of an undressed deer-skin . . . deer . . . antlers . . . I am very fond of deer, they are so gay and lively." Deer represented manliness to him, as he remarked next.

I would call attention here to the idea of a "hide," which will play an important part in a later dream interpretation. Behind this kleptomania was clearly the castration wish, which, as the analysis revealed in other ways, was directed first and foremost against the father's genital organ. The clever boys were well-suited by their industry and mental superiority to reactivate at the beginning of the second puberty period the first and earliest feelings of jealousy.

I will make use of this material to point out a surprising difference between the attitude of my patient and that of women with the classical type of kleptomania, who steal obsessively, regardless of whom they are stealing from. They steal on the principle of stealing for stealing's sake, without any affective impulse to injure someone else; I should say they steal without any object transference. By their thefts they are trying to make good the cosmic injustice of their bodily configuration; their thefts have more of a narcissistic tone. Since there is no intention to injure there is also no sense of guilt; their actions are directed against an impersonal injustice. In my patient's obsessive thieving, however, it is just the transference factor, the choice of those who were to be stolen from, which is characteristic. He stole only from superior schoolfellows; he envied only a bigger penis, and not, like women, the penis in itself.

I do not suppose that this single observation suffices for us to draw any contrast in principle between male and female kleptomania in regard to the presence or absence of transference factors (absolute and relative kleptomania) and of the sense of guilt.[15] I know that hardly a single analysis goes through without revealing minor kleptomaniac tendencies in childhood and that in women too the person stolen from often plays an important part. It seems to me, however, that the above considerations explain why the classical objectless kleptomania is met with *only in women.*

In the development of the patient's castration complex this kleptomaniac episode marks an important period; for it shows in its active form the same impulse that, by a reversal into a passive form, later on expressed itself in the peculiarity of his neurotic character. The

[15] In a conversation I had with Dr. Abraham, he informed me that he had often found in analysis other determinants of obsessive stealing, besides the envy of the penis mentioned by me, such as the impulsion to take by force the parent's love which was not forthcoming or any unobtainable pleasure of any kind. This last motive is obviously the ruling one in the habit very common among children of stealing good things to eat. The longing to take the mother from the father also unconsciously plays an important part. In the course of this conversation we came to the conclusion that in all these cases the ultimate impulse to obsessive stealing comes, at the deepest unconscious level, from the longing for the first source of pleasure; it is the unwillingness to be parted from the mother's breast. The nipple is the first love token, the first source of pleasure to the child; this oral origin is evident in thefts of sweetmeats. Stealing because love or pleasure is not forthcoming merely shows that the first refusal of the mother's love, the withdrawal of the nipple, has not been overcome. Obsessive stealing would thus always arise out of an active castration wish, if we take the castration wish in Stärcke's extended meaning.

intense sense of guilt shows the struggle for repression which the
conscience was waging against the envious attitude toward the father
or his representatives—an attitude which in earliest childhood (the
first puberty period) had been overcome, but was revived again shortly
before the second puberty period. And in the course of further analysis
an even earlier kleptomaniac episode was actually recalled. As a boy
of five or six he often stole money from his father's pockets, and also
other things like those he stole at school; even at that time, however,
he did not keep the stolen property, but gave it away to his playmates.

Repression of this asocial impulse was not successful, and so an
attempt at defense was sought by means of other mental mechanisms
—first of all by *projection.* We see this method of defensive warfare
in his behavior under temptation to steal, and in his impulse generally to put himself into situations where the temptation to dishonesty is strong. As early as his fourteenth year he obtained by his
honesty a position of great personal responsibility in a shop. After
severe resistances in the analysis a series of recollections with a strong
affective tone in regard to this period of his life came out; they were
memories of the attempts of the customers to bribe him and of his
strongly ambivalent feelings toward the head of the firm. He fought
the temptations, remained honest, and projected the struggle between
his conscience and his own aggressive tendencies outward, dispatched
the enemy within him in his struggle with the dishonest customers.
His better nature, his ego ideal, played the part of the head of the
firm by identification; the repressed (or better, to-be-repressed) part
of his personality was identified with the customers. He dealt with
his ambivalence by dividing his ego into two by means of projection
and identification, and thus satisfied both the repressed and the repressing tendencies. For this solution (the paranoid mechanism) of
his conflict he required situations in which he met with temptation.
He kept up this defense-mechanism until his twenty-second year, when
the affair of the embezzlement occurred; then for the first time this
form of defense against his asocial tendencies failed him. He delivered
up the thief and withstood the temptation, but yet he fell ill with
hypochondriacal and conversion symptoms in the whole alimentary
canal. Eating solid food was given up, as an oral representation of the
castration wishes; the formation of a hard stool, affectively overcharged
on account of its penis significance and so rendered suspicious to the
repressing tendency, was prevented by diarrhea. While in these symptoms the fluid contents of the bowel served the purpose of the higher
repressing ego system, the repressed active castration wish obtained
expression in the form of a hypochrondriacal sensation of a stick in
the throat—he had swallowed a penis. These symptoms strengthen the
surmise that the patient was suffering from a latent narcissistic neuro-

sis, which was replaced by neurotic behavior in life and thereby prevented from breaking out. These symptoms did in fact reappear during the analysis at a time when his impulse-ridden behavior came to light, and when he was coming to believe that the unhappy end of all his friendships and the stereotyped repetition of material losses was due not to the cruelty of fate but to his own impulses to self-injury, by which he relieved the burden on his conscience and from which at the same time he extracted a passive masochistic pleasure.

His recognition of this had a far-reaching effect. He suddenly began to review all the relationships with friends that he had at the moment, which were very numerous, and discovered that he had invested the remnant of his fortune again systematically in his friends' business undertakings, in such a way that all control over it and insight into the inner conduct of affairs was out of his hands. The examination of things showed him that he had again suffered serious losses in several directions. His attitude now underwent a very sudden and unnatural change. He who had never been capable of exercising any control over his own financial affairs, who regarded it as an insult to ask a friend for an account, now became suspicious and demanded balance sheets; he changed completely, to the utter astonishment of all his friends and their circle. It was at this time, after the passive satisfaction that he had previously obtained in life had been brought under the control of the censorship and become impossible, that the hypochondriacal and conversion symptoms appeared as a substitute. The analysis and interpretation of these symptoms brought, as has been said, a mass of forgotten memories back into consciousness, and led to the rapid disappearance of these symptoms; only to be followed very shortly, however, by the paranoid symptoms, which had already been heralded by the sudden change of character shown in his suspicious attitude (character regression, as Ferenczi has called it).

Among the memories unearthed at this time one was accompanied by especially strong feeling; as a child of six he had flung himself sobbing upon the body of his dead father, kissing his face, and had cried out: "I will do everything I can to make up for all that I have done against you!" The revival of this memory gave the impression of a cathartic abreaction; the repressed displaced affect broke out during the analytic session in all its original intensity. Sobbing and crying he saw before him with hallucinatory clearness the completely forgotten face of his dead father.

We may pause for a moment over this memory and consider that in it we have found the actual experience which was for ever being reproduced again by the repetition compulsion, and which brings sense and meaning into the patient's senseless behavior in life. His whole life literally consisted in "making up" for a dark mysterious sin, in perpetually discharging an oppressive unpayable debt. The oath that he swore by his father's dead body he literally carried into action in life; driven by a truly demonic compulsion, he paid back the pennies he had taken from his father's waistcoat pocket to any and every father substitute who crossed his path in life.

These memories and the recognition they brought sufficed to effect the astonishing change of character described. But these analytic discoveries merely exposed the reaction of the conscience that, under the pressure of the sense of guilt, had turned the impulse to its passive form; behind it there lay, for the present still concealed, the necessary reconstruction of the aggressive active impulse—surmised and theoretically inferred, except for the transitory kleptomaniac episodes in school. Corresponding to this was the too sudden appearance of the change of character and the way in which it grew more and more marked: it replaced (with a character regression) the memory of the repressed aggressive attitude. He became more and more suspicious, quarreled with all his friends, and could no longer endure their superiority which before he had sought so eagerly. He scented fraud in everything; was at one moment furious, at the next depressed; he went so far as to make a scene with one friend in a public place. His condition came continually nearer to paranoia.

One day he told me he had been put on the Bolshevists' black list and was living in fear of the world revolution that was soon going to take place; he would be one of the first victims, for he was already being watched. Now that he could no longer pay the world by damaging himself, by being deceived and stolen from, anxiety had developed. His neurotic behavior, like every neurotic symptom, had served as a protection against anxiety, forming as it did the passive discharge of an originally active libido. He felt guilty and paid, let himself be stolen from, in order to avoid a worse fate; he paid *in order to be able to keep his penis*. And then analytic recognition took away this defense against his neurotic fear of the community and the anxiety broke out in ideas of persecution. Indeed he had not been persecuted before because he had paid out money to prevent it.

One day, during the analysis of a dream, quite unmistakable paranoid symptoms appeared; they bore, however, a strong transference character.

Dream. He was in a stable and saw hidden in a corner (perhaps behind a wall) a bear; it was on two legs like a human being. The bear went up to a dark heap which he could not see clearly and *very carefully* picked up a furry hide off the heap; then went slowly along, and *very carefully* put the skin down in another place on the stable floor. In the background he saw two horses, one of which moved (perhaps it kicked out its hind leg) while the bear was carrying out this performance.

The first associations came without difficulty. The bear made him think that as a child he was called "Bear," and that his baptismal name meant "bear" in his own language. Then he remembered an incident of his childhood. He was perhaps five or six years old when a bear came into his father's stable-yard and tried to get into one of the stalls; it disappeared again, however, without taking anything. Then followed memories about being overtaken and robbed by gypsies. When I asked him for associations to a "hide," he became irritable. Nothing came to his mind . . . then a hesitating mutter . . . "Perhaps it was a wild boar's skin." The next association was . . . "Fur collar." Then he was silent a long time; suddenly he broke out:

"I feel something cold streaming on to me from you. You're sending out electricity on to me!"

Intense anxiety came over him; he was quite convinced of the reality of his delusional ideas. ("The man has electricity in his body!")

To complete the account in full of the course of this transitory paranoid condition I will interpolate here that interpretation of these delusional ideas led during this very session to relief of the anxiety and to understanding on the part of the patient. The way had been well prepared by the foregoing analysis. The dream was interpreted in the following sessions, and in a relatively short time we arrived, through a series of memories with a strong affective tone (among which was that, already mentioned, of stealing money from the father), at a practically complete mastery of his castration complex. The paranoid attitude also gave way and the exaggerated change to suspiciousness relaxed, but without any return of the impulse to self-injury. The character change showed itself also externally; his expression, his manner, his handwriting, and above all his gait, altered conspicuously. He started a new business undertaking, and for the first time since his breakdown he again achieved success in it.

The meaning of the dream, however, was revealed fully only when the significance of the "very careful" operations of the bear came to light.

The bear steals the hide and goes about it very carefully like a thief (please refer to the memory of the bear, followed by that of being attacked by robbers). The hide obviously serves as a penis symbol, as it did it in the former chain of associations: schoolbag—hide—deer—maleness, and as is indicated too by the first associations to it; wild boar—fur collar. His next associations explain the intense anxiety that supervened together with the paranoid ideas of reference (the physician was sending out electricity on to him) when I first

asked him for associations to "hide." As a child he was once terrified
by a wild boar and another time by an otter. The next association to
otter was: "Men often wear fur collars of otter skin" . . . "It was a
big powerful otter" (otters are smooth, long, and cylindrical in shape).
He had once as a child of five seen a stableman having intercourse
with a peasant girl in the stable which he saw in his dream; it frightened him intensely because the girl screamed horribly. This brought
memories of observing parental intercourse.

In the dream the hide stands for the greatly feared penis of the
grown-up man (stableman, father); it is strongly endowed with affect,
as is the chain of associations throughout: penis—fright—wild boar—
otter, and it is to be noted that the exaggerated impression made by
these animals is due to association by similarity of shape (otter and
penis. In the dream, however, these terrifying animals are condensed
into a *hide*, that is, are *dead;* and in the appearance of the bear as a
body snatcher (hide = corpse) the repressed wish is gratified—the
wish that threatened to break forth from the unconscious at the moment when he stood by the dead body of the father he had feared and
envied and who was now so harmless—*the wish to rob the dead father
of his penis*. Instead of this wish there appeared in consciousness the
sense of intense guilt: "I will do everything I can to make up for all
that I have done against you!"

At the sight of his father lying dead, the conflict in the ambivalence
surged up, if not for the first time, yet certainly with greatest intensity,
when the death wishes of fantasy were suddenly realized.

In the dream the hide is also a symbol of feces; the bear picks it up
from a "heap." The first association to heap was "dungheap"; a heap
in a stable is obviously a heap of horse dung. The word hide (*Fell*)
also made him think of refuse (*Abfall*). At the moment that the bear
picks up the hide the horse makes a threatening movement. The connection is clear: the bear steals horse dung (money) from the horse
(father). Directly after relating the dream the patient himself interpreted the two horses as the two parents. I should also like to emphasize that in the dream the bear behaves in the same way as the
patient had behaved in life as a child when, because of his sense of
guilt, he did not keep the things he had stolen from his father, but gave
them away to his playmates. The bear puts the hide carefully back on
the floor. As we have seen, he too in later life cannot keep the money
he has earned and is impelled to give up some of it again.[16]

We saw that by the dream work of condensation the hide has acquired a central significance. Besides this, the dream makes use of the

---

[16] His unconscious, which was in this respect so unusually sensitive, perceived only too plainly the structure of present-day commercial organization,
i.e., that the money a man earns is taken away from someone else.

(paranoid) projection mechanism. The division of the ego into two is clear: conscience (ego ideal) is hidden behind a wall (endopsychic perception of repression) and looks on at the bear's operations; the latter at the same time stands for himself, the repressed part of himself which he projects into the outer world. The complete interpretation of this dream amounted to an explanation of the neurotic trait in the patient's character. The envy of the father's penis was displaced on to money, and then under the weight of the conscience was turned against himself in the form of an impulse to self-injury. Behind this last line of defense, by displacement, projection and reversal of the instinct, against the primitive aggressive castration wish, there lies as an intermediate stage the passive homosexuality, which comes to expression during the interpretation of the dream in the transitory paranoid delusion: the physician is sending out electricity on to him. A complete account of this transformation of the libido would be as follows:

1. *Primary attitude of envy directed against the father: the positive castration wish* (stealing money from the father).

2. *Institution of an ego ideal identified with the father* (introjection of the father as the ego ideal). As a result of this ambivalence a conflict of the conscience ensues (scene by the father's dead body). Under the pressure of the sense of guilt a transformation of the active castration wish into a passive one takes place by "turning upon the self" (talion punishment). Together with the passive castration wish appears the passive homosexual attitude to the father as a punishment, by identification with the suffering partner (sadistic-masochistic conception of coitus: the sexual act witnessed in the stable). This passive homosexual current of feeling undoubtedly proceeds mainly from heterosexual libido dammed up by prohibitions against incest and parricide. It cannot remain in this crude homosexual form, however, because of fear of castration and fear of homosexual assault; it is therefore sublimated as:

3. *Passive submissive attitude to superiors and friends* (passive homosexuality) and *passive kleptomania* (castration wish). This last phase serves as an outlet for the libido at the same time sanctioned by conscience, and serves also as a defense against anxiety. The object of this anxiety was originally the paternal penis; later the anxiety takes the form of a dread of the community.

The defense formula against the aggressive impulses runs therefore: It is not I who wish to castrate my father and possess my mother, but *he* who wishes to castrate me and do to me what I should like to do to her. This defense formula leads to anxiety, nevertheless; only after displacement from the penis to money and only after social sublimation of the passive homosexuality does it become adapted to keep the anxiety in check. At the moment when the analysis was undoing this whole process backwards, when the wishful tendency behind the apparently accidental money losses was exposed and had been renounced, the anxiety which lay concealed behind this defense mechanism broke out as dread of the Bolshevists. The analysis went deeper, however, and in the interpretation of the "bear" dream substituted castration for the money losses, by bringing up the equivalence of money and penis. The anxiety which by displacement and sublimation had been disguised as dread of the community regressed to the naked dread of the homosexual assault that was now expected as a consequence of castration: "You are sending out electricity on to me!"

This quite unambiguous analysis of the mechanism by which a transitory paranoid anxiety developed will perhaps enable us to add a small contribution to the theory of paranoia or, rather, of delusions of persecution. This contribution becomes possible when we regard the result of this analysis in the light of Freud's recent more extended investigations into the ego system.

The homosexual genesis of the paranoid ideas is quite clear in the case described, but we also obtain an insight into the original evolution of homosexuality—namely, projection of the aggressive castration wish and thereby division of the ego into two. The ego ideal which arose out of introjection of the father is saved by a projection of the aggressive tendency incompatible with it; this latter then directs itself against the ideal. This aggressive side of the ego system, which remains at this primitive level, after projection gratifies its castration wish against the higher side which is identified with the father, against the ideal. So that, by being deceived and stolen from by his friends, he was not merely punished for his aggressive covetous tendencies, but was also—as the man in possession who could be defrauded and robbed—their superior; and thus he acquired a father's position toward his friends. This contradiction made the passive attitude to his friends more tolerable. The whole mechanism, therefore, is similar to that described by Freud for melancholia; it is only less narcissistic, because the aggressive side remains projected. The incest wish is also at the same time guarded against by a similar process which, however, appears to be independent of the first process described; the active wishes in regard to the mother are resolved into an identification with her, through the passive homosexual attitude to the father. Both the active impulses which have been turned upon the self pass over together into passive homosexuality: the aggression against the father and the heterosexual impulse toward the mother turn into a passive female attitude in regard to the father (this entails at the same time self-punishment).[17]

[17] My speaking of the incest wish in connection with the castration wish is only apparently an arbitrary digression; for the latter already includes the former. The envy of the father's penis is only intelligible when the incest wish

To sum up, in the libido development under investigation three great stages are distinguishable:

1. The primary, sadistic, active, heterosexual. (Primal crime of incest and castration wishes.)

2. Following this, a defense against these asocial impulses by transformation of them into masochistic, passive homosexual.

3. A defense by displacement and sublimation against the passive homosexual outlet for the libido.

I should wish not to go further without pointing out that Freud has already described these three great stages as occurring in the evolution of civilization and particularly in the evolution of religion. The primal crime is the *first* stage. The passive submissive attitude to the totem animal and later to the god is the *third* stage. The *second* stage of unsublimated homosexuality is not manifest; it is repressed, as also in the character development I have been describing, only to appear after displacement from the father to the totem animal or after sublimation from the father to the god. Freud has shown the supreme importance of repressed homosexual tendencies for the origin of religion in his paper, "The History of an Infantile Neurosis," [18] which constitutes a confirmation out of individual psychology of the theory developed in *Totem and Tabu*. The part played by the unconscious passive homosexuality, which provokes anxiety and is guarded against, is the same in his case as in mine. In his case, in so far as it is not worked off in hysterical bowel symptoms, it leads to a caricature of religion, in my case to a caricature of the morals of capitalism.

The neurosis which expressed itself in the patient's whole career in life did not, however, constitute the entire solution of the father-conflict. He further made use of a more narcissistic mechanism: of the sense of inferiority, which also had its root in the castration complex.

Exaggerated feelings of inferiority strike the analytic eye at once as an intermediate stage on the way to delusions of inferiority, and it is not difficult to recognize in them a wishful tendency: i.e., the tendency to self-punishment for a primary attitude of envy. The feeling of inferiority has indeed always an envious attitude inherent in it, and relates reciprocally to it; envy is sadistically toned and inferiority masochistically. "I am too weak" means also "Another is stronger than I." The craving to create situations in which inferiority is felt is the same process that Freud has described as the repetition compulsion to conjure up again and again a traumatic situation that had not been

---

is already in existence to give cause for this envy. With regard to the patient's tendency to identify himself with his mother, I may mention that he had since childhood had a habit of pinching his right nipple, which had grown considerably larger in the course of years as a result.

[18] S. Freud, "The History of an Infantile Neurosis," *op. cit.*

overcome. In feeling himself weaker than someone else, whether justifiably or not, a person with feelings of inferiority is recreating the father-son situation which he has never overcome. The later course of this conflict is known: identification with the father and introjection of the father as ideal. The solution of the conflict is now attempted within the ego system and the feeling of inferiority represents a feeling of tension between the ideal and the ego, as Freud remarks in his latest work.[19] Solution of the conflict is attempted narcissistically, as in melancholia. One part of the ego is raging against the other; to the ego ideal this is a sadistic solution and to the ego it is a masochistic one. The ego envies the ideal and is punished for it by torturing feelings of inferiority, but it obtains masochistic pleasure from the punishment. This is the well-known sadistic-masochistic game of such characters; it takes place within the ego system and absorbs the primary aggressive impulses which would otherwise be sublimated and applied in useful occupations. Delusions of grandeur are an extreme form of the outcome of this conflict; in them ego and ideal have combined; the ideal is cannibalistically incorporated into the ego, in the way that Freud has described in maniacal insanity.[20] Thus the tension is relieved and therefore this condition is so frequently a final one. These two ways or solving the conflict are well known to us in a milder form as character traits; they are the "inferiority" character, with his shy, anxious manner (melancholic type), and the exuberant character, with his self-confident, unrestrained manner (hypomanic type).

In my patient this origin of the feelings of inferiority in rivalry with older persons, in penis envy, was clearly visible. His first recollection of strong feelings of inferiority dated from his schooldays, when he envied the cleverer boys and stole from them. Later the feeling of inferiority took a particularly tormenting form: "I've learned nothing; I don't know anything." Since he tried to soothe this envy by stealing penis symbols, it is clear that the mechanism was one of displacement and sublimation (of the envy on to the cleverness of the boys).

The other manifestation of his feeling of inferiority was his shame

[19] S. Freud, *Group Psychology and the Analysis of the Ego*, New York: Liveright, 1940; (originally published in 1922).

[20] *Ibid.* I should only be following Freud's train of thought if I described the coincidence of the ego and the ideal as a cannibalistic form of identification, for he compares fits of mania with the festivals originating in the totem feast, which is a cannibalistic act with an identification tendency. Mania would then be a further step on the way to the narcissism which is entered upon in melancholia. In the latter the love object is absorbed into the ego system; in mania the splitting within the ego system itself disappears, the cannibalistic identification of the ego with the object is then completed within the ego system and an even more complete narcissism is thus achieved.

about his Jewish birth. This shame was so pronounced that he concealed the fact from his greatest friends and even from his wife (he had been baptized). The connection between this form of inferiority feeling and the castration complex is well known. The two circumstances, that he had had little education and was a Jew, were his most painful conscious conflicts, and they expressed nothing else but the envious attitude of his early years which had never been overcome. When we reflect that the source of the ego ideal is the identification with and introjection of the father, it is easily comprehensible that the inferiority feeling, the conflict between ego and ego ideal, should assume the form of the primal conflict between father and son. The way in which he relieved this tension, at times by an arrogant hypomanic manner and fantastic pseudologia, at times by depressive self-torturing, is a good illustration of the applicability of the Freudian melancholia mechanism as an explanation of feelings of inferiority. Perhaps one might venture the assumption that the difference between delusions of grandeur and delusions of inferiority, on the one hand, and mania and melancholia, on the other, consists simply in this: that in the first pair of neuroses it is *homosexual* libido that is narcissistically introverted and sadistic cannibalistically gratified within the ego system (between ego and ego ideal), whereas in the second pair of neuroses the *heterosexual* libido undergoes the same fate.

A primal form of castration

In the course of my discussion of this case the patient's castration complex has been found to represent the castration wish against the father turned upon himself, as a self-punishment in order to relieve the sense of guilt. We know that this is only one root of the complex, the one proceeding from the father conflict. We cannot forget, though, that the father conflict is only one side of the Oedipus complex, that is, it is the consequence of an incest wish. Castration is not merely the talion punishment expected for the penis envy directed against the father; it is also the punishment for the incest wish. In fact, the latter source of it is the best known and best recognized.

The part played by the incest wish in the formation of this patient's castration complex was followed back very far. Analytic recognition was again linked up with the solution of transitory symptoms; understanding of them did not advance our knowledge of his social character traits, which were, as we have seen, fully explicable from the father conflict, but they explained his behavior in his marriage.

The transitory symptoms which replaced memories in this connection were again hypochondriacal—feelings of strangulation in the throat, quite different from that of the stick in the throat already mentioned, and feelings of pressure on the chest and back. All these sensations felt as though the pressure was an external one. These symptoms lasted for some days and were peculiarly trying during the analytic session. Analysis of them brought to light a mass of memories belonging to the period from his fourth to his seventh year, which I can relate shortly in view of the traumatic character which recurred monotonously in them all.

One day in the engine room he put his finger into the machinery and was severely injured. Another time he swallowed a fish bone and barely escaped choking to death. When his father beat him he used to run to the water mill and listen in a melancholy mood to the water rippling; on one such occasion he fell into the water and was nearly caught by the mill wheel. Once in the open he was badly frightened by a mouse that ran up on to his leg; he caught it on his thigh under his knickers (a patent falsification of memory and screen memory!). As a boy of six he often rode bareback without saddle or stirrup; on one occasion his horse shied and bolted into a wood, where his neck caught in a low bough and he was left hanging. Another time his horse shied and bolted into a stable and he only escaped by ducking his head in the nick of time, so as to get through the low door, and even so his back scraped against the door jamb and his throat was pressed tight against the horse's neck. After this last memory had emerged the feelings of pressure on his throat, chest, and back disappeared suddenly. While he was relating this adventure he became very much moved, and suddenly he said with tears: "I wish I was alone in a small dark place now or near some water."

I will not now try to decide how far these recollections represent actual experiences or how far they are the products of fantasy. It is not important for us whether they were actual faulty actions on the part of the child which constantly brought his life into danger, or creations of fantasy: in any case they were the products of his unconscious (faulty actions are also determined by the unconscious). What is conspicuous in all these recollections is the mortal danger and the *form* of the threatened death—*suffocation;* among them are interpolated some memories of the castration type (finger cut off, mouse in knickers, hanging by the neck—the last also a danger of suffocation).

I should like here to refer back to my earlier remarks on the subject of *affective association*, in order to bring in the evidence of these other observations in support of them. Behind the anal and the oral loss of a pleasure-giving part of the body there lies the *first* traumatic experience, the act of birth: the loss of the enveloping womb, accompanied by strangulation in the throat, feelings of pressure on chest and back, and the danger of suffocation. The earliest affective experience of pleasure followed by "pain" through the loss of a part of the body is unquestionably the act of birth, and it is thus suited to express the expectation of castration in the manner of the most primitive level of the unconscious. *The patient's transitory hypochrondriacal sensations of pressure were repetitions of the sensations present during the act of birth.* These hypochondriacal sensations were resolved in the analysis partly by memories of faulty acts in childhood dangerous to life entailing similar sensations, and partly by memories of the castration type. Hanging by the neck, falling into water, riding into a small space through a narrow passage in danger of strangulation are clear representations of birth, the last two, indeed, in the reverse direction: representations of a return into the womb.

The double meaning so characteristic of unconscious processes here comes clearly to expression. The meaning of all these transitory bodily sensations, memories, faulty acts, and associations replacing one another is at once incest wish and castration wish, return into the womb and birth. The unconscious equations run: castration = birth, incest wish = return to the womb[21] The incest wish and the punishment for it are carried through in one and the same process, expressing the compromise between ego and libido with which we are so familiar. Falling into water and being drowned, riding into a small closed space through a narrow passage and thereby being strangled, serve, by their element of suffering, as punishments for the wish which is at the same time symbolized in these performances: the return into the womb = incest.

A few more remarks about the equation "return to the womb = incest."

During coitus a part of the body, which in dreams, as we know, so often stands for the whole personality, presses up against the womb; further, through cell division the germ cells, detached particles of the body which also biologically correspond to an extract of the personality—one remembers the fact of heredity—also reach the womb. On the genital level the libido is indeed, speaking biologically, an impulse to introduce the germ cells into the uterus. The pressure of the penis against the uterus can in this light be regarded as the symbolic representation of the wish to return to the womb. Reality, however, necessitates two deprivations: the mother is replaced by another woman and the return is accorded only to a part of the organism, the germ cells.

On the basis of the compulsion to repetition discovered by him, which seems to be the fundamental fact underlying all mental and biological processes, Freud conceives the sexual instinct to be an im-

---

[21] Freud has interpreted the fantasies of rebirth as wishes for incestuous intercourse with the mother. "The rebirth fantasy is probably always a milder form, a euphemism, so to speak, of the fantasy of incestuous intercourse with the mother." ("The History of an Infantile Neurosis," *op. cit.*)

pulse toward the reunion of matter which has at some time become divided.[22] I have attempted[23] to equate this division with the cell-splitting which ensues upon growth, and to identify the impulse to reunion with the impulse to re-establishment of the mature state before division. As an act preparatory to the union of the two products of division (the germ cells) coitus is the first step on the way to this re-establishment of the mature state. The germ cells and the complete individual are actually the asymmetrical products of cell division and correspond essentially to the two equal halves of the single-cellular protozoa which reproduces itself by division.

In conclusion, I will sum up the essential points of this paper. In the castration complex two self-injuring tendencies met in one stream: on the one hand, the talion punishment for active castration wishes, out of the father conflict; on the other hand, the punishment for incest wishes. Further, in this second source the expectation of castration is only *one* manifestation of an expectation of a general narcissistic wound. It is the deposit of an ontogenetic experience—that every pleasure has its outcome in loss, in pain.[24]

The patient's behavior in his marriage now becomes completely comprehensible. His impulse to give, to pay for every act of intercourse, is a need to give out a substance of narcissistic value and thus a sublimated anal representation of his castration wish, by which he allays his sense of guilt in regard to coitus. In spite of depreciating her by payment the wife remains to him the superior being—the mother. He thus behaves exactly as in his youth when he did penance for his incest-fantasies by his blunders, whose double meaning was at once castration and incest, a guilty impulse to death by water and by suffocation: to birth and the return into the womb.

The castration wish stood as the central point of his whole character formation and that is why he was such an unusually favorable object in which to study this complex. The analytic solution of it led

22 S. Freud, *Beyond the Pleasure Principle*, New York: Liveright, 1961.

23 Franz Alexander, "Metapsychologische Betrachtungen," *Int. Ztschr. Psychoanal.*, VII (1921), 270.

24 The uncanny sense of expectation, often felt by neurotics but also by the healthy, that an indefinite vague misfortune will follow just when great success has been achieved or when life seems for a moment to have granted perfect happiness, also rests upon the affective expectation of a narcissistic wound, deeply imprinted by the affective experiences of ontogenetic development. Polycrates throws his ring into the sea at the moment when he has attained complete happiness, in order to ward off, by this symbolic self-castration, the envy of the gods and the misfortune it brings. This symptomatic act too has its reverse meaning: he throws the ring into the water and thus expresses the wish to return to the womb.

not merely to a complete change in his social character traits, but also to a change in his sexual character. This change too did not take place without disturbance. The dissolution of the sense of guilt led at first to an unbridled longing for a mother instead of a wife, only later on to be gradually brought into adjustment with reality.

Dreams in Pairs
or Series

◄ 1925 ►

It very often happens that two or more dreams in the same night stand in some sort of relation to one another. In the *Traumdeutung* Freud speaks of the way in which successive dreams which all contain the same latent content grow progressively clearer. Often, however, the relation between pairs of dreams is still closer: not only is the content connected but there is also a dynamic or, more correctly, an economic connection. A certain dynamic relation between pairs or series of dreams which express the same wish is nearly always present. The following is the simplest type of a relation of this sort. The first dream may, for instance, express the incest wish, the sexual act being disguised symbolically. For example: "I am driving in a carriage with my mother." In the second dream the act is disguised less, or not at all, but the incestuous object is replaced by a harmless one. The two dreams are then complementary to one another and permit, as it were, a complete gratification of the wish in two stages, by which it escapes the notice of the censor. The obvious economic gain for the repressed tendency is that through dividing the gratification into two stages a fuller satisfaction is rendered possible, though the economic work of the censor remains the same. Both the symbolically disguised sexual intercourse with an incestuous object and the manifest sexual act with an indifferent person are, if taken alone, capable of entering consciousness; they express the real wish, however, only incompletely. But taken in connection with each other, the second dream having reference to the first, they constitute a complete representation of the repressed tendency. If we look out for it, we come across this mode of representation so frequently that it is superfluous to give examples.

There is another more interesting and more complicated mecha-

This article was originally published in German; the English translation was not done by the author.

nism, very like the one I have just mentioned. Here the economic connection is still closer: the second dream arises out of the first and
is conditioned by it. We see this mechanism plainly in the following
pairs of dreams:

Dream I. "A wedding-feast is in preparation. My brother is going
to marry my *fiancée*, but the clergyman fails to appear and so the
wedding cannot take place. I say to my brother that probably we
could find another clergyman. However, nothing happens and the
wedding cannot take place."

Dream II (the same night). "We and a girl whom we know are
looking at photographs together. Among them we see the photograph
of my brother-in-law's mistress. We both begin to laugh because she
is so plain, and I say that my brother-in-law would certainly maintain
that she looked very interesting."

The patient had the day before brought to the analysis a dream
which, as we shall soon see, had a similar latent content, but which we
did not discuss during the analytic hour. "A Chinaman and an English
woman who live in the same boardinghouse as myself wish to have
intercourse. I should have to be present because there is no other
room available, but it would be extremely embarrassing to me to be
forced to witness the act. Fortunately, however, nothing happens."

Different as their manifest content is, all three dreams have the
same meaning. In the first the brother's wedding is frustrated (there
is no clergyman there) but, in order to shift the blame from himself and
to hide his malicious joy over the disaster to the marriage, it is the
dreamer who is the person to say, with a gesture of hypocrisy, that
they could probably find another clergyman, as though he himself were
very anxious for the wedding to take place. In discussing the dream
the patient soon remembered a scene in which his elder brother had a
quarrel with his wife and said that he would get a divorce. On that
occasion the patient detected in himself a secret joy and was ashamed
of his own malice.

The meaning of the second dream is expressed more directly and
is almost undisguised. In this dream the patient is laughing at a girl
whom his brother-in-law had already thrown over and who was very
plain; moreover, he was doing this together with another girl who
also disliked the one at whom they were laughing. The question is:
why does the second of the two girls appear in the dream and why
does he need a companion in giving way to his malicious satisfaction?
The answer to this question reveals the real meaning of the dream.
The girl in whose company he laughs at his brother-in-law's former
mistress shares his antipathy to her. And it is the reason for the dislike displayed by the girl who appears in the dream which is the
essential *tertium comparationis:* the two girls are rivals. Thus the

dreamer chooses this girl to share in his derisive laughter because he hates the brother-in-law's mistress from a similar motive, namely, from jealousy. This reveals his passive homosexual fixation to his brother-in-law, which gives rise to the wish to separate him from his mistress. Or, to put it more accurately, it shows his malicious satisfaction in the separation which has already taken place and in the fact of the girl's ugliness. Similarly, the desire to frustrate his brother's wedding arises out of a passive fixation to him.

The difference between the two dreams is this: in the second, the dream about the brother-in-law, the malice is openly expressed and its homosexual motives are clearly indicated in the part played by the girl who shares his feelings, while in the dream about his brother the only thing manifest is the interest, ego-syntonic but none the less hypocritical, in his brother's wedding taking place. To put it quite shortly: in the first dream the latent wish is more strongly repressed. Or to express it in another way: the dream about the brother corresponds more closely to the demands of the superego, even though this is really deceived by the dreamer's hypocrisy, for after all the wedding cannot take place. Now the economic reason for this difference is obvious: feelings against the illicit relations of his brother-in-law are less strongly condemned by the censor (superego) than similar feelings against his brother's legal marriage. And in the main the homosexual fixation to the brother-in-law, being less incestuous than that to his brother, is not so strongly repressed. But there is another dynamic factor which I wish to emphasize, and it is just this which interests us now. In the first dream the patient behaves in a most lofty manner; only in the second dream does he reap the benefit of this hypocritical self-mastery. For, having done his best to promote his brother's marriage in the first dream, he is able in the second to indulge with a quiet conscience in malicious feelings against his brother-in-law's mistress. In the first dream he satisfies the moral demands of the superego; in the second he is free to transgress again. The moral credit which he acquires in the earlier dream is used to pay for his guilt in the later, and release an uninhibited gratification of the repressed tendency. His untroubled enjoyment of his malicious feelings in the second dream is made possible by his moral behavior in the first.

I would now recall that the patient had brought to the previous sitting a dream the latent content of which was similar to that of the pair of dreams. It is only from this first dream that we can understand the deepest unconscious basis of the other two. Here sexual intercourse between the Englishwoman who lived in his boardinghouse and the Chinaman is frustrated. The meaning is clear. The boardinghouse corresponds to his home. The circumstance in the dream that he was obliged to be present during coitus, because there was no other room available, is an allusion to his parents' bedroom, where he slept as a little child; and the alien inhabitants, the Chinaman and the Englishwoman, are contrast figures for his nearest relations, his father and mother. The most deeply repressed wish in all three dreams is that of hindering his parents' coitus and separating them from one another. The wish to separate which recurs in all three dreams—the brother-in-law from his mistress, the brother from his wife, the Chinaman from the Englishwoman, refers ultimately to the parents. Here we observe a certain sequence. The more the persons are disguised the less does the action need to be masked. Thus, in the dream of the foreigners the sexual act is clearly retained, while the incestuous objects are not only disguised but actually transformed into contrast figures. In the dream about the brother-in-law the wish to separate appears in a modified form as malicious delight in the ugliness of the woman. In the dream about the brother, where an incestuous object (the brother) makes his appearance, the wish to separate is directly denied. This is an example of the mechanism I described at the beginning.

The mechanism by which the allaying of the feeling of guilt in the first dream makes it possible for an otherwise repressed wish to be gratified without inhibition in the second is plainest in pairs of dreams of which the first is a punishment dream and the second a wish fulfillment, sometimes actually ending in a pollution. I will give an instance of two such dreams.

Dream I. "I am on the seashore. My brother comes up in a row boat. He gets out but immediately jumps back into the water by the boat. The boatman is very angry with him for jumping back into the water and begins to abuse him, but my brother pays no attention to him. Now my brother is out of the water again and we go off together. The boatman behind us continues to shout and I say to him that he has no right to abuse me, for I have done nothing. We run toward the town and the boatman pelts us with stones from behind. Curiously enough, it is only I who am in danger and not my brother, for he has suddenly vanished."

Dream II. "I am with a little girl of about eleven or twelve years old. She says that I may kiss her arm on a certain place at her elbow (as if it were difficult to do). But I am able to do it and kiss her all over the upper part of her body."

The details of the analysis of these dreams are of no importance at the moment. The first is a punishment dream, in which the punishment affords at the same time gratification of a passive homosexual wish (being pelted with stones from behind by the boatman). The essential feature, however, which was emphasized in the telling of the dream, is that the dreamer was punished though quite innocent, for it was his brother and not he who jumped into the water. He is punished for his brother's act. The brother's sinful act is incest (to spring back into the water = back into the maternal uterus). The boatman who punishes is the father, who has placed him on the seashore (brought him into life) and separated him from the mother (the water). The compensation for the injustice suffered in this dream is enjoyed in the second dream, which ends in a pollution. An experience from the day before suggested the little girl whom he kissed. He had met on the previous day at the analyst's house a little girl of five or six, accompanied by her mother. He had been struck by the precocious, boastful manner and speech of the little girl. His association to kissing the arm at the elbow was that it was there that he and his brother loved to kiss their mother when they were little children. He even thinks that he copied his brother in kissing his mother in this way. Thus the pollution dream is clearly a mother incest dream. Having been unjustly punished in the first dream for his brother's offense, he thereby justifies himself for committing incest with full gratification in the second, and this in the same way as his brother, for he kissed the little girl in the way in which his brother kissed his mother.

The connection between the two dreams is obvious, and we see that the punishment dream serves as a sop to conscience, so that it may not disturb the gratification in the second dream. We can see at once that this mechanism corresponds to that of the obsessional neurosis, in which activities displaying a masochistic tendency to self-punishment serve to liberate other, sadistic tendencies. The account must balance. And the same principle is at the bottom of the manic-depressive mode of reaction, in which the torturing period of depression and self-condemnation is followed by the period of mania with its freedom from inhibitions. Punishment and license are here divided into two successive phases; in the obsessional neurosis they exist simultaneously side by side. In the manic period conscience is quite powerless; it has exhausted its oversevere control in the melancholic phase.

I will quote another short but very characteristic example of a pair of dreams.

Dream I. "I ask someone to give me a newspaper. He is an unknown man, who scolds me and will not give me the paper."

Dream II. "Someone is giving me change. He gives me the right change but I do not give him the equivalent in return."

Both dreams are clear allusions to the analysis. The day before, the patient saw a newspaper in my room and asked me to let him look at it. I refused his request with some noncommittal remark. The relation of the second dream to the analysis is also clear. When he was last paying his fee he remained in my debt for a small sum which was

left over in changing a larger note. In the first dream I insult him unjustly—the unknown man is a familiar allusion to the analyst. In the
second dream he is able to do me a material injury without incurring
any guilt. The unconscious train of thought which underlies these two
dreams is: "As the analyst was so disobliging as not to let me look
at his paper I will not pay what I owe him." In this pair of dreams
we see most clearly and simply the mechanism which I have described.
The patient makes me guilty, in order to be free from a feeling of
guilt toward me. Thus the analyst takes on the role of the superego
in the pairs of dreams that I quoted earlier. In the first of those the
superego has its account paid: it even receives more than is owing. It
can give undue play to its punishment tendencies and inflict unjust
punishment, in order that it may be disregarded in the second dream.
We have an exactly similar procedure in politics where each party
waits for the opposing party to compromise itself by going too far.

The last pair of dreams, in comparison with the earlier ones, shows
us the genesis of the superego as postulated by Freud. Here the patient's unconscious behaves in relation to an actual person in authority
(the analyst) as it did toward the superego in the other pairs of dreams.
This is the reversal of the original process of introjection which led to
the setting-up of the superego.

The Need for Punishment
and the Death Instinct

◄ 1929 ►

The problem of the need for punishment leads us to the most remarkable aspects of the psychic life of man. It leads us to those actions, unintelligible to rationalistic psychology, which harm the agent himself, cause him pain and hurt, and reveal a plainly self-destructive purpose. These actions appear paradoxical to our ordinary thinking, because we are accustomed to assume, from self-knowledge and the observation of others, that actions are in general performed to avoid pain or to gain pleasure. Actions and other psychic manifestations clearly intended to procure suffering seem to contradict this general principle. The investigation of such occurrences, not subject to the pleasure principle, or not exclusively so, led Freud to the assumption of an instinct which operates in the direction of death, the aim of which is destruction. In his view it is of secondary importance whether this instinct is directed outward, sadistically, to the destruction of other life, or inward, masochistically, against the subject himself; in both cases it is the same instinct.

Freud assigns primary significance to the impulse toward self-destruction, the death instinct, and derives outwardly directed destruction from this primary death instinct. Other investigators, e.g., Jones[1] and Reich,[2] believe, however, that self-destructive human behavior can be derived from the turning inward of the destructive instinct originally directed outwardly; i.e., masochism from sadism, and not *vice versa*. This second view dispenses with the concept of a death

This article was originally published in German; the English translation was not done by the author.

[1] Ernest Jones, "The Origin and Structure of the Super-Ego," *Int. J. Psycho-Anal.*, VII (1926), 303.

[2] Wilhelm Reich, "The Need for Punishment and the Neurotic Process," *Int. J. Psycho-Anal.*, IX (1928), 227.

37

instinct and contents itself with the assumption of a destructive instinct which can also, in suitable circumstances, turn inward.

A great deal of psychic happening with a self-destructive purpose can certainly be explained—since the time when Freud grasped the meaning of melancholia—by aggressions directed inwardly which were originally intended for an external object and only later turned upon the ego itself. My present point of view will, perhaps, throw light upon some of the circumstances which tell in favor of a primary death instinct, apart from destructive tendencies which are *secondarily* turned within.

I should like to consider in the first place how far it is possible to understand the manifold expressions of the self-destructive or self-injuring trends in a purely psychological way, without any theoretical assumptions. These trends appear indeed in the most diverse manifestations. If we start from suicide, and go on to other phenomena in which self-destruction comes out less plainly, perhaps through mitigation by other trends, we can establish a scale of constantly-diminishing effectiveness of self-destruction. The trend shows particularly plainly and strongly in moral masochists and melancholiacs, whose life appears perpetually endangered by it. From a purely phenomenological point of view, a similar impression is produced by the criminal who is such from sense of guilt, and who intentionally gets himself into jail. The latter, however, already represents a special easygoing kind of moral masochist in whom the need for punishment clearly serves for the avoidance of pain. Both the action and the punishment free him from anxiety of conscience; they signify an unburdening for him, an economic gain in the pleasure-pain balance. In this obviously self-injuring behavior, the contribution of the pleasure principle, the striving for avoidance of pain, is clear. Naturally the pleasure principle manifests itself even more plainly where punishment or suffering are bound up with pleasure; as in the masochistic perversion. Here the punishment scene, or the infliction of the pain, appears to be only a comedy; in certain cases indeed it is only a precondition of the sexual act performed normally. In one case I suceeded in obtaining confirmation of Freud's supposition that the masochistic perversion represents an erotization of the same self-destructive tendencies which so seriously endanger the life of moral masochists.[3] The sexualization of these aggressions directed against the self makes them less dangerous, neutralizes their destructive efficacy.

Besides these strongly marked expressions of the destructive instinct directed against the self, we know from daily life of a wide range of human actions and behavior which consist in seeking out

[3] F. Alexander, *Psychoanalysis of the Total Personality*, New York: Nervous and Mental Diseases Publishing Co., 1930.

painful situations. Such behavior is indeed to be found in everybody almost all the time. We have learned from Freud of the development from the pleasure principle to the reality principle. The essence of this development consists in the ability not merely to endure instinctual tensions at times, but even to seek out directly situations of pain or suffering, in the interest of a future and assured pleasure gain, or of the avoidance of a greater pain. One is acting in this way, for example, when one submits to the painful operations of dental treatment, in order to save oneself still greater distress in the future.

It will, perhaps, be objected that I have no right to liken such a rational quest for pain in the obvious interest of the self to the self-destructive tendencies or processes previously described. The development from the pleasure principle to the reality principle is, of course, in the highest degree in the interest of the individual, while the procedures previously described are entirely against his interest. It is, however, easy to show that the development from the pleasure principle to the reality principle enables us to find the transition to the paradoxical self-injuring actions already described, and so to understand more readily that complicated relation between ego and superego, the need for punishment.

Freud has described the reality principle as the pleasure principle tested and improved by reality. It stands for an intelligently organized conduct of the instinctual life directed by the aim of obtaining the greatest possible ultimate sum of pleasure and the smallest possible sum of pain. The way in which this is achieved is that the ego, with the aid of its testing of reality, confronts with one another external facts and possibilities and instinctual demands. In this function the ego is partially a representative of reality, even though at bottom it may sympathize with the instinctual demands of the id. Under the pressure of a more powerful reality, it has had, willy-nilly, to identify itself in part with this, and now it demands in turn from the instinctual life due regard for this factor of paramount power. If then it voluntarily seeks out painful situations, it does so in the interest of a pleasure gain, or, at least, of lessened pain. The ego thus originates from the id as a differentiation product of the latter, through identification with external reality, but only for the purpose of thus securing a more complete satisfaction of instinctual demands. The differentiation of the superego from the ego, which comes later in the history of development, involves, however, a very similar process, an identification with a special part of reality: with social requirements. The relations of the superego to the ego constitute a parallel phenomenon to the relations of the ego to reality. Just as the ego arose from the id, in so far as the psychic apparatus, turning at least one of its parts toward external reality, acknowledged the distinctive characters of this, i.e., came to resemble it, so the superego arose out of the ego through identification with social demands.

It is, therefore, also not surprising if the ego applies the same methods in relation to the inner representative of the social demands, the superego, as it had learned to practice in relation to the external world. It gives in to the superego, where necessary, just as to external reality, and, if required, it takes suffering on itself in order that elsewhere it may thus be enabled to carry the instinctual demands through triumphantly. But upon the same principles rests the relation of the child to his educators, who behave to the child's instinctual demands in exactly the same way as impersonal reality. They inflict pain on the child if he does not obey, and reward him with pleasure prizes if he will make the needed instinctual renunciations. It is therefore only a matter of course that the behavior of the ego to the superego will conform to the same principles as are at the basis of its relations to external impersonal reality and to its educators.

The behavior of the ego to the superego is therefore in accordance with the *reality principle*. We can best study this behavior in the pathological states in which ego and superego are sharply opposed to one another, and in which the superego is like a foreign body within the ego. In such cases the ego must give way to the demands of its superego in exactly the same way as to external reality, and must subject itself to instinctual restrictions, and indeed even to direct suffering, in order to secure certain instinctual satisfactions. The remarkable principle of purchasing the right to instinctual gratification through suffering derives from the period of development from the pleasure principle to the reality principle. Here, and without as yet any moral rationalizations, the law is that pleasure is to be attained only through temporary endurance of pain. Reality in its indifference does not concern itself with our instinctual demands, and so we must take account of its characteristics. These characteristics are unfortunately only too often such that if we want to enjoy anything, it means a sacrifice, and this sacrifice consists always of pain. If the tourist wants to enjoy the fine view from a summit, he must first toil up perspiringly, and moreover he has to pack his knapsack full if he does not want to freeze on the top, nor to have to enjoy his view in a hungry state. And in the same way every enjoyment on this planet of ours is tied up to a heavily loaded knapsack. The ego has learned this proposition thoroughly and early enough never to be able to forget it again. It is only too understandable if the ego, in its struggle for pleasure gratifications, also keeps on offering to the curbing superego (that internalized piece of reality) suffering and renunciation in return for pleasure, as it learned to do throughout the development from the pleasure principle to the reality principle. The need for punishment would thus be an anthropomorphic form of the reality principle.

It is not to be wondered at if we have not immediately recognized the origin of the reality principle in this anthropomorphic or, I could say, criminal form, in which the punishment expiates the sin and entitles to new pleasure gratifications. One looks hopefully for some impressive situation of childhood which could be held responsible for this connection.

I do not believe, however, that this remarkable causal nexus of pleasure and pain can be explained by any one single situation, as for example by the situation of the infant during the period of sucking, which according to Rado's investigations would appear specially significant for melancholia. However important the experience may be that hunger is always followed by satisfaction, the affective connection that pleasure follows pain, and conversely pain pleasure, has a wider basis. It is supported by the entire development of the psychic apparatus from the pleasure principle to the reality principle. Indeed, this connection between pleasure and pain constitutes the foundation of the reality principle, which in turn is the foundation of ego formation. Precisely through the acceptance of this principle the ego has developed out of the id. From the moment of birth onward, the psychic apparatus is continually encountering the painful experience that the world is no longer shaped so exactly to its subjective demands as was the maternal womb. The sucking situation is perhaps still the most similar to the intra-uterine one. The more independent the child becomes, however, the more he learns that the way to pleasure leads through endurance, renunciation and suffering. While during the sucking period he only has to bear *renunciation* in the *passive* form of hunger, he learns later that he has often to seek out suffering *actively* in order to attain pleasure. And this active quest for suffering on tactical grounds, which often seems so paradoxical to us, is what is characteristic of the ego in its relations to reality and to the superego.[4] These relations, which I have already indicated in another place, are here set out in such detail because I have met with the reproach that I have indeed noted this deeply anchored character of the mental apparatus, the inability to bear pleasure without pain, but have failed to give any causal explanation of the fact.

We have been able to trace back to the pleasure principle a wide

---

[4] In an article of which the train of thought coincides at many points with mine, Ferenczi holds with justice that we must grant the psychic apparatus the ability to estimate quantities of pleasure and pain (a "mental computer"). Sandor Ferenczi, "The Problem of Acceptance of Unpleasant Ideas," *Int. J. Psycho-Anal.*, VII, 312.

range of psychic processes having an intention injurious to the self. We need not, therefore, at once think of masochistic gratifications or of the destructive action of the death instinct in the case of every action or piece of behavior of a human being which in a seemingly irrational way causes him physical suffering or some other form of pain, since we have seen that even the need for punishment stands in the service of pleasurable instinctual gratifications. It is a matter of indifference whether the suffering is undertaken in the interest of reality adaptation, or whether it serves to work off the inhibiting effect of the superego upon gratification. Our first question about such seemingly paradoxical self-injuring tendencies must always be whether they might not after all have such a rational meaning. It is not always easy, especially in the case of the complicated inner psychic relationships between ego and superego, to divine the economic meaning of the occurrences in question, i.e., to tell in which way the apparently self-injuring behavior of gratification of the need for punishment serves instinctual gratification after all, or permits the lessening of pain. I have tried to establish this point of view for the neuroses and to show that neurotic suffering is the general condition of neurotic instinctual gratification. The question is now how far one can get with such a point of view. The investigation of the neuroses has shown that neurotic suffering, apart from playing this economic part in the service of gratification, mostly signifies *in itself* a feminine masochistic or passive homosexual gratification. And the further a neurosis progresses, the more suffering becomes an end in itself. As Freud has put it, the ego strives to adapt itself to the neurosis.[5]

This readiness of the ego to turn the suffering at first forced upon it into a gratification and to exploit it masochistically must however give us pause. For a new principle thus enters into the otherwise so rational course of psychic events. In any case, the suffering, which has thus become an end in itself and a gratification, has changed its original part. If we see the climber drag his heavy load even up mountains where there is a well-provided restaurant at the top—and one may see many such climbers—we must tell ourselves that the original purpose of the knapsack has here undergone a material change. While it is dragged up a deserted mountain for the purpose of avoidance of pain, in the present case it serves apparently only to make the ascent harder. Ought we in such a case to think immediately of a manifestation, even if harmless, of the death instinct? Anyone who knows the mentality of the climber will soon guess that we are here dealing first of all with the gratification of the demands of the "tourist superego": to stand firmly on one's own feet, as independently as

[5] S. Freud, "Inhibition, Symptom and Anxiety," in *The Problem of Anxiety*, New York: Norton, 1936.

possible of all help, and to defy the forces of nature. The case is really one of a narcissistic gratification, with neglect of the primitive bodily narcissism of the ego in favor of the higher moral narcissism of the superego, a transfer of self-feeling from the ego to the superego, a displacement of accent within the psychic apparatus, not altogether unlike Freud's description of what happens in the case of humor.[6] Only, in humor the superego is cathected in its generous, superior, benevolent character, while in the above spartan behavior it is the hardness and discipline of the superego that makes itself felt. Even though the two procedures obey a similar principle formally, topographically and dynamically, their psychic contents stand in polar contrast. This spartan mentality drives one to despair by its stiffness, i.e., *lack of humor;* it constitutes in its content the direct antithesis to humor. It originates indeed from an opposite situation. While by means of the superior solace of humor one raises oneself above a desperate situation, the Spartan wantonly and needlessly goes in quest of a state of suffering. By means of humor one creates the semblance of a superiority not present in the situation, while the spartan-puritan attitude makes a show of superiority which is entirely superfluous in that situation. The heavily loaded tourist who pants up by the side of a mountain railway acts as if he were in a desert. Both reactions are paradoxical and not appropriate to the objective situation. In the one case, the seriousness of the situation is underrated, in the other it is taken more seriously than called for. In the case of humor one is laughing while waiting for the gallows, in the other one is beating a false alarm. In humor the life principle prevails in spite of the desperate situation, will not let itself be beaten and overcompensates for the external danger, while in the spartan reaction a nonexisting danger is simulated. Here the death principle makes its appearance, even if only in play.

I willingly admit that in the instance here considered we are concerned with the gratification of a superego demand of a narcissistic character. Obviously the sense of what he can do counts as more valuable for the climber than the bodily discomfort hurts him. He is acting according to the pleasure principle. The only question is why he is choosing this irrational mode of gratification which is bound up with the endurance of needless suffering. A masochistic compliance of the ego may be sufficient ground for the choice of this peculiar gratification. In this masochistic readiness of the ego we are already looking in vain for a rational factor; suffering has become an end in itself.

The operation of this factor which is independent of the rational

[6] S. Freud, "Humour," *Collected Papers*, New York: Basic Books, 1959, Vol. V, 215-221.

pleasure principle becomes still plainer when we discover our moun-
taineer engaged in perilous crag work, where he is exposing his life to
serious risks. The narcissistic gratification derived from one's powers
of achievement may indeed still play a certain part here, but nobody
will fail to see the impulse, completely independent of this narcissistic
gratification, to play with death, to expose one's life to serious risks.
Here we may conjecture something like a forepleasure in relation to
the death instinct.

It we take such observations as the remarkable attraction many
people feel to situations of danger, or the fact of the masochistic
readiness of the ego which even without any tactical purposes seeks
suffering as an end in itself, do these facts necessitate the assumption
of an endogenous death instinct? This much emerges unequivocally
from what has already been said, that the rational principle of undergoing suffering for the purpose of avoiding greater pain or gaining
pleasure, operates even in processes in which one would readily assume
a masochistic gratification or the self-destructive action of the death
instinct. It does not matter whether the case is one of obstacles in
external reality or of inhibitions of the superego; the ego is able to
take upon itself active restrictions and suffering in order the better to
overcome these inhibitions and obstacles. For these restrictions of the
instinctual life, the ego utilizes the aggressive or destructive forces
which have been defeated by the obstacles of reality and are now
turned back against the instinctual life of the self. It is necessary to
yield to the more powerful enemy at least at times or in certain places,
but the blind instincts have to have this tactical insight brought home
to them by force. The dynamic picture is not altered because the suffering which the ego could not help taking upon itself is eroticized secondarily, because the ego puts the best face on the matter and tries to
give a pleasurable turn to this arduous struggle. Freud's view as to
instinctual fusion makes possible the concept of an admixture of erotic
quantities even in destructive processes, and this should then explain
masochistic pleasure.[7]

However, the fact of masochistic pleasure alone does not prove the
endogenous character of these self-destructive processes. In any event,
these processes issue in part—and, in the opinion of many, altogether—
from the destructive strivings originally directed outward and then
turned back. We are indeed made somewhat dubious by those cases in
which that masochistic need of the ego plays an outstanding part, in
which one does not get the impression that the suffering is only sought
for tactical reasons, but rather that it seems itself to be a primary factor.
An unequivocal answer to this question as to the presence of a primary

[7] S. Freud, "The Economic Problem in Masochism," Collected Papers, New
York: Basic Books, 1959, Vol. II, 255-269.

death instinct cannot, however, be obtained by the method of direct clinical observation. Even if it were there, it would always be fused with destructive trends which have been turned back secondarily, and we have no qualitative diagnostic procedure available for distinguishing them. Perhaps, however, an economic consideration will bring us closer to the problem.

We picture the improved pleasure principle, the reality principle, in this way: that the psychic apparatus only takes upon itself the precise amount of self-restriction and suffering that is necessary, just as much as is absolutely essential for the attainment of instinctual gratifications. If the external pressure or resistance of reality against our instinctual gratifications has no internal ally in the shape of a death instinct, these externally imposed self-injuries should only amount to as much as the resistance of reality demands. If, however, there were present a constant endogenous factor such as the death instinct, then its effect would have to make itself apparent in a larger amount of externally imposed self-injuries than the reality principle demands. That would mean that human beings do not merely die of attrition against the resistance of reality, and that this attrition receives an endogenous support in the death instinct, which in turn again hails an ally in the resistance of reality, because this supports its deadly work. An ego governed exclusively by the pleasure principle and entirely dominated by the will to live, would have to behave like a government which under compulsion by an external, more powerful enemy, formally punishes certain offenders who have acted from purely nationalistic, patriotic motives, but not a whit more than is just necessary to preserve outward appearances. The moment, however, that the government goes further, it is already injuring itself. If we are negotiating with an opponent and objectively put ourselves in his place, we are betraying our own interests. If the ego pays greater regard to the demands of reality than is needed in the interest of instinctual gratification, it is betraying the interests of the id. If the ego turns its capacity for testing reality into an end in itself and does not merely apply it to the service of instinctual demands, if it looks for objective truth, it is giving up its original attachment to the instinctual life and placing itself on the side of reality. The philosophy of the young and vital American nation will not, from its pragmatic standpoint, acknowledge any other than a pragmatic truth, which is in the service of instinctual demands. Too much knowledge can be as harmful as too little knowledge. Too much knowledge means inhibition, and paralyzes the aggressive vigor of the id.

This play of forces between the life instinct and destruction can readily be watched in its process of development. Every scientific theory is to begin with a crude approximation, an inadequate provisional battle formation in the struggle for the domination of the facts. The facts and the critical negations representing them force us to supplement and complete the theory. And so scientific theory grows organically under the double pressure of the negations of the ego as representative of reality, and the affirmations of the id eager for conquest. If, however, the "no" came too early, if the investigator knew at the beginning the whole sum of the negative facts which become known in the end, he would never have had the courage to form a theory; he would have broken down in discouragement under the crushing weight of the facts. On the other hand, however, without his boldness we should never have known the facts which later turn against him. We are only too familiar with the two types of scientists who in their development deviate one-sidedly from the optimum instinctual fusion of the life and death instincts. We know the romantic, usually young, in whom affirmation is predominant, and the critic whom the harshness of the facts has already made despondently defeatist. Either alone could not survive in the struggle for the truth. The critic who seeks absolute truth independently of his own instinct to dominate reality is already offering death his hand. If this death pact does not succeed, he owes this solely to the errors of the romantics.

> *Nur der Irrtum ist das Leben,*
> *Und die Wahrheit ist der Tod.*[8]

But not only in its tests of reality does the ego show the tendency to ally itself in greater measure with the external world than would be called for in the interests of instinctual life. We can see that its socially adapted part, the superego, may in suitable circumstances be able to represent the interests of the community against those of the instinctual life up to the point of destruction of the life of the self. The question is naturally again whether this identification with social reality is stronger than is unconditionally demanded by the interest of the individual. It is, of course, obvious that as against the community, the individual is the weaker party who must put up with certain restrictions, and that when the superego demands these, it serves in the first place the interests of the individual. But if it proves that the superego, although it belongs to the psychic system, often in renegade fashion acts more in the interest of the community than in that of the individual and is ready to sacrifice the latter to the former, this seems to argue in favor of the presence of the death instinct.

The investigator's impetus towards the absolute truth and the self-sacrifice of an individual for the community point to the existence of the death instinct, even if only by way of circumstantial evidence. It

[8] "Only errors are life,/ And the truth is death."

can, however, easily be objected to this circumstantial evidence that in these cases the psychic apparatus is greatly impoverished in narcissistic libido through the strong object attachment to reality or to its fellow men, and therefore succumbs more readily to the hostile pressure of the external world and of its own aggressions turned back upon itself. It would then love the external world more than itself and that would lessen its power of resistance. That again would thus not be a proof of the death instinct. While eros in the form of sublimated object libido flows out into the external world and binds men to one another in a society, the inner arena of the psychic apparatus remains in far greater degree exposed to the effect of the destructive instinct which has been turned back, and this can now turn more strongly against the original instinctual demands and in such a roundabout way further the growth of social institutions. Whether this process is supported by a primary death instinct, which by its convergence with the resistance of the external world makes the individual more tractable for social demands, is again a question of relative quantities. We have to allow for four quantities: the *resistance of reality, the sum of the aggressions that have been turned back,* and the relative amounts of *narcissistic libido* and of *object libido.* The operation of the death impulse would only be proved beyond cavil if the equation between these four quantities failed to tally, if the self-destructive effect of the destructive forces checked and turned back by the resistance of the external world and by object attachments proved greater than the calculation led one to expect; and this too after taking into account the neutralizing effect of narcissistic libido. If it appears that in many cases men turn against themselves *in greater degree* than the pressure of reality and their love for the outer world demand, this will unequivocally testify to an endogenous self-destructive factor. Because of the impossibility of measuring psychological magnitudes, we begin to doubt whether we shall ever be able to solve the problem of the death instinct empirically.

What can, however, be affirmed is that two factors condition the turning of the destructive instinct against the self: the resistance of reality, and object love—the latter when anyone loves a part of reality more than himself, as the scientist loves truth. Through object love the loved portion of reality is received into the enlarged circle of narcissism, and thus the hostile, destructive aims of the introjected portion of reality succeed in finding their way into the psychic apparatus. The superego of the small boy which develops on the basis of a narcissistic identification with the father includes also the inhibitory characters of the father. If the son wishes to be like his father, he must likewise take over his inhibitory characters, his prohibitions. And so the child makes a thoroughly bad bargain: the advantages of the identification signify a promise for the future, "when he is grown up"; the inhibitions, however, enter into force immediately. Any identification with reality is a dangerous thing; one is taking into oneself the obstacles and even the hostile tendencies of reality, at the same time. In this way a tendency of the external world directed against the psychic apparatus is internalized.

In a similar fashion, however, the death instinct postulated by Freud arose already in the formation of the first living molecule, from the disintegrative nisus of those chemical combinations which were ingested and incorporated by the growing, living molecule. In its growth the living molecule is constantly taking in explosive combinations, charged with disintegrative tendencies, just as the psychic apparatus admits destructive tendencies from without by every act of identification. The living substance uses the energies originating from disintegration for further building up, but finally in death the disintegrative tendencies triumph, and the biological molecule dissolves into its elements. It certainly does not die solely by the external pressure of reality, it does so by the disintegrative nisus of its own constituents—just as the drop of liquid, which biologists are fond of regarding as the prototype or even as the precursor of the living molecule, breaks up not only under the operation of gravity, but because of its endogenous surface tension which strives for contraction of its surface.

I am aware that the psychological side of my demonstration only has the value of circumstantial evidence. For the disputable death instinct, and the destructive instinct broken against the resistance of reality and turned back, operate in the same direction, so that it is impossible to distinguish them. The only strict demonstration would, as stated, be to show that the self-destructive activities are often more intense than the resistance of reality and object love demand, that we cannot explain the intensity of every observed self-destructive process from the counterpressure of reality, without assuming an endogenous force acting in the same direction, viz., the death instinct. To put this in the language of psychology: it would have to be shown that the sadism of the superego, which is of course the internal representative of the dynamic pressure of reality upon the instinctual life, is not sufficient, without a primary masochism, to explain suicide and many other self-destructive processes. We have no scales in psychology, and never shall have any. If biology does not come to our help, we are dependent on estimates. It is true, however, that these estimates tell in favor of the existence of a death instinct.

When we watch the severe self-aggressions of the melancholiac, we can indeed often interpret them, in accordance with the causal pleasure-pain nexus here described, as *tactical preliminaries* for the outbreak of mania, as attempts to disarm the superego, but we must not forget that many melancholias are not punctuated by manic phases and that many melancholiacs actually carry out suicide. The so obstinate involutionary melancholias of advanced age likewise do not appear to us as such psychologically conditioned preliminaries for a manic phase. In these the picture is dominated by the enhanced effect in old age of the endogenous death instinct. Biological considerations, however, demand the assumption of a death instinct in an unequivocal way. From the beginning of life the disintegrative nisus of the elements of the highly complex biological molecule is active within it. It constitutes the core of the self-destructive tendencies upon which the later ones of the ego and the superego are deposited. It is then merely a question of convention from what point onward one talks of a death instinct.

The controversy about an endogenous death instinct reminds me of the discussions whether the downfall of the Austro-Hungarian monarchy was due to the pressure of the external enemy or the disintegrative trend of its many heterogeneous parts. Under the magnifying glass of sociology, the problem is easier to solve, and no one questions the answer that both factors were operative. The continuance of the psychic apparatus, exactly as of a state, is the more endangered the more complex it is, i.e., the more identifications it has carried through without organic union of the identification products.

Psychological experience shows that the superego, this last product of identification with reality, marks the greatest source of danger for the continuance of the psychic apparatus. It has not yet been organically absorbed into the ego, and, highly charged with the aggressions of the external world, it betrays forcibly that it belongs to external reality. The superego is the part of the psychic apparatus which displays least solidarity with it. But the ego, too, represents such an identification product, originating from the id by partial identification with reality, and in part taking into itself the resistance of reality against the id. This internalized resistance manifests itself as the primary masochism of the ego. Still deeper down there is the disintegrative trend of the body, active since the beginning of life.

The surface tension which arrests the growth of the drop of liquid and disrupts it, the decomposition of the biological molecule into its elements during the catabolic phase of metabolism, the self-destruction of the psychic apparatus, the breaking up of states and cultures: all these are expressions of the same regressive dynamic principle, which counteracts growth and life just as the momentum of inertia opposes the formation of higher dynamic units, and which we should like to forget or deny in its biological manifestation, namely the death instinct.

About Dreams with
Unpleasant Content

◄ 1930 ►

It has become almost a tradition in our science that new results and conceptions should be confronted with the theory of dreams which is without doubt the best founded portion of the whole psychoanalytic theory. I feel it as a gap in the psychoanalytic literature of recent years that new views of the ego have not yet been tested by the dream theory. Until lately we knew very little about the role of the ego in contributing material to dreams as a dream was considered a manifestation of repressed wishes. According to this view the function of the ego is only a distortion of the repressed psychic content which is incompatible with the conscious personality whereas the material of the dream is the creation of repressed wishes. The theory is that the latent meaning of the dream is the product of the repressed mental forces and that only the transformation of this despised latent content into the harmless manifest dream is due to the repressing ego which, however, does not itself contribute to the latent meaning of dreams. Nevertheless Freud suggests, not, to be sure, in his book, *Interpretation of Dreams,* but in the later additional chapters on dream interpretation—that in the formation of dreams with unpleasant content, for example of so-called punishment dreams the ego may participate to a larger extent than in other kinds.

Dreams with unpleasant content are often in apparent contradiction to the wish fulfillment theory of dreaming. In many cases, however, it is easy to show that behind the manifest unpleasant content there is hidden a repressed wish. Since we know the important role of self-punishing tendencies in mental life, there is no difficulty in understanding many unpleasant dreams as fulfillments of

This article was originally published in German; the English translation was not done by the author.

such tendencies and these punishment dreams are very instructive for the study of the exact nature of self-destructive tendencies. The general conception, however, is that in dreams the pleasure principle has a much wider influence than in the mental processes of the day and that the dream is the domain of wishes which reality and our inhibitions hinder in their realization. Therefore, it is hard to imagine that in this domain of wish fulfillments the inhibiting and restricting mental forces can play a creative role. We have learned that these repressing forces are merely disturbing factors responsible only for the distorted representation of genuine wishes. Yet it seems that we have underestimated the dynamic possibilities of the socially adjusted part of personality and that we have also underestimated the degree to which this part—I mean the superego—has become an organic part of the mental apparatus. We have always known that not even in dreams can we escape from the inhibiting influence of the superego but what I want to show you now is that the superego has not only a distorting function in dreams but is also able to create dreams as are the repressed tendencies of the id.

In the system of total personality the superego lives its own life, having tendencies of its own, which if inhibited in their satisfaction may disturb the sleep as well as repressed asocial tendencies do. Thus we can speak of dammed-up tendencies of conscience as well as of a dammed-up libido.

May I bring you a simple example to illustrate these facts.

Probably everyone of you has had as a schoolboy a typical kind of dream which Freud assigns to the class of "comfort dreams." One has to go to school early in the morning and after being awakened one decides to remain in bed for some minutes longer, then one falls asleep again and in dream one sees himself in the school room in which the lesson is just beginning. Freud calls these kinds of dreams "comfort dreams" and assumes that they arise on the same principle as thirst dreams and urination dreams. In the latter an organic need such as thirst or the tension of the bladder disturbs the sleep and the dream has the function of protecting the sleep through a hallucinatory satisfaction of the disturbing needs. In the school dream not an organic need but the sense of duty to get up and to go into the school is the factor which disturbs sleep. This sense of duty is, however, not a repressed wish at all; on the contrary it is a pronounced social motive, a typical case of a demand of the superego. This dream protects the sleep through a hallucinatory fulfillment of a disagreeable duty or on other words of a demand of conscience.

This example alone would be sufficient to prove that conscience tensions may create dreams as well as repressed or unsatisfied wishes.

Nevertheless I should like to cite two more complicated examples.

The first dream I am going to describe was reported during a psychoanalytic treatment by a young business man, a hypochondriac, who lost his money during the inflation in Germany and at the time of his dream was just on the way to re-establishing himself. To understand the dream it is necessary to know his actual circumstances. After his financial breakdown his older brother helped him and in the weeks preceding the dream he was in a difficult conflict with his conscience. He played with the idea of buying a new motor car since he had to sell his own beautiful car when he lost his money. The conflict in him was caused by the fact that his brother had lent him money for business investments and not for the purpose of buying a new car. Finally the devil gained the upper hand and he bought a small car. Just on the day following the dream he planned to make his first trip in it with his wife and on the night preceding the excursion he had the following dream:

"I am driving in my wonderful big white car which I owned before my breakdown. My wife is with me; we are just passing the market place of a small provincial town and we have to drive slowly. I hear people in the market place speaking about me, they point with fingers at me saying: 'That is the profiteer, Mr. B.' It was a terrible experience."

He woke up in anxiety bathed in cold perspiration. The first feeling he had after waking up was the intense relief that it was only a dream and next came the thought of the planned motor car trip with a pronounced pleasure which he expressed in the following way: "How silly this dream was since tomorrow I am going for a drive anyway but in my small new car."

In the further associations the patient described his feelings toward his older brother and we succeeded in tracing the deeper sources of his sense of guilt connected with the motor car. It became evident that this was a reaction to the repressed envy he felt toward his successful brother who owned a beautiful and powerful car. The car was but a symbol of everything for which he envied his brother, that is, his abilities, money, success with women, etc.

This dream is a clear case of a punishment dream and was produced merely by the claims of his conscience. He went to sleep with an intense sense of guilt provoked through the planned excursion which he was going to make in the new car, that is in the symbol of his negative affects toward his brother. The dream served to relieve this sense of guilt through putting him in a painful situation. While the tension of repressed wishes can be relieved through hallucinatory pleasurable satisfactions, the demands of the conscience can only be fulfilled by punishment, by suffering or by sacrifice. The advantage the dreamer had from his dream was that he quieted his conscience in a fairly comfortable way. In his dream he lived in the past and fantasied a painful situation as a profiteer which was no longer the case with him.

Besides that, he succeeded in his dream in exchanging the severe sense of guilt he felt toward his brother for another but milder conflict, that is, with the social guilt feeling of a profiteer which he had had in the period of inflation on account of making much money in an easy but somewhat disreputable way.

To sum up: The dream was an attempt to get rid of his sense of guilt in the easiest possible way. He had to suffer, that was unavoidable, for his conscience was stirred up by the purchase of the motor car and the tendency of the dream was to reduce the necessary self-punishment as much as possible. The influence of the pleasure principle in such a mental situation can only be toward the diminishing of unavoidable psychic pain. As a matter of fact his dream succeeded in restoring his disturbed mental balance so that he could make his excursion the next day with an easy conscience, having paid the price for it by the painful experiences of the preceding night.

Another dream may serve to elucidate even more the purpose which unpleasant dreams have of relieving conscience and thus permitting sleep. It was dreamed by a puritanical young married man in a period of his analysis in which he began to become aware of his repressed extramarital wishes. He had lived since his marriage in the belief that no woman except his wife existed for him and denied even the possibility of extramarital wishes. This was the dream:

It seemed that I was rather a small boy and that I and a small girl of the same age were about to get into bed. I believe that the bed was the same one in which I used to sleep about that age. A man was already lying in the bed. As I put my right foot up to the bed in preparation to get in the man pointed to my toes which were rather dirty and I felt ashamed that I did not wash them. My foot then was its present size rather than that of a small boy.

He associated to the dream at first an advertisement for cornplasters which consisted of a foot with small electric lights in the toes to represent the corns. There was also a hand pointing to one of them. He saw this cornplaster advertisement on the street the day preceding the dream. The small girl reminded him of a girl cousin with whom he had his first puppy love affair in his childhood. They kissed and hugged and on one occasion practiced mutual exhibition. Another girl stood on guard to warn them if anyone should approach.

As already mentioned the patient dreamed this dream at a time when he began to recognize his extramarital wishes which until that time he had succeeded in repressing. These wishes, brought nearer to consciousness, provoked a conscience reaction that is a fear. He also remembered that the evening before on going home late he was accosted by prostitutes. He passed the same corner almost every night but this was the first time that he had been accosted. It is easy to assume that he was accosted because this was the first time that he had looked at the women and that this gave them the courage to address him. He had this dream at a time when the conflict between his puritanical ideals and his repressed extramarital wishes was stronger than ever. In the dream he imagined an old forbidden sexual situation, namely, the first one of his life instead of his present one. He was in a similar mood when he went to bed as he was in his childhood when he had his first sexual experience with his cousin for which he felt guilty. He did in his dream something similar to the man with the motor car dream, namely, he substituted a conflict of the past for his present conflict situation.

The second purpose of the dream consists in the replacement of an expected severe punishment of unknown character by a trifle. The man in the bed points to the dirty toes and the boy is ashamed that he did not wash them. In the dream he is just about to commit a forbidden sexual act with the girl, but he was not rebuked for this offense but for a much smaller sin, that is, of having dirty toes. Knowing the symbolic meaning of toes we understand that the menacing finger pointing to his toes refers to the genitals which he replaced by the toe. Although this dream was a very unpleasant one connected with fear and shame, it nevertheless saved him from a much worse fear of being attacked in his genitals on account of his forbidden sexual wishes.

The tendency of the dream was to comfort himself by saying that his aroused extramarital wishes have no greater significance than that of having dirty toes. The dream was produced by the sense of guilt which he had on going to sleep after having met the prostitutes. Thus guilty feeling was a repetition of similar fears of his childhood, namely the fear of castration, and he succeeded through the dream in substituting for this fear a milder form of an unpleasant affect, namely the shame of being dirty. Both of these unpleasant dreams had the tendency to save the sleeper from a fear reaction. The conscience which is aroused demands like a hungry divinity his rights and the best the dreamer can do with his unexpiable conscience is to give it the cheapest possible satisfaction.

I hope that I have succeeded in proving that not only repressed wishes but also the socially adjusted part of the personality, that is, our normal feelings, are able to produce dreams which are in a larger sense wish fulfillments, although not fulfillments of asocial repressed wishes but of the claims of conscience. Guilt feelings or the sense of duty disturb the sleep as well as any genuine wish, which I could demonstrate in the simplest way by the school dream.

To do justice to this fact we have to choose the most general of the Freudian formulations, namely that the dream is an attempt to protect sleep by the aid of hallucinatory processes which are suitable to relieve disturbing tensions. We have to add, however, that these tensions may have quite different sources such as organic stimuli, unfulfilled or repressed genuine wishes as well as the claims of conscience.

These considerations may corroborate the conception which I tried to work out in another place, that the socially adjusted part of our personality, the superego, has to be considered as an organically assimilated part of the mental apparatus with dynamic effects similar to those of the original, unadjusted impulses of the id.

The Neurotic Character

◄ 1930 ►

The tendency which psychoanalysis has been showing of late is that of laying emphasis upon the patient's personality as a whole. This newer orientation presents the fundamental condition for understanding or therapeutically influencing that group of people whose difficulties manifest themselves, not in the form of a circumscribed set of symptoms, but in the form of a typical behavior pattern which is clearly a deviation from the normal. In contradistinction to true neurotics who squander their energy in futile inactivity, these individuals live active and eventful lives; the essential characteristic of neurosis, the autoplastic mode of instinct gratification, is often entirely absent. Another feature of neurosis, which since Freud pointed it out we have learned to regard as fundamental, is substitutive gratification in the form of a symptom of those impulses which are condemned by the ego. This feature is totally absent in the group of individuals under consideration. Instead they live out their impulses, many of their tendencies are asocial and foreign to the ego, and yet they cannot be considered true criminals. It is precisely because one part of such an individual's personality continues to sit in judgment upon the other, the manifestations of which it is too weak to control, that his total personality is easily differentiated from the more homogeneous, unified and antisocial personality of the criminal. The singular and only apparently irrational drive to self-destruction met with in such people indicates rather definitely the existence of inner self-condemnation. Thus one characteristic of neurosis, the presence of a mental conflict, or more explicitly, of an unconscious battle between two conflicting parts of the personality, is clearly discernible in this group. We deal here with a definite characteristic which betrays the splitting of the personality in two parts; one giving in to its impulses and the other reacting upon it in a moral,

This article was originally published in German; the English translation was not done by the author.

even overmoral way, doing this not only by means of restraining the ego, but also by means of punishing it. It is this characteristic that justifies us in placing such individuals in the class of pathological people.

We owe to psychoanalysis the fact that we are now able to approach the crude asocial behavior of these people without the usual evaluative, i.e., condemnatory attitude, but with a sense of medical understanding to which we are accustomed in dealing with neurotic or organic symptoms. Their conduct arises from unconscious motives which are not directly accessible to their conscious personality. This fact justifies the contention that in principle such an individual is afflicted with his conduct in the same sense that the man who has a neurotic or an organic complaint is afflicted with his symptoms. Admonition, encouragement or punishment coming from the environment is as useless as his own resolution, "I am beginning a new life tomorrow"; and his resolution is as useless as would be the attempt to cure oneself of diabetes by one's own will power. The impossibility of overcoming the tendency to act out neurotic impulses by a conscious effort of will, even when the tendency is condemned by the individual himself, is the characteristic which it has in common with organic and neurotic conditions. At any rate the path which leads from organic symptoms to antisocial or even irrational attitudes to life is rather long. This is easily explained, even though psychoanalysis and medicine are not as yet unified into one whole. The scientific study of such individuals is comparatively new even in psychoanalysis. It is therefore not at all surprising that this type of people are not recognized from the very beginning as pathological; depending on their respective ages, they are turned over to the custody of the reformatory or the judge rather than to that of the physician. We are still accustomed to consider disease as something independent of the conscious will of the individual, as a *vis major* which the sick person must endure. On the other hand, we are also accustomed to hold the personality of the individual accountable for all his apparently conscious acts, making an exception only for those acts which are performed in a state of clouded consciousness (as, for instance, in paragraph 51 of the German Criminal Code). It is difficult to hold a man responsible for his gastric ulcer; it is much easier, as the experience in the war showed us, to hold him responsible for his hysterical symptom; and still easier to blame a man for his irresponsibility, his gambling, and his incapacity to engage in serious work. To have the right to consider such people as pathological, we should have to extend and redefine considerably our concept of disease. One might regret that in doing this one places the organically sick in rather bad company.

From the structural-dynamic point of view, such an irrational style of life, dominated as it is by unconscious motives, stands nearest to the class of obsessional acts in which the underlying impulse no longer appears in the form of wholly nonsensical symbolic operations, but rather simulates rational acts. Thus it resembles kleptomanic behavior, where the theft has a highly subjective and richly symbolic meaning, and is not carried out for the rational purpose of mere acquisition, as might first appear. In the obsessional neuroses an impulse which is alien to the conscious personality appears to the conscious like a foreign body; in such borderline cases as kleptomania the impulse breaks through and finds expression in conduct. In the cases with which we are dealing, the repressed tendencies are invariably carried out, even though in the process of motor expression they appear in a modified form. These tendencies stream into the ego, and permeate it much more thoroughly than the circumscribed compulsive acts; they influence the total behavior of the person. At times they master the ego to such an extent that a conscious conflict and insight into one's illness can be totally absent. Yet the never-failing tendency to self-punishment is present in such individuals, an unconscious conflict and an unconscious rejection of their drives is unmistakable. Those who fail to show this unconscious moral reaction will not be spoken of here as neurotics, but as criminals or some other social misfits.

The great medico-legal importance of the cases in question is at once apparent. A large proportion of such individuals, neurotically driven by unconscious motives, now to commit a transgression, then to seek punishment, sooner or later fall foul of the law. Their unmistakable differentiation from true criminals, with whom they are almost invariably confused in current judicial practice, is one of the most important tasks of psychoanalysis, a task the practical fulfillment of which will only become possible when psychoanalysis finds its way into the courts. If neurotic criminals are to benefit from enlightened judicial understanding, the whole question of responsibility must be reconsidered on the basis of an entirely new set of principles, for to this day unconscious motives are beyond judicial cognizance. Only the recognition of unconscious motives in a given crime will enable the law to rid itself of its present day spirit. Some modern trials are reminiscent of the spirit of the witch trials; this stands out with particular clarity when a transgressor, driven by unconscious impulses, is subjected by the judge and prosecuting attorney to the bombardment of a cross examination which attempts to insinuate a host of conscious motivations.

Some years ago I made an attempt to delimit nosologically this group of pathological characters. Following Freud's terminology, who described some typical cases in his "Some Character Types Met With in Psycho-analytic Work," I proposed to designate them as neurotic characters. This designation was intended to convey the idea that the neurotic element manifested itself in these individuals not so much in the form of circumscribed symptoms as in their characters—that is to say, it permeates the patient's personality and thus influences his total behavior. The tragedies that lurk behind the theatrical exaggerations of the hysteric, the wild excesses of brutality and remorse which are related in the seemingly ridiculous symbolism of the obsessional neurotic, and which read like the weirdest detective story to him who can translate them—all are brought to dramatic expression by the neurotic character in real life. Neurotic characters succeed in actualizing their world of fantasy, despite the fact that most of them by so doing bring disaster upon themselves.

In addition to the forensic significance of this group, I should like to point out two more reasons which justify our interest in this subject. The first is the purely practical side, which concerns psychoanalytic therapy, for a large proportion of our patients belong to this category. The second reason which prompts my return to the subject is the impression, which harmonizes entirely with that expressed by Glover in his stimulating paper, "Einige Probleme der psychoanalytischen Charakterologie," that the nosological delimitation of these cases, in spite of valuable contributions, has not yet been made with sufficient clarity.

My statement about the high frequency of these individuals will be amply substantiated when we come to the clinical description of cases, and therefore I shall first devote a few words to the problem of classification.

When I suggested the importance of distinguishing from the symptom neuroses those individuals whose lives, when viewed as a whole, reveal a typical pattern which is determined by neurotic motives, that is, by motives which are foreign to the ego and unconscious, I did so under the influence of Freud's description of neurotic character types, and of his masterly formulation in *Beyond the Pleasure Principle* of the unconscious determination of neurotic careers, which I had had opportunities to appreciate in the course of my clinical practice. Valuable contributions to the subject have subsequently appeared, such as Aichhorn's book *Wayward Youth*, which familiarizes us with the social and psychological circumstances out of which a large proportion of such characters come. Abraham furnished us with an exemplary delineation of the classical case of an impostor. Only Reich, in his volume on *The Instinctual Character* has made an attempt to make a nosological demarcation. His starting point, in agreement with my own, is the very pertinent formulation of Freud's, that there appears in these cases, in the place of autoplastic symptom formation, the alloplastic acting-out of neurotic impulses. Reich, however, takes the concept of neurotic acting-out in another and far more general sense than Freud gives to it in *Beyond the Pleasure Principle*. What we find, then, in Reich's case histories are isolated and unsublimated manifestations of instinct, such as extraordinary forms of masturbation. But in my opinion these direct and unsublimated instinctual expressions are precisely the ones which are the best calculated to prevent the development of the dynamic pattern which is characteristic of the neurotic character. Whenever tendencies which are incompatible with reality are short-circuited into masturbation, or whenever a patient can gratify his thirst for self-punishment by accentuating the masochistic component in masturbation, which was true of one of Reich's women patients, the enormous tension produced by these drives is abolished, and their dynamic capacity to irradiate the whole life pattern is lost. The acting-out of neurotic impulses in such a form as masturbation is far more autoplastic than the acting-out of neurotic impulses in life; and in this respect it stands close to the neurotic symptom, which it resembles in that it is a private affair of the patient's with which the people around him may be wholly unconcerned. The implicating of the environment in the gratification of neurotic impulses, however, is an especially typical characteristic of the group which I have in mind, as Glover quite correctly emphasized. Excessive masturbation is notoriously frequent among all pathological individuals who are conspicuously indifferent to what goes on in the outer world, a group of which the obsessional neurotic may be taken as representative. Reich's case histories show a congeries of neurotic symptoms, psychotic symptoms and perversions, which, as he himself says, is a grotesque symptomatology. Now the case history of a neurotic character reads like a novel with plenty of action, for the most characteristic trait in the behavior of such individuals is eventful action. I am not disposed to question the fact that certain isolated expressions of unsublimated drives play a far more important role with some neurotics than with others, and that it is perhaps possible to classify certain cases from this point of view. However, the principle which lends coherence to Reich's cases has not been made sufficiently clear, and it applies, as well, to another type of individual than Freud had in mind in *Beyond the Pleasure Principle*. Reich's cases are of a different order than the "criminal from a sense of guilt," or the person who is destined to collapse with success, or the group whose clinical definition I am seeking to establish. If Glover detects contradictions in our conceptions, I believe this is attributable to the fact that Reich called his collection of quite distinctive cases the "impulse-ridden characters," which was an expression I used as a synonym for the neurotic character in my first formulation.

I shall attempt to sketch a unified clinical picture of this group, holding fast to the main outlines and avoiding structural subtleties, for the sake of bringing into the foreground certain clear principles upon which definite diagnosis must depend. My theoretical discussion will be confined to the major dynamic and structural relationships.

Who, then, are the neurotic characters? I refer to those cases of neuroses without symptoms whose pathological nature the trained psychoanalytic glance is readily able to detect, but for which there is no place in accepted nosological categories. I do not refer to those individuals whom we are accustomed to call obsessional neurotic characters, but who on closer scrutiny so frequently turn out to be true obsessional neurotics whose symptoms have been especially well disguised and rationalized. Nor do I refer to those individuals whose compulsive impulses are so adequately gratified in religious ceremony or bureaucratic routine that they are not driven to invent their own symptoms. Unquestionably these groups offer a transition to the one with which I am concerned, but none of the classical cases is found among them. Such neurotic types often succeed in isolating their unacceptable impulses and their drive for self-punishment from the general pattern of their lives, and in confining them to harmless expression in a restricted sphere. I do refer to those individuals whose lives are full of dramatic action, to whom something is always happening, as if they were literally driven by the demonic compulsion which Freud once metaphorically imputed to them. These are the individuals whose whole lives can be interpreted as clearly as an isolated neurotic symptom, for every transformation and permutation remains the unmistakable manifestation of the same unconscious conflict. Here is where the adventurers belong whose manifold activities give expression to an underlying revolt against public authority. They always manage to be punished unjustifiably, from their highly subjective point of view, by the father surrogate, the State, and thus to put the State in the wrong.

A representative of this group, whose acquaintance I owe to Herr Staub, his lawyer, by whom I was consulted in his preparation of the defense, had no medical degree, but learned surgery so well that he was made an assistant in a surgical clinic. He performed operations and wrote scientific articles until he was exposed and indicted. No mere symptom can yield a scintilla of the satisfaction which this degree-less though by no means ignorant physician experienced when, in the midst of his legal difficulties, he was consulted by a loyal woman patient, who even insisted that he should operate upon her. He experienced the same glow of satisfaction when he was arrested for the theft of some scientific books and of a few microscope parts, all trifling objects which he could easily have obtained legitimately. He had what he wanted. He had stolen in the interest of scientific research, and he had been arrested for it. He had triumphantly demonstrated to himself the absurdity of a criminal code under which such a thing could happen.

But this triumph had not come to him so easily. Since his theft of the books was discovered through what was obviously an intentional clumsiness on his part, the police wanted to let him go. But he proceeded to confess the microscope theft, which had not been discovered and about which no questions had been asked, so it was necessary to hold him. In general, it is safe to say that this particular kind of a neurotic delinquent has an easy time of it. The guardians of the law, not excluding the medical experts, are only too easily taken in by their provocative conduct, which, of course, originates in the unconscious.

Another impostor, who came from the Jewish quarter of a great metropolitan center, seemed to have made it his goal in life to make another authority, in this instance, the Church, ridiculous. He was baptized and became a Catholic priest, and compromised himself, and, of course, the Church, in an array of strange scandals. His favorite amusement was to flout his priestly garb before new acquaintances in a gambling hall or a questionable nightclub, where he flagrantly misconducted himself. Finally, after he had made himself absolutely impossible in his own country and in his own denomination, he succeeded in obtaining a high ecclesiastical office abroad. Just how and just when he will disgrace his calling this time only the future can tell.

The obsessional neurotic who suffers from a repressed father hatred of the same intensity discharges his affect in fantasies or in nonsensical compulsive ceremonies, but this priestly adventurer succeeded in impressing his superiority upon one of the greatest powers in the world, the Catholic Church. But even his pleasure is not unalloyed. Every time he strikes out against authority, the blow recoils upon his own head. He plays fast and loose with his own reputation, which he never hesitates to sacrifice if only he can thereby injure the father imago.

In these anti-individualistic times, such modern Casanovas, who dramatize themselves in the process of traducing State, Church and constituted authority in any shape and form, are few and far between. They are anachronisms today. They belong in the leaden chambers of the Doge's palace rather than in the drab cells of a penitentiary. Even as our prisons have grown prosaic, the neurotic character of our modern adventurer has lost its color. Today he is a political doctrinaire, safely regimented within a political party. Or more often he appears in the business world as a captain of industry and an unscrupulous profiteer who is remorselessly driven by the same self-destructive impulse which moved his more heroic predecessors. The alternating phases of rise and abrupt collapse, which characterize the doings of these individuals in the financial world, reveal the aggressive and self-destructive tendencies which run along together. I have had occasion in the course of an analysis of a neurotic character extending over some years to observe these unconsciously determined oscillations, which conformed to the manic-depressive mechanism. The patient's cleverly timed losses gave precisely the manic release which was indispensable to his next successful flight.

More common and perhaps better known to the psychoanalyst are those neurotic characters who, in contrast to the foregoing, act out their neurotic impulses in their love relationships. I want, however, to warn in advance against attempting to draw a sharp line of demarcation between neurotic characters whose impulses are chiefly expressed in social life and those whose main outlet is in love relationships. My impression is that neurotic conduct in one sphere is usually associated with disturbances in the other, although it is not to be denied that in many cases the one or the other is more conspicuous. It is unnecessary to depict the typical representative of this group in detail. The Don Juan types who are in hot pursuit of eternally unattainable ideals are as familiar to the psychoanalyst as are the slaves, tinged with masochism, whose need for punishment is not confined to a definite masochistic perversion, but is rather woven into the warp and woof of their whole erotic life. Self-sacrifice on behalf of a woman whom they serve with unswerving devotion is for them as much a prerequisite of love and potency as are the more tangible forms of punishment for the true masochists.

More complicated and perhaps more rare are the cases of those who are attached to two women at the same time, and who find it impossible to choose between them. I want to dwell a little on the structure of such a case, for it shows with particular distinctness the close connection between occupational and intimate life to which allusion has been made.

In this man I found a splitting in the fundamental impulses, similar to that which we see in the obsessional neuroses, in which passively feminine demands were present alongside aggressively masculine drives. The passive tendencies were sternly repressed, and instead of passive homosexuality there appeared, as a result of a well-known regressive process, a pronounced oral fixation on the wife, who had to take over the role of the mother completely. However, the oral fixation absorbed the homosexual trends. As a reaction against the infantile-feminine desires, one could see a tremendously exaggerated aggressive masculine drive. This conflict pervaded his whole personality. Energetic and ruthless in his professional life, always striving for independence and a position of leadership, he was at the same time a lover of nature, an amateur in music, with a sentimental penchant for beauty and perfection of form. With almost clairvoyant power he represented himself in a dream *as a giant automobile of incalculable horsepower, whose body, however, was a light French coach of the rococo period.*

He vacillated continually between the two incompatible and reciprocally influencing tendencies of his personality. The major problem of his existence was to satisfy his passive desires without doing violence to his ideal of masculinity. In business he was active, avid of responsibility, and readily shouldered every difficulty; but in the atmosphere of his home he leaned on his wife in a state of total child-like irresponsibility. His philosophy ran like this: "The demands that business make on me are so heavy that I must have a perfectly indulgent wife." His wife was supposed to anticipate his wishes, and he regarded it as the greatest insult when he had to express a desire in words. In business, however, he carried a sportsmanlike share of the load. This side of his nature was disclosed in a very simple dream. *He was pushing a needle through a thick piece of pasteboard, and kept demanding new layers. He succeeded in penetrating very thick layers.* This was what he was actually like in business, and the dream shows as clearly as possible that his business life was a sublimation of his aggressively tinged sexual drives. Masculinity was a point of honor for him. Only when he had indulged the masculine component of his nature sufficiently, did it become permissible for him to live out the feminine-infantile tendency. But the moment he had satisfied a feminine desire, he had wounded his masculine narcissism, and was scourged into activity once more. This equilibrium between activity in business and infantile-feminine passivity in marriage was upset when he entered a concern where, for the first time in his life, his soaring ambitions were checked. The head of the enterprise, a very able man, knew how to keep him in hand and turn his abilities to his own ends. For one who had struggled his whole life against unconscious passive homosexuality, it was unbearable to be subordinated to a leader. As the patient's active sexual tendencies were no longer gratified on the sublimated level, they broke through into the specifically sexual sphere. Thwarted by his superior, he was obliged to give double proof of his capacity. He not only committed adultery, but in taking the wife of another, he committed the Oedipus crime. From then on he was chained to both women. To keep his mistress became a point of honor. The mistress became the object of his actively masculine desires, and the wife was the object of his passive homosexuality. It was impossible to dispense with either woman without losing his equilibrium. Just as the equilibrium was formerly maintained between his wife and his business, so now he distributed these two conflicting tendencies between the two women.

We were successful in tracing this remarkable cleavage in his personality back to his earliest childhood. At the age of four he was already the same individual. Memories from the fourth year showed that he still drank milk from a bottle and stubbornly refused to be weaned from it. *But*—and he told me this recollection with the same accentuated "but"—he was at the same time an unusually alert and independent youngster who rode a bicycle out on the public highway all by himself. At the age of four this individual who drank milk from a bottle and rode a bicycle alone exhibits precisely the same antithesis, and with exactly the same psychological interconnection, as he showed as an adult who combined infantile dependence upon his wife with unbridled impetuosity in business. It is not difficult to reconstruct his childhood situation. The stubborn youngster who refuses to give up his bottle is teased by everybody, including parents and elder brothers, and twitted as a "baby." As a reaction to this he excels every one in keenness and self-reliance, thus procuring for himself the right to remain infantile in one particular, and to indulge his oral craving to his heart's content. So in spite of this infantile retardation, he was able to overcome his inferiority feelings, and to salve his masculine narcissism. And this solution remained the prototype for his whole life. The role of the bottle was later taken over by the wife, whom he often really treated like an inanimate object made expressly to minister to his whims; while his business and later his mistress were the successors to the bicycle, by means of which he vindicated to himself and the world his claims to independence and masculinity.

Unfortunately, I cannot go into the interesting details of the deeper analysis, which showed how the early childhood supervision of his infantile masturbation favored the oral fixation through the castration fear which it aroused, and how this oral fixation came into collision with the constitutionally strong masculine genitality, and laid the foundation for a remarkable cleavage in character formation.

In an obsessional neurotic these incompatible tendencies would have produced a number of passive and active symptoms. In an hysteric such passive oral demands might have led to an array of gastric symptoms covering pregnancy fantasies. Such symptoms played a role, though a subordinate one, also in this case, and during the treatment they assumed much larger proportions as the progress of analytic insight substantially restricted the acting-out of neurotic tendencies in the real world. This is not unlike the experience in a case which I reported several years ago. In neither of these cases did the conflicting tendencies lead to the formation of neurotic symptoms, for they were able to come to full fruition in the principal spheres of real life, in marriage and in business. In the present case the neurotic splitting in the personality found expression in the life pattern.

From all that has gone before, I believe that we have a working conception of the cases which I call the "neurotic characters." Now that the main outlines of the clinical picture are clear, I should like to make more detailed theoretical distinctions between these cases and other kinds of pathological material.

Our best starting point is the theory of the neurotic symptom. At the Salzburg Psycho-Analytical Congress I undertook to formulate three universally valid characteristics of neurotic symptoms, which I still consider sound. The neurotic symptom is first, regressive in nature; secondly, it is autoplastic, and thirdly, its latent content is rejected by the ego. It is regressive because it is continually reaching back for infantile objects and methods of instinctual gratification, which is precisely why it is rejected by that portion of the ego which has adapted itself to the demands of reality. This rejection expresses itself in the disguise of the meaning of the drive, in the reactive appearance of the need for self-punishment, which is an indispensable condition of all neurotic gratification, and in the autoplastic type of instinctual gratification. Gratification is restricted to the world of fantasy.

Regression to an earlier level of instinctual gratification appears throughout the whole range of psychopathological phenomena, for this is the only mode of expression for those impulses which are not adapted to reality. Either one or both of the other two characteristics of the neurotic symptom, autoplasticity and rejection by the ego, may be absent in regressive behavior. In such cases we are dealing with different psychopathological expressions. If, for example, autoplasticity is absent, though the other two characteristics, rejection by the ego and regression, are present, we are dealing with a neurotic character. The regressive and rejected impulses are not gratified by means of autoplastic symptom formation, but by means of alloplastic activity which influences the relation of the individual to the environment. Even in those cases where there is no conscious protest against an impulse, its rejection by the ego is evidenced by the never failing reaction of a guilty conscience, and by the modified and relatively milder form in which the unconscious goals are arrived at. So in the place of hostility against the father, there may be bitter hatred of the State. The self-injuring component is indispensable to the gratification of the fundamental impulses of the neurotic character, just as the suffering is indispensable to the gratification of the impulses of the neurotic who produces symptoms.

Let us consider another possibility. The rejection by the ego failed; autoplasticity and regression are present, however. We are then dealing with a psychosis. In other words, the regressive tendencies find undisguised expression. The defensive apparatus of the ego, such as disgust and sympathy, and the reality testing are in abeyance. The ego is helpless against the onslaught of impulses from the id. Only the autoplasticity betrays the presence of a conflict. The incomprehensibility of the symptoms is due to the particular depth of the regression and not to concealment. We merely deal with a primitive language of the instincts which the adult has long since unlearned. The autoplasticity is also a partial consequence of deep regression. The intrauterine wish is hardly susceptible of alloplastic realization.

Finally, if autoplasticity and rejection are absent, and only the regression remains, we have pure criminality. The asocial tendencies, which the neurotic represses and confines to substitutive gratification, and which the neurotic character, at the cost of much self-inflicted punishment, is able to live out in radically modified form, are all given free rein by the true criminal without the presence of inner conflict. Of course there are many grades of criminality, and patricide is exceedingly rare in our day. Most criminals find it necessary to content themselves with substitutive acts which they can perform without conflict. This is a sign that in the modern world even criminality has become domesticated. As a matter of fact, I am convinced of the opinion that on closer examination most of our criminals will turn out to be neurotic characters, and that the notion of pure criminality must be looked upon as a theoretical concept akin to the theory of a limit in mathematics.

On the basis of these considerations we shall distinguish four major psychopathological groups: the *neuroses,* the *neurotic characters,* the *psychoses,* and *criminality.* The dynamic and structural evaluation of the perversions is not so simple. From one point of view they seem to be partial psychoses in which the psychotic element is limited to the sphere of unsublimated sexuality, manifesting itself in sexual aberration. The regressive impulses are accepted by the ego, but they are expressed solely in relation to the sexual object. On the other hand, these manifestations are more alloplastic than the psychoses, and the ego is preserved intact. That is why masochists often stand rather close to neurotic characters and sadists to criminals.

The problem of evaluating the perversions from the structural and dynamic standpoint has convinced me of the unexpected fruitfulness of some of the conceptions developed by Ferenczi in his theory of genitality. Ferenczi sees in the physical manifestations of sexuality a series of efforts to relieve unassimilated tensions of the most varied character which have been diverted according to the conversion principle of symptom-formation. In a case of masochistic perversion previously reported,[1] I was able to establish with almost experimental certainty that the perversion grew out of the sexualization of the need for punishment, which was itself rooted in the father conflict. This

[1] Franz Alexander, *Psychoanalysis of the Total Personality,* New York: Nervous and Mental Disease Publishing Co., 1930.

need for punishment, which means a certain amount of destructive tendency directed against oneself, found ample sustenance, of course, in the anal erotic fixation and in the feminine component of the bisexual organization. The decisive factor in the development of the perversion, however, was the uncontrollable need for punishment arising from the Oedipus conflict. If the self-destructive impulses are not expressed in the cruder manifestations of sex, we have a moral masochist, which is one type of neurotic character. I presume that in sadism we are dealing with murderous impulses against the parents which are diverted toward the sexual object, and which find expression in a form which is modified by the strength of the erotic component of the object relation. In borderline cases, where the strength of the erotic element is small in comparison to the magnitude of the destructive drive, we have the picture of murder with assault.

This assumption is strengthened by the common observation that sexual sadists are often weak and inhibited natures, for their aggressiveness is wholly absorbed in sexuality. It is also true that masochists who work off their sense of guilt in their sexual activities are unscrupulous egotists in everything else. Thus one may say that every sadist is an abortive criminal, and every masochist an abortive neurotic character.

It is evident that the perversions seem to have no definite place in our classificatory scheme. The reason is clear enough. The distinction between neurosis, neurotic character, psychosis and criminality depends upon the different ways in which desexualized impulses are gratified. A varying quantity of desexualized impulsive energy is fundamental to the neurotic symptom, the neurotic acting-out, the psychotic symptom, and the criminal act. The essence of a perversion, however, is the gratification of a frankly sexual tendency. Following Ferenczi, we can look upon the perversions as the result of successfully diverting into explicitly sexual channels the tensions which would otherwise overflow the ego, where they would have received expression in one of the four pathological forms previously described. Thus the perversions can be said to be the non-desexualized antitheses of the four categories. It quite often happens that one of the four classes is mixed with a perversion, which means that while part of the total impulsive tension is desexualized, another portion is diverted into sexual expression. So it is not surprising to find that a perverse sexuality often goes with an impulsive life in which the desexualizing processes are disturbed. The less the impulsive tensions are diverted into sexual forms of gratification, the more they will encumber the ego and seek new outlets, and this means that they will produce neurotic symptoms, neurotic acting-out, or psychotic and criminal behavior. This adds little to Freud's formula that the neurotic symptom is the reverse of a perversion; it merely extends the application of this conception to other psychopathological phenomena, in particular to neurotic acting-out, as well as to psychotic and criminal manifestations. I beg you to regard this schematic arrangement as little more than a rough effort at orientation in respect of the manifold perplexities of psychopathological phenomena. This reservation should be borne even more distinctly in mind in considering the chart which I have drawn up to furnish a visual perspective over the field.

Chart of Fundamental Psychopathological Reactions
(*The Dynamic-Structural Point of View*)

⟶

The arrow indicates the direction taken by the ego in its growing incapacity to reject unconscious impulses

Psychological manifestations with conflict present		*Psychological manifestations with conflict absent*	
The ucs impulses are displaced and manifest themselves autoplastically	The ucs impulses manifest themselves by means of neurotic acting-out	Failure of defense with breaking down of the ego organization	Failure of defense with ego organization preserved
Substitutive gratification	True, although disguised, gratification	Undisguised gratification of id. Mainly autoplastic manifestations	Unmodified and uninhibited gratification
Autoplasticity Neuroses	Alloplasticity Neurotic character	Autoplasticity Psychoses	Alloplasticity True criminality

Addiction (?) (to drugs, etc.)

Partial failure of defense
Repressed impulses are expressed only by means of modified forms of sexual expression. True gratification
Perversions

I must admit that I am no friend of the use of charts in psychology. But on this particular occasion it is a valuable timesaver. Let it be clearly understood that most cases will never fit neatly and completely into a single pigeon hole. Neurosis minus neurotic acting-out, neurotic characters minus symptoms, and both minus perversions are rarities. How far there is such a thing as pure criminality, I have already considered questionable. Only the direction pointed out by the arrow is definitely important. Starting from the classical neuroses and moving in the direction of the psychoses and criminality, we can say with perfect assurance that the successful defense of the personality against tendencies which are incompatible with reality decreases.

Two principal groups emerge, on the one side the neuroses and the neurotic characters, where active conflict is evident in repression and in conscience reactions, and on the other side the psychoses and criminality, where no sign of conflict is visible. To be sure, the conflict is present in the psychoses, but only before the illness has fully developed. They resemble battles in which all the defending troops have fought and fallen. In the pure criminal the functions of the ego and of all its institutions remain unimpaired, but in view of the absence of a social reaction, the asocial elements are accepted without conflict.

Of course there are many equally justifiable standpoints from which other perspectives may be obtained. On this occasion we have only asked whether and in what measure the ego is successful in defending itself against those impulses which are incompatible with reality, and at the same time in providing for their gratification, and we have not considered either the depth of regression or the psychological content of the various impulses. From the standpoint of content, criminality and the psychoses would constitute two opposite poles. The regression is the deepest in the psychoses, for it is a biological regression, while the criminal is merely unsocial, and his instinctual life is on the plane of normal adults, considered from the biological point of view, or at least is perfectly capable of reaching this level.

Let us summarize the main points which have been made in discussing the neurotic character. Its most essential characteristic is the great expanding power of the tendencies which are alien to the ego. They will not permit themselves to be confined, as in neurosis, to the purely subjective sphere of symptoms, but crash through into the world of reality against the protest of the socially-adjusted portion of the ego. The relative strength of the ego is obviously less than among the neurotics, not on account of its absolute weakness, but *on account of the tremendous expanding power of the fundamental impulses.* I believe that it is decisively significant whether or not an individual is inclined toward the autoplastic gratification of his impulses. Without an autoplastic disposition no neurosis is conceivable. Unquestionably a specifically constitutional factor is primarily responsible for this quality of the fundamental impulses. The expansive force of his impulses brings the neurotic character closer to the healthy individual than to the neurotic. He really acts, and does not permit society to coerce him into a fantasy world of symptoms. The healthy individual would rather modify his impulses than renounce substantial gratifications in the world of reality, but the neurotic character tries to hold on to his fundamental drive. Because a part of his own ego is hopelessly at variance with certain of his impulses, he is bound to make war on himself.

The expansive living-out of impulses is the differential point which delimits the neurotic character from the person suffering from a neurosis, and brings him closer to the healthy person. We find this in the therapeutic process, too. Here we find it unnecessary to compel the patient to make the difficult step from introverted autoplasticity to acting, a step which in cases of severe neurosis is frequently impossible. The therepeutic goal in the case of neurotic characters is merely bringing the individual's acts under the domination of his conscious personality. That is why these cases present such satisfactory material for analytical success once they come to the analyst. In their youth they have no sense of personal difficulty. They present mostly the picture of vigorous, joyful daredevils who only after a series of bitter experiences awaken to a sense of difficulty. That is why we see them come to analysis only after they have reached mature age.

It is now entirely comprehensible why the neurotic character has fired the literary imagination since time immemorial. Neurotic characters are nearly all strong individualities who struggle in vain to hold the antisocial tendencies of their nature in check. To put it more sharply, they are individualists who are fettered by social sentiments. The eternal struggle between man and society is exemplified, not in elusive intrapsychic processes, but in the visible drama of their own lives. That is why they are born heroes who are predestined to a tragic fate. Their fall is the victory of society, and the spectator who has the same conflict within his breast—and who is without it?—is enabled to live out both the rebellious and the social tendencies of his personality by sympathetically feeling himself into the lives of the vanquished.

I might have brought out all that has gone before in a form much less abstract and scientific, but much truer to the palpitating reality of life had I chosen one of the masters of world literature to portray the neurotic character. I could very well have inscribed the name of one of the four Brothers Karamazoff under each of the captions of the chart. In that novel Dostoevsky did nothing less than exhaust the whole field of psychopathology, for he assigned each of the four fundamental types of pathological reaction to the Oedipus situation to one of the four brothers.

That Dostoevsky was thoroughly aware of the universality of what he had written is shown by the words which he spoke through the mouth of the prosecuting attorney, who alluding to the Karamazoff family, said, "Perhaps I am prone to exaggerate, but it seems to me that some *fundamental elements* in our intellectualized society have found expression in this family." I might have entered under the first heading in the chart the name of the neurotic Alyosha, in the second the neurotic character Dimitri, and in the third the psychotic Ivan, and in the fourth Smerdiakov, whose criminal tendencies appeared during his epileptic twilight states. It is noteworthy that Dostoevsky permitted true criminality to occur only under exceptional pathological conditions.

For a thorough understanding of the neurotic character it would be worth more to study Dimitri than the most interesting case history. Dimitri is not *a* neurotic character, but *the* neurotic character, in whom every conceivable dichotomy, good and evil, sadism and masochism, mawkish sentimentality and arrogant licentiousness, heroism and pusillanimity find wildly uncoordinated expression. Dimitri's confession to his brother Alyosha is a precious document for the comprehension of the splitting inherent in such a character: "No, man is planned on too lavish a scale. I would cut him down. An offence to the intellect may be a thing of beauty to the heart. . . . It is horrible to reflect that beauty is more than terrible; it is inexplicable. There the devil wrestles with God, and the battlefield . . . is the human heart."

The fate of Dimitri is typical of that of the neurotic character. He never committed parricide, though he tottered on the brink of it. His sense of guilt, which fed on his wishes and not on his deeds, brought him under suspicion. Any judge who views the circumstantial evidence exclusively on the basis of the psychology of the conscious mind would believe him guilty. Only a psychology of the depths can rescue the all too numerous fellow sufferers of Dimitri from miscarriages of justice. Every problem connected with "Neurosis, Psychosis, and the Neurotic Character" is epitomized in the contrasting personalities of the expansive Dimitri, of Ivan, who intellectualizes, rationalizes and projects his problems on to the outer world, and of Alyosha, who sternly represses everything.

Had my principal interest been the interrelationship of neurosis, neurotic character and organic disorder, I might appropriately have selected the incomparable figure of the Parisian art collector whom Balzac immortalizes in his *Cousin Pons.* Cousin Pons is a neurotic character of the kind we call an eccentric. This art collector and gourmand, who completely disguised his sublimated anal erotism and freely expressed his unsublimated oral erotism, fell ill with melancholia when his scruples suddenly put an end to his oral indulgence. Apart from collecting, all that mattered in his life was the round of sumptuous and exclusive dinners to which he was invited by his rich and snobbish relatives, whose art advisor he was. Once he chanced to overhear the servants call him an "old plate-licker," and suddenly see-

ing himself as others saw him, his lethargic superego awoke and for-
bade any further culinary indulgence. Presently old Cousin Pons could
endure it no longer, became melancholic, and on the basis of this melancholia developed a gall bladder complaint which brought on his
death. This is a case history painted against the background of Parisian
society. Balzac's medical clairvoyance not only transcended the knowledge of his own day but of our own. We are already in a position to
recognize the relationship between oral erotism and melancholia, and
we suspect (though the internist doesn't yet, or perhaps doesn't any
longer suspect) a relation between melancholia and gall bladder diseases. Balzac delineates this connection with the naive assurance of the
intuitive genius in a case history which, since it took into account the
total situation, is fundamentally more veracious than the most exact
case history, with all the indices of all the body humors, which has
ever been put together in a medical clinic in a gall bladder case.

In Balzac's novel a neurotic character falls victim to a narcissistic
neurosis, which leads to an organic disease when he undertakes to deny
himself. I could have set forth the connection between the neurotic
character and neurosis by examining in detail the sad story of Cousin
Pons, but such an undertaking would far exceed the space at my disposal. The principal merit of science is brevity, even at the cost of
doing some violence to the facts.

Perhaps, as our psychological knowledge develops, we may advantageously replace the story of Cousin Pons by a medical treatise with
a title something like this: "A Contribution to the Understanding of
the Interrelationship of Oral Erotism, Melancholia, and Gall Bladder
Diseases, with Observations on the Mutual Replaceability of Neuroses,
Neurotic Acting-out, and Organic Disorders." Today such a treatise
is not yet possible; medicine can still learn from Balzac.

Buddhistic Training as an Artificial Catatonia

The Biological Meaning of Psychic Occurrences

◄ 1931 ►

When I review the subject matter of this paper, I find that I could just as accurately have announced as its title "The Psychic Meaning of Biological Occurrences," instead of the reverse, as I have done. This reciprocal relation forms my thesis, the consistent elaboration of which is my task today, namely: that psychic processes have a biological validity just as biological processes have a psychic one. Today, however, I do not wish to prove this principle upon the basis of individual analytical experience, but rather to turn to the understanding of a definite mental condition. I, therefore, do not start upon the same deductive path which philosophy has always traveled in order to penetrate its fundamental problem, the connection between body and mind. The solutions of the problem by the philosophers have been not a little varied and even at present are not uniform. For example, in the radical materialistic conception of Vogt thoughts are regarded as products of brain secretion, whereas the idealism of Berkeley completely denied the existence of the material world and regarded it as an appearance, as mere mental content. Only one of the philosophical solutions interests us especially. I refer to the identity theory of Spinoza which for the first time expressed the idea that mental events are at the same time physical, and vice versa. *"Ordo et connexio idearum idem est ac ordo et connexio rerum."* The solution of Spinoza is so simple and matter of fact. It is a metaphysical egg of Columbus, and one can only wonder how it is that, after long wanderings through labyrinths of epistemological specula-

This article was originally published in German; the English translation was not done by the author.

tion it was left for Schopenhauer alone to reiterate the thought of Spinoza, albeit in a new form, modified by the theory of evolution. However, it is probably not accidental, and shows us the trend of development, that Spinoza designates his first principle, his *causa sui*, whose Janus head is at one and the same time body and mind, by a physical expression, "Substance," whereas Shopenhauer equates it with the psychological phenomenon of "Will." Actually the dynamic conception of force, of power, is the only one which is common to physical and psychological experience.

Physics and biology have shown that, aided by a scientific method, one can learn more of this *"causa sui,"* while the attempt of psychology to discover anything of value by direct introspective means for a long time remained without success. Freud first pointed the way through the discovery of free association and the art of interpretation, which extends the circle of consciousness inward and makes it possible for us by way of immediate knowledge to understand biological happenings. In this way the metaphysical concept of will receives a scientific content in the concept of instinct and establishes a connection with biology.

One kind of introspective knowledge was known to Indian philosophy in a remarkable form long before the discovery of the psychoanalytical method. Just as psychoanalysis, in order to understand the unconscious, prescribes a certain mental condition which eliminates conscious criticism, so the Buddhistic doctrine of self-absorption worked out a psychotechnique in order to turn "knowing" from the outer world inward, and through this to achieve the emotionless condition of Nirvana. With this, I come to my task of today: namely, to elucidate the self-absorption phenomena of Buddha upon the basis of the principle of the identity of biological and psychological processes. From our present psychoanalytical knowledge it is clear that Buddhistic self-absorption is a libidinal, narcissistic turning of the urge for knowing inward, a sort of artificial schizophrenia with complete withdrawal of libidinal interest from the outside world. The catatonic conditions of the Hindu ascetics in self-absorption prove quite clearly the correctness of this contention. The mastery of the world is given up and there remains as an exclusive goal of the libido the mastery of self. In the older pre-Buddha Yogi practice the aim is clearly a mastery of the body, while the absorption of Buddha is directed toward the psychic personality, i.e., the ego. We know, however, that in Hindu fakirs the connection of the conscious will with the depth of bodily processes is never completely successful. They carry out their wonderful performances in the Yogi absorption, which, in contrast to the Buddhistic practice, takes place in a condition of autohypnosis. They are undeniably capable of quite extraordinary feats;

they can consciously regulate, even though incompletely, fundamental physiological functions, otherwise inaccessible to the will, or at least they can consciously initiate a regulating interference. Let us repeat this again and see what it means: to regulate physiological processes consciously. It means nothing else than an increase in analytical ability, a longed for but never mentioned goal of psychoanalytical science: the exploration, perhaps the cure, of organic illness through the expansion of the regulatory activity of consciousness to the physical libido which governs the coordination of cells. Up to now, a conscious mastery of the object libido, which lies nearer to consciousness, is the successful result of analytical research. Unquestionably the next step is the therapy of the narcissistic neuroses, and after this the investigation of organic illness of the neuroses of the cell bodies, the organs— and last the investigation of the regressive phenomena of cell functions; I mean by this, tumors.

The Yoga self-absorption, however, has no therapeutic goal; the mastery of the body is an end in itself. Likewise, in Buddhistic self-absorption the turning of the perceptive consciousness inward is an end in itself, a narcissistic-masochistic affair, shown by the fact that the way to it leads through asceticism. Psychoanalysis turns inward in order to help the instincts to accommodate themselves to reality; it wishes to effect an alliance between consciousness and instinct, in order to make experience with the outer world useful to the instincts. The Buddhistic theory sets itself an easier task: it eliminates reality and attempts to turn the entire instinctual life away from the world, inward, towards itself.

Freud expressed the difference between the artist and the neurotic thus: The artist, in contrast to the neurotic, establishes contact with reality by a fantasy satisfaction of his libido, and to this extent acts socially. In this sense self-absorption is a kind of narcissistic neurosis and psychoanalysis is its scientific counterpart. I should like to try and show you that this neurosis, through its incomparable depths of narcissistic regression, has a special meaning for us, and deserves our attention.

In what does the nihilistic theory of Gatama Buddha consist, and what influence has it upon his disciples, who follow his teaching?

The common factor in the various Indian self-absorption methods is the goal-conscious systematic withdrawal of all libidinal interest from the outer world, and the attempt to dispose narcissistically of all such freed quantities of libido. The important and interesting thing for us is that in self-absorption the intellectual functions are also drawn in. Even in Buddha's teaching the chief accent falls upon this inward perception. "Where there is no self-absorption there is no wisdom, and no wisdom where there is no self-absorption, and he who has both self-absorption and wisdom is near to Nirvana," says Buddha.[1]

The actual mental absorption is introduced by a general ascetic training, which consists in a systematic suppression of all emotional life. The chief conditions are freedom from hatred, ceasing to desire property, denial of all fleshly pleasures, and sexual continence. Analytically regarded, this means that not only every genital but also every sadistic, oral erotic, and anal erotic outlet must be closed, in order to lead the libido to the ego, in its most primitive functions. The external means of accomplishing these demands consist in isolation, a peaceful composure of the body, and the observation and regulation of breathing. It is clear why breathing plays this special role. It is the only constant periodical function which is accessible to the conscious will. After this ascetic preparation the first mental absorption sets in, which leads to Nirvana through the four steps of Jhana. The first Jhana step consists in a turning aside from the variety of external perceptions and inner imaginations, and in the limitation of fantasy activity—concentration of thought upon a single theme. The objects of these meditations are different, yet are exclusively such as tend to depreciate the world and life in its entirety, meditations on the brevity and futility of human existence. Gradually these meditations pass over to increasingly gloomy observations of the hideousness and impurity of the human body, death, and the corruption of the flesh. These observations are bound with feelings of lively disgust with the body. The melancholic coloring is the chief feature of these sadistic, self-directed self-observations, the first stage of absorption, as emphasized by Heiler, in his research into religions. "In this phase of absorption the cosmic picture of the meditating monk is amazingly simplified, the entire world still only the inscrutible symbol of universal metaphysical evil . . . deep sorrow shakes the meditator, bitter contempt of the world fills him . . . all these transitory worldly desires and wishes die." It is thus that Heiler describes this phase of absorption, which in the light of our clinical psychoanalytical knowledge, is exceedingly clear and especially interesting, inasmuch as it presents an experimentally induced melancholia. It is caused through the world, with all its multiplicity, ceasing to be a libido object, after every worldly interest is artificially withdrawn, during the ascetic preparatory training, and now the entire withdrawn libido is directed to the individual's body. The body assumes the role previously taken by the world and becomes the sole object. The libidinal interest of the ego is, at this stage, purely sadistic. The passionate frenzy against itself does not differ in any way from the well-known clinical picture of melancholia. This con-

[1] Heiler, *Die Buddhistische Versenkung*, Munich: 1922.

dition is, however, far removed from the desired goal of absorption. The monk still feels disgust with his own body, and even this feeling must be conquered. If the conquest of disgust is successful, then the sadistic attitude towards the body will be replaced by a positive attitude. To put it clearly, the barrier erected during individual development, the feeling of disgust, the dam which is to protect the libido from narcissistic regression, is broken down and the entire libido, which until now found an outlet only in its sadistic component, streams back into the large resevoir of the ego. After the barrier of disgust is broken down no inhibiting factor is there to stop the transformation of object libido into narcissistic libido, that is, to stop the regression of libido into its primary form, self-love. This phase of positive attitude towards the ego is described in the Buddha text in the following words:

In this condition the monk is like a pool, fed from a source within himself, which has no outlet, neither to the east, nor to the west, north, nor south, and which also is not replenished by rain from time to time. This pool is fed from the cool stream of water within itself, with cool water streamed through, filled and flooded entirely, so that no single corner of the pool remains unsaturated: just so does the Bikkhu drink from his physical body, fills and saturates himself completely from all sides with the joy and pleasurable feelings born out of the depths of absorption, so that not the smallest particle remains unsaturated.

This is the second Jhana step. I think no analyst can more fittingly describe the condition of narcissism than is done in this text, if we substitute the word "libido" for "stream of water." For this reason this description seems to me especially interesting and important, because it is the description of a condition which we have theoretically reconstructed and named "narcissism." The person's own body and, indeed, his entire body, becomes his sole object. This feeling of pleasure, a consummate voluptuousness of all organs, tissues, and cells, a pleasure completely freed from the genitals, an orgasm diffused through the whole body, is a condition which we ascribe to the schizophrenic in his catatonic ecstasy. We can consider the Buddhistic wording an introspective description of the mental situation during catatonia. This text justifies me methodologically in regarding Buddhistic absorption and Nirvana as psychological documents rather than as products of metaphysical speculation. Freud's conception of the development of object libido from ego libido is confirmed, point for point, in the artificial regression of absorption, and becomes an experimental truth. Furthermore, Freud's melancholia mechanism receives substantiation by the finding in the preceding melancholy stage of Jhana, which occurs when the world as object is lost, becomes sadistically depreciated, and when this sadism turns against the ego, which again recaptures its former developmental object role from the outer world. The narcissistic step corresponds to the next further regression in that the barriers of disgust are broken down and the whole organism is flooded with positive libido. Perhaps the only new thing that we learn from this is in what sense a schizophrenic regression is deeper than one in melancholia. The deeper regression in schizophrenia comes about when the sadistic investment of the ego is replaced by a positive one. The protective role played by disgust, the disappearance of which is an old and well-known symptom of schizophrenia, comes clearly to expression: the conquest of disgust is the precondition for entering the second step of Jhana. Hate, disgust of the body protects against love and is employed in the construction of the ego system in the form of feelings of disgust. If, then, schizophrenic regression corresponds to the narcissistic phase of individual development, melancholia must correspond to that post-narcissistic stage in which a critical agency is set up for the purpose of fighting the narcissism of the ego, which negatively invests the nucleus of the ego. In the self-accusations of the melancholic we hear the voice of the strict educator, whose criticisms and punishments are a pattern for a negative attitude of the ego against itself.

We have thus far seen that absorption systematically reverses the direction which development took in a constructive path, and then strives to demolish the entire physical and psychic personality. We may well be curious to learn where this regressive path can still lead, after the stage of narcissistic orgasm.

The third step of Jhana consists in a constant diminution of the feeling of pleasure of the second stage with a gradual transition into apathy. The narcissistic orgasm of the entire body is followed by a state of detumescence. The fourth stage is the condition of complete mental emptiness and uniformity. "Exalted above pleasure and pain, free from love and hate, indifferent to joy and sorrow, indifferent toward the whole world, toward Gods and Men, even toward himself, the monk lingers on the heights of *sancta-indifferentia*, on the threshold of Nirvana." Thus Heiler describes the last step of absorption. It is not difficult for us to recognize in this condition the last stage of schizophrenia, schizophrenic dementia, but it *is* difficult to evaluate and establish to which period of individual development it corresponds. According to Heiler, this condition is only quantitatively different from that of Nirvana; Nirvana means only its intensification.

We have several ways of approaching the analytical understanding of this state. First of all, physical behavior. Complete immobility with scarcely perceptible breathing; a limitation of metabolism, a kind of trance. In the final condition of the older autohypnotic Yoga absorption this physical effect is much more striking than in the Nirvana of the Buddhistic absorption. The unbelievable miracles of the fakirs, which seem to mock at all physiology, take place in this autohypnotic state of Yoga practice. When we consider these miracles, we are struck by the remarkably stereotyped position of the body. Crouched together, the extremities folded up, with the head down, hanging from a tree, and similar things. Yet the greatest miracle is allowing oneself to be buried alive. It is not our province here to determine to what extent the stubbornly repeated rumors of forty-day burials rest upon truth. Sufficient other acts have been proven and the remarkable capacity of the fakir to influence his physiological function, even metabolism, has been established.

We are chiefly interested in the meaning of these customs, the meaning of which is involuntarily forced upon the analytical eye. Immobility, a remarkably uncomfortable position of the body, restriction, indeed almost cessation of breathing, burial. The sense is clear, a regression to the condition before birth, immobility, being folded together, without breathing, lying in the mother. The end effects of Yoga practice which Buddha employed, only spiritualized, makes it very probable that the end conditions of his absorption, Nirvana, likewise means the deepest regression to the condition of intra-uterine life, the more so since the physical characteristics are the same, immobility, being folded together, breathlessness,—think of a Buddha statue. Nirvana is the condition in the mother's womb. "Without perception, without wishes, the peace in which there is no death nor being reborn, no Here, no Beyond, only an intermediate kingdom, that is even the end of sorrow," says Heiler.

But the intra-uterine meaning of Nirvana will be much more obvious if we regard its psychic content and follow Buddha step by step through the four stages of Jhana into Nirvana. Here our analytical interest begins. The absorption was until now purely affective, yet Buddha promises his disciples knowledge, which is the true goal of absorption. Parallel with the physical and affective absorption runs the intellectual, the perception of the concealed connections of existence in the self to be attained by turning all intellectual power inwards. In the fourth stage of Jhana, Buddha recognized the eternal law of Karma, the cycles of eternal reincarnation. In birth, Buddha sees the cause of the threefold evils, age, sickness, and death. In the legend of the young prince who thrice sets forth upon a journey, Buddha explains to his followers the cause of his religious strivings, the cause of which leads him to turn away from the world, back into his innermost being. On first venturing forth, the young prince is induced to return by the sight of a helpless old man; at the second, the sight of sick people who are wallowing in their own excrements, and the third time by a funeral procession. The conquest of age, sickness, and death is the expressed goal of Buddhistic teaching and we may rightly call it a narcissistic religion in opposition to the transference religion, Christianity, which attempts to regulate the social life of humanity in its affective relation. We can even express it more forcibly. The aims of Buddhistic teaching are therapeutic, the conquest of age, sickness, and death. Their way is that of regression through introversion, and their cure Nirvana, the conquest, or nullification of birth. In his legend of the threefold exodus, Buddha three times curses birth: "Oh, shame, say I, of birth, that at birth age appears, sickness appears, death appears." [2] The cause of the threefold evil is birth, the cosmic law reincarnation, and Nirvana means its conquest. " 'In Nirvana the power is annihilated which leads to existence, no longer is there reincarnation'—says Buddha. 'Man has regressed; sunk back into pure Being which is nothing but itself.' " [3]

I hope that I have succeeded in making it seem probable to you that the end goal of Buddhistic absorption is an attempt at psychological and physical regression to the condition of intra-uterine life. We saw the introspective description of the different steps of the regressive absorption scale which correspond to the various steps of individual development, that the way to Nirvana can be likened to a cinema film which is turning in the reverse direction. Beginning by liberating the libido from the world, and leading through melancholy and then through the narcissistic catatonic phase, it finally attains the apparent alibidinous condition of Nirvana, the intra-uterine state. We can understand this regression in the light of the libido theory until we reach the narcissistic phase. Analytical understanding is an equation which expresses the relation of the ego to the libido. The equation of the melancholy phase runs: sadistic investment of the ego as object; the equation of the narcissistic phase: positive investment of the ego as object. The question which remains open, according to the libido-ego equation of Nirvana, is that of the intra-uterine condition, which, according to the description in the Buddhistic texts, appears to be alibidinous. The difference between object and subject vanishes, says Heiler in regard to this state. "The Complete has sunk back into pure Being, which is nothing but itself." Thus says Buddha. A distinction between subject and object is truly necessary to an understanding of the libido concept, and even the narcissistic libido takes the ego itself as object. This apparently alibidinous condition of Nirvana, pure existence, can be nothing other than the most complete restriction of the ego impulses and of the libido, one such as Freud

[2] Leopold Ziegler, *Der ewige Buddho,* Darmstadt: 1922.
[3] Heiler, *op. cit.,* p. 40.

assumes for single-celled protozoa, or, like the original narcissism of the sperm cells which, according to his conception, were purely narcissistic.[4] According to this, the sensation of Nirvana would be identical with the complete coincidence of ego impulses and libido. This assertion, however, is a biological theory. What has it to do with psychological sensation?

First of all, the intra-uterine state is not a single moment in time, but comprises the developmental period from the fertilized cell up to the time of birth. In which phase of intra-uterine life does Buddha discover the conquest of the cycle of reincarnations, the sinking back into pure existence? Indeed, where does Buddhistic regression really end?

We could easily form a picture of the melancholy phase of absorption. We found the description of the second stage of Jhana an excellent presentation of narcissism in the classical sense. In this state we could even recognize the catatonic ecstasy of schizophrenia. The psychological meaning of Nirvana, the sensation of the condition in the mother's womb, is difficult to imagine. That this condition is meant is entirely clear. Buddha himself calls it the conquest of birth, the conquest of eternal reincarnation. What does the expression "eternal rebirth" actually mean? For this we must seek some solution. One might easily get the impression that these statements about Nirvana are pure metaphysical conceptions, the fruit of some type of philosophical speculation. Yet we can at once discard this assumption. All other phases of absorption were psychological conditions and the path to them led through systematic, chronologically exact workings of the personality. The psychotechnique of Buddha made it possible voluntarily to trace this regressive path. The Yoga practice makes possible the physiological miracle, the voluntary restriction of metabolism; the absorption theory of Buddha produces a complete psychic regression. We are justified in assuming that the end state of this regression corresponds to a psychic experience as nearly related to the intra-uterine condition as narcissistic absorption is to the actual narcissistic period of individual development. Yet I have a still more weighty proof that Nirvana really is a psychological regression to the intra-uterine state, more precisely into a condition whose libido-ego equation is identical with that of the embryological period, a proof which I have withheld until now. I refer to the interpretation of Buddha's "salvation knowledge" in the fourth state of Jhana, which makes possible the entrance to Nirvana, the knowledge of the eternal repetition of rebirth. The meaning of these laws, the central core of Buddhism, can be understood in its deepest meaning only in the light of psychoanalytical in-

[4] S. Freud, *Beyond the Pleasure Principle*, New York: Liveright, 1961.

terpretation. However, the philosopher Ziegler comes very near to this in his interpretations. Let us turn to his profound work, *The Eternal Buddha.*

According to Ziegler, the whole way to self-absorption through the four steps of Jhana serves to free psychic processes from every tone of emotion, pleasurable as well as painful. All the painful feelings of the first state and all the pleasurable ones of the second stage of Jhana which could induce the worshipper to persist at one of the stages must be overcome. Only in the fourth stage, when thought is cleansed of every pleasurable or painful undercurrent, can the liberating recollection of the reincarnations enter. We analysts are also acquainted with two kinds of resistance in our patients: those which depend upon unpleasurable affects and those tenacious defenders of the borders of narcissism which are based upon a tendency to persist in a pleasurable condition. The absorption scale corresponds to the chronological path of a well-conducted analysis. In conquering the melancholy phase the unpleasurable resistance is overcome and only then in the second stage ensues the conquest of narcissism.

Permit me to repeat the therapeutic meaning of the four-fold absorption in Ziegler's words:

In the same measure, as the monk becomes more absorbed within himself, and the sources of each external experience are dammed up upon which we Occidentals are accustomed to base almost all our knowledge, and surely all our science,—in just the same measure sources hitherto unknown to him begin to well up within him, the very distant whispering murmur of which his unusually sharpened ear ever more clearly perceives. He who has become strong in four-fold self-absorption has actually tempered and annealed for himself a new sense, which he can use as a drill is used by a geologist. Grown wise in himself and of himself—this monk is able above all things to recollect himself. This knowledge is recollection, and indeed in distinction and opposition to mere memory, is to be understood throughout as *anamnesis* in distinction and opposition to mere *mneme.* . . . That the ascetic shall remember most verifically and vividly all the circumstances of his life down to the least detail is the most important outcome of the four Jhanani; that is the first relatively holy wisdom.

I leave it to you to draw the parallel with psychoanalysis.

Shall we believe that the pious monk who followed Buddha's prescriptions was capable of such recollections? In the three first Jhana stages we saw that in case he did not recollect, he reenacted, formed transitory symptoms in Ferenczi's sense, a passing melancholia, a passing schizophrenia; he repeated the stages of his earlier development. It is theoretically conceivable that in the affectless, resistance-free fourth state conscious memories arise. But how far this remembered knowledge, as Buddha calls it, goes is hard to establish. If we may believe Buddha, it goes very far. He halts not at all at the threshold of individual existence but passes over into a continuous state of regression. Let us hear what Buddha says of the condition of the fourth stage.

In such a zealous state of mind, refined, cleansed, purified, free of dross, supple, pliant, steadfast, invulnerable, I directed the heart toward recollected knowledge of previous forms of existence. I recollected many different forms of existence as if one life, then two lives, then three, then four, then five, then ten, then twenty—then a thousand, a hundred thousand, then times when many worlds were created, then times when many worlds declined, then times when many worlds arose—vanished.[5]

The meaning of those regressive recollections of all forms of existence, of all reincarnations until there is no more rebirth, until rebirth is finally dug out by the roots, until man is annihilated, can no longer remain in doubt. The regressive absorption, the turning of the film of life in a reverse direction, goes further, goes beyond birth and passes all stages of intra-uterine life, and unrolls embryological development, which is nothing other than a short repetition of all forms of life in the geological rise and fall of many worlds of early times since the first birth. The question previously put, Where does the Buddhistic regression end? can now be answered. Absorption goes back to the beginning of embryonic development.

I am perfectly aware of how improbable this sounds. Yet if you have followed me along the regressive path of absorption perhaps you will not deny that this path, which is a chronologically true demolition of ontogenetic development, finally leads to a primitive condition where ego impulses and libido completely merge, similar to the state which we can assume, according to Freud, to obtain for the germ cell. We know that neurotic symptoms make use of archaic forms of expression; it is really then only a quantitative question as to how old this form is. Whether it arises from the extra- or intra-uterine condition is no fundamental matter. In the form of action, of repetition, every regression is thinkable, and I hope I have made it probable that the condition of Nirvana in Indian ascetics who have mastered the regression technique and whose entire libido through years of practice is withdrawn in this introverted narcissistic direction, can be expressed as a libido-ego equation which is identical with that of the germ cell. But Nirvana means not alone a complete regression to the beginning of development, but at the same time a knowledge. The clairvoyant knowledge of eternal reincarnation, the recollection of all forms of life, all geological periods, which Buddha perceived after go-

[5] "Die Reden Gotamo Buddhos," from the collection *Majjhimanikajo des Pali Kanons*, translated by Karl Eugen Neumann, Munich: R. Piper, 1922, Vol. I.

ing through the fourth step of Jhana, is nothing more than our fundamental biogenetic law, except that Buddha discovered it by a completely different approach. He knew this law experientially by reliving
in his affective regression, his embryological existence. The difficulty
we cannot resolve is how consciousness, or, as Buddha maintains,
memory, can follow this deep regression so far. Here we meet our
most difficult problem, whose solution is hardly possible, and which I
shall in no way undertake. Nevertheless, permit me to point out that
we meet the same problem daily in analytical practice and that just
this commonplaceness explains why we have accustomed ourselves
not to think about it.

This problem begins with Freud's thesis, that the neurotic is always right. Our entire analytical striving rests upon this truth . . .
that we listen to the neurotic and seek to trace a meaning in his symptoms. Freud's statement really means that the *unconscious* is always
right. Now the above problem is brought somewhat nearer if we re-
formulate the sentence, "the unconscious is always right," more pre-
tentiously: The unconscious knows everything—knows all that concerns the inner world. Ignorance of that which is within first begins
with the censorship. We find this thesis proven every day. The unconscious knows the "primal scene," knows of the amniotic fluid, and
knows the fact of fertilization. Freud shows that it is unnecessary, in
order to understand the unconscious, to search for actual observations
or even for early fantasies. He predicates the conception of inherent
fantasies and with this predicates a phylogenetic knowledge. This
knowledge is a sort of recollection. And as the memory of living matter
is unlimited—in embryonic development are repeated even the occurrences of primeval times—so also the recollective knowledge of the unconscious is unlimited in time. The deepest layer of the unconscious
cannot be other than the psychic reflection of those early biological
events which we group together in the designation embryological development. Upon this deepest layer, which we can designate as phylogenetic knowledge, Buddha strikes in his regressive absorption. For
this embryological period a capacity for unlimited recollection is characteristic. Biologically regarded, it *is* nothing else but recollection. And
yet it remains a riddle, this discovering of biogenic law by introspective
means the discovery, or rather the direct experiencing of it. This deepest layer of the unconscious, which is pure recollection, is furthest of all
from consciousness, and with Buddha this is said to become conscious!

We can hardly picture that the recollected knowledge of Buddha
retraces and psychologically reproduces embryological development.
We know what a piece of work it is to make a neurotic symptom, and
archaic regression, conscious, even aided by the entire stock of our

analytical experience. It seems implied that Buddha, while in his schizophrenic regression, presents a symptom, interprets it at the same time, and in this way substitutes memory for repetition. Yet if we deny this there then remains only the other possibility, that Buddha found this law not by subjective means, but by the usual kind of objective knowledge, and then fantasied this into its theoretically correct place in the scale of absorption. The truth may be midway between these extremes. The dogma of rebirth is contained in the old Indian Atman. It appears in the theory of the transmigration of souls, a primitive intuitive presentiment of the theory of evolution, but in part, perhaps chiefly based upon the objective observation of death, birth, and of the similarities between men and beasts, and representing a deductive conclusion from such observation. We may also be dealing with a sort of "fausse reconnaissance," as Heiler assumes, without recognizing the deeper meaning of that term. Heiler says: "We Occidentals can with difficulty picture to ourselves this anamnesis, this memory of previous existences. We can, however, psychologically understand how a person all whose desires and strivings focus on a flight from the painful recurrences of birth, in moments of highest spiritual tension, might, by a sort of fausse reconnaissance process, take the visual images which arise to be memories of previous reincarnation." But through Freud we know the deeper meaning of *fausse reconnaissance*. We recognize something which we know unconsciously, which we have repressed, or which is present in us as unconscious knowledge. The emerging fantasy pictures, in Heiler's explanation, arise from the unconscious. They enter during the repetition of embryological development, similar to a dream, or a free association, and are the last tributaries of the unconscious to surge into consciousness. However this may be, it is clear that Buddha has in some manner experienced the fundamental biogenetic law; his experience has not alone biological but also geological validity. Yet this subjective experience is contained in every kind of knowledge, also in our seemingly purely objective type of knowledge of the outside world. Every intuitive comprehension of a truth, if it is accompanied by the subjective feeling of its being a discovery, or of having self-evidence, is a kind of fausse reconnaissance, a recognition of one's own self mirrored in the outside world. The connections within the self are just the same as in the external world—the self is only a special part of reality. "*Ordo et connexio idearum idem est ac ordo et connexio rerum.*" And now I am again at my point of departure. I did not wish to prove the reciprocal validity of biological and psychological occurrences, but to use this concept to illuminate the phenomena of Buddha's self-absorption. The oldest problem in philosophy reappears in this individual case. Yet all our sense of wonder vanishes if we accept Spinoza's solution. There are two roads to all knowledge. One can experience the world as an object, or experience it directly, know it endopsychically. If the methods of both forms of knowing are correct, then they must lead to the same result, and this is the only true control. Indian culture has brought the subjective method of self-submersion to completion, while our occidental culture fosters the method of objective knowledge. Only in psychoanalysis do the two methods meet. Here I recall a statement of Groddeck that human intelligence is nothing but the stupidity acquired through repression.[6] I should like to amplify this sentence to the effect that in a certain sense our entire consciousness is based on such a relative stupidity upon ignorance of that which is within. We leave the regulation of our instinctual life to more primitive processes and agencies than our critical consciousness such as conscience, the consciousness of guilt. The regulation of deeper biological happenings are left to agencies which lie still further from consciousness and whose existence we are only beginning to appreciate.[7] With this stupidity in regard to our inner life we gain our knowledge of the external world. This freedom comes from inner processes, which take place automatically without the necessity of conscious interference and permits us to direct all our attention toward the world.

When Buddha announced his absorption theory a number of autohypnotic absorption methods, which one knows as Yoga practice, had already been discovered. Seeking the truth, Buddha had at first chosen autohypnotic absorption and later discarded it as not leading to his goal. His main methodological discovery was that absorption must take place under completely conscious circumstances in order to reach Nirvana. I will not again point out the striking similarity between the analytical method and the doctrine of Buddha. The overcoming of affective resistance and of narcissism, so that one is able to recollect instead of repeat the extension of consciousness in a regressive direction toward the past, this is the doctrine common to Freud and Buddha. Can we regard as accidental this remarkable repetition in the history of both spiritual creations whose founders both at first attempted to use hypnosis, which they found at hand as prescientific practice? And was it also accidental that both then arrived at the conclusion that the chief and really difficult task is to establish the connection with consciousness?

Yet there remains an insurmountable difference between the two doctrines, deeply founded within the difference between Indian and

[6] G. Groddeck, "Ueber den Symbolisierungezwang," *Imago*, VIII (1922), 72.
[7] One thinks of the "ego-memory-system" of Ferenczi in "Psychoanalytical Observations on Tic," *Int. J. Psycho-Anal.*, VII, 1921. *Selected Papers*, New York: Basic Books, 1955.

European culture. Buddhistic absorption goes much deeper in the direction of regression, yet it must pay dearly for this depth. Through this it allows the entire outside world to pass into oblivion, conquers the self, but loses the world thereby. The objective of psychoanalysis is more pretentious, it strives to conquer self without losing the outside world. The Buddhistic doctrine is more asocial; we find in the causes of absorption only biological factors such as age, sickness, and death, but no social factors such as the Oedipus complex. The world is given up, and the cure consists in regression to the condition where ego and libido, no longer driven by outer necessity, reach their ultimate boundaries. Buddha does not seek an adjustment to the world, as psychoanalysis seeks to achieve a new compromise, to establish a new boundary between ego and libido, adjusted to reality. This asocial feature of his doctrine also spelt its end, which came with a tragic crash. The Neobuddhists overlook this failure if they expect from his doctrine a new salvation.[8]

Buddha denies himself the eternal life, which he has achieved through the conquest of death, by the entrance to Nirvana. Here is the first contradiction in the completely self-contained Nirvana philosphy. Buddha, voluntarily parting from life, directs the following words to his favorite pupil, Ananda:

If to thee though, Ananda, the Perfect One has given an important sign, an important suggestion, thou hast not been able to see it, hast not prayed for the Perfect One . . . may the Exalted persist throughout the ages, may the Welcome One exist throughout the ages, for the good of many, for the healing of many, out of pity for the world, for the use, welfare and succour of gods, and men. Hadst thou, Ananda, prayed for the Perfect One, so had thy words been twice unheeded, the third time answered. For this reason thou hast overlooked it, hast missed it.[9]

Here we see, heavily shrouded, in the dark background, the Oedipus complex, the father conflict. Buddha departs, because his followers have not understood him, because he has remained alone, because even his favorite pupil, Ananda, does not seek to keep him from going. This incomprehensible "not asking to remain" means nothing other than an unresolved father conflict. According to Oldenburg, the silence of Ananda is explained by saying that the death god, Mara, had confused his reason.[10] Yet Buddha understands Ananda's silence. He does not want to believe what he sees, and hints to Ananda that he expects from him a request to remain. But Ananda remains silent and Buddha departs. The attempt to eliminate reality

[8] I think first of Leopold Ziegler.

[9] Ziegler, op. cit., pp. 159-160.

[10] Oldenburg, Buddha; sein Leben, sein Lehre, seine Gemeinde, Stuttgart-Berlin: Gottasche Buchhandlung, 1921, p. 356.

completely has failed. He begins his analysis at a point which lies behind the Oedipus complex. He begins where we leave off, at the narcissistic boundary, at the borders of the organic.

And thus he instructs his disciples. He must go because his followers under the pressure of the unconquered father complex desire his departure. Buddha has not analyzed but repressed the object transference. Had he remained consistent, he would never have been able to announce his doctrine.[11] He completely withdrew from the world, yet one thread he left unsevered—his spiritual connection with his disciples. Here it is that he receives his mortal blow. He denied the world, and the denied world revenged itself upon him in the form of the unconscious parricidal wishes of his followers.

[11] Buddha actually doubted whether he should keep his teachings to himself or announce them to mankind (Oldenburg, *op. cit.*, p. 159). Nowhere in the Buddhistic literature has sufficient account been taken of the deep contradiction between the absorption doctrine and Buddha's practical ethics, so far as I am able to follow. The goal of absorption, Nirvana, is a completely asocial condition and is difficult to combine with ethical precepts.

The Relation of Structural
and Instinctual Conflicts

◀ 1933 ▶

Definition of the concept of structural and instinctual conflicts

The structural differentiation of the mental apparatus is only one of the factors that lead to psychic conflict. Older, in respect of development, and more elementary is the factor known as the polarity of instinctual processes. The structural relations of the mental apparatus, as they appear in dreams and symptoms, have been the object of more study and are better understood than the more fundamental fact that instinctual processes are manifested in pairs of opposites, such as the pair, active-passive, or expulsive-receptive, or masculine-feminine, or sadistic-masochistic, or exhibitionistic-voyeur. This polarity is considered generally as if it were a fundamental scientific fact, an irreducible phenomenon for which there is no chance of causal explanation. Empirically, in psychology, we must simply accept this polarity and preserve the hope that biology will some day provide us with its explanation. The opposed polar strivings, despite their apparent intimate mutual relationship, furnish an ever-present possibility of psychic conflict.

The study of mental phenomena from a structural, dynamic and economic point of view is by no means incompatible with the qualitative study of the instinctual forces that participate in our metapsychological equations; rather, the two points of view supplement each other. The validity and utility of both modes of approach is evident, for example, in our formulation of the compulsion neurosis: the symptoms can be understood and described as the expression of a dynamic equilibrium between repressed and repressing forces; but they can be described and understood equally well as sadistic and masochistic reactions, or in many cases as the expressions of the patient's bisexual strivings. Up to now we have usually preferred to use separately either the more formal metapsychological, or the qualitative point of view; and quite naturally, since the picture becomes incomparably more complex if we consider both categories of variables—the qualities of the mental forces and their topographic, dynamic, and economic relations—at the same time.

In reality, however, structural and instinctual relations are interwoven, and if we study them separately we are merely availing ourselves of a traditional scientific privilege to find an orientation in a complicated field: we may select certain categories of variables and neglect the rest for the time being. My presentation, however, is an attempt to bring the two points of view mentioned into a more intimate relation, by showing the advantages to be gained from the simultaneous application of both principles. There is no gainsaying that this combination will increase the complexity of our formulations, and my sole excuse for this sacrifice of simplicity is the greater completeness of this combined approach, by means of which, known psychological relations may be more precisely described, and the causal connection of clinical facts hitherto isolated may be established.

To begin with, it is necessary to define the difference between structural and instinctual conflict. I speak of a structural conflict when an instinctual striving is rejected by the ego not because the quality of the striving is incompatible with the ego's own attitude, but because it has been condemned by the superego, which, as we know, represents an incorporated external rejection. For example, a heterosexual striving consciously acceptable to, and even desired by the ego may be inhibited merely because of fear. In this instance, the ego finds nothing to object to, but is forced to reject the striving by the superego or by an external situation.

In contrast to this structural conflict, based as it is on the difference between the various parts of the personality, I speak of instinctual conflicts when a striving is rejected because it is incompatible with another, ego-acceptable one which determines the ego's actual attitude. The best-known example of such an instinctual conflict is seen in the repression of passive homosexual strivings when these clash with the masculine aspirations of the conscious personality. Even though both types of rejection are due to castration fear, there is an important difference between the two types of conflict. In the first case, as when a man's heterosexual strivings are inhibited by the superego's attitude, the fear responsible for the inhibition referred, originally, to an external danger—the punitive father—that became introjected secondarily as superego. In the second case, the fear arises from a wish to be a woman, which creates self-castrative impulses and endangers the symbol of masculinity, the penis. To limit ourselves for a moment to the problem of the male castration complex, a man's castration fear usually has both the more external, structural basis and the internal, instinctual basis: it is the expression of his incorporated fear of the castrator, and of the inner fear of his own female wishes. The relative importance of these two sources of castration fear varies in different individuals.

The practical clinical advantage of this distinction, apart from any theoretical value, is obvious. If a patient's castration fear turns out to be chiefly the result of external intimidation, the prognosis will be better than if the castration fear was related to a bisexual conflict —that is to say, where the patient feels his masculinity threatened mainly by his own deep female desires. In the first case, although external intimidation may have found structural expression as fear of a harsh superego, this incorporated fear of a castrator represents a much more flexible, superficial conflict than that caused by the deep incompatibility of female and male strivings. The prognosis will naturally be most favorable in those cases in which the external fear is not yet incorporated—that is to say, in which an instinctual gratification is blocked because of painful experiences or threats which were not yet able to force themselves upon the personality powerfully enough to lead to a structural differentiation within the mental apparatus.

We many distinguish between three degrees of conflict: 1) external conflict based on external inhibitions, 2) structural conflict based on internalized inhibitions—that is, superego reaction, and 3) instinctual conflict based on the incompatibility of coexistent opposed strivings. The first two categories of conflict we may consider more superficial as compared with the third category, which lies on the borderline of the psychic and somatic.

The special value of this distinction between structural and instinctual conflict becomes evident, however, only when we realize that in the course of time structural conflicts may intensify existing instinctual conflicts. It is well known, for example, that the early inhibition of active masculine tendencies is apt to lead to a vicarious re-enforcement of passive homosexual strivings. I refer to the mechanism which Freud described as homosexuality resulting from overcompensated competition with the father. The inhibition of aggression leads to a passive homosexual attachment to the powerful and unconquerable competitor. The same mechanism is responsible for the progressive erotization of superego reactions in the evolution of compulsion neuroses, in which the originally self-punitive symptoms tend to acquire gradually a more and more masochistic or passive homosexual significance. The tendency of the mental apparatus to make the best of deprivations and to gain pleasure in any possible way is responsible for this process. The masculine gratifications being blocked, the potentialities of female gratifications become more important and emphasized. Whether a mere structural inhibition is able to change the factual proportions of the bisexual organization, we do not know, but we do know that in the course of time a permanent inhibition of masculine gratifications is apt to increase the intensity of the bisexual conflict in the ego.

The interrelation of structural and instinctual factors appears even more involved if we turn our attention to the subsequent results of an increased bisexual conflict such as is generated by an originally external, secondarily structuralized inhibition. Female strivings, increased through inhibition of masculine tendencies, supply a new material for conflict, because they offend the masculine aspirations of the ego, contribute to the fear of castration and must consequently be repressed or sublimated.[1] In neurotics this repression usually does not take place without causing considerable secondary disturbance, and evoking in the patient various manifestations of flight from these re-enforced, repressed female strivings. I refer to the great variety of exaggerated displays of masculinity which are reactions to a sense of inferiority, and to the notorious masculine protest, which Adler considers a basic fact not capable of further analysis. But the masculine protest and the exaggeration of masculinity are merely the external clinical manifestations of this instinctual conflict, which in most cases has a long previous history beginning with the external conflicts of the Oedipus situation and leading to the secondary re-enforcement of female tendencies.

The "sense of inferiority" and the "masculine protest"

Let us study more intimately these well-known phenomena, which have been somewhat neglected in psychoanalysis—perhaps through a distaste for the oversimplifications and platitudes with which Adler has overloaded this field. Taking as our point of departure the male personality after the pregenital period, we can schematically differentiate between a primary active masculine phase, a secondarily re-enforced passive feminine phase (resulting from the inhibition of masculine wishes), and lastly a third period—the return of secondary masculinity, characterized by exaggerated active aggressive manifestations. Between the first and third masculine phases, then, is interpolated a phase of female strivings referring to the father, reactively re-enforced through the familiar mechanism of overcom-

---

[1] As has been mentioned above, in the present state of our knowledge it is impossible to decide whether the female component of sexuality factually increases through the inhibition of masculine strivings. What can be observed is only an intensification of the bisexual conflict, probably due to the fact that through the repression of masculine features, the male ego is more exposed to the inner danger of becoming effeminate. In the woman, repression of female trends exposes the female ego to the danger of becoming masculine and thus intensifies the bisexual conflict.

pensation for primary rivalry. Freud considers the first two phases in the development of the male personality a universal feature of our civilization and relates the second intermediate phase, the passive attitude to the father, to the origin of religions and social organization.

When we compare the secondary masculine manifestations with the masculine strivings originally inhibited, we usually observe that these tendencies on returning from repression have diverged considerably from their original character. They display the typical features of reaction formations, as if they were intended to deny something which is present in the unconscious. To take a typical example: after the period of the Oedipus conflict, in which the boy's infantile masturbation was inhibited by threats of castration, a period follows which is often characterized by a somewhat masochistically colored passive relation to authorities. In analyses, typically, patients tell us (and often corroborate their assertions by the statements of relatives) that up to their fifth or sixth year they were lively, vigorous little boys, but that they then became shy and retiring. In puberty, however, they showed signs of resurgent masculinity, but this masculinity often had a pronounced sadistic-aggressive form inacceptable to the ego, had therefore to be repressed anew and could be expressed only in symptoms. The sadistic quality of this returning masculinity is a reaction to the feminine masochistic desires and a denial of their existence. As we know, most compulsive symptoms and ceremonials are either disguised expression of, or mechanisms of defense against, these sadistically distorted masculine strivings. Apart from the production of symptoms, however, there are many and various manifestations of this revived secondary aggressive masculinity, which I should like to discuss in more detail.

But let us for the moment turn to the question: what has happened in the depths of the personality during the period which begins with the first intimidation and inhibition and ends with the return of the repressed tendencies from repression? What is responsible for the altered character of the returning instinctual tendencies? The repressed strivings and the strivings which return from repression are not the same; a definite regression to pregenital characteristics has taken place. The passage through the unconscious has evidently led to a defusion. The masculine tendencies have lost a certain amount of erotic charge and hence show a predominance of destructive qualities. But what has happened to the erotic quantities? In a series of analyses, I could establish that this erotic charge, which was present to a greater degree in the early incestuous strivings of the five or six year old boy, had been reconverted into narcissistic libido. The psychological explanation of this regressive re-enforcement of narcissism is not difficult, since it is obvious that the intimidation of the masculine drive, with the resulting increase in passive homosexuality, acts like a narcissistic injury. The little boy does not renounce his masculine aspirations; he loses their instinctual background. The emptiness of these aspirations, with their instinctual power markedly diminished, is felt by the ego as a narcissistic injury and becomes manifest clinically as a *sense of inferiority*. This leads to the withdrawal of cathexis from objects and increase in narcissism—the usual result of narcissistic injuries—for the ego now needs more erotic charge to cure its narcissistic wound. The resurgent masculine manifestations, deprived of a certain amount of eroticism, must necessarily be more sadistic. Their chief purpose is to relieve the sense of inferiority; they are intended to save inner prestige rather than to establish real erotic relationships with objects. Interest in objects is diminished, proportionally to the enhanced narcissistic need of self-assertion of the ego, and in consequence, adolescent sexuality gives the impression of proving to the youth that he is a man. The stronger the primary aggression against the father, the stronger will be the passive female reaction; and the stronger the passive female reaction, the greater will be the inner need for narcissistic compensations. The fulfillment of this need leads to greater defusion—that is to say, to a greater deficiency of erotic elements in the resurgent masculine manifestations. To some degree this process is universal; from it arise the adolescent's typical insecurity and awkward exhibition of masculinity.

The metapsychological analysis of these well-known phenomena may be excused because it will help us to understand the subsequent destiny and various manifestations of the reactive masculinity, which we shall discuss in greater detail.

Instinctual conflict in exhibitionism

Most transparent is the role of the repressed female strivings in male exhibitionism. I agree with Fenichel's statement[2] that exhibitionism is mainly a denial of castration, but the castration fear which the exhibitionist desires to overcome is chiefly a reaction to an inner danger—the pervert's own female passive tendencies. In the analysis of a case of criminal exhibitionism (which I had occasion to supervise) the dream life of the patient was replete with evidence of extreme masculine aspirations. In one of his dreams he was the leader of a military organization and directed strategic operations of great importance. In the actual life of the patient, acts of great violence, committed chiefly against persons in authority, played an important part. The irritation at authorities and the ambition to play-act as an authority had both

[2] Otto Fenichel, "The Psychology of Transvestism," *Int. J. Psycho-Anal.*, XI, 1930.

been reactions against his own passive homosexual strivings, the denial of his female tendencies. But exactly the same purposes were served by the exhibition of his penis.

I had an excellent opportunity to study the psychology of exhibitionistic tendencies in the case of an extremely modest, but, in life, very successful patient, who justifiably could call himself normal to a considerable degree. The only abnormal acts of his harmonious life were two exhibitionistic incidents, the first of which he committed as a student, the second when mature. Both times he felt a sudden impulse to exhibit himself naked; the second time to exhibit his body and his genitals to an unknown woman who was standing naked by an open window across the street. As has been mentioned, one of this man's most characteristic traits was his great modesty, which did not, however, assume the form of shyness. Early memories revealed strong heterosexual aspirations towards the mother during his fourth or fifth year, but the concomitant admiration and jealousy of his father could only be reconstructed, though from quite convincing material. The business failure of the father, during the patient's latency period, turned his admiration into pity and criticism. In puberty, the patient showed signs of a strong inner uncertainty, and he fled from a painful sense of inferiority, taking an exaggerated interest in physical training, pursuing intellectual ambitions, devoting himself to hard work, and in addition almost consciously repudiating all sexual feeling. The analysis of a long series of dreams and direct recollections enabled me to reconstruct the psychological events which occurred between his Oedipal period and adolescence. His easy victory over his father led to intense guilt reactions, which sharply interrupted the straightforward development of his masculinity. His father being eliminated as a competitor, he had to apply the brakes for himself. However, just because of this early and easy victory, his impulse to exhibit his own success was most rigorously inhibited. In one of his transference dreams, he participated in a ski race; he and a childhood competitor (who represented the analyst) reached the finish almost simultaneously. After crossing the line, when he passed the judges he shouted his own name to show that he had won, but then immediately returned and as if to correct himself, told the judges that his rival had really come in first. Thus, the crucial trait of his character, modesty, was revealed as his reaction against his competitiveness.

Another pair of dreams, however, showed that the reaction to the primary competitive conflict with his father affected his instinctual development more profoundly than the mere overcompensation of his competitive exhibitionism. In the first dream of this pair, a man was kicked on the head and collapsed; in the second dream a woman was standing, exhibiting her erect, well-developed penis. This pair of dreams contained, in a fascinating condensation, the history of his instinctual conflict. In the first dream, he clearly expressed his own self-destructive wishes, and referred to their origin as aggression turned from his father back on to himself. In this dream he destroys the masculine side of his personality. The second dream of the pair expressed his reaction to the self-castration of the first dream, as if to say: "Although I was forced to restrain my own masculinity because of my father, and therefore feel as if I were a woman, nevertheless I am not castrated." This second dream of the female exhibiting a penis shows us clearly that its psychological determination is identical with that of the patient's own exhibitionistic deed in the "window episode." His first association to the woman with the penis was his own exhibitionistic incident. An extremely modest man all his life, he did not even allow himself sublimated gratification of the exhibitionism which found explosive discharge at that time. But it was his flight from his own passive tendencies that gave the exhibitionistic impulse sufficient dynamic power to overthrow the control of his otherwise harmonious ego. Weighty analytic evidence showed, moreover, that in this case the patient's passivity was chiefly determined by oral regression, even more than by his female desires. The abrupt exhibitionism at the window was chiefly a reaction against oral receptive tendencies stimulated by the sight of the breasts exposed by the woman at the window. Breasts were the most important objects of his sexual interests, and as objects of his love he always chose women who were "nutrient mother" images.

This case leads to the consideration of another typical instinctual conflict, the conflict between male active tendencies and oral receptiveness. Although receptive oral tendencies usually accompany the passive homosexual ones, a thorough analysis almost always permits one to distinguish between a more *oral* character and a more *female* character in the receptive tendencies—between *oral receptiveness* and *female passivity*.

In several analyses of homosexual patients, I repeatedly found a strong oral fixation, which was the deepest pregenital basis of the passive female genital tendencies which arose later. Often, however, castration fear directly forces instinctual activity to revert to the passive oral relation to the mother, which, it seems to me, is somewhat more easily acknowledged by a male ego than the female form of passivity. The conflict between oral receptiveness and masculine activity usually has a somewhat different clinical appearance from the bisexual conflict, although in both cases exaggerated masculinity dominates the picture.

Instinctual conflict between masculine ambitions and oral receptiveness or female passivity in criminals

The importance of the tendency to display one's masculinity by criminal behavior is one of the striking findings in the study of delinquency undertaken by myself at the Judge Baker Foundation in collaboration with Dr. William Healy.

The heroic exhibitionistic evaluation of criminal deeds, in America perhaps even more than in Europe, plays an important part among the motives for breaking the law. In spite of official condemnation, not only unconsciously but even consciously the public surrounds criminality with a kind of adolescent hero worship. Thus the commission of a crime can easily endow a young man with an inner prestige that he of necessity loses under the pressure of an oversevere puritanical education which curtails his primary masculine manifestations. Apart from this puritanical atmosphere the highly developed mechanization of the economic life, which does not leave much leeway for the individual striving of the ego, contributes to a standardization of thought and emotion. Finally, this incarceration of the personality is completed by that tyrant of all democracies, public opinion, which suppresses all individual strivings, less spectacularly, perhaps, but more powerfully than the most absolute dictators. *Vox populi* pretends to be *vox dei*, as kings pretended to rule as God's representatives on earth. Thus criminality in the New World even more than in Europe, impresses us as a desperate pathological revolt of the individual against a mechanizing and levelling machine civilization which threatens to strangulate individuality, and which, with the help of puritanism and public opinion, inexorably compels the individual to become a part of the collective unit. This anti-individualistic trend of civilization is perceived by the ego as an attack upon its masculine sovereignty, and criminality is one form of the ego's attempts to regain its lost freedom.

One of the toughest of my criminal patients, a real gangster, displayed in his very first dreams a distinct uncertainty regarding his sexual potency. In the first dream reported, the bullet of his revolver would not go far enough, and he tried to raise the revolver to an oblique position in order to obtain a greater ballistic curve. His fear of impotence very soon evinced itself as the result of a strong oral trend—the wish to be dependent, to be loved and taken care of. Parallel with this oral dependence upon his mother, there was a passive homosexual attachment to his older brother. Though strongly repressed, both passive tendencies were the chief determinants of his overt behavior, which was the antithesis of his unconscious attitude. In life, he was aggressive, foolhardy, independent, and chivalrous and made self-sacrificing gestures towards his mother and oldest brother. He had been arrested for a crime committed by his older brother, for which he had taken the blame. His chief conscious ambition was to be entirely free of obligations towards everyone and to be independent of everyone. He disliked accepting any help, nor would he borrow money, which he preferred to obtain by theft or robbery. This increased his self-confidence and gave him the tough exterior that he needed to cover up his unconscious sentimental longing for dependence. He soon transferred the same superior attitude to me, and in his dreams it was *he* who helped me, or I was working for him under his direction. Other determinants of his criminal behavior may be neglected in this connection—for example, his need for punishment which sprung from the rivalry with his brother. The most powerful motive, however, was his flight from his oral receptive and from his passive female tendencies. Whereas his passive homosexual attachment to the brother was a transparent overcompensation of original rivalry, his oral regression was a reaction to a series of real deprivations. From his eighth year on, he was sent from one foster home to another, where he usually had to do hard work. He was really undernourished in his receptive demands and the oral regression originated out of the lack of those sublimated gratifications which other boys under better conditions enjoy in family life. The lack of real interest and love on the part of the environment threw him back to the original claims of being fed by the mother. This regression was indeed the manifestation of his thirst for being loved and cared for, which he had definitely to renounce from his eighth year on. But the tough atmosphere of his environment was not the best place to display any emotion which even remotely resembled sentimentality. Nothing had to be more concealed in this environment than softness and thirst for dependence. The display of exaggerated toughness and independence, courage, and generosity, loyalty to his comrades, were the results of the instinctual conflict between pregenital receptive and passive female longings on the one hand, and masculine aggressiveness on the other. It was really a fascinating and unexpected result of the analysis to detect in the depths of this young Robin Hood's personality the desperate little boy crying for his mother and seeking help from his older and stronger brother.

In another twenty-six-year-old delinquent, the repression of the passive strivings was not so complete as in the above case. This boy was the youngest in the family, the pet of four older sisters and an older brother. Whereas, in the former case, the undernourishment of passive gratifications was the basis of the oral regression, this delinquent patient was overfed with love and attention. There was little to wonder at if he found it difficult to renounce the privileged position of the baby of the family. But in fact he never really did renounce this position and always remained the favorite of women. Even in jail, he received the visits of several women, all interested in his welfare and fate. Nevertheless, the conflict in this case was no less violent than in the other. He committed almost all of his delinquencies under the influence of alcohol, usually in the form of acts of violence. When he was fourteen years old, he enlisted in the Navy, chiefly to show the sister with whom he lived that he was not a baby and was not afraid.

The following incident, which happened when he was a sailor, may illustrate his way of dramatically exhibiting his aggressiveness. On one occasion, in Shanghai, he went ashore to a notorious bar frequented by sailors. In front of the barroom he saw a young American sailor weeping. On learning that this American had been thrown out of the bar by a group of English sailors, he went in and asked for the man who had attacked his comrade. The first one who responded he knocked out, and he then attacked the others. A violent fight ensued. Our sailor's energy was stimulated not only by the presence of an external enemy, but also by his need to deny the passive tendencies which he had to overcome. He had to demonstrate to himself that he was not a little baby, the pet of his big sisters, and this inner conflict worked like "dope" in the ear of a race horse. The fight ended in a complete victory and he was hailed as "the brave American sailor." Now that he had proven what a great fellow he was, he could allow himself to give in to his passive tendencies. In fact, ten minutes later, he invited two of the hostile English sailors to have a drink, and the drinking party resulted in a great friendship.

Similarly determined was his relationship to his best friend, with whom he had at least a dozen violent fights, always while drinking. The fights usually ended in a common excursion to a house of prostitution. His fighting spirit had a long history. When he was twelve years old and an usher in a theater, he attacked a man who had insulted a young lady in the audience. Yet, at the same time, in contrast to the other patient, he indulged his dependent tendencies, accepted aid from women and liked to be cared for in every way.

We see here a most interesting interplay between, and alternating gratification of, both sides of his nature. In the criminal case previously described, the passive homosexuality and the oral dependence were both repressed and entirely eliminated from the ego, which showed reaction formations only. In this delinquent, however, prolonged indulgence in the pleasant role of the petted baby of the family did not allow this solution of the instinctual conflict. Here the conflict had to be fought out in the same structural part of the personality —namely, in the ego—for the ego had acknowledged many of its passive strivings, even though it could not yield to them entirely because of its masculine ambitions. The result was a kind of alternating gratification of both categories of tendencies. One had the distinct impression that the patient could indulge in his dependent tendencies only if from time to time, he proved to himself that he still possessed his aggressive masculine potentialities. This pattern of the solution of the instinctual conflict betrayed itself in his sexual life as well. Not only passive dependent tendencies but passive homosexual strivings, also, could enter the ego. He was overtly bisexual and played in his sexual relations to men both the active and the passive role. The active role, which, especially in fantasies, took the form of rectal intercourse, was manifestly a reaction to passive gratifications which hurt his masculine pride. He could accept the female role only after he had proved that he could be a man, also, if he wanted to. In his homosexual fantasies, he made a woman of his sexual partner, whereas in reality he often took the passive role.

His sensitiveness which arose when he accepted the passive role can best be seen in the following episode. While still in young adolescence, he was picked up in New York by an older homosexual. In the park they passed two men who made some remark. Our patient immediately turned around, knocked out one of the two men and attacked the second. A long and violent fight ended finally in the patient's victory.

Although these two cases are so different in their clinical appearance, they display the same instinctual background, and only the combination of both points of view—the instinctual and the structural—can account for their phenomenological difference. The instinctual conflict in both cases is the same: a conflict between passive female and oral receptive tendencies on the one hand and masculine activity on the other. In the first patient of the Robin Hood type, however, the conflicting tendencies are distributed between two different systems, since the ego rejects the passive trends and shows only reaction formations against them; whereas in the second case, the conflict is fought out in the same system—the ego—which is dominated both by passive and active tendencies. The explanation of this difference may be found in the historical fact that in the first case the oral regression was a reaction to deprivations, whereas in the second case the passive receptiveness was the result of spoiling and the direct continuation of the patient's early infantile family situation, which in reality was never changed. In the second case, the ego had much reason to accept this passive situation, a situation which yielded so many pleasures and advantages.

A similar solution of the instinctual conflict was observed in another patient to whom I have already referred in a previous publication.[3] In contrast to the sailor, however, in this man only the oral receptive and the active masculine tendencies were included in the ego, while the passive female tendencies were rather successfully repressed. Another difference was that the gratification of the oral receptive and the active masculine tendencies was separated more thoroughly in this case, although, as in the sailor, both kinds of instinctual strivings were contained by the ego, and had to fight out their conflict in the ego. This patient was dependent only upon women, especially upon his wife, but extremely independent and a real leader in his profession. Toward his son, he had a nearly conscious jealousy, since the relation to his wife was almost exclusively the attitude toward a mother. One of the first and most violent disagreements in their marriage developed from what seemed to be a trifle. His wife was of another nationality, but the patient spoke his wife's mother tongue with a fair readiness, although much worse than she spoke his mother tongue. His wife disliked speaking her own language with her husband, which he resented extremely, and he tried to force her to carry on their conversation in the wife's native language. Peculiarly enough, the wife, who otherwise submitted herself to his wishes, stubbornly refused to use her own mother tongue at home. This fact infuriated him and evoked the most violent scenes. This conflict was one of the most usual reasons for his temper tantrums, in which he would lie in bed for days refusing to work, talk or take part in any kind of activity. As the analysis showed, he had obviously desired to revive the mother-son situation of those days in which he could not yet speak as well as his mother. He wanted to look up to his wife as to a powerful and omnipotent mother. She had to read his thoughts and he was resentful if she did not guess correctly. This man was the respected and acknowledged leader of one of the greatest commercial enterprises in Germany; a fact strikingly inconsistent with his behavior at home.

In this patient the instinctual tendencies could be traced back to his fourth year, when he still drank milk from a bottle but at the same time was a fresh and bold youngster, who drove his bicycle alone on the road. One of his earliest memories was of an incident in which, in extreme rage, he threw a spoon away that he was supposed to use for eating. The unusually prolonged indulgence in the ways of a suckling baby obviously was incompatible with his equally strong masculine *Anlage*, and he could solve this conflict only by overemphasizing and proving his independence and masculinity, so that he could indulge in his oral receptive gratifications without being disturbed by feeling his inferiority.

[3] F. Alexander, "The Neurotic Character," *Int. J. Psycho-Anal.*, XI, 1930, and in this volume.

His oral receptive and active tendencies, however, were most thoroughly separated and distributed between his psychosexual attitude to women and his sublimated relations to men. He was orally dependent upon his wife but a leader among men. As has already been mentioned, parallel with his oral dependence on women, there were also signs of passive receptive tendencies toward men, which, however, were strongly repressed and which only accidentally, and in sublimated form, came to the surface and influenced his overt behavior. A striking similarity with the behavior of the sailor is to be found in an incident which the patient, in order to give me an example of typical behavior, told me in his first analytical session.

He commuted between two cities, traveling at night in an ordinary continental railway compartment. Disregarding the passengers who were asleep in the darkened compartment, he would begin to whistle, pull the shades from the lamps and commence to read his newspaper, rustling it as noisily as possible. Usually he succeeded in provoking one or two of the passengers to protest. An interminable and violent argument would then begin, an argument in which he would prove that by paying for his ticket he had, technically, acquired the right to read, and he would strongly advise all who felt themselves disturbed by his reading to buy a ticket for the sleeping car. As a rule this violent argument would end in complete amity, and at the terminal station the whole party would celebrate their newly found friendship with a glass of beer. After he had proved to his own satisfaction, and to everyone else, that he was independent and hard, he was able to indulge himself in the sublimations of the softer feminine side of his nature.

Bisexual conflict in homosexuality

In a long and most instructive analysis of a case of homosexuality I was able to discover an extremely deep-seated instinctual conflict, with a somewhat different basis. The patient was a man of thirty with an alarming type of dipsomania; his homosexuality was characterized by repeated violent fights with the sexual partner, and a series of compulsive ceremonials which interfered seriously with his freedom of activity. A progressive deterioration of his behavior, which consisted in yielding more and more to sudden impulses, led to the complete collapse of his career and compelled his hospitalization. The most salient psychological fact presented at the beginning of his analysis was his almost religious adoration of the memory of his mother, who had died a few years previously. Another signal feature was his denial that women possessed any sexual attraction for him, although the very first general account of his life, as well as his dreams, betrayed his heterosexual interest.

Most of the details of his analysis may be omitted, as I wish to indicate only the main facts in his instinctual development. He was the only son of a socially distinguished family, a family entirely dominated by the strong personality of the mother, and in which the father, a mild and unassuming person, was dependent upon the mother in very much the same way as his little son. Competitive feelings in regard to the father, for which the son had indeed little reason, could be discovered only in the last period of his analysis. Up to that time, as we have said, he consistently denied any masculine aspirations. All active heterosexual tendencies were covered by a deep layer of oral dependence upon the mother. His refusal to be heterosexual also determined his compulsive symptoms. These were all symbolic self-castrations and at the same time reactions against his desire to castrate himself. It was on this basis that we may explain a stubborn, uncontrollable tearing of his fingernails, usually carried out in his sleep. Similarly, obsessional fears of forgetting things and losing his mind were manifestations of this same refusal to be masculine: in the typical fashion of compulsive neurotics, he had to make sure of the contents of his pockets, and see whether his money, his checkbook and other objects were still where he had put them. He could scarcely read anything because when he did, he would immediately be obsessed by the idea of forgetting some data connected with the reading. He was forced to interrupt his reading and consult an encyclopedia or textbook to make sure that he remembered the facts accurately. These symptoms were all reactions against his wish to dispense with masculinity. However, this self-castrative tendency was not primarily self-punitive, a reaction of the superego; it had a deeper instinctual basis. He wanted to get rid of his genital sexuality because it disturbed his passive relation to his mother, whom he adored as a goddess in an extremely passive way. He entirely renounced his masculinity, since heterosexual impulses would have disturbed this attachment, which he succeeded in endowing with a completely sublimated religious character. The incompatibility of active male tendencies with this oral passive dependence was the instinctual basis of his wish to do away with all manifestations of his heterosexuality. Only late in his analysis, after he had begun to tolerate his masculine tendencies, could we discover the chronologically older source of his castration fear, its origin in his conflict with his father. This phase of the analysis, in the second year of his treatment, started with a confession that in his early twenties he had had a violent love affair with a socially inacceptable woman. The unwillingness with which he confessed this was striking, since it disavowed his previous contention of lacking all real interest in women. During his narration of this love affair, a latent resentment against his mother came to the surface, a resentment due to her having been the cause of the abrupt ending of the affair. The mother, as is so common, fostered the son's passive attachment by her own possessive attitude toward him, her only son, whom she did not wish to lose to another woman.

A violent exacerbation of his compulsive fears of losing things appeared during the same period of the analysis, in which the fight between the active heterosexual and oral receptive tendencies had been revived to an utmost degree. Each progressive step in the direction of heterosexuality was followed by a violent wave of self-castrative tendencies, for a long while without any signs of father conflict or sense of guilt. The transference was still exclusively a passive oral mother transference; he blamed me for each success in the line of activity, and he resented such success as an attempt on my part to get rid of him and resolve his passive dependence.

However, his violent self-castrative tendencies inevitably generated castration fear as a response. In turn, this fear evoked manifold symbolic evidence of his masculinity. It was interesting to observe his almost simultaneous wish to lose and to have a penis, his rapid vacillation between the wish to castrate himself, his castration fear and the ensuing display of masculinity. He would lie on the couch (for him, a passive gesture) only if he held in his hand objects symbolic of the phallus; then a little later he would place near the genitals some other object which represented symbolically the female organ.

The most striking reaction against his self-castrative tendencies was an unusual hysterical conversion symptom, marked polyuria, which set in periodically during these weeks of intense instinctual conflict. Sometimes his bladder filled every two hours, and the urge was particularly harassing during the analytical session. Conclusive analytic material left no doubt as to the meaning of the symptom. It was an attempted denial of the castration which he nevertheless wished to inflict upon himself at the time, chiefly for instinctual reasons. During the period of this polyuria, he dreamed not of urinating but of having water poured on him. His wish to be a woman was very similar in meaning to the self-castrative behavior of one of Abraham's patients, a drug addict who injected his genitalia with cocaine and expressed thereby his wish to be castrated so that his oral relation with his mother would remain undisturbed.[4]

As our patient progressively acknowledged his heterosexuality, his conflict increased in intensity. He succeeded in having sexual intercourse with a young woman—at first, however, with relatively little emotional meaning. As he gradually began to display more signs of masculinity and an increasingly competitive attitude, he began to feel

[4] This case was reported at a meeting of the Berlin Psychoanalytic Society.

a marked sense of guilt in reference to his father. At the same time, wishes to identify himself with the analyst began to dominate the material of his analytic sessions. The transference assumed for the first time the character of the competitive father transference, though he constantly tended to fall back into the passive receptive attitude. Only then did the other source of his castration fear come to light: his superego's reaction against his wish to be competitive and aggressive in regard to his father. In this period of the analysis, his homosexual interest—a classical example of mother identification and projection of the oral receptive tendency on to the sexual partner— had almost disappeared.

In this analysis I was able for the first time to distinguish clearly between the two different sources of castration fear; because the in-stinctual foundation of the fear—the incompatibility of his oral recep-tive and masculine active tendencies—predominated and entirely overshadowed the conflict concerning his father. But it would be falla-cious to assume that this extreme oral dependence was a sign of de-ficient masculinity. Only the simultaneous presence of aggressive masculinity and passive dependence can explain the history of his symp-toms and their development.

Besides merely differentiating between the two sources of castra-tion fear, I was also able to reconstruct their chronological sequence and the involved interplay of structural and instinctual conflicts. An early renunciation of competition with the father, who gave the pa-tient so little opportunity for a masculine identification, led to a com-plete regression to the oral level. This regression was at the same time effectively supported by the possessive attitude of the mother.

The instructiveness of this case is due to the fact that the instinc-tual conflict developed during the analysis before my eyes, after the treatment had succeeded in stirring up his deeply buried masculinity. Before the analysis, his short but violent love affair, the only revolu-tionary attempt at overcoming his oral dependence, was easily sup-pressed by the strong personality of the mother.

Solution of the conflict between retentive and expulsive tendencies in anal eroticism

A discussion of instinctual conflicts would be incomplete if it omitted a consideration of the role played by the anal organization in their solution. At present, however, I should like to call attention to merely one point—to the function of anal eroticism in the solution of the conflict of active and passive strivings, or more precisely, of recep-tive and expulsive strivings. After the first deprivations on the oral re-ceptive level, the child soon detects at the other end of the alimentary tract the possibility of obtaining a pleasurable sensation of a similar character. This pleasure sensation, though physically related to the oral sensation, differs from it in one important respect: it is based, not on a receptive function like oral pleasure, but on a retentive function, on the retention of the child's own bodily product. This, as we already know, explains why the feeling of independence is so typical of the anal character. The anal pleasure is the first one which the child can obtain not only independently of the environment—this is also true of thumbsucking—but in a way that cannot be so easily detected or interfered with. Perhaps an even more important feature of anal eroticism is that it gratifies at the same time both passive receptive and active expulsive tendencies and is therefore extremely suitable for balancing these opposed conflicting trends. Thus anal regression often serves as the solution of this most fundamental instinctual conflict between active and passive, receptive and expulsive tendencies and explains the patient's stubborn adherence to it.

Instinctual conflicts in the female ego

Whereas the exclusively structural dynamic analysis of mental processes permits formulations which are equally valid for men and women, the combination of the metapsychological approach with the qualitative analysis of instinctual forces makes a separate study of female psychology necessary. It is not my present purpose to go into details regarding the structural and instinctual relations in women. I shall content myself with a few general conclusions.

In the male, the Oedipus situation finds structural expression in the development of the superego. This structural differentiation in turn gives rise to an instinctual conflict which results from the inhibition of the masculine tendencies and consequent re-enforcement of passive female or regressive oral receptive tendencies. In female development, according to Freud's recent studies, the instinctual conflicts of the late pre-Oedipal period determine the Oedipus relation, which then leads to the structural differentiation in the personality. The instinctual conflict, the flight from the female role expressed in the penis envy of the little girl, has to be settled before the girl can identify herself with her mother, and thus form the basis of the structural differentiation of the female personality. The little boy's castrative attitude towards his father finds a stronger structural expression than the same conflict during the phallic phase of the little girl. The little girl's phallic aspiration, according to this view, is relinquished mainly on account of frustration, whereas in the case of the little boy, the external frustration is very soon supported by guilt reactions based on a positive father indentification.

In spite of the great attention paid to this field in recent years, much in this pre-Oedipal phase of female development is still obscure.

As soon as the mother identification has taken place, however, the structural and instinctual relations become more transparent. Here again, the structuralized mother conflict influences the character of the female strivings; it increases their masochistic quality, according to the principle described by Freud in his article, "The Economic Problem in Masochism." The need for punishment called "moral masochism," which results from the mother conflict, intensifies the original female masochism and thus increases the masochistic quality of the female role, as if the little girl intended to emphasize the suffering element of her incestuous wishes in order to diminish her guilt feelings toward the mother. In the analysis of the very common masochistic fantasies of little girls, the aggressor can be easily identified as the father. The sexual fantasy itself contains the punishment and thus eliminates the sense of guilt. Now a new difficulty arises, however, on account of the fear of this overmasochistic character of the female role. In this overmasochistic form the ego cannot accept the female attitude and a new flight from the female role sets in. The masculine tendencies of the female ego, which are held over from the phallic phase, support this flight, and this new wave of masculinity fortifies the pre-Oedipally prepared female castration complex and creates a variety of new difficulties in the relation to men. In order to avoid guilt feelings toward the mother, the little girl tends to imagine that the sexual act is pure suffering and considers the man a brutal aggressor. Both the fear of the penis and resentment against the man in the form of castrative wishes are necessary reactions to this masochistic distortion of the sexual functions. I have repeatedly found that the little girl adheres so stubbornly to the theory that she has lost a penis because this gives her justification of her own castrative tendencies. It is a paranoid mechanism: "He took mine and therefore I am justified in wanting his penis."

Thus in female psychology we see a similar interplay of structural and instinctual factors. The structural factor representing the mother conflict modifies the character of instinctual strivings, increasing their masochistic nature in a way which ensures their rejection by the ego. This rejection leads to aggressive castrative wishes which are the basis of new structural and external conflicts. As in men, the structural conflict leads to an instinctual one, which in turn again leads to new structural and external conflicts.

Conclusion

We may now attempt to compare the results of this study with those structural dynamic formulations with which several years ago I tried to give a generally valid description of neurotic symptom formation.[5] We see in both men and women an instinctual factor active and responsible for the return of repressed tendencies that is different from the structural factor which alone was taken into account in the older formulation. According to the previous formulation, suffering, self-punishment or any kind of compliance with the claims of the superego, by diminishing the ego's fear of the superego, facilitates the gratification of repressed tendencies. The same formulation also took into account that the self-punishing reactions coincide with and serve for the gratification of female masochistic tendencies. Comparing the results of the present investigation with this older view, we find now in addition another factor responsible for the return of repressed tendencies: the reaction against passive female wishes or oral receptive strivings which have been increased under the influence of the repression of masculine active strivings. The repression itself creates a force which acts in the opposite direction. This reactive force has two components—the well-known pressure of the repressed tendencies for return, but in addition to this, a reactive or compensatory tendency to deny the polar opposed striving (female passive or oral receptive) which has increased as a result of the repression. *In the case of men the repressed masculine drive tends to return not only in order to express itself, but also to deny and outweigh female strivings.* The return of the repressed tendency consequently has a double dynamic basis: (1) The formerly described diminished dependence of the ego upon the superego through suffering, and in addition (2) the reaction of a repressed tendency against its polar opposite, which increased through the mere fact of the repression. While suffering impairs the superego's veto of the returning tendency, the instinctual conflict increases its expressive power.

Psychologically these phenomena manifest themselves somewhat differently in men and women. In both men and women, the tension between superego and ego is manifested in the psychological phenomenon of the sense of guilt. The resulting instinctual conflict, however, appears in men more as a sense of inferiority, in women more as fear. To avoid guilt, the male ego flees either to a female or pregenital attitude, but pays for this with an increased sense of inferiority. In fleeing from this sense of inferiority into an intensified aggressive display of masculinity, the guilt conflict is again increased and consequently new repressions are required. At the same time the exaggerated overt masculinity and independence intensify the thirst for femininity and dependence in the unconscious. This vicious circle of the neurotic conflicts can be best compared with a decompensated

[5] F. Alexander, *Psychoanalysis of the Total Personality*, New York: Nervous and Mental Disease Publishing Co., 1930.

heart disease in which the insufficient heart function leads to increased tension in the tissues, which in turn adds to the dynamic obstacle to be overcome by the contractions of the heart.

In women, the immediate consequence of the mother conflict is not to increase the opposite masculine tendency, but to intensify the very quality of the female role, its masochistic nature. This creates primarily fear of and resentment against men rather than a sense of inferiority, since the masochistic tendency is not so intensively in conflict with the female ego's attitude as are passivity and masochism in man. Even oral regression is nearer to female sexuality (which, at least in relation to men, is receptive) than to male sexuality, which is an expulsive, giving function. However, the more the female ego has retained from its pre-Oedipal phallic aspirations, or, in other words, the stronger the masculine identification of the female ego, the more sense of inferiority is apt to mingle with fear and resentment.

This flight of the masculine ego from female tendencies, which have been increased under the influence of the intimidations of the Oedipus period, and the similar flight of the female ego from the feminine role, which under the pressure of guilt feelings assumed an overmasochistic character, does not justify the Adlerian concept that the masculine principle is the only effective factor in the personality both of men and women. The repudiation of female strivings and masochism is only one side of the total picture. It is true that male patients, in denying their passive female or receptive dependent tendencies, are apt to overload themselves with responsibilities and emphasize their masculinity and therefore cannot indulge in any receptive gratifications. Yet just because of this exaggeration of their masculinity and independence they develop an unconscious wish for infantile dependence and passive receptiveness. They live a more masculine life than they really can afford. Many of their neurotic symptoms covertly satisfy their repudiated passive strivings which on account of this repudiation are even increased in the unconscious. Similarly, women with a pronounced masculinity complex always remain unsatisfied because their passive female longing is not abolished even though it be rejected by the ego on account of its too intensely masochistic component. In psychology there is no possibility of measuring quantities, and therefore we cannot determine the relative intensity of different psychic quantities. What we can say with certainty is that both in the male and female personality, apart from the wish for domination and masculine activity, the regressive tendency for infantile dependence or female passivity is a powerful factor. The fact that in the masculine personality these tendencies cannot appear in the conscious ego without causing a conflict is no proof of their ineffectiveness.

In conclusion, we may say that the structural differentiation, which is the result of adjustment to the environment, has a double effect upon the personality. By excluding certain impulses from motor discharge, it creates a tension of the restricted strivings. But in addition it has an even deeper effect upon the instinctual life. It disturbs the balance of conflicting tendencies, increases the bisexual conflict, changes the proportion of pregenital and genital strivings, and that of the destructive and erotic elements in the object relation: furthermore, it changes the quantitative distribution of narcissistic and object libido. We have learned that the ego has a double function; it brings the instinctual life into harmony with the situation given in external reality, and it brings harmony into the original chaos of the instinctual strivings of the id. We see now that the performance of the first function, the adjustment to the environment, creates difficulties for the solution of the second problem, the equilibrium of the instinctual life. It was not my purpose to give a complete account of all possible instinctual problems which arise secondarily from the stuctural differentiation of the personality during the process of adjustment. In discussing its universal effects upon the instinctual life, I tried to demonstrate a possible method of approach, which consists in the combination of the metapsychological with the qualitative analysis of mental processes.

It was especially instructive for me to observe that like neurotic behavior, a criminal behavior also is often not simply an expression of the unadjusted nature of man, but on the contrary a reaction of protest against certain effects which adjustment entails upon the instinctual life. Indeed, most of the criminals I have studied were not simply unadjusted, but in a sense overadjusted, intimidated or spoiled individuals, and their criminality was the ego's protest against the disproportionate consequences of intimidating or spoiling, such as loss of masculine characteristics and regression to infantile cravings. The loss of masculinity and adult qualities act like narcissistic injuries and are responsible for the aggressive, antisocial nature of the ego's compensatory reactions. So long as society's methods of adjusting the child's ego to collective life remain either intimidation and deprivation, or spoiling (instead of a scientifically founded, adequate combination of both), criminality will be an unavoidable by-product of social life.

Concerning the Genesis
of the Castration Complex

◀ 1935 ▶

I want to describe the psychological conditions relative to which one of my patients remembered an important dream of his childhood, the connection of which with a significant experience of his childhood furnishes a convincing confirmation of our representation of the genesis of the fear of castration. The dreamer was a young artist who suffered from temporary impotence. A childhood dream, which he had completely forgotten, he remembered during an analytic session in which a recent dream was being analyzed. The recent dream, which brought back to his consciousness the dream of childhood, was as follows:

"I see an acrobat or boxer with a yellow vest in the typical posture which an acrobat would assume, in order to demonstrate his physical power or strength. He held his legs straddled in a particular manner."

To "boxer" there came into his mind the gymnasium apparatus which he had bought the previous day for exercising and to strengthen his muscles. The great significance which the patient attached to physical strength had become known to us in a previous hour. The wish to be strong was in him a substitute for the lessened sexual potency and was to help him overcome the unpleasant feeling of inferiority. The overestimation of bodily strength is quite frequent in patients who suffer impotency.

With "yellow vest" he associated gold and gold money. Money filled for him the same role as physical strength; it was a substitute for genital potency and a means of overcoming the inferiority caused by the impotence. This method also, i.e., using money to overcompensate for inferiority feelings, is frequently met with; for example, in parvenus who seek to make compensation with money for personal qualities which are lacking.

112

The peculiar straddled position of the legs called to his mind the position of the legs of the woman during coitus. He added that he imagined himself as a woman, i.e., castrated, because he could not use his genitals.

The signification of the dream is evident: the patient appears in the dreams as an acrobat, as if to say, "In spite of the fact that I am impotent and like a woman (the legs spread or placed in a womanly manner) yet I am strong as a boxer and have much money (yellow vest)." The dream is a device for comforting him in his impotency. The mechanism used in the dream is regression to anal and muscle erotism by means of which the impaired genital erotism is to be replaced.

The dream gave me a good opportunity to show him these connections and to gather up the analytic disclosures hitherto gained. While I was in the act of showing him the psychic methods with which he wished to compensate for his impotence he interrupted me with a childhood recollection and a dream of his childhood which suddenly came to him. When he was three years old a servant girl had compelled him to look at the genitalia of a little five-year-old neighbor girl whose legs she had forced her to spread apart. This first knowledge of the anatomic sex differences has frightfully upset him. In the night following this experience he saw in a dream *this same little girl, out of whose genitals there hung a fairly long cord. He himself was sucking on this cord.*

The meaning of this dream reveals itself openly as the belying of the fact which he had observed about the little girl the day before —namely, that she had no penis. Apart from that, the boy denied the oral deprivation, in that in the dream he was sucking at her genitals as at a nipple.

His knowledge of the female genitals increased his castration fear and he responded thereto with a reaction which was intended to entirely destroy in like manner an earlier disillusionment, the loss of his mother's breast. The source of his castration fear was, hence, an earlier sustained loss, the separation from the breast of the mother. He had fears of losing his penis because he had once before entirely lost a source of joy—the breast of the mother. The view of the genitals of the little girl greatly increased the fearful expectation. The dream then comforted him, in that he asserted that the girl nevertheless had a penis; "It is not true that there are persons without penises; therefore it is not true that a person may lose his penis." The dream goes even further and says, "It is not only true that you cannot lose your penis; you have, in fact, lost nothing and you have even the satisfaction of your suckling pleasure, the loss of which no one will ever force you to undergo."

The only detail of the dream which I could not explain was the representation of the female genitalia—condensation of (breast) nipple and penis—by means of a long cord. It is to be observed as a curiosity that the patient associated with this cord the umbilical cord, but since he had this association thirty years after the dream, we cannot find any relationship to the dream. At three years of age he certainly had no knowledge of the existence of the umbilical cord.

If we compare the recent dream with that of his childhood, of which he again became conscious through the analysis of his recent dream, we find a striking similarity between them. In the recent dream he sought to comfort himself for his impotence, which represents a kind of castration, by an anal satisfaction—by money—and in the dream of his childhood he allayed his castration fear by an oral satisfaction. One cannot escape the conclusion that these three experiences—the weaning from the feeding breast, the curtailing of the anal satisfactions and the castration fear—are emotionally bound together and belong to the same emotional category. We can further assert that the two pregenital deprivations, the oral and the anal, prepare an emotional basis upon which grows the castration fear. When the child has learned in his early pregenital development that every pleasure has an end, then the expectation of the unhappy losses take deep root in him and thus he learns to react to the genital pleasures with castration expectations. This explains the universality of the castration complex, which is found in all cases, even where actual castration threats never occurred. The castration fear is deeply rooted in the typical pregenital experiences of infantile disillusionments and deprivations.

The conditions under which this infantile dream was remembered have also a technical significance and serve to illuminate a fundamental principle of our technique of treatment. As is evident, both dreams have the same emotional basis. After the analysis of the actual dream, after its latent content became conscious to the patient, he remembered the infantile dream. I am convinced that this is the typical way to get at the repressed infantile material. By bringing into consciousness a repressed unconscious thought content of the present time, we open the way for similar or identical infantile repressed material. After my patient understood the mechanism by means of which he sought to comfort himself concerning his impotence, he could remember the mechanism by means of which he had endeavored to govern his infantile castration fears.

This circumstance is the foundation of a universal technical principle. It asserts this: the analysis of the actual situation (in the first place, naturally, the transference as an experimental example of the actual psychic situation) is the best way to bring infantile material into consciousness. An economic consideration may clarify this fact. The repressions of adult life are conditioned by infantile repressions; that means, one represses as an adult, similar material (similar emotional qualities) as one repressed when a child. The distinguishing difference between the situation of the adult and that of the child lies in the relationship between the strength of the ego and the repressed impulses. The weak, helpless infantile ego must repress the same conflicts which the grown-up ego could easily resolve. Therefore, the chances of being able to make conscious the recently repressed material are much greater than those of remembering the corresponding infantile material. In other words, the understanding of recent unconscious material enlarges the permeability of the ego for repressed affects. In the transference situation the patient repeats his repressed infantile situation but instead of an infantile ego, the grown-up ego has to cope with the same emotions. In addition, the emotions active in the transference are less intensive than the corresponding infantile emotions, because they are only experimental examples of the latter. All repressed material cannot be remembered during an analysis, but that which can be remembered we will get mostly only after the emotional content of the transference and actual life situation have been made conscious.

The Logic of Emotions
and Its Dynamic Background

◄ 1935 ►

Emotional syllogisms

Our understanding of psychological connections is based on the tacit recognition of certain causal relationships which we know from our everyday experience and the validity of which we accept as self-evident. We understand anger and aggressive behavior as a reaction to an attack; fear and guilt as results of aggressiveness; envy as an outgrowth of the feeling of weakness and inadequacy. Such self-evident emotional connections as "I hate him, because he attacks me," I shall call emotional syllogisms. Just as logical thinking is based on intellectual syllogisms, the "logic of emotions" consists of a series of emotional syllogisms. The feeling of the self-evident validity of these emotional connections is derived from our daily introspective experience as we witness these emotional sequences in ourselves, probably from the first moment after birth until death. Just as the logic of intellectual thinking is based on repeated and accumulated experiences of relations in the external world, the logic of emotions is based on accumulated experiences of our own internal emotional reactions. The logic of intellectual thinking is the crystallized product of external, the logic of emotions is crystallized in the same way out of internal, experiences. As such, the logic of emotions is more ancient than logical thinking, which probably explains its ability to overpower intellectual processes.

It is quite justifiable to call these emotional causal sequences "the logic of emotions" because they seem to us almost as binding as those intellectual relations which are the basis of logical thinking. We say, for example, "It was quite logical that A gave such an emotional answer to B because we heard that B had insulted him."

The psychoanalytic method has extended the possibility of such casual explanations also to psychic phenomena which seemed previously irrational and inexplicable. It showed that often in the chain of

116

metal processes some of the links are not conscious and that in such cases unconscious links can be reconstructed which are connected by the same kind of psychological causality as conscious mental processes. The reconstruction of unconscious emotional links made a wide range of seemingly irrational psychic processes, such as neurotic symptoms, accessible for psychological explanation. Every psychoanalytic reconstruction of the patient's psychic development consists of such emotional syllogisms. Psychoanalytic interpretations are to a great extent applications to unconscious processes of emotional syllogisms which we know from our conscious mental life. If we investigate closely any of our psychoanalytic concepts, we recognize that they are based on these tacitly accepted connections in emotional life. Thus, for example, the Oedipus complex consists of a number of such syllogisms. *Because* the little boy feels that the father interferes with his possessive attitude toward the mother, he develops aggressive feelings against the father. Another feature of the same complex reveals a different emotional connection. *Because* the little boy feels that he is small and the father is big, he envies the father's strength. That possessive love does not tolerate competitors, and that envy is a reaction to weakness, is, in this case, the logic of emotions which is exemplified by the Oedipus complex.

Though many such emotional connections are well known and tacitly accepted as universally valid characteristics of man's nature, psychoanalysis has also described emotional relations which are not so self-evident and which we do not know from our everyday life without some reflection. Thus, from everyday experience one is acquainted with guilt feelings, but the understanding of a guilt reaction is not so self-evident because it is not entirely a conscious reaction. However, after some reflection, everyone can understand from his own experience that a sense of guilt arises when hostility is directed toward a person for whom at the same time love and gratitude is felt. On the other hand, even the most careful introspective reflection could not establish the fact which pyschoanalytic technique has revealed—that the hostile intention might be even entirely unconscious and yet provoke a sense of guilt that a person consciously feels without knowing its origin. This explanation of guilt feelings from unconscious hostilities is based on an emotional connection which we know from the psychology of conscious processes, the validity of which, however, is then extended to include unconscious processes.

In studying unconscious processes, especially dreams, it soon became obvious that the emotional logic of unconscious processes, though similar to the logic of conscious processes, is not entirely identical with the latter. In his *Interpretation of Dreams*, Freud has shown that unconscious thinking does not follow the rules of conscious thinking, that the strict rules of logic are not valid for unconscious thinking. Simple logical postulates, such as that if a thing is in one place it cannot be in another place at the same time, are not recognized in the dream. Freud also showed that in dreams causality is expressed by temporal sequence, that the difference between assertion and negation is much less distinct, and that a statement can be expressed by its opposite. Moreover the critical faculty of differentiating between objects is not so highly developed in the unconscious. In dreams one object can be substituted for another, even if there is very little essential similarity between them. All these differences refer, however, to intellectual faculties and show that the dream processes are characterized by less precision of the intellectual functions. It seems that the fundamental emotional connections which I call "the logic of emotions" are about the same in consciousness and in the unconscious. Fear and guilt as a reaction to hate and attack, envy as a reaction to the feeling of weakness, jealousy as a reaction to possessive love, govern both conscious and unconscious processes. If anything, these emotional syllogisms appear in the unconscious even more frankly because they are less disturbed by the correction of rational critical insight. One can express this difference by saying that conscious mental processes are characterized by fuller development of certain critical intellectual functions, by a more precise differentiating faculty, whereas the logic of emotions seems to appear more frankly and forcefully in the unconscious. Furthermore there are a series of emotional reactions or syllogisms in the unconscious which to the conscious mind of the adult appear somewhat strange and peculiar. The principle of talion, eye for an eye, tooth for a tooth, has a much more strict validity for the unconscious than for the conscious mind of a civilized adult. The civilized adult will still recognize this emotional syllogism as human but it appears to him somewhat primitive or archaic and he will not apply it with the same naïve certainty as a logical law. For the unconscious, however, the principle of talion is just as binding as is for the conscious mind the logical syllogism that if A is equal to both B and C, then B is equal to C.

The strangeness of some of the emotional syllogisms governing unconscious processes is one of the reasons why psychoanalysis seems to the lay mind so abstruse. One often hears the layman saying that people do not feel and react as psychoanalysts state; that the psychology of psychoanalysis is not human. The study of children or primitive people, whose behavior is still frankly governed by these primitive emotional syllogisms, shows, however, that they are not only human but even more fundamental than the later acquired modifications of the emotional life.

To a large extent the development of psychoanalysis consisted in the discovery and formulation of different archaic emotional syllo-gisms which rule the unconscious processes. I refer in the first place to one of the most brilliant discoveries of Freud: the emotional syllo-gism that underlies the paranoid delusion of persecution in men.[1]

"I do not love him, I hate him," is the first part of the syllogism de-termined by the rejection of female tendencies felt toward a man, a rejection which is based on the wounded narcissism of the mascu-line ego.

The second link of the syllogism is, "I hate him because he perse-cutes me."

The emotional logic of this mechanism is obvious: hostility can be accepted by the ego if it seems a justified reaction to being attacked.

The psychology of conscience, of which we speak in structural terms as the relation of ego and superego, can only be understood on the basis of such primitive emotional reactions. So, for example, the foundation of the compulsion neurosis is the principle that suffering is felt by the ego not only as an atonement for guilt but even as a source of justification for indulgence in forbidden gratification. This emo-tional syllogism which underlies the complicated system of obsessional and compulsive symptoms, is often referred to as the bribery of the superego by suffering. It can be verbalized as follows: "Since I suffer and submit myself to extreme restrictions, I have the right to indulge in forbidden gratifications."

Rado has described a somewhat similar emotional syllogism as of fundamental significance for the understanding of depression. Here suffering and self-inflicted punishment are used not only for atone-ment and as a justification for transgressions (as in the compulsion neurosis) but also as an appeal for love, "because I am suffering so much, therefore I deserve to be loved by you." [2]

Another type of emotional logic forms the basis of a more compli-cated mechanism which Freud described as homosexuality resulting from overcompensated rivalry. This reaction can be divided into a series of partial emotional reactions. The whole emotional process is about the following: envy, hostile rivalry against the competitor, causes guilt which requires humiliation before the competitor. If this need for humiliation is connected with the feeling of weakness toward the powerful competitor, it results in a female submission which is the

[1] S. Freud, "A Case of Paranoia," *Collected Papers*, New York: Basic Books, 1959, Vol. II, 150-161.

[2] Sandor Rado, "The Problem of Melancholia," *Int. J. Psycho-Anal.*, IX (1928), 420-437. The emotional syllogism: suffering as an appeal for love, is even more clearly worked out in Rado's address, "Unconscious Mechanism in Neurotic Depressions," delivered at the Annual Meeting of the American Psy-chiatric Association in Boston, 1933.

basis of a passive homosexual attitude. This emotional syllogism, which is nearer to the female than to the male psychology, can be expressed as follows: "You are too strong; I cannot overpower you, but at least I wish to be loved by you."

The vector analysis of psychic processes

If we deprive these emotional sequences of their ideational content and only pay attention to the dynamic quality (direction) of the tendencies which participate in these emotional syllogisms, we come to simple dynamic relations similar to those in physics and chemistry. It is probable that such simple relations constitute also the fundamental dynamics of biological processes.

In many of these emotional syllogisms a common and striking feature is a certain polarity. It appears that the expression of a tendency is apt to provoke and strengthen its polar opposite: for example, suffering increases the tendency toward gratification and vice versa, indulgence in a pleasurable gratification increases guilt which then gives rise to an inhibitory reaction against the gratification. Furthermore extreme masculine aggressive competition is apt to strengthen the polar opposite passive female tendency; and passive female tendencies again by wounding the masculine narcissism stimulate the masculine attitude. Dependence stimulates the opposite tendency toward independence; effort and struggling increase again the polar opposite wish to be helped and to lean upon a strong helper.

This polarity of the mental life which can be compared with the law of action and reaction in physics is, as we will see, by no means the only dynamic principle expressed in these emotional syllogisms.

In the investigation of psychogenic organic disturbances it has proved of great value to study psychic processes according to their general dynamic direction (vector quality), while temporarily ignoring the manifold variety of their ideational content. During the analysis of organ neuroses we soon learned that very different psychological impulses with quite different specific content may lead to the disturbance of the same organic function. At first sight it seems that these psychogenic factors are not at all specific, that the same disturbance can be caused by a great variety of different psychological contents, seemingly unrelated to each other. Further analysis of these apparently unrelated psychic factors showed, however, that they had one important feature in common, namely, the direction of the general dynamic tendency expressed by them. So, for example, organs with the functions of incorporation are apt to be disturbed by very different repressed tendencies. These tendencies, however, have one dynamic feature in common, namely, that they all express receiving or taking something. It has been observed that this general dynamic quality of a psychological content determines which kind of organ function will be disturbed by it: the stomach functions can be disturbed for example by any one of the following heterogeneous group of repressed wishes: the wish to receive help, love, money, a gift, a child, or the wish to castrate, to steal, to take away something. The same group of wishes may also disturb other organic functions which involve incorporation, such as, for example, the inspiratory phase of the respiratory act or swallowing. The common feature in all these different tendencies is their centripetal direction; they express receiving or taking something.

During our studies we have learned that it is necessary to differentiate between two forms of incorporation, between passive receiving and aggressive taking. Taking by force, the aggressive form of incorporation, develops as a rule as a reaction to thwarted receptive tendencies. The emotional syllogism underlying this process is: "If I do not receive something, I have to take it by force." Though for the purposes of psychological understanding it is of great importance to differentiate between the two qualities of passive receiving and aggressive taking, nevertheless with regard to their dynamic effect both of these tendencies belong to the larger category of intaking tendencies and are therefore suitable to influence the incorporative organic functions of both the gastrointestinal tract and the respiratory system.

Another dynamic quality of similar importance is the eliminating tendency. This dynamic category also includes an enormous variety of psychological contents: to give love, to make an effort, to help to produce something, to give a gift, to give birth to a child, on the one hand, but on the other hand also the wish to attack someone (especially by throwing something at him). Any of these impulses, if repressed and excluded from voluntary expression, are apt to influence eliminating organic functions such as urination, defecation, ejaculation, perspiration, the expiratory phase of respiration. Here again, for purposes of psychological understanding it is of primary importance to differentiate between an aggressive form of elimination (anal attack) and a more constructive form consisting in producing and giving something of value (giving birth, for example). Thus we found that a psychogenic diarrhea may be an unconscious substitute for an attack (described by Abraham), but it also may have the meaning of giving birth to a child or may be a substitute for a gift. Both the aggressive and the gift meaning of the excremental functions are well known in child psychology; they retain also the same infantile significance in the unconscious of adults.

A third dynamic quality, the significance of which has forced itself upon us during the analysis of gastrointestinal neuroses, is that of retention. Here again a great variety of different psychological contents share the one common dynamic quality—that of retaining or possessing. Collecting different objects, ordering and classifying them (as a sign of the mastery of them), also the fear of losing something, the rejection of the obligation to give something, the impulse to hide and protect things from being taken away or from deterioration, and the mother's attitude toward the fetus—all these may find expression in retentive physiological innervations. The best known of these is constipation, but it seems also that the retention of urine, retarded ejaculation and certain features of the respiratory act can express the same tendencies. Within the category of retentive urges, it is more difficult to differentiate between a destructive and a more constructive quality, as we have been able to do in the case of the receptive and eliminatory tendencies. For a long time I did not find a satisfactory criterion for differentiating between constructive and destructive forms of retention. Suggestions of Thomas M. French helped, however, to formulate a satisfactory discrimination which corresponds well with the observed psychological material. Retention can be thought of as a constructive process, if it means assimilation as represented in the process of organic growth. Retentive tendencies expressed in the mother's attitude toward the fetus and certain tendencies which we usually call anal erotic, such as a careful classification and organization of material or other protective tendencies, can be considered as more constructive manifestations of this dynamic quality, whereas the tendency to withhold from others, to hide something spitefully, as a revenge or with the tendency to hurt others, is a destructive manifestation of the retentive tendency.

Thus we differentiate three larger categories of psychological tendencies, *intaking, eliminating* and *retaining*. In each of these categories we differentiate again between a positive constructive and a negative destructive manifestation of the same tendency: in the first group, passive receiving and aggressive taking; in the second group, giving of a value and elimination for the purpose of an attack; and in the third, retaining in order to build up and withholding something from others. It is evident that the three main classes express fundamental urges, whereas the six subclasses are more complex tendencies which express not only the direction of the tendency but also a certain attitude (love or hate) toward external objects.

After having differentiated between these general dynamic tendencies, it was no longer difficult to recognize certain emotional syllogisms which express in psychological terms the dynamic relations between these three fundamental tendencies. Only the recognition of these emotional connections has made possible the understanding of the psychological determinations of disturbed organ functions.

I shall discuss those emotional syllogisms which we have studied most thoroughly. I have already mentioned one of them. "I do not receive and therefore I have to take by force." This emotional reaction has been most important for the understanding of the origin of guilt feelings on account of oral incorporating tendencies. This guilt reaction to oral aggression, as I have shown previously, plays an important role in gastric neuroses and in the formation of peptic ulcers.[3]

Vector Analysis of Psychic Tendencies

Tendencies classified according to their fundamental dynamic quality. (Direction)	Tendencies in relation to objects
Incorporation	$\begin{cases} \text{To receive} \\ \text{To take} \end{cases}$
Elimination	$\begin{cases} \text{To give a value} \\ \text{To eliminate in order to attack} \end{cases}$
Retention	$\begin{cases} \text{To retain in order to build up *} \\ \text{To withhold from others} \end{cases}$

*This tendency does not express an object relation but a relation to the self as an object.

An emotional syllogism which is not so well known expresses another dynamic relation between aggressive taking and passive receiving. This is the inhibition of the desire to receive after the receptive urge has taken the aggressive form of wishing to take. The underlying emotional syllogisms can be formulated as follows: "I cannot accept anything from a person whom I really want to rob." This type of guilt reaction plays an important role in the child-parent relations. The castrative tendencies of the little boy toward the father make him unable to receive favors from the father, and become an obstacle to a positive identification with him. This same emotional syllogism is of primary importance also in gastric neuroses and in peptic ulcer formation; it explains the inhibition of oral receptive tendencies as a reaction to an extreme aggressive demanding attitude. These two emotional sequences concern dynamic relationships between two different subgroups within a single dynamic group, the receptive tendencies.

[3] F. Alexander, "The Influence of Psychologic Factors upon Gastro-Intestinal Disturbances"; Catherine Bacon, "Typical Personality Trends and Conflicts in Cases of Gastric Disturbances"; Harry B. Levey, "Oral Trends and Oral Conflicts in a Case of Duodenal Ulcer," *Psychoanal. Quart.*, III (October, 1934), 501-588.

Let us now turn our attention to the relationship between two different categories of dynamic tendencies, the intaking and the eliminating. Indulgence in receptive tendencies often leads to the compensatory tendency to give. Abraham spoke of generosity as a reaction to oral receptive tendencies. The underlying emotional logic of this reaction can be described by three more or less independent emotional syllogisms: (1) "I prefer to give rather than to receive because the giver is in a superior position," (2) "If I am the giver, I am not so dependent upon the good will of others as I should be if I must receive from them," and finally (3) "Because I received so much, I must give something in return." The first syllogism has a narcissistic basis; the second is based on fear; the third is a guilt or superego reaction. All these partial emotional reactions lead to strengthening the giving attitude as a reaction to indulgence in the receptive role.

A similar increased urge to give can also arise as a reaction to strong aggressive taking tendencies. We found that this "compensatory giving" is the emotional basis of many neurotic diarrheas (mucous colitis).[4]

The following emotional syllogism expresses a relation of opposite character between receptive tendencies and the urge to give: "I give so much and therefore I have the right to receive." This is a mechanism which is also of fundamental importance for the understanding of certain psychological features and predominating character trends in cases of psychogenic diarrhea. The diarrhea is evaluated by the unconscious as a form of giving and is utilized to justify a strong and demanding attitude in life. Patients suffering from gastric neurosis or peptic ulcer are more apt to compensate for their strong unconscious receptive-dependent attitude by assuming responsibilities and by concentrated efforts in work; the compensatory mechanism of the colitis cases on the other hand is merely symbolic: the diarrhea is often a substitute for real compensatory giving in life.

Also the relation between receiving and retaining is governed by several emotional syllogisms. "I do not receive and therefore I must hold on to my possessions" is the best known example. This has been described by several authors who have written about the anal character. This emotional reaction has proved in our studies to be an important causative factor in psychogenic chronic constipation.[5]

[4] Alexander, op. cit., George W. Wilson, "Typical Personality Trends and Conflicts in Cases of Spastic Colitis"; Maurice Levine, "Pregenital Trends in a Case of Chronic Diarrhea and Vomiting," Psychoanal. Quart., III (October, 1934), 501-588.

[5] Alexander, op. cit., and The Medical Value of Psycho-Analysis, New York: Norton, 1932, p. 197; George W. Wilson, "Report of a Case of Acute Laryngitis occurring as a Conversion Symptom during Analysis," Psychoanal. Rev., XXI, No. 4 (October, 1934), 408-414.

Our study of cases of chronic constipation have revealed also a more complicated emotional syllogism which also leads to increased retention. This emotional syllogism connects four different dynamic impulses: receptive, giving, aggressive eliminating, and retaining tendencies. "I receive so much that I must give something in return" is the first part of the syllogism. This strong urge to give, however, is rejected by the narcissistic nucleus of the ego. "No, I do not want to give, and if I must give, then it shall be nothing better than excrement." This expresses the resentment and the aggressive tendency against the one to whom one feels obligated. This aggressive attitude finally leads to fear of retaliation and to increased retention. Apart from this complicated dynamic connection, the strong urge to give directly increases the retentive urge by stimulating the fear that one will suffer loss by giving too much.

In studying these dynamic relationships, the principle of polarity is most striking. Inhibition in receiving stimulates retention, but on the other hand extreme retentive tendencies increase the sense of obligation to give. The principle of polarity is, however, not the only dynamic relationship. We saw, for example, that the positive form of elimination, giving, stimulates the aggressive form of elimination because the obligation to give causes resentment against the one to whom one gives (or has to give) so much. The well-known unconscious hostilities against those whom we love are based on this emotional relation. In this case it is not the polar opposite tendency that is stimulated but rather a parallel tendency. Similarly we see that the inhibition of receiving increases the urge for taking: both these impulses have the same direction and belong to the category of intaking tendencies.

The emotional connections within the retentive group are more obscure than those in the first two groups. The relationships between constructive and aggressive forms of retaining cannot yet be formulated in simple psychological terms. We see, however, that both biologic and social organisms increase their inner cohesive forces if attacked by external enemies, and often grow and flourish better when attacked than in peace. If there is a strong need for protection against loss the opposite tendency not only to holding on to possessions but also to inner consolidation and growth is stimulated. On the other hand, in a peaceful atmosphere the tendency to inner consolidation—probably a function of the retentive urge—often relaxes. Dynamically this means that the destructive form of retention stimulates its constructive form, but it is difficult to translate this dynamic relation into psychological terms. The psychology of the retentive urges still needs further clarification.

The significance of this kind of vector-analysis of psychological impulses which attempts to recognize behind the variety of psychological content its fundamental direction, consists in the fact that those emotional syllogisms which connect these vector quantities are of a general validity and are equally applicable to a great number of different psychological connections. They can be compared to algebraic equations in which different values can be substituted for each other provided they possess the same vector quality. I refer to the publication of the Chicago Psychoanalytic Institute on "The Influence of Psychologic Factors upon Gastro-Intestinal Disturbances," regarding clinical examples illustrating the validity of vector analysis, i.e., that different psychological impulses possess the same vector quality (for example, giving a gift, birth to a child, giving love, taking care of) have a similar influence on the corresponding organic functions.

The usefulness of the vector analysis of psychological impulses is, however, not restricted to the understanding of gastrointestinal disturbances. Experimental studies in which I am engaged, together with Leon Saul, suggest that psychic influences on the lung functions follow the same dynamic principles. It seems that receptive and aggressive taking tendencies can be expressed by the inspiratory act, and eliminating tendencies by the expiratory act. We hope that the psychological background of certain types of asthma can be understood by means of this type of psychodynamic studies.

Psychological influences on still other excretory processes can be understood upon a similar dynamic basis. In one of my patients, for example, a marked perspiration of the palms expressed hostile tendencies; it was similar to psychogenic diarrhea: a substitute for an attack. These mechanisms throw light on such general psychophysiological reflex phenomena as increased peristalsis and increased perspiration (cold sweat) in reaction to fear. We know that fear always provokes aggressions; the coward who "has no guts" substitutes diarrhea and "cold perspiration," a sort of symbolic attack in place of an effective attack on his enemy. These mechanisms, loosening of the bowels and "cold perspiration" in face of danger, though very common, must nevertheless be considered neurotic reactions because they do not fulfill a useful purpose. We may contrast this reaction for example with the increased adrenalin production in reaction to fear, which has physiological consequences of so much value in mobilizing the energies of the individual for defense or flight.

In the light of this dynamic insight, those organ neuroses which consist in a disturbance in the biological functions of intaking, retaining, and eliminating, can be considered as the outcome of a disturbance of the normal balance between these psychological tendencies. Within a certain range of individual differences, there seems to be a certain proportion between these fundamental tendencies which may be considered as normal. It is *probable* that these proportions are different in men and women, but it is *certain* that the normal ratio between giving and receptive tendencies in a little child is different from the corresponding ratio in a fully developed adult. In the little child, still in the process of mental and physical development, receptive urges are stronger in relation to giving tendencies than in adults. We consider it as evidence of neurosis if an adult retains the receptive dependent attitude of a child, because this does not correspond to his psychological and biological status. The psychological manifestation of this is seen in the sense of inferiority with which the adult ego reacts to such an infantile distribution of receptive and giving tendencies.

It is my conviction that this dynamic equilibrium between the three vector quantities, intaking, eliminating and retaining, is biologically conditioned, and represents the fundamental dynamics of the biological process: "life." Emotional syllogisms like those above cited are the reflection in consciousness of this fundamental biological dynamics which can be understood and described both in psychological and in biological terms.

The genetic study of the life history of patients with organ neuroses impressively demonstrates the sensitiveness of the dynamic equilibrium between these three fundamental tendencies. No one of them can be disturbed without upsetting the harmony of all of them. So for example if the receptive demands in childhood are met with continuous deprivations, this may lead to a deeply imprinted fear and to a pessimistic, defeatist outlook, which increases the retentive urges. "I have never received sufficiently, so I must hold on to my possessions. I cannot give anything away because I never shall receive a substitute for it." This strong withholding attitude may then increase a sense of obligation to give, and this sense of obligation as a rule causes deep resentments and consequent withdrawal from the environment. In other cases again we observe that early intimidations cause aggressions, which in turn through guilt reactions make it impossible for the individual to accept support. This inhibition to receive increases the longing for help in the unconscious and at the same time may lead to an extreme compulsion to give in order to placate the guilt feelings.

The most important regulator of the balance between intaking, eliminating, and retentive tendencies is genital sexuality, which constitutes a potent means of drainage for those fundamental psychodynamic urges which cannot find relief in social relations (sublimations). This draining function of the genital sexuality which Ferenczi postulated in his "Theory of Genitality" can be best demonstrated in the extreme case of perversions. Accumulated, unsatisfied aggressions against external objects may lead for example to a sadistic distortion of the sexual urge; unrelieved guilt feelings similarly to a masochistic perversion and inhibited and accumulated curiosity to voyeur tendencies. This draining function of genitality explains why so often "Lustmörder" and pedophiliacs are extremely inhibited, crushed, and weakly individuals who never can give expression to their aggressions in life. All these accumulated aggressions find a vent in their sexual activity. Similarly sexual exhibitionists are usually extremely modest and shy individuals who cannot give expression to their wish to impress others through the ordinary channels: through speech and gestures. They relieve all their pent-up narcissistic urges to show off by exhibiting the penis, i.e., in form of their sexual gratification.

I am convinced that this draining function of genital sexuality is responsible for the central significance of genital disturbances in the etiology of neuroses and psychogenic organ disturbances. The genital system and the voluntary muscular system together take care of those impulses which are directed toward external objects. Genitality relieves those impulses which cannot be handled through the voluntary system. Vaginal gratifications certainly are the most effective relief for accumulated, unsatisfied receptive tendencies in life, ejaculation is correspondingly the most powerful expression of the tendency to give. Both the genital and the voluntary systems are concerned in the external policies of the organism in contrast to the vegetative organs which manage the organism's internal affairs. If both the genital and voluntary outlets are obstructed, other artificial outlets must be developed: the vegetative functions become overcharged by being used for the expression of impulses which should normally be directed toward external objects and which do not constitute real vegetative aims. The neuroses of the gastrointestinal tract and probably those of the respiratory system are just such artificial outlets for accumulated receptive, taking, giving, attacking, and retentive tendencies which, because of inhibitions, are unable to find normal outlet through either the voluntary or the genital systems. The intaking or eliminating or retentive nature of these inhibited tendencies, their vector quality, then determines the type of vegetative organ function which will be disturbed.

Remarks about the Relation
of Inferiority Feelings
to Guilt Feelings

◄ 1938 ►

It is no exaggeration to say that there are no other emotional re-actions that play such a permanent and central role in the dynamic explanations of psychopathological phenomena as guilt feelings and inferiority feelings. Since guilt feelings can be considered as a variety of anxiety—fear of conscience—their outstanding significance in psy-chopathology is self-evident, anxiety being generally recognized as a central issue. The importance of inferiority feelings becomes on the other hand obvious if one thinks of the close relation to envy, com-petitiveness, and ambition. In our literature inferiority feelings and guilt feelings are often dealt with rather summarily as more or less parallel manifestations of a tension between certain ideals and the actual personality, as a kind of tension between what one is and what one would like to be, between what one does and feels and what one should do or feel. In structural terms we speak of tension between su-perego or ego ideal and ego, and consider both inferiority and guilt feelings as different but very closely related expressions of this same tension.

In the following I will try to demonstrate that in spite of the fact that in structural terms inferiority feelings and guilt feelings can be described with the same formula as a tension between ego and ego ideal they are fundamentally different psychological phenomena, and as a rule their dynamic effect upon behavior is opposite. Individuals under the pressure of guilt feelings are apt to behave, with other factors remaining the same, in an opposite way than under the pres-sure of inferiority feelings. I go so far as to call these two types of re-actions dynamic antagonists, comparable in physiology with the sym-pathetic and parasympathetic systems or with extensor muscles and contractors.

129

In making certain generalizations about the relationship of inferiority feelings and guilt feelings to each other, I shall use the method
of approach which seems to me most promising in describing psychodynamic correlations. This is the method of establishing certain elementary emotional sequences for which I have proposed the term
emotional syllogisms, the sum of which constitutes the logic of emotional life. Just as rational thinking can be reduced to a few logical
syllogisms also the more primitive emotional sequences in the mental
apparatus can be reduced to a few elementary emotional syllogisms
which are universal and characteristic for man. I am inclined to see in
these universal emotional sequences the fundamental principles of the
biological process of life as they reflect themselves subjectively in the
individual mind. Guilt reactions and inferiority feelings, or in other
words the psychology of conscience and narcissism, can also be reduced to such elementary emotional equations. We get acquainted
with these emotional sequences during the study of free associations
and dreams and transference manifestations of our patients because
all these phenomena are to a higher degree subject to elementary
emotional dynamisms than the phenomena of rational thinking and
therefore reflect the principles of emotional life in more or less undistorted fashion.

What we call the psychology of conscience in fact consists in a
series of such primitive emotional sequences, the most important of
which is the syllogism that is known as the principle of talion. This conscience reaction can be defined as the expectation of retaliation provoked by one's own hostile aggressions. This expectation is a fearful
one, therefore it belongs to the category of anxiety and properly can
be called fear of conscience. All shadings of the sense of guilt are only
quantitatively different: the sense of guilt is always felt as a pressure,
as an unpleasant tension, the expectation of an impending evil, of a
deserved punishment. It has been sufficiently demonstrated in psychoanalytical literature that the fear of conscience is nothing but the
intrapsychic reduplication of the fear of an external danger, the fear of
retaliation on the part of those persons whom one has attacked, is attacking, or wants to attack. If the fear is directed against external persons we speak of retaliation fear, if the fear is independent of external
objects and is an internal reaction to one's own hostile tendencies,
then we speak of guilt feelings or fear of conscience. We speak also of
an unconscious sense of guilt. This expression however is not quite
adequate. What might be unconscious in this phenomenon is not the
anxiety element in it. There is always the sense of either free-floating
anxiety, a pressure, a fearful expectation, an uneasiness. What is often
unconscious is the underlying repressed hostile aggression, the cause
of the anxiety. All conscience reactions can be reduced to this syllo-

gism: "Because I wish to hurt someone, I shall be hurt and should be hurt." The discussion of its origin, of those experiences from which this emotional axiom has crystallized itself, does not belong to the scope of my present study.

As a form of anxiety, the fearful expectation of an inevitable and deserved suffering, the sense of guilt is primarily an inhibitory phenomenon. Under its pressure the individual is apt to avoid the expression of those impulses which have evoked and contributed to his guilt feelings. At present there is little doubt that these impulses are probably exclusively of a hostile destructive nature.

In certain forms of neuroses and psychoses, especially in paranoia, guilt feelings may have a paradoxical, not inhibitory but excitatory, influence upon the expression of hostile impulses. The emotional logic which makes these paradoxical reactions intelligible can be described about as follows: "It is true that if I wanted to hurt him I should deserve punishment—but I do not want to attack him—he attacks me, he is the guilty one; I act only in self-defense." This emotional syllogism eliminates the inhibitory effect of guilt feelings and makes out of them a source of aggressive behavior. The phenomenon of guilt projection is therefore not contradictory to our more fundamental statement that guilt feelings have an inhibitory effect upon the expression of aggressions. The projection of guilt is one of those mechanisms by which one rids himself of the inhibitory influence of guilt feelings. Other equally common and important mechanisms by which guilt feelings are relieved are self-inflicted punishment and provocative behavior by which others are incited to aggressive behavior.

The psychological content of guilt feelings can be verbalized about as follows: "I am not good. What I want to do (or what I did) is mean or low. I deserve contempt and punishment." In this feeling, in a way, always a sense of justice is implied. One feels guilty because one wants to attack or has attacked somebody who does not deserve it. Such a sense of justice must be present if we are to speak of genuine guilt feelings because whenever one feels that a hostile intention or attack is justified, guilt feelings disappear. Therefore self-defense is never connected with guilt feelings. Without the feeling that one's hostilities are unjustified, there is no guilt feeling. Otherwise the phenomenon of guilt projection would be unintelligible. Whenever one can convince oneself that the object of one's hatred deserves the hate by giving adequate reason for being hated, the feeling of guilt is abolished. This also explains why the most severe guilt feelings develop in sons of loving, understanding, and mild fathers who do not give any justification for hostile feelings.

In summary: guilt feelings belong to the category of fear. They have an inhibitory effect upon the expression of hostile tendencies. This inhibitory effect implies a sense of justice. The different types of reaction to guilt feelings are: 1) the avoidance of the expression of hostile tendencies; 2) self-inflicted punishment; 3) provocative behavior; and 4) guilt projection. All these mechanisms presuppose a sense of justice or in other words the feeling of one's aggressions being unjustified.

Comparing this dynamic analysis of guilt feelings with the psychology of inferiority feelings we find that inferiority feelings on the contrary have as a rule a stimulating and not inhibitory effect upon the expression of hostile aggressions. Inferiority feelings seem even to create directly hostile aggressions. It is true that at first sight the self-condemnation which is at the basis of inferiority feelings sounds similar to the self-condemnation contained in guilt feelings. Also inferiority feelings are a type of self-criticism. The feeling as in the sense of guilt is: "I am no good, I am contemptible." But further inquiry shows an important difference. This feeling of inadequacy is not connected, like guilt feelings, with any sense of justice. The feeling is not so much not being good in a moral sense but being weak, inefficient, unable to accomplish something. In inferiority feelings it is not implied, as it is in guilt feelings, that the self-condemnation is the result of wrongdoing. It is a self-accusation based on a comparison, on the simple fact that one feels weaker than another person. This explains why inferiority feelings stimulate competition. From guilt feelings one tries to rid oneself by renouncing further aggressions or by atoning for them. From inferiority feelings one tries to free oneself by just the opposite type of behavior, by ambitious competition, by trying to take up the fight again, to take revenge on the one who has no other fault than being stronger than oneself.

The common neurotic reactions to inferiority feelings are 1) increased hostile aggressiveness, 2) an attempt to depreciate the competitor, and 3) fantasying oneself as superior, as in megalomania. It is important that in all these reactions aggressive behavior is stimulated and not inhibited as in the case of guilt feelings. Comparing the common reactions to guilt feelings with those to inferiority feelings we see that the former consist of an inhibition against expressing hostile aggressions, the latter consist in a heightened expression of aggressiveness.

The objection might be raised that this distinction between inferiority and guilt feelings is artificial and hair-splitting. One may say that in both cases one accuses oneself of some kind of deficiency. In the case of inferiority feelings one says to oneself, "Are you not ashamed that Bob is stronger than you and licked you?" In the case of guilt feelings: "Are you not ashamed that you steal chocolate from the drawer?" In both cases the same expression is used, "Are you not ashamed?" Closer inquiry shows however that here the use of language is somewhat loose, and the same expression "shame" has a different connotation in the two cases. Shame for being licked by Bob stimulates hostile competition and ambition, or will lead to an attempt to depreciate Bob. The effect of guilt for stealing chocolate is paralyzing. The first type of shame can be eliminated by licking Bob, that is to say by aggressive behavior. The second type of shame can be eliminated only either by atonement or by future avoidance of stealing, that is to say by a higher inhibitory pressure upon the instinctual life.

If doubt still remains that we deal here with two entirely different emotions a brief reference to a clinical example will clearly demonstrate the antithetical dynamic effect of these two forms of self-criticism. The structure of many neuroses consists precisely in the conflict into which the coexistence of strong inferiority and guilt feelings brings the patient. In a case of chronic alcoholism this conflict became evident shortly after the beginning of the analysis. This middle-aged man, the middle child of three brothers, showed from the beginning of his remembered life up to the present age an extremely pronounced self-consciousness connected with vivid sensations of inferiority. He always compared himself unfavorably with his brothers and others, had great athletic ambitions in competitive sport but never had confidence in himself. In the course of years he developed an extremely modest and submissive personality. His ambitions to excel and compete remained restricted to fantasy. In life he was a retiring type, nonconspicuous, conformist, always polite, avoiding contradiction, with the tendency to minimize his abilities. This overt attitude of modesty and submissiveness however put him under extreme pressure and created intense inferiority feelings in him. These became most tormenting in relation to his chief. The patient never would contradict his chief, would follow his suggestions, accept blame while talking with him; but after he left the office he was filled with self-contempt and would tell himself, "You should have answered. You should have said *no*. You should have demonstrated to him that he was not right. You are no good and you never will be any good." This self-depreciatory attitude usually became so unbearable that he would have the urge to drink. Alcohol dissipated his sense of weakness and inefficiency. As soon as the alcohol began to make its effects felt his spirit was lifted; he felt courageous and strong. But apart from the effect of the drug, the act of drinking itself had the significance of a rebellious act for him. He secretly enjoyed the feeling that in the middle of the day during office hours he escaped his duties and indulged in a forbidden activity. In this alcoholic mood he would also indulge in promiscuous sexuality in a rebellious spirit against limitations imposed upon him by external social standards, by the voice of his otherwise so strict conscience. Obviously these alcoholic and sexual escapades relieved his sense of inferiority because under the influence of alcohol he dared to commit such offenses which he would never have ventured without alcohol.

But soon after he thus successfully escaped the pangs of inferiority feelings he ran into a new conflict, that of guilt. The most interesting part of this observation pertains to this second phase of his alcoholic spells. As soon as the effect of the alcohol began to wear off, he began to feel guilty—guilty and not inferior. Now after he had committed all these forbidden sexual and nonsocial acts in order to show his independence and thus escape his inferiority feelings his conscience began to work and make itself felt in the form of remorse. To get rid of this remorse he again had to turn to alcohol which had also the effect of ridding him of his guilt feelings. An ingenious physician whom I analyzed used to call the superego the alcohol-soluble portion of the human personality. In this case certainly the alcohol dissolved both types of reactions, inferiority feelings and the sense of guilt. The emotional sequence however was unmistakable: First an extreme sense of inferiority and self-contempt because of his conformist, submissive attitude, and then as a reaction to this, aggressive uninhibited behavior, and finally sense of guilt in the form of remorse. While the victim of guilt feelings he would make up his mind never to drink again, to stop illicit sex relations; while tormented by inferiority feelings his attitude became just the contrary. "Why not drink? Why not do forbidden things? Only a weakling gives in to every external or internal pressure!"

In this connection I may also refer to a similar vicious circle caused by the antithetic dynamic effect of inferiority and guilt feelings which I have demonstrated in certain criminal cases. An intensely ambitious and competitive hostile attitude towards brothers and father in the little boy leads to strong guilt feelings and retaliation fear. Under the pressure of guilt feelings and fear the competitive attitude gives place to a submissive attitude by means of which the inhibited and intimidated boy tries to gain the love of his dangerous and powerful competitors. This submissive inhibited attitude now creates intense inferiority feelings, hurts the male pride, and leads to aggressive criminal behavior by means of which a tough, independent, stubborn unyielding attitude is demonstrated and every dependence denied. This attitude becomes a new source of guilt feelings which lead to new inhibitions which cause again inferiority feelings and stimulate again aggressive behavior. This mechanism finds a simple explanation after one has recognized the antithetical effect of guilt feelings and inferiority feelings. In order to escape inferiority feelings the criminal is driven to commit acts which give him the appearance of toughness, bravado and aggressiveness. But this behavior which seeks to avoid the Scylla of inferiority feelings drives him into the Charybdis of guilt feelings.

In a previous paper I tried to define inferiority feelings as an expression of deeper instinctual conflicts and contrast them with guilt feelings which derive from the later structural differentiation of the mental apparatus. The deepest source of inferiority feelings consists in the childhood conflict between the progressive wish to grow up and be like the adults on the one hand and the deep regressive force towards the early dependent forms of existence on the other hand. Whenever this regressive wish makes itself felt the ego which identifies itself with the progressive attitude reacts to it with the feeling of inferiority. This conflict becomes further intensified when the first genital cravings develop around the Oedipus period. These genital tendencies are not only in conflict with the oral dependent attitude of the child but are also connected with the feeling of frustration on account of the discrepancy between instinctual cravings and somatic maturation. Accordingly inferiority feelings are presocial phenomena, whereas guilt feelings are results of social adjustment. It is noteworthy that under the pressure of guilty conscience the human being may assume such an amount of inhibition and may be driven so far back towards a dependent and help-seeking attitude that it becomes incompatible with his narcissism. To remedy this narcissistic injury caused by very strong dependence, he may recourse to extreme forms of independent and aggressive behavior. In this way social inhibitions may become the very source of nonsocial behavior.

Very recently Horney again described this vicious circle which is created by the conflict between love- and help-seeking attitude and competitiveness.[1] She considers this conflict as a typical phenomenon of our present competitive civilization.

It seems to me most probable that sociological factors may contribute to the intensity of this fundamental conflict. One would expect that in a civilization in which masculine aggressiveness, competitiveness and independent accomplishment are highly esteemed this conflict would be accentuated. Horney has correctly pointed out that in our civilization the one requirement of social adjustment which demands a certain amount of subordination of individual interests stands in an obvious contradiction to another social asset, namely to ambitious competitiveness. In other civilizations in which not individual initiative and achievement but subordination, obedience and

[1] Karen Horney, "Culture and Neurosis," *Am. Soc. Rev.,* I, No. 2 (April, 1936), 221-230.

submissiveness are considered as great social virtues, this conflict may be less intense. Where giving in to authority, accepting a submissive attitude or even one of self-humiliation are not felt as shameful by the group, such attitudes will not cause such an extreme narcissistic injury as we observe it in most of our patients. On the other hand psychoanalytic experience shows that originally the human being is an individualistic creature and his social inhibitions are later acquirements. In the Oedipus situation every boy still has a competitive attitude. The conflict between inferiority and guilt feelings, competitive individualism versus dependence and submissive subordination (or at least cooperation) is a universal conflict and corresponds to two sides of the basic instinctual structure; to the progressive tendency toward growing up and becoming an independent biological organism on the one hand and to the regressive tendency toward the dependent forms of infantile existence on the other hand. Standards prevailing in different civilizations may increase or diminish the individual's difficulty in solving this universal conflict. It would be erroneous however to attempt to explain it entirely as a phenomenon of our individualistic competitive era. It would be a challenging undertaking if it were possible to compare the intensity and frequency of this conflict situation during different phases of historical development, for example during the individualistic periods of the renaissance, compared with the medieval centuries in which a rigid hierarchic social order prevailed, based on acceptance of authority. Perhaps even cultures existing at present would offer opportunity for such comparative studies.[2] The individualistic competitive West and the introverted East with its rigid caste system would represent possibly the greatest extremes in this regard. It is noteworthy however that in the analysis of a Chinese student conducted in the Chicago Psychoanalytic Institute by Dr. Saul the conflicts between aggressive ambitious competitiveness and submissive dependence were most conspicuous. The question whether or not this should be explained by the fact that the far East is in rapid process of accepting Western ideology can hardly be answered on the basis of this one experience. There is no doubt, however, that the structure of civilization contributes only in a quantitative manner to this fundamental conflict of individualistic independence and narcissism versus fear, guilt and dependence. But this leads us to a question to which at present there is as yet no answer: to the question as to the degree of socialization of which the species homo sapiens is capable, and as to how far—under any form of culture—man necessarily retains his individualistic nucleus.

[2] Since the publication of this article, a study has appeared which undertakes to differentiate between "shame and guilt cultures." Gerhart Piers and Milton B. Singer, *Shame and Guilt*, Springfield, Illinois: Charles C. Thomas, 1953.

Psychoanalysis Revised

◄ 1940 ►

The human setting of the development of ideas

Progress in every science is based on two processes: discovery of new facts and the gradual improvement of the conceptual mastery of these facts. The second of these processes involves the critical evaluation of current views, establishing what they accomplish and where they fail and need modification. In the natural sciences this continuous discarding of older views and replacing them with new constructions which are better adapted to the observations is considered a natural course of development. It is seldom connected with violent emotional attacks or with the foundation of inimical schools competing with and disparaging each other. The revision of theory in physics is mainly a question of intellectual argument, an unemotional evaluation of factual evidence. The more removed a discipline is from its observational basis the greater opportunity there is for emotions to enter into scientific discussion. In the nineteenth century almost all German philosophers were fighting each other, the idealists viciously attacking the materialists and the positivists trying to discredit the followers of all other schools. Every professor of philosophy felt that he had the ultimate and unique key to the sanctuary of truth. Also in young and less developed fields of science emotional issues are of great influence. Thus, in the social sciences and in psychology the admixture of such emotional impurities mars the rational evolution of ideas. The strictly intellectual process, the consistent and gradual adaption of theoretical constructions to the ever-growing observational material makes the study of the history of physics, however, a thrilling experience well-nigh aesthetic in nature.

Naturally, every fundamentally new scientific discovery is apt to arouse emotional rejection both among experts and laymen. Every science consists of the continuous struggle of objective knowledge against wishful thinking. Since the world is not as we want it to be, every new recognition of a factual situation arouses emotional resistance. Apart from this emotional resistance, the inertia of the intellect also has a retarding influence. One adheres to ideas which have proven helpful in the past. Every alteration of ideas requires new learning, new effort, a new intellectual adjustment. While wishful thinking and the inertia of the mind are universal phenomena, there are also some more individual emotional issues frequently involved. Every originator of an idea has a partiality toward his own accomplishment. We know how sensitive authors are even toward small editorial changes in their manuscripts. No wonder that this sensitiveness appears in exaggerated fashion when a change of fundamental ideas and theories is required. But it is not only the originator of ideas who is emotionally involved in scientific progress. So also is the critic who requires changes and suggests minor or major improvements upon the theory. Often he has a more critical than creative mind and unconsciously resents the genius' creative capacity. And should he himself possess a productive intellect and have ambitions for originality, he might feel envious of the giant with whom he is unable to compete. Then he will be apt to exaggerate the defects of the theory of the originator and emphasize the novelty and significance of his own contributions. And finally there is the inert mass of blind followers who uncritically apply the views of an authority, who laboriously have learned the ideas of the master and now desperately defend them from every innovation which would demand new intellectual investment. Since they seldom have judgment or courage for critical evaluation they feel confused and helpless if the critic begins to undermine traditional views and thus shakes their blind belief in the authority, a belief which they so direly need. They therefore dislike the innovator who is capable of emancipating himself from the spell of the master. Of course apart from these three extreme groupings among scientists, there are many who represent transitions, mixed types, who may have the qualities of all three groups. In fact the majority belongs to this mixed type.

As in all fields of scientific life, so also in psychoanalysis these are the actors in the drama of scientific development: the creative genius, his critics, the mass of followers and, of course, all the intermediary types. All these together, despite their human frailties, are responsible for every step in scientific progress. One purpose however unites them all: the search for truth. In the long run the intellectual strivings for understanding outweigh the emotional impurities; or at least let us hope that this is the case.

Evolution and revolution of ideas

Attempts to revise psychoanalytic views and to improve upon the psychoanalytic technique of treatment are almost as old as psychoanalysis itself. Indeed Freud's life work consisted in a continuous struggle for the adjustment of his theoretical concepts to the rapidly increasing factual material which had been discovered by means of his novel technique of studying human beings. He revised even his most fundamental concepts several times and it was no easy matter for his pupils—most of them more or less uncritical followers —to keep step with the ever-changing views of the master. Only a few of them offered a fundamental revision of Freud's views. Some of them succeeded in founding new schools, none of them in improving the theory. And yet apart from these radical innovators and dissenters, a slow and gradual change of ideas took place which, however, has not found systematic expression in psychoanalytic literature. Horney's new book, *New Ways in Psychoanalysis*,[1] is one of the very few systematic attempts at a critical evaluation and revision of the theoretical constructions of psychoanalysis.

Much of what the author offers as fundamental innovation is nothing but the more or less successful formulation of precisely such gradual changes in traditional concepts which almost tacitly—certainly without much ado—took place during the natural course of development as a result of the interchange of ideas between many different workers. Due to a prevailing worship of authority, or perhaps only to an instinctive respect for the sensitiveness of the master, only a few of these more or less widespread modifications were stated explicitly and then always in an unsystematic fashion without emphasis upon the deviation from older concepts. Mostly these changed attitudes were expressed in clinical discussions, in case seminars, thus gradually pervading psychoanalytic teaching.

All of this, of course, does not detract from the merit of Horney's attempt to review systematically and to describe explicitly changes which took place more or less tacitly in the course of many years. It is more a question of taste and perspective, how much credit an author is willing to give himself for changes which gradually have occurred and were unsystematically expressed by a number of others. Thus, for example, Horney's emphasis on the actual life situation had already been voiced in 1924 by Ferenczi and Rank[2] who, like others—among them the author of this article—criticized the search for infantile memories as a therapeutic aim in itself. Furthermore, Horney's stress upon understanding the total dynamic configuration of personality in relation to the environmental situation is today indeed a commonplace. It would be a difficult task to single out those publications which have contributed to this synthetic point

[1] K. Horney, *New Ways in Psychoanalysis*, New York: Norton, 1939.
[2] S. Ferenczi and Otto Rank, *The Development of Psychoanalysis*, New York: Nerv. and Ment. Dis. Pub. Co., 1925.

of view. Anyone who wanted to arrogate to himself alone the recognition of this methodological principle would do a grave injustice to the majority of experienced analysts. Another view which Horney makes a target of her polemic passion is the attempt to explain overt behavior as the mechanical repetition of previous situations. This was discarded by Freud as soon as he abandoned the universal traumatic explanation of neurotic symptoms, although the occasional, almost unmodified repetition of earlier experiences in the form of psychotic and neurotic symptoms remains a valid observation.

Many of Horney's critical comments are directed against such antiquated views as if they were still current. On the other hand, she often claims for herself innovations which have been current for a long time. Her book contains, however, other less obvious criticisms, and also problematic yet significant suggestions. She subjects the problem of the role of sexuality in neuroses and the whole libido theory to a most timely scrutiny and although she cannot offer any satisfactory new solution to replace old concepts, she stimulates a discussion of these taboos of psychoanalytic theory which in the course of time have lost much of their magic quality.

If Horney's book did not contain more than a systematic review of more or less generally accepted, but not explicitly formulated changes in psychoanalytic thinking, as well as discussion of more problematic views, the only criticism against it could be that it is somewhat lacking in perspective towards her own contribution. This of course is only a secondary issue. But certainly a more detached historical presentation, showing the gradually increasing trend toward more dynamic and less mechanical views, would have been more convincing and its educational value for the so called "orthodox followers" considerably greater.

Her polemic ardor involves the author, however, in greater difficulties and more serious issues than those of questionable taste and lack of perspective. As is often the case when one attacks an enemy, one is likely to adopt the enemy's worst weaknesses. Horney attacks the libido theory and replaces the idea of a vague and mystical biological substance—the libido—with an equally empty sociological slogan—culture. She tries to expel Satan with Beelzebub. Just as human behavior cannot be explained satisfactorily by a solely biological principle which is immanent in the organism (libido), neither can it be explained by a sociological principle alone (culture). Cultural influences obviously act upon a highly complex biological system which has to an amazing degree a preformed individual structure. Furthermore, culture itself is originated from the dynamic qualities of biological systems. Obviously we deal here with a complex interplay between biological systems (men) which create a society and become modified by their own creation.

Horney would have had a wonderful opportunity to present historically the development from the more static and material concept of libido—this mystical substance which circulates in the body —to a more dynamic psychology of individual tendencies which have to be understood in their total configuration and in relation to the environment. She could have shown the striking parallel between the development of physics and psychoanalysis. Physics also starts with the mechanical substance idea, then develops the concept of the Proteus-like energy which appears in different forms, only to arrive at the field theory in which the energy quantities are no longer dealt with in isolated systems but in relation to each other. Also in psychoanalysis a more materially conceived libido was replaced by more dynamic concepts. Increasing attention was paid to the great variety of individual tendencies and strivings. Referring to them as libido manifestations became more a matter of speech than anything else. In the last ten or twelve years in what is called ego psychology the interest was focused on these individual tendencies in their complex interrelationship with each other and the environment. This point of view Horney introduces now as a fundamental deviation from Freud.

To this Horney may reply that such a historical representation is impossible because in the psychoanalytic literature these consecutive phases cannot be so clearly distinguished. This may be true; but the task would then be only more difficult, not impossible. Anyone who really cares to undertake this important work can find classical examples in such historical studies as Mach's *Science of Mechanics*[3] and *History of Thermodynamics*[4] and Einstein's and Infeld's *Evolution of Physics*.[5] In these presentations the authors' efforts are not directed towards minimizing the value of older concepts in order to make the new ones appear more significant. On the contrary, they try to show the beauty and the accomplishments of older views—how gradually latent inconsistencies in the theory and new observations require changes, thus demonstrating the organic growth in scientific thought—its step by step adaptation to the observational substratum. A polemic attitude does not allow such a detached historical approach.

[3] Ernst Mach, *Science of Mechanics,* trans. by J. McCormick. Illinois: Open Court Publishing Co., 1914.

[4] E. Mach, *Die Prinzipien der Wärmelehre, Historisch-Kritisch entwickelt.* Leipzig: J. A. Barth, 1896.

[5] Albert Einstein and Leopold Infeld, *The Evolution of Physics,* New York: Simon & Schuster, 1938.

Horney's polemic dialectic approach is responsible for the fact that whenever she goes beyond sheer criticism and offers a new solution she is apt to replace an old error with a new one. How could it be otherwise? The antithesis is always the opposite of the thesis but truth is seldom the diametric opposite of an error. Therefore, if the thesis is erroneous, it does not ncessarily follow that the antithesis will be right. To correct these errors in both directions requires a laborious synthesis. The dialectic approach may be a successful outlet for polemic passion, but it is a detour in scientific development. It is not necessary that one first fall into the opposite error before one find the right solution. There is an evolution, not only a revolution of ideas. All this will be demonstrated with a few examples of Horney's dialectic procedure.

The pitfalls of the dialectic approach

SOCIOLOGY VERSUS BIOLOGY; CULTURE VERSUS LIBIDO

Horney accuses Freud of being an instinct theorist who has a one-sided biological orientation: "In so far as he [Freud] is convinced that psychic life is determined by emotional drives and in so far as he assumes these to have a physiological basis, he belongs to the instinct theorists. . . . Freud conceives instincts as inner somatic stimuli which are continually operating and which tend toward a release of tension." Horney also criticizes Freud because "he is mostly interested in the ways in which the family in particular and culture in general molds these emotional tendencies which have a physiological basis." It is obvious to anyone who is schooled in scientific methodology that this type of dialectic argument which Horney uses, such as not physiology but environment, is empty and lacks any real sense. There is no sense in denying the biological foundation of processes that take place in a living organism no matter whether one studies the circulation of the blood or emotional tensions. All manifestations of the patient's behavior are naturally the expressions of fundamental underlying biological dynamics. If Freud is interested in how this complex biological system acts under the influence of environmental influences, he does exactly what the physicist does who is observing the behavior of a system in a field of forces. It is pointless to try to deny that a biological organism itself has its own phylogenetically predetermined dynamic structure. It is true of course that the behavior of animals is much more predetermined than that of human beings. The spider does not learn how to make a complicated web. It prepares its first web in all the minute geometric details exactly as its ancestors have done. Probably a spider's behavior is very little modified by later experiences. No sociology is needed to understand its behavior. In human beings the opposite extreme is true. Very little behavior is predetermined in detail yet the fundamental dynamic structure is to a high degree similar in all races and cultures. The psychodynamic structure of man is certainly molded to an extremely high degree by later experiences and the study of these molding experiences is precisely the fundamental contribution of psychoanalysis. Reading Horney's book, one might get the impression that Freud was an old style psychiatrist who believed that all later mental changes in life are rigidly predetermined by constitutional structure. Freud's significant contribution to psychiatry is just the opposite view. He demonstrated the extreme formative significance of later experiences, especially of family life, as the medium through which cultural trends exert their influence upon the individual. For dialectic reasons Horney must create the effigy of a one-sided biologically oriented Freud. Then in order to destroy this effigy, she becomes extremely one sided in the opposite (antibiological) direction. Thus she overlooks some quite fundamental facts of human psychology: that not only is the human being born with a psychophysiological dynamic structure but that even his later development is influenced to a high degree by the quite rigidly predetermined biological growth. Such biological changes as the postnatal myelinization of certain nerve tracts, the advent of dentition, the further development of the central nervous system which enables the child to learn to walk and talk, the physiologically determined development of the functions of intelligence, the maturation of the sex glands, senescence—these are all biological phenomena and constitute the most fundamental crises in emotional development. The individual has not only to adjust himself to a complex external environment but also to an ever changing internal environment which follows the unchangeable course of biological growth and deterioration. To try to understand the psychology of puberty or senescence without paying attention to the biological changes in the organism would be a procedure just as one-sided as to try to understand an individual as a complex structure of innate libidinal drives which operate in him without regard to external influences.

We see that for the sake of argument, Horney is driven to a theoretical position which is just as untenable as the imaginary position which she attributes to the imaginary straw man, Freud. Instead of attacking an imaginary one-sided biological orientation she could have restricted herself to her extremely valuable critical statements concerning certain primitive notions which prevailed in the original views of genital and pregenital development. In her chapter on libido theory her contention that possessiveness and greediness are not the results of anal habits and pleasure sensations or that dependence is not the result of an oral libido are certainly valid statements. She is right in stating that the fact that the infant's dependence is involved mainly with its nutrition does not prove that dependent feelings of the adult are the sublimation of oral libido. The correct formulation is that while the little child manifests its dependent needs in the wish to be fed, in being carried around and taken care of by the mother, the adult feels this longing in a different, that is to say an adult way, in the wish to receive financial or emotional support or advice. The form of the expression of dependence changes but the dependent attitude, which is not the result of the process of nutrition, is the primary factor. The interesting phenomenon which Freud, Abraham, and others discovered was that the early oral way of satisfying a dependent longing or the infantile way of manifesting independence or spite becomes a model for later behavior. Horney, however, has to deny the significance of this intimate relation between adult and childhood behavior for the sake of attacking the concept of the repetition compulsion. I shall come back to this controversy.

I do not know whether or not some analysts still maintain these early views of libido theory according to which the bodily pregenital activities are considered as the basis of fundamental emotional tendencies, dependence being the manifestation of an oral libido; cruelty, stubbornness, or independence as manifestations of anal libido; ambition, the sublimation of urethral libido. Certainly for those who still believe in these anatomical, nondynamic concepts Horney's book will have an excellent educational value. In this connection the following passage of Horney's book deserves quotation:

. . . a person does not have tight lips because of the tenseness of his anal sphincter, but both are tight because his character trends tend toward one goal—to hold on to what he has and never give away anything, be it money, love or any kind of spontaneous feeling. When in dreams an individual of this type symbolizes persons through feces, the libido theory explanation would be that he despises people because they represent feces to him, while I should say that representing people in symbols of feces is an expression of an existing contempt for people.

I agree fully with this view of Horney which I have expressed in a very similar way in the concepts of "vector analysis." [6] If Horney, instead of a wholesale attack upon the biological bases of the instinct theory, had singled out this confusion about the relation between infantile behavior patterns, pregenital activities and emotional attitudes on one hand, and later adult behavior patterns and emotional atti-

---

[6] F. Alexander, "The Influence of Psychological Factors on Gastro-Intestinal Disturbances: A Symposium," *Psychoanal. Quart.*, III (1934), 501-588; and "The Logic of Emotions and Its Dynamic Background," in this volume.

tudes on the other, she would have avoided an untenable theoretical position. Of course by restricting herself to the clarification of this single issue the whole sensational effect of her dialectic attack under the slogan of "sociology versus biology" would have been lost.

How untenable Horney's antibiological attitude is, is best shown by the fact that she comes into glaring contradiction with herself. In her chapter on feminine psychology when she validly questions Freud's explanation as to why the girl turns away from the original object of attachment, the mother, towards the father, Horney uses against Freud a biological argument. She writes: (p. 102) "Not recognizing the elemental power of *heterosexual attraction*,[7] Freud raises the question as to why the girl has any need at all to change her attachment to the father." Here, when she needs it, Horney is obviously not averse to taking refuge in a fundamental biological instinct (heterosexual attraction) for the explanation of certain aspects of human behavior.

ACTUAL SITUATION VERSUS CHILDHOOD SITUATION
DYNAMIC STRUCTURE VERSUS REPETITION COMPULSION

In her book Horney makes a somewhat belated attack against a one-sided interest in the childhood situation and against uncritical hunting after childhood memories. She emphasizes that the goal of therapy is to give the patient an understanding of his actual emotional problems and thus to enable him to master his emotional difficulties. Although this seems to be a commonplace, one must concede that for a long time there was a tendency among analysts to neglect the exact study of the actual emotional situation and to concentrate upon those early childhood events which can be brought into etiological relationship with the present. The recollection and reconstruction of these early experiences were considered the main goal of therapy.

This whole argument hinges, of course, on the difficult question of the therapeutic significance of the recovery of forgotten memories, a question which has been repeatedly discussed in the analytic literature. Ferenczi and Rank, although by different reasoning, came to a similar conclusion. They too stressed the detailed study of the actual life situation and minimized the significance of remembering and of reconstruction of the past.[8]

I believe that years ago I found the correct answer to this controversy and have expressed it in different publications.[9] My sug-

---

[7] This author's italics.

[8] Ferenczi and Rank, *op. cit.*

[9] "Concerning the Genesis of the Castration Complex," and "The Problem of Psychoanalytic Technique," both in this volume.

gestion was that whenever a patient is able to recollect a forgotten infantile situation this will always take place when he is able to face a repressed tendency directed towards a person who plays an important role in his actual life. For example when he becomes able to recognize a hostile impulse against his benefactor then he will also be able to remember hostile impulses against persons who played a similar role in his past life (father or brother). I also emphasized that the transference emotions being less intensive and less realistic than those felt towards real objects in life, the recognition of such a repressed impulse most likely will take place in the analytic situation. Such an uncovering of a latent transference emotion makes it possible for the patient to remember similar and repressed emotional attitudes of the past. One could say the ego becomes permeable for a certain type of repressed affects. Remembering, accordingly, is more an indicator of a successful removal of a repression than anything else. It is more the result or a sign of the progress of the analysis than the cause of it. I wrote:

By bringing into consciousness a repressed unconscious thought content of the present time, we open the way for similar or identical infantile repressed material. . . . The analysis of the actual situation (in the first place, naturally, the transference as an experimental example of the actual psychic situation) is the best way to bring infantile material into consciousness. . . . One represses as an adult, similar material (similar emotional qualities) as one repressed when a child. . . . The understanding of recent unconscious material enlarges the permeability of the ego for repressed affects. . . . In addition, the emotions active in the transference are less intensive than the corresponding infantile emotions, because they are only experimental examples of the latter.[10]

In another place I stated: "Although the direct therapeutic value of the process of recollection may be questioned, the removal of the infantile amnesia must be considered as a unique indicator of the successful resolving of repressions." [11]

It is obvious that this evaluation of recollection does not necessarily deny that the recovery of infantile memories is also of therapeutic value. It seems that a comparison of his actual neurotic reactions with those earlier emotional situations after which these are patterned helps the patient to recognize their inadequacy.

For minimizing the value of genetic understanding, Horney sets up another dummy, a Freud, who in a simple-minded mechanistic way tries to explain adult behavior as the unmodified repetition of childhood behavior under the influence of a mystical repetition com-

[10] "Concerning the Genesis of the Castration Complex," loc. cit.
[11] "The Problem of Psychoanalytic Technique," in this volume.

pulsion. After she sets up this imaginary adversary, Horney defends the opposite thesis: that what is aimed at in analysis is to help the patient understand his present life situation and to recognize his neurotic ways of handling his "basic anxiety" (actual character structure).[12] Then he will be able to correct them. In spite of the fact that many of her contentions are partially correct and significant, perhaps in no other place does Horney get into a more hopeless confusion than in this argument. She gets trapped in the pitfalls of dialecticism.

It is obviously correct that the patient should understand his actual emotional entanglements through which he gets involved in conflict with the environment and with himself. It is also true that the adult behavior patterns are not unmodified repetitions of childhood situations. On the other hand, there is no doubt that past experiences have a determining influence upon the later personality structure. The question is only one of how past experiences shape character formation. A careful analysis of this question: in which way the emotional experiences of the past mold the dynamic structure of the personality is however entirely lacking in Horney's book. She is satisfied with emphatic and repetitive statements that the present is not an unmodified repetition of the past. She is interested only in proving that Freud overestimates the significance of the past and does not try to understand the present situation of the patient in its totality. After she has thus erected the imaginary one-sided thesis that Freud explains behavior on the basis of repetition compulsion, that is to say, by the mechanical automatic repetition of the past—then in order to win the battle she has only to discredit the concept of repetition compulsion.

My intention here is not to defend a philosophical concept of repetition compulsion as the basis of every drive or instinct. Such a concept is an abstraction and has but little to do with the understanding of the emotional problems of patients. What is of interest for us are those observations from which, correctly or incorrectly, the concept of repetition compulsion has been abstracted. We may entirely disregard this abstraction itself and deal with the factual material. This consists of a vast variety of observations showing that there is a tendency in the living organism to repeat certain behavior patterns which it has learned in the past for the gratification of its needs. The

[12] When Horney on page 143 states that "the patient's own character structure is entirely neglected in Freud's considerations," one can only ask oneself whether she understands the Freudian theory. Freud's concept of the superego formation is based precisely on the assumption of a structural change within the personality—the result of a complex developmental process—which has a definite influence upon behavior. That structural changes of similar nature may take place during the whole of life is a valid statement of Horney.

best evidence for such a repetitive tendency is offered by a study of the learning process.[13]   The violin player has the greatest difficulty in giving up old faulty movements which have become automatic by faulty practice. Even with advanced technique he is apt to relapse until new, stronger innervation patterns are established. The same principle holds true for the adjustments which the child has to perform during his emotional development. After the child has discovered that thumbsucking is a method of relieving emotional tension, later, after he has given it up, he may under certain conditions have recourse to this old habit. A female patient, whenever her advances were repudiated by her husband, fell asleep with her thumb in her mouth. This is a simple demonstration of a regressive way of trying to satisfy a craving for love, security, and sexual gratification.

The genetic significance of such observations cannot be argued away by any dialecticism. It is the well established phenomenon which Freud called regression which Horney tries if not to deny, at least to minimize in its significance. The dynamic process underlying similar clinical observations can be formulated as follows: if an individual is thwarted in the gratification of a need there is a tendency to regress to an earlier way of gratifying the same need or a similar one which can be substituted for the thwarted longing. The above clinical observation is an extreme example of an almost unmodified repetition of an old behavior pattern. Psychotic and some neurotic symptoms often are such isolated repetitions of early experiences. When patients suffering from hallucinations hear the same words with which their mother used to admonish them, this also is a faithful unmodified repetition of a past experience. If Horney had said that such unmodified repetitions are only characteristic for certain isolated symptoms which are like foreign bodies in the personality but that the totality of the patient's behavior is very far from being a mere repetition of the past, she would have made an irrefutable statement. The patient is struggling to adapt his emotional needs to the given situation; whenever the integrating power of his highest centers (in psychoanalysis we call them ego) fails to find a satisfactory solution he is apt to return to old techniques and methods of gratifying his needs.

One of the most significant contributions of Freud to psychiatry has been to show that the seeming irrationality of certain neurotic behavior and symptoms disappears with the discovery of the phenomenon of regression. So long as the patient's behavior is a rational response to his internal needs and external situation one can understand it from the knowledge of the actual situation alone. The be-

[13] Thomas M. French, "Clinical Study of Learning in the Course of a Psychoanalytic Treatment," *Psychoanal. Quart.*, V (1936), 148.

havior of an ideally rational being—who of course does not exist—who could adjust his subjective needs precisely in the most efficient manner to any given situation, could be understood without knowledge of his past. Every reaction of his would be a consistent rational adaptation to the given situation. Knowing the situation and the actual emotional needs the problem of his behavior could be completely solved at any given moment without any knowledge of the past. Human beings, however, are far from acting so rationally because, to put it simply, they are the victims of their habits—of those adaptive mechanisms they learned in the past. Unconscious mechanisms are just such residues of the past in contrast to the ever flexible rational behavior which is under the control of the conscious ego. The inadequacy of symptoms to resolve emotional tensions lies just in their regressive nature, in the fact that they represent solutions which were adequate in the past but are no longer so. Clinical experience shows that they usually represent a very early behavior pattern of childhood. The thumbsucking of the woman who is rebuffed by her husband will not solve her despair for being rejected, whereas the thumbsucking of the child might be a quite adequate solution of an emotional tension—its feeling of being thwarted. It is scarcely believable that Horney can have forgotten these elementary and fully substantiated facts of psychological dynamics.

Of course the repetitive nature of a neurotic symptom is not always so transparent as in the above quoted case. It is more difficult to understand the dynamic process of regression in patients who return not to an early form of gratification but to a painful situation of the past. The phobia of the patient who is afraid of leaving his home and feels safe only in its vicinity offers a typical example of an irrational, inexplicable symptom which puzzled psychiatry for so long. Such a patient is afraid in a situation which entails no danger for him. The symptom becomes intelligible only when one realizes that the patient has regressed to an early emotional attitude of childhood. As a child he felt safe only near to his home and was afraid to go far from it. At that time, of course, his anxiety might have been quite rational because as a child he had not the capacity for sufficient orientation. The question in such a case is: why does the patient regress to such an unpleasant experience of his past? The analytic study then shows that this patient uses the symptom to barter a lesser evil for a greater. What he is really afraid of is not being far away from home but of loneliness and lack of human contact. He does not have the confidence that he can solve this problem in his actual life situation; his symptom, fear when on the street, helps him to deceive himself about this seemingly insoluble issue. He persuades himself that he is afraid of the street and thus saves himself the painful realization of how alone and isolated he is in his life. He also saves himself from the effort to build up human relationships for which he feels inadequate and unwilling. This symptom has an additional determination. The patient craves to be back in the past as a child when his dependent feelings were satisfied; however putting himself back into childhood in fantasy he must also face the unpleasant side of childhood: childish insecurity and fear. This is a similar psychological mechanism to that which one can observe when a little child plays with a toy representing a wild animal. The more he believes in his fancy of dealing with a wild animal, the more he will get into a real fearful excitement. If he wants to enjoy the thrill of hunting a tiger in his fantasy he must also experience the fear that goes with it. The tragedy of the neurotic patient can be found in this mechanism. After he has said "A" by regressing emotionally into the past, he must also say "B" and accept the sufferings of the past as well.

A neurotic symptom is a foreign body embedded in the texture of rational behavior. In order to grasp its significance, one must first (as Horney validly requires) understand in all detail the actual emotional situation. Yet without knowing the past emotional patterns which it repeats the symptom remains unintelligible. What Horney might reasonably have criticized is the faulty conception of regression that attempts to explain the totality of the patient's behavior as a mechanical repetition of the past. In this connection it is also important to emphasize that the retracing of an isolated symptom to an early behavior or emotional pattern is quite unsatisfactory. The important issue is to understand the symptom in its dynamic relation to the totality of the actual personality structure. One must understand what gap the symptom fills in the emotional situation; what kind of a rational, acceptable human relationship is replaced by it.

Horney's error lies in erecting an antithesis between the analysis of the actual dynamic structure of the patient (Horney calls it horizontal analysis) as opposed to the genetic point of view (Horney's vertical analysis). Only both points of view together can give a satisfactory understanding of human behavior.[14]

14 In her chapter, "The Emphasis on Childhood," Horney herself feels that her discussion may appear as a controversy of "actual versus past" and in the summary of this chapter (pp. 152-153) she comes to a valid formulation of the relationship of the present to the past. This makes it even clearer that her whole preceding pointed discussion in the chapter was directed against an imaginary opponent who wants to explain the whole of an adult patient's behavior as a mechanical repetition of past experiences. Though the formulation at the end of the chapter is correct, in the previous heated discussion of the repetition compulsion the fundamental significance of the recognition of regressive phenomena is lost.

FEAR OF THE HOSTILE WORLD VERSUS FRUSTRATION

Horney involves herself in controversy even where her ideas are not only confirmatory of Freud's views, but where they represent a valuable contribution to existing knowledge. Following Freud she considers anxiety as the central dynamic issue in neuroses. She correctly states that apart from seeking satisfaction one of the most powerful driving factors in behavior both of adults and children is the tendency to avoid insecurity, to alleviate that free floating anxiety which is based on a feeling of insecurity. (Peculiarly Horney tries to postulate a fundamental difference in this respect between neurotics and normals, a difference which is obviously only a relative one.) Also Horney assumes that this insecurity, a "basic anxiety," develops in childhood. Freud distinguishes two main factors in this childhood anxiety: fear of retaliation and of loss of love. Horney using somewhat different terminology comes to a similar conclusion. So far so good. The further discussion of anxiety, however, involves Horney in a controversy with certain views of Freud which she has to repudiate if she wants to remain faithful to her antiphysiological orientation. There are in particular two things which she does not like, 1) the psychoanalytic emphasis upon the biological helplessness of the child as the ultimate reason for his anxiety and 2) the view that anxiety might result from the frustration of fundamental instinctual tensions.

Careful analysis of the infantile situation leads, however, precisely to these two factors. The human infant is indeed helpless and fully dependent in the satisfaction of all his vital needs upon the help and good will of the adults. Whenever he is repudiated and left to his own resources, an unbearable tension of necessity develops in the child; he feels threatened in his vital existence and probably experiences something like a panic. Thus both frustration and the biological helplessness of the child are in a most intimate causal nexus with the primary anxiety of the child. This cannot be argued away by any pettifoggery.

Frustration of subjective needs is still in another, more indirect way connected with anxiety. The gratification of certain forbidden impulses brings the child into conflict with adults and leads to punishment or withdrawal of love. Such impulses consequently are felt as threats because if it gives in to them they involve the child in conflicts with the adults. They represent an internal danger because of their painful consequences which the child has experienced before.

A third causal connection between frustration and fear is that frustration provokes in the child hostile impulses which by necessity lead to fear of retaliation. Horney has to combat or at least minimize the importance of this intimate connection between frustration and anxiety because it has a biological foundation. This however does not keep it from existing.

What Horney mostly stresses is the part which the environment by its "unreliability and unfairness" plays in making the child feel insecure. This, of course, is a highly productive point of view. Yet this like every problem of human behavior has its two sides. 1) There is the field of forces to which the biological system is exposed: the environmental influence; 2) but there is also the biological system itself with its own complex structure. The primary interest of psychoanalysis is the individual, and what it studies are processes within the individual in his relation to the environment. Anxiety is a process within the individual, and as such it must ultimately be described in psychological and physiological terms.

To consider the individual as an inert, infinitely pliable system is methodologically just as incorrect as the procedure of Melanie Klein who tries to understand neurotic phenomena in the child from the interplay of immanent endogenous forces which are strictly phylogenetically predetermined and unfold themselves automatically during development.[15] Therefore Klein is so little interested in the nature of the environment to which the child is exposed she does not even find it necessary to get acquainted with the parents of the children she studies. The counterpart of this one-sidedness is however, to try to understand the child from the exclusive study of those external influences to which it is exposed without making reference to the complex internal structure of the child and the immanent phylogenetically predetermined main lines of development. Horney's one-sided stress on the analysis of the environmental factors (the sociological point of view) might be excused as a reaction against one-sided concentration upon the individual without sufficient and detailed reference to his environment, a trend which in fact has been current in some analytic circles. But in as much as Horney goes to the other extreme, her statements require correction. An anxiety theory not based on physiology is a scientific anomaly.

CULTURAL INFLUENCES VERSUS SPECIFIC FAMILY CONSTELLATIONS

The short history of the relationship of psychoanalysis to sociology unquestionably is marked by grave methodological errors. Freud committed one of them which he did not correct in his later writings when he applied individual psychological mechanisms in an over-simplified manner to primitive societies. That this error has been repeated by some of his followers is well known. I have characterized

15 Melanie Klein, *The Psychoanalysis of Children*, London: Hogarth, 1932.

this methodological error as "psychoanalyzing society." [16] In such attempts the psychoanalyst considers a complex society as if it were nothing but a magnified individual, overlooking the fact that an organized society is not a homogeneous unit, but consists of highly differentiated groups that have intricate interrelationships. These interrelationships form a cultural pattern determined by a variety of historical, geographical, climatic and other factors acting upon those universal psychological mechanisms which operate in the individual. The specific form of a culture can never be explained by psychological mechanisms alone; the knowledge of the history of the group is indispensable. Group behavior is not the creation of a single individual, like an unconscious fantasy, but is primarily an historically determined phenomenon, a result of the complex interaction between human beings in an organized society. In her latest book Horney pays little attention to this most vulnerable point in Freud's writings but criticizes Freud's "limitations in understanding of cultural factors" on another basis:

How little weight Freud ascribes to cultural factors is evident also in his inclination to regard certain environmental influences as the incidental fate of the individual instead of recognizing the whole strength of cultural influences behind them. Thus, for example, Freud regards it as incidental that a brother in the family is preferred to the sister, whereas a preference for male children belongs to the pattern of a patriarchal society (p. 170).

Here Horney again puts herself into a false position. She falls into an error opposite to that of Freud's. To apply individual mechanisms unreservedly to group phenomena obviously is a grave mistake, but it is just as incorrect to try to replace the highly specific psychological influences existing within each individual family with general cultural factors. The specific family in which the patient has been raised might be an atypical family, a dissenter within the group. Horney quotes as an example the cultural trend current in our society of preferring boys to girls. She warns analysts to take into account such cultural trends in dealing with their patients. But what if the patient's father and mother are exceptions and both had an atypical predilection for girls? Psychoanalysis deals with individual human patients and not with groups. It is a more microscopic method than that of sociology. It is interested in the specific actual influences upon the growing individual rather than general cultural trends. I have subjected this problem to methodological scrutiny and because I cannot say it more concisely, I quote:

Much confusion is brought into this field by the lack of precise definition of what is meant by the expression, "environmental influences."

16 "Psychoanalysis and Social Disorganization," in this volume.

For the sociologist this expression means mainly certain traditionally transmitted cultural patterns that determine the individual's behavior in almost every manifestation of his life. It determines not only the social attitude in a broader sense but also an individual's eating habits, his excremental habits, the way he raises his children, and the way he treats his wife, economically and even sexually.

For the psychoanalyst this expression means something even more specific. . . . He cannot be satisfied with speaking of such general influences as are represented by cultural patterns. He must look for more specific factors which vary from family to family and which have a different significance even within one family for the different children. For example, the environment of an only child is entirely different from that of another child who is a member of a large family, although both may belong to the same social group. The environment of the oldest child is different from that of the youngest and from that of the middle child. Of course we speak here of a subjective or psychological environment. For the anthropologist or sociologist whose interest is focused on culture as a whole system, these differences are not so interesting. He studies the civilization of some part of Africa and compares it with one in central Australia. For the psychoanalyst, the object of study is the individual with his specific emotional problems. . . .

The attempt to substitute such generalizations as "cultural patterns" for the specific details of the environmental influences upon the individual actually found in each individual case is not permissible. "Cultural patterns" is a generalization of certain types of behavior which are typical in certain groups. But we know that the individual differences can be enormous within the same civilization. In our Western civilization, for example, certain children may be trained by nursing habits that are typical only in some of the so-called primitive civilizations. This may contribute to the development of a personality type which in our civilization would be infrequent and yet would be the most common type in another civilization. In the clinical psychoanalytic approach the main aim is to understand each individual in terms of his own life history. The sociologist is interested in the cultural system as a whole, the clinical psychoanalyst in specific individuals.[17]

This methodological criticism of an uncritical application of the sociological point of view clearly shows what a tremendous amount of thought and energy is wasted by the dialectic vein of reasoning. Freud erred by applying individual mechanisms to group phenomena without sufficiently considering other factors. His dialectic adversary must necessarily go into the opposite error by applying the sociological point of view adequate for studying group phenomena but not sufficiently refined for the study of the fates of specific individuals within the group.

[17] "Psychoanalysis and Social Disorganization," in this volume.

The summing up

Horney's argument is written in a most conciliatory style, but its effect is to create an imaginary, exclusively biologically oriented Freud who single-mindedly tries to explain adult behavior as the mechanical repetition of early instinctual (biological) patterns. But her badly mutilated psychoanalysis has lost both its legs: its biological foundation, and the stress on the genetic understanding of the present from the past. The antibiological and antigenetic Horney proposes a theory which one-sidedly deals with the complex dynamic structure of the adult personality suspended in a vacuum and robbed both of its physical body and its genetic past: a scientific nightmare.

Although theory is not its *forte*, the book has considerable assets. It is full of excellent descriptions of typical emotional conflict situations within different personality organizations. Horney's masochistic, perfectionistic and narcissistic characters are clinical pictures masterfully abstracted from a wealth of observations. This article, however, is devoted to the question of the revision of theory which is also the main topic of Horney's book.

Fortunately the predominance of her interest in theoretical polemics did not entirely suppress the clinical orientation of the author. Her book is motivated by the keen recognition of certain shortcomings of psychoanalytic theory. It is written by a born clinician who by nature is only at home when dealing with psychological realities and not with theoretical abstractions. She should not have undertaken the difficult job of revising the theoretical foundations of psychoanalysis. Yet her book will have a healthy influence in making us realize even more than we already do that the theoretical superstructure of psychoanalysis has not kept pace with our rapidly improving understanding of the psychodynamic structure of our patients' total personalities. But Horney opposes an imaginary psychoanalytic theory which never even in its very beginnings was so one-sided as she depicts it. Because she opposes this imaginary theory in an antithetic fashion her theoretical solutions contain errors which are precisely the opposite of those she is combatting. Thus the theoretical views she offers are often considerably weaker than those which are actually current although unfortunately not yet systematically formulated.

In one respect however, Horney's book deserves unreserved praise: the validity of her attempt to understand patients in terms of detailed psychological realities instead of theoretical abstractions cannot be overemphasized in our field in which there is such a temptation to replace with theory a real understanding of the living person.

The need for a revision of psychoanalytic theory

Freud was primarily a great observer and only secondarily a great theoretician. His theories sometimes lack strict consistency, contain contradictions, and are avowedly of a preliminary nature. One must realize that he did pioneer work in an almost virgin territory. He developed an extremely refined instrument for psychological investigation, accumulated novel observations, and it is only natural that his first formulations were groping attempts to bring some order into the chaos of the newly discovered field of the dynamics of human personality. He was perfectly aware of the shortcomings of his theoretical concepts and laboriously and consistently worked on their improvement. He justifiably stated that it was too early to create a pedantic and strictly defined conceptual system because this would hamper further development. He intentionally kept some of the fundamental abstractions somewhat vague and undefined—like those of libido, of narcissism, of sublimation—because he was keenly aware of the fact that these concepts must be kept in flux in order to become gradually adjusted to the increasing wealth of observations. This vagueness of some of his concepts has often been held against him by those who would have preferred a simple clearcut "textbook-psychoanalysis" which might easily be learned by reading a few books. Psychoanalysis thus remained a fertile field for the empirically minded, clinically oriented person who could dispense with precise and logically consistent theoretical systems. Therefore psychoanalysis attracted good clinicians and observers rather than keen theoreticians, which might partially explain why psychoanalysis during its rapid development has dragged along theoretical concepts belonging to its different phases. This led to an extreme redundance of theory. The original materialistically conceived libido theory—the theory of the pregenital zones—coexisted with the more dynamic views of psychological conflict, vector concepts, the structural view of the human personality, the fully dynamic anxiety theory, and that of the ego defenses. There was, however, a constant trend towards a more synthetic dynamic approach, away from more analytic mechanistic and materialistic concepts.

As has been mentioned before, this development strikingly parallels the development of physics from Newtonian mechanics through Maxwell's electromagnetic field theory to the concept of relativity.

Fortunately, this coexistence of older and newer theoretical views belonging to the different phases of psychoanalytic theory has had little influence upon actual dealing with the patients. It has not helped therapy but has not harmed it much either. There are many excellent psychoanalytic practitioners who do not care much for theoretical finesse and, while in their clinical work they represent the most advanced dynamic point of view, in their theoretical thinking they may still adhere to early libido concepts. Nevertheless a well-formulated and conceptually clear theory becomes more and more imperative. The more a discipline advances the more it needs such conceptual order brought into its findings. In an increasing degree further advancement will depend upon a well-defined theory.

Therefore the aim which Horney sets for herself in her book, namely, to purify psychoanalysis from some traditional views of the past which are no longer consistent with its present status might have been welcome had she done it in a critical historical instead of in a polemic dialectic fashion. She certainly would have more successfully filled an urgent need. Even so, her book—though it does not always do justice to current views—at least shows up the weaknesses of earlier concepts. If only she had not fallen into exaggeration to an unnecessary degree!

In order to revise a theory it is necessary at first to take stock of what are those well established fundamentals upon which one can build a superstructure. In her remarkable first chapter which is free of polemics, Horney tries to reconstruct these solid fundamentals. First she mentions the introduction of psychological causality into psychiatry, then the discovery of the dynamic effect of unconscious tendencies, and the dynamic conception of the structure of the personality. Furthermore she includes among the immovable cornerstones of Freud's theory the concept of repression and other forms of defenses of the ego: reaction formation, projection and rationalization; also the concept of displacement of emotions and their turning towards the self. She also includes Freud's dream theory.

This is a fair though somewhat narrow evaluation of the fundamentals. Many important Freudian concepts she must repudiate in order to remain faithful to her dialectic premises. So we do not find among the fundamentals recognized by Horney such extremely valuable concepts as regression and fixation which are based on the best factual evidence. By admitting these, Horney would have lost her freedom to militate against the genetic approach. As has been pointed out above, without the concept of regression neurotic and psychotic symptom formation and some neurotics' automatic repetitive behavior would remain entirely unintelligible. Horney gives somewhat more consideration to Freud's structural concept of personality. What she does not like here are only the instinctual factors implied in the theory of the ego and superego. It is only natural that the concept of an instinctual reservoir—the id—could not find any toleration in the antibiological orientation of Horney.

The value of these approximate structural generalizations can however hardly be questioned. The concept of the ego representing the highest integrating center of the mental apparatus and having the function of adapting conflicting subjective needs to each other and to the external environment is one of the most valid formulations in psychoanalytic theory. This concept fully coincides with the modern dynamic views of the physiology of the central nervous system. Freud's and Fechner's stability principle, according to which the ego's function is to reduce excitation within the organism, is identical with Cannon's physiological theory of homeostasis. The most encouraging fact is that psychology and physiology arrived at these parallel formulations entirely independently of each other. The controlling functions of the ego which have been postulated by Freud are corroborated by the inhibitory effect of the highest integrating cortical centers; moreover the twofold receptive surface of the ego which enables it to mediate between internally perceived subjective needs and externally perceived outward situations coincides with the twofold sensory apparatus in the central nervous system, the capacity of the cortex to register internal and external stimuli. The concept of a superego as the lastest acquired inhibitory function is also in good accord both with clinical observation and physiological thought. In fact the concept of the superego is one of the most successful abstractions of psychoanalytic theory and even Horney would have nothing against it if Freud had not explained its dynamic force on a biological (instinctual) basis. The id, which nobody has directly observed, is of course still a theoretical conclusion based on the observation that the integrative synthetic function of the ego develops only slowly from a more disorganized dynamic state. But here the physiological facts at least are not contradictory since it has been established that the lower midbrain centers (hypothalamus) seemingly have some relation to emotional expression on a less highly integrated level than the cortex.

So far then, in reviewing psychoanalytic theory we do not find any need for a fundamental revision. What is needed is further elaboration and refinement. If Horney requires an elimination of the biological point of view, what psychoanalysis requires is a much greater correlation of psychological dynamics with the functioning of the central nervous system. Future development obviously lies in this direction.

What are those views in psychoanalytic theory that require fundamental revision? I too like Horney believe that it is our instinct theory which is most unsatisfactory; but unlike Horney, I consider the instinct theory unsatisfactory not because it is too biological but because it is not sufficiently so. Its most vulnerable spot is the evaluation and definition of the role of sexuality.

The coordination of psychological and physiological dynamics

The concept of sexuality has undergone fundamental changes in Freud's thinking. Originally he distinguished two basic drives—the instinct for self-preservation (ego instinct) and sexuality, and extended the concept of sexuality to other phenomena which have nothing to do with reproduction. He made this extension on the basis of phenomenological evidence. The child obviously has sexual sensations when other parts of the body are stimulated in connection with such vegetative processes as nutrition and excretion. Furthermore, the study of the perversions has demonstrated that almost any strong emotion can become the content of sexual desire such as curiosity in voyeurism, pride and boasting in exhibitionism, hostility, cruelty and the wish for domination in sadism, and guilt feelings, notably the wish to be punished and disciplined, in masochism. One spoke of displacement of sexual energy or transformation of pregenital libido into genital libido and vice versa. Similar figurative expressions were used which had no satisfactory meaning. Later, Freud introduced—in place of a multiform sexuality and an ego instinct—the theory of the eros and death instincts. They represent the two fundamental vectors in the process of life, the one towards upbuilding and growth, the other towards destruction, decomposition and death. In order to explain such phenomena as sadism which is both destructive and at the same time sexual, he proposed the idea of erotization of the destructive instinct.

This dualistic theory may explain such phenomena as sadism and masochism but it is too abstract a concept to be useful for understanding and describing the tremendous qualitative wealth of sexual and nonsexual psychological phenomena. Its advantage is that it is strictly a dynamic vector concept.

Ferenczi then made a valuable suggestion by calling attention to the draining function that sexuality fulfills in the energy system of the organism. Every excitation the ego (the central nervous system) cannot discharge through activity by voluntary goal-directed behavior may find a kind of short circuit outlet in sexual excitement and release. He considered the genital apparatus to be the executive organ for draining such unrelieved tensions.

This can best be demonstrated in the field of perversions. Accumulated but never expressed hostile feelings against adversaries may lead for example, to a sadistic distortion of the sexual urge. I had the opportunity to make the interesting observation that lust murderers and pedophiliacs are often extremely inhibited, crushed and weakly individuals who never could give expression to their aggressions in life. All these accumulated aggressions find a vent in their sexual activity, in attacking the weak. Similarly those persons are apt to develop voyeurism whose intellectual curiosity, for some reason or other, is inhibited. Sexual exhibitionists are usually morbidly modest and shy individuals who cannot give expression to their wish to impress others through ordinar channels: through speech and gestures. They relieve all their pent-up boastfulness by showing off in exhibiting their penes, which is connected with a sudden release of tension and is felt as sexual gratification. I have demonstrated that unrelieved and accumulated guilt feelings may find an outlet in masochistic perversion.[18]

According to this concept, sexuality is the expression of a surplus excitation within the organism which it is unable to relieve in other ways. It does not seem to be related to any specific quality of impulse because the sudden gratification of any pent-up emotional tension may be connected with sexual excitement and pleasure sensation. Horney correctly emphasizes that this does not at all mean that all these emotions are sexual in nature. The confusion comes from our using the term sexuality in two different ways: we call sexual 1) certain pleasure sensations connected with genital excitement and also 2) the process of reproduction.

The correct formulation is that every biological or emotional tension, whether or not it is connected with reproduction, might be relieved by a genital excitation and release connected with a pleasure sensation. In the young individual, pre-eminently emotional tensions related to the vegetative processes of growth are connected with such pleasure sensations and release (oral and anal pleasure sensations). In the mature individual, primarily the emotions centering around reproduction are connected with genital pleasure sensations and outlet. It would possibly be advisable to restore to sexuality its original meaning and restrict its use to psychological and physiological processes connected with reproduction. The so-called pregenital manifestations are connected exclusively with the process of growth even though surplus tensions belonging to the growth process (for example nutrition) may also find a release through the genito-urinary system. The question now is: what is the biological relationship between pregenital tendencies centering around the process of growth on the one hand, and the genital tendencies centering around reproduction on the other hand?

Ever since I took up the study of psychoanalysis, I have struggled with this problem. In my earliest publication I subjected this

[18] F. Alexander, *The Psychoanalysis of the Total Personality*, New York: Nerv. and Ment. Dis. Publ. Co., 1935, pp. 128-138.

question of the relation of growth to reproduction to an inquiry[19]; also in other writings, although never in a systematic fashion, I tried to correlate the fundamental psychological tendencies with the basic processes of life.

I came to some approximate formulations. The main phases of life are growth towards maturation, reproduction after having achieved maturation and, finally, decline towards death. The life process itself is based on incorporation of energy and substance from the environment, their retention and elimination. During the three different phases of life (growth, reproduction, and gradual decomposition) the balance between the incorporation of energy, its retention and its elimination, varies. In the young maturing individual, more energy and substance is retained than eliminated; hence it grows. The psychological expression of this phase of life appear in the form of so-called pregenital tendencies which all center around incorporation and retention. Eliminative tendencies appear only in connection with waste products. The young individual in order to grow must take in from the environment and retain whatever he can use for his growth. This is clearly reflected in the egocentric help-seeking dependent attitude of the child. Only after the child has reached or has approached the limit of individual growth, that is to say maturity, does a new physiological phenomenon appear: reproduction, together with a new psychological orientation, love of others in the mature sense. The surplus energies which can no longer be used for growth create a tension which the individual resolves in the form of reproduction. Reproduction in multicellular organisms follows the same principle as in primitive monocellular organisms: basically it is an asymmetric form of cell division. In the monocellular organism, after the limits of the individual growth are reached cell division takes place. The corresponding process in the complex polycellular beings is the elimination of the germ cells.

Seen in this perspective, reproduction is nothing but the continuation of growth overstepping the limits of the individual. Growth and reproduction being thus connected in the biological sense, it is quite natural that the psychological expression of growth, the so-called pregenital sexuality, should be related to sexuality in the restricted sense (genital sexuality and reproduction).

The important fact is that all these processes which are connected phenomenologically with sexual pleasure and which primarily are released through the genito-urinary tract are manifestations of surplus energy or surplus tension. Thus for example, an oral incorpo-

[19] F. Alexander, "Metapsychologische Betrachtungen," *Int. Ztschr. Psychoanal.,* VII (1921), 270.

rating urge that goes beyond the need for food appears in the form of thumbsucking which causes, by the artificial stimulation of the mouth, a sexually tinged pleasure sensation, often accompanied by genital excitement (oral erotism). A surplus of aggressiveness which goes beyond its natural aim of defending the organism against an enemy, appears in the form of sadism: this is cruelty for its own sake and is connected with genital excitement and pleasure. Thus sadism is the manifestation of an accumulated aggressiveness which either is not useful to the organism at the moment or which the organism (as in neurotics), on account of inhibitions, cannot express sufficiently in attacking adversaries. Then it is drained by the sexual apparatus. Finally, propagation appears when the individual is saturated and his surplus energies cannot be usefully employed any longer for the maintenance of life or further growth. The physiological expression of this surplus energy is the drive towards reproduction. Its psychological manifestation is the turning away of interest from the individual's own person towards external love objects. From the physiological point of view this form of elimination is no longer elimination of waste products but of germ cells; from the psychological viewpoint it is giving real affection to others which replaces mere self-love.

Only this last specific manifestation of surplus energy is what we should call sexuality. All the pregenital manifestations belong to the great chapter of growth. Since sexuality is growth beyond the limits of the individual, pregenital and genital manifestations are related to each other.

Today our criterion for the sexuality of an emotional process lies in the phenomenological fact that it is accompanied by pleasure sensation in the genitals. It might be hoped that in the future we will be able to correlate more precisely sexual pleasure sensations with certain quantitative factors (possibly with the suddenness of the release of an emotional tension) rather than with the quality of the tension.[20]

These biological considerations throw a somewhat different light upon the significance of sexuality in neuroses. Ferenczi's drainage theory offers the clue. Whenever this draining through genito-urinary release is inhibited for psychological reasons (neurotic conflicts and inhibitions), the central nervous system is robbed of one of its most important means of relieving tensions. Thus an unrelieved tension is sustained. In neurotics, the normal acceptable expression of emotions

---

[20] In one place Freud suggests that the sexual pleasure sensation might be dependent upon a certain time relationship between excitation and release (rhythm). See "The Economic Problem in Masochism," in *Collected Papers*, New York: Basic Books, 1959, Vol. II, 255-269.

in personal relationships is inhibited and a regression to earlier forms of emotional expression takes place. In the place of mature human relationships, childish dependence mixed with spite and hostility appear. Thus disturbed human relationships and not disturbed sexuality is the primary cause of neurosis. Horney correctly emphasizes this in her book. Disturbed sexuality is rather the result of the regression from mature emotional expression to infantile forms. If these infantile attitudes are drained off by sexual expression, we speak of perversions. In those cases in which even this immature sexual expression is blocked, neurotic symptoms appear in order to relieve the emotional tensions. This is the real meaning of the old formulation of Freud that perversions and neuroses have a vicarious relationship to each other ("the neurosis is the negative of the perversion").

However this is not the place to evolve in detail a new instinct theory. I have wished only to make a few suggestions as to lines along which an adequate dynamic theory of the fundamental drives might be further developed. The requirements which such a theory must fulfill are that it be in accordance with the fundamental observations of physiology as well as with dynamic psychology of human and animal behavior.

It is possible that only through experimental methods will these issues be clarified. The study of the relation of hormones to instinctual tendencies is most promising in this respect. We are already able by the experimental introduction of hormones into animals to intensify fundamental instinctual attitudes, for example the maternal instinct. One can also produce homosexual behavior in animals by the introduction of sexual hormones. It would be false on the basis of such experiments to return to the substance theory of libido, since hormones are nothing but catalyzers and can only accelerate or intensify certain phases of the life process. They are certainly not carriers of libido. The importance of these observations is that they open the way for an experimental study of the fundamental instincts. They may also serve as a reminder for those who tend to forget that human impulses have a biological basis.

In summary, the further elaboration and revision of psychoanalytic theory must come from the correlation of psychological observations with the facts of physiology and general biology. It is most encouraging, as Grinker has pointed out lately, that the principal dynamic and structural concepts of psychoanalysis such as repression, regression, ego and superego functions, are in close accord with the present findings of neurology.[21] Now also our instinct theory must be correlated with the fundamental dynamics of the life process.

[21] Roy Grinker, "A Comparison of Psychological 'Repression' and Neurological 'Inhibition.' " *J. Nerv. and Ment. Dis.*, LXXXIX (1939), 765-781.

The attempt to make psychoanalysis more sociologically and less biologically oriented is unsound because psychoanalysis must integrate both with biology and sociology at the same time. We must understand the biological structure of the organism as well as the nature of those external influences to which it is exposed. The creation of such an artificial antithesis as "sociology versus biology" might be useful in political life—it has some demagogic appeal to the emotions —but it has no place in science. Man is a complex biological organism, and individual personality, and a member of a highly organized social group. He must be understood and described in physiological, psychological, *and* sociological terms.

Three Fundamental Dynamic Principles of the Mental Apparatus and of the Behavior of Living Organisms

◄ 1951 ►

The principle of stability

The basic function of the mental apparatus consists in sustaining the homeostatic equilibrium within the organism which is continuously disturbed by the very process of life and by changing environmental influences. This principle of stability has been formulated by Freud who attributed it to Fechner. The core of the mental apparatus is the ego which performs the homeostatic function through coordination of the biological needs with each other and with the existing and everchanging environmental conditions. It accomplishes this biological task through four functions: (1) by internal sensory perceptions it registers internal disturbances of the physicochemical equilibrium, perceiving them as needs and sensations. (2) Through external sensory perceptions it registers environmental conditions upon which the gratification of its needs depends. (3) Its third function is the integration of the data of internal and external perceptions in a way which makes adequate coordinated voluntary execution possible. (4) Finally, as the center of motor control, it performs its executive function. A further function of the ego is the protection from excessive external stimuli.

The principle of economy or inertia

The second fundamental principle which governs the adaptive functions of the ego I call the principle of economy or inertia. Every organism is born with unconditioned reflexes which are useful for maintaining those constant conditions within the organism which are necessary for life. All internal vegetative functions such as digestion, the circulation of the blood, breathing, and excretion are

165

such automatic mechanisms. They do not require conscious effort and, with the exception of certain alimentary and excretory functions, are not acquired by learning but belong to the hereditary equipment of the organism. In contrast, the functions which regulate the relation of the organism to its environment, must be learned through trial, error, and repetition. Behavior patterns adequate for maintaining biological and psychological homeostasis are repeated until they become automatic and are performed with minimum effort. Accordingly, learning consists of two phases: 1) groping experimentation through trial and error and 2) repetition of the adequate behavior patterns which have been found useful by trial and error. Next to the principle of stability the most common and basic tendency of the organism is to replace adjustments requiring effort inherent in experimentation by effortless automatic behavior. This general tendency is of great importance for psychopathology.

The second phase of learning merely consolidates the newly acquired learning by repetition. The stability principle expresses the tendency of the organism to maintain constant optimal conditions for life, and alone it is not sufficient to describe animal behavior. The tendency toward stability is further defined by the principle of inertia —namely, that the organism tends to perform the functions necessary for maintenance of constant conditions with minimum expenditure of energy. This energy-saving tendency I call interchangeably the "principle of economy" or the "inertia principle." To a large degree, though not completely, it corresponds to the so-called "repetition compulsion" of Freud. These two principles together are the most universal dynamic principles of life.

The advantage to the organism of the principle of economy is obvious. The energy saved by automatic behavior can be utilized to meet novel situations which require strenuous groping experimentation.

It is important, however, to realize certain disadvantages in automatic behavior. Conditions change, and owing to growth the organism itself changes. Changed conditions require fresh adaptation. The adult cannot, like an infant, satisfy his needs by relying upon maternal help. He must learn independence and become active instead of passive. He must walk and eat and ultimately satisfy many other needs on his own. Growth requires continuous learning. The principle of economy appears in this connection as inertia which impels the organism to cling to automatic behavior which was satisfactory in the past but which is no longer adequate. This is what Freud called *fixation*. He also discovered that when conditions become difficult and novel or threatening situations present themselves, earlier patterns of behavior tend to reassert themselves. This disposition, which he called *regression*, has proved one of the fundamental factors in psychopathology.

Changing conditions require *flexible behavior* or, in other words, rapid *ad hoc* responses which are suitable at the moment but might be inappropriate in another situation. The capacity for sudden shifts of conduct belongs to the most highly developed functions of the personality: the integrative functions of the ego. It rests on the ability to learn from past experiences and to exercise reason in abstraction and differentiation. By memory and reason man is able not only to continue behaving in ways he has found useful but to change as actual situations require. Life is thus a continuous struggle between the organism's tendency to retain old patterns on the principle of inertia and the challenge of growth and changed circumstances to adopt new ones.

The principles of stability and inertia can explain only those biological phenomena which consist in the preservation of life by useful adaptive responses. Another principle, that of surplus energy, is required for understanding growth and propagation.

The principle of surplus energy

Every organism undergoes a biologically predetermined course of development. After birth, however, the influence of the external environment becomes more important. Nevertheless the principal phases of postnatal development are also predetermined. In the human being the completion of the myelinization of the nervous pathways occurs in a certain phase; coordination in grabbing, walking, speaking, etc., occurs in a more or less uniform way; the intellect begins to function at approximately the same age in all; the maturation of the sex glands and the termination of skeletal growth takes place similarly in everyone; and senescence, though with variations, sets in at approximately the same period in all cases.

The progression from birth to maturity can be viewed as a series of steps toward the mastery of functions which make the human being independent of its parents. Man first learns to masticate food and focus his eyes, then to coordinate movements which make grabbing possible. He then learns to walk, speak, and take a reasoned view of the world, and finally achieves maturity in his sexual development. The child, however, clearly resists his own progress toward maturity and clings to acquired adjustments in accordance with the principle of inertia. Whenever he is tired of the arduous task of constant readaptation or is confronted with new and difficult situations, he tends to fall back on earlier modes of behavior. Particularly successful previous adjustments serve as fixation points to which he regresses in times of emotional stress.

This resistance to growing up is a most conspicuous trait in all children, but it is only one aspect of the total picture. Growth, of course, is biologically predetermined, and the organism has no alternative than to accept it as an unalterable fact and adjust itself to it. There are, however, many psychological factors as impressive as inertia and regression which point toward growth and independence. Everything which the child learns is acquired originally through spontaneous playful experiment. Activities such as the moving of the limbs, focusing the eyes, and experiments in walking are not at first utilitarian but merely pleasurable. The young colt exuberantly racing in the meadow illustrates spontaneous pleasurable exertion. It is true that by these playful exercises the organism prepares itself for the serious struggle for life which begins when parental care is outgrown and the organism is thrown on its own resources. In learning spontaneously and playfully to master the body, however, no such practical foresight governs the behavior. The child plays and exercises its voluntary body functions merely for the sake of the pleasure derived from these activities. The hands grab for the sake of grabbing and not to obtain food, the eyes focus for the sensation of seeing, and the legs are used in walking and running because this is enjoyable. One of the fundamental discoveries of Freud was that these playful exercises, along with the mature manifestation of sexuality, belong to the same category which he called "erotic." This was the rediscovery of a fact known intuitively to the ancient Greeks. The Greek god, Eros, was the god of both love and play and was represented appropriately by a child.

Erotic phenomena do not follow the principle of inertia. They are designed not to save energy but to expend it spontaneously. They are creative and progressive and serve as the dynamic motor power behind growth and propagation. They do not represent automatic repetitions or utilitarian adjustments but lead the organism toward new ventures and experiments. The practical utilization of the faculties which the organism has acquired by pleasurable experiment is a secondary step. The faculties must first be acquired separately before they can become integrated in a sensible manner for adaptive purposes. The energy spent in this lavish experimental and playful manner is surplus energy, not used for preserving homeostatic stability or survival. Its discharge, however, is one specific manifestation of the homeostatic principle. Excess of unused energy disturbs homeostatic equilibrium and must therefore be discharged.

In order to consider the origin of surplus energy I introduced the vector analysis of the life process. From the point of view of energy, life can be viewed as a relationship between three vectors: 1) the intake of energy in the nutritive substances and oxygen; 2) their partial retention for use in growth; and 3) the expenditure of energy to maintain existence, its loss in waste, in heat, and in erotic playful activities. In the mature organism the erotic activities assume the form of propagation. This occurs first in puberty as a new kind of eliminating function: the production of germ cells. Propagation may be understood as growth beyond the limits of the individual biological unit. It follows the pattern of propagation in monocellular organisms. The process of growth has a natural limit when the cell reaches maturity. Thereafter reproduction occurs through the division of the cell. When a biological unit reaches a certain size, addition of substance and energy becomes impossible because its capacity to organize living matter has reached its limit. Individual growth then stops and propagation serves as a means of releasing surplus. Otherwise the homeostatic equilibrium would be disturbed.

Energy which is not needed to maintain life, I call surplus energy. This is the source of all sexual activity. In the infant, whose needs are satisfied by adults, the incorporating and retentive vectors outweigh the elimination. Hence the rapid growth. In spite of retention in the form of growth there is still much surplus energy neither stored nor used to maintain existence. The residuum is released in erotic activities. This explains the preponderance of erotic over self-preservative behavior in the child. When the child expends energy erotically he discovers at play new uses for his organs and exercises them until mastery is achieved and their different functions become integrated in a utilitarian fashion for independent existence. Erotic play for the sake of pleasure is the first phase, and the utilization of the functions acquired during erotic play is the second. This may appear paradoxical, but the prolonged dependence of the child upon the parents permits him the luxury of playful erotic activities. Thus the energy-saving principle and the creative use of surplus energy are interwoven and combine to maintain life and permit propagation. Repetition makes useful functions automatic and saves energy which can be used for growth and procreation.

Psychoanalysis in
Western Culture

◄ 1955 ►

After about 300 years of extroverted interest in the surrounding world, Western man has arrived at the phase of self-scrutiny. Following his spiritual awakening in the Renaissance he began to explore the globe, then the solar system, and the human body. Man's place in the animal kingdom was recognized as late as the middle of the nineteenth century. Around the same time increasing interest in understanding society signaled a gradual shift of scientific curiosity from the cosmos to man himself. The last step in this turning toward the self was Freud's theory of the human personality.

Once before in the history of thought a similar sequence of shifting interests took place. In ancient Greece a long period of cosmological speculation was followed by an increasing interest in psychology, ethics, and politics. It appears that this withdrawal of interest to the self signalizes a critical point in cultural development. It occurs when the traditional social mechanism no longer functions smoothly because of rapid changes in the social structure and when the first signs of decline appear. Socrates, Plato, and Aristotle came on the scene when Athenian democracy began to show the first signs of crisis. In our present era, too, interest in psychology, skepticism in absolute truths and epistemological relativism are in the process of replacing the naive and carefree preoccupation with the world around us, coinciding with the crisis of our free societies.

This historical coincidence of social crisis with awakening interest in the self is not surprising to the psychoanalyst. A person becomes aware of himself when the automatic gratification of his subjective needs is interfered with. Self-awareness is a result of the interruption of automatic gratifications which do not require any cognitive effort. Consciousness is neither unmixed pleasure nor a futile luxury of nature. It is the result of frustration which mobilizes those complex

170

processes we call thinking. The function of the ego is to gratify subjective needs which are not gratified automatically but require specific adaptive responses. So long as previously acquired and stabilized automatic patterns work well we do not need to take cognizance of our internal processes.

A burst of interest in social theory accompanied the industrial revolution. It influenced the ideas of Malthus, Adam Smith, Bentham, Ricardo, Marx, and others. As a final response to the rapidly changing society, psychoanalysis appears as a self-protective measure of man when his reliance on automatic, traditional behavior patterns fails him. To paraphrase Freud, where superego was, now conscious ego ideals must be. Self-knowledge becomes imperative and the bliss of self-forgetful curiosity in the surrounding world belongs to the past.

Another response to stress caused by the changing social scene —in a sense an opposite response—is a trend away from individual freedom toward what Toynbee calls the universal state, toward increased central planning and control, toward the type of social system which relieves the citizen from the increasingly difficult free choice, takes care of him but at the same time prescribes his activities, his social functioning, and even his thoughts. Whether this is an unavoidable phase of cultural development, as Toynbee assumes, is an open question. Whether or not free societies can remain free and can solve the problems which they themselves have created by rapid change, rendering individual choice more and more unreliable, no one can tell. The dilemma in which contemporary man of the West finds himself, however, is unmistakable. Free societies recognize and favor individual differences. These are considered the sources of all progress. The center of gravity in free societies is the individual person. Society's function is to give maximum opportunity for self-expression and at the same time guard the members of society from infringing on one another's interest by insisting that everyone keep the accepted rules of the game. This type of system under favorable conditions, such as during the last 300 years of Western culture, through encouraging individual expression in the sciences, arts, and technology, can be highly productive. At the same time, because it accelerates social change and as a result complicates the problems of individual adjustments, it creates insecurity. Self-regulating mechanisms, such as the supply and demand principle in economics, no longer function smoothly, and the urge for central planning appears. Traditional value systems lose their categorical force and this throws individuals back to their own choices. This results in a flight from free choice and enterprise toward the security of steady jobs, preferably in large, depression-proof companies, or in state employment.

Social behavior of man is always governed by two trends, one

toward stability and security; the other toward adventure, exploration of the unknown, and creation. The trend toward security is the
manifestation of self-preservation which we define today more precisely as the homeostatic principle. It is expressed in man's striving to
secure the basic necessities for survival with a minimum amount of
expenditure. The trend toward new ventures into the unknown is
the manifestation of an equally basic biological principle, that of
growth and propagation. Neither of these two trends is more fundamental than the other. They constitute life. Growth and propagation
result from that surplus which remains over and above what is needed
to survive. Whatever is left over from that amount which is needed
for maintaining the homeostatic equilibrium is retained in the form of
growth. Growth, however, has its limitations when maturity is reached.
After maturity the surplus is expended in the form of creativity—
both biological and social. A great deal of this surplus is discharged
playfully or for the sake of meeting the challenges of obstacles in
adventurous pursuits. Both motives, the quest for security and the
lust for adventure and mastery, are always present in the social
aspirations of man, although they do not always have the same distribution. In certain historical periods, like the Middle Ages, the security
motive dominated. Other periods are characterized by an experimental spirit. American democracy, particularly during the pioneer
era, is one of the most dramatic examples of a rapidly changing free
society driven by the spirit of mastery of challenges. It is an extreme
case of a dynamic free society whose spiritual origins go back to the
Renaissance.

In the last 20 years we witness a reversal of this trend in this
country, a reversal which was preceded by several years in Europe.
Public opinion polls have shown that the overwhelming majority of
American youth prefer jobs which pay low income but offer continuity,
and only a very small percentage still prefer to take the risk of
depending upon personal ability to make a great success or lose
everything. A number of contemporary sociologists, anthropologists,
and psychiatrists have not only recognized this profound personality
change in our present generation but given some indications of its
deeper psychodynamic background.

Margaret Mead [1] impressively describes the difficulties which the
present American youth has to face to find his own formula of life.
The young man or woman cannot learn from their parents because
from generation to generation the patterns of behavior change to fit
the ever changing condition. They must learn from each other

---

[1] Margaret Mead, *Male and Female*, New York: Morrow, 1949.

and in groping experimentation find their own organizational principles of behavior.

Erik Erikson[2] came to similar conclusions in describing the difficulties of contemporary youth in finding what he calls their ego identity.

David Riesman[3] refers to the same transition when he speaks of a change from the "inner-directed" personality structure of the past to the "other-directed" personality of the present.

A closer scrutiny reveals that the difficulties of social adaptation which these authors describe in different terms are the same ones to which psychoanalysts attribute etiological importance in neuroses. Neurosis is a condition in which the ego fails in its task to harmonize subjective needs with one another and with the internal standards of the personality which are the imprints of the prevailing social value system. Neurosis indeed is the characteristic disturbance of our age, just as infections and plagues were in past periods when people began to congregate in large cities before they knew how to master the biological hazards of such close coexistence. Psychoanalysis fulfills the same function today that bacteriology did in the past. It helps to replace traditionally sanctioned patterns with *ad hoc* adaptive responses.

From this perspective psychoanalysis appears as a self-curative reaction of Western society to the immense complexities of adjustment. Psychoanalytic treatment aims to replace the individual's automatic, traditional internalized patterns with the ability to find his own formula of life based upon a fuller understanding of himself.

One of the conventional arguments against psychoanalysis has been that analysts consider it their task to help the patient adjust himself to the environment no matter what this environment may be. According to this argument psychoanalysis is a conserving factor opposing change. This argument collapses if one considers that the basic feature of our heterogeneous Western culture is giving opportunity to the individual to change his own environment by actively participating in the social process. Moreover, it is a culture characterized by "social mobility." In fact, psychoanalytic treatment often results in helping a patient to choose an environment more suited to him than the one in which he developed his neurotic difficulties. As a result of treatment he may change his occupation, his human contacts, he may divorce his spouse and he may even emigrate into another country with a different idiology.

Suppose psychoanalysis would have existed in the days of the

2 Erik Erikson, *Childhood and Society,* New York: Norton, 1950.
3 David Riesman, *The Lonely Crowd,* New Haven: Yale Univ. Press, 1950.

Pilgrims. If applied successfully to the protestors, it would have helped them to accept the conditions under which they lived, and the great experiment, "The American Dream," would not have come about.

Considerations of this kind may suffice to illustrate the complexity and the ambiguity of the concept of mental health. The thesis that psychoanalysis is a method which helps the individual accept his environment is more than an oversimplification. It is erroneous because it neglects one fundamental aspect of psychoanalytic treatment. Psychoanalysis aims at something more than merely helping the patient adjust himself to the social system in which he lives. Psychoanalysis is a true product of that phase of Western civilization which had deep respect for individual differences that people actually have in our complex free societies. It aids a person in the integrative task in which he failed: to reconcile his own basic personality with his environment without sacrificing that intangible something which makes him a person different from all others. Psychoanalysis is the most individual type of treatment which medical science has ever produced. Each case is a unique problem. What the therapist is primarily interested in is not the nosological classification of a person, not in what way he is similar to others but in what way he differs from them. Every person has his own potential formula of adjustment. Psychoanalysis aims at an adjustment which takes cognizance not only of a given social environment but also of the uniqueness of every person. From this perspective psychoanalysis gives reality to the expression "the respect for the dignity of the individual," a term which is often used in a vague and well-nigh meaningless fashion. This respect for individual difference explains why psychoanalysis is unthinkable and is therefore prohibited in totalitarian societies. The psychotherapist who sees the salvation of the patient in recreating him according to his own image, even if such a thing were possible, certainly does not practice anything which is even similar to psychoanalysis.

Both analyst and patient belong to the same culture, which believes in and values individual differences. This belief translated into therapeutic practice means that patient and therapist are allied in a joint venture to find a solution for the patient which might be similar to solutions of many others but still is designed to emancipate his unique potentialities. Environment is not considered immutable in all its aspects but as something which itself can be changed. A nonconformist solution might be the best therapeutic result for a given person. Neurosis and nonconformism are not identical. Neurosis is a self-crippling, ineffectual way of expressing and trying to realize the highly individual aspirations of a person.

If psychoanalysis were a procedure which merely helps a person to adjust himself to existing conditions, it would be most desirable and favored in totalitarian societies. That the opposite is true shows that the policy makers know intuitively that its underlying philosophy by no means promotes conformism. Stated in a somewhat oversimplified form, psychoanalysis tries to help a person to remain an individual in a complex society and to express his individual inclinations on a realistic and socially constructive level by becoming a dynamic actor in the social process, by creative participation in it.

In distinction from the rest of the animal kingdom, man creates his own environment.[4] In this light psychoanalysis and the social sciences, better understanding of himself and of the social process appear as possibly the last efforts of Western man to save his individuality from yielding to growing insecurity which drives him toward the universal state. If this effort fails, the only remedy left is a social system in which individual choice is reduced and responsibility for biological and spiritual survival is transferred from the individual to the community. No one can predict the outcome of this race between the increasing trend toward the universal state and the valiant effort of the social and psychological sciences to help man remain master of his fate.

The proponents of the universal state argue that a highly differentiated industrial society does not necessarily increase insecurity. They like to adduce the biological organism, as an example of a highly differentiated system in which the cells have no doubts or uncertainties about their functions or their survival so long as the total organism functions properly. The cells' biological role is restricted to a particular function and their supply of energy and working conditions are secured by automatic regulatory processes. The only organ which has to worry is the highest coordinating center of the organism. Theoreticians who play with these analogies conclude that in the universal state the central government in a similar fashion takes over all the chores and problems of human society. The rest of the people do not have to worry about anything but to perform their specialized and prescribed functions.

If this analogy were correct, the inevitable conclusion is that our present insecurity stems from the fact that we are victims of a cultural lag, still living in the past, adhering to what Mannheim[5] called the "liberal-democratic, bourgeois ideology," worshipping the false gods of individualism introduced into Western history in the Northern Italian cities in the early Renaissance. It was then perpetuated and further developed in the hero worship of the explorer, the scientific

[4] Nests of birds and spider webs can hardly be compared with the creation of cultural environment. These are strictly predetermined, inherited performances.

[5] Karl Mannheim, *Ideology and Utopia*, New York: Harcourt, Brace, 1953.

discoverer, the artist, the protestant who makes man the ultimate arbiter of his values; in the adoration of the laissez faire free trader and the creative but often unscrupulous entrepreneur. Their argument continues as follows: All these basically narcissistic but admittedly imaginative and gifted individuals were useful in their own times. They may have helped us to explore our habitat, to master time and space. They are certainly responsible for the tremendous rapidity of social change. They outlived their usefulness. In their creative or predatory fervor they built up such a thoroughly novel cultural environment that our present task in the West consists in bringing order into the chaos created by this unregimented if imaginative flight of ideas. Not only is self-expression for its own sake outdated but at present it is disruptive, dangerous, contributing to further chaos. The social tasks of our culture have changed. They consist in consolidation and in the rational use of the achievements of the creative genius of our forefathers. This is the next logical and inevitable step in social evolution. Our ideological outlook and values must be adapted to these new cultural tasks and the individual must yield his place to the mass man.

It is true that this sequence of events—periods of creative self-expression followed by a period of consolidation in which the previously exalted individual yields his place to the exalted state—has repeatedly occurred in the course of history. Yet the question arises whether this is an inevitable sequence of events. Is this the only possible outcome of the fact that man through his creative abilities so radically changed his environment that for a time he must busy himself with learning how to live in it? Is this blind dialectic of history the swing of the pendulum between periods of creative change followed by consolidation, and finally by decline, a universal law or only a special case among other possibilities?

When I confronted Freud with this question, whether the wave of the future lies in the direction of the totalitarian state, he gave another reply:

Why do cells reorganize themselves into higher units? Only in order to survive and become more effective in defending themselves against external dangers. Termites are the weakest creatures on earth. They have not even a protective hard shell like ants. No wonder they seek to survive by cooperation and sacrifice their freedom for the sake of mere existence. But man is the crown of creation, the master who dominates the world. Why should he give up his freedom to the same extent as the weak and helpless termites? Against what enemy must he organize himself in so rigid a fashion? [6]

---

[6] Whether or not external danger and pressure are the only factors promoting collaboration, which of necessity always requires some curtailment of individual freedoms, is not a point for discussion here.

The obvious answer is: against his only serious enemy, his fellow man. And from here on the argument may go on like this: Because of his alloplastic genius man constructs machines and other labor-saving devices which relieve him from the greatest part of the burden of procuring the necessities for survival. Extrapolating this trend towards the utilization of labor-saving devices into the future, we may reasonably expect that the economic problem of supplying food, shelter, locomotion will be relegated to the machine and man will have to face the problem of what to do with this liberated energy. There is no logical reason why such a development should require increasing restriction of man's freedom of expression and degrade him to an insect-like automaton. That technology creates insecurity and through it a trend toward the universal state is obviously a paradoxical phenomenon which requires specific explanation. By no means is it self-evident that industrialism must necessarily lead to an unproductive phase of human history, a return to a kind of tribal society in which each individual's place and function are rigidly predetermined. I do not propose a full explanation for this paradoxical phenomenon. Its solution might give us the way out of the throes of the crisis which manifests itself in the ideological split between Western culture and the rest of the world.

Man made the machine but instead of remaining its master he is gradually becoming its slave. Under the impact of machine civilization, man becomes more and more machine-like himself. Instead of leaving to the machine those functions which can be performed with automatic repetition, he is in the process of automatizing and routinizing those functions which require choice and inventiveness. In his admiration of the calculating machine, he proposes to rewrite Hamlet by a machine which can reshuffle all the words of the English language in all permutations until finally it will eject an immaculate copy of the story of the Danish prince. Instead of evaluating a person as a unique combination of his constituent elements he tends to disregard the unique features for what is common and measurable. He deals with his fellow man on the basis of crude categories such as race, social group, height and body weight, number of credits which he received in his classes, man hours and all the data which can be counted and put on a punch card. Instead of using the machine for what it was invented—to give him freedom to use his creative faculties—he wants to organize society, taking the machine as a model. It must be obvious that technology does not need to lead to a loss of spiritual freedom, a loss of respect for individual differences, and to increasing security. On the contrary, it could be used for increasing freedom and encouraging the luxury of individuality. The universal state is by no means a logical, inevitable outcome of industrial civilization.

My lament that man is shaping his own personality to become machine-like is not an explanation but simply a statement of fact. The motivational background of this social trend still awaits explanation.

One of the customary answers is that the destructive utilization of technology for conquest and exploitation creates precisely the type of emergency situation in which social control and rigid organization of society becomes imperative. The atmosphere of the cold war, the constant preparation for the ultimate showdown of power requires strict organization of material and human resources, and prohibits the luxury of individual freedoms. In our times the expectation of the day of doom, of the last judgment, has been replaced by the expectation of the atomic war. The abuse of the machine for destructive purposes at a time when it could be used for relieving the struggle for existence for all inhabitants of the earth is obviously one of the factors.

In spite of our potential abundance we behave as if we were still living in a world of scarcity in which the competitive struggle for natural resources is the only answer for survival. We still adhere to the old method of war for solving conflicts of interest. We have not yet adjusted ourselves to the new situation which our rapid conquest of natural forces poses. We do not recognize all the potential, peaceful utilizations of our technological knowledge, which could solve constructively all those problems we now try to solve by mutual destruction. This, however, is only a partial answer which considers merely the economic factors. Of equal or greater significance are ideological issues which are more or less independent of our basic vegetative needs.

The materialist theory of history which explains in unilinear fashion all human profiles by the economic structure of society—or to use synonymous expressions, which explains from economic structure the ego ideals, basic personalities, ego identities or ego representations characteristic for an era or for a culture—is one of the great and dangerous fallacies of the past, a fallacy from which not all contemporary social scientists have extricated themselves. The influence of the economic substratum is, of course, powerful and conspicuous and therefore more readily recognized. However, it is well known that traditional value systems, social attitudes, and institutions, which once came into being largely under the influence of economic factors, exert their influence even after the conditions which produced them have changed. In the past these social attitudes and institutions might have been adaptive reactions to existing conditions but they

retained through tradition their dynamic power long after they outlived their adaptive usefulness.

This temporal lag, however, is not the only noneconomic determinant of personality formation. No one to my knowledge has stated
the fallacy of this narrow economic determinism more convincingly
than one of the few true philosophers of our aphilosophical era, Ortega y Gasset.[7] According to him, necessity for survival does not explain man's whole behavior. It explains only what is least interesting
and least characteristic for man as a culture-building species. Behavior for survival is more rigidly determined by the specific survival
problems than behavior which takes place after the basic needs are
fulfilled. Adaptive responses to basic necessities leave less choice open
than those self-expressive modes of behavior which are not dictated
by immediate survival needs. In other words, man shows his human
qualities more in his leisure than in his struggle for survival. What he
does with his faculties after he has secured his basic needs, how he
plays, how he daydreams, how he uses his creative capacities, distinguishes him as a personality. In his routine, utilitarian, economic
performance, whether he is pushing a button, or tilling the soil, he is
like the next person. His behavior is determined by his social role and
function. By this I do not imply that behavior in leisure, in play and
fantasy, are not determined but they are determined by other than
survival needs; they are more varied and characteristic for the person
as an individual. The homeostatic, or self-preservation functions of the
ego are less characteristic for a person as an individual than the
manifestations of his libido. What makes man different from all other
species is that he uses his creative forces not only for biological
growth and propagation but alloplastically for building different
forms of culture which are not solely determined by survival needs.
On the contrary, in his playful, nonutilitarian but libidinous, exuberant exercise of his faculties, man makes discoveries, the utility of
which is only later discovered. Anthropologists, particularly Roheim,
have shown that such practical inventions as agriculture, gardening,
and cattle raising, which marked the beginnings of human civilization, originally were not invented planfully for utilitarian aims. On
the contrary, this useful occupation developed from playful activities
of man from idle hobbies, and were exploited only secondarily for
economic purposes. While playfully acting out primitive fantasies concerning propagation, he discovered gardening. Cattle raising stems
from the totemistic rites in the religious practices of the primitives.
Domestic animals served at first for the representation of father,
mother, and children and not until later was their practical usefulness

[7] Jose Ortega y Gasset, *Toward a Philosophy of History*, New York: Norton,
1941.

discovered. Utility was certainly not the primary motivation of the pioneers in aviation but the yearning to rise towards the skies, which often appears in our dreams to express our wish for mastery, power, and freedom. Flying originally was invented neither for the sake of future passenger traffic nor for throwing bombs at our enemies.

We come then to the seemingly paradoxical conclusion that culture is the product of man's leisure and not the sweat of his brow. His productive abilities become liberated when he is relieved from the necessities of the struggle for survival. Without being familiar with the psychoanalytic theory of ego and libido, Ortega y Gasset with the visionary intuition of the true philosopher came to similar conclusions. He writes:

The ancients divided life into two spheres. The first they called *otium*, leisure, by which they understood not the negative of doing, not idling, but the positive attitude of seeing to the strictly human obligations of man, such as command, organization, social intercourse, science, arts. The second, consisting of those efforts which meet the elemental necessities and make *otium* possible, they called *nec-otium*, with apposite stress on the negative character it has for man.[8]

It is a sad commentary on our times that man, when technology potentially and to a degree actually relieves him from the chores of his homeostatic or life-preserving burdens loses his *raison d'être*, cannot find new goals, cannot find new values, a new ego identity. As Ortega y Gasset says succinctly: "Desiring is by no means easy." He reminds us of the quandary of the newly rich man.

With all wish-fulfilling means at his command he finds himself in the awkward situation of not knowing how to wish. At the bottom of his heart he is aware that he wishes nothing, that he himself is unable to direct his appetite and to choose among the innumerable things offered by his environment. . . . If it is so difficult to wish for objects which are already available, one may imagine how difficult the properly creative wish must be, the wish that reaches out for things yet non-existent and anticipates the still unreal. If a man is unable to wish for his own self because he has no clear vision of a self to be realized, he can have but pseudo wishes and spectral desires devoid of sincerity and vigor.[9]

One cannot help thinking of our contemporary youth—whom Riesman calls "other-directed"—devoid of an internalized system of values. Ortega y Gasset suggests that "it may well be that one of the basic diseases of our time is a crisis of wishing and that for these reasons all our technical achievements seem to be of no use whatever."[10]

[8] *Ibid.*, chap. 3, p. 118.
[9] *Ibid.*, p. 119.
[10] *Ibid.*, pp. 120-121.

Many feel that our crisis consists basically in losing faith in science, a faith which animated us in the last 300 years. Some thinkers, as Niebuhr or Maritain, want to fill this gap with return to supernaturalism and mysticism.[11] Is this loss of faith in scientific method justified, however? We may well have recognized by now that the methods and concepts of the natural sciences cannot resolve the social dilemma of our times. We have taken, however, the first steps toward the scientific exploration of man's complex motivational dynamics and the nature of his specific culture-building potentialities. Sociology and psychology are the emerging sciences of our times. August Comte, the father of sociology, was born 234 years later than Galileo; Freud 288 years later. Natural sciences have over a 200-year headstart on the social sciences. To catch up with this discrepancy is a worthy goal. The specific cultural significance of psychoanalysis lies in helping Western man to find his ego identity. I do not have in mind only psychoanalytic therapy and its derivatives but the over-all influence of psychoanalytic thought and knowledge about childrearing, educational practices, parent education: its influence upon contemporary literature and art, transmitted rapidly through all the new channels of communication. I refer particularly to the fact that psychoanalysis is becoming before our eyes an integral content of the collective consciousness of the West.

The all-pervasiveness of this influence can give us hope that through understanding himself and the society in which he lives, the poor-rich man of the West may find new aspirations for the future.

The understanding of the dynamic interaction of the self with the social environment is in itself a goal so stupendous that it could occupy the productive capacities of many generations to come. Faith in the progress achieved through the natural sciences of the last centuries may be duplicated by a new faith—in what the social sciences may do for the further progress of man.

The mechanical philosophy of the *vis-a-tergo* which explains *what is* from *what was* is not sufficient to understand man. Man has the unique ability to create something which is not yet existing. He does not live *from* his past alone but he lives *for* his future. Although past, present, and future represent a dynamic continuum, a person best reveals his unique identity in what he strives for. Technology has relieved him, at least potentially, from a great part of the burden which is needed for merely existing. Is there any cause to doubt that the new social sciences and psychology in particular, will give him guidance in finding what to live for, a content for wishing what is appropriate to his own individuality and to the world in which he lives, or

[11] Sydney Hook, John Dewey, and Ernst Nagel, "The New Failure of Nerve," *Partisan Review,* January-February, 1943.

better said, in which he wants to live? If we believe in this cultural function of our discipline and if we believe that our aim can be reached, this will serve as a vision which is the moving power behind every productivity. This is my credo as a psychoanalyst.

Unexplored Areas in Psychoanalytic Theory and Treatment—Part I

◄ 1958 ►

Theory

Divergent views about the structure and functioning of the personality and the nature of the therapeutic process resulting in heated arguments and occasional schisms has been characteristic for our field since its inception. Although these differences often were expressed in polemics, resembling religious disputes of past centuries, it is reassuring that concerning the fundamental principles of psychodynamics they mainly consist in different emphases. Or they are of semantic nature, resulting from the difficulties in communicating with each other abstract and often vaguely defined concepts. It is not facetious to say that often we ourselves do not know what we mean, and therefore it is not surprising that we cannot precisely communicate our ideas with others. We use terms and concepts which lack the precision of the abstractions current in older disciplines. We are experiencing to a much larger degree the same difficulty as the physicist when he applies mathematical abstractions to actually observed phenomena. The geometrist operates with points which have no extension in space. The physicist applies these geometrical abstractions to matter which has extension. A discrepancy is thus unavoidably introduced. In our field abstractions are incomparably farther removed from the actual things to which we apply them. I shall illustrate this gap between current psychoanalytic abstractions and observational data and the unclarities of these abstractions themselves with examples concerning our most fundamental theoretical views.

THE MENTAL APPARATUS

We speak of ego, superego and id existing as distinct structures within a cohesive system. What we actually observe are only certain

183

functions which we attribute to certain organized structures distinct from others within a larger unit we call the mental apparatus. Since psychoanalytic theory attempts to be self-contained, it prefers not to include in its scheme physiological concepts. The mental apparatus is not considered as something existing in space—for example, in the brain—but is conceived as a functional system, an organization of certain psychological elements such as impulses, instincts, notions, ideas and values. In a vague fashion we of course assume that this psychological system is in some manner connected with the brain, but in building our psychological models we are not concerned further with the nature of this connection. And yet we speak of ego boundaries and use other spatial notions, such as excluding impulses from the system we call the "conscious" and relegating it to the "unconscious." Such analogical schemes are, of course, quite permissible aids to help the visualization of a system of abstractions. The danger lies in the fact that at the same time we deal with the mental apparatus as a system of psychological functions, we also use terms and concepts of structural nature, referring to spatial arrangements. The statement, "An impulse is unconscious," means, strictly speaking, that the impulse lacks a certain quality of conscious impulses, but shares with the latter certain other qualities. If we think strictly in functional terms, we may say that under certain conditions an impulse may lose or acquire the quality of consciousness. In structural terms we state that an impulse, as soon as it passes the conscious ego's boundary—a spatial reference—it acquires the quality of consciousness. The point is not whether one or the other description is correct, but only that it is necessary to recognize explicitly that the structural approach supposes a spatial theory, and therefore it combines strictly psychological (dynamic) and brain-physiological models. It is a hybrid, a psychophysiological model without being explicitly so. I mention this only in support of my previous remark that we do not always know precisely what we are talking about.

It appears to me that if we want to construct a pure *psychological model* of the mental apparatus, we shall have to restrict ourselves to strictly functional, or if you prefer, "dynamic," concepts and visualize the personality as a system of interacting impulses, inhibiting and motivating forces. How useful such a model would be is another question, but we must never forget that most psychological phenomena are perceived in time but not in space. This need not prohibit us from structural speculations, but we must frankly state that in doing so we trespass into brain anatomy and physiology. This is no sin, and I am convinced that the future model of the mental apparatus will be built on a frankly recognized combination of psychological and physiological concepts. Since the functions of the mind and the brain are connected or even synonymous, this conclusion is nothing but stating something which is self-evident. It is so self-evident that if it were not for our almost compulsive avoidance of mixing psychology with physiology while actually we are constantly mixing them, this statement would be superfluous. We in the field of psychology need not be ashamed to admit that the knowledge of personality functions requires both psychological and physiological observations, and psychological concepts are not sufficient to reconstruct a final model of the mind. If for example, we speak of action we deal with a physiologically observed phenomenon. When we speak of motivation resulting in action we refer to something about which we have only psychological knowledge. Accordingly, even such a basic concept as action cannot be described in its totality in purely psychological or purely physiological terms. One part of action, namely its motivation—at present at least—can be described only psychologically; the motor behavioral results only in physiological terms. The biceps contracts responding to a nerve impulse from the motor cortex at the moment a person wants to slap someone's face. Without stating both the psychological impulse to slap and the slapping itself, the phenomenon is not fully described. I shall not enlarge on the opposite error of the behaviorists, who compulsively avoid dealing with motivation, which they cannot directly observe.

This constant unavoidable mixing of physiological and psychological data is clearly seen if we review the psychoanalytic theory of ego functions. We differentiate between perception of external and internal stimuli as one of its basic functions. We find the anatomical and physiological substratum of these psychological functions in the structure of the sensory apparatus, which conducts and registers stimuli originating outside and inside of the organism. We speak of the integrative function of the ego and recognize its anatomical and physiological substratum in the cellular architectonics of the brain, in an hierarchical system of coordinating centers and communication lines. We speak of the executive functions of the ego and find its anatomical and physiological implementation in the motor apparatus. Is it not high time that we try more systematically to reconcile psychological with physiological data and abstractions, and give up the traditional attitude that while it would be nice if physiology were in accordance with psychological notions, yet we do not need to be seriously concerned with physiology in constructing a psychological model of the ego.[1]

Undoubtedly we know little of the physiological basis of such phenomena as repression, substitution, sublimation, turning impulses

[1] In collaboration with Ralph Gerard, we had made the beginnings of such a reconstruction which we plan to complete in the future.

against the self, etc., and our first task is to describe them in psychological terms as we observe them or conclude to their existence. What has to be kept in mind, however, is that these are but phenomena within a complex communication system as visualized by the cyberneticists, and eventually they will be expressed in general principles which prevail in all communication systems. We are not rivals, but collaborators with the representatives of this new branch of science.

INSTINCT THEORY

The distance between actual observation and theory becomes even larger when we begin to hypothesize certain forces responsible for the constant dynamic activities going on within the structure we refer to as the mental apparatus. It is true we experience in ourselves forces at work in the form of motivations, and are aware of causal sequences between these motivating forces and certain biological functions. This is an excellent starting point, at least as good as the Cartesian edict *"cogito ergo sum."* We feel hunger and as a result we walk toward the icebox. We can justly say that the sensation of hunger is in causal relation to our motor behavior, the steps we took toward the icebox. We feel an impulse we call curiosity and open the newspaper to learn about the satellite. The difficulty arises when we attempt to construct abstractions concerning these different impulses. As in every science, we begin with classification. We lump together activities motivated by hunger, self-defense, and our other goal-directed and structured activities, by which we try to satisfy our survival needs, such as going to school, then to college, then to a professional school. All such activities we attribute to a self-preservative (or ego) instinct. We differentiate them from sexual impulses, and from all those idle, nonutilitarian curiosities and play activities, which are pursued, as it appears to us, for their own sake for the pleasure we derive from them. We have thus constructed our first two categories: the self-preservative and the erotic impulses. We soon discover the difficulties of making clearcut distinctions. Nature is not willing to be fitted into our neat categories. Being curious about the content of an icebox is obviously different from the curiosity we have about the structure of the atom. The one is highly practical and is aimed to eliminate a basic need—hunger—which is obviously a self-preservative goal. On the other hand, even the most rabid pragmatist, the representative philosopher of our utility-oriented era, would concede that the curiosity about the structure of the atom originally was not directed primarily toward any practical aims. It was a *l'art pour l'art* kind of curiosity, even though the satisfaction of this curiosity later proved to have undreamed of practical applications. It is more similar to a child's prying open a clock to see how it works inside. We arrive then at two kinds of curiosity, one subordinated to survival, the other a curiosity for its own sake, which has some erotic or at least playful connotation. Our classification system is now seriously threatened. We have to place the impulse "curiosity" into both of our pigeonholes. Sometimes it appeaars as self-preservative, sometimes as erotic. We may draw some consolation from theoretical physics, where light in some relations appears as corpuscular, in others as undulatory. But we meet the same difficulty even with simpler motive forces. We clearly recognize that to crave for a piece of bread when we are hungry, and to yearn for some culinary concoction are two different things.

Our dilemma increases when we proceed in our abstractions and try to conclude to some kind of a substratum behind these two kinds of impulses. We call them the instinct of self-preservation and libido. How to apply this classification, however, when the same impulse to ingest food and liquid once appears as self-preservative and the next moment as libidinous? Have they two kinds of material substrata, for example, two kinds of fluids or hormones, or do we deal here with two kinds of nerve impulses only in a quantitative, not qualitative sense? Lust for culinary pleasure and hunger mostly appear together in everyday life: we eat both to satisfy hunger and enjoy the taste of food. One is rarely only hungry or only a glutton. As a solution, a kind of fusion of two instincts was assumed; Freud speaks of the erotization of an impulse: self-preservative and sexual impulses may mix and our job becomes to account for the proportion in which each of the two instincts participate in the fusion.[2] The impossibility of making such a quantitative analysis sufficiently precise shows that this is little more than a *façon de parler*.

A new difficulty arose when the two instincts were conceived as polar opposites. Freud always considered ego instincts and libido more or less as antagonists, and in his later instinct theory this antagonism became essential.[3] He distinguished between life and death instincts opposing each other, and spoke of their fusion in terms of neutralization, the upbuilding life instinct neutralizing the destructive effect of the death instinct. Hunger now implicitly became a manifestation of eros as a biological urge to maintain life. It is true that hunger and the erotically tinged culinary satisfactions coexist peacefully and do not disturb or counteract each other. Yet a valuable distinction between hunger and the erotic pleasures of the sense of taste was lost when hunger became an expression of eros.

Since both kinds of impulses, eros and thanatos, appear in the

[2] Sigmund Freud, "Instincts and their Vicissitudes," in *Collected Papers,* New York: Basic Books, 1959, Vol. IV, 60-83.

[3] S. Freud, *Beyond the Pleasure Principle,* New York, Liveright, 1961.

organism, they must have some kind of a biological substratum, and if so do these two instincts have basically different biological substrata or only differ in their direction, two forces with opposing vectors? Freud's reference to anabolism and catabolism as the basic biological substrata of the two instincts implies a vector concept. Physiologists speaking of anabolism and catabolism do not assume two fundamentally different processes; they think of two phases of a physicochemical process called metabolism, which consists of building up more complex organic compounds and their simultaneous decomposition, which is connected with transformation of chemical energy into mechanical energy and heat.

It would be indeed attractive if one were able to reduce the great variety of purposeful and utilitarian activities preserving life, together with all playful erotic and frankly sexual phenomena on the one hand, and destructive hostile impulses on the other hand, to anabolic and catabolic processes; to understand hate and love, life and death as the ultimate manifestations of these biological antagonists. This dualistic theory has a grandiose metaphysical sweep in accounting for the two most fundamental biological and psychological phenomena: life and death and love and hate, as the results of a force operating in the direction of growth and organization, and another one aiming at destruction and disorganization. This theory, however, just because of its lofty abstraction can hardly satisfy those more concrete intellectual needs which led to the original differentiation between self-preservative and erotic phenomena. It hardly can account, for example, for the two forms of curiosity, one motivated by survival needs, one by a detached urge to find out something only for the sake of understanding it without any useful purpose. Neither of them can be attributed to the death instinct. Similarly, hunger and culinary desire, both satisfied by ingestion of food, hardly can be traced back, one to a death instinct, the other to eros. This impasse is seen most strikingly when we examine the phenomenology of the aggressive-destructive impulses.

Historically, the phenomenon of sadism was the stumbling block in Freud's original view, differentiating between erotic and self-preservative forces. Aggression can be both self-preservative and, in the form of sadism, erotic. As will be seen, Freud's solution of this difficulty led to new problems. The fact that pregenital manifestations of sex are not race preservative induced Freud to make one of his most lasting generalizations. Propagation, the mature genital act and the corresponding psychological attitude, the love felt for the sexual partner, is only one, the most advanced form of sexuality. It is the result of a development from immature pregenital, autoerotic activities to mature race preservative manifestations of sexuality.[4] Although not explicitly stated by Freud, the pregenital manifestations of sexuality are the psychological expressions of organismic growth. They consist of playful and pleasureful practices of the different functions of the body, oral and anal practices, exercise of the muscle system and of the sensory organs. They do not directly serve survival; they, however, prepare the organism for independent existence. During these pleasurable playful practices of the different organic functions, the child not only derives "functional pleasure" but at the same time learns how to use these functions. A common example is muscle eroticism. In the mature organism these functions largely, though not entirely, lost their erotic nature and the sexual sensation became gradually tranferred and restricted to the genital organs.

In his earlier instinct theory, not considering any longer propagation as an indispensable part of sex, Freud was able to enlarge the category of sexual phenomena and include into it pleasure-yielding practices of the body which have no race preservative function, yet experientially have a distinct similarity with genital pleasure. This way, phenomenologically at least, he arrived at two distinct categories —libido which includes all those impulses which are connected with a pleasurable sexual kind of gratification, and those useful activities by which we preserve our existence: the ego instincts. The dilemma, which this first instinct theory never could resolve was in which category should aggressiveness be placed. In the form of sadism it obviously has a sexual connotation. Sadistic acts do not serve survival needs—they are practiced as a source of sexual gratification. Aggression, however, may be devoid of any sexual connotation, as in a man struggling to overcome an obstacle which prevents him from obtaining food or wanting to eliminate a foe who threatens his survival. Yet, aggressiveness which was the prototype of an ego instinct, under certain conditions which were never clearly defined, may appear as sadism, a frankly sexual phenomenon. A similar contradiction appeared with the introduction of the concept of narcissism. Self-love, as the classical reference to Narcissus clearly indicated, is placed into the category of libidinous phenomena. At the same time it is clearly an ego instinct. Obviously, the transition of an impulse from the self-preservative to the sexual category is a rather common phenomenon, and as long as the theory does not account for the factors which are responsible for the transformation of rational self-interest into erotic self-love—narcissism—or vice versa, nor for the factors responsible

[4] S. Freud, "Three Contributions to the Sexual Theory," *Basic Writings*, New York: Modern Library, 1938.

for the way rational self-preservative aggression assumes a libidinous appearance in the form of sadism, it is not a satisfactory theory. Freud's newer life and death instinct theory tried to solve this dilemma by substituting for the original pair—ego instinct versus libido—another antagonistic pair of impulses: eros and thanatos. Eros includes the self-preservative functions, growth and those functions which phenomenologically appear as erotic.

Now, narcissism, object love, all manifestations of pregenital and genital sexuality, creative activities on a sublimated level are all considered erotic; aggression, whether directed against others or the self, is the manifestation of the death instinct. To account for the fact that self-destructiveness in masochism may be the source of sexual gratification, or destructiveness directed against others may frankly become sexual, Freud retained the auxiliary hypothesis of instinct fusion which he used already in his earlier theory. Here again the theory fails to tell about the factors responsible for such fusion. If ultimately the destructive and love instincts are manifestations of two polarly opposite vector quantities, such as catabolism and anabolism, it is difficult to conceive of any other kind of fusion but an arithmetical one, addition or subtraction. Destructiveness becomes accordingly sadistic by an admixture of eros which minimizes the effect of thanatos. All the self-preservative functions now become by definition, erotic, since they are serving life and growth. If they are all erotic, what then differentiates hunger from thumbsucking, practical from creative curiosity, muscle exertion for survival from the erotic enjoyment of muscle action? What is fused here with what? Obviously, not eros with thanatos, since neither the frankly erotic nor the phenomenologically nonerotic manifestations of these functions can be considered as expressions of the death instinct.

It is needless to belabor the point further that from these global abstractions there is no return to the concrete facts of observation.

The Freudian dual instinct theory has, however, a nucleus which, if differently stated, resembles recent formulations of communication theory. Instead of assuming two kinds of instincts, one toward life and one toward death, it is more promising to speak of a trend toward organization, which counteracts the entropy principle, the most universal law of all natural process: the trend from more organized toward less organized states. As was pointed out by Wiener[5] and Schroedinger[6] some kind of device similar to the demon which Maxwell thought up to illustrate the entropy principle actually operates in living organisms. Maxwell's imaginary demon is located in a con-

[5] Norbert Wiener, *The Human Use of Human Beings*, Boston: Houghton Mifflin, 1954.
[6] E. Schroedinger, *What Is Life?* Cambridge: Cambridge Univ. Press, 1956.

tainer filled with gas, watches the molecules and separates them according to their velocity by opening a trap door for the high speed molecules and closing it against lower speed molecules. This way he could increase the temperature on one part of the container and create order in the randomly distributed molecules with different velocities. This results in increasing free energy (negative entropy) of the gas. The internal organizing principle is obviously information about molecular velocities which enables Maxwell's demon to bring order into a chaotic conglomeration of elementary particles. In living organisms through all kinds of feedback mechanisms such informations are actually received by a central agency, which makes it possible for the organisms not only to maintain stable conditions but even to grow and progress toward higher and higher states of organization. A living organism is one which actually possesses a Maxwell demon operating in it.

All this at first seems contradictory to the general entropy principle. The obvious answer to this paradoxon is that the law of entropy is only valid for closed systems. The demon depends on external sources of energy and his activities themselves involve at least as much increase of entropy as they save. In open systems—and actually all existing systems are open except the universe as a whole—temporary local deviations from the law of entropy are quite possible. Only the whole of the universe is running down toward thermodynamical equilibrium, in which there is no longer any free energy and no change occurs anymore, a state of a completely random distribution of all constituent parts within the universe. Communication theory now defines the instrument by which this continuous progress toward increasing entropy, that is to say, toward disorganization, can be at least locally and temporarily reversed in certain systems. This instrument is information. Shannon[7] has introduced a quantitative yardstick of information, one bit of information being equal to what is necessary to decide between two *a priori* equi-probable alternatives. This is indeed an exciting discovery because it connects entropy with communication theory; it connects two seemingly completely separate fields; thermodynamics and communication theory. This connection is, however, not surprising. Weaver explains it by reminding us that information in communication theory is measured by the amount of freedom of choice we have in sending messages. In a highly organized state the degree of randomness of choice is low and also entropy is low. By means of information, that is to say by self-regulating feedback mechanisms, we can decrease the freedom of choice; in other words, we introduce order into a disorganized

[7] C. E. Shannon and W. Weaver, *The Mathematical Theory of Communication,* Urbana: Univ. of Illinois Press, 1949.

state just as Maxwell's demon can do. Information, operating within a system, accordingly acts against the law of entropy, is capable of destroying a certain amount of it, even though it in itself depends on external sources of energy. Along these lines of reasoning, communication theory might be able, if not to explain but at least to measure quantitatively, the degree of organization. Since organization achieved by means of information is an indispensable property of life, the degree of organization appears to be the proper yardstick for the quantitative study of the life process. The significance of this yardstick is that it has been found useful both in communication theory and also physics. As we shall see, it may have in the future an equally meaningful application in the study of instinctual discharge phenomena.

INSTINCT THEORY, COMMUNICATION THEORY AND THE LAW OF ENTROPY

No matter how stimulating this formulation of the most basic property of the phenomenon of "life" may be at the first blush, in itself it does not seem to help us to describe and understand better the relationship of sexual to nonsexual instincts. No such contribution came as yet from this source. The replacement of eros and thanatos with the more operational concepts of thermodynamics and communication theory is gratifying indeed, yet the gap between communication theory and instinct theory is still unbridged. In the following no attempt is made to close this gap in an operational sense; only a perspective of future possibilities is suggested.

I attempted in past writings to describe the relation of sexual to nonsexual phenomena.[8] Thomas French independently came to quite similar conclusions[9] I took as a starting point the fact that an extreme variety of functions, such as ingestion of food and all oral activities, elimination of waste material, curiosity, love, aggressive behavior, self-assertion, the wish to be noticed, can assume a sexual connotation, but also may appear as nonsexual under other circumstances. In other words, almost every emotion and voluntary function may become the content of sexual excitation. This is most clearly seen in the field of sexual perversions.

As stated before, aggressive hostility may appear as a completely nonsexual striving, but also may assume a distinct sexual character in the form of sadism. The same is true about curiosity which in

---

[8] Franz Alexander, "A Note to the Theory of Perversions," in S. Lorand (ed.), *Perversions, Psychodynamics and Therapy*, New York: Random House, 1956.

[9] Thomas French, *The Integration of Behavior*, Chicago: Univ. of Chicago Press, 1952, I, 147ff.

sexual form appears in the voyeur. The wish to attract attention, to impress, in its sexual form appears as exhibitionism. In the history of passive homosexuals we often find an early frustration in the form of the longing for a strong father figure. Here the passive longing finds a sexual expression.

At this point I should like to call attention to another observation which throws further light upon the relationship of the non-sexual and the sexual expressions of the same impulse.[10] A quantitative complementary relationship exists between these two kinds of manifestations. Persons who have manifest perversions frequently show a conspicuous lack of the nonsexual expressions of the same trend which appears openly in their sexual behavior. Sexual exhibitionists are often highly inhibited in their ability to make an impression on the nonsexual level. They conspicuously neglect their external appearance and are inhibited in such expressive innervations as gesticulation and modulation of speech. Although I have no statistical data available, I found a number of stammerers among them. Others did not have a definable speech defect but had marked difficulty in verbal expression. It appears that the crude exhibition of their genitals is the only way in which they can gratify their need to be noticed.

Another example for this complementary relationship between sexual and nonsexual manifestation of the same drive is offered in sadism. It is commonly known that sexual sadists are often weaklings, incapable of forcefully asserting themselves in their relationship to others. Their aggressiveness is pent up because its normal expression in interpersonal relations is inhibited; it is discharged—short circuited—in their sexual behavior.

A similar observation pertains to pedophiliacs who are extremely inhibited toward women of their own age because of excessive inferiority feelings. Their only outlet, in many cases, is sadistically distorted sexual approach to minors.

In the analysis of voyeurs, I have been impressed by the conspicuous absence of any nonsexual curiosity. A counterpart of this observation was provided by a scientist who devoted himself to basic research. His passion to uncover and disclose the secrets of nature took the place of sexual curiosity which had become inhibited at an early age; only in late adolescence did he discover the anatomical difference between men and women.

In the case of masochism, such a correlation was explicitly stated by Freud: "An individual may, it is true, preserve the whole or a certain amount of his morality alongside his masochism, but, on

10 Alexander, op. cit.

the other hand, a good part of his conscience may be swallowed up by his masochism."[11] Giving heed to this statement, I was impressed to find an extreme, sometimes blatant, selfishness sexual masochists display in their nonsexual human relationships. Their need for punishment finds sexualized expression in their masochism and this frees them from the inhibitory effect of their conscience.

Practically every emotional trend, love, curiosity, the need to call attention to one's self, aggressiveness and the need for suffering can be expressed either nonsexually or sexually. I have suggested in other writings that when an impulse is discharged in an isolated fashion without being subordinated to a more complex goal structure, it assumes a sexual connotation and that such isolated emotional discharges occur in states of excess excitation, when there is a surplus of motivational cathexis beyond that which is necessary for co-ordinated utilitarian, self-preservative functions.[12] An excess of oral craving, beyond what is physiologically conditioned by hunger, is precisely what we call oral eroticism. Excessive accumulated aggressive impulse which is not needed for utilitarian aims—aggressiveness which is not necessary for survival, may be discharged in the form of sadism.

Such an excess excitation occurs mainly under two conditions: 1) when there is an amount of excitation in excess of what is needed by the organism in its survival activities, and 2) when excitations which could not be absorbed and included in the structure of the ego, because of a neurotic interruption of normal maturation, find isolated discharge either in the form of perversions or in neurotic symptoms.

The same surplus theory of sexuality applies well also to the genital manifestations of sexuality. It is in accordance with current biological concepts to consider reproduction as growth beyond the limits set by individual growth potential. This theory is in accordance with the biological view that growth and sexuality are closely related phenomena. Gerard, for example, defines the relation of growth to reproduction:

Clearly the defining line between growth and reproduction . . . is uncertain and broken. Reproduction of cells constitutes growth of the individual; reproduction of individuals . . . growth of the community. Indeed, reproduction might be looked upon as a form of discontinuity or a critical point dividing an otherwise continuous growth process into a series of separate quanta. . . . The simpler forms of reproduction, the division and

[11] S. Freud, "The Economic Problem in Masochism," in *Collected Papers*, New York: Basic Books, 1959, Vol. II, 255-269.

[12] F. Alexander, *Fundamentals of Psychoanalysis*, New York: Norton, 1948.

separation of cells commonly but not always with mitosis, are merely such a punctuated protoplasmic increase.[13]

In a sense, reproduction is the manifestation of an excess of "growth energy," of which no further use can be made in individual development after the organism reached the limit of its maturational process.

The fact that germ plasm remains isolated and does not become an integrated part of the total organism also accords well with our psychological formulations. According to these, the sexual nature of an emotional discharge depends upon a special condition: whether the discharge takes place as an isolated gratification of a tendency which serves as a goal in itself, or whether it becomes a component part of a goal structure which serves the interest of the total organism. Although in genital sexuality the partial drives become integrated and subordinated to the goal of propagation, genital sexuality remains a goal in itself and is not necessarily subordinated to other goals. Genital impulses may also become desexualized and, like any other emotional trend, integrated into the total personality; they then find expression in nonsexual love, creativity or some other sublimated form. This desexualization, however, does not mean losing an admixture of another instinct—libido—but rather a different form of discharge of the same impulse.

Without trying to speculate about a special substratum such as two instincts of different quality, we ask the question, under what circumstances does an emotional content assume the quality of sexual excitement. The answer which our observational data give us is of great simplicity. Every gratification of an impulse has an erotic character if it is performed for its own sake and is not subservient to the needs of the organism as a whole. This can be considered as a surplus of excitation.

This view can be subjected to empirical scrutiny and does not need to remain the result of merely deductive speculation. If the statement is correct, we do not need to postulate two kinds of instincts of different quality. We consider sexuality in all its multiple manifestations as a special form of discharge of any impulse. The same impulse of the same quality can be discharged sexually or otherwise. It loses the quality of sexuality as soon as it becomes a constituent part of a complex structure—which French appropriately called a goal structure.[14]

This concept of sexuality, though it was previously not stated quite as explicitly and comprehensively, is not quite original. Its

[13] R. Gerard, *Unresting Cells*, New York: Harper, 1940.
[14] French, *op. cit.*

sources can be found in some of Freud's early views on the nature of sexual phenomena, and more specifically in some of Ferenczi's writings.

Freud in his earlier writings several times raised the question whether sexuality was not merely characterized by a quantitative factor. In his "Three Contributions to the Sexual Theory," he wrote ". . . sexual excitation arises as an accessory to a long series of internal processes when the intensity of these processes has exceeded certain quantitative limits." [15] Later in his "Instincts and Their Vicissitudes" he asked:

Are we to suppose that the different instincts which operate upon the mind but of which the origin is somatic are also distinguished by different qualities and act in the mental life in a manner qualitatively different? This supposition does not seem to be justified; we are much more likely to find the simpler assumption sufficient—namely, that the instincts are all qualitatively alike and owe the effect they produce only to the quantities of excitation accompanying them, or perhaps further to certain functions of this quantity. The difference in the mental effects produced by different instincts may be traced to the differences in their sources.[16]

Here Freud, however, did not recognize that in addition to intensity the mode of discharge is essential. He refers, however, in addition to intensity, to rhythm. A more explicit statement comes from Ferenczi:

. . . whenever an organ fails to indulge its pleasure tendencies directly but renounces these in favor of the organism as a whole, substances may be secreted from this organ or qualitative innervations be shifted to other organs and eventually to the genitals, it being the task of the latter to equalize in the gratificatory act the free-floating pleasure tensions of all the organs. [Sexuality consists in] . . . all those accumulated amounts of unpleasure which, side-tracked during the utility functioning of the organs, were left undealt with, undisposed of. In ejaculation all those (autotomic) tendencies are summated, the carrying out of which was neglected by utility functioning. Every organ has its own individuality, its physiology of pleasure in contrast to its physiology of function. The summation of those excitations which have no utility constitutes genital sexuality, which releases accumulated, unused energy.[17]

Ferenczi's formulation, if one disregards the nonessential statement about hypothetical fluids, is identical with the view here proposed.

This view concerning the relation of sexual to nonsexual phe-

[15] S. Freud, "Three Contributions to the Sexual Theory," *op. cit.*

[16] S. Freud, "Instincts and Their Vicissitudes," in *Collected Papers,* New York: Basic Books, 1959, Vol. IV, 60-83.

[17] S. Ferenczi, *Thalassa, a Theory of Genitality,* New York: Psychoanal. Quart., Inc., 1949.

nomena has still one other commendation. The introduction of this theory closely resembles certain developments in the theory of heat and electricity. The earlier theories in both of these fields were substance theories, both heat and electricity were considered a special kind of fluid. In the course of time both of these "substance" theories gave place to purely dynamic concepts, the kinetic theory of heat and the field theory of electricity. In these newer theories heat became the manifestation of molecular movements; temperature depended upon the velocity of the movements, and similarly the electric field with its purely quantitative (geometric) characteristics replaced the fluid concept. Also the concept here presented no longer requires the assumption of two underlying qualitatively distinct instincts. We operate only with two modes of discharge of any excitation which can be characterized by two variables: intensity and, what is more important, a configurational variable. The latter depends on whether the discharge is a part of a structure of impulses subordinated to the survival interests of the total organism, or remains isolated and is discharged as an individual impulse.

The anatomy and physiology of the genito-urinary apparatus and the biology of propagation are strongly in favor of this interpretation of sexual phenomena.

Phylogenetically in the cloacal state there was one common organ for the elimination of waste products and germ cells; later it became divided into a urinary and genital portions, but its basic function was retained: all products which were not utilized for self-preservation, waste products and germ cells were drained by it. In addition, the genital apparatus discharges not only germ cells but also excitations which are not subordinated for the aim of survival. In the early phases of development, sexual excitation is pregenital and often extragenital and can be relieved locally, in the mouth, anus, etc. Gradually more and more of the erotic excitations are discharged through the genito-urinary tract. Every gratification has intrinsically an erotic character, which is satisfaction of a tendency for its own sake and not subservient to the needs of the total organism. It serves only to relieve surplus tension. Every surplus excitation which the organism cannot use or does not need for its own preservation is erotic and most of it is drained through the genito-urinary tract.

The view here presented accounts for the fact that every mental content can have a sexual and nonsexual expression and states precisely the conditions under which an impulse is discharged sexually or nonsexually. It makes superfluous to assume two specific instincts underlying the great variety of impulses.

It must be by now obvious that this view uses a somewhat

similar concept as the one which has been found so productive in communication theory and physics: the degree of organization. It attributes the erotic nature of a discharge to its degree of freedom versus its being a part of a system of discharges. This can be also seen in society which gradually is losing its playful hedonistic qualities as it becomes more and more organized and thus restricts the freedom of the activities of its members. As Huizinga in his *Homo Ludens* so aptly stated, our present industrial civilization compared with earlier centuries is becoming more serious and less playful. As he puts it, in the nineteenth century all Western humanity donned the "boiler suit." Play requires utmost freedom of choice, which is lost when the activities of man become closely knit into a social fabric.[18]   Cats and dolphins are great individualists and at the same time the most playful animals—ants the most collective and most organized and the least playful.

The maturation process of the growing child displays the same principle. As I pointed out before, the infant at first practices most of his biological functions playfully for the mere pleasure he derives from them (1). The hands grab for the sake of the pleasure derived from it, the eyes focus on objects, not to espy useful objects in the environment, but for the sake of the sheer fascination derived from the act of seeing. The same is true for locomotion. The young colt, as the child, is romping around aimlessly for no practical reason but as a pleasurable expenditure of overabundant energy. In all these playful activities there is a great freedom of choice; they are not directed toward specific utilitarian goals which limits choice because the act is subordinated to and prescribed by the specific goal. Gradually all these separate nonutilitarian functions become integrated into rational planful activities and at the same time they lose their erotic quality. Our previous formulation about the nature of erotic discharge can be quantitatively expressed by saying that the *erotic value of an action is inversely related to the degree to which it loses the freedom of choice and becomes coordinated* and subordinated to other functions and becomes a part of an organized system, of a goal structure. If this is true and if the essence of life consists in the entropy reducing capacity of the organism, we cannot refrain from saying that the process toward increased organization or less freedom of choice takes place at the cost of erotic gratification of the individual members of a system, be these organic functions of the body or members of a social organization. In the insect states, for example, in termite society, organization progressed so far that the majority of the members became asexual and what erotic ex-

---

18 Johan Huizinga, *Homo Ludens*, Boston: Beacon Press, 1950.

pression remains for them consists in an occasional communal ritual-
istic performance consisting in to-and-fro rhythmic movements col-
lectively performed. Does the increasing trend toward spectator sports
in our society express the same trend? From this perspective it appears that decreasing entropy is a rather costly process, costly for
the constituent individual members or a system. It is not costly in
the terms of energy consumption since communication processes
operate with small quantities of energy, but costly in another sense,
because the individual members of a system must sacrifice much of
their freedom of choice and with it much of erotic pleasure. Sexual
functions in insect societies are restricted to the small number of
sexual types, in the organism to the genital tract and the germ cells.
The latter remain isolated from the rest of the organism, are not influenced by the events within the organism to a great degree and
are not interacting parts like other cells of the total system. With the
individuals—cells in the organism, persons in society—sacrificing their
freedom, the whole system's free energy, or to use a current expression, negative entropy, increases. Of course this increased negative
entropy eventually will have to be lived down in the course of life.
Moreover, according to current views, the organizational process itself takes place at the cost of negative entropy.

I shall stop here, no matter how tempting it may appear to
work out a quantitative formula in which erotic discharge, or more
precisely, erotic potential is measured by entropy, the same concept
which was found valid for information. The difficulty to arrive at
such a formula is that in the field of information theory we can
precisely state the degree of choice, which we cannot do precisely
at present in the case of impulses.

At our present state of knowledge operationally the loss of freedom of choice in impulse discharge cannot be measured, and therefore this type of reasoning may be considered as idle speculation.
A quantitative formula increasing loss of freedom of choice in behavior where not simple messages but meanings are involved would
account for the basic rhythm of the life process which consists in
the parts continuously losing freedom during maturation in favor of
the total system's freedom. This latter, appears, for example, on the
social level as the emergence of the sovereign state, monarch or
dictator, a particularly characteristic feature of the highly organized
and centralized nations.[19]

The degree of freedom of choice in instinctual discharge we may
call the "erotic potential." In view of the lack of an operational
definition of this concept it would be premature to relate this to

[19] It is essential to distinguish between freedom of the constituent parts
and the freedom of the system as a whole.

free energy (negative entropy). It is, however, not premature to consider the essence of life in the faculty of living organisms to reduce temporarily entropy by organization achieved through intercommunication between parts which reduces the freedom of their action. By this device organisms are able at least temporarily to postpone the unavoidable eventual decay of internal order, leading to a random distribution of their constituent parts.

I do not feel competent to answer the objection that all this is nothing but analogizing. Loss of freedom of choice of the constituent parts has a concrete quantitative meaning and can be measured in a variety of systems, such as a conglomeration of molecules in a gas or in an electronic communication system. At present it has no operational application to instinctual organization in a biological organism or to society. If a common quantitative operational definition of the degree of randomness actually could be forged, which would be also applicable to organismic behavior, this would unify all the different fields which are dealing with complex organized systems.[20]

It would be a naive conclusion, however, to state that since organization is so essential to life, the more organization the better. It is a different matter when certain privileged individuals may retain freedom of expression and thought or that of propagation and form an intellectual elite of scientists and artists or breeding types— a kind of brain cells and germ cells of society. The rest of the population is restricted to prescribed functions as, for example, muscle cells, which can only do one thing, contract and extend, or liver cells, which can only secrete more or less of a chemical substance.

At this point a highly subjective remark may be at place. From the point of view of the individual person, he is fully entitled to resist the trend toward increasing negative entropy achieved by organization, as far as he can afford it in view of the fierce competition between societies. Let us not forget that highly complex structures are apt to explode and are subject to a continual natural decay. At this point, the vistas of science and values diverge. Science cannot decide for you whether it is preferable to be the single electron of a hydrogen atom or one of the many that circle the nucleus of

[20] In a highly contestable writing on logical and general behavior system theory, R. C. Buck criticizes efforts of Gerard and Miller to find common principles prevailing in systems of different levels. This criticism would also apply to the here proposed general principle. I do not intend in this paper to discuss the heuristic value of this type of inferences. (See R. C. Buck, "On the Logic of General Behavior Systems Theory," in H. Feigl and M. Scriven (eds.), *Minnesota Studies in the Philosophy of Science*, Minneapolis: Univ. of Minnesota Press, Vol. I, 1956.

uranium; whether it is a more preferable existence to be one of the many identical liver cells enjoying complete routine and security or to live the exciting life in being a part of the brain tissue constantly facing change and being called upon to make fateful decisions, or a germ cell which through the completely random process of mutation can playfully produce an immense variety of fantastic new combinations of genes—a truly creative act of nature.

It appears that the need for increasing organization is superimposed from the outside upon all systems. Nations, we know from experience, organize and restrict freedom in war. It is true that Maxwell's demon rests within the system and performs his nefarious activities of ordering around the freedom-loving molecules on his own account, but as has been pointed out, he has to rely on external sources of energy for his own functioning. Moreover, the demon only directs and thus organizes the movements of the corpuscles, the individual momenta of each particle which they do not receive from the organizer. These dynamic quanta form the raw material of which the demon can build up his system. Organization is only one part of the creative act, there must be something to be organized and this is the unalienable property of each individual part. In any case, organization on all levels of systems, atoms, cells and societies, has to contend constantly with the basically never fully renounced trend of these elementary parts to regain their lost freedom for random activity. If this were not so, the universal trend in nature toward increase of entropy would not exist.

If the universe as a whole is considered a closed system, this means eventual thermodynamic equilibrium or death. For pessimists, who assert this, however, there is one consolation, namely, that for all existing organized systems after their disorganization there is always a new beginning. External sources bring about a new impetus for the particles to form a new order only to be lived down again. The eternal rhythm between upbuilding and destruction goes on, if not forever, long enough for the inhabitants of this planet not to be concerned. And finally, is the universe a closed system?

Be it as it may, so far as the human race is concerned it appears more likely that it will become extinct not as a result of the law of entropy, but as the result of becoming progressively organized into two opposing camps bent to destroy each other. It is difficult to decide which one is the evil spirit, the individualistic fervor of the constituent parts of a system or the order-loving demon of Maxwell. Certain it is that even the best demon needs the individual molecule's contribution: the momentum of each corpuscle. Both have a share in creation and destruction.

◄ *Two* ►

Psychoanalytic Treatment

A Metapsychological Description
of the Process of Cure

◄ 1925 ►

The object of the present paper is to describe in metapsychological terms the alteration in the mental systems which we seek to effect
by means of psychoanalytical treatment. The change in question is
the result of a process whereby an original condition of psychoneurosis is terminated by recovery of health. Before going further,
however, some orientation of a general kind is necessary. Throughout
this metapsychological analysis of the ego changes aimed at during
treatment, I am guided by Freud's topographical-dynamic doctrine
concerning the structure of the mental apparatus, which doctrine I
regard as the ultimate result of our collective clinical experience. In
attempting to refer these conclusions once more to their empirical
substratum, I propose to retrace the difficult path traversed by the
founder of this theory during its gradual formulation. In speaking of
changes during treatment, I imply of course treatment in accordance
with the technique as laid down by Freud himself; as opportunity
occurs I shall examine from the metapsychological point of view recent
suggestions and advances in technique.

Taking as a starting point for our investigation the neurotic
state as observed at the beginning of treatment, let us see if we can
find a general formula which will be valid for all neuroses. We select
this starting point not because it comes first chronologically, but because experience shows that it is easier to understand the normal
from a study of pathological states than vice versa. Disease supplies
a dynamic motive power for research; accurate understanding is a
prerequisite of successful treatment. Preanalytic psychology was
really a hobby or pastime; it lacked the dynamic factor which has
aided us in our deeper investigations, namely, the ultimate aim of

This article was originally published in German; the English translation was
not done by the author.

effecting cure of disease. It was only the pressure of necessity encountered in pursuing this aim that enable the investigator of the mind to overcome the obstacle of those states of resistance with which we are so familiar, not only during the analytic session, but in the attacks on our science.

Keeping then to the dynamic principle which has been the basis of the success of psychoanalysis, we shall find our general formula by means of general dynamic considerations, by setting out the relation of the mental system as a whole to the outer world—to reality. Since this relation is obviously disturbed in every neurosis, it provides an excellent starting point. A dynamic standpoint is the more justified in that the essence of psychoanalytic theory consists in a dynamic conception of mental processes. In its latest and most general formulation as a topographical-dynamic theory of the ego, the principle of psychoanalytic theory is a dynamic principle: that of keeping stimuli at a constant level. This principle, first laid down by Fechner, implies that there exists in the mental system a tendency to reduce as far as possible or at the least to keep constant the amount of stimulation and tension in that system. Freud formulated this principle more precisely by distinguishing two sources of stimulation, outer and inner sources. We called those from without, *stimuli*, from within, *instincts*: these will be first considered from the dynamic standpoint apart from any difference in quality. The foregoing can be regarded as a preliminary step in the description of dynamic activity in the mental system: this consists in the mastering of stimuli and the mastering of instincts. When we come to investigate the more obvious of these two activities, the mastery of stimuli from without, two mechanisms differing in principle are to be found; on the one hand, adaptation of the psychic, or more correctly of the psychophysiological, system to outer sources of stimulation and, on the other, actions which are intended to abolish these sources of stimulation. In the former instance the psychic system is itself altered in an expedient way, it is adapted to the source of stimulus from without; in the latter a change is effected in outer reality by means of suitable action which abolishes the particular source of stimulus from reality. To take a simple example: in the case of a fall in temperature, two defense mechanisms differing in principle are possible: outer reality can be altered by means of heating, or the discharge of warmth from the body can be lessened by reduction of the exposed surface, in the case of constant exposure to cold by the gradual development of hair. Adopting Freud's and Ferenczi's terminology, we can describe this suitable alteration of the outer world as an *alloplastic* modification and the alteration of the psychophysiological system as an *autoplastic* modification; from this point of view the biological type of development is seen to be mainly autoplastic, while human cultural development is mainly alloplastic.

In investigating the complicated process of mastering instincts we again meet with these same mechanisms. Psychoanalysis has taught us that the instinctual needs of the mature, fully developed organism are directed for the most part toward reality. Gratification solely by means of changes in the system itself is only possible for sexual instincts, in the form of autoerotisms, and then only during immature stages of development; fully developed instincts are attached to objects outside the system. Since, however, the sources of excitation lie in this case within the system, it is obvious that the excitation can be abolished only by an alteration within that system. This alteration necessary for relief from instinct tension necessitates, however, actions directed toward without: in carrying out these actions both autoplastic and alloplastic mechanisms are involved. In order to seize and incorporate nutritive material, biological development has created autoplastic apparatus—limbs, teeth, alimentary mechanisms, etc., while human civilization has developed alloplastic means—weapons, agriculture, the art of cooking food, etc. The reproductive instinct has in part, in association with the self-preservative instinct, adopted this autoplastic molding of the body apparatus, together with alloplastic modifications, through civilization, by creating new objects. We can find a libidocomponent in every product of civilization, as in every part of the bodily apparatus. Male libido in the final stage of genital maturity pursues the most extreme alloplastic course, in that it actually creates objects for itself. Agriculture, industry, science, and art are newly created objects for the libido. Pursuing Ferenczi's ingenious train of thought we can regard the female sexual apparatus, uterus and vagina, as an alloplastic result of active masculine sexual instinct. Just as it created art and science, this instinct created the female body as an object for itself, a fact which for some years now we might have deduced from the biblical story of creation.

We must not, however, allow ourselves to be diverted from our main task, viz., the discovery through dynamic considerations of a formula common to all neuroses. Summarizing, we may say that in carrying out its function of abolishing inner tensions by the mastering of stimuli and instincts, the mental system makes use of autoplastic or alloplastic mechanisms. Either it attempts to modify reality to suit its own requirements or, unable to withstand the pressure of reality, it adapts by altering itself: and this not only when reality appears as a source of stimulation but also when instinctual necessities are directed toward the circumstances of reality. At the very outset we found that biological development consisted in the products of mainly autoplastic processes, civilization in those of mainly alloplastic processes. The same line of thought indicates the ontogenesis of libido, namely, the replacement of an intrapsychical narcissistic object by extrapsychical objects of autoerotic libido discharge by genital activities directed toward objects. Applying these considerations to the problem of neurosis, we see that neurosis constitutes an antithesis, a protest against the developmental tendency toward alloplastic modification. We are immediately reminded of a statement made by Freud[1] in his *Introductory Lectures:* he regards the neurotic symptom as an unsuccessful attempt at adaptation in place of a suitable action. We might express this principle as follows: every psychoneurosis is an attempt at autoplastic mastering of instinct. It consists in changes within the system having the tendency to mastering of instinct. It is only partly successful, since the desired freedom from tension affects only one part of the system, the id; it gives rise to fresh tension in another part of the system, the ego, as is seen in the latter's rejection of the symptom. Instinct tension which has disappeared from one part of the system appears in another part in a different form, as an ego conflict, the feeling of illness. We know from Freud that this new tension, the effort to reject the symptoms, is due to the heterogeneity of the two parts of the mental system. The conscious ego has already reached the mature stage of genital object libido, has prepared itself for activities toward sublimated objects; the symptom, on the other hand, consists in an autoplastic modification in a substitution of incestuous, introjected objects for actual objects, and, with the exception of hysteria, in the substitution of pregenital relations for genital forms. These autoplastic and regressive processes signify the gratification of instinctual needs for one part of the mental system, whereas the more developed part demands *actual* non-incestuous objects and genital discharge.

The general formula therefore runs as follows: the dynamic task of neurosis is not accomplished; the discharge of total mental tension miscarries; the attempted *autoplastic* and *regressive* mastering of instinct relieves one part of the system only and leads to fresh tension in another part. In places of instinctual tension there arises a repudiation of the symptom which is expressed in the form of a feeling of illness.

This formula provides us merely with a description of the dynamic results of neurosis; the introduction of the topographical point of view, i.e., that of two heterogeneous part-systems, explains symptom repudiation; but we have still to discover the more immediate cause of regression, the dynamic factor which drives the mental ap-

[1] S. Freud, *Introductory Lectures on Psycho-Analysis,* London: 1922.

paratus to master instinct in a way which is not in keeping with the more developed part, the ego, but corresponds to immature periods of ego development.

That a dynamic pressure in the direction of symptom formation exists, one which is stronger than the counterpressure of symptom re. pudiation, can be seen when, in the course of treatment, we attempt to free the mental system from this conflict, i.e., when we attempt to enforce the ego's standpoint by undoing the neurotic discharge of instinct and the symptom. The object of the treatment is clearly to reverse the symptomatic gratification repudiated by the ego, to re-establish the original instinct tension and to force the mental apparatus to make a fresh attempt at instinct gratification, one in consonance with the requirements of the ego. The mind of the neurotic struggles against this by producing resistances to the treatment. In the last resort, therefore, resistance is directed against the form of instinct gratification required by the ego, i.e., against genital activities directed outward toward actual non-incestuous objects. We can call this struggle against actions of this kind a *flight from reality*, since other activities are not permitted by social reality. The cause of this flight from reality will provide us, therefore, with the general etiology of neurotic formations.

At the very earliest stage of its formulation psychoanalytic theory provided us with an answer to this question: frustration, disappointment, trauma, in short, bitter experiences in the fight with reality induce the mental system to abandon attempts to alter reality and to seek the blissful state of freedom from tension by inner avenues of discharge, thereby avoiding the dangerous outer world. Reverses suffered during the struggle constitute then the general etiology of neurotic formations. If we regard *disposition* as the sum of traumatic experience in the first years of life, birth included, and the inherited experiences of forebears as *constitution*, it would seem possible to explain all neuroses from a traumatic point of view. The expression of unfavorable experiences is anxiety: anxiety is nothing more or less than the expectation of a "painful" increase of tension in the system, the lasting impression of a defeat in an attempt to discharge tension. It follows on miscarriage in the mastering of instinct or stimulus, when instead of the expected relief from tension an actual increase occurs. Anxiety is directed therefore against instinctual demands or against outer stimuli and is a reminder, both inward and outward, of miscarried attempts to overcome instincts and stimuli, i.e., attempts which have not led to the relief anticipated.

We see then that anxiety is the ultimate cause of resistance against our therapeutic efforts. Anxiety causes the flight from reality, the reluctance to deal once more with reality; it explains the tendency to cling to autoplastic mechanisms of discharge: it explains introversion. Nevertheless it explains only the autoplastic nature of the symptom without clearing up entirely its second characteristic, the element of regression, that harking back to old ways of mastering instinct, which constitutes the second fundamental character of the symptom. It is of course clear that difficulties met with, the defeats experienced, in these new processes of mastery which arise during the compulsive course of development, failures in the attempt to master a new instinctual organization will favor regression to a stage that has already been successfully attained. Yet, just as failure and trauma induce regression, so success, i.e., successful exploitation of a stage of organization which ensures instinct mastery, provides a point of attraction, a fixation point for later regressive movement. Anxiety commences the regressive process of symptom formation and operates in the same direction as the attraction of the fixation point.

To understand the character of regression more fully, we must now consider the second main principle of the mental apparatus. The Freud-Fechner principle enabled us to regard the mental processes as a whole as efforts toward relief of tension, but does not tell us why any one out of many possibilities of relief is chosen; it does not explain the regressive nature of neurotic relief mechanisms; it does not at present take into consideration developmental factors. This second principle which determines the *tendency* of discharge processes is the *repetition-compulsion* or the Breuer-Freud principle—which as we shall soon see has the identical content—viz. a definite relation between free and tonic mental energy. In investigating this principle we shall once more consider separately the mechanisms of mastering stimuli and instincts respectively.

States of tension induced in the mental apparatus by outer stimuli always give rise to motor innervations, intended either to render the source of stimulation harmless or to establish some means of protection by modification of the system itself. Against typical forms of outer stimulation the system protects itself by typical reflex innervations, which occur without any mental operation, but which are adapted to deal with certain definite sources of stimulation. Where the stimulus is of an unusual kind, protection can only be achieved after a tentative, experimentation, involving mental operations of a kind we describe as "reality testing," has been undertaken, and it depends on the discovery of innervations suited to the source of stimulation. It is easy to see that during this experimental work, which requires both time and energy, the mental system remains in a state of continuous excitation until the correct defense is established. Incorrect attempts do not lead to discharge of tension; they may indeed increase the amount of excitation. There can be no doubt that all reflex mechanisms were once phylogenetically tentative attempts to cope with reality, attempts from which the correct response was gradually formed and stereotyped. The mental system tends toward these sure methods of defense by reflex mechanisms; they operate without expenditure of mental energy and are certain to be successful in an appropriate situation. At the same time the mental apparatus resists fresh situations, alterations in reality which require fresh struggles and testing of reality. It is fixation upon mechanisms which are already well practiced, upon its memorials of successful combat with reality, and it strives to avoid fresh situations, seeking to deal with these with previously acquired patterns. We recognize here the Breuer-Freud principle of the relation of free and "bound" mental energies. The mental apparatus tends to convert free into tonic energy, to substitute automatisms for actual labile processes, for tentative, experimental examination of reality, for the comparison by means of memory of the present with past situations. It prefers to repeat automatically what has been learned in the past by its forefathers or itself in the exhausting work of "reality testing," to use available automatisms which do not require any fresh effort. These automatisms preserve in tonic form the achievements of previous "reality testing." Freud has recently characterized this principle as the most fundamental of our conceptions concerning the nature of the mental apparatus: it forms the basis of all our further investigations.[2] The flight from reality, which was found in the investigation of neurosis to be of cardinal importance, is the expression of this principle. Reality is only accepted so far as it can be mastered by automatisms: anything that is new or unexpected is rejected by means of flight. Only when automatisms fail to act and the system is subjected to intolerable stimulation, is the latter prepared to rectify these and

[2] In this presentation the compulsion to repeat is derived from fixation upon successful attempts at mastery of instinct. Nevertheless the manifestations which led to Freud's discovery of the compulsion to repeat as a general principle are of a different nature: they consist in the repetition of unadjusted situations in which no successful mastery of the stimulus took place. From this point of view the mental apparatus is fixated, not only on states where successful discharge of tension has been achieved, but also on unmastered states of stimulation. We believe, however, that this latter mode of fixation with its compulsive harking back to states of tension is not in the strict sense of the term a repetition. We must rather regard these manifestations—as Freud himself does—as an indication that the mental apparatus is in a constant state of stimulation, as the result of traumatic rupture of the barrier against stimuli as well as of unmastered instinctual demands. Hence in reality it repeats only the stimulus situation and is in a state of constant tension from excitations which have not been bound, which it then attempts to bind by means of repeating the original stimulus or wish. We might regard these as instances of *protracted* attempts to master stimuli or instinct excitations. On the other hand, the above-mentioned repetitions of former successful mastery mechanisms are genuine regressions to states which have already been given up. In traumatic repetitions the mental apparatus has never really emerged from a state in which stimuli have broken through the barrier.

once more come to grips with reality. The principle finds expression also in the topographical structure of the mental apparatus. This is divided into two parts, viz. into the system Cs, the organ of reality testing, of labile energic processes, and into the corporeal or spinal mind, the organ of automatisms: in the language of anatomy, the cerebral cortex and the spinal cord.

Now this same principle and a similar topographical division into ego and id applies to processes of mastering instinct; confirmation of this is provided by collective psychoanalytical experience, by the theory of fixation and regression. As we know, the history of instinct development represents the succession of various mechanisms of instinct mastery—we call these stages of organization—and later on the succession of a series of objects. We find a marked tendency to regression, a clinging to stages of organization which have already been successfully reached and to familiar, accepted objects. Every innovation necessitated by the compulsive processes of development, and later by change in the circumstances of life, is rejected. Every stage of organization attained forms a fixation point which is abandoned for the next only after resistance. Nevertheless, every fixation point is a source of relative protection against deeper regressions. The nature of a neurosis is determined by the relative strength of fixation points, by the degree of regression. In catatonia, as Nunberg has shown, the regression reaches back to the intra-uterine situation.[3] Rank imputes this deepest regression to all forms of neurosis.[4] He does not, however, deal with the economic factor of this deepest regression, with the role of later fixation points in the different neuroses. Yet, in the case of the obsessional neurotic, the main part of the libido is satisfied with a regression to the anal sadistic stage, the melancholic with an oral regression, while the hysteric actually remains at the genital stage. The cause of regression is in all cases the same, a rejection of the exogamous object choice demanded by reality. Neurotics appropriate the incestuously chosen object by the alloplastic method of introjection, but the hysteric alone preserves a genital relation to this object; in all other neuroses a pregenital is substituted for a genital relation. Intra-uterine life constitutes the earliest of these pregenital relations. Rank, in his ambitious work, has succeeded in showing that all subsequent organizations of the libido, including the final genital stage, are attempts to compensate for the loss of the blissful intra-uterine existence. In this sense he is justified in holding the view that all neuroses are attempts to reproduce this state. Nevertheless, in the choice of neurosis it is of the utmost significance which of the later stages of organization is

[3] Nunberg, "Der Verlauf des Libidokonfliktes in einem Fall von Schizophrenie," *Int. Ztschr. Psychoanal.*, VII, 1921.

[4] O. Rank, *The Trauma of Birth*, New York: Basic Books, 1953.

picked out. In proportion to the degree of success with which the individual recaptures this vanished happiness in one of the postnatal mechanisms of libido discharge, to that extent does fixation to a particular stage of organization occur, which then acts as a protection against further regression. We shall have occasion to return to this point later.

The foregoing considerations enable us to complete the dynamic formula for neuroses in the following way: from the point of view of the Freud-Fechner principle, the neurotic symptom is an attempt to discharge instinct tension. It has three main characteristics: it is *autoplastic, regressive* and is *repudiated by* the conscious part of the mental apparatus, *the ego.* We can explain its autoplastic nature on the grounds of an exaggeration of the flight from reality, as the result of trauma, of failure. The regressive character is the expression of the Breuer-Freud law, viz.: the general tendency in the mind to avoid new encounters with reality, and consequently to substitute for the fresh forms of instinct mastery the automatic repetition of defense mechanisms which have already been abandoned. Following Freud, we can regard this factor as *organic inertia.* We have already said that the third characteristic of the symptom consists in its rejection by the ego; this brings us to the problem of mental topography, with which we are especially concerned in this paper, and which leads to the description of the healing process.

Brief reference has already been made to Freud's explanation of this repudiation of the symptom: it arises from the different stages of development of the two component systems. While the ego shares fully in the process of adaptation to reality, the id lags behind in development and provides a great reservoir for archaic modes of instinct mastery. This dissociation of instinct gratification from the ego, its autoplastic regression from reality to the interior of the system, is made possible through the separation of the two systems by a boundary formation which Freud has called the *superego.* This institution was first recognized by psychoanalytic theory in the form of the dream censorship: its function is to relieve the ego from the burden of investigating instinctual demands. This it does by taking over the function of perception inward, but also the dynamic task of regulating instinctual life. Thus the superego forms the executive organ of the Breuer-Freud inertia principle. As the deposit of earlier adaptations to reality it tends to hold the mental system fast to earlier schemata of instinct mastery. It is an introjected legal code of former days which makes it possible to avoid encounters with reality by adherence to its ordinances, and by a system of rigid categorical imperatives obviates the necessity of fresh "reality testing." Yet not only has reality altered in the course of development, but instinctual demands, too, have altered;

hence its laws now require revision. The superego has nevertheless no access to reality and behaves as if nothing had altered; it performs its task automatically and with the monotonous uniformity of reflexes. Like the reflex, it represents mind which has become body. True to its developmental history in childhood, it operates with primitive methods of reward and punishment. And just as the superego has no access to reality, so the representative of reality, the ego, has no access to the instincts: this has been taken over by the superego at the inner boundary of the ego. In this way the ego has been relieved of the task of inner perception and so is better able to perform the work of testing reality. The ego is blind to what goes on within and has forgotten the language of the instincts.[5] The superego, however, understands this instinctual speech only too well and demands punishment for tendencies of which the ego is quite unaware. In this way the superego divides the mental system into two parts, one of which is in excellent touch with reality but cannot communicate its information to the instincts, and the other of which has no direct access to reality. The superego itself has only out-of-date information about reality and cannot perform the function of adaptation to reality; on the contrary, by reason of its obsolete, inexpedient sort of adaptation, the work it does runs counter to reality, since it holds instincts to earlier kinds of adaptation and exempts them from any new attempts. In the interests of the incest prohibition it curbs the whole of genital sexuality and puts obstacles in the way of real sexual satisfaction even with non-incestuous objects; through its punishment mechanisms it permits autoplastic gratification of precisely what it has itself forbidden, namely, the incest wishes. This gives rise to the neurotic symptom, which represents a discharge of tension in the id that is tolerated by the superego but is regarded with disfavor by the ego. In the matter of symptom formation the ego is not consulted: it has delegated its function of instinct regulation to the superego and the superego abuses its power. The latter enters into a secret alliance with the regressive tendencies of the id and by the ostensible severity of its self-punishments permits gratifications of a kind which, although only autoplastic, are none the less alien to reality.

We now see that our therapeutic endeavors must be directed against this two-faced overlordship on the part of the superego: hence it is necessary to make brief reference to the role of the superego in symptom formation, the nature of which has been described by Freud in his latest work.

The neurotic activity of the superego is twofold: it disturbs and

[5] See also my paper, "Der biologische Sinn psychischer Vorgänge," *Imago*, IX, 1923.

inhibits ego-syntonic behavior, which is *a priori* in conformity with the requirements of reality, by equating this, as the result of faulty reality testing, with actions which it has learned to criticize in the past and by dealing with it in the way it dealt with them. At the same time, by means of self-punishment, it permits autoplastic, symbolic gratification of precisely those condemned wishes. In the form of impotence, for example, all sexual wishes are equated with incest wishes and as such are interfered with. The superego behaves, in short, like a dull-witted frontier guard who arrests everyone wearing spectacles, because he has been told that one particular person is wearing spectacles. It behaves like a reflex which can only produce one innervation. The corneal reflex is almost always an expedient reaction which protects the eyes from foreign bodies, yet on occasion it can prove a hindrance, as during medical examination by an eye specialist. It would be simpler if this reflex action could be avoided by conscious effort, instead of having to be overcome by the use of eyelid retractors. In this case some communication between consciousness, which tests reality, and the "spinal mind" is desirable: in other instances the reflex defense is more prompt and more certain. In a similar way the strict categorical imperative of a superego which is functioning well is frequently adapted to the requirements of social life: nevertheless there are occasions when, owing to new situations and alterations in reality, a more direct relation between the reality testing faculty and the instinctual world is necessary, between the ego and the id, excluding the superego which is out of touch with reality.

It may at first seem paradoxical that this rigid inhibiting institution, the superego, should actually favor instinctual gratifications which have been condemned by the ego to be realized. We know, however, that the superego can easily be hoodwinked; once its punishing tendencies are gratified, its eyes remain shut. It is one of the oldest findings of psychoanalysis that a symptom represents a compromise between the need for punishment and the crime itself. It is in principle a matter of indifference whether these two tendencies are gratified in one phase as in hysteria, or in conjunction as in the obsessional neurosis, or in two stages as in the manic-depressive neuroses. It is striking to observe how meticulously the conscience of the obsessional neurotic records, like a careful shopkeeper, all debts and claims, all punishments and aggressions; with what sensitiveness it demands new punishments when the limits of the wrongdoing that is covered by punishment are overstepped. Similarly, in the melancholic phase of manic-depressive neurosis, conscience gives expression to acts of glaring tyranny and injustice only to be thrown over without any guilt feeling during the maniacal phase. We might compare it with a struggle between two utterly antagonistic political parties, where one provokes the other to excesses in order to compromise the latter and justify its destruction.

Herein lies the twofold role of the superego: knowing nothing of reality, it frequently inhibits activities that are actually ego-syntonic and, by overseverity toward the inner world, it permits condemned instinctual gratification along the autoplastic route of symptom formation. The results of its activity constitute the expression of the Breuer-Freud principle. As an automatic organ, as the tonic deposit of bygone adaptations to reality, it obviates fresh testing of reality, and when it becomes neurotically diseased these bygone attempts prove inefficient protection against the regressive tendencies of the id.

The superego, therefore, is an anachronism in the mind. It has lagged behind the rapid development of civilized conditions, in the sense that its automatic, inflexible mode of function causes the mental system continually to come into conflict with the outer world. This is the teleological basis for the development of a new science, that of psychoanalysis, which, be it said, does not attempt to modify the environment but, instead, the mental system itself, in order to render it more capable of fresh adaptations to its own instincts. This task is carried out by limiting the sphere of activity of the automatically functioning superego, and transferring its role to the conscious ego. This is no light task; it implies the conscious creation of a new function. The ego of those living under conditions of Western civilization has been instituted solely for the purpose of testing reality. It is an appreciable increase of the burdens of consciousness to take over the investigation and regulation of instinctual activities, to learn the laws and speech of the id in addition to the laws of reality. Quantities of energy which are tonically "bound" in the automatic function of the superego must once more be converted into mobile energy, a part that is now body must again become mind. The resistance against this reversal is well known to us from the analytic resistances during treatment and the general resistance against the science of psychoanalysis.

Here we have the solution of the problem set in this paper. The curative process consists in overcoming resistances to the ego's taking over of the function of the superego. Neurotic conflict, that state of tension arising from repudiation of the symptom, can be solved in two ways only: either the ego's rejection of the symptom must cease, in which case it must abandon reality testing, together with those forms of instinct mastery which are already adapted to reality, and take part in homogenizing all the mechanisms of instinct mastery in the direction of disease; or it must put into force the point of view adapted to reality. This homogenization of the mental system in the direction of disease is familiar to us in the psychoses, where the ego abandons reality testing and remodels reality in an archaic sense, in accordance with the stage of instinctual gratification preferred. Psychoanalytic treatment drives in the opposite direction: it seeks to effect a homogeneous system by bringing the whole system nearer to the conscious level, by opening communication between the ego and the id, which had been previously barred by the superego. The ego is now called upon to settle the claims made by instinct, to *accept or reject* them in accordance with the results of reality testing. As Freud expressed it, the aim of treatment is to substitute judgment for repression. The repressive activity of the superego only bars the road to motor discharge of any instinctual demand: it does not imply the abandonment of that demand. On the contrary, it allows a secret gratification. For the ego there are two possibilities only: *accept and carry out* or *reject and abandon*. The task during treatment is to eliminate gradually the repressing institution, the superego: from the two component systems, the ego and the superego, a homogeneous system must be constructed —and this must have a twofold perceptual apparatus, one at the outer surface directed towards reality, and one at the inner boundary directed towards the id. Only in this way can a mastery of instinct be achieved which is free from conflict and directed towards a single end.

The transfer to the ego of the role of superego takes place in two phases during treatment. Making use of the transference, the analyst first of all takes over the part of superego, but only in order to shift it back on to the patient again when the process of interpretation and working through has been carried out; this time, however, the patient's conscious ego takes it over. The achievement of analysis is a topographical one involving dynamic expenditure; it displaces the function of testing and regulating instinct to a topographically different part of the mental apparatus, viz., the conscious ego. To do this, it must overcome the inertia principle, i.e., the objection to exchange an automatic function for a conscious activity. The role of the analyst therefore consists in at first taking over the supervision of instinctual life, in order to hand back this control gradually to the conscious ego of the patient. By means of the transference he gains the patient's confidence and produces the original childhood situation during which the superego was formed. So long as the whole mental system of the patient is freed from the supervision of instinctual life, so long as the analyst is responsible for the entire instinctual life, the process goes on without interruption. Once the role of superego has, with the help of this projection mechanism, been taken over in entirety, so that the previous intrapsychical relation between id and superego has been converted into a relationship between the analyst and the id, the more difficult dynamic task begins, namely, to shift back on to the patient once more this role of supervision. This returning of the role of superego takes place for the most part during the period of becoming detached from the analyst. In terms of this schema the psychological processes involved in treatment are very easily described, but it falls to me yet to go more fully into the universal applicability of this description.

The nature of transference from this point of view is that the intrapsychical relations between id and superego are transferred from superego to analyst. To understand this, we must think of the origin of the superego and compare it with the phenomena of transference. Put briefly, the superego is an organ of adaptation which has arisen through a process of introjection of persons (or, more correctly, of the relationships to persons) who originally enforced the first adaptations. By this process a formation is set up in the mental system which represents the first requirements of reality; these consist of introjected educative parental regulations. The superego is made up to an important degree of parental commands and prohibitions; hence it is mainly an acoustic formation, as the auditory hallucinations of melancholics show. The commands and prohibitions were conveyed through the auditory apparatus. As Freud has shown us, the relations between id and superego are nothing more or less than a permanent crystallization of the bygone relations between the child and its parents. This can be best studied in the case of personalities which are neurotically split, the superego functioning as an utterly foreign body. The entire complicated symptom structure of the obsessional neurosis is a play enacted by an obstinate, untrained child and its parents; and just as all French comedies deal with monotonous regularity with the theme of adultery, so in every neurosis we come across the identical theme in varying guise. Even the methods of the "id-child" remain unchanging—always to provoke the parents, the superego, to unjust and oversevere punishment, in order to do what is forbidden without any feeling of guilt, precisely as in the triangle play the conduct of one partner is represented in a way which seems to justify the adultery of the other.

In the course of transference this intrapsychical drama is converted into a real one between the id and the analyst. It is not necessary to enter into further details: the patient seizes with extraordinary alacrity the opportunity of realizing in relation to the analyst his former relations with his parents, which he has been forced to introject only because he was unable to realize them in reality. In this way he is able to cancel that piece of adaptation to reality which has been forced upon him and is represented by the superego. He soon observes, however, from the attitude of the analyst—who works counter to the pleasure principle—that while these tendencies can be understood they are not gratified. The new educative process then begins. The demands of reality are, however, not communicated by means of orders and prohibitions, as previously happened under the sway of the superego, but by an impersonal method, by logical insight, by accurate testing of reality. In this way the reliving of his past becomes abandoned by the patient himself, and the original instinctual demands, which can no longer be experienced in the transference situation, appear in the mind as memories. Tonic discharge is blocked, automatic repetition is prevented; the former demands of instinct become active once more; they become problems of the immediate present, and as such form part of the content of consciousness. Instead of automatic repetition, memory appears. From now on discharge must be not only ego-syntonic but in accordance with the demands of reality, since it can only be effected in agreement with the organ of reality testing.

So events run in theory, but not in practice. Every analyst has, time after time, observed that when a transference situation has been resolved and brought into a genetic relation with the original childhood situation, in no instance does an immediate orientation in the direction of normal libido control occur, but instead a regression to still earlier stages of instinctual life. The libido eludes analytic endeavors by a backward movement, and retires to positions it had previously abandoned. Each fresh interpretation brings about a still deeper regression, so much so that the beginner often imagines he has driven a hysteric into a state of schizophrenia. I must confess that the desire to be clear in my own mind as to the nature of these processes was stimulated to a large extent by certain uncanny moments during analytic work, when to my dismay symptoms of conversion hysteria which had already been carried over into the transference gave place to paranoid and hallucinatory symptoms. Further progress in the analysis, however, showed that each new symptom is carried over into a new transference situation, so that every deep analysis runs through a whole gamut of artificial neuroses, ending regularly, as Rank has shown us, in a reproduction of the prenatal state. I have been able to trace the same gradations of regression in the contemplative states of Buddhism.[6]

Analysts cannot dispense with recognizing and appraising this ultimate mode of regression in order to be able to drive the libido from this most inaccessible hiding place forward in the direction of genitality. We owe much to Rank for having called attention to the general significance of this deepest form of regression; above all that he has shown this regression during treatment to be an affective repetition of actual experience and not only of a preconscious fantasy. I cannot emphasize too strongly that those who oppose this view are making the same mistake that Jung made many years ago. One would

[6] *Ibid.*

have just as much right to regard all oral or anal erotic regressions as the products of regressive fantasy.

On the other hand, it is clear from the foregoing considerations that this regressive movement ensuing upon analysis of the transference situations—which arise spontaneously and are characteristic in each individual case—is to be regarded as resistance.[7] Observation during treatment of this continually backward flowing regression provides us with an extraordinary picture, one which lays bare the entire complicated process of the construction of the superego. The picture is made up of a consecutive series of transference situations, in which the analyst plays ever-changing roles taken over from the superego. The consecutive series of regressive transference rolls is a picture of the layers of the superego seen upside down. It is a gathering together of imprints from the various stages of development. The deepest layer represents the biological relation between mother and child, and merges gradually more and more into social relations with the father. The mother represents the first demands in instinct development: through the act of birth she first demands abandonment of the state of passive nutrition by the bloodstream and requires the substitution of nutrition through the alimentary canal and active employment of mouth and lungs. Later she calls for the abandonment of breast feeding and is usually the first to disturb the child's autocratic command over its excretions. Gradually the father and the whole father series take over the larger part in the education of instinct and represent the demands of the community. The father, however, takes on the earlier mother role not only in regard to frustration experiences but in a positive way: just as the mother was the source of bodily nourishment, so the father provides mental pabulum. The passive homosexual attitude toward the father found in every analysis is the repetition and substitute for the passive suckling situation; the paternal penis is the substitute for the breast, as Freud showed in his analysis of Leonardo da Vinci. We find the most strongly repressed ideas of oral incorporation of the penis and of the father as a whole, in a form with which we have been familiarized by Abraham's accurate descriptions.[8] Roheim has shown us in his admirable study of primeval history how the sons tried to transfer the mother role to the father, by devouring him and defecating on his grave, on the parallel of suckling at the maternal breast.[9] The same history in reverse order is faithfully reproduced dur-

[7] I wish to lay the greatest stress on this point in contradistinction to Rank's point of view; in his presentation the resistance character of intra-uterine regressions is by no means clear.

[8] Karl Abraham, "The First Pregenital Stage of the Libido," *Selected Papers*, New York: Basic Books, 1953.

[9] Roheim, "Über das melanesische Geld," *Imago*, IX, 1923.

ing treatment. The father role, which at the beginning is invariably transferred to the analyst, is more and more displaced by the mother transference. On this point I can fully confirm Rank's observation. Repeated attempts in a progressive direction disturb the picture often enough, nevertheless the regressive tendency predominates. Although not really free from conflict about the father the patient regresses to times when the latter was not a source of disturbance and when the only battle he had to fight was a biological one with the mother. The cause of the regression is now clear: it is the expression of the Breuer-Freud principle, the automatizing tendency to solve new problems according to an old plan. The mind attempts to solve the father conflict on the model of the suckling situation: the father is to be destroyed by way of oral incorporation, in this way providing new strength for the struggle for existence, just as the mother's milk provided strength for physical development.

The patient is under the influence of the same tendency to automatize when he attempts to meet the task of detaching himself from the analyst by a fantasy-reproduction of the birth trauma. He has already solved the problem of birth: the most conclusive evidence for this is that he is alive. Before the end of treatment, however, he is faced with the entirely unsolved problem of doing without analytic aid. It is small wonder that he feels this to be similar to the severance from the mother's body. On that occasion also he had to learn the use of organs entirely *ab initio*, when taking over the nutritive role of the mother. Now at the termination of treatment his consciousness, which hitherto has been adapted only to testing reality, has to face new tasks. Having learned during treatment the language of instinct, it must take over responsibility for the regulation of instinctual activities, a regulation which has previously been exercised by the superego operating automatically. During treatment the analyst has thought and interpreted instead of the patient: indeed, by reconstructing the past he has done some remembering in his stead. From now on all this must be the patient's own concern. In bidding goodbye to his superego he must finally take leave of his parents, whom by introjection he had captured and preserved in his superego. He has indeed been ignominiously hoodwinked in analysis. The analyst seduced him into giving up the introjected parents, by himself taking over the role of the superego, and now he wants to saddle the patient with the burden. The latter protests and attempts in return to score off the analyst by sending him in the long-since-closed account for his birth, and this often by way of somatic symptoms. He feels, as did one of my patients, a circular constriction around his forehead, the pressure of the pelvic canal by which his head was so shamefully disfigured at birth: he is breathless and feels a heavy pressure around the chest.

Only when all this has been proved mere resistance against detaching himself from the analyst, against independence, does he consciously attempt to do without further analytic help. The patient is not overcoming his birth trauma by means of these birth scenes; on the contrary, he is countering detachment from the analyst with them; he is substituting an affective reproduction of the birth which is an accomplished fact, for the separation from the physician with which he is faced. Now he reproduces the past instead of performing the task in front of him. Even after treatment he will not have overcome the birth trauma. Rank himself has shown us in the most convincing way that man never gives up the lost happiness of prenatal life and that he seeks to re-establish this former state, not only in all his cultural strivings, but also in the act of procreation. These forms of representation are, however, egosyntonic; in analysis the patient must give up only such attempts at repetition as are autoplastic and dissociated from reality; he must give up symptoms, relations to the superego in which he has perpetuated his whole past and which finally he aimed at rescuing for good in the analytical transference situations. In the same way as he repeats in analysis the severance from the mother's body, he repeats all other difficult adaptations of his instinctual life which have been forced upon him during development, all with one end in view, to avoid a new adaptation to actual reality.

We are at one with Ferenczi and Rank in thinking that every subsequent stage of libido organization is only a substitute for the abandoned intra-uterine state: we have already accepted this idea in the analysis of the castration complex.[10] Nevertheless each successfully established stage of organization represents a fixation point: the intra-uterine state is the first, but, dynamically speaking, by no means always the most significant of the long series of fixation points. The period at which an individual utters the negation which sets up a neurosis varies widely; yet it is precisely this point which determines the form of his subsequent neurosis. When in the course of treatment his special fixation is analyzed, subsequent regression represents resistance against the consequences of this analytic solution, against the demands of the ego, against activity directed outward.

We have here corroborated in principle Rank's significant conception but have had to amplify it by a necessary quantitative (economic) evaluation of intra-uterine fixation. For analytic treatment the task remains to convert the tonic energy "bound" in automatic repetitions into the labile energy of conscious mental activity, in order that the struggle with reality may be taken up. The energies "bound" in the acquired automatisms of the superego are freed through recollec-

---

[10] See "The Castration Complex in the Formation of Character," in this volume.

tion. To compare memory material with the testing of reality is the highest achievement of the mental apparatus. Only the ego can remember: the superego can only repeat. The dissolution of the superego is and will continue to be the task of all future psychoanalytic therapy.[11]

The criticism will undoubtedly be advanced that I have been a little unfair to the superego. It will be said, and with justification, that in meeting the demands of reality the conscious ego is in principle very similar to the superego. The superego is merely a part of introjected reality from the past, an introjected educational code. Inner codes arise from outer. Now the conscious system, too, possesses a similar code. Logical thought in terms of reality is a product of adaptation. The laws of logic are copied from the laws of nature: they, too, represent a fragment of introjected reality. Leibnitz, who was not familiar with the theory of evolution, postulated a divine, pre-existing harmony between the laws of nature and the laws of thought. We know that the superego as well as the conscious ego are the inner representatives of reality, but not of reality alone; the id, too, is represented by them. We have indeed imputed tainted motives to the superego, in that its overseverity represents a secret alliance with the id and permits expression of the latter's tendencies without sense of guilt. Now the same charge might be brought against the ego. The laws of logic are more strict than the laws of nature; they admit of no exceptions. The ego, too, falsifies, renders inaccurately and caricatures reality in its logic, in order to master reality more easily; in this way the ego serves the ends of the id.

Our investigation of the inner structure of the mental apparatus has revealed in it a petrified imprint, as it were, of actual bygone struggles with environment: we saw the superego as a stereotyped mind, a mind which has become body. The laws of logic, too, have already become automatisms. Perception is mind: a logical law is

[11] I am aware that in the foregoing presentation the concept of the "superego" has been somewhat schematic and therefore more narrowly defined than in Freud's descriptions. I limit the "superego" to the unconscious alone, hence it becomes identical with the unconscious sense of guilt, with the dream censorship. The transition to conscious demands, to a conscious ego ideal, is nevertheless in reality a fluid one. We might regard these parts of the "super ego" which project into consciousness as the most recent and final imprints in its structure, as constituents of the "superego" *in statu nascendi*. They are not so fixed as the categorical, unconscious constituents of the conscience, and are more accessible to conscious judgment. This schematic presentation has been adopted in order to throw into sharper relief the dynamic principles concerned. I have compared extremes, the completely mobile apparatus of perception with the extremely rigid unconscious part of the "superego." Freud's conception and description, which takes into account the complete "superego" system, is nevertheless psychologically more correct.

mind stiffened into body. Psychoanalysis leads back from body to mind.

A few comments on the nature of these considerations may be appended here. I have attempted to trace the manifestations of pscho-analytic therapy as a whole to two main principles: to the Fechner-Freud principle of equilibrium and to the Breuer-Freud principle of inertia. This is synonymous with tracing all mental activity to these two fundamental dynamic laws. Here we have the basis of a system of mental dynamics which is of general validity independent of the quality of instincts and stimuli, and which can serve as a sure guiding line in research. The two fundamental principles of the mind bear a strong resemblance to the two dynamic basic principles of physics, to the first and second principles of thermodynamics. Whereas the Fechner-Freud principle merely implies the equalization of states of tension, the inertia principle describes the tendency of psychic processes. In this sense it resembles the second principle of thermo-dynamics which, of the many possible conceivable transformations of energy, describes the only one possible in nature. This, too, is a law of tendency and includes the inertia factor, in that it implies the constant reduction of "free energy," just as the principle of mental inertia implies the continuous "binding" of *free, mobile* energy into *tonic* energy. Future investigation will decide whether we deal here merely with a formal analogy or with an identity.

The Problem of
Psychoanalytic Technique

◄ 1935 ►

The general principles of psychoanalytic technique, as formulated by Freud in his five articles between 1912 and 1914, have often been subjected to careful reconsideration by various authors. Yet, and it is remarkable, these authors have failed to make any important innovation or modification. Many of the authors in developing their ideas of technique do so with the honest conviction that they are suggesting radical improvements over the standard technique. Others, more modest, maintain that their discussion calls attention to certain principles developed by Freud but for some reason or other neglected by the majority of analysts in their practical daily work.

There is an obvious reason for this constant urge to improve upon the analytic technique. Psychoanalytic therapy is extremely cumbersome, consumes the time and energy of patient and analyst, and its outcome is hard to predict on the basis of simple prognostic criteria. The desire to reduce these difficulties and increase the reliability of psychoanalytic treatment is only too intelligible. The difficulties, the time and energy consuming nature of psychoanalytic therapy, are by no means disproportionate to its ambitious aim: to effect a permanent change in an adult personality which always was regarded as something inflexible. Nevertheless, a therapist is naturally dissatisfied, and desires to improve upon his technique and to have precise definite rules of technique in place of indefinite medical art. The unremitting search to reform the technique therefore needs no special explanation; what needs explanation is the frequency with which pseudo-reforms are presented by their authors, under the illusion that they are discovering something new. This illusion originates in the complex nature of the psychoanalytic method. Psychoanalytic technique cannot be learned from books. The psychoanalyst must, so to speak, rediscover in his own experience the sense and the details of

225

the whole procedure. The complex behavior of the patient as it is presented to the therapist simply cannot be described in all details, and the understanding of what is going on emotionally in the patient's mind is based on an extremely refined faculty usually referred to as intuition. In a former article I tried to deprive this faculty of the mystical halo which surrounds it by defining it as a combination of external observation with the introspective knowledge of one's own emotional reactions.[1]

Freud's articles on technique were published between 1912 and 1914, at least fifteen years after he had started to treat patients with the method of free association and they may therefore be considered a resumé of at least fifteen years of clinical experience. These technical discoveries, for which a genius needed fifteen years, every student of psychoanalysis must recapitulate on the basis of his own experience. Though his study is now facilitated by general and simple formulations and by the precise description of those psychological processes which take place during the treatment, nevertheless the material which presents itself in every case is so complex and so highly individual that it takes many years for the student to achieve real mastery of the technique. Transference, resistance, acting out, removal of the infantile amnesia—these things he learns to appreciate only gradually. In consequence, he will be especially prone to emphasize those particular points of technique whose validity and importance are beginning to impress him. This alone can explain so many tedious repetitions and reformulations of the principles of technique reformulations, moreover, that are usually one-sided and much less judicious and clear than Freud's original formulations.

The general principles of the standard technique are consistent adaptation to the psychological processes which are observed during treatment: the phenomena of transference, resistance, the patient's increasing ability to verbalize material previously unconscious and the gradual removal of infantile amnesia. In the procedures that deviate from the standard, either one or another of these phenomena is overrated from the standpoint of therapeutic significance and is dealt with isolated from the others. The controversy is always centered around the therapeutic evaluation of (1) *emotional abreaction,* (2) *intellectual insight,* (3) *appearance of repressed infantile memories.* Those who consider emotional abreaction as the most important therapeutic factor will emphasize all those devices that may produce emotional eruptions resembling the abreactions in cathartic hypnosis: certain manipulations of the resistance, or the creation of emotional tensions in the patient, for example by avoiding interpretation of

[1] See "Psychoanalysis and Medicine," *The Harvey Lectures,* 1930-31 Baltimore: Williams and Wilkins Co., 1931.

content. Those who believe that the best permanent therapeutic result comes from the patient's complete insight into the nature of his emotional conflicts will stress technical devices which have this aim; they will concentrate upon the analysis of content. Finally those who consider the most effective therapeutic factor to be the removal of infantile amnesias will be inclined to stress the reconstruction of the infantile history. Now in reality all these therapeutic factors are closely interrelated and dependent upon one another. For example, the occurrence of infantile memories is often, though not always, connected with emotional abreaction; intellectual insight on the other hand may prepare the way for emotional abreaction and recollections; and emotional experience, if not overwhelmingly intense, is the only source of real insight. Without recollection and emotional abreaction, intellectual insight remains theoretical and ineffective. The close interrelation of these three factors is clearly recognized in Freud's papers on technique, and his technical recommendations are based upon knowledge of these interrelationships.

All innovations up to today consist in an undue emphasis upon one or another of these factors—an overemphasis which is based on an insufficient insight into the dynamics of therapy.

One can roughly differentiate between three trends in technique: (1) neocathartic experiments, (2) reconstruction and insight therapy, and (3) resistance analysis. It should be stated, however, that none of these innovations or technical procedures have ever found general acceptance, and I suspect that the actual technique used by most of the innovators themselves in their daily work remained closer to the original than one would assume from their publications. Most psychoanalysts expect progress in technique to come not from one-sided overemphasis of one technical device but from an increasing precision in our knowledge, especially our quantitative knowledge of mental processes. Such greater knowledge should make possible a more economic procedure which will spare us much wasted time—the greatest weakness of our therapy. I shall try to evaluate critically some of these technical procedures in the perspective of the development of the technical concepts of psychoanalysis.

The therapeutic efficiency of abreaction of emotions in connection with recollection during hypnosis was the starting point of psychoanalysis both as a therapy and as a psychological theory. This led Freud to assume that the symptom disappeared because the dynamic force which sustained it had found another outlet in the hypnotic abreaction. The next step in the development of therapy was derived from the observation that emotional abreaction has no permanent efficacy, because the phenomenon of abreaction does not alter the constant tendency of the ego to eliminate certain psychic forces from motor expression. The state of hypnosis only temporarily created a situation in which such an outburst of emotionally loaded tendencies could take place, but this abreaction was dependent upon the state of hypnosis and the disappearance of the symptom depended upon the emotional relationship of the patient to the hypnotist. From this Freud came to recognize the phenomenon of resistance and discovered the technical device of free association. To eliminate one of the most important manifestations of the resistance he devised the basic rule, namely, the involuntary directing of the train of thought away from the repressed material. The last step in the development of the technique consisted in the recognition of the role of the patient's emotional attitude toward the analyst. What appeared on the surface as the patient's confidence in the analyst revealed itself as the repetition of the dependent attitude of the child on its parents, which by correct handling allows expression of deeply repressed material.

The insight gained from experience with cathartic hypnosis and then later with the method of free association may briefly be summarized as follows: The mere expression of the unconscious tendencies which sustained the symptom is not sufficient to secure a lasting cure. The rehearsal of individual traumatic situations of the past during treatment is not as important as the building up of the ego's capacity to deal with those types of tendencies which it could not face and deal with in the pathogenetic childhood situations. The original repressions create certain repression patterns, according to which, in later life, tendencies related to the original repressed ones become victims of repression. The cure consists in a change in the ego itself, an increase in its power—one might say its courage—to deal with certain emotional problems which it could not deal with early in life. The expression, an increase in the courage of the ego, is appropriate; for as we know now, fear is the motor of repression and courage is the faculty of overcoming fear.

But another expression requires explanation. What do we mean by increasing the ego's capacity to deal with repressed tendencies? A symptom obviously is not cured by the fact that the tendency which produced it enters consciousness. The mere fact of its conscious appearance cannot be of curative value unless we assume that when the preconscious and ultimately unconscious content becomes conscious, the process of becoming conscious consumes the same amount of energy as was represented by the symptom itself. That this is not the case is clearly seen by the fact that to become conscious of the formerly unconscious content does not always or necessarily relieve the symptom. Gradually it became clear that the appearance of a repressed tendency in consciousness is only one necessary condition of the cure; it opens a new outlet for the symptom bound energy, namely, the outlet through voluntary innervations. Whether the process itself by which an unconscious tendency becomes conscious consumes at least a portion of the repressed energy quantum is still an open question. The dynamic equation of the process of cure is that the energy bound in a symptom before analytic treatment equals the energy spent in certain voluntary motor innervations afterward. It is possible that a smaller amount of symptom-bound energy is consumed in the process of its becoming conscious, that is to say, in the psychological processes which constitute conscious thinking.

The dynamic formulation that the energy which was bound in the symptom, after treatment takes up a new dynamic allocation needs further qualification. The new appropriation of energy, in voluntary innervations, must be in harmony with the forces already residing within the ego. If this condition is not fulfilled, a conflict is created within the ego which inhibits the free disposal of the formerly symptom-bound energy. This harmonizing or integrating function of the ego, however, is generally considered a faculty on which the analyst has to rely but to which he cannot contribute much by his therapeutic activity. This limits the indication of psychoanalysis to patients who possess an ego of sufficient integrating power, because the process of integration and its end result, a conflictless disposal of formerly symptom-bound energy, must be left to the patient himself.

Nunberg subjected this integrating or synthetic function of the ego and its role in therapy to a careful investigation and showed that the process of a repressed content's becoming conscious itself represents an integrating process in the ego.[2] I shall return to this problem later. It is certain that with or without the analyst's cooperation the formerly repressed energy, which during the process of the treatment becomes a part of the dynamic inventory of the ego, must become reconciled and harmonized with the already existing forces in the ego.

The fundamental validity of this formulation of the process of therapy has been corroborated in particular by recent developments which have shifted the emphasis from the analysis of symptoms to the analysis of character or of the total personality. We have learned that apart from neurotic symptoms, in many patients an even more important expression of repressed tendencies takes place in so-called neurotic behavior. This is a more or less stereotyped automatically fixed and unconsciously determined way of behavior, which in contrast to voluntarily guided behavior is beyond the control of the conscious ego. There is even a group of neurotic personalities whose sickness consists mainly or exclusively in such impulsive or stereotyped

[2] Herman Nunberg, "The Synthetic Function of the Ego," *Int. J. Psycho-Anal.*, XII, 1931.

behavior without any pronounced symptoms. Gradually it became an aim of our therapeutic endeavors not only to cure neurotic symptoms but to extend the ego's administrative power over this automatic and rigidly fixed expression of instinctive energies.

The aim of the therapy can thus be defined as the extension of conscious control over instinctual forces which were isolated from the conscious ego's administrative power, either as symptom or as neurotic behavior. We may now investigate by what means those who deviate from the standard technique hope to achieve this aim. In order to evaluate these deviations, we must consider the part played by the three therapeutic factors in the analytic process, *abreaction, insight,* and *recollection.* We saw that abreaction without insight is insufficient. We understand now why. The process of integration, by which the repressed tendency becomes an organized part of the ego, does not take place without insight; insight is the condition—perhaps the very essence—of this integrating process. Equally obvious on the other hand, insight without emotional experience, that is to say, without abreaction, is of little value. Something which is not in the ego cannot be integrated into it, and emotional experience is the sign that the tendency is becoming conscious. Therefore theoretical knowledge of something which is not experienced emotionally by the patients is perforce therapeutically ineffective, though it must be admitted that in certain situations a merely intellectual insight may prepare the way for abreaction. It is not advisable to think of these processes too schematically. Abreaction without insight and insight without abreaction are two extremes, between which in practice there are all degrees of combination and analyses do in fact consist of such differently graded mixtures of insight and emotional experience. Abreactions, small in quantity, take place throughout any analysis conducted by the standard technique and each successive abreaction is attended by more and more insight.

Whereas there is considerable agreement concerning the relation of insight to emotional experience, there is much controversy about the effectiveness of infantile recollections. The concept that the energy contained in a symptom can simply be transformed and absorbed by the process of recollection, is obviously erroneous. Nevertheless, recollection seems to be an indispensable precondition if a repressed tendency is to be thoroughly intergrated into the ego system, in that it is recollection which connects the present with the past. Although the direct therapeutic value of the process of recollection may be questioned, the removal of the infantile amnesia must be considered as a unique indicator of the successful resolving of repressions. Therefore the removal of infantile amnesia might be required as a sign of a fully successful analysis, even though a cure and the removal of infantile amnesia may not necessarily be directly causally related.

We see now that all three factors, abreaction, insight, and recollection, are required in order to obtain the goal of psychoanalytic procedure, which is, the removal of certain repressions and the subsequent integration of the formerly repressed tendencies which makes their ego-syntonic disposal possible. Whereas insight and abreaction are in direct relationship to the process of relieving repressions and of integration of the repressed forces, the importance of recollection may be a more indirect one. It serves as an indicator of the removal of repressions.

A brief survey will illustrate our point that the divergence from the standard procedure usually is a one-sided overemphasis of one of these three factors. So far as one can reconstruct the evolution of analytic technique, Freud, after he gave up hypnosis, began to lay more and more stress on insight and the reconstruction of the infantile history. This was quite natural. He tried to reproduce in the waking state the phenomenon he and Breuer observed during hypnosis, namely, the patient's recollection of forgotten traumatic situations. The main goal became to make the patient remember during the process of free association, and, so far as this was not fully possible, to complete the gaps in memory through intellectual reconstructions. Around 1913, however, when Freud first formulated systematically the principles of the technique as we use it today, we see that he was already fully in the possession of the above described dynamic concepts and considered analysis by no means a merely intellectual procedure. Yet once he had recognized the importance of the patient's intellectual insight as precondition of the integrating activity of the ego, in contrast to many of his followers, he never lost sight of its significance.

It seems that at some time between the introduction of the method of free association and the publication of the technical recommendations of Freud in 1912, 1913 and 1914, there must have been a period in which analysts overrated the importance of an intellectual reconstruction of the infantile history. This can be seen from the fact that even after Freud's publications on technical recommendations many analytic pioneers apparently persistently overintellectualized the analytic process, and stressed the interpretation of content and reconstruction of infantile history, overlooking the more dynamic handling of resistance and transference. This explains the joint publication by Ferenczi and Rank of *Entwicklungsziele der Psychoanalyse*, which may be regarded as a reaction against this overintellectualized analysis.[3] Ferenczi and Rank, as I tried to show when their pamphlet

[3] Sandor Ferenczi and Otto Rank, *The Development of Psychoanalysis*, New York: Nerv. and Ment. Dis. Pub. Co., 1925.

appeared in print, went to the other extreme.[4] According to them the whole analysis consists in provoking transference reactions and interpreting them in connection with the actual life situation. The old abreaction theory began to emerge from the past. Ferenczi and Rank thought that after the patient had reexperienced his infantile conflicts in the transference neurosis, there was no need to wait for infantile memories; they believed that insight was possible without recollection merely through the understanding of the different transference situations which are modeled upon the forgotten conflictful childhood experiences. Much of the originally repressed material they held had never been verbalized in the child's mind, and therefore one could not always expect real recollection of those situations upon which the transference reactions are modeled. Assuming that Ferenczi and Rank were right, and that one does not need to wait for the infantile amnesia to be dispelled, the obvious practical value of their concept would be a considerable abbreviation of the treatment. In this concept obviously the ego's integrating function is neglected, together with the corresponding technical device, the working through. The tedious task of helping the patient to bring his transference manifestation into connection both with the actual situation and with his former experiences plays a less important role in this technique. After the transference manifestation becomes clearly expressed and understood by the patient, even though the connection with the original patterns of the transference is not established, the analysis could be terminated on a date set by the analyst.

The further developments are well known. Rank more and more centered his attention on the actual life situation, and considered insight into the infantile history as merely a research issue with no therapeutic significance whatsoever. Ferenczi, however, soon discovered that the artificial termination of the analysis did not work out therapeutically, dismissed it from his technique and tried to enhance the effectiveness of the therapy by increasing emphasis upon the abreaction factor. Though he did not return to the method of cathartic hypnosis, he frankly admitted that he considered abreaction, as it takes place during cathartic hypnosis, to be the really effective therapeutic factor, and he tried to reproduce it in the method of free association by creating artificial emotional tensions, at first through his active technique, later through his relaxation method.[5] With the help of the

[4] F. Alexander, Review of Ferenczi and Rank's *Development of Psychoanalysis, Int. Ztschr. Psychoanal.*, XI, 1925.

[5] S. Ferenczi, "The Further Development of an Active Therapy in Psychoanalysis," in *Further Contributions to the Theory and Technique of Psychoanalysis,* London: Hogarth, 1926; "The Principle of Relaxation and Catharsis," *Int. J. of Psycho-Anal.*, XI, 1930, 428-443; "Child-Analysis in the Analysis of

ingenious technical device of relaxation, in certain cases he succeeded in creating semihypnotic states, in which the patient in a twilight state repeated his infantile emotional conflicts in a dramatic fashion.

Both the joint attempts of Rank and Ferenczi and Ferenczi's later technical experiments can be classified as abreaction therapies, in which the element of insight, that is to say, the process of integration, is neglected. These technical reforms imply a regression back toward cathartic hypnosis with a reintroduction of all the therapeutic deficiencies of this period. They represent an emphasis of intensive transference analysis and neglect of the intellectual integrating side of therapy, the working through.

Another technical trend is represented by Reich's resistance and later analysis.[6] According to Reich the aim of therapy is the transformation mainly into orgastic genitality of energy bound in neurotic symptoms and character trends. The discussion of this narrow theoretical concept does not lie within the scope of this study. Our present interest is his technical motto, the stress on certain hidden manifestations of resistance, which according to him are not recognized by most psychoanalysts, and his strict distinction between interpretation of resistance and interpretation of content. According to Reich certain hidden manifestations of resistance must first be analyzed and only afterwards can the analysis deal with the content which the patient's ego is resisting. The important things are not the familiar open manifestations of resistance, but those secret manifestations which the patient expresses only in a very indirect way in characteristic behavior, for example, in pseudo-cooperativeness, in overconventional and overcorrect behavior, in affectless behavior, or in certain symptoms of depersonalization. The emphasis on hidden forms of resistance is unquestionably of great practical value. Glover[7] mentions in his treatise on technique the importance of these hidden forms of resistance which one easily overlooks, and Abraham in one of his classical contributions described the pseudo-cooperative attitude of certain patients as a specific form of hidden resistance.[8] Reich's emphasis on understanding the patient's behavior apart from the content of his communications is largely a typical example of the rediscovery of one of the many therapeutic revelations that every analyst encounters

Adults," *Int. J. Psycho-Anal.*, XII, 1931; "Reflections on Trauma," *Int. Ztschr. Psychoanal.*, XX, 1934.

[6] Wilhelm Reich, *Charakteranalyse*, Vienna: privately published, 1933.

[7] Edward Glover, "Lectures on Technique in Psychoanalysis," *Int. J. Psycho-Anal.*, VIII, 1927.

[8] K. Abraham, "A Particular form of Neurotic Resistance against the Psycho-Analytic Method," *Selected Papers*, New York: Basic Books, 1953.

during his development, as he gradually becomes more and more sensitive to the less obvious, more indirect manifestations of the unconscious. However, Reich's distinction between resistance which is expressed in the patient's communications and that expressed by his gestures and general manner of behavior is quite artificial. All of these expressions complement each other and constitute an indivisible unity.

Reich's other principle of the primacy of resistance interpretation over content interpretation is based upon a similarly artificial and schematic distinction. As Fenichel has correctly pointed out, the repressing tendencies and repressed content are closely connected.[9] They constitute one psychic entity and can only be separated from each other artificially. The patient's resistance, for the careful observer, always displays at least roughly the content against which the resistance is directed. There is no free-floating resistance. At least the general content of the repressed can be recognized at the same time as the fact of the resistance itself. The more the analyst is able to help the patient to understand his resistance in connection with what it is directed against, the sooner the resistance itself can be resolved. Mostly the verbalization of what the patient is resisting diminishes the resistance itself. Strachey has convincingly described this reassuring effect of correct and timely interpretations, which can best be witnessed in child analysis.[10] It is true, as Fenichel states in his critical discussion of Reich's technique, that in the interpretation of the content the analyst can go only slightly beyond what the patient himself is able to see alone at any given moment. Yet every resistance should preferably be interpreted in connection with what it is directed against, provided of course that the content interpretation corresponds to the status of the analysis.

Reich's concept of layer analysis is similarly a product of his overschematizing tendency. That unconscious material appears in layers is a familiar observation. Freud operates with this concept as far back as the "History of an Infantile Neurosis," and in *Totem and Taboo* he shows that the primary aggressive heterosexual phase is as a rule concealed by an overdomestication of these tendencies, by a masochistic passive homosexual phase. Following Freud's lead, I

[9] Otto Fenichel, "Zur Theorie der psychoanalytischen Technik," *Int. Ztschr. Psychoanal.*, XXI, 1935. As a matter of fact Fenichel mentions this argument as expressing not his own views, but those of the advocates of content interpretations, including Freud. He writes: "They [these advocates] think that because of the persistent interweaving of defensive forces and rejected tendencies, it is impossible to verbalize the ones without at the same time verbalizing the others." (Author's paraphrase.)

[10] James Strachey, "The Nature of the Therapeutic Action of Psychoanalysis," *Int. J. Psycho-Anal.*, XV, 1934.

tried, in an early paper, "Castration Complex and Character," to reconstruct the history of a patient's neurosis as a sequence of polar opposite phases of instinctual development.

The existence of certain typical emotional sequences, such as: early oral receptivity leading under the influence of deprivations to sadistic revenge, guilt, self-punishment, and finally to regression to a helpless dependence are generally known. The validity of such typical emotional sequences, which make the material appear in "layers," is sufficiently proven, and every analyst uses this insight as a useful orientation in the chaos of unconscious reactions. This, however, does not change the supreme rule that the analyst cannot approach the material with a preconceived idea of a certain stratification in the patient, for this stratification has individual features in different patients. Though certain general phases in the individual's development succeed others with universal regularity, the different emotional attitudes do not necessarily appear during the treatment in the same chronological order as they developed in the patient's past life history. Moreover, the pathogenetic fixations occur at different phases in different cases, and the fixation points determine what is the deepest pathogenetic layer in any given case. Often we find an early period of sadism leading to anxiety and covered consecutively by a layer of passivity, inferiority feelings, and secondary outbreak of aggression. In other cases we see that the deepest pathogenetic layer is a strong fixation to an oral dependent attitude, compensated then by reaction formations of overactivity and aggressiveness, which in turn are covered by a surface attitude of helpless receptivity. It is not uncommon that a patient in the course of the first two or three interviews reveals in his behavior and associations as sequence of emotional reactions belonging to different phases of his development. As Abraham many years ago emphasized during a discussion in the Berlin Psychoanalytic Society, it is not advisable to regard the different emotional reactions as they appear during the treatment in a too literal, too static sense, as though they were spread out one layer over the other, for in the unconscious they exist side by side. During development, it is true, they follow each other in temporary sequences, one emotional phase being the reaction to the preceding one. During treatment, however, probably due to as yet unknown quantitative relationships, they do not repeat exactly their historical chronological order. I have often observed in more advanced stages of an analysis— sometimes even in the early stages—that patients during one analytic session display almost the whole history of their emotional development. They may start with spite and fear, then take on a passive dependent attitude, and end up the session again with envy and aggression. The analyst can do no better than follow the material as it presents itself, thus giving the lead to the patient, as Horney[11] has again recently emphasized. Reich's warning against premature deep interpretations is correct, to be sure; Freud emphasized this point in his technical recommendations, and it is implicit in the general principle that interpretation should always start from the surface and go only as deep as the patient has capacity for comprehending emotionally. But in Reich's overschematic procedure, the danger resides in that the analyst instead of following the individual stratification of emotional reactions in the patient, approaches the material with an overgeneralized diagram of layers, before he is in a position to decide which emotional attitude is primary and which should be considered as reaction. The chronological order of the appearance is by no means a reliable criterion. An observation of Roy Grinker and Margaret Gerard in the Department of Psychiatry of the University of Chicago clearly demonstrates that the order in which the transference attitude of a patient appears is determined also by factors other than the chronological order in which it developed in the patient's previous history. As an interesting experiment they had a female schizophrenic patient associate freely for a few days alternately in the presence of a male and a female psychoanalyst; they observed that the patient's attitude was influenced by this difference of the analyst's sex. When the male analyst conducted the session, the patient was constantly demanding and aggressive; to the female analyst she complained and was more confiding, seeking for reassurance. This experiment clearly shows that the chronological sequence of transference attitudes does not follow rigidly a historically predetermined stratification of infantile attitudes, and is determined also by other factors.[12]

The slogan of the primacy of resistance interpretation over content interpretation found its most consistent expression in an extreme distortion of the analytic technique, in Kaiser's resistance analysis, from which every interpretation of content is pedantically eliminated. The analysis is reduced to an extremely sterile procedure of pointing out to the patient his resistance manifestations.[13]

After Fenichel's excellent critical analysis of this technique, there is little call for comment. Its most paradoxical feature consists in the fact that Kaiser, who limits the therapeutic agent of analysis to dramatic abreactions entirely, reminding us of the latest experimentation of Ferenczi, attempts to achieve such abreactions by a merely in-

[11] K. Horney, "Conceptions and Misconceptions of the Analytical Method," *J. Nerv. and Ment. Dis.*, LXXXI, 1935.

[12] I wish to thank Drs. Grinker and Gerard for permission to refer to this interesting observation.

[13] Hellmuth Kaiser, "Probleme der Technik," *Int. Ztschr. Psychoanal.*, XX, 1934.

tellectual procedure—namely, by convincing the patient of the irrationality of his resistance behavior and resistance ideas. This intellectual insight, Kaiser thinks, can break down the resistance itself and allow the repressed material to appear in a dramatic fashion. In order to create strong emotional tensions, he carefully avoids every interpretation of content and goes so far as to condemn every indirect allusion of the analyst to preconscious material, even if this is so near to consciousness that it needs only verbalization in order to appear on the surface. It is not the intellectual insight into the resistance, but the avoidance of all content interpretation, that creates in the patient such tensions as to provoke dramatic abreactions. The reassuring effect of verbalizing preconscious material, which encourages further expression of repressed material, has been mentioned above. To call the child by its name divests much of the patient's fear of the uncanny tension that comes from the pressure of preconscious material when it is merely felt as some unknown danger. The analyst's objective discussion of such material eliminates the infantile fear of the condemning parents and of their inner representative, the harsh superego. Verbalization of repressed content has for the patient the meaning of a permission; careful avoidance of it means condemnation.

Obviously here the fascination of the analyst by the fireworks of emotional rockets is what leads to such a distortion of the analytic technique, which is quite without logical justification and contradicts our dynamic concepts of the analytic procedure. The ideal of the standard technique is just the opposite—a permanent, steady, uninterrupted flow of repressed material, undisturbed by sudden dramatic advances that necessarily lead to new regressions, which often neutralizes the effect of many weeks' or many months' work. This steady flow can, however, only be obtained by a judicious economic use of resistance and content interpretations in such connections as they appear, by helping the patient connect the emerging material with the rest of his conscious mind and with his past and present experience.

Without attempting to advance any radical reforms or lay down new technical rules, I shall try in the following to investigate the question as to how far and in what way the analytic method aids the integrating or snythetic process in the ego, which, as Nunberg has correctly claimed, is an integral part of the analysis.

The process of the cure we described as the combination of two fundamental psychological processes, (1) the inviting of unconscious material into consciousness and (2) the assimilation of this material by the conscious ego. To the first phase our literature refers by different expressions: *emotional experience, abreaction, transformation of unconscious into conscious material;* the second phase is called *insight, digestion or assimilation of unconscious material by the ego* or *synthesis and integration.* Seen in this perspective it is obvious now that the technical reforms and innovations which we have been discussing in detail are all primarily concerned with the first phase and are reactions to an early overintellectualized period of psychoanalytic treatment, in which intellectual insight was overstressed, and in which reconstructions and interpretations were made by the analyst upon material which had not yet appeared in the consciousness of the patient. Ferenczi and Rank stress the emotional experience in the transference, and Reich's and Kaiser's main interest is focused upon methods of mobilizing unconscious material by manipulating and interpreting the resistance. In all these experiments with technique the first problem, the mobilization of unconscious material, is considered the crucial one; the assimilation of the unconscious material is left to the integrating powers of the psychoneurotic's fairly intact ego. The question is now in which way this ultimate aim of the therapy, the integration in the ego of the material previously unconscious, can be supported by the correct handling of our technique.

Nunberg's analysis of the process by which unconscious content becomes conscious clearly shows that this process itelf is an integrating act of the ego.[14] The quality of consciousness in itself involves an integrating act: a psychological content in becoming conscious becomes included in a higher, richer, more complex system of connections. The preconscious material's becoming conscious has long been considered by Freud as the establishment of a new connection: that between object images and word images. Obviously what we call abstractions, or abstract thinking, represent again a higher grade of synthesis between word images. Although we do not yet know much about its details, what we call conscious thinking consists mainly in the establishment of new connections between conscious contents. It must be remembered, however, that these new connections of higher grade cannot be established arbitrarily by the ego. The connections must be correct, that is to say, they must be in conformity with the results of the reality testing of the ego. Therefore generalizations, the establishing of connections between different conscious elements is permanently counteracted by the critical or distinguishing faculty of the ego, which it uses, however, only under the pressure of reality. Without the pressure of the reality testing functions, the synthetic function would run amuck as it does in many philosophical systems. Nunberg convincingly demonstrates all this and considers the delusional system in paranoia to be the result of such a faulty overstressed synthetic effort of the ego, by which it desperately tries to bring

[14] Nunberg, *op. cit.*

order into a personality chaotically disorganized by the psychotic process.

Nunberg also called attention to the fact that every neurotic system and most psychotic symptoms are synthetic products. In fact all unconscious material, as it presents itself to us during the treatment in its *status nascendi* of becoming conscious appears in certain synthetic units; fear together with guilt and hate, receptive wishes and dependence overreacted to by aggression appear to us as two Janus faces of the same unit. We discover the synthetic nature of the unconscious material also in such generalizations as connect or identify the objects of sexual impulses in the unconscious. The extension of the incest barrier over all individuals of the other sex is the simplest and best known example of this generalizing tendency of the mental apparatus. The process by which an unconscious content becomes conscious consequently consists in the disruption of primitive synthetic products and the reassembling of the elements in the higher synthetic system of consciousness, which is more complex, more differentiated and consequently more flexible. Thomas M. French's recent studies of consecutive dreams clearly demonstrate that during the course of the treatment a progressive breaking up of primitive emotional patterns takes place, together with a building up of new more complex relationships between the elements. This new synthesis allows behavior more flexible than the rigid automatic behavior which is determined by unconscious synthetic patterns. It is the ego's function to secure gratifications of instinctive needs harmoniously and within the possibilities of the existing external conditions. Every new experience requires a modification in the previously established patterns of instinct gratification. The unconscious consists of psychological units, expressing more primitive, usually infantile connections between instinctual needs and external observations. These primitive units as we know are not harmonized with each other, nor do they correspond to the external conditions of the adult. Therefore they must undergo a new integrating process into higher systems: a new adjustment between instinctual needs and external reality must be accomplished, in which process the ego plays the part of a mediator. The establishment of these new connections, however, necessitates the breaking up of the old units—in other words, of symptoms or fixed behavior patterns which correspond to earlier phases of the ego development. What must be given emphasis, however, is the fact that all unconscious material appears in synthetic units, which constitute certain primitive patterns that connect instinctual demands with the results of reality testing.

According to this concept the process by which an unconscious content becomes conscious corresponds to a recapitulation of ego development, which consists in a gradual building up of more and more complex and flexible systems of connections between different instinctual needs and sense perceptions.

We are now prepared to discuss the technical question: in what way does our technique contribute to the breaking up of the primitive psychological units as they exist in the unconscious and help their elements to enter into the new, more diversified connections in the conscious ego? The main function of psychoanalytic interpretations obviously consists precisely in the establishment of new correct connections and in the breaking up of old overgeneralized and more primitive connections. The effect of interpretation can most simply be compared with the process of the child's learning to connect and differentiate objects. At first, when the child learns the word "stick," it begins to call every longitudinal object a stick, and then gradually learns to differentiate between stick, pencil, poker, umbrella, etc. When a neurotic patient learns to differentiate between incestuous and nonincestuous objects, that is to say, to react differently toward them, he essentially repeats the same process.

In his current systematic study of patients' consecutive dreams during the process of cure, French subjects this learning process to a thorough investigation, from which we expect to learn much of the nature and details of this learning process. At present we know only its general principle, namely, that it consists in a gradual establishment of new and more differentiated connections between the psychic representatives of instinctual needs and the data of sense perception.

What does this insight teach us with regard to our analytic technique? It is obvious that our interpretations must fulfill both purposes: they must break up the primitive connections and help to establish new, more differentiated ones that are in harmony with the reality with which the adult is confronted. The standard technique, as it was described in its basic principles by Freud about twenty years ago, still serves this double purpose better than any of those reform procedures, which neglect to give aid to the synthetic functions of the ego and take into account only the mobilization of unconscious material. What we call "working through" has the function of aiding the integrating process. Its therapeutic value is sufficiently proven by experience. My contention, however, is that every correct interpretation serves both purposes: mobilization of unconscious material and its integration into the system of consciousness. The *synchronization* of the two functions of interpretation into one act, inducing abreaction and insight at the same time, may be considered a fundamental technical principle, which I should like to call the *integrating principle of interpretation*. I disagree with every attempt which tries artificially to isolate these two processes, most extremely represented in Kaiser's technique, because the best means still of overcoming a resistance is the correct interpretation of its not yet verbalized background. The basis of the ego's resistance is its inability to master or to assimilate unconscious material. Everything which the patient can understand, that is to say, everything which he can connect with other familiar psychological content of which he already is master, relieves fear. In other words, every new synthesis within the ego, by increasing the ego's ability to face new unconscious material, facilitates the appearance of new unconscious material. The longer the patient is exposed to material which puzzles him, which seems strange, and appears to him as a foreign body, the longer the analysis will be retarded and the appearence of new unconscious material blocked. The ideal we strive for in our technique is that whatever unconscious material appears in consciousness should be connected at the same time with what is already understood by the patient. This makes of the analysis a continuous process. Therefore, whenever it is possible interpretations should refer to previous insight. To be sure, as has already been emphasized, interpretation does not consist merely in the creation of new connections but also in the breaking up of primitive infantile connections. This can be done only if the material as it appears in its totality is exposed to the patient's critical judgment. Umbrella, walking cane, poker, lead pencil, must be demonstrated together in order to break up their faulty identification and generalization as a stick. The interpretations must point out these connections, formed by the mind in infancy as they appear in the presenting material. We know that these connections, as they occur in symbols, for example, often seem extremely strange to the mind of the adult, who has forgotten and overcome this primitive language of the unconscious. It is too much to expect that the patient will be able to recognize without help the infantile generalizations as something self-evident. I do not doubt, however, that after the old primitive connections are broken up, the patient, because of the integrating power of his ego, would in time establish the new syntheses alone. Here, however, is the place where the analyst can help and accelerate the integrating process. Interpretations which connect the *actual life situation* with *past experiences* and with the *transference situation*—since the latter is always the axis around which such connections can best be made—I should like to call *total interpretations*. The more interpretations approximate this principle of totality, the more they fulfill their double purpose: they accelerate the assimilation of new material by the ego and mobilize further unconscious material.

This principle of totality should not be misunderstood and used in a different sense than it is meant. Totality does not mean, for ex-

ample, that all deep overdeterminations in a dream should be interpreted. Totality does not mean an unlimited connection of material
which though in fact related is still far from the surface. It means
totality not as to depth but as to extension—the connecting with each
other and with previous material of elements which belong together.
It cannot be emphasized too much, however, that these connections
should center around the emotionally charged material, usually the
transference manifestations. Fenichel's formulation regarding the penetration of the depth is valid, to wit, that the interpretation can only
contain just a little more than the patient is able to see for himself
at the moment.

The supreme requirement for the correct handling of the technique, however, more important than any principles and rules, is
the precise understanding in detail of what is going on at every moment in the patient. It is needless to say that all the formulations here
given should be considered not as rules but as general principles to
be applied always in accordance with the individual features of the
patient and the situation.

The isolation of resistance from content interpretation is not a
desirable aim though at times it is necessary, in particular when the
tendency against which the patient has resistance is not yet understood by the analyst. Probably the only effective way of permanently
overcoming resistance consists in helping the ego to integrate, that is
to say, to understand new material. Therefore in the long run all those
technical experiments which aim at sudden abreactions of great quantities of unconscious tendencies fail. These techniques expose the ego
not to a continuous flow but to sudden eruptions of new material and
necessarily must cause new repressions, repression being a phenomenon which Freud has explained as resulting from the infantile weak
ego's inability to deal with certain instinctual needs. The reproduction of such an inner traumatic situation in which the ego is exposed
to overpowerful stimuli cannot be a sound principle of our technique.
Many, not all, roads lead to Rome. In analytic therapy our main allies
are the *striving of unconscious forces for expression and the integrating tendency of the conscious ego.* Even if we do nothing else,
if we do not interfere with these two dynamic forces, we will be able
to help many patients, and if we succeed without therapeutic activity in aiding and synchronizing both of these two fundamental agents,
we will increase the efficiency of our technique.

Nunberg's thesis that the psychoanalytic treatment is not only an
analytic but simultaneously a synthetic process as well is fully valid.
It has often been maintained that psychoanalysis consists mainly in
the mobilization of unconscious material and that the integration of
this material must be left to the patient's ego. The standard technique,

as it is used since Freud's technical recommendations, consisting in interpretations centering around the transference situation, really involves an active participation of the analyst in the integrating process. Through our interpretations, without fully realizing it, we actually do help the synthesis in the ego. Doing it consciously and understanding this integrative function of our interpretation may contribute to developing the art of analysis into a fully goal conscious, systematically directed procedure. Always keeping in mind the function which our interpretations fulfill in the treatment eventually will help to bring us nearer to the ultimate goal, the abbreviation of the psychoanalytic treatment.

"The Voice of the Intellect Is Soft . . ."

◄ 1941 ►

In *The Future of an Illusion*, Freud wrote: "The voice of the intellect is a soft one but it does not rest until it has gained a hearing." [1] There are few statements which pertain more closely to the central problem of analytic therapy—indeed to the essential problem of man —the guiding influence of the intellect over the impulses, the struggle between Dionysus and Apollo.

The first part of this statement expresses the greatest difficulty of analytic therapy, namely, that the voice of the intellect is so soft; the second part of the statement expresses the strength of psychoanalysis, namely, that this voice, although soft, is permanent. Once a clear insight is reached, it is impossible to get rid of it completely.

The study of painful dreams has shown us that even in our dreams, where wish fulfillment rules, we cannot get rid of the voice of our conscience. Before we can satisfy ego alien wishes in dreams, we must pay a price in the form of fulfilling, at least to some degree, the claims of the conscience, in the form of suffering or other methods of bribery. [2] More recently, French has demonstrated that not only can we not rid ourselves of the voice of conscience in dreams but we cannot even fully disregard the external obstacles interfering with our wishes. [3] Both observations are based on the same principle, since the conscience is nothing but a part of the environment's attitude which has been incorporated within the ego. The principle is that the impression of the external reality upon the mental apparatus in the form of recognition of the factual situation or in the form of the norms of

---

[1] S. Freud, *The Future of an Illusion*, New York: Liveright, 1949.

[2] "About Dreams with Unpleasant Content," in this volume.

[3] Thomas M. French, "Reality and the Unconscious," *Psychoanal. Quart.*, VI (1937), 23; and "Insight and Distortion in Dreams," *Int. J. Psycho-Anal.*, XX (1939), 1.

the conscience is not fully reversible. The effectiveness of the impression may vary, but it is an irreversible process which never is erased entirely.

The ego's function is not only to grasp the external situation, but also the internal situation; to mediate between conflicting impulses. There is ample evidence that once the ego has grasped the internal emotional situation, such an insight is never fully erased again. It is common knowledge that during the course of a psychoanalytic treatment, many of the patient's dreams are responses to interpretations given in a previous session. French in his microscopic dream studies has convincingly demonstrated that the patient even in his dreams cannot fully disregard what he has grasped about himself while awake.[4]

The grasp of the internal emotional constellation is the main object of the analytic procedure. One can well describe the analytic therapy as a continuous struggle of a patient against insight which the analytic work is constantly bringing about. The patient tries to reject or disregard again and again this insight and uses all the methods of self deception at his disposal—rationalization, falsification of the internal and external reality or disregarding certain disturbing elements of them. The analyst tries to drive home a correct appreciation of external and internal reality and uses the transference as his greatest ally in this endeavor. Not infrequently the strange situation arises that the patient recognizes the factual situation both internal and external under the influence of positive transference but whenever the analysis is interrupted, he attempts to work himself free from the chains of the intellectual insight in the direction of wishful distortion. Frequently even during weekends or a few days of interruption the processes of repudiation of the analytic insight can be observed. The long duration of the psychoanalytic therapy is due to precisely this fact, namely, that the pressure of intellectual insight is relatively weak in comparison with those dynamic forces which are opposing it. That an analysis ever progresses at all is due to the fact that no matter how small this pressure of insight is, once it is gained, it has a dynamic influence. This comes to expression in the typical course of a psychoanalytic treatment; two steps forward and two steps backward but the two steps backward are somewhat shorter than the two forward have been. A careful study of regressive material shows that even during a relapse the patient carries with himself, and cannot fully disregard, what he has clearly grasped. Should the psychoanalyst overlook these slight but significant manifestations of the fact that insight had influenced the patient, he would often have to despair. The well-

---

[4] French, "Insight and Distortion in Dreams," *op. cit.*

known dreams of resistance are the best examples. Such dreams are direct responses to interpretations given previously and are attempts of denial; they show an internal struggle against the interpretation. This struggle itself is the best proof that the new insight contained in the interpretation took hold of the patient. So long as such a gradual process, interrupted by relapses, can be observed in a kind of spiral progression, the therapist feels encouraged to continue with his strenuous task. The only encouragement he has lies in the fact that no matter how soft the voice of intellectual insight is, it is indelible. The patient may repudiate most violently insight which he accepted some time before, yet there is evidence that it left indelible traces in his mind. In fact, the violence of the repudiation is the best sign that the patient has to struggle against something forceful. The violence of the resistance is the sign of the intensity of the pressure exerted by insight.

This indelible nature of analytic insight came to an unusually clear and convincing expression in a patient's dream which he had when the struggle between resistance and insight reached its height, one might say, at the most critical phase of his analysis.

The patient was a forty-year-old man, happily married, the father of two children, who came to the analysis with a complaint, somewhat unusual for a man of his age. He came to my office with tears in his eyes, complaining that nobody loved him and he felt isolated in life. From time to time this feeling took the form of real depressions. He was a successful man who enjoyed the highest reputation among men of his profession and others. His life was more or less uneventful and smooth and yet he stated he had never been happy for one moment in his whole life from early childhood.

For the sake of this discussion, we may disregard most of the details of his life. What we shall need in order to understand the point in question is the description of the nature of the patient's emotional problem and the historical background of his suffering.

Characteristic of this patient was that his suffering, although intensive and permanent, was not known to his environment. He had a "poker face" and kept his suffering to himself. On some occasions, however, tears would roll down his cheeks but even then his face did not contort but remained calm and expressionless.

He was the older of two sons of a successful and able father. His mother was a practical minded housewife, entirely devoted to household economy and raising her two sons. She placed all her ambition in her first son whom she loved unconditionally. The second son was given much less attention and affection. The influence of the mother upon her older son could be expressed best in a sentence which in this form probably never was uttered: "You must become a great man, a leader in your field, not only to follow your father's footsteps, but surpass him; you are able, smart and you can do it if you want to." From early childhood the boy's orientation to life was according to his mother's influence. There was only one aim in his life—knowledge, success—to be on top. He became an extremely studious boy, inferior in physical competition, but always a bright student. He was determined to follow father's profession and outdo him in his own field. There was never any hesitation or deviation from this one circumscribed goal. Relaxation or play was always felt by him as a waste of time and he never could indulge in it freely with a good conscience. But actually, there was no occasion for such guilt feelings, because there was no temptation. What he loved was only study, increasing his knowledge—the pursuit of his career. While the relation between mother and son was close and the parents' life was harmonious, the patient never got along well with his father. He disliked him and, at times, even hated him. He thought that father was too severe with him and really did not like him.

As the analysis progressed an entirely different emotional picture presented itself concerning his relations to his parents. Underneath, a desperate desire for father's love and guidance was his strongest emotion—something which he could not admit to himself. The ambitions of his mother drove this boy prematurely and excessively into competition with his father and at the same time the mother obviously overwhelmed her first son with love which was taken from her husband. This corrupting mother love, however, failed entirely to allay the boy's deep feeling of insecurity; on the contrary, it increased it. As a defense measure against this premature maturity towards which his mother pushed him, he developed the unshakable conviction that he was really not very able; that he never would come near his father in knowledge and efficiency. In fact, it appeared to him as a totally impossible idea that he could ever compare with his father. The same attitude he retained toward all father figures in his life. Later as an adult, in spite of his great ability and expert knowledge, secretly he always felt that he never could match other experts in his field. Emotionally, he remained always a little boy; secretly admiring his father, wanting his love and guidance. Nevertheless, he pushed forward and nobody except him could even surmise his deep emotional insecurity. Outwardly he had an authoritative appearance of great self-confidence. Yet his neurotic conflict was centered around the tremendous passive longing towards his father, which in fact never was satisfied in his life. He reacted in the polar opposite reaction to the mother's desires. Mother wanted him to become a hero and he wanted nothing more than the guidance of a strong father figure. This is not astonishing in the least, if we realize that because of his mother's influence he never enjoyed a warm, confidential relationship as a young boy; he and his father became emotionally competitors at an age when the boy needed father's leadership.

It was not difficult to reconstruct during the analysis that his father reacted to the mother's admiration for the son with an unconscious jealousy. At the same time he loved his son, wanted him to become successful and taught him what he could. However, the relation between father and son was strained on account of the manifest hatred of the boy toward his father, as well as on account of the father's unconscious jealousy. Thus, these two men in the family lived beside each other in a never resolved mutual ambivalence.

In the boy the frustrated wish to be loved by the father created a strong feeling of inferiority. This passive longing was like an open wound and made him aware of his weakness. As a result he reacted with hatred and aggression. Under mother's instigation he had to compete with the father. This overstrong competitiveness, as well as his reactive hatred, caused intensive guilt feelings. These interfered with his wish to be loved by the father. An emotional impasse developed which he was absolutely unable to resolve. In spite of his father's ambivalence he could have received some love from him, but even this he could not freely accept on account of his guilt feelings. Therefore, he had to develop the conviction that father did not love him at all. Only this made his competition and aggression bearable. If father didn't love him, he was justified in hating him. He exaggerated the manifestations of the father's jealousy and interpreted them as a proof of his conviction that father was rejecting him. This pattern persisted throughout his life and his tremendous competitiveness and selfish aggressiveness did not allow him to feel that anybody could love him. At the same time he was insatiable in his thirst for love.

This patient is an exaggerated example of that inherent paradox of western civilization to which Sumner refers by the telling expression—"antagonistic cooperation." We have to compete with each other but at the same time we need each other's mutual help to a high degree. This problem of the men of our present age grew to an unsolvable neurotic conflict in this patient under the influence of the family situation which I have tried to describe.

All this became clear during the first eighteen months of his analysis. The insight into the nature of his difficulties became clearer and clearer. At first, merely a verbal insight, it became more and more emotionally absorbed. The deeper this understanding grew, the greater became his desperate resistance. It was obvious that the patient was fixated to this emotional configuration—no matter how painful it was for him. In one analytic session he exclaimed desperately "without competition and racing my life would be empty and aimless." He was a typical exponent of our times, the race of success was the only goal he was trained for in all his life. Yet at the same time he could not renounce having a loving father. As an adult he always sought for such father figures but inevitably sooner or later came into this typical ambivalence conflict with them and lost them. He could not renounce either side of the conflict—the desire to be loved or the narcissistic passion to win in the race of life.

In this phase of his analysis, it became obvious that only a thorough emotional reorientation could solve this conflict. One could not go on living with the all-exclusive, cold determination to reach the top, entirely devoted to his advancement, considering everyone as a competitor and at the same time desiring and expecting love and warmth from just those whom he felt must be run down in the race. It became clear to him that either he must accept emotional isolation and loneliness or give up his blind and vicious ambition. He could not do either. In his dreams he became exclusively occupied with this insoluble conflict. In some of these dreams he cynically and more or less openly gratified his ambition and grabbed everything for himself. In one dream he had a brain tumor and was incurable. In such dreams he obviously declared, "I cannot change. I am an incurably grabbing and ambitious person and must remain so; it is an organic condition like a brain tumor." What he really meant was that he did not *want* to give up his desire to have everything for himself.

Another series of dreams again expressed the other major tendency—the longing for being loved. As it is often the case in such an advanced state of the analysis, his dreams became simple and did not need any interpretation. The insight has too deeply penetrated and not even in the dreams could he get rid of it. Thus, in one of his dreams, he ardently asked the analyst, "Do you love me?" This analytic session was filled by expressing tearfully his wish for being loved and forgiven for his murderous ambitions. This wish was so frankly brought forward that the patient could not help but smile about it in the midst of all his tears.

This emotional impasse, after the analysis denuded it from all secondary ornaments and elaborations, in its simplicity very much reminded one of those conditioning experiments in which the experimental animal becomes confused by contradictory stimuli and develops neurotic symptoms. After a few futile attempts which appeared in dreams to repudiate the conclusion that without an emotional change and fundmental reorientation he would not be able to get rid of his loneliness, the patient dreamed the following:

I was in my dentist's office and he put an apparatus in my mouth which had a continuous buzzing sound and which worked constantly and automatically. I was afraid but he said even little children have this done. In another room I saw the dentist's little boy who was sad because he did not get sufficient feeling and attention from his father. I consoled him. Then I went back to the dentist to plead his son's case. The dentist became very angry at my return and said that he had been working eighteen months on my case and felt he was finished with me.

Patient, who just at that time was under dental treatment, in his associations, connected the dentist, who was an old friend of his father's, with the analyst and the dental treatment with the analytic therapy—the eighteen months referred to the duration of his analysis up to that time. Then patient expressed his exasperation about not being able to solve his problem and the fact that understanding it so clearly made his condition even more unbearable. This feeling obviously was expressed in the dream with the machine which the dentist (analyst) put into his mouth (mind) which works automatically and from which there is no escape. Even the ending of the analysis would not change this. He cannot get rid of the intellectual insight and its permanent voice. Its voice in the dream is not even so soft, it buzzes incessantly inside of him. He still fights the inevitable conclusion that he must grow up emotionally. His conflict is that of the little boy who prematurely under mother's instigation must fight father and yet needs father's love and guidance. He sees clearly that he must grow up. In the dream the dentist says that even little children can be treated this way. He feels an immense pity with his infantile self-represented by the dentist's little boy, whom he consoles. But the conclusion is inevitable: he is no longer a little boy but an adult at the peak of his career; both the excessive hunger for being loved and the relentless ambition fed by inner insecurity are incongruous with his present status.

The further course of the analysis was a fascinating spectacle of the continuous struggle between an ingrained emotional pattern and insight which had taken deep hold of the patient. In fact, to mature emotionally in a few months is not an easy task. We must realize that at this time the patient was a successful man, ranking among the first in his profession, teaching and guiding students and was himself the father of two children. But emotionally, he was still the small boy prodigy competing with his father, feeling very small and weak in relation to him and secretly longing for father's love and guidance, which he never allowed himself to possess.

Before he could accept the role of a mature person and that of a father, still another emotional problem had to be solved. Driven so early toward achievement and accomplishment, patient deep down had a tremendous envy for the role of his younger brother who could indulge in a passive careless existence, a role which was granted to him by both parents. They did not expect much of him and allowed him to grow up in a happy-go-lucky indifference. Recoiling from the strains of ambitious efforts, patient unconsciously longed for the brother's role but only with one part of his self. At the same time he was almost drunk with ambition. This envy of his younger brother's position was the other obstacle against maturation. He could not easily assume an unambivalent father role toward his students, younger professional colleagues, and his own son because he begrudged and envied their position, although in actual life he was helpful and concerned in their welfare. From time to time, however, his resentments broke through and his behavior toward his inferiors became unreasonable. He wanted to be the son and the father at the same time and these two wishes never have been fused in him to a chemical alloy. They remained a physical mixture in which each component retained its own quality.

Although at the time when the patient had the dream of the dentist his behavior had already changed considerably and his depressions were less frequent, less intensive and of shorter duration, still he had a long road ahead of him. However, the main analytic problem was accomplished. It was now a question of time for the insight to gain hearing for its soft but permanent voice and enforce an emotional reorientation.

It is not my purpose at present to describe in all detail the process by which, slowly but progressively, intellectual insight gains more and more foothold and ceases to remain a merely verbal insight. These details may vary from case to case but the dynamics of this process follow some general principles. The firmer the insight takes hold of the patient, the less he is able naively to express certain conflictful tendencies in his actual behavior. Thus, gradually, a situation arises in which the patient's objective behavior noticeably improves and the expression of the neurotic conflict becomes more and more limited to the dream and wakeful fantasy life. This state of affairs may become somewhat confusing for both patient and analyst: the patient actually behaves more and more controlled, while his dreams express franker and franker the neurotic conflict situation. Often there is also a discrepancy between the patient's subjective feeling and objective behavior.

Also this patient reported how miraculously he changed so far as his actions were concerned. His feeling tone, however, was not yet up to this objective change. Sometimes it appeared to him as if it were not *he* who acted so normally. This feeling has in principle much in common with depersonalization, but it corresponds to an opposite dynamic situation. While depersonalization feelings occur when deeply repressed tendencies rather suddenly break through and directly influence manifest behavior or the conscious thought processes, in the situation to which I refer, the influence of the conscious control becomes stronger than it ever was before. This gives the patient the peculiar subjective feeling of strangeness. In both cases, in depersonalization as well as in this curative metamorphosis, the patient does not recognize himself as he used to know himself: in the first case he is more in the second, less under the influence of unconscious emotional tensions.[5]

Another characteristic feature of this advanced phase of the analysis is that the patient assumes an almost objective and understanding attitude toward the products of his fantasy life no matter whether these fantasies appear in dreams or in a wakeful state. As I have mentioned, the dreams frequently become extremely simple and frank. Sometimes even during dreaming the patient looks with some understanding and distance upon his dream. When the feeling of forgiveness is mixed with this feeling, the patient assumes the attitude of humor toward the products of his own fantasy. This patient had this sensation at the occasion of the frank and simple dream in which he asked the analyst whether he loved him or not. The hour was filled with an oscillation between tearful longing for love and a humorous and understanding attitude toward his own childishness. His tears were a mixture of those of a longing child and of an adult who looks with some humorous resignation upon the past golden days of childhood. Humor requires the capacity of looking at something which deeply concerns us from a certain distance. This emotional attitude can be observed in children, when they desperately weep over the loss of a toy or being reprimanded or some other little tragedy of their life and are consoled by an understanding adult, who tries to point out to them that they are taking the adversity too seriously, that such a "big boy" or "big girl" should not be so childish. The smile between tears which appears on their faces, like a sun breaking through dark clouds, is the first indication that they begin to accept a more mature conciliatory, in fact humorous attitude and are ready to laugh about their own childishness.

The whole end phase of the analysis can be described as that under the pressure of insight the neurotic conflict situation becomes more and more circumscribed and isolated from the rest of the per-

---

[5] This explanation of depersonalization feelings corresponds to that of Freud's in his "Disturbance of Memory on the Acropolis," *Collected Papers*, New York: Basic Books, 1959, Vol. V, 302-313. Oberndorf tries to explain depersonalization from the opposite process, namely, from repression and not as Freud from the failure of repression. See C. P. Oberndorf, "On Retaining the Sense of Reality in States of Depersonalization," *Int. J. Psycho-Anal.*, XX (April, 1939), 138.

sonality. I like to refer to this phenomenon as a process of *sequestration*.

In this patient this process was very marked. At that time he perceived this unresolved wish to put himself simultaneously in his father's and in his younger brother's place as a foreign body which should be excised from his person. It was still existing in him but it was no longer an integral part of his personality. At this phase of his analysis it was only when he became drunk that he could freely indulge in acting out his old neurotic patterns. Under the influence of alcohol this newly acquired conscious integration became eliminated again and the old neurotic patterns had a chance to reassert themselves. Once in a drunken state he tried to make love in brief succession to the wives of five of his friends. It was an orgy of narcissistic competition but also of seeking for maternal love. The next day after this wild night he felt of course tired and sleepy. While dozing off during the day in his half-sleeping state he had a fantasy that in the neighbor's courtyard, the ground contained gold which he tried to appropriate during the night. Under the cover of darkness, he took out big rations of gold from the ground and hoarded it in the back of his car. He was only half asleep and immediately the idea came to his mind: "what can I do with all this gold—gold hoarding is prohibited. Moreover I have enough; why do I want to accumulate more and more of something which I cannot use?" This immediate afterthought shows that not even in the fantasy can he gratify freely his wish to have everything for himself. Immediately, the critical reaction appears that this insatiable drive for acquisition is out of place. He feels that as a fully grown adult there is no place in him for this type of infantile emotional orientation, for the wish to incorporate and retain in order to grow. The mature organism rejects these pregenital tendencies which naturally have their legitimate place in the growing organism. Here the sequestration process can be observed in its actual operation. To his naive and frank acquisitive fantasy he immediately reacts critically and this reaction contains all elements of a valid insight.

Another manifestation of this process of sequestration was a dream in which *he was to make a post-mortem study on the body of an idiot. The idiot was, however, not quite dead yet and reached out toward him. He felt some anxiety.*

The patient recognized immediately that the idiot represented a part of himself, those irrational emotional patterns which he learned to understand so well which, however, were not yet quite dead and still represented a threat for him. Indeed, it was only a few days ago when he, under the influence of alcohol, behaved in such an irrational fashion toward the wives of his friends. The process of sequestration, however, can be clearly observed. One part of his person is sharply circumscribed as a person living outside of himself and just about dying. The dominating portion of himself is the intellectual person who looks upon the neurotic mechanisms with curiosity, yet from a distance.

In this connection, it is important to emphasize that not every dream in which an ego alien tendency is projected or in which the dreamer is both acting and at the same time observing himself should be evaluated as a sequestration dream. Both projection and the split between an acting and observing self may be present in schizophrenic conditions. In such cases, however, the dynamic relationship between the split parts of personality is just the opposite to that in sequestration. In the schizophrenic projection a weak ego is exposed to a conflictful tendency which it cannot repress and therefore must project; and in schizophrenic self-observation an anemic weak ego is powerlessly observing the dynamically preponderant acting self. The ego is degraded to a pale, helpless onlooker. In the curative process of sequestration the power relationships are just the opposite. The conscious ego is steadily gaining in dynamic power, the conflictful emotional patterns become sharply delineated and the ego is able to look upon them from a distance as upon a foreign body. The relation between schizophrenic projection and self-observation on the one hand and sequestration on the other, is the same as that between neurotic depersonalization and the strange ego feeling observable during the satisfactory progress of the analysis. In depersonalization which follows a sudden breaking through of repressed tendencies the power relation between conscious control and ego alien tendencies shifts in the favor of the latter. The strange ego feeling observable when the patient, beyond his own expectations and against his usual habit, begins to act in a more controlled way, is the result of a changed power relationship between conscious control and neurotic patterns in the favor of the former.

The favorable therapeutic significance of sequestration dreams should not be overevaluated. One must not forget their wish fulfillment function. In representing the neurotic pattern as an alien and dying being the patient gives a more optimistic interpretation of his situation than is warranted. The dream expresses the wish of being already cured. It is significant, however, that such a wish should be the motive force of a dream. In a period of analysis when the patient, under the pressure of insight, is desperately struggling for mastery over his behavior and feelings, the appearance of such dreams is quite natural. They indicate, however, the direction in which the wind blows. Moreover, the personification of a neurotic emotional pattern by a dying person distinct from one's own self, is not a full distortion, merely an optimistic exaggeration.

It is important to distinguish these sequestration dreams from those which might be called pseudo-sequestration dreams. These may have a similar structure as the real ones, but in these, the patient tries to mislead the analyst—he flatters the analyst's therapeutic narcissism by pretending an improvement of his condition. The patient expresses something which he thinks his analyst would like to hear in order to escape his vigilance. In order to consider a dream as the manifestation of the progressing process of sequestration, it is necessary to take into account the whole behavior and feeling tone of the patient and not only the dreams in themselves. Particularly significant are some other reliable signs of the changing internal equilibrium, such as the paradoxical relatonship between actual behavior and dream life, a streak of humor in the patient's attitude toward his own neurotic material and the strange ego feeling, resulting from a metamorphosis in the direction of cure.

In fact, because of their wish fulfilling function, dreams alone are not quite reliable indications of the actual changes in the balance of power between the higher integrating functions and ingrained emotional patterns. Changes in the feeling tone are in this respect perhaps more revealing. The more the patient becomes accustomed to his changing self, the more the old attitudes are apt to be felt as foreign bodies which the patient wants to eliminate. This emotional reorientation is reflected both in wakeful life and also in sequestration dreams —in the latter often in a wishfully exaggerated manner. It is a challenging problem for microscopic dream studies to work out more precise criteria for evaluating both this wishful distortion and a real shift of internal power relationships during the emotional process of sequestration. Progress can be best judged by observing which of the attitudes, the newly acquired ones, or the old patterns, are dealt with as foreign bodies. For a long period, the patient may oscillate between these two sets of attitudes. In one session he may resist the change as something foreign, and the attempt at sequestration is directed against this newly won insight. This was the case when the patient whom I have described represented analytic insight in his dream actually as a foreign body, a buzzing apparatus in his mouth. The next time, however, the patient may treat not the new insight, but his old neurotic patterns as a disturbing foreign element as this patient did by representing them as a dying idiot reaching out towards him. In a well-progressing analysis with the increasing assimilation of insight by the ego, the attempts of sequestration will be more and more directed against the old conflictful patterns, rather than against the newly acquired insight.

In evaluating this well-observable process of sequestration another consideration is important. Without question the ego owes its unity to the successful elimination of the dynamic forces which it cannot reconcile with the dominating emotional patterns. When this integrating capacity is very low, the ego must use excessive measures to exclude alien tendencies. It behaves like a bad colonizer, who cannot assimilate the alien elements and must violently suppress or even exterminate them. Hysterical repression, delusional projection, compulsion neurotic isolation are examples of such excessive defense measures. When these defenses break down psychotic states of ego disintegration may ensue. On the other hand, if these methods of exclusion, particularly repression, succeed too well, an impoverishment of the ego's dynamic resources will be the result. Everyone knows some well integrated and rational, but pale and uninteresting persons among his intellectual friends. This type is eternalized in the person of Ivan Karamazov, the tepid intellectual, in contrast with the neurotic but colorful Dimitri. They pay for their self-control with the paucity of fresh and earth-bound emotional forces. Their personality is like a bureaucratically run state—orderly, but pallid. Moreover, the calmness of such a bureaucratic state is always threatened by the revolution of repressed forces.

All this explains why our therapeutic effort is aimed not at the elmination of dynamic forces from the ego, but at their incorporation in new dynamic patterns. In fact, there are no neurotic tendencies per se, only the quantitative distribution of tendencies and their dynamic organization should be called morbid. Both a morbid and a healthy ego is built of the same dynamic elements, only their quantitative distribution and combination differs. The curative processes of sequestration which I consider a common occurrence in the ending phase of the analytic therapy must be understood in this sense; not single tendencies become eliminated by sequestration but ingrained dynamic patterns which account for automatic modes of behavior. What the patient personifies in a sequestration dream as a dying being is not a single neurotic tendency, but an automatic pattern of feeling and behavior. The constituent elements of such dynamic patterns will be taken up and utilized by the ego in a new, more harmonious and flexible organization.[6] This process of reintegration is also reflected in the dream life. French called attention to the fact that dreams may be considered "premonitory of a real conflict solution that the patient will achieve perhaps very soon, perhaps only after a period of weeks or months."[7] One might refer to such dreams as dreams of resolution. Dreams of sequestration and of resolution are in a close dynamic

---

[6] See also "The Problem of Psychoanalytic Technique," in this volume.

[7] Thomas M. French, "Reality Testing in Dreams," Psychoanal. Quart., VI (1937), 1.

interrelationship to each other. This is a problem, however, which deserves a special discussion.

Although I consider the process of sequestration and its reflection in the dream life a general occurrence during progressing analytic treatment, in fact a phenomenon which is based on the dynamic principles of analytic therapy, this type of dreams may be much more pronounced in certain cases than in others. Only careful comparative studies will be able to establish in which type of patients such dreams are particularly frequent. If I try to review my experience, I would be inclined to say that they are most characteristic for the neurotic acting-out personality. Here the unconscious tendencies are not circumscribed in symptoms but diffusely permeate the total personality and find direct expression in overt behavior. These are the cases in which the patient's increasing understanding of the unconscious background of his behavior reflects itself most clearly in the dream life as a process of sequestration. What hitherto was a constituent dynamic element of the ego becomes separated and the patient can look upon it more objectively from a distance. Neuroses in which the neurotic tendencies are circumscribed in the form of pronounced symptoms, this process of sequestration is less clear. In a sense the neurotic symptom can be considered as a sequestration product, an attempt of the patient to isolate conflictful alien tendencies and drain them by symptoms. Obsessional ideas for example are felt by the patient as foreign bodies disconnected from the rest of the thought processes. Thus, symptom formation which is in itself an unconscious attempt at self-cure and the curative process of sequestration, have much in common: the difference being that symptom formation can be considered as a halted curative process. It is an isolation of neurotic tendencies which, however, is not followed by reorganization. Conflicting dynamic forces remain rigidly tied up in the symptom. For the curative process which I have discussed here, I proposed the expression "sequestration" because it consists both in the isolation and subsequent elimination of the conflict. Of course this elimination does not consist in the ejection of a diseased part as in bone sequestration, but it is a reorganization of the dynamic components of a neurotic pattern: it is not so much elimination as resorption. Sequestration is the sign that the personality is ready for such a reorganization.

During the treatment of a symptom neurosis, at first the symptoms become dissolved and transformed into neurotic behavior in the form of a transference neurosis. The transference neurosis will then be gradually undermined by insight. In this phase of the analysis, also in symptom neurosis, the process of sequestration can be observed. This explains why transference cures are so unstable. They consist in the replacement of a symptom neurosis by a neurotic attachment of the patient to the analyst. The conflictful dynamic pattern instead of being isolated in symptoms, now permeates the ego and influences interpersonal relations. Before the patient can be cured, it must be isolated again by insight, sequestered and then resolved.

Viewing the analytic procedure as such a struggle between deeply penetrating intellectual insight and ingrained emotional patterns, the technical question of termination of treatment appears from a new angle. The beginnings of psychoanalytic therapy go back to the period of cathartic hypnosis. The development of scientific concepts follows similar principles as organic evolution. Due to a certain amount of inertia in rational thinking, vestigial concepts are carried over into later phases of the evolutionary process. Even the development of a mechanical device like an automobile follows the same principle. An early model T Ford, with its short high body, still resembled a horsewagon without a horse. Gradually, the construction of the body, the wheels, the steering wheel became more adjusted to the fact that the car is not pulled by a horse but driven by a motor. Yet for a long time until the last models of streamlined cars were introduced, the running board was retained as a vestigial organ, which had only a function when the wagon was high and could not be reached with one step. Also in our analytic thinking we did not get entirely rid of the concepts of the cathartic period. One often hears analysts saying about a patient who is undergoing an analysis of two or more years duration, that he will probably "be finished" in two or three weeks from now. Long ago we dispensed with the idea of a dramatic ending in most of our cases and yet did not clearly draw the necessary conclusions from our changed views. At the beginning in cathartic hypnosis, one expected the patient to become free of his symptoms, even be cured after his pent-up emotions have been abreacted and removed in one or a few sessions. The procedure was conceived almost as an operation. Some cases of monosymptomatic hysterias and traumatic neuroses may be relieved from their symptoms in such a dramatic fashion. Shock therapy, too, attempts a similar mode of cure. In a character analysis as it is practiced at present, we visualize the therapeutic process quite differently. Insight becomes deeper, more and more comprehensive, slowly enforcing its verdict, until the emotional patterns yield and its components are gradually forced into new more satisfactory combinations. This process has no sharply limited termination. The patient does not get up one day from the couch cured. Therefore it is difficult to form an opinion as to when this process should be terminated. Since the tension between insight and emotional patterns is never resolved completely and the therapeutic process has the shape of a parabolic curve, the analysis could be continued indefinitely. On the other hand, after an insight has deeply penetrated—the patient cannot get rid of it any more—its voice is soft, its effect slow, but permanent.

Many analyses reach a phase in which the continuation of the analytic situation has, if anything, a retarding influence. After insight has taken deep roots in the personality, it is often easier for the patient's emotions to struggle against an external representative of this insight, the psychoanalyst, than against his own newly gained but deeply penetrating intellectual understanding. Reliable indications, showing that this phase of the analysis has been reached still wait for precise formulations. Such methods as the microscopic study of dreams and the careful evaluation of the patient's feeling tone, offer valuable leads to decide when a long character analysis should be terminated. The appearance of the above described type of frank and simple sequestration dreams with their latent content in sharp contrast to the improved objective behavior, is a helpful sign that the analysis has entered its final phase, particularly if such dreams occur together sometimes with a feeling of strangeness at other times with a humorous mood. Certainly such emotional reverberations of deepening insight are more vaulable indications of progress, than verbal formulations which the patient may be able to recite by heart.

Closely related to the question of termination is the device of correctly timed interruptions, recently becoming more and more popular. Long years of practice has taught me that in many cases interruptions at the right moment are not only advisable but necessary for therapeutic success. While the patient is still in analysis he is inclined to delay converting his new orientation into action. He is still a patient and this makes him feel entitled to have a neurosis. The patient and unfortunately sometimes even his analyst are still waiting for some more or less dramatic ending—the turning up of an old missing memory or the violent expression of hostile impulses or something of the like. Mostly this expectation is tacit and vague, both with patient and analyst. Yet it allows the patient to procrastinate and the physician to continue the treatment and to hope for the better. During an interruption, especially if it is of sufficiently long duration, and the resumption of the analysis is promised only conditionally, many patients become more determined to overcome their difficulties. It is true that not having the pressure of the analysis, they may be tempted to try once more living according to the old patterns. The result of such regressions of course is the revival of old neurotic suffering without the relief of the daily analytic sessions. The analyst is not there but the insight which the patient has won during the analysis *is* there and he cannot discard it. In his emotional stress he must enforce his insight alone without the support of the analyst. This increases the feeling of freedom and independence. The analyst is not there but the insight which the patient has won becomes practical reality. This is comparable with the situation of a swimmer who has learned the strokes theoretically and then finds himself in the water and has to make use of what he has learned. It is important that he be left alone to his own resources. Of course, we may find it often necessary to continue the analysis after an interruption. My experience is that after such a resumption of the treatment, frequently more is accomplished in a few weeks than has been in many months in the last period of the analysis. During the interruption the patient becomes convinced that he must reorient himself if he wants to get rid of his neurotic suffering. This is often necessary to break down deeply rooted defenses. A long drawn out analysis often lulls the patient into a pseudo-wellbeing. The insight is still somewhat of a platonic nature and the neurotic suffering, particularly anxiety, is relieved through the transference situation. The interruption disturbs this equilibrium. Of course it must be correctly timed after insight has taken deep hold of the patient.

Viewing the analytic procedure from this point of view we clearly realize that the struggle of old emotional patterns against newly won insight is never ended either in normals or in neurotics. Psychoanalysis introduces new insight which will exert its influence upon the patient long after he has left the couch. He is not cured on the couch. The effect of psychoanalysis continues after he left his analyst. In fact, in most cases, the greatest part of the curative process takes place after the treatment.

Analysis of the Therapeutic Factors in Psychoanalytic Treatment

◄ 1950 ►

Observations made during the therapeutic procedure are the primary source of psychoanalytic knowledge. Most of our knowledge of psychodynamics stems from this source. Precise understanding of the therapeutic factors is significant both for improving our therapeutic techniques and also for increasing our theoretical knowledge. Between theory and therapy there is a reciprocal relationship: observations made during treatment are the main source of our theoretical knowledge, and we apply our theoretical formulations to improve our technique.

This presentation is based on the premise that much in our therapeutic procedure is still empirical, and that many of the processes which take place in patients during psychoanalysis are not yet fully understood.

In particular, there is divergence of opinion concerning 1) the relative therapeutic value of the patient's intellectual insight into the origin and nature of his neurosis; 2) the relative value of emotional discharge (abreaction); 3) the role of emotional experiences during treatment as they evolve in the transference; 4) the role of parallel experiences in life; 5) the significance of the time factor (frequency of interviews, technical interruptions, length of the treatment). The last question is practical and the answer to it depends both on clinical experience and on the clarification of the first four.

One of the basic observations on which Freud's theoretical structure was built was the therapeutic value of emotional abreaction in hypnosis. Emotionally charged, forgotten memories appeared with dramatic expression of the repressed emotions. Substituting barbiturates for hypnosis, this principle was widely applied to war neuroses during and after the recent war.

261

The second step was the recognition that abreaction alone has no permanent curative value; that the ego must face and learn to handle the repressed emotions. The emphasis was on insight. There followed then the period in which Freud's therapeutic interest was focused on reconstructing the traumatic events of the past and making the patient understand and remember them. Reconstructions and interpretations of past pertinent events had to be understood and accepted by the patients in order to be cured.

The third step was the discovery of the transference which shifted the emphasis again to emotional experience and expression. This is, of course, an oversimplification. Actually, abreaction, insight and transference have long been considered in their interrelationships, and only the emphasis has changed from time to time with different authors. One element, however, was common to all these views: the insistence upon the necessity of making repressed material conscious. In hypnosis, repressed material was mobilized by reducing the ego's defenses. During the period in which free association was used, but before the importance of the transference was clearly recognized, the therapist's intellectual understanding was imparted to the patient in the hope that this intellectual insight would enable the patient to face what he repressed. The recognition of the transference led to a better understanding of the therapeutic processes as well as a more effective therapy. In the transference, the original pathogenic conflicts of the early family relationships are repeated with lesser intensity. This is what is called the "transference neurosis." The emotional re-enactment in relation to the therapist of the crucial conflicts gradually increases the ego's capacity to face these conflicts. One may say, it increases the ego's permeability to the repressed material. Freud's formulation was that in the transference the stronger adult ego faces the same but less intensive conflicts which the weaker infantile ego had to repress. This dynamic equation represents the essence of our present views of therapy: in childhood the weak ego faces overwhelming emotions; in the transference the adult's stronger ego faces a weaker edition of the original conflict. Accordingly, the treatment ultimately aims at changing the ego to enable it to resolve conflicts with which it could not cope before. The method by which this change in the ego is achieved is a kind of gradual learning through practice—by exposing the ego, step by step, to conflicts as they emerge in the course of treatment. At the same time the defenses of the ego against repressed material are reduced by making them explicit by precise verbalization. This process—commonly termed "working through"—can be described as a kind of emotional gymnastics.

The course of most successful treatments can be visualized as a gradually increasing capacity of the patient to recognize and express repressed psychological content. The simplest example is the depressive patient who gradually becomes able to recognize and express his hostility directed toward an ambivalently loved person. This increased ability to express repressed material is achieved primarily by the analyst's recognizing and verbalizing the slightest manifestations of the patient's repressed emotions and of his defenses against these emotions. An interpretation of hostility expressed against the analyst, which is given objectively and without any resentment, encourages its freer expression by the patient. By helping the patient to verbalize without judging and evaluating what the patient could not express, the analyst encourages the patient's becoming conscious of repressed content. The original repression of hostility was a response to parental influences. The analyst assumes a role different from that of the parents. He is emotionally not involved. This difference makes possible what we have called the corrective emotional experience.[1]

According to this view, the intensity of the transference should have a certain optimal level. This is supported by the common observation that if the emotional involvement of the patient is insufficient, the treatment may be greatly retarded and the analysis becomes merely an intellectual exercise. If, however, the transference neurosis becomes too intense, the patient's ego may face a situation similar to the one which it could not meet originally. It is well known and well demonstrated by Köhler's[2] and French's[3] contributions that the ego's integrative functions are impeded by excessive emotion. Violent anxiety, rage, or guilt may become so formidable that the ego's coordinating functions cannot master them. From this it must be evident that one of the aims of therapy is to keep the transference on an optimal level.

A common type of unsuccessful analysis is due to the development of a too intensive dependent transference from which the patient cannot be dislodged. The analyst's hope that further working through eventually will resolve this dependent attachment, as well as the patient's own procrastinating tendency, collaborate to produce this therapeutic impasse. The neurotic is inclined to side-step renewed attempts to cope with life, retreats into fantasy, produces symptoms. During the treatment he exchanges symptoms for a

[1] Franz Alexander, Thomas M. French, et al., "The Principle of Corrective Emotional Experience," in Psychoanalytic Therapy, Principles and Application, New York: Ronald Press, 1946, p. 66.

[2] Wolfgang Köhler, The Mentality of Apes, London: Kegan Paul, Trench, Trubner, 1931.

[3] T. M. French, "A Clinical Study of Learning in the Course of a Psychoanalytic Treatment," Psychoanal. Quart., V (1936), 148-194.

neurotic transference relationship but resists abandoning this newly acquired substitute for his neurosis for new attempts in life. Thus the situation develops to which Freud tersely referred by saying that the patient's wish to be cured gradually changes into his wish to be treated.[4] Since with certain types of chronic neurotics this development is a common one, the problem how to avoid this danger is obviously one of the important problems of psychoanalytic technique.

The question how to keep the analysis on a transference level of optimal intensity, particularly how to avoid a too intensive dependent relationship resulting in an interminable analysis, leads us to the quantitative aspects of the psychoanalytic treatment. These we shall discuss in the light of the previous formulation of the therapeutic process and of the corrective emotional experience.

We start from Freud's emphasis on the fact that in the transference the patient's adult ego is given opportunity to face those emotional situations which it could not manage in childhood when the ego was weaker. The weak ego had to repress these emotions which therefore remained excluded from the ego's integrative activity. The emphasis is on the difference between the integrative powers of the adult and the immature ego. The other important fact, according to Freud, is that the repetition of the old conflict in the transference is of lesser intensity. Its intensity is reduced because the transference emotions are reactions to previous experiences and not to the actual patient-physician relation. The only actual relationship between the patient and doctor is that the patient comes to the physician for help. It is only in the patient's mind that the therapist assumes the role of the father or mother or of an older or younger sibling. The most important consideration in this connection is that neurotic patterns do not develop in a vacuum; they are adaptive reactions to parental attitudes. In the transference the original interpersonal relationship between child and parent is re-established only so far as the patient is concerned. The crucial therapeutic factor is that the analyst's reactions are different from those of the parents. The simplest example is the repression of self-assertive and aggressive attitudes due to parental intimidation which encourages dependence and causes all kinds of inhibitions in human relations. In the transference the therapist's attitude must reverse that of the intimidating parent. The fact that the patient's aggressions are met objectively without emotional response or retaliation on the part of the analyst corrects the original intimidating influence of the parent. The parental intimidation is undone by the more tolerant and sym-

---

[4] Sigmund Freud, "Further Recommendations in the Technique of Psychoanalysis," in *Collected Papers*, New York: Basic Books, 1959, Vol. II, 342-366.

pathetic attitude of the therapist who replaces the authoritarian parent in the patient's mind. As the patient realizes that his modest self-assertion will not be punished, he will experiment more boldly and express himself more freely toward persons in authority in his daily life. This increases the ego's capacity to deal with aggressive attitudes which anxiety had previously repressed. This is actually a much more complicated process but this simple example may serve to explain the principle of corrective emotional experience. Parental intimidation, however, is not the only form of pathogenic experience. Parental overindulgence, emotional rejection, and ambivalence are of equal importance.

As soon as we clearly recognize the specific problem of the patient, it becomes possible to work consistently toward the right kind of corrective experience. It is generally assumed that the objective and understanding attitude of the therapist alone is sufficient to produce such a corrective emotional experience. No doubt, the most important therapeutic factor in psychoanalysis is the objective and yet helpful attitude of the therapist, something which does not exist in any other relationship. Parents, friends, relatives, may be helpful but they are always emotionally involved. Their attitude may be sympathetic but never objective and never primarily understanding. To experience such a novel human relationship in itself has a tremendous therapeutic significance which cannot be overrated. The old reaction patterns do not fit into this new human relationship. This explains why the patient's behavior in the transference becomes a one-sided shadowboxing. The old patterns developed as reactions to parental attitudes and lose their sense in the transference relationship. This compels the patient gradually to change and to revise his neurotic patterns. He deals with someone who neither resents his aggressions nor feels guilty like a parent who overindulges the child because of his unconscious rejection of the child. Under the influence of his unimpaired critical judgment, which we assume in a non-psychotic individual, the patient will be gradually forced to learn new emotional patterns which fit into this new experience. The old reactions fitted and had sense only in the family. No doubt, therefore, the objective, understanding attitude of the analyst in itself is a most powerful therapeutic factor. This attitude, combined with correct interpretation of material which is about to emerge from repression, together with the analysis of the ego's defenses, is primarily responsible for the therapeutic effectiveness of psychoanalysis. This effectiveness, in comparison with all other methods in psychiatry, is so impressive that it is easy to be satisfied with all this and forget about those aspects of therapy which require further improvement. What I mean primarily is the question, how economic is this procedure? In other words, can its effectiveness still be increased and the length of treatment reduced?

My experience is that the objective and helpful attitude of the analyst allows, without any artificial play acting, ample opportunity for modifying the patient-therapist relationship in such a way that it will facilitate and intensify the corrective emotional experience. I have described the treatment of a forty-two-year-old patient suffering from hysterical convulsions, impotence and a severe character neurosis which was about to break up his marriage.[5] The essential factor in this case was an overbearing, tyrannical father who succeeded completely in undermining this patient's self-confidence and normal self-assertion. The patient had, as a defense, developed an overbearing attitude in his home and treated his family, particularly his son, as he was treated by his own father. The treatment consisted of twenty-six interviews over a ten-week period with satisfactory results. Not only have all his symptoms disappeared including the convulsions and his impotence, but his attitude toward his son and wife has changed. The wife, who had decided to divorce him, reversed her decision. This patient's case has been followed up. After four years he is still married, his symptoms have not returned and there are only occasional relapses into irritability and impatience toward his son, an attitude which he is able to control. I do not quote this case because of the therapeutic result, unusual because of the small number of interviews. I quote it because it is a simple example of corrective emotional experience. This was achieved by creating an emotional atmosphere in the transference which was particularly suited to reverse the original intimidating influence of the patient's father. My attitude was not simply objective and helpful; it was consistently tolerant and definitely encouraging, exactly the opposite of his father's attitude. While the father was overbearing and omniscient, the analyst emphasized repeatedly the limitations of psychiatry and of his own knowledge, encouraging the patient to express his disagreement with interpretations. The father had been extremely critical of the patient; the analyst openly displayed admiration of certain of the patient's qualities. This was of course all within the limits of the usual attitude of the analyst, but I gave a definite emotional coloring to the transference, which might be criticized as not psychoanalytic but psychotherapeutic because of its openly encouraging connotation. This entirely new situation which he had never encountered was most embarrassing for the patient. He did not know how to react to it. At first he tried in his dreams to make the analyst a replica of his domineering father. In one, the

[5] Alexander, French, *et al.*, *op. cit.*

analyst smashed glassware the patient had manufactured which reminded him of the time his father, a glass manufacturer, in violent rage had smashed glassware because he had not liked the design. After these distortions had been interpreted, the patient desperately tried to provoke the analyst to act as his father did. When all this failed he gradually began to change his own behavior.

In another case, the corrective emotional experience was provoked by a different departure from the conventional psychoanalytic attitude on the therapist's part. The patient was a young university student who was unable to apply himself to his studies. He idled about, spent a great part of the day in bed, masturbated excessively, read cheap detective stories and was unable to form any meaningful social relations. He had no attachments to women, frequented poolrooms and felt quite miserable about his purposeless way of living. His "laziness" was the symptom of a latent compulsion neurosis. During his first consultation he justified his idleness by stating that his father never loved him and never gave him anything of value; therefore, his father should support him. In his first analytic session he reported a dream: *"I wanted to sell my diamond ring but the jeweler after testing the stone declared it was false."*

He immediately remarked that the dream was silly because he knew that his ring was genuine. In the course of further associations it transpired that the ring was a present from his father. The dream expressed transparently the patient's defensive formula that he had never received anything of value from his father; hence, the motive for proving in his dream that his father's gift was spurious. His whole neurotic structure was founded on the belief that he owed nothing to his father.

External circumstances forced him to move from the city and he was transferred to another analyst who died after a short period. He continued with another analyst, and a few months later he asked me for an interview. He complained that his analyst disliked him because, continuation of treatment was impossible. The analyst was always polite and kindly, but he felt that this was all calculated play acting. In reality, he said, the therapist hated him. I talked with his analyst who, to my surprise, substantiated the patient's story: he felt a strong aversion to the patient which he tried his best to conceal. He urged me and I agreed to continue the treatment. I soon understood my predecessor's prejudice. The patient did everything to make himself disagreeable. He usually arrived unwashed, unshaven and unkempt, bit his nails, spoke in a scarcely intelligible mumble, criticized everything, and paid a very low fee. If I kept him waiting a minute he immediately accused me of doing so because he paid less than others. He was so unpleasant in every possible way that it was difficult to tolerate him. One day I spoke to him somewhat impatiently. He jumped up from the couch and exclaimed, "You are just like your colleague. Do you deny that you dislike me and do you call it analysis being impatient with your patient?" I realized that I had better admit my dislike of him. He was extremely perturbed by this admission. I explained that his behavior was unconsciously calculated and succeeded in making him disliked. He wanted to prove that just as his father supposedly disliked him, the analyst also rejected him; this allowed him to feel hostile and continue his old neurotic pattern of life. I reminded him of the dream about the diamond ring. This session became a dramatic turning point of this analysis, which before had begun to appear a stalemate. He became well groomed, and tried to be as pleasant as possible. He started to apply himself to his studies and to organize his daily activities.

In this case the corrective emotional experience was, in a sense, opposite to the one previously described. This patient had an indulgent father to whom his son was the apple of his eye. He supported him freely without reproach, although during his schooling he did not apply himself to his studies. This paternal indulgence created intolerable feelings of guilt in the boy who, as a defense, tried to persuade himself that his father really disliked him.

In the dramatic interview in which he discovered my dislike for him, it suddenly became clear to him that the situation with his father could not be repeated; that it was a unique relationship, and that no one but his indulgent father would love him despite all his provocations. He realized that to be loved he must make himself worthy of love; furthermore, the guilt feelings resulting from his father's goodness diminished with the analyst's open admission of his dislike. At the end of his analysis this patient was very appreciative, presenting the analyst with a photograph of his new self. Years later he called on me. He had become successful and was married happily. Every experienced analyst has had similar experiences. The case is noteworthy because of the dynamics of the patient's remarkable improvement which was induced not by the usual understanding objective attitude of the analyst but by an involuntary display of his irritation.

The analyst's reaction was not calculated to be different from that of the patient's father. He simply lost, for a moment, the type of control which we consider so important in psychoanalytic therapy. I do not want to imply that in general this control is not necessary. My point is that the knowledge of the early interpersonal attitudes which contributed to a patient's neurosis can help the analyst to assume intentionally a kind of attitude which is conducive to provoking the kind of emotional experience in the patient which is suited to undo the pathogenic effect of the original parental attitude. Such intensive revelatory emotional experiences give us the clue for those puzzling therapeutic results which are obtained in a considerably shorter time than is usual in psychoanalysis. The important question facing us is whether it is possible in many cases to manage the transference in a way to precipitate such intensive revelatory experiences. At present it is difficult to generalize about how such intensive revelatory experiences can be provoked. One thing is obvious: the corrective emotional experience is possible only after the intrapsychic conflict has been reconverted into an interpersonal relationship in the transference and the introjected parental influences are projected upon the analyst; in other words, when the original neurosis has been transformed into a transference neurosis. This aim is most difficult to achieve in severe compulsion neurotics in whom the original child-parent relationship is completely incorporated in the personality in a complex intrapsychic conflict between the different structural parts of the personality. This keeps the intensity of the transference on a relatively low level and the whole therapeutic procedure tends to become overintellectualized. In such cases, patient, prolonged preliminary work is often required before the intrapsychic neurotic system is disrupted and transformed into a neurotic interpersonal relationship.

This whole problem is closely related to the countertransference. The proposition made here is that the analyst should attempt to replace his spontaneous countertransference reactions with attitudes which are consciously planned and adopted according to the dynamic exigencies of the therapeutic situation. This requires the analyst's awareness of his spontaneous countertransference reactions, his ability to control them and substitute for them responses which are conducive to correcting the pathogenic emotional influences in the patient's past. Occasionally, as in the case of the student, the spontaneous countertransference reaction of the analyst is accidentally the desirable attitude, but this is a rare exception. As a rule spontaneous countertransference reactions of the analyst resemble parental attitudes. The analyst, like the parents, is apt to react with positive feelings to the patient's flattery, with helpful attitude and sympathy to the patient's suffering, and with resentment to the patient's provocative behavior as the parents did. Even if he does not give overt expression to his countertransference, the patient may sense it. Since the phenomenon of countertransference has been recognized, we know that a completely objective attitude of the analyst exists only in theory no matter how painstakingly he may try to live up to this requirement. The main point is, however, that within the framework of the mainly objective atmosphere of the psychoanalytic situation, there is sufficient opportunity for replacing the spontaneous countertransference reactions with well-defined and designed attitudes which facilitate the patient's own emotional reorientation. In this connection, it should be considered that the objective, detached attitude of the psychoanalyst itself is an adopted, studied attitude and is not a spontaneous reaction to the patient. It is not more difficult for the analyst to create a definite emotional climate, such as consistent permissiveness or a stronghand, as the patient's dynamic situation requires.

Having presented the corrective emotional experience as the dynamic axis of the treatment, let us turn to the other well-established therapeutic factors and first examine the therapeutic importance of recovered memories.

After Freud abandoned hypnosis, his main interest lay in reconstructing the early emotional development by resolving the "infantile amnesia." When he substituted free association for hypnosis, he tried to induce the patient to recall repressed traumatic memories. At this time all his interest was focused upon tracing the genesis of neurosis and of personality development in general. He had first to understand the natural history of neuroses in order to develop a sensible method of treatment. It was a lucky circumstance that this etiological study of the individual's past history coincided, partially at least, with therapeutic aims. Both required recovery of forgotten memories and this became for a time the main therapeutic device. He came only gradually to realize the therapeutic significance of transference and the importance of the patient's reliving, not merely recalling, his early conflicts. His first impression, however, was so strong that the belief in the primary therapeutic significance of genetic reconstruction was perpetuated.[6]

We know now that the recovery of memories is a sign of improvement rather than its cause. As the ego's capacity to cope with repressed emotions increases through experience in the transference, the patient is able to remember repressed events because of their similar emotional connotations. The ability to remember shows the ego's increased capacity to face certain types of psychological content. This change in the ego is achieved through the emotional experiences of the treatment, although it cannot be denied that remembering and understanding the origin of neurotic patterns have a therapeutic influence and help the reintegration of repressed psychological content into the total personality.

The therapeutic evaluation of intellectual insight is probably

[6] The importance of genetic understanding in relation to emotional experience is discussed further on.

one of the most difficult problems of the theory of treatment. We used to distinguish three therapeutic factors: abreaction, insight, and working through. *Abreaction* means the free expression of repressed emotions. *Insight* was considered to be effective only when it coincided with emotional abreaction. As Freud expressed it, "An enemy cannot be licked who is not seen." The patient must feel what he understands, otherwise he could be cured by a textbook. *Working through* refers to the repetitive, more and more precise verbalization of all the details of the emotional patterns, including abreaction and insight, during analysis as the ego's defensive measures are gradually reduced. It consists of experiencing and understanding each aspect of the neurosis as it is revealed under treatment and as the patient's resistance to self-expression diminishes.

In evaluating the mutual relation of these three factors in therapy, it is important to realize that often quite definite changes in the emotional pattern can be observed in patients without intellectual formulation by the analyst or patient. The corrective emotional experience in the transference alone may produce lasting therapeutic results. A purely intellectual understanding of the neurosis has seldom much therapeutic effect. On the other hand, intellectual insight based on and combined with emotional experiences stabilizes emotional gains and paves the way for new emotional experiences. The ego's basic function is mastery of impulses through integration. This is the essence of the function we call understanding. Understanding gives the patient a feeling of mastery, and this in turn encourages mobilization of repressed material which before could not be mastered by integration with the rest of the conscious personality. Through insight the ego is prepared to face emerging unconscious material and is not taken by surprise when it actually appears in consciousness. This explains the common observation that the same interpretation which was given repeatedly during treatment and which seemingly has left the patient completely unimpressed, one day provokes a revelatory emotional response. This happens when the previous, merely intellectual understanding of repressed material becomes combined with emotional experiences of the same material as it emerges from repression. The previous interpretations were, however, not without effect: they paved the way for the emotional experience. Intellectualization by interpretation of content, however, in certain cases must be avoided as much as possible. The substitution of understanding for feeling is one of the principal defenses of the compulsive personality. In such cases the corrective emotional experiences must be achieved without too much intellectual preparation. The patient must experience his basic ambivalence toward the analyst which can be facilitated if the analyst's own spontaneous emotional reactions, which the patient's ambivalence has provoked, are kept under control and are replaced by a well-planned attitude.

It is universally accepted that the central therapeutic issue consists in the mobilization of unconscious material. Only if the ego is actually confronted with those impulses which it could not handle before except by repression, can the patient learn to handle such impulses. The defenses of the ego originally developed under the influence of personal relationships: parental intimidation, overindulgence, guilt, ambivalence, rejection, and unconscious seduction are the most common etiological factors. Intellectual insight into the nature of the ego defenses alone is not sufficient to abolish their influence. The emotional content of the patient-physician relationship, the fact that the therapist's attitude is different from the original parental attitudes, is the major dynamic factor which allows repressed material to become conscious.

In the light of this discussion, certain quantitative factors in therapy—those therapeutic measures by which an optimal level of the transference neurosis may be achieved—can be evaluated.

Experience shows that the transference neurosis develops spontaneously as the result of continued contact with the therapist. The outlook for a prolonged treatment favors the patient's procrastination and disinclination to face the problems from which he escaped into neurosis. The transference neurosis soon loses many of the unpleasant features of the original neurosis because it is seen to be a necessary part of the treatment, and the conflicts provoked by the regressive tendencies are reduced by the analyst's attitude. This allows the patient to be neurotic during treatment without too much conflict. Reducing the frequency of interviews is one of the simplest means of preventing the transference from becoming too powerful an outlet for the patient's neurosis: by frustration, the dependent strivings become conscious and the patient is compelled to resist them consciously.

Whenever the patient's ego shows signs of need for emotional support, increasing the frequency of interviews may be indicated. In doing so, however, one must be aware that allowing the patient a greater dependent gratification is a tactical concession which the therapist has to make at the moment, but which will increase some time later the task of weaning. It is unwise to generalize, and experience and skill are required to estimate when and how to reduce or increase the frequency of the sessions. In many cases it is advisable to see the patient once, twice, or three times a week, instead of daily, to prevent too much dependence.

Reducing the frequency of the interviews is probably the most effective application of the principle of abstinence. It prevents the unnoticed hidden gratification of dependent needs thus forcing them to become conscious. This principle was most consistently developed by Ferenczi, who pointed out that denying the patient just that satisfaction which he most intensively desires has proven most useful in producing pertinent unconscious material.[7] According to this principle, the patient's dependence upon the analyst becomes conscious through curtailing its gratification. Were a person fed every half hour, he would never become conscious of feeling hunger. The patient's dependence upon the analyst, gratified by the routine of daily interviews on which the patient can count indefinitely, may never become conscious with sufficient vividness if the sessions are not reduced in some phase of the analysis. Everyone knows the stimulating influence of an unplanned cancellation of an interview upon the production of unconscious material. Vacations which are undertaken in the therapist's and not in the patient's interest may also have such an effect. My point is that we should not leave this important therapeutic tool to chance but use it systematically whenever the patient's analytic situation requires.

Longer interruptions have a somewhat different therapeutic function. In the early twenties Eitingon made experiments with interrupted analyses in the outpatient clinic of the Berlin Psychoanalytic Institute. Since then this device has been systematically tested in the Chicago Institute for Psychoanalysis.[8]

Interruptions of shorter or longer duration have the function of increasing the patient's self-confidence. During the interruptions he will have to apply independently in life what he gained during the treatment. The tendency of the neurotic is to avoid renewed attempts to cope with the life situation from which he retreated into fantasy and symptom formation. Interruptions counteract the patient's tendency to postpone indefinitely the solution of his problems. They are one of the strongest weapons against perpetuating the transference neurosis indefinitely. Interruptions must be imposed tentatively, since there is no way of telling exactly when the patient is ready to accept them without relapsing.

One must remember that the patient, while he is being analyzed, continues his ordinary life. It is true that many of his neurotic needs will be gratified in the transference. This as a rule allows the patient to behave less neurotically outside. On the other hand, the

[7] Ferenczi, S., "The Further Development of an Active Therapy in Psychoanalysis," in *Further Contributions to the Theory and Technique of Psychoanalysis,* London: Hogarth, 1926, 201, 202.

[8] Alexander, French, *et al.,* "The Principle of Flexibility. Interruptions and Termination of Treatment," *op. cit.,* 35.

therapist must not allow the patient to withdraw his attention from his outside relationships and to escape completely into the therapeutic situation. Originally the patient came to the therapist with current problems. The transference allowed him to relieve the pressure of these current problems by retreating from life into the shadow world of the transference. There must be a constant pressure to keep the patient in contact with his actual problems in life from which he only too readily has withdrawn into the transference. It is not realistic to expect that a patient, who has postponed the solution of his real problems for months or years and withdrawn into the relatively isolated world of transference, will one day suddenly return a well-adjusted person to the world of reality. While the patient works through his resistances and becomes able to express more and more frankly in the transference his neurotic attitudes, he learns gradually to modify them at first in relation to the analyst and later also in his extra-analytic human relationships. The latter takes place to some degree automatically but the neurotic tendency is to delay the attack upon his actual problems. A steady pressure must be exerted upon the patient to apply every analytical gain to his life outside the analysis. The analytic process cannot be divided into two separate phases: first, one which encourages the development of the transference neurosis and, second, one in which the patient is induced to return with modified attitudes to the solution of his actual problems. The two must take place more or less simultaneously.

Another significance of extratherapeutic experiences was first explicitly emphasized by Edoardo Weiss.[9] The transference cannot always repeat all the neurotic patterns of a patient. Some aspects of his neurosis he will of necessity re-enact in his life; moreover, it is often advantageous to relieve too intensive positive or negative emotional attitudes within the transference by taking advantage of corresponding extra-analytic interpersonal relationships. In the Chicago Institute for Psychoanalysis, some of the members of the staff believe that in some cases most of the patient's problems can be worked out by the analysis of the extratherapeutic experiences, and that a real transference neurosis can be avoided. I personally lean toward the view that a well-defined transference neurosis is not only unavoidable but desirable in most cases.

Summary

The need for re-evaluation of the psychodynamic factors operative during treatment is emphasized. According to the view pre-

[9] Weiss, Edoardo, "Emotional Memories and Acting Out," *Psychoanal. Quart.*, XI (1942), 477-492.

sented, the dynamic axis of psychoanalytic therapy is the corrective emotional experience which the patient obtains in the transference. The significant factor is not only that the patient relives his original conflicts in his relationship with the analyst, but that the analyst does not react as the parents did. His reactions should correct the pathogenic effects of the parental attitudes. The objective, understanding attitude of the analyst in itself is so different from that of the parents that this alone necessitates a change in the patient's original atitudes. If the analyst succeeds in reconstructing precisely the original pathogenic parental attitude, he may facilitate the occurrence of intensive corrective emotional experiences by assuming an attitude toward the patient opposite to that of the most relevant pathogenic attitude which prevailed in the past. This does not consist in artificial play acting but in creating an emotional atmosphere which is conducive to undoing the traumatic effects of early family influences. The corrective emotional experience is the most powerful factor in making the patient's original ego defenses unnecessary and thus allowing the mobilization and emergence into consciousness of repressed material. It helps the patient's ego to assume a modified attitude toward hitherto repressed or inhibited impulses. Other important technical measures serve to keep the transference on an optimal level, such as changing the frequency of interviews according to the state of the analysis, correctly timed interruptions, and encouraging the required kind of extratherapeutic experiences.

Our experience in the Chicago Institute for Psychoanalysis is that with the consistent observance of these principles and technical measures the treatment becomes more effective and economical.[10] Although the total duration of the treatment as a rule is not spectacularly shortened, the actual number of interviews can be substantially reduced in the great majority of cases. The principle which is stressed is that of flexibility in preference to routine. Briefness, in so far as the total duration of the treatment is concerned, does not characterize this approach.

Naturally the personality of the analyst and his sex are of great importance for creating the kind of emotional atmosphere and experiences in the transference which are most conducive to reversing the adverse influences in the patient's past. The selection of an analyst for each patient is an involved problem and requires special consideration.

Reasons are submitted for the urgent need for a careful reexamination of the therapeutic process.

[10] Alexander, French, et al., op. cit.

Current Views
on Psychotherapy

◀ 1953 ▶

Psychotherapy as a systematic method of treatment based on a knowledge of mental illness is one of the latest developments in medicine; psychotherapy as an emotional support offered to a suffering patient is as old as medicine itself. In fact, emotional support is a universal component of human relationships. Everyone who tries to encourage a despondent friend or to reassure a panicky child practices psychotherapy. These common measures employed in daily life are not merely empirical—as are the home remedies for bodily ailments, which are used without any understanding of the symptoms they are intended to cure. Psychotherapeutic home remedies are based on a common-sense understanding of human nature.

People have always known intuitively that they could calm down a worrying person by listening patiently to his story, even though it is only recently that the relief obtained from such an unloading has become known as abreaction, in scientific jargon. People have long known that a reassuring, friendly, and somewhat authoritative attitude toward a confused, frightened person was helpful; they have known, as a matter of common sense, that such a person needed to lean on someone else. Today psychiatrists formulate this knowledge by saying that the ego's integrative capacity is lowered under the influence of fear. In the same way, it has long been recognized that an enraged person may be more reasonable after he has given vent to his feelings; today, the psychiatrist would say that rage, like fear, narrows the integrative capacity of the ego, and that it can be relieved by allowing the person to express it. The point which I want to stress is that prescientific knowledge of human nature is a well-developed faculty which every healthy person possesses without any systematic learning. In fact, without it one could not survive in social life.

Every science consists in the improvement of common-sense

276

knowledge. For example, physics and chemistry are based on improvements of both common-sense observations and common-sense reasoning; however, the improvements in these sciences were so fundamental that the results are often directly contradictory to the pre-scientific knowledge of nature, as is best exemplified by modern cosmology. Similarly in psychology the results of systematic observations and reasoning are steadily increasing the gap between common sense and scientific knowledge. It is often overlooked, however, that psychology, while it still has many real methodological shortcomings, started from a more advanced level of common-sense knowledge than did the physical sciences, since in psychology the observer and the observed are of the same kind. In physics and chemistry, when the observer deals with the behavior of material objects in time and space, he must rely entirely on his observations, because he does not know from firsthand experience how the objects will behave. If he throws an object into the water, he cannot, by means of common sense, predict whether it will sink or float. He must know its specific weight, and the establishing of this requires a long series of systematic measurements plus a hydrodynamic theory.

When we observe another person's behavior, however, because the object of our observation is another human being, we can put ourselves in his place, or, as we say today, we can "identify" ourselves with him; and thus we can predict with fair accuracy what he will do next because we know how we would act in a similar situation. This is one of the reasons why psychotherapy can be practiced with a fair degree of success even by a person who does not know much about the theory of personality and psychoneurosis, so long as he has what is called a "good common-sense knowledge of human nature." This is why the field of psychotherapy, until very recently, has been a free-for-all. Only very recently has there been a definite transition from common-sense psychotherapy, practiced by anyone who thinks he can do it, to so-called scientific psychotherapy as a medical specialty. Even today, the claim of medical psychotherapy that it is superior to the emotional help given in everyday life is still questioned by many people, whether well-educated or ignorant. This claim is based, however, on the fact that a systematic knowledge exists today of human personality and its disturbances—a knowledge which is derived from systematic and refined methods of psychological observation and reasoning.

With these introductory remarks I have referred to a new and fundamental trend—namely, the use of psychotherapy as an etiologically oriented method of treatment which requires specific knowledge and training. The fact that this knowledge is derived from psychoanalysis has occasioned heated disagreements among psychoanalysts regarding the relationship of psychoanalytic therapy to other forms of psychotherapy. The fact that psychoanalysis has developed outside of academic medicine and psychiatry so that some rivalry of necessary exists between psychoanalysts on the one hand and academic psychiatrists and physicians on the other is only partially responsible for the high emotional temperature characteristic of these controversies. Another element in these controversies is the fact that many psychoanalysts grew up in an era in which psychoanalysis was regarded with mistrust and emotional bias by academic psychiatry, so that these analysts in turn have come to feel a mistrust of academic psychiatry and have preferred to practice and develop their science apart from the medical fraternity. They have felt that psychoanalysis could not be accepted in an undiluted form by those outsiders who were not psychoanalyzed themselves, because of emotional resistance. These psychoanalysts have felt that they must keep the teaching and practice of psychoanalysis under their own control. They have lost sight of the fact that psychotherapy is older than psychoanalysis and is the traditional domain of the psychiatrist. Thus it has been difficult for many of us as psychoanalysts to recognize the radical changes which have gradually transformed the whole scene around us, so that psychoanalysis is no longer regarded with the same mistrust. In fact, Freud, who is said to have disturbed the sleep of humanity, has in our own time thoroughly succeeded in awakening a great part of it.

Psychiatrists have come to recognize more and more the fundamental nature of Freud's discoveries; and psychiatric practice is at present highly influenced both directly and indirectly by psychoanalysis. Many of us as psychoanalysts feel that this change in the cultural climate has changed our role and responsibility. Now, when psychiatry is not only ready but eager to assimilate in an undiluted form the teachings of Freud and the work of his followers, we feel that it becomes our responsibility to guide and facilitate this process of incorporation. For this process is steadily going on in this country, and, aside from sporadic resistances, the emotional barriers are rapidly disappearing. Thus it is now rather generally accepted, both by analysts and by nonanalytic psychiatrists, that psychoanalytic concepts—the theoretical knowledge of psychodynamics and neurosis formation— are necessary for every psychiatrist and make up one of the basic sciences of psychiatry. Since psychoanalytic theory has become the common property of the whole of medicine, the identity of psychoanalysis as an isolated discipline now rests almost exclusively on the ability to distinguish the specific nature of psychoanalytic therapy.

I am one of those psychoanalysts who firmly believe that the absorption of psychoanalytic theory and techniques into the field of psychiatry, in particular, and medicine, in general, will become com-

plete in the not-too-distant future, for this course of events is dictated
by the immanent logic of the field. Yet I must admit that there are
great practical problems to be solved before this unification can be
consummated. First, the preparation for psychoanalytic practice requires more than theoretical instruction and experience; it requires the
personal analysis of the student as a preparatory step in order that he
may master the technique intellectually, and be free from disturbing
emotional involvements of his own in handling patients. Yet the inclusion of the personal analysis in the academic curriculum of all psychiatrists offers many complications which are well known and needs
no further discussion here.

A related difficulty arises from the practical dictates of policy on
the part of the psychoanalyst. The psychoanalyst, because of his different training background, feels it important to preserve his identity,
and for practical reasons justly insists on doing so. But a sharp distinction between psychoanalytic treatment and other methods of psychotherapy used by so-called traditional psychiatrists which are based
on the utilization of psychoanalytic observations and theory is becoming more and more difficult. In their actual practice, all psychiatrists
are becoming more and more similar, even though some may practice
pure psychoanalysis and others may practice psychoanalytically
oriented psychotherapy. This in itself should not be disturbing; on
the contrary, the basing of all psychological approaches to psychiatric
patients on solid foundations—on the theoretical knowledge of the
disturbance—is a healthy sign. But however desirable the trend toward
uniformity of all psychotherapy may be, the psychoanalyst who wishes
to retain his identity as such is faced with a practical problem.

In the past, I have repeatedly expressed myself in favor of the
present trend toward the unification of the whole profession dealing
with human behavior and its disturbances. At the moment, however,
I should like to consider the difficulties of such unification from all
sides, from the point of view of both practical policy and logic. My
high regard for the integrity and intellectual acumen of those of my
colleagues who in the past have opposed my views induces me to try
to appreciate their concerns and reservations, particularly their desire
not to allow the dividing line between pure psychoanalysis and other
psychotherapies to disappear.

It is not difficult to show the logical cogency of the position that
since we possess today a basic understanding of human behavior, all
treatment of personality disturbances should rest on the same scientific principles, no matter who undertakes the treatment and what
particular technique he employs. There is no particular kind of anatomy or physiology, no particular theory of antisepsis which is consid-

ered applicable to abdominal surgery as opposed to brain surgery, or, for that matter, to major surgery as opposed to minor surgery; the basic principles are the same and must be taught to every surgeon. While it is customary to divide psychotherapeutic procedures into two categories—the supportive and the uncovering—it must be borne in mind that supportive measures are knowingly or inadvertently used in all forms of psychotherapy; and conversely, some degree of insight is rarely absent from any sound psychotherapeutic approach. Thus in this complex field pedantic distinctions do not do justice to the actual happenings.

In general, all uncovering procedures aim to increase the ego's ability to handle emotional conflict situations which are entirely or partially repressed and therefore unconscious. Such conflicts usually originate in childhood and infancy, but are precipitated in later life by actual life situations at that time. In the uncovering procedures, the therapist tries to re-expose the ego in the treatment situation to the original conflict which the child's ego could not handle and therefore had to repress. Repression interrupts the natural learning process and does not allow a corrective adjustment of the repressed tendencies. The aim is a new solution to the old, unresolved or neurotically solved conflicts. The principal therapeutic tool is the transference, in which the patient relives his early interpersonal conflicts in relation to the therapist. Regression to the dependent attitudes of infancy and childhood is a constant feature of the transference, and, in the majority of cases, the central one. This regression in itself has a supportive effect. It allows the patient to postpone his own decisions and to reduce the responsibilities of adult existence by retiring into a dependent attitude toward the therapist resembling the child's attitude in the child-parent relationship. In many instances the greatest therapeutic effect of psychoanalysis is found precisely in this kind of support, which the patient is then unwilling to give up by terminating the treatment. The so-called interminability of such treatment indicates that, no matter what the therapist originally aimed at, the treatment is supportive in nature, for as soon as the treatment is interrupted, the patient relapses. On the other hand, many so-called rapid transference cures persist, even though in the therapist's judgment they are not based on real change in the personality. Such favorable transference results occur when the ego's integrative capacity has been only temporarily impaired by acute emotional stress, so that once the emotional support provided by the therapeutic situation reduces this stress, the ego is able to regain its functional capacity without any further activity on the part of the therapist. The ego's natural function is to master internal tensions by its integrative function. Emotional support relieves emotional tension and thus increases the natural integrative capacity of the ego and accounts for improvements which are not due to particular therapeutic measures.

In spite of this overlapping of uncovering and supportive effects in all forms of psychotherapy, it is not difficult to differentiate between the two main categories of treatment—primarily supportive and primarily uncovering methods. Primarily supportive measures are indicated whenever the functional impairment of the ego is of temporary nature caused by acute emotional stress. In such cases the therapeutic task consists, first of all, in *gratifying dependent needs* during the stress situation, thus reducing anxiety. Another important therapeutic device consists in reducing emotional stress by giving the patient an opportunity for emotional *abreaction*. A more intellectual type of support consists in *objectively reviewing* the patient's acute stress situation and assisting his judgment, which is temporarily impaired under the influence of severe emotional tensions; the patient thus becomes able to view his total situation from a proper perspective. In addition to these three forms of support, the therapist occasionally will have to *aid the ego's own neurotic defenses*. This is indicated whenever there are definite reasons to mistrust the ego's capacity to deal with unconscious material which threatens to break into consciousness through the weakened defenses. Finally, whenever the neurotic condition results from the patient's chronic involvement in particularly difficult external life situations which are beyond his ability to cope with, the *manipulation of the life situation* may be the only hopeful approach. This is, of course, indicated only in cases when, for external or internal reasons, there is no hope for increasing the ego's functional capacity by prolonged treatment.

These five procedures—gratification of dependency needs, abreaction, intellectual guidance, support of neurotic defenses, and manipulation of life situations—constitute the essence of supportive measures. They may require a shorter or longer series of sessions; occasionally they may be accomplished in only one or two interviews. There is no way to predict precisely the duration of such treatment; the therapist must proceed empirically, basing his judgment upon the therapeutic progress.

It is widely but erroneously held that supportive psychotherapeutic methods require less technical and theoretical preparation than psychoanalysis. I believe that every psychotherapist should be able to understand the underlying psychopathology and to apply the different therapeutic tools according to the specific needs of each patient. Supportive measures, if undertaken without such understanding, not only may be ineffective in certain cases, but may jeopardize the chances of recovery by undermining the patient's confidence in the efficacy of any psychiatric treatment. Not infrequently, even such common-sense procedures as giving consolation to a depressed patient or urging the phobic patient to overcome his fears may, if improperly applied, result in aggravation of the condition. Similarly, illtimed provocation of emotional abreaction in an acting-out neurotic may have serious consequences; and the strengthening of existing neurotic defenses in certain cases may not only be superfluous, but may unduly prolong recovery. All forms of psychotherapy must, therefore, be based on a knowledge of personality development and psychodynamics.

Chronic conditions in which the ego's functional impairment is caused by unresolved emotional conflicts of childhood require a systematic and more prolonged type of treatment, in which the ego is re-exposed to earlier pathogenic experiences. No hard and fast rules exist to predict the length of such treatment, which may vary from a few months to several years.

Because of the recent concern lest the identity of psychoanalysis be lost, there is a strong tendency to try to differentiate sharply in *quantitative* terms between psychoanalytic therapy proper and other uncovering procedures utilizing the principles of psychoanalysis. For a while this controversy appeared to center around such spurious issues as the frequency of interviews, the duration of the treatment, and whether the patient should lie on a couch or sit face to face with the analyst; these were considered as the crucial criteria.

Some of us maintained an opposing view. We felt that the frequency of interviews and the whole duration of treatment depend on several factors which cannot be precisely appraised quantitatively, in our present state of knowledge. The therapist in each case must feel his way and find the optimal intensity of treatment. Anticipation of duration at the beginning of treatment is seldom possible; certainly no accurate estimations can be made in advance.

From all this it should be clear that a rigid distinction between the different uncovering methods is not possible. The length of treatment or any external criteria are certainly not the most suitable bases for classification. As long as the psychological processes in the patient are the same and the changes achieved by these processes are of a similar nature, it is not possible to draw a sharp dividing line between psychoanalysis proper and psychoanalytically oriented psychotherapy. Accordingly the only realistic distinction is not between briefer or longer treatments with less frequent or more frequent interviews, but is the distinction between primarily supportive and primarily uncovering methods.

Obviously the great variety of patients makes necessary variations in approach. This being the case in all fields of medicine, one might expect that such a flexibility would prevail also in the field of psychoanalysis. The fact that most psychoanalysts have used precisely the same so-called classical procedure for all their patients has been due to various circumstances. For many years the general practice among psychoanalytic therapists was to accept those cases for therapy which appeared suitable for the classical procedure and to advise the others not to undergo psychoanalytic treatment. In other words, the patients were selected to fit the tool.

Moreover, psychoanalytic treatment is the primary source of psychoanalytic knowledge, and the original procedure is best suited for research. Since in the early phases of psychoanalysis, the primary concern was quite naturally that of increasing basic knowledge, the classical procedure was rather universally used. Some of us have come to the conviction, however, that the time is now ripe to utilize the accumulated theoretical knowledge in different ways, so that not only those patients who appear suitable for the original technique, but the whole psychoneurotic population as well, may benefit from our present knowledge. This extension of psychoanalytic help to a great variety of patients is another important new trend in our field.

One can understand why this distinction between analysis proper and analytically oriented therapy has been such an important issue only if one considers its practical implications. First of all, the identity of the psychoanalyst, particularly in the eyes of the public, is threatened by the flexible use of analytic principles. It would appear that now anyone may claim recognition as a psychoanalyst who uses analytically founded psychotherapeutic methods, since the psychoanalyst can no longer be easily identified by the external criteria of his technique.

One psychoanalyst, in the heat of a recent discussion of this problem, exclaimed that insistence on daily interviews in every case is important because this clearly distinguishes the psychoanalyst from other psychiatrists! "Other psychiatrists see their patients once a month, once in two weeks, or maybe once a week. Some of them," he continued, "might see their patients twice a week—but the psychoanalyst sees them five or six times!" While this may sound thoroughly nonsensical, it has a kernel of sense. A product which cannot be easily identified by external criteria can be easily confused with other products which are essentially different but which appear similar. In some instances, a trademark is only a name for a drug which does not differ in its chemical properties from other drugs; in other instances, however, the name designates a product which is different from others in principle.

At the present moment, when psychotherapy is such a comprehensive term for all psychological methods—some of them based on common sense, others on various theoretical concepts—the feeling of psychoanalysts that their procedure should be identified by its name is quite justified. On the other hand, this practical consideration should not be an impediment to the natural evolution of the field. Psychoanalytic principles today are being applied in various forms. The only logical solution is to identify as similar all these related procedures which are essentially based on the same scientific concepts, observations, and technical principles, and to differentiate them from intuitive psychotherapies and those based on different theoretical concepts.

In this connection it should be emphasized that using psychoanalytic principles in a more flexible way requires not less but more knowledge. A student who follows in every detail the classical procedure does not have to face the problem of evaluating what kind of deviations should be used and when and how. Routine protects him from making independent decisions, which would have to be based not only on the general understanding of the case but also on the precise appreciation of the momentary psychodynamic situation. For example, the analyst who is not protected by routine may at a given time have to consider whether he should try to reduce the intensity of the patient's emotional involvement; he may decide that the patient's dependency can be counteracted by making it more conscious, and so reduce the frequency of the interviews or interrupt the treatment temporarily, so that the patient will be on his own for a while and will be made to feel that he need not rely continually on his therapist. Such considerations require evaluations which are not necessary if the psychiatrist proceeds according to a rigid procedure.

One may feel that the question of classification and semantics does not deserve as much attention as I have given it. I would agree that the scientific import of this question is negligible. Yet this issue has kept the psychoanalytic community in a turmoil in the last few years. This is the result of the changes which psychoanalytic and psychiatric practice are undergoing. Knowledge is universal, and we must recognize that the tendency on the part of psychoanalysts to set boundaries is not dictated by conceptual needs; but the trend arises mainly from the practical necessity for identifying a group of practitioners who have had a specific kind of training, in order to protect the general public from misrepresentation.

I would now like to turn to some current developments in the psychoanalytic field. For a long time very little was added to Freud's original formulations concerning the therapeutic effect of psychoanalysis. According to Freud, the essence of psychoanalytic therapy consists in exposing the ego during the treatment situation to the original emotional conflicts which it could not resolve in the past. This revival of pathogenic emotional experience which takes place in the patient's emotional reactions to the analyst is called the transference neurosis. The resolution of this artificial neurosis is the central therapeutic tool. Freud emphasized two quantitative factors to account for the therapeutic effectiveness of psychoanalytic treatment: first, that the repetitive reliving of the original conflicts in the transference are less intensive than were the original conflicts; and, second, that the ego of the adult, which is exposed to this weaker edition of these conflicts, is stronger than was the ego of the child which could not resolve the original conflicts. In other words, in the transference the stronger ego of the adult has a better chance to solve the less intense conflicts.

After several years of experimentation with the quantitative aspects of therapy, the Chicago group has formulated a third therapeutic factor. In the classical technique and theory, this factor was implicit but was not formulated with sufficient clarity. We think that for the transference experience to have a corrective value, it must take place under certain highly specific conditions. How to establish these conditions is the main technical problem of the psychoanalytic treatment. First, one must realize that the new settlement of an old, unresolved conflict in the transference situation becomes possible not only because the intensity of the transference conflict is less than that of the original conflict—as Freud expressed it, the transference is only a shadow play of the original conflict—but also because the therapist's response to the patient's emotional expressions is quite different from the original treatment of the child by the parents. The therapist's attitude is one of understanding, but at the same time it is emotionally detached. His attitude is that of a physician who wants to help the patient. He does not react to the patient's expression of hostility either by retaliation, by reproach, or by showing signs of being hurt. Neither does he gratify the patient's regressive infantile claims for help and reassurance. He treats the patient as an adult in need of help; but this help consists merely in giving the patient the opportunity to understand his own problems better. He does not assume the role of an adviser, nor does he assume practical responsibility for the patient's current activities. He gives the patient no opportunity for blame or gratitude other than that which one might realistically feel toward someone who has rendered a professional service. In the objective atmosphere of positive, helpful interest, the patient becomes capable of expressing his originally repressed tendencies more frankly. At the same time, he can recognize that his reactions are out-of-date, that they are no longer adequate responses to his present life conditions, and—most important—that they are not reasonable reactions to the therapist. Once, of course, in the past, these reaction patterns made sense; they were the reactions of the child to the existing parental attitudes. The fact that the patient continues to act and feel according to outdated patterns, whereas the therapist's reactions conform to the actual therapeutic situation, makes the transference behavior a kind of one-sided shadowboxing. The patient has the opportunity to understand his neurotic patterns and at the same time to experience intensively the irrationality of his own emotional responses. The fact that the therapist's reaction is different from that of the parent to whose behavior the child adjusted himself as well as he could by his own neurotic reactions makes it necessary for the patient to abandon and correct these old emotional patterns. After all, this is precisely the ego's function—adjustment to the existing external conditions. As soon as the old neurotic patterns are revived and brought into the realm of consciousness, the ego has the opportunity to readjust them to the changed conditions. This is the essence of the corrective influence of those series of experiences which constitute the transference; thus we refer to it as a corrective emotional experience.

This formulation has far-reaching consequences for the technique of the treatment. It takes into consideration not only the transference but also the analyst's attitude toward the patient, the countertransference. Freud's original concept was that the analyst, through his neutral attitude, functions as a blank screen upon which the patient casts his emotional reactions; these reactions are characteristic for him, are determined exclusively by his past experiences, and are not influenced by the analyst's personality. In recent years, this concept has come to be considered an abstraction; there is now general agreement that it does not describe quite precisely the emotional phenomena actually occuring in the course of treatment. The relation between patient and therapist is a two-way street. The analyst, to whom the patient attributes the role of important persons of his past, nevertheless remains for the patient at the same time a real personality. There is no doubt that the analyst has an emotional reaction toward the patient which is determined by his own personality structure. This countertransference may not be openly expressed, yet it contributes to what I call the emotional climate of the interviews. These countertransference reactions become particularly marked after the patient's transference neurosis has fully developed. It is at this time that the analyst's own spontaneous emotional responses become most important; if they are identical with or resemble the parents' original attitudes, the transference experience loses much of its corrective value, for the original neurotic patterns were adaptive responses of the child to parental attitudes. The most important therapeutic element is precisely the fact that the therapist's reactions are different from the pathogenic parental reactions, and the whole self-revelatory process in psychoanalysis is made possible by this very principle. An attitude on the part of the analyst which is not evaluative or restrictive favors the emergence of unconscious material which was repressed in childhood, primarily because of the condemnatory attitude of the environment.

On the basis of several years' experimentation I have proposed that the omnipresent spontaneous countertransference attitudes of the analyst should not only be controlled—on this there is general agreement—but should also be replaced by a type of response which is most suitable to bring out the irrationality of the patient's neurotic patterns. For example, if the patient in his self-assertiveness was originally intimidated by a tyrannical father, the most suitable analytic climate is an outspokenly permissive one. If, on the other hand, the patient's father was overindulgent and by his doting love evoked an oppressive type of guilt in his son, the analyst may advantageously behave in a more detached manner; at the same time, he can be helpful without losing the basic nonevaluative attitude. In accordance with the patient's needs, the analyst can change the interpersonal climate from a more to a less detached one, or from a more to a less permissive one.

Some analysts have contested these recommendations with the argument that if these assumed attitudes are artificial, they will fail to achieve their purpose; the patient will sense their insincerity. My answer to this is that the detached objective attitude of the analyst required by classical theory is also highly studied. Certainly it is not a spontaneous attitude in human intercourse. Moreover, since the therapist's whole orientation is to help a suffering human being, trying to act in a manner which is in the interest of his patient is by no means artificial. Every educator should do this; we as psychiatrists require such changes in attitude in a psychiatric nurse, for instance.

I cannot leave this topic without referring at least briefly to another recent development which pertains to one of the central difficulties of psychoanalytic treatment—the occasional extreme prolongation of treatment. In the past, psychoanalysts did not face this fundamental difficulty with the necessary courage. We fell into the habit of dissipating our concern for the excessively long duration of some treatments by excuses which were not always valid. For example, we said that if the so-called period of working through was handled with sufficient patience and tenacity, eventually even an unusually prolonged treatment could be successfully terminated. If this failed, we declared that the patient was incurable. But are these interminable patients really incurable, and must psychoanalytic treatment be considered a life-long crutch for them? Or is the prolongation of the treatment in many cases due to a lack of full understanding of the quantitative aspects of our procedure? Freud discovered this central problem of psychoanalytic treatment rather early in his career. He said that his initial difficulty was to help his patients remain under treatment; later he encountered the opposite difficulty—that his patients' desire to recover became outweighed by their desire to be treated.

In the light of present theory this difficulty is easily understood. We know that the patient sooner or later will replace his original neurosis—which consists primarily of intrapsychic conflicts—with the transference neurosis in which the intrapsychic conflicts are reconverted into interpersonal relations between the patient and the physician—which are replicas of his early neurotic involvements in the family. This transformation contains elements of gratification for the patient. He is allowed to keep his neurosis as a necessary part of the treatment and can retain his dependence which causes less and less conflict in the permissive and understanding atmosphere of the analytic situation. In other words, the transference gradually loses the quality of suffering. The original neurosis was a conflictful combination of gratification and suffering; the transference neurosis at first retains both of these features, but in the course of the treatment the conflictful elements diminish and the gratifications increase. Soon a stationary equilibrium sets in. Many a patient comes to the analyst when he is at the end of his rope, when his subjective state has become well-nigh intolerable; but once the transference neurosis has replaced the original one, the patient may go on in a fairly comfortable subjective state for years, provided he can see his analyst regularly. In such cases, a scrutiny of the nature of transference gratifications reveals that they consist primarily in the satisfaction of the patient's dependent needs.

After years of experimentation, many of us in the Chicago Institute became aware of the necessity to put a brake, from the beginning of the treatment, on the regressive dependent component of the transference. No matter how valuable and indispensable a factor it may be, only by making it conscious and keeping it conscious can it serve an optimal value. This must be done by frustrating it, for interpretation alone does not always suffice. One of the most powerful frustrations consists in well-timed reduction of the frequency of the psychoanalytic interviews and well-timed shorter or longer interruptions. Routine continuation of the treatment in daily interviews over years may favor the regressive tendencies to such a degree that some patients will never be able to renounce them.

This problem of how to handle the patient's dependent needs is a central issue of psychoanalytic therapy and it will remain, in the future, one of the most difficult technical issues. In order to cure the patient, the analyst must allow him some regression to an infantile state. The price of this powerful therapeutic device is the difficulty of terminating the treatment. Thus the medicine of artificial regression in the transference can be given in overdoses. Like radiation therapy, it is a powerful weapon, but not without danger, for it can become the source of a new illness. In order to improve the therapeutic procedure, we must become aware not only of its beneficial aspects but also of its hidden dangers. There is no use in denying that the history of psychoanalysis includes many interminable patients, along with its brilliant successes. But I believe that not all of these cases are incurable, and that we will be able to help many of them by learning how to handle, in terms of desirable quantities, the most effective factor of psychoanalytic therapy—the revival of the infantile neurotic conflicts in the transference situation.

Many experienced analysts have expressed their reservations toward these quantitative variations of the so-called classical procedure and are inclined to consider them as dilutions of the classical procedure. Only time will decide the practical usefulness of these variations. One thing is certain: the mere repetition of routine—and the rejection of new suggestions as a threat to the purity of psychoanalysis—can lead only to stagnation. Further improvements of therapeutic technique can come only from a persistent re-examination of our theoretical premises and from relentless experimentation with technical modifications.

Two Forms of Regression and
Their Therapeutic Implications

◄ 1956 ►

Freud originally described regression as a tendency to return from a later acquired, more advanced form of organization of ego and intinct to a more primitive phase. It usually occurs when the ego is confronted with a conflict it cannot master. The ego seeks security by returning to a phase when, in its development, it was still successful. In other words, it returns to a preconflictual state. The formerly successful adaptive patterns to which the ego returns, Freud called points of fixation. Since the adaptation of the ego is never complete, these older points of fixation retain some cathexis. Freud illustrated this concept by a simile: an advancing army in enemy territory leaves troops at strategic points to which it may return if it is forced back by an overwhelming enemy. According to this view there is a reciprocal relationship between fixation and regression. The greater the cathexis of a point of fixation, the more likely will be regression to it if later conflicts arise. Regression serves the gratification of needs that remain unsatisfied in a new conflict which the ego has not yet mastered.

Considerably later, Freud described another type of regression and fixation: fixation to an unresolved traumatic conflict. The best known examples are traumatic dreams, in which the dreamer conjures up, often in full detail, a traumatic event. The recognition of this phenomenon—fixation to an unresolved trauma—was crucial for Freud's theoretical constructions after 1921. These observations necessitated recognition of a principle that does not follow the pleasure-pain formula. The revival of these unsettled traumatic situations does not serve any gratification. They are painful and cannot be explained by the assumption that the organism is always motivated by a need to avoid the unpleasant tensions caused by the pressure of unsatisfied instinctual needs which it tries to eliminate by seeking

290

gratification pleasurable in itself. Freud offered an explanation for phenomena of this kind. The fundamental task of the ego is to maintain a stable equilibrium within the mental apparatus. This task it cannot achieve under traumatic conditions; it therefore returns again and again to the traumatic event in order to achieve a mastery of it. A trauma is a situation in which the ego is overwhelmed by stimuli that it cannot reduce to an optimal level, thus failing in its basic function. The compulsive return to such unsettled traumatic experiences of the past is a second kind of regression, fundamentally different from the regression first described which accomplishes quite the opposite result, a return to a previously successful form of adaptation. In regression to a previously successful adaptation, the mental apparatus is seeking gratification according to an old pattern; in the regression to a traumatic situation, however, it attempts mastery of an unresolved tension. It seeks a solution for something that was not solved in the past.

Fenichel pointed out that the concept of repetition compulsion should be revised in the light of these new formulations. He showed that the term repetition compulsion refers to several quite different phenomena, of which he described three: first, repetition compulsion based on periodicity of instinct; second, repetitions due to the tendency of the repressed to find an outlet; third, repetitions of traumatic events for the purpose of achieving a belated mastery. The theoretical significance of this principle of mastery, supplemental to the pleasure-pain principle, is sufficiently well known and I will not further discuss it. Its application to understanding the therapeutic process, however, has not been made fully explicit. I will describe some of its technical consequences, which are in no sense new but have not, I believe, been systematically presented in psychoanalytic literature.

The reactions of patients in the transference provide the best known examples of the repetition compulsion. In the psychoanalytic situation the patient emotionally re-enacts relationships with persons who played important roles in his past. The question immediately arises: to which category of repetition do transference manifestations belong? Do they represent a trend to return to positions of ego and libido that were satisfactory in the past, or do they belong to the category of regression to a traumatic situation, that is to say, attempts at belated mastery? It is obvious that categorizing them is important for therapy. Careful scrutiny of transference manifestations suggests that the two types of transference reaction occur with equal frequency. The simplest example of the first kind, the return to a once satisfactory point of fixation, is the development of a positive dependent transference in which the patient attributes to the analyst the role of the good mother image. Most often this type of transference has the connotation of an oral dependent relationship. Although this kind of regression is motivated by the urge to return to an old type of gratification, it never can be realized without conflict. One reason is that these regressive trends contradict the standards of the adult ego. Oral dependent gratifications are disguised, and they are defended against by overcompensations; and these disguises and defenses reveal the conflict between more mature standards and pregenital attitudes.

This same conflict originally arises in early childhood when the growing child is driven from its pregenital positions by the inexorable law of biological maturation and also by the pressures exerted by the parents. Accordingly, regression to a pregenital phase during treatment may contain both components: it may represent a return to an old satisfactory position of instinctual gratification and it may simultaneously contain an element of struggle for belated mastery of an unresolved conflict resulting from maturation. Only this second component makes regression in transference an ally of our therapeutic aims; the regressive evasion of an unresolved conflict must be evaluated as resistance. Inasmuch as the patient regresses to a pregenital position he is resisting the solution of another later conflict, usually the Oedipal conflict; nevertheless, by regressing he again has to face unsettled conflicts of the past and is given opportunity during the treatment to master such conflicts.

In order to evaluate to what degree a regressive manifestation of transference is evasion of a conflict and to what degree it is an attempt at belated mastery, Freud's original concept of fixation appears to be helpful. He believed that the relationship of regression to fixation is determined by the amount of original cathexis retained by the points of fixation. If this cathexis is relatively great, the patient probably must resolve the unsettled pregenital conflict before he can progress in his treatment. If, however, the regressive return to a once satisfying pregenital position was mainly an evasion of another transference problem, the Oedipal one, it must be considered to be the manifestation of resistance.

As a rule both components are present. Estimation of the relative importance of the two components is often difficult or even impossible. This dilemma has long been known. It usually takes the form of an argument: which is the real therapeutic issue, the oral conflict or the Oedipal conflict? Does the patient hide his anxieties concerning the Oedipal relationship by his emphasis on the oral conflict or are we dealing with a so-called pseudo-Oedipal conflict, the main issue being the still unresolved pregenital situation? It is evident that no generalizations can be made. In some cases the first, in others the second formulation is the correct one. It is equally obvious that the correct evaluation of these alternatives is of great help for the therapist in coping with this sort of problem. Since we deal here with a continuum ranging from cases in which the Oedipal involvement is the central pathogenic issue to others in which the pregenital fixations are paramount, the extreme examples at the ends of the continuum are most suitable for illustration of this theoretical problem.

The analysis of a thirty-eight-year-old university teacher began with aggressive and competitive ideas. The patient expressed doubts about the scientific nature of psychoanalysis in general and contrasted it with the greater exactness of his own work. The undertone of his behavior was polite scepticism which he expressed with a somewhat condescending attitude. His first dreams were of a phallic nature. For example, *in an airplane flight he took over the pilot's role from the official pilot, in whom he had lost confidence, and thus succeeded in avoiding a crash.* At the same time he began to talk about a rather recent extramarital sexual affair. He appeared punctually at the interviews and followed the basic rules conscientiously. The discrepancy between his underlying dependent gratification and the aggressive content of his associations made it clear that his competitiveness was a defense against his strong passive involvement. I pointed out to him that in spite of his scepticism he seemed to put great faith in the treatment; otherwise he would not cooperate so conscientiously. This remark called his bluff and he left the interview with manifest embarrassment. In the next interview I called his attention to the fact that the previous day upon leaving he had avoided shaking my hand, a habit I still retain from my continental background. I raised the question whether this should not be interpreted as retreat from personal involvement. This sufficed to provoke an intense resistance.

Within a few interviews the character of the transference was changed. The patient assumed the somewhat boyish attitude of a pupil and his dreams assumed an oral content. The dreams of flying which had occurred almost every day of the first week gave place to pregenital fantasies. Animals began to appear in the dreams, soft woolly animals such as a llama or a shaggy dog; in them he represented an early pregenital attitude. He regressed from a passive, homosexual position to an oral receptive one that was more acceptable. There was to be sure a conflict about his oral demands, which had been frustrated in the past by a cold, rejecting mother. The hostility resulting from oral frustration was expressed by pregenital soiling. *In a dream he represented himself as a teenager urinating against a wall.* In another dream he openly expressed a tendency to anal soiling. This transference of pregenital character lasted for more than two years. Occasionally feeble attempts were made to return to Oedipal problems, only to withdraw from them as fast as he had after the first week of treatment.

His life history gave us the clue to this trend of the analysis. He had turned away from a cold and somewhat rejecting mother and during his preadolescence and most of his adolescence had had a close relationship with his father, whom he admired and who expressed much interest in the patient, the oldest of three brothers. It was only in his fifteenth or sixteenth year that this positive relationship changed into a highly critical and rebellious attitude, not expressed openly but manifested by the patient's following his own interests and by his passive resistance against the father's aspirations for him. This adolescent attitude was a revival of his earlier Oedipal rivalry and hostility against the father for which, however, he had become completely amnesic.

The therapeutic problem was to cause the patient to face the first appearance of his Oedipal involvement. We may reasonably ask, however, whether or not the pregenital interests revived in the analysis were equally pathogenic. It is well known that the outcome of the Oedipal conflict depends at least partially upon the development in the pregenital phases. It is difficult to distinguish clearly those cases in which ill-resolved pregenital conflicts are responsible for the unsuccessful outcome of the Oedipal phase from those in which unfavorable experiences at the height of the Oedipus complex are of primary importance. Theoretically every developmental phase has an influence upon the later ones. If we are to pursue this argument consistently, however, we must take into account not only the pregenital phase but also its determinants, the constitution, and possibly also the events of the intra-uterine period. The developments of instinct and ego are determined by a large number of variables, and we have good reason to believe that in some patients the genetic factors are so all-important that, no matter how favorable the later development, the constitutional vulnerability will always assert itself. In other cases unfortunate experiences during the pregenital development are outstanding and predetermine almost irreversibly the outcome of the Oedipal period. In a third category of patients the nature of the Oedipal period, which is highly dependent upon parental attitudes and the structure of the family, constitutes the first serious obstacle in development.

My first recognition of this crucial problem I can trace back to an early phase of my analytic experience. I discussed with Freud a patient whom he had referred to me. Freud interrupted my presentation by saying, "You must ask yourself the question: what was the first time the patient said 'no'?" He meant, at what period in his life did the patient first encounter a situation to which he could not or would not adapt himself? Once such a genetic reconstruction is made, we are in a better position to evaluate the therapeutic significance of the shifting phases in the patient's transference. If we consider that first "no" as representing the conflict situation which the patient could not successfully resolve, we can speak of *regressions to the preconflictual phase*. These are defensive evasions of the pathogenic conflict. I hasten, however, to qualify this statement and deprive it of its attractive simplicity. As a rule, we do not deal with one pathogenic conflict but with a series of conflicts whose pathogenic nature is of necessity influenced by what happened earlier in the patient's development. In most cases in which the Oedipal conflict is of central significance, its pregenital precursors are also important. Accordingly, the analysis of pregenital material is not wasted time. Yet it is obvious that if the defensive nature of pregenital regression is not recognized, the therapist may lose sight of the total picture and may expect therapeutic results before the later Oedipal involvements are clarified. In other words, antiquity is not always equivalent to depth from the point of view of pathogenesis.

Considering the psychoanalytic literature with this in mind, one might be tempted to make the generalization that pregenital problems have recently become more popular, whereas in earlier days the significance of the Oedipus complex was emphasized. I have repeatedly heard and read the statement that in recent decades the nature of neurosis has changed under cultural influences: hysterias with their phallic and genital origin are less frequent and we see today more organ neuroses in which the pregenital factors are out standing. I have even heard the argument that neuroses are like bacteria; as bacteria may become adapted to antibiotics and produce strains no longer susceptible to them, so psychoneuroses adapt themselves to our efforts to eradicate them and withdraw from the well-advertised Oedipal conflict to the depths of pregenital history. I am somewhat sceptical of this analogy. Cultural influences may very well affect statistically the incidence of the various types of case. We are nevertheless confronted with the task of reconstructing the pathogenetically significant experiences in each individual case, and in doing so we find that to analyze so-called deep regression toward pregenital material is not always to penetrate into the truly pathogenic events.

The emergence of such early material means, as often as not, that the ego is by regression evading the struggle over a later pathogenic conflict. In my experience, at least in psychoneurotics, the most common central conflict is today, just as formerly, the Oedipal conflict. I do not doubt the significance of earlier relationships between child and mother; they are particularly outstanding in the field in which I am most interested, the theory and treatment of organ neuroses. Perhaps my preoccupation with this type of case makes me too cautious about generalizations. This caution has proved particularly well justified in the study of peptic ulcer. In these cases frustration of oral tendencies has been constantly found to be a central issue. Sustained but frustrated oral receptive and oral regressive tendencies have a stimulating effect upon stomach secretion. In the psychoanalytic study of such cases, however, it becomes increasingly clear that the oral regression is not always due to a particularly strong oral fixation, although this may be true in a number of cases; often it is the result of regression from an unresolved Oedipal conflict. So far as the organic symptom is concerned the oral regression is of specific importance. The oral regression is, however, often induced by the Oedipal barrier. In male patients I have repeatedly observed that as the analysis progresses the patients become involved more and more in transference conflict representing the Oedipal phase. The oral regression serves as a defense, substituting oral dependence for passive homosexual wishes. The homosexual wishes are, in turn, reactions to originally competitive, hostile tendencies; yet it is also true that the Oedipal rivalry in such orally fixated patients is a mixture of phallic competitiveness and oral envy.

We arrive then at the conclusion that we cannot expect a simple "either-or" answer concerning the significance of pregenital and genital conflicts; the relationship between the two types of conflict is complex. By attacking the pregenital position, the analysis may drive the patient to deal with his phallic Oedipal problems; but he does so only to retreat again when the battle becomes hot in the Oedipal arena. This should not prevent us, however, from trying to form a quantitative estimate of the balance of pregenital and Oedipal cathexes.

A correct estimate of this balance of powers proves of great help in the conduct of the treatment. In the case mentioned above, for example, it took two years for the analysis to lead us back to the crucial Oedipal phase from which the patient had retreated after the first week. Only after the Oedipal phase had been worked through could the treatment be terminated. The relative ease with which the pregenital material appeared even in the second week of the analysis and the consistency with which the patient substituted pregenital precursors of Oedipal involvements should have made me aware earlier of the defensive nature of his preoccupation. It has been known for a long time that the patient senses the analyst's interest and exploits it for his resistance. The material in which the analyst shows interest and which he emphasizes in his genetic interpretations may be used by the patient as a defensive weapon, using such material as a bait. In case discussions one often hears such statements as, "You mistake this material for Oedipal involvement; it is only a pseudo-Oedipus complex hiding the real pathogenic material." The reverse argument we hear less frequently: that one overrates the importance for pathogenesis of pregenital material, which really is only a regressive evasion of the Oedipal conflict. Either argument may be correct in a particular case. When Rank proposed his theory of the trauma of birth, it was soon recognized that intra-uterine dreams are as a rule regressive distortions of incestuous wishes. The same may be true —although to a much lesser degree—of some pregenital material. The following excerpt from an analysis may serve as an illustration of these theoretical considerations.

The thirty-eight-year-old head of a business corporation consulted me because of a generally depressed state of mind, lack of interest in his job, difficulty in getting up in time to catch the train, and increased irritability toward his children, especially toward his youngest daughter. His speech was retarded, his facial expression a mixture of sadness and anxiousness. His blood pressure was markedly elevated. He had been employed at his present job about a year and a half, when he had moved to Chicago from the East, where he had held a similar job but in a smaller firm. The present job gave him greater income and more prestige, and it was also somewhat easier in its demands on his time. The patient had five children. The youngest daughter was born shortly after they moved to Chicago, where they bought an attractive house in the suburbs. His relationship with his wife he described as very satisfactory. He characterized her as an understanding and mature person.

During the very first interview the patient became tearful when he told how much he loved his youngest daughter and what a wonderful child she was. He wept again when he mentioned that his youngest sister had given up a well-paid job to become a missionary and had departed a few weeks before for the Belgian Congo. On both occasions his voice shook and he scarcely could finish his sentences. He became disturbed again when he mentioned a seventy-year-old man, a member of the company for over twenty years, who caused the patient a great deal of trouble. This old man, he said, was not very competent, yet he made decisions without consulting the patient and got credit for accomplishments to which the patient was entitled. The patient felt helpless in the matter, for although he was himself administrative head of the company, the other man had served the company for many years and had greater influence with the board and was the real power behind the scenes. Speaking about him, the patient was not tearful but expressed irritation verging on anger.

I called his attention to these three topics that upset him. In response he reiterated how cute his daughter was, how annoying the seventy-year-old man was, and how helpless he himself felt in that situation. Of his sister he said, "How pathetic it is that she is giving up a good job to take up so hazardous an assignment as that of a missionary." He added that his father was a minister as had been his grandfather and great-grandfather. He continued to talk about his own family, which consisted of seven children—he had two older sisters, an older brother, and three younger sisters. The patient's mother had died when he was six years old. He spoke of his father in terms of highest regard and emphasized how selfless a person he was. The spirit of the family was harmonious. All the sisters and brothers liked each other and there was no dissension among them. The patient's older brother was a successful businessman; one sister became a welfare worker and was killed in the line of duty; the other sisters were married and had children. The patient was puzzled to explain why he became so upset about the youngest sister's becoming a missionary. He could not understand it and asked me to explain to him how a person could give up a well-paying job for such a hazardous assignment.

In his second interview the patient said that he felt much depressed and spoke mostly about the annoyances at the office. He mentioned that his term as president of a national organization had just expired. He confessed that since becoming depressed he had regularly been drinking in the evenings until he went into a torpor and finally fell asleep. Whenever he drank he felt quiet and relaxed.

It soon became evident why he was so upset by his sister's becoming a missionary. He described his intense ambition, his pride in his position, and the importance to him of obtaining credit for his work. He contrasted these qualities with the altruism of his sister, who gave up material goods and a fine salary to expose herself to the dangerous life of a missionary in a primitive colony. The sister followed father's principles, for whom to do good was the sole purpose of life; he had accepted a parish in a poor rural district where he felt he could do more good than in a large city. In fact the patient felt that his father had neglected the material welfare of the family to devote himself to humanity. The patient became more and more bitter over the material deprivations caused by his father's overly humanitarian attitude; he told with growing indignation of his having had to go to school in mended clothes and of other similar deprivations. The seven children had been a heavy economic burden, yet the family had lived in complete harmony. The prevailing attitude of the family had been neighborliness and consideration for others. It was clear that the patient's determination to become a successful businessman must have been—at least in part—a reaction against economic want as well as against father's ideals. As soon as he left home he began with all his energy to promote his career and became increasingly successful in improving his economic status. He never relaxed, never felt any conflict about working hard, until very recently after he had been promoted to his job in Chicago. Just after this event his youngest daughter was born.

It was clear that this patient reacted with depression to success. Our problem was to explain the unconscious basis of this paradoxical reaction.

Early in the treatment he revealed intense unconscious guilt mobilized by the simultaneous occurrence of three events. 1) His competitive, hostile feelings and unconscious death wishes toward the seventy-year-old man who, in interfering with his ambitions, revived deeply repressed Oedipal rivalry and death wishes toward his father. 2) His sister's altruistic act brought into sharp relief his own self-centered ambitions and impressed upon him how blatantly he had betrayed his father's principle of subordinating his own economic advantage to the good of others. 3) The birth of his youngest daughter added to his family responsibilities and further deprived him of his wife's attention. One of his complaints when he came for analysis was a growing irritability toward his children. This conflict manifested itself by an urge to spend more time with the family and less in his office. He decorated the children's room himself and began to neglect his business. The unconscious guilt connected with his business activities, in which the conflict with the senior man was central, was another important cause of his withdrawal from business. All this, however, was only half of the picture. The other factor was the regressive return to a pregenital position.

In the first days of his treatment he was from time to time irritable with the therapist and showed signs of recalcitrance and hostility. In the fifth interview, however, he reported that an entirely new interest in his past had preoccupied him during the last few days. He started to reminisce in a sentimental way. He had always looked forward energetically and never thought of his past life; but now he was thinking about the happy days of his early adolescence on an uncle's farm. He recalled with tears in his eyes the creek in the pasture; then after a pause added, "Mother was born on that farm." This started a train of thought about his mother's death. He could remember nothing of her except her death as a result of an acute illness when he was six years old. He knew that he had cried all night after her death, and that for half a year thereafter he did not go back to school. Although he could not remember how he had felt about mother and her death, he accepted as plausible my suggestion that he must have been very much disturbed by it, for he had at once discontinued going to school. The lack of emotion and memory about mother was in striking contrast with his sentimental feelings about the farm. Obviously he repressed all feelings concerning his mother and his bereavement and substituted for the attachment to mother nostalgia for the farm. In this way he protected himself against the unbearable feeling of losing mother.

A period followed in which pregenital material appeared with increasing clarity. At the same time the transference became strikingly dependent in character. *He dreamed that he lost the key to his office which prevented him from entering it. In another dream, he lost his coat; and in yet another, he forgot the number of the room. In another dream he saw himself teaching his little son to play the drum.* Music had always been one of his greatest relaxations. *Then he dreamed he was in a hotel in Atlantic City at a convention but had to take care of his little daughter who was with him.* He had in reality spent a few days in this hotel at a convention in great luxury, all expenses paid. He understood immediately that the dream expressed a self-indulgent trend. He got vicarious gratification from taking care of his daughter, with whom he identified himself. During this period he began more and more to stay away from his office to play with the children, participating in their games as if he were a child himself. He felt more relaxed, and after a few weeks resigned from his job. I reminded him of our agreement not to make irreversible decisions during the treatment. He excused himself by pointing out that he would have been fired anyhow because he had been neglecting his duties and that an inquiry was pending, initiated by his enemy, the old man. He decided not to look for another job for at least half a year. He was assured of his salary for that period. His depression lifted, he felt relaxed and content; his blood pressure went down to normal.

This material, particularly the self-castrative dreams of losing his key and his coat, indicated that the patient had retreated from his competitive ambitions to a pregenital position. He played the role of a mother with his children, vicariously enjoying the mothering and at the same time re-establishing in himself the lost object by identification with mother. Regressive dreams continued. *In one he was climbing down from a high office building.* He interpreted it as the expression of his urge to give up his business career and his ambition for a high position. In another dream *he was driving in a Communist country. Someone tried to impress upon him how well off the country was. They all had a sumptuous dinner. The patient was sceptical and thought he should warn his staff that they were closely watched.* In this dream he expressed his discomfort over the fact that I was watching his regressive evasion. He was disturbed by my constant demonstration that he was evading his problems, particularly the problem of his future and of the conflict that had started his illness: the conflict with the old man. Whenever this topic came up he refused to recognize his own rivalrous tendencies and tried to explain the conflict as his reaction to the old man's nefarious strategy.

A second dream of the same night clearly expressed his concern about his economic future. *He came out of a restaurant and the hat check girl, before giving him back his hat and coat, gave him a manicure and a massage which cost him only three dollars.* In his associations he tried to reassure himself that he might safely take a half year's vacation witout getting into financial trouble. He recognized witout my help the self-indulgent, passive trend expressed by this dream in which he gave me the role of the girl who took care of him. Three dollars was a fraction of the fee he paid me. We may assume that a passive homosexual trend was another factor producing this dream.

About ten days after this dream the patient discontinued his treatment with the excuse that the analyst would soon leave for summer vacation anyhow, and that he felt well and was no longer depressed; his blood pressure was down and he had stopped drinking. In the fall, he said, he would look for a job and then would return to his treatment. Fall came but the patient did not return. He called to say that he would not start working before the first of January and that he continued to feel relaxed and contented. By the first of January I had left Chicago; but I was informed that the patient had called up again, saying that he had received several good offers, felt well, and would start working soon. He thought he would not need treatment immediately and would await my return. I believe that even if I had stayed in Chicago he would not have returned at that time for further treatment.

The treatment came to an end before the patient became conscious of the central pathogenic conflict, centering around his death wishes against the father substitute. As I have said, in the transference his negative feelings appeared only at the very beginning of the treatment and gradually yielded to a dependent positive attitude which lasted until treatment was interrupted.

How shall we evaluate the relationship of the two outstanding dynamic factors operative in this case: the withdrawal from the conflict with father, and the fixation to a dependent oral position? A conclusive solution of this question is not possible because of the incompleteness of the analysis. The fact that I have extensive notations about every session, allowing a careful reexamination of the material, can hardly make up for this incompleteness. The patient interrupted his treatment in the phase of pregenital withdrawal, still influenced by both positive and negative aspects of his conflict with his father,

before we had an opportunity to attack this central conflict. There
are strong indications that the pregenital regression did not represent a return to an unsettled pregenital conflict but was a regressive
evasion from Oedipal involvement. The patient's depression, which
was the first he had ever had, appeared shortly after the beginning of
the tension between him and the senior member of the corporation.
There is, of course, evidence that the patient had a strong oral attachment to his mother. He reacted to his mother's death with a severe
disturbance which kept him from school for a half a year. He succeeded
in repressing his reactions to that bereavement by developing amnesia
for the whole happy period of his first six years in order to save
himself from frustration.

This early period before mother's death constituted a fixation
point to which he regressed when in his business career he had to
face the never resolved father conflict, precipitated by his unconscious
death wishes toward the senior man. The regression was not to an
unresolved conflict as occurs in traumatic neuroses; most probably
it was a regression to a once successful and gratifying period of adjustment. This regressive retreat was favored not only by the conflict with
the senior man, but also by increased responsibilities and by deprivation of his dependent needs after the birth of his fifth child. An
additional deprivation was moving into a new environment. His guilt
over his destructive ambitions *pushed him back* toward the dependent
pregenital attitude; at the same time he was *pulled back* by his fixation
to the oral dependent gratification that had been successful in the first
six years of his life.

It is not possible to evaluate precisely the relative strengths of the
pullback exerted by the oral fixation point and the pushback resulting
from Oedipal guilt. The fact that until his recent breakdown he had
consistently, vigorously, and successfully pursued a steadily rising business career induces me to believe that the unresolved Oedipal conflict should be considered the primary pathogenic factor. If this assumption is correct, we may predict that his improvement will be
only temporary and he will relapse as soon as he becomes involved
in some other competitive struggle with a father image in his new job.
It also follows that should he resume his treatment, the primary therapeutic goal will be resolution of the father conflict and not of an
unsettled early pregenital involvement. This does not mean that the
patient did not retain a great amount of cathexis on the oral level. It
can be assumed, however, that the pregenital regression would
never have occurred if he had not encountered the Oedipal barrier
when his ambitions were thwarted by the senior member of the company.

Only further treatment can decide with certainty whether or not this evaluation of his conflict is valid. I submit this case not because I can answer the question with certainty, but to illustrate the technical consequences of differentiating between two types of regression during treatment: one to an unresolved conflict for the purpose of mastering it; the other to a once satisfactory phase of development. I want moreover to call attention to the fact that chronological depth of regression is not always equivalent to pathogenic depth; also that to find one general formula valid for all cases is impossible.

Summary

Originally Freud described regression as a trend to return from a later acquired, more advanced form of ego and instinct organization to a more primitive phase. This occurs when the ego is confronted with a conflict situation it cannot master and returns to a phase of its development which was still successful: it returns to a preconflictual state ("fixation points"). The greater the cathexis of the fixation point, the more likely will be a regression to it if later conflicts arise. Later Freud described another type of regression and fixation: fixation to an unresolved traumatic conflict. Traumatic dreams are common examples. The return to such unsettled traumatic situations does not serve any gratification. They are painful and cannot be explained by the assumption that the organism is always motivated by avoiding the unpleasant tensions caused by the pressure of unsatisfied instinctual needs which it tries to eliminate by seeking gratification which in itself is pleasurable. Freud's explanation for this type of phenomena was that the ego's fundamental task is to maintain a stable equilibrium within the mental apparatus; if it fails to fulfill this task, it retains a tendency to achieve a belated mastery. It again and again returns to the traumatic event in order to resolve the tension.

Fenichel has pointed out that the concept of repetition compulsion should be revised in the light of these new formulations. He showed that the term repetition compulsion refers to quite different phenomena. He describes three of these: first, repetition compulsion which is based on periodicity of instinct; second, repetitions due to the tendency of the repressed to find an outlet; and finally, repetitions of traumatic events for the purpose of achieving a belated mastery. In spite of its theoretical significance this principle of mastery has not yet been applied for the understanding of the therapeutic process.

The transference manifestations of the patient are the best known examples of the repetition compulsion. In this paper it is demonstrated that the regression in the transference can follow both types of regression described by Freud: a regressive evasion of an unsettled conflict by returning to a preconflictual adaptation or a return to an unresolved conflict in the past. The significance of these two types of transference mechanisms is quite different from the point of view of therapy. Evasive retreat to preconflictual adaptations is in the service of resistance, while return to an unsettled conflict for its belated mastery runs parallel with our therapeutic effort. A differentiation between these two kinds of transference manifestations is important from the point of view of our interpretations. It has been known and repeatedly described in psychoanalytic literature that patients often dwell upon a type of material for which the analyst shows interest. If the analyst interprets evasive regressive material as pathogenically significant, this gives the patient opportunity to use such material as resistance: by dwelling on it he procrastinates, turning to chronologically later but pathogenically more important material. In other words, our interpretation should express our judgment concerning the nature of a transference manifestation: whether it is regressive evasion or an attempt at belated mastery.

Pregenital material is often evasive regression from the Oedipal conflict. In some cases, however, it may signify a return to early unsettled pregenital conflicts, but in most cases this is not an "either-or" situation. A patient seldom returns to a *completely* conflict-free period but regresses to a *relatively* conflict-free period. In other words, he chooses the lesser evil. In these situations the analysis of such defensive material contributes to our therapeutic goal: it gives opportunity to resolve earlier conflicts of pathogenic significance which contributed to the central conflict of later origin. In this paper it is demonstrated that the two types of regression are mostly mixed and the therapist's task consists in estimating their relative significance in the transference manifestations of the patient.

Two general conclusions are made: 1) chronological depth is not always equivalent to pathogenic depth; 2) it is fallacious to attempt to find one general formula valid for all cases.

Current Problems in Dynamic
Psychotherapy in Its Relationship
to Psychoanalysis

◄ 1959 ►

The current trend toward applying psychodynamic reasoning to psychotherapy which in certain respects differs from the standardized form of psychoanalytic treatment is one of the most signficant developments in psychiatry. Freud foresaw this development in his often quoted statement in which he compared psychoanalysis with gold and other psychotherapeutic procedures with its alloys. This unmistakably implies a value judgment, and permits certain reflections concerning the underlying reasoning. It obviously stems from Freud's conviction that the aims of psychoanalytic treatment and research run parallel. Psychoanalysis aims at the genetic understanding of the patient's complaints. According to Freud, insight into these origins is the primary therapeutic agent. Etiological research and psychoanalysis accordingly have the same objective: to understand the origins of a disease. Referring to psychotherapy, Freud obviously meant that the latter was not an attempt to penetrate into the early determinants of the patient's current complaints. It tries to alleviate them with procedures which are not etiologically oriented, at least not to the same degree as classical analysis. In it the pure gold of etiological understanding is mixed with less valuable practical objectives.

There is growing doubt among many experienced analysts concerning such a complete parallelism between the aims of genetic research and psychoanalytic therapy. Freud's parallelity statement is only approximately true. It was, however, a most fortunate position at the time when Freud pronounced it. It was a logical outcome of his conviction that in order to cure a disease one must understand its causes. Therefore, his first interest was in understanding the nature and the origins of neurotic illness. This was the first indispensable step towards attempting to cure it. To this basic conviction of Freud we

305

owe the development of his personality theory, of psychodynamics as a basic science of psychiatry and of all disciplines which are concerned with man as a social being. It replaced the hit and miss type of psychotherapy, which lacked any sound theoretical foundation and an etiologically oriented treatment.

It was indeed fortunate that for a long time the theoretical interest in etiology outweighed therapeutic ambitions. Freud, according to his own testimony, never was a therapeutic enthusiast. His overwhelming curiosity to understand the genetic background of his patient's problems is clearly reflected in his earliest technical recommendations, which stressed the significance of insight.

The first serious challenge to the thesis that the patient's own genetic understanding of his neurosis is the primary therapeutic factor occurred when the transference phenomenon was discovered. Freud then proclaimed that the patient, in order to be cured must not only understand his neurotic past, but re-experience it in relation to the therapist. Emotional reliving of the past, in addition to insight, now took an important place in the theory of the therapeutic process.

The relation of the emotional reliving of the past to intellectual insight is still an open question. Freud never changed his view that remembering of repressed traumatic situations is the ultimate goal. Only remembering those early events in which the neurotic patterns originated enables the patient to terminate their compulsive repetition in the transference and in his life. Ferenczi and Rank challenged this theory and maintained that re-experiencing during treatment of previous dynamic patterns alone without remembering the original events in which they originated, permits the patient to recognize their irrational nature and replace them with attitudes appropriate to the present. This view was rejected by most analysts as well as by Freud, although it was never subjected to a detached empirical evaluation. This emphasis on emotional experience by no means questioned the postulate that the therapist must understand the genetic background at least intuitively, but preferably consciously, in order to conduct the treatment effectively.

In a series of writings I revived this old unsettled issue by pointing out that the repeating of the old interpersonal reaction patterns during treatment constitutes a corrective experience, because they are repeated towards the therapist who does not behave in the same way as those original objects behaved towards whom the patient's original patterns were directed.[1] I emphasized, as did other psychoanalysts,

---

[1] Franz Alexander, Thomas M. French, et al., *Psychoanalytic Therapy, Principles and Application*, New York: Ronald Press, 1946; *Psychoanalysis and Psychotherapy*, New York: Norton, 1956. (See also "Analysis of the Therapeutic Factors in Psychoanalytic Treatment," in this volume.)

that neurotic reactions do not develop in a vacuum, but are the child's unsuccessful adaptive reactions to environmental influences. The repetition of old patterns in a new setting, to which they do not fit, serves as a challenge to the patient's ego for readjustment, to exchange old patterns with new appropriate ones. One of the ego's basic functions is the constant readjustment of behavior to the everchanging external and internal situations. The neurotic ego lost this flexibility and remains fixated or easily reverts to old modes of feeling, thinking and acting. The transference situation is a unique experience, inasmuch as the therapist's behavior is different from that of the original significant persons in the patient's past life, but it also differs from the behavior of other persons who react to the patient's fixed behavior patterns and mostly reinforce them. The therapist's uninvolvement mobilizes the ego's basic function to attempt a new appropriate adjustment.

It is obvious that from this perspective the cognitive act, namely the intellectual *recognition* of the difference between past and present is secondary to the actual *experiencing* this difference in interacting with the therapist. In this view the emphasis shifts from insight to experience, although the role of insight as a secondary but often powerful consolidating factor is by no means denied. This emphasis on emotional experience has been earlier made by others, particularly Aichorn in his treatment of delinquent youth. The therapist's permissive, yet uninvolved, behavior is perceived by the patient as a quite novel experience, and induces him to change his own responses. The old controversy between Plato's and Aristotle's learning theory—learning through logical insight versus learning through practice—is revived in this current argument. It appears to me that we deal here not with a question to which the answer is either/or. Both principles—experience and insight—are operative in every form of learning, also in the specific form of re-education we call psychoanalysis, and, if I may add, also in dynamic psychotherapy. If some analysts choose to call this new emphasis on emotional experience a dilution of the true concepts of the classical theory, I can only answer them that the phenomena in nature seldom can be understood from one single principle. Even the phenomenon of radiation could not be adequately described by the undulatory theory of light alone and required the revival of the older corpuscular theory. Certain aspects of radiation require the undulatory, other aspects of it the corpuscular theory. The emphasis on the emotional events during treatment may dilute the purity of the single-minded emphasis on insight, but only the two together do adequately describe the actual therapeutic process.

Here is the point where the aims of etiological research and treatment begin to diverge. As long as insight into the origins of the disease were considered as the principal therapeutic factor, the aim of genetic research and psychoanalytic treatment indeed coincided. The stress on emotional experience alters the absolute validity of this contention. It is quite possible that by focussing attention upon the emotional interaction between therapist and patient, the cognitive reconstruction of past events will lose its primary significance, although I believe that in many treatments this will always remain a potent factor. At present it would appear to me that intellectual insight mostly follows rather than precedes corrective emotional experiences. It is made possible by the latter. Bluntly stated, profound therapeutic results may arise from merely corrective experiences even if they are not followed by the revival of repressed memories. Cognitive reconstructions alone never have penetrating therapeutic effect. The appearance of repressed memories is the sign rather than the cause of an emotional change which has already taken place.

This is the crucial point where dynamic psychotherapy and classical psychoanalysis merge. The creation of an appropriate interpersonal climate which fosters that type of emotional experiences which induce the ego to replace old patterns with new ones is the predominant factor in all dynamic psychotherapies, including psychoanalysis. Our current studies in the Mt. Sinai Hospital, in which we observe the therapeutic interaction between therapist and patient, both in psychoanalysis and psychotherapy, convinced our research team that the cognitive and emotional events can only be artificially separated. Moreover, it is becoming clear to us that the influence of the individuality of the therapist is a crucial, although yet almost completely unexplored, factor.

According to the blank screen model of the classical theory, the analyst functions incognito as a neutral intellect who masters the psychoanalytic theory. This concept is being amended by growing consideration paid to the analyst's countertransference reactions as a significant factor in the therapeutic process. A further crucial question is how much, apart from his specific countertransference reactions, the therapist as a distinct individual enters into the therapeutic process. Or, in other words, would the course of the treatment be the same if the patient were treated by a different analyst with the same theoretical orientation and practical experience, but having a different personality—for example, had the patient been treated by a woman instead of by a man, by a younger man instead of an older man, by a reserved rather than an outgoing personality? How are the specific personality features of the therapist, including his own value systems, perceived by the patient even if the analyst tries to keep his incognito, and how does all this influence, if at all, the transference and the whole course of the treatment?

These and many other vital questions are today unanswered.

What seems to be certain is that the patient does not perceive the analyst only as an abstract intellect, but as a distinct person. This fact must be included in an adequate theory of the therapeutic process.

It also appears to be certain that the emotional and the cognitive factors are organically connected. This fundamental fact makes the efforts to divide psychotherapeutic procedures, including psychoanalysis, into rigid categories, both artificial and futile. Knight lucidly expressed this view in 1949 in emphasizing that fundamentally there is only one psychotherapy which "must rest on a basic science of dynamic psychotherapy."[2] The patient's condition and the spontaneous course of the therapeutic process, and not our own preconceived artificial categories, prescribe our activities and interventions. Even emotional support alone may introduce spontaneous insight by decreasing anxiety which interferes with insight. In fact, I suspect that the supportive effect of the psychoanalytic process has been not sufficiently recognized as one of the main factors favoring both insight and the emergence of new emotional patterns. Quite rapid puzzling transference cures may find their explanation precisely in this circumstance: the emotional support which the patient derives from the treatment situation may restore the ego's temporarily impaired integrative capacity, and thus introduce a spontaneous healing process.

This view, if it is valid, unavoidably must have an effect upon our training practices. Knight's tersely stated principle did not yet affect our educational policies sufficiently. Psychoanalysis and dynamic psychotherapy can only be taught and practiced together as one comprehensive field. To implement this principle is extremely difficult at present because of our traditional customs and status considerations, and above all because of the current trend in all aspects of our civilization towards organization and standardization.

Our field is too young to be allowed to be frozen prematurely by this organizational fervor, which demands clearcut, standardized, but often quite artificial, professional categories. In spite of this, because of its practical effectiveness and theoretical soundness, dynamic psychotherapy is in the process of introducing a new fresh point of view in psychiatry, which is not weighted down by a heavy load of traditional beliefs and practices. Gradually it will transform not only the education of psychiatrists, but psychoanalytical training itself.

[2] R. P. Knight, "A Critique of the Present Status of the Psychotherapies," *Bull. N.Y. Acad. Med.*, 2nd Series, Vol. XXV, No. 2 (1949), 100-114.

Psychoanalysis and Psychotherapy

◄ 1960 ►

To speak about psychotherapy and say something which has not been said before on this topic by others and myself is a most difficult assignment. The more we practice psychotherapy, the more we write and speak about it, the more we recognize how much we do not know about its workings, and how little can be stated clearly and with conviction. The same is true for that special form of psychotherapy we call psychoanalysis. Because what is known in this field has been so often stated, I shall this time try to call attention to what we do not know and needs further investigation.

It is a characteristic feature of this field that our practical results are greater than our theoretical knowledge would warrant. We help many patients, both by formal analysis and by the less formalized utilization of psychodynamic principles, without being able to account precisely for our successes and failures. The unpredictability of our results is one of the most conspicuous and also the most disturbing fact in this field.

It is no overstatement that our reputation for a long time was better than we deserved. If I ask myself what is most disconcerting in my relation to my patients, I can say without hesitation that they expect more from me than I feel I can deliver. They come to my office and expect to find answers for their most complex problems, which are the ultimate result of an immense variety of factors: their basic personality equipment, their early experiences, their physical health, the vicissitudes of their fate and their present life involvements, in all of which fortuitous events play an overwhelming role. It is not possible to evaluate precisely how the multiplicity of these variables contributed to their present state. Most of our judgments are primarily intuitive; we can only guess the relative share of these different factors.

The suffering patient has no conception of our relative ig-

310

norance. The emotional nature of the doctor-patient relationship in all fields of medicine is the same. The patient who needs help is inclined to invest the physician with omnipotent qualities, just as primitive man regarded the medicine man as a magician whose healing powers were unlimited. However, the discrepancy between actual knowledge and the patient's expectations differs greatly in the various branches of medicine.

We face our first dilemma: Shall we disillusion the patient by emphasizing our limitations, or shall we make therapeutic use of his exaggerated confidence, allowing him to regress freely to a child-parent relationship, which in itself often has an immediate therapeutic effect on the supportive level? We know from experience only too well that the initial relief which many patients obtain from accepting the role of the helpless child toward the omnipotent parent-physician cannot be perpetuated indefinitely without utilizing this emotional dependence as a vehicle for achieving permanent changes within the patient's personality by insight and corrective experience.

But no generalization is possible. With certain patients an immediate confrontation with their wishful distortions concerning psychiatry in general, and the psychotherapist in particular, would mean jeopardizing that reassuring patient-physician relationship which might be imperative in some cases to save the patient from self destruction or from further regression. In other cases, allowing exaggerated hopes and a magical distortion of the therapist's image to develop undisturbed may lead later to a therapeutic dilemma, which we will not be able to resolve by relying on the faint voice of the intellect. Lacking psychological yardsticks, we can rely at present only on our intuitive appraisal of the patient's ego strength to decide how far we can permit such a regression to go. A misappraisal may have serious consequences. Having permitted for supportive reasons excessive regression toward magical expectations, we shall have the greatest difficulty in countering the patient's tacit or open accusation that we have misled him and promised him more than we can deliver. Many patients when asked years after completed treatment what they got out of it will say: "It helped me some—probably it did—but I still have my problems. I could not even say whether the improvement was due to the treatment or to fortuitous circumstances." Many will add: "At the beginning there was a great relief and improvement, then it became less and less, and then for years nothing much happened." That is, of course, nothing but the reflection of the fact that the first relief came from the supportive effect of the therapeutic realtionship which was not followed up by substantial permanent change. It is, of course, true that the persisting changes derived from gradual insight and corrective experiences in the transference develop more slowly and are less spectacular than the initial relief was. Yet the effect of the frequently almost miraculous initial relief achieved without any effort on the patient's part can hardly be erased. Nothing is more harmful for the ultimate outcome than to accept tacitly the role of the all-knowing magician which most patients force upon us at the beginning of the treatment. A dogmatic pseudoscientific attitude, and particularly the ritualization of the treatment procedure in its external formalities powerfully supports the patient's blind confidence in our knowledge. Often we delude ourselves that we are giving solid insight to the patient when really we mainly perpetuate the parental role. To these aspects of psychoanalysis Rado called attention with the term parentalizing therapy.

On the larger social level this attitude toward psychotherapy, and particularly toward psychoanalysis, appears in the public's overestimation of the potentialities of treatment, surrounding the analyst with an aura of sacred knowledge. Many experienced therapists are seriously concerned with this overselling of psychiatry. Essentially it is not overselling in any active sense. Psychoanalysts do not need to promote such notions actively; their silence and lack of emphasis upon our relative ignorance suffices to allow this overvaluation of our therapeutic knowledge to grow. History teaches us that the need to believe in miracles, in supernatural help for his miseries, is perhaps the strongest motive force in man. Without such illusions and hopes most people could not maintain their emotional equilibrium. It is fortunate that the advent of psychoanalysis made these hopes somewhat more realistic. And yet, to correct unrealistic hopes and reduce them to their proper level is imperative. If hope is a powerful integrating factor, betrayed hopes have a most disintegrating effect. In a great many cases the patient's and often the therapist's uncritical belief in the magic of the therapeutic procedure both prolongs the treatment and permits false, unrealistic hopes to substitute for accepting the realistic limitations both of the patient and of our procedure. It prolongs the treatment and leads eventually to disillusionment and rejection of psychiatry. The number of interminable cases which finally had to be terminated without producing magical results is increasing daily, and contributes to a growing opinion that psychoanalysis is really not the answer to neurotic illness. The previous overestimation of our therapeutic procedures gradually gives place to an underestimation, and the public following its imminent emotional needs looks for new illusions as we are witnessing it today in the advent of miracle drugs.

This unjustified public reaction can only be corrected by a realistic appraisal of what we really know about the therapeutic process, and what we really can expect from its practice. Taking stock of where we stand today is, however, not enough. Spelling out the opaque areas is imperative, but this must be followed up by bold and relentless therapeutic experiments, as well as a radical re-evaluation of our traditional theoretical beliefs. A blind acceptance of untested assumptions, both concerning technique and theory, can only perpetuate the status quo: a limited unsatisfactory understanding of the healing factors and of the shortcomings in our present day procedures.

I shall very briefly try to delineate the major limitations of our knowledge as I can see them.

We know that neurotic behavior is the result of an interrupted emotional and cognitive learning process, a fixation or regression to early patterns of feeling, thinking and acting which have been acquired in the very early phases of life. This perseverance of early reaction patterns is the basis of the central psychotherapeutic phenomenon, the transference. What we try to do is to allow these reaction patterns to express themselves clearly in the transference, to make them fully conscious and to help the patient to recognize their origin in those early interpersonal situations to which the immature ego has been exposed.

Perhaps the most important fact we have learned in the course of fifty years or more is that such genetic understanding alone is seldom, if ever, sufficient to help the patient to readjust his early modes of reactions to his present internal and external situations. We have learned that insightful re-experiencing of the infantile neurotic patterns in relation to the therapist is needed. We also know, however, that emotional re-experiencing still does not answer the crucial question of how and why this re-experiencing should lead to an *alteration* of the original patterns. The transference is as we well know by no means a unique phenomenon restricted to the therapeutic situation. It is the patient's habitual reaction in all of his interpersonal reactions. What then precisely brings about a change in the course of the treatment?

Our current notion is that the therapeutic situation, in contrast with all other interpersonal relationships in life, has a highly specific nature. In the transference situation the old patterns appear in an almost unadulterated form, only slightly modified by the reactions of the therapist. In all real life situations people respond to the patient's reactions with their own patterns and the patient perceives his feelings and his behavior as the responses to the other person's behavior. In psychoanalytic treatment the therapist does not react with his own spontaneous responses, does not evaluate but remains neutral, impersonal and merely interprets the patient's material. This never-before-experienced objectivity of the therapist highlights the inappropriateness of the transference reactions, their past-determined nature, and induces the patient to replace them with more appropriate responses.

This conceptualization of the therapeutic process is reflected in the theory of the therapist being a blank screen. There seems to be an agreement today that this concept is an oversimplification and does not correspond to reality. The fallacy of the blank screen concept is clearly admitted by the recognition of countertransference phenomena. It is, however, assumed that by recognizing and controlling countertransference reactions, the blank screen model can be approached. Here is, I think, where the first unexplored gap appears in our theoretical construction. Apart from his countertransference reactions, the therapist's actual personality as a whole, his individuality in all its manifestations represents an unknown but highly significant variable. There is every indication—and I do not need to substantiate this statement since I do not think it is controversial—that the individual features of the therapist as a person have a decisive influence upon the course of the treatment. In other words, the course of the treatment of the same patient by two different therapists would evolve in different ways, although the two therapists may have the same or nearly the same theoretical convictions and equal experience. There are sufficient indications, mostly derived from supervisory work with candidates, that the individuality of a therapist may be therapeutically more favorable with one type of a patient than with another. This personality factor is a highly elusive one. It can be studied only by outside observers of the therapeutic process, and certainly not by the therapist himself. The recognition of this factor requires also a modification of our views about the transference. There can be no doubt that the transference manifestations of the patient are not undistorted repetitions of past patterns, but combinations of the repetitive predetermined patterns with the patient's reactions to the personality of the therapist. I do not need to emphasize further that these considerations open up questions of extreme theoretical and practical significance, questions for which we have no answers at present. Our ignorance concerning the influence of these personality factors is at least partially responsible for the unpredictability of therapeutic results.

At this point the objection may be raised that obviously I am speaking of psychoanalysis and not of psychotherapy in general. The repetitions of old patterns in the transference and their modification belongs to the armamentarium of psychoanalysis. How do these considerations apply to other forms of psychotherapy? Particularly, how does this affect supportive therapy in which our goal is restricted to giving relief in emotional stress situations and offering the patient gratification for his dependency needs for an indefinite period of time? As long as the therapist appears in the role of authority in whom the patient can confide, and from whom he gets consolation and advice, his individuality should not make a great difference. Yet, it is often of decisive importance whether the patient turns for help to an older or younger man or to a woman; the supportive value of such a therapeutic interaction will primarily depend upon the specific emotional needs of the patient, and on such imponderabilia as the degree of his initial confidence and of the personal attraction he feels for the therapist. Since mostly we cannot match patients and therapists, and even if we could we do not know in advance how to match them, all these factors are beyond our control and must be considered as chance factors.

I shall only briefly refer to other blank areas on the map of our psychotherapeutic knowledge. The actual interaction between patient and physician is an almost unexplored area. Our categories by which we try to describe this complex phenomenon are too vague and general to give even an approximate idea of what is really going on between patient and therapist. We know about the cognitive content of the interpretations in the version in which the analyst remembers them after the interview. How this cognitive content is transmitted to the patient, what he absorbs, what he rejects or misinterprets, and how all this influences his associative processes has never been observed on the spot and studied in sufficient detail. It is encouraging to know that in a great many centers of psychoanalytic research direct observational investigations are being undertaken at present. As one who is engaged in such a study and who knows its complexity, I expect that it will take several years before some general conclusions can be drawn from these types of investigative ventures.

But the greatest obstacle against studying this issue with an open mind lies not alone in the complexity of the therapeutic process itself, but in our preconceived ideas which are perpetuated through professional status consideration and outmoded educational practices. This problem is too vital; it cannot be met by beating around the bush and trying to avoid stepping on professional toes. Our young and immature field is rapidly becoming the victim of premature standardization, institutionalization and organization, which is a general trend in our present historical era. Our interest in practical application of knowledge is so compelling that we cannot wait for acquisition of further basic knowledge. We are justly concerned in good training standards, and try to enforce them by institutional measures. These bona fide efforts, however, lead to rigidity and interfere with the necessary continuous revision of training standards, and particularly of the subject matters we teach. In fact, we become afraid of new knowledge, lest it disturb our neat professional categories and training standards. All social institutions have the tendency to resist change. Our field is too young, however, to be allowed to become the victim of premature standardization

A careful observational study of both formal psychoanalytic and psychotherapeutic procedures indicates that in all psychotherapies which are based on psychodynamic principles, all the therapeutic factors—support, emotional experience and insight—are operative and that our distinctions of the different kinds of psychotherapies are artificial. In all fields of science, the first inclination is toward distinguishing clear categories. To think in terms of continua requires more sophistication and does not give that type of certainty which Aristotelian dichotomies do: for example, psychoanalysis in sharp contrast to psychotherapy. In our field this trend to categorize sharply manifests itself both in our treatment procedures and in teaching. It is hardly possible to decide in advance what therapeutic factors will be used throughout a whole treatment. Often the therapist begins with establishing a firm supportive relationship, and only very gradually strives for more and more insight. In other treatments both patient and therapist have the illusion that it is insight which helps the patient when in reality their mutual intellectual problem-solving activities are but subterfuges to justify the continuation of the treatment, which primarily consists in giving support by satisfying regressive needs. Again, there are treatments in which we initially feel that the patient's ego cannot tolerate insight, and yet we find that after the patient gains security in a firmly established, dependent relationship, he spontaneously will gain insight beyond our initial expectations and often without our active help. The ego's intrinsic function is an integrative one. If this function is impaired, this is mostly due to excessive anxiety or excessive instinctual pressure. Often the mere relaxation of these tensions restores the ego's integrative capacity and a natural curative process may be introduced.

If this view is correct, it should have a far-reaching influence upon our teaching practices. It is not sound teaching to try to restrict a resident rigidly to use only one type of approach, for example, to limit himself to only supportive measures. Not our preconceived categories, but the patient's ever changing psychodynamic condition prescribes the nature of our approach. A second year resident who had not yet started supervised analysis in his psychoanalytic training was strictly advised by his instructors not to use genetic interpretations with his clinic patients in psychotherapy who were under his charge as a resident. He conscientiously followed these instructions until he got into serious difficulty with a neurotic patient. The latter bombarded the resident with his dreams, by which he desperately tried to express and communicate to the therapist his unconscious conflicts. His anxiety mounted, and the dreams as well as the rest of the material became clearer and clearer. In one of his dreams the patient compared himself with an engine which was getting hotter and hotter, and finally exploded. This dream introduced a deterioration of his condition. The resident, as it turned out in my seminar, clearly understood the material but felt bound by his pledge not to act as an analyst and interpret unconscious material. The patient reacted to this disregard for his unconscious material precisely as a child does who knows intuitively and from hearsay where babies come from, but correctly interprets his parents' evasion of this subject as a prohibition. Everything pertaining to this field is tabooed and the child's guilt and anxiety mounts. I absolved the resident from his pledge, and a few correct transference and genetic interpretations saved the resident from losing his faith in psychiatry, and the patient from a pending psychotic episode. This is only one of the many examples of similar occurrences. They show that at present residency training and psychoanalytic training are far from being intelligently integrated with each other.

We cannot deal with patients according to our status categories. One who undertakes the psychotherapy of a patient must be capable of using all the existing knowledge and techniques. Not we, but the patient's ever changing condition decides what approach he needs. The strict distinction between therapeutic factors, such as support and interpretation and division of therapies according to their exclusive reliance on only support or only insight, and the corresponding division of psychiatrists into general psychotherapists and psychoanalysts are unscientific and illogical.

The same consideration pertains to the question of training analysis. In all forms of psychotherapy the personality of the therapist is his primary instrument. To increase the knowledge of this instrument is the purpose of training analysis. It is indispensable for everyone who wants to dedicate himself to psychotherapy. The exceptions—those who have an unusually high degree of native introspective knowledge of themselves and do not need a thorough training analysis—are so rare that they do not contradict this requirement.

Psychotherapy in all its forms, with all the improvements it derived from advancing psychodynamic knowledge and from the compulsory training analysis of prospective analysts, is still a highly unpredictable field, in which intuition and that intangible something we call the total personality of the therapist are paramount therapeutic factors.

Partial teaching of psychotherapy is an artificial procedure. Psychiatrists must know themselves as well all that is known in this field. To teach them according to artificial categories which correspond to our professional pigeonholes may promote organizational aims and reassure those who are worried about their status and prestige but will not promote the development of psychotherapy.

Unexplored Areas in Psychoanalytic Theory and Treatment—Part II

◄ 1958 ►

Treatment

In recent years there is increasing awareness of the fact that the therapeutic process, the main source of all our dynamic knowledge of personality, has not yet been adequately observed in its totality. Hence we do not yet understand precisely the psychodynamics of the treatment procedure. To understand a process, it must be observed. This simple dogma which is the credo of science in the last 300 years has sufficiently proved its validity. It appears, indeed, a banal statement, and yet physics began as a science with the actual systematic observation of motion. Before Galileo, philosophers such as Parmenides, Heraklites and Aristotle talked about stability, motion and change, but never subjected to a methodical observation the things of which they were talking. The same is true for anatomy, which began when the dissection of the human body replaced idle speculations about its construction. And what is for us of greatest interest, the knowledge of personality, began with the banal, yet most significant, historical fact that Freud decided to listen patiently to his patients' complaints, something which strangely enough never was done before in a methodical fashion. All this shows that people seem to have a deep aversion to observe the phenomena they are curious about; they prefer to speculate, or what is worse, to talk about them.

One cannot, however, accuse psychoanalysts of neglecting observation. True, we too talk a great deal about things we did not observe directly—instincts, for example—but certainly the theory of the therapeutic process is based on a most extensive accumulation of observational data. We never really observed, however, the therapeutic process itself in its entirety. We have observed the patient over and over

319

again, but not the therapist in action. We had to be satisfied with the highly selected and certainly anything but objective material, which the therapist could offer us concerning his own activities, reactions and feelings during treatment. In my belief, the next advancement in the realistic understanding of the therapeutic process will come from an approach in which both therapist and patient in their interaction will be studied by a group of trained observers.

I must hasten to state that the impetus for this type of study, which I am at present conducting, came to me first from my contact with David Shakow and soon afterward from a few psychologists and psychoanalysts including Drs. Hilgard and Gill.

What can we hope to learn from this type of investigation? To outline these expectations first I shall have to turn to our current notion of the therapeutic process.

I shall try to reduce the theory of treatment to a few basic propositions, from which an integrated basic therapeutic model, or as we shall see, some alternative models can be constructed. This makes unavoidable repeating briefly our current notions on this subject, although I do not necessarily subscribe to all of them.

THEOREM 1

During therapy, unconscious (repressed) material becomes conscious. This increases the action radius of the conscious ego: the ego becomes cognizant of unconscious impulses and thus able to coordinate (integrate) the latter with the rest of conscious content. As a result, the ego can modify hitherto unconscious impulses so that it can include them into conscious voluntary behavior without internal conflict.

This theorem is based on our notions about ego functions. By internal perceptions the ego registers internal disturbances of physiochemical equilibrium, perceiving them as needs and sensations; by external sensory perceptions it registers the conditions existing in the environment upon which the gratification of internal needs depends. Through its cognitive function it reconciles these two kinds of data with each other and finally, as the center of motor control, it executes cognitive decisions in the form of coordinated voluntary behavior.

While these four ego functions—internal, external perception, integration and execution—are usually explicitly recognized, the importance of one component of the integrative act is somewhat neglected, namely, the omission of perceptory data. An adequate amount of loss of information, to use a term current in communication theory, is a necessary part of the integrative act as well as of the conduction of messages. Otherwise, the communication channels would be hopelessly jammed, and the coordinating function would become impossible by an excessive load of useless—at the moment useless—information. In our empirical era this point cannot be overemphasized. Many "research projects" die from the plethora of indiscriminately collected data. This is due to the erroneous belief that in a "really scientific" study everything must be registered and correlated with everything else. It is quite true that in both the theory of repression and of apperception the principle of loss of information is implicit. Repression is defined as excluding from awareness material with which the ego cannot deal at the moment. It is apt to become a pathological phenomenon, because the loss of information is emotionally conditioned, and therefore valuable information is lost. And similarly, apperception consists in the transformation of the crude data of perception into a meaningful Gestalt which does not contain everything which was perceived. A similar process Freud described by his analogy of the spotlight of attention turned upon readily available but not consciously registered material, through which preconscious material becomes conscious.

THEOREM 2

According to the basic model, mobilization of unconscious material, eventually leading to its becoming conscious, is achieved mainly by two therapeutic factors: (a) free association and (b) the patient's emotional interpersonal experiences in the therapeutic situation (transference). The therapist's objective, nonevaluative, impersonal attitude is the principle factor in mobilizing unconscious material. This objective, impersonal, nonevaluative attitude is the essence of the blank screen concept and is the core of the basic model.

Theorem 2 is based both on the *theory of free association* and the *theory of transference*. We shall discuss them separately.

The theory of free association. It is assumed that as a result of the patient's eliminating conscious control over his train of thoughts, preconscious and eventually unconscious material appear in his consciousness. This expectation is based on the assumption that there is an ever present tendency of repressed material to enter into consciousness, which tendency is counteracted by resistance emanating from the ego. This assumption is consistent with the view that the ego is the central controlling agent of voluntary goal-directed behavior and therefore every impulse which seeks expression necessarily seeks admittance to this central executive agency.

According to the basic model, the technical device of free association requires the patient's full conscious cooperation. The so-called basic rule to abandon conscious control over trains of thought and to tell without any distortion everything at the moment it occurs is explained to the patient before the analytic treatment begins. Moreover, the therapist explains to the patient the rationale of the basic rule. This way the patient is made a partner in the therapeutic venture, and from the beginning shares the responsibility for the therapeutic work which is a teamwork between patient and therapist. Without such cooperation between the patient's conscious ego and the therapist, psychoanalytic treatment is not possible. This precondition serves as the criterion for selection of patients who are suited for analytic treatment.

The theory of transference. It is only natural that the neurotic patient will sooner or later direct his typical neurotic attitude toward his therapist. In psychoanalysis this repetition of neurotic reactions is favored by the therapist's encouraging the patient to be himself as much as he can during the interviews. Free association is by no means merely an intellectual procedure for the patient, because he is increasingly encouraged to express freely repressed emotions and turn them toward the analyst.

According to the basic model, the therapist's objective nonevaluation attitude is the main factor in mobilizing unconscious material during the process of free association. At the same time, it facilitates the manifestation of transference.

It is important to keep in mind that the most significant repressions took place as a result of parental influences. In the course of analytic treatment, because of the prevailing permissive objective atmosphere, this material which has been repressed, or at least checked by inhibitions, is encouraged free expression.

The expression of unconscious material, however, does not take place in a vacuum. The mobilized unconscious tendencies of the patient become expressed in an interpersonal situation; the analyst becomes the object of the hitherto repressed tendencies. This is what is called transference. By its definition the transference is a regressive phenomenon. At the same time, according to the prevailing view, the transference is an ever changing phenomenon. With the mobilization and free expression of different layers of unconscious attitudes, the transference changes. Its content corresponds to previous attitudes of the patient. As these infantile patterns become revived during the therapeutic process and are expressed toward the analyst, the transference neurosis appears.

In the case of chronic neurosis, much of the original parent-child relationship has become internalized. The external struggle between child and parents, the expression of hostility and sexual impulses, of guilt, of expiation by suffering and punishment—all this complex interplay between the child and his environment has been transformed into an internal struggle. The parental images become incorporated as part of the personality, and the external battlefield of emotional interplay becomes transplaced into the internal arena of the personality. The emotional interplay between the child and parents becomes an internal conflict between differentiated attitudes within the personality. During psychoanalytic treatment the *intrapsychic conflict becomes again transformed back into its original interpersonal form as an interaction between the patient and the physician as a parent or sibling substitute in the transference situation.* Only after this externalization of the intrapsychic conflict has taken place and the transference neurosis has developed can the real therapeutic task be undertaken—the treatment and cure of the transference neurosis.

THEOREM 3

The central therapeutic task consists in the resolution of the transference neurosis. In Freud's view the transference neurosis is a less intensive repetition of original neurotic patterns and consequently consists of infantile reactions but is experienced in relationship to the therapist. Its intensity is reduced because the transference emotions are reactions to previous situations and not to the actual patient-physician relation. The only actual relationship between the patient and doctor is the fact that the patient comes to the physician for help. When in the patient's mind the therapist assumes the role of the father, mother, or older or younger sibling, he is actually none of these, and the transference relationship reflects the distortions in the patient's fantasy of the real situation. The nonpsychotic patient whose ego retains its capacity to test reality is aware of the imaginary character of the transference, and this serves to reduce its intensity. Infantile conflicts are viewed openly in the personal relations with the analyst and are faced by the adult ego. Originally, when they were first repressed, the child's weak ego could not cope with them. These quantitative factors, the stronger adult ego facing a weaker edition of the original conflicts, constitute according to Freud the rationale of the treatment.

According to the basic model then, the confrontation of the irrational repetitive predetermined transference reactions (predetermined by the patient's earlier development) with the realistic interpersonal situation in treatment is the principal therapeutic agent in psychoanalysis. This confrontation is a cognitive act leading to insight, but must take place when the patient actually experiences his repetitive reactions in relationship to the therapist. Giving insight into what the patient actually experiences during treatment is called *emotional* insight. To give such emotional insight is the actual accomplishment of the therapist during the whole treatment procedure. Emotional insight, however, pertains not only to the content of the repetitive patterns, but includes also the patient's resistance. Interpretations of the patient's resistance against this type of insight are a major function of the analyst.

According to the basic model, this type of emotional insight resulting from the confrontation of transference patterns with the past and current reality situations is sufficient in itself to accomplish the therapeutic task. *It requires the revival of repressed memories of events in which the transference patterns originated.*

Ferenczi and Rank[1] introduced a modification of Theorem 3, maintaining that the repetition of earlier childhood patterns in the transference situation and their interpretation alone suffices to accomplish the therapeutic task, without reviving the memory of those previous situations in which the transference patterns originated. This theory stressed the significance of the emotional experiences in the transference situation, and did not consider essential the full understanding of their early genetic basis. The main therapeutic agent consists in the interpretation of transference reactions without necessarily connecting them with past memories. This modification never gained full acceptance, although its validity was never rigorously tested.

These three theorems are the foundation of the basic model of treatment. They represent a condensed summary of Freud's views on psychoanalytic treatment as he proposed them in his technical papers published between 1912 and 1915.[2] These three theorems constitute the basic principles of psychoanalytic therapy which fundamentally remained the same up to the present date.

This model disregards, however, two important facts. To begin with, the transference neurosis is not projected on a blank screen on which only the outlines of the objective therapeutic situations are visible, but on a screen with a design of its own which favors certain interpersonal events and which differs in each treatment according to the specific personality makeup of the therapist. The latter determines his spontaneous unconscious countertransference reactions and

---

[1] S. Ferenczi and O. Rank, *Developmental Goals of Psychoanalysis,* New York: Nerv. and Ment. Dis. Pub. Co., 1925.

[2] Sigmund Freud, "Further Recommendations in the Technique of Psychoanalysis: On Beginning the Treatment; The Question of the First Communications; The Dynamics of the Cure," in *Collected Papers,* New York: Basic Books, 1959, Vol. II, 342-365.

"Further Recommendations in the Technique of Psychoanalysis: Recollection, Repetition and Working Through," *ibid.,* 366-376.

"Recommendations for Physicians on the Psychoanalytic Method of Treatment," *ibid.,* 323-333.

"The Dynamics of the Transference," *ibid.,* 312-322.

"Further Recommendations in the Technique of Psychoanalysis: Observations on Transference-Love," *ibid.,* 377-391.

to a degree also his conscious reactions, which are determined not only by his theoretical preparation and practical experience in therapy, but also by his manifest personality traits. Furthermore, the interpersonal relationship in therapy is also influenced by the daily variation of the therapist's subjective state of mind, which is determined by the current experiences in his life. According to the blank screen concept, the analyst functions only as an abstract intellect who helps the patient's insight and serves as an impersonal target of the patient's transference reactions. Although the basic model did not exclude explicitly the influence of the analyst's distinct personality upon the interpersonal relationship in therapy, it did not account for this influence in detail. Freud as early as 1910 speaks about countertransference. The far-reaching consequences of this phenomenon, however, were never systematically studied.[3] The other factor which the basic model disregards is that the therapist actually does more than simply make the patient recognize the inadequateness, the past-determined, and not present-reality-determined nature of his neurotic patterns. He may introduce new value systems by suggestion (re-education) or simply by the fact of what he is as a person. In other words, he offers new identification possibilities to the patient.

I have to apologize for imposing on the reader's patience in outlining the basic assumptions on which the classical therapeutic model is based. My excuse is that I tried to reduce the verbosity with which these views are habitually presented, but a brief statement of these theoretical abstractions is unavoidable if we want to delineate the unexplored areas. This we can do by establishing those points where the theoretical model deviates from the actual events of the therapeutic process. Before trying to identify further the obvious shortcomings to the basic model, a few words should be said about important variations of the basic model as formulated by different authors, who sensed these inadequacies.

Many authors emphasized the significance of the patient's indentification with the analyst as an important noncognitive factor in bringing about a change in the patient's feeling patterns and behavior. This was perhaps most explicitly stated by Strachey in 1934.[4]

The essence of this view is that the analyst serves as a new superego inasmuch as the patient identifies himself with the analyst's attitudes. Interpretations are not only effective by convincing the patient intellectually, but also because the patient adopts wholesale—

[3] S. Freud, "The Future Prospects of Psycho-analytic Therapy," *ibid.*, 285-296.

[4] J. Strachey, "The Nature of the Therapeutic Action in Psychoanalysis," *Int. J. Psycho-Anal.*, XV (1934), 127-159.

not because he became convinced by reason—the therapist's attitude, whom he trusts and admires. Freud was aware of this component of the treatment when he admitted the role of suggestion.

Another variation of the basic model appears in Rado's adaptive technique.[5] He stresses that the therapetuic process to be successful must include more than helping unconscious material to become conscious by the standard procedure; it should also consist in the therapist's helping the patient to readapt himself to his actual life situation by a kind of active reeducational "emotional" process. This emphasis implies, as the identification theory, a not purely cognitive factor. "Insight alone has little if any therapeutic effect." The patient . . . "can learn to change his faulty emotional patterns in one way only: by practice; he must begin to do this before the eyes of the physician." Rado stresses the principle as French and I did in previous writings,[6] that the exploration of the past is not an aim in itself, but must be used for the understanding of the current difficulties in life from which the patient has retreated into his neurotic patterns, which are determined by his past experiences. Rado's criticism of the "parentifying type of psychoanalysis," however, is not a criticism of the accepted theory of treatment, but of its misinterpretation and abuses. The constant confrontation of the transference patterns, with the realistic physician-patient relation, as well as current life situations, is an accepted principle of standard analysis. On the other hand, Rado's admonition that the regressive evasion of the present should be constantly curbed and the patient must be brought back to "the adult level" is identical with my contention that regressive material is not always useful therapeutically. When the patient regresses emotionally to the pretraumatic phases of his life, this must be considered as resistance against working through the pathogenic conflicts; it must be evaluated as a sign of resistance, and accordingly must be counteracted.[7] Essentially Rado's contribution consists of his emphasis that the aim of the treatment is not the exploration of the past, but readjustment to the current problems of life which requires an active collaboration between therapist and patient.

Finally a third variation of the basic model is the theory of corrective emotional experiences which I have proposed and elabo-

[5] Sandor Rado, *Recent Advance of Psychoanalytic Therapy*, Vol. XXI of *Psychiatric Treatment*, Baltimore: Williams & Wilkins, 1953; "Adaptational Development of Psychoanalytic Therapy," and "Adaptational Psychodynamics: A Basic Science," in *Changing Concepts of Psychoanalytic Medicine*, New York: Grune & Stratton, 1956.

[6] Franz Alexander, Thomas M. French, *et al.*, *Psychoanalytic Therapy, Principles and Application*, New York: Ronald Press, 1946.

[7] "Two Forms of Regression and their Therapeutic Implications," in this volume.

rated in recent years.[8] This model requires the introduction of Theorem 4.

THEOREM 4

The essence of the therapeutic process consists of the difference between the physician's reaction and that of the parents, parent substitutes and/or siblings. The objective nonevaluating attitude which has the emotional connotation of helpful interest is certainly a most significant factor in allowing the emergence of repressed material and its revival in the transference situation. Equally important, however, is the recognition on the patient's part that these reactions are not suited to the analyst's reactions, not only because he is objective but also *because he is what he is, a person in his own right.* They are not suited to the situation between patient and therapist, and they are equally unsuited to the patient's current interpersonal relationships in his daily life. The patient is no longer a child, and the persons with whom he has to do are not parental or fraternal figures. This recognition is not merely intellectual insight, but is at the same time an emotional experience. Simultaneously recognizing and experiencing this discrepancy between the transference feelings directed toward the original objects in the past, and the reactions of the therapist, who is a distinct personality and is experienced as such by the patient, is what I called the corrective emotional experience.[9] I shall briefly deal later with some technical conclusions derived from this fact.

This formulation, as also the two above-mentioned variations, do not require, however, *essentially* different therapeutic procedures. They spell out therapeutic factors which actually are operative in the usual psychoanalytic procedure, but are not explicitly stated in the original model. So far as Strachey's position is concerned, no one would deny the fact that identification with the analyst in addition to conviction arrived at by a cognitive process plays at least an intermediary role in every treatment. The patient accepts at first interpretations not only like geometrical deductions through becoming convinced by his own insight of their validity, but at first he accepts them because the analyst says so, knowing that the analyst is an expert with specific preparation and knowledge and also because of his positive transference. And as to Rado's model, no one would deny that most therapists—whether the textbook prescribes it or not—apart from assuming the role of a detached intellect, also approach the

8 F. Alexander, "Some Quantitative Aspects of Psychoanalytic Technique," *J. Am. Psychoanal. Assoc.*, II (1954), 685-701; *Psychoanalysis and Psychotherapy*, London: Ruskin House, 1957; Alexander and French, *et al., op. cit.*
9 *Ibid.*

patient's current life problems with a kind of collaborative reasoning and help him to draw some practical conclusions from the insight gained during the treatment. And finally, concerning the theory of corrective experience, it is hard to question the corrective influence of the fact that the analyst not only does not evaluate but he *is* a concrete person, different from the parental images toward whom the patient's transference reactions are not suited (nonadaptive).

The theory of the corrective emotional experience only spells out explicitly a factor which is an unavoidable component of every treatment.

According to this view, the fundamental therapeutic factor consists in *transference experiences* which are suitable to undo the pathogenic experiences of the past. In order to give these new experiences a corrective value, they must take place under certain highly specific conditions. How to establish these conditions is the main technical problem of the psychoanalytic treatment. According to the basic model, the desirable emotional climate of the treatment situation is achieved by the nonevaluative objective and impersonal attitude of the therapist. The basic model emphasized the patient's emotional insight into the *similarity* between transference reactions and the original infantile patterns. We add now the emphasis on experiencing emotionally the discrepancy between transference reactions and the analyst's actual behavior and personality.

In most chronic cases the re-experiencing of the injurious interpersonal relationships of the past under more favorable conditions, e.g., in the transference situations, is not alone sufficient. The patient must also obtain an intellectual grasp and recognize the past sense and the present incongruity of his habitual emotional patterns. The relative significance of emotional experience versus intellectual grasp is probably the most difficult and most controversial part of psychoanalytic treatment.

We may complete now Freud's formulation of the therapeutic function of the transference.

The new settlement of an old unresolved conflict in the transference situation becomes possible not only because the intensity of the transference conflict is less than that of the original conflict, but also because the therapist's actual responses to the patient's emotional expressions are quite different from the original treatment of the child by the parents. This difference is twofold. First of all, the therapist's attitude is understanding and at the same time emotionally detached. The second factor is that he is actually a different person who does not elicit the same reactions as the original persons in the patient's life did. The important part in this view is that it becomes necessary for the patient to abandon or modify his old patterns. This becomes necessary because the therapist's reactions are different from those early responses on the part of the members of the family. The ego's basic function is precisely this: adjustment to the actual prevailing conditions. As soon as the old neurotic patterns are revived and brought into the realm of consciousness, the ego is challenged to readjust them to the changed external and internal conditions. This is the essence of the corrective influence of those series of experiences which constitute the transference experienced toward a person, who otherwise, if it were not for the distortion resulting from transference, would elicit quite different responses in the patient. There is no disagreement that this is the essence of psychoanalysis, although the personality factor was not explicitly stated in it.

From all the three variations of the therapeutic model, certain technical conclusions follow. Strachey did not draw technical conclusions from his emphasis upon identification. The obvious conclusion, however, is that no matter how powerful a weapon the identification with the analyst may be, the ideal goal remains gradually to transform identification into conviction based on real insight. The question remains, however, unanswered: how does genuine insight make the patient change his ways? Rado's emphasis on the therapist's active help in readjustment and my emphasis on corrective emotional experience are attempts to answer the well-nigh universal question which some time during his treatment every patient asks: "Well, I know now what is the background of my disturbance. How does this knowledge help me to change myself?" Rado takes up this challenge and helps the patient actively to apply insight to those actual problems of his actual life from which the patient withdrew to neurotic symptoms or neurotic behavior. No one would deny the value of such a procedure which to some degree, particularly at the end phase of treatment, is used by most experienced therapists.

The theory of corrective emotional experience leads to still another technical conclusion. This concerns the most opaque (in my opinion) area of psychoanalysis, the question of the therapist's influence on the treatment process by the virtue of being what he is: an individual personality, distinct from all other therapists. The evaluation of this most elusive element in the therapeutic equation is at present quite beyond our ken. We know only that the blank screen model is an abstraction, which is too far removed from the actual events during treatment. The therapist, himself a participant in the process, cannot properly evaluate the influence of his own personality. The supervisory situation gives us some vague notions. We observe that certain candidates handle certain types of patients better than others. We have no systematic knowledge, however, about this factor, not even a general hypothesis.

The concept of corrective emotional experience, however, allows some probable assumptions, which are supported by clinical observations. If it is true that the analytic relationship is a unique one, dissimilar to all previous experiences of the patient, and that this dissimilarity is the most central therapeutic agent, certain conclusions become cogent. What does this dissimilarity consist of? First of all, there is no known human relation with an equal amount of objectivity and lack of emotional involvement, a relationship which on the therapist's part consists only in the wish to understand and help. This ideal, however, is never completely realized as the much discussed phenomenon of countertransference clearly demonstrates. The assumption that the well-analyzed analyst recognizes and controls his own emotional involvement and thus approaches the ideal of a blank screen—a detached intellect communicating with an impersonal voice—is never fully realized. This can be best illustrated by an experiment of thought (Gedanken-experiment): to visualize a treatment in which the patient never meets his therapist as a concrete person, but is received by a microphone through which the therapist is talking with a sound-filtered voice. That such an attempt never was made may indicate that with our practical or intuitive sense we never fully believed in the desirability of the blank screen even if it could be realized. It clearly shows that although our theory does not account for it, we recognize that the therapeutic situation is a highly personal one, in which two unique personalities interact and not as the original model assumes, one real person, the patient, with the therapist, a depersonalized intellect who has mastered psychoanalytic theory. The discrepancy between the patient's past interpersonal experiences, which he repeats in the transference, and the therapeutic situation is accordingly not only due to the objectivity and relative uninvolvement of the therapist, but also to the fact that he is a person in his own right.

A number of clinical examples I described in other writings showed that the "corrective"—or "reconstructive"—value of the therapeutic experience, is enhanced if the analyst's spontaneous reactions, the specific nature of his countertransference attitudes, or his studied attitudes are quite different from the original parental responses.[10] Conversely, if the past parental attitude resembles that of the therapist, an interminable treatment results. The reason for this is quite transparent. The neurotic patterns are adaptive, though unsuccessful, responses to the interpersonal experiences in the family. It is to be expected that if the therapist's countertransference reactions resemble— not, of course, in intensity but in quality—those which contributed to

10 *Ibid.*

the formation of the neurotic patterns, the patient will continue to use them. Toward a doting father the son may respond with guilt, and consequently has to repress or project his hostilities. A paternal warm countertransference of the therapist will perpetuate this pattern, while a more detached therapist who has not quite as warm a response to the same patient would create a therapeutic climate in which free expression of the patient's negative feelings become possible and their repression or projection is no longer necessary. Moreover, the patient will recognize more readily the inappropriateness of his own transference reactions and will feel the need to replace them with more appropriate ones.

I do not need to elaborate this principle further, although I am fully aware of the vagueness of this type of observation and reasoning. My point is that this factor—the influence of the therapist's own personality upon the course and outcome of the treatment—requires further investigation. Neither is this the occasion to discuss in detail my previously made technical suggestions concerning the possibility that the therapist can do more than recognize, control and reduce the effects of spontaneous countertransference attitudes, in case they happen to be similar to those of the patient's parents or other members of his family, but he can replace them by purposefully lending a favorable kind of emotional climate to the interviews.[11] I fully recognize the fact that the analyst cannot change himself and not every analyst is a good enough actor to create convincingly an atmosphere he wants. Here seem to lie the limitations of our technique, and we may have to accept the fact that every therapist is better suited to one type of patient than to others. Yet, I am convinced as a result of many years of experience that by planful behavior the therapist can considerably enhance his repertoire and can have good results even in cases in which his spontaneous reactions would not have a corrective value.

In a current investigation our team in the Mount Sinai Hospital in Los Angeles tried to formulate those questions which appear most unexplored in the therapeutic process, in the first place this personal equation. We developed a procedure of observation and processing of data, from which we expect to obtain some clarifications of these opaque areas.

The main questions we ask can be listed as follows:

Is it true, and if so to what degree, that the patient repeats previously established reaction patterns toward the analyst?

Is it true that the patient's neurotic reaction patterns change as a result of the fact that he intellectually recognizes and emotionally experiences that these patterns had a meaning in the past (were re-

[11] *Ibid.*

actions to family members) but are not adequate reactions to the analyst and his current life situations?

What is the significance of the repetition of such insights and experiences during a prolonged treatment? (working through).

Is the change in the patient's reaction patterns also influenced by the specific personality of the analyst?

Another unexplored area pertains to what is called psychoanalytically oriented psychotherapy.

Can psychoanalytic psychotherapy be defined as a method which in certain quantitative aspects differs from psychoanalysis proper, but fundamentally elicits similar psychological processes in the patient as does psychoanalysis?

What other factors enter into psychoanalytically oriented psychotherapy?

Is identification with the analyst as significant in psychotherapy as it is in psychoanalysis?

Are the direct educational influences of the analyst more important in psychotherapy than in psychoanalysis?

How do concurrent extratherapy events in the patient's life influence the therapeutic process, both in analysis and psychotherapy?

And more specifically, what is the relation of therapeutic experiences to life experiences in the course of the treatment?

Does therapy facilitate certain life experiences which in turn have effect on the therapeutic process?

For example, is a patient who becomes less inhibited as a result of treatment more apt to get involved in an affair, which may influence beneficially his development?

In which way should such a reciprocal effect between therapy and life experiences be included in the technique of treatment?

What is the role of pure chance? (Occurrence of therapeutically favorable or unfavorable life experiences.)

The essence of our investigative procedure consists in the direct observation and recording of the therapeutic process and a carefully planned processing of these data.

The therapeutic process is recorded and observed through a one-way mirror arrangement by three psychoanalytically trained observers who dictate into a microphone on the spot or after the interview their observations which are clustered in pre-established categories, such as content of the verbal exchange, nonverbal communications, transference manifestations, past and current events in relation to each other, dreams, manifestations of resistance, etc. One of the observers serves as audio-visual observer; the two others focus on nonverbal communication, the one on expressive movements, the other on the tonal qualities of speech. In addition, the therapist has a signaling device by which he can register five kinds of observations about himself, whenever they spontaneously catch his attention. These are: bodily sensations, feelings about the patient, wandering away of his thoughts to his own affairs, the sensation of suddenly recognizing some connections in the patient's material, and finally his thinking of the observers. All the material coming from the therapist and on the spot dictations of three observers are synchronized on a tape. Also, certain physiological responses, such as sum total of body movements, pulse rate, skin temperature and electric skin resistance, are recorded both in therapist and patient. After the interview the whole team independently dictate their evaluations of the hour according to a prepared structured pattern. These synchronized records are finally studied by the coordinators who try to reconstruct all occurrences of the interview as an integrated whole. There is no feedback from observers to the therapist, who had no access to any other material than the records of the interviews and his own post-interview dictations.

We try by this procedure to record every visible and audible event, and also the analyst's own thought processes. Yet the whole study is focused around the appraisal of the influence of the analyst's personality upon the process.

Our principal questions are:

How does the analyst's individual personality influence the therapeutic process and how should this factor be included into a revised theoretical model?

And how does the analyst's theoretical orientation influence the therapeutic process?

These two questions necessitate that every member of the team, both therapists and observers, submit himself to preliminary tests and also prepare self-appraisals concerning his own values and attitudes and his own theoretical views about psychoanalytic therapy.

Finally, we wish to throw some light upon the recently so much belabored question:

What are the differences and similarities between psychoanalysis proper and psychoanalytically oriented psychotherapy?

Our pilot experiments already indicate that a valuable and hitherto neglected source of information about the affective interplay between therapist and patient consists in the observation of non-verbal communication.

One example. In our pilot study a female patient during an interview, by provocatively expressing her doubts of my interpretations, induced me to become more explicit and emphatic. After the interview I read the remarks of the observers which they dictated on the spot. This is what one of them reported: "analyst picked up pencil and is pointing it directly at the patient. Patient sticks her right index finger in her ear. After a while the analyst became less emphatic and smiled. Soon the patient took her finger out of her ear. Then the analyst began to point the pencil again toward the patient as he was explaining something to her. The patient now closes the top of her blouse." I was completely unaware of this nonverbal communication between the patient and me. Occasionally, of course, in everyday practice the therapist notices conspicuous nonverbal behavior in the patient, but seldom, if ever, recognizes it as a reaction to his own nonverbal behavior.

The main objective of this study is to learn more about the influence both of the therapist's personality and of his theoretical orientation upon the therapeutic process. To appraise the influence of the therapist's personality as distinct from his theoretical orientation, we are devising ways and means how to differentiate between the effect of the cognitive and noncognitive—the experiential—components of the process. We shall have to observe at least two treatments conducted by therapists whose theoretical orientations and personality profiles have been previously established, and can be further reconstructed by the observers as the treatment progresses. This is facilitated by the device that the therapists, in their post-interview dictation, have to account for all their interventions.

We are keenly aware of the danger inherent in this type of research: namely, being swamped by an enormous amount of data. We know that we must avoid the compulsive urge to try to observe everything and try to correlate everything with everything else. The success of this type of study depends upon asking the correct questions and making a sensible selection of data to be processed.

Our main hope is that the device of exposing all therapeutic events to several trained persons—three observers and several co-ordinators—will allow us to subject the elusive material we are dealing with, if not to the same rigorous standards of scrutiny which prevail in the natural sciences, but at least to more objective control and more detailed work-up than is possible in the private practice of psychoanalysis.

This last reference to the prevailing research in psychoanalysis as it is conducted in private practice, should not be interpreted in a derogatory manner.

It is appropriate at this point to stop and to realize that practically all our psychodynamic knowledge was acquired in this fashion, private practitioners making scattered observations, which never could be fully reproduced, studied and precisely communicated to others. And yet the results of their unsystematic studies revolutionized psychiatry and the social sciences and produced the first comprehensive theory of personality. This accomplishment is most impressive. At the same time it is equally impressive that since the discovery of the role of transference and resistance as proposed in Freud's technical papers between 1912 and 1915, no great technical advances have been made. Whether the therapeutic effectiveness of the treatment has increased at all in all these years is hard to establish. Comparing this stagnation with the great advancements in organic medicine during the same period of time, the striking contrast cannot be simply ignored. The obvious explanation is that we continued to use the same methods of observation and became too complacent and therefore averse to try out new avenues of approach. Primarily this is due to the fact that psychoanalytic research remained outside of academic publicly supported institutions and continued to be carried out as an accessory of private practice. This explains at least partially the fact that we omitted to observe the totality of the therapeutic process. The intimate nature of the material was our excuse. No doubt privacy in matters of personality is even greater than the privacy of the body, and the difficulty of penetrating the privacy of the analyst is perhaps the greatest obstacle. In order to expose the whole therapeutic process to adequate objective observation by others, the therapist must be willing to expose himself. I shall not further elaborate this delicate subject. The analyst, unlike any other physician, has been in the enviable position of being able to expose from his activities only as much as he was willing to expose. I should like to add: even if he is willing to tell everything, he cannot tell what he is not aware of and cannot observe, namely, the manifestations of his own idiosyncratic qualities. Therefore, it appears to me not too exaggerated a hope that the mere fact that analysts are willing to expose their activities to the direct observation of their confreres will give opportunity to learn more about the therapeutic process.

◄ *Three* ►

Psychosomatic Medicine

Zest and
Carbohydrate Metabolism

◄ 1950 ►

Between 1921 and 1929 Petenyi and Lax,[1] and Lax and Petenyi,[2] and Szondi and Lax[3] showed, first, that adrenalin caused latterly a marked fall of blood sugar which, in cases of tetany fell as low as 3 mgm. per cent without any initial rise; second, that these falls in blood sugar were not accompanied by any of the symptoms of fatigue, prostration, apathy, palpitation, vertigo, anxiety, tremulousness and perspiration, that constitute the "hypoglycemia syndrome" produced by the injection of insulin; and, third, that the average rise of blood sugar half an hour after the ingestion of 50 grams of dextrose in 26 normal men was 69 per cent, and in 31 neurasthenics was 31 per cent. They concluded that the most conspicuous symptoms of neurasthenia were analogous with the "hypoglycemic syndrome" but not causally dependent upon it, for neurasthenics do not show hypoglycemia. Although they regarded the flat sugar tolerance test as pathognomic of neurasthenia and held that adrenalin protected a man against the toxic (neurasthenic) symptoms produced by insulin, there is nothing to suggest that they ever inquired whether the adrenergic sympathetic system was underactive or the vagal-insulin parasympathetic system was overactive in neurasthenia.

The work of Alexander and Portis[4] has not only confirmed the

---

Written in collaboration with Warren S. McCulloch, M.D., and Helen B. Carlson, M.D.

[1] Geza Petenyi and Heinrich Lax, "Über die Wirking des Adrenalins auf Blutzucker," *Biochem. Ztschr.*, CXXV (1921), 272-282.

[2] Heinrich Lax and Geza Petenyi, "Beitrag zur Kenntnis der Hypoglykamischen Reaktion," *Klin. Wochschr.* III, Jahrgang (1924), 678.

[3] L. Szondi and H. Lax, "Über die Alimentare Glykamische Reaktion bei Nurasthenie," *Ztschr. Ges. Exper.*, LXIV (1929), 274-280.

[4] Franz Alexander and Sidney A. Portis, "A Psychosomatic Study of Hypoglycemic Fatigue," *Psychos. Med.*, Vol. VI, No. 3 (July, 1944), 191-205; Portis, "The Medical Treatment of Psychosomatic Disturbances," *J.A.M.A.*,

findings of Szondi and Lax but has shown that the principal "neuras-thenic" or "hypoglycemic" symptoms can be much alleviated or en-tirely prevented and the blood sugar curves restored to normal by atropinizing the patient.

Let us describe briefly the kind of patients we have in mind. They are apt to have been energetic with a closely knit system of values centered on some one goal that became not merely unattain-able but unapproachable. Such anxieties as they have seem to be irrelevant, and real hardships and dangers sometimes put a stop to their sysmptoms. This syndrome has been called "vegetative retreat," for the symptoms suggest the under-activity of the sympathetic and/or overactivity of the parasympathetic outflow we all suffer when we must work without zest. Even if the patient is able to do his daily chores, he feels fatigued, sleeps too much, eats too much, often grows fat, and an hour or so after eating is frequently tremulous, sweaty and weak.

Because we were not convinced that the minor fluctuations of zest, from interest to boredom, were able to disturb a system so well governed by many reflexes, we began to study it by measuring the blood sugar at intervals of 5 and 15 minutes in healthy nurses and interns, 1) at rest, 2) watching a moving picture, and 3) playing games, often chess, in which the players became sufficiently involved to show some sweating of the hands and quickening of the pulse. Under none of these circumstances was there a consistent shift in either direction but there were fluctuations and there was a marked difference in the mean value of the differences between successive samples.

1) at rest	Av. 4.4	S.D. 2.0
2) at movies	Av. 8.9	S.D. 3.1
3) at games	Av. 11.0	S.D. 3.0

The differences between these average differences are statistically significant at the level of 1 per cent. The erratic nature of these fluctuations is perhaps best indicated by this, that in 1), 2), or 3) the average difference on 15 minute sampling is not significantly different from that on 5 minute sampling.

We then determined the responses to intravenous glucose in 27 patients who complained of loss of zest and compared them with those of 21 normals on nearly the same diet. Fasting blood samples were taken. 0.6 cc. of 50 per cent glucose solution per kilogram was injected and blood samples were drawn 5, 10, 15, 20, 25, 30, 45, 60,

CXXVI (October, 1944), 413-417; Portis and Irving H. Zitman, "The Mechanism of Fatigue in Neuropsychiatric Patients," *J.A.M.A.*, CXXI (February, 1943), 569-573.

90, and 120 minutes thereafter. Total reducing substance was determined using a micromodification of the Hoffman tungstic acid technique.

At the 15th, 20th, 25th or 30th minute we often encountered a single value so high as to cause a shelf or sometimes a spike on the curve of descent. We could detect no preceding or accompanying autonomic change although the spike did seem to be larger and more regularly present when patients were anxious. We make no attempt to explain it but note that its occurrence prevents us from comparing our findings at 30 minutes with Alexander and Portis' figures.[5] It is clear that by the 60th minute the patients' blood sugars are at least 10 mgms. per cent below those of the controls, a difference which is barely significant. The main difference between normals and patients is apparent in the average nadir regardless of when it occurs, for in the normals it is only 5.5 mgms. per cent (standard deviation, S.D. 4.23) below the fasting value, whereas in the patients it is 21.3 mgms. per cent (S.D. 5.08) which gives a Student's t of 10.7.[6] Obviously this is a statistically valid difference between the groups.

The same difference is best seen by comparing four most apathetic patients with six particularly zesty normal subjects. Under resting conditions the former produced the lowest, the latter the highest, of the curves in Fig. 1. They then played a game of chess in which both were obviously interested. The normals, but not the patients, had fast pulse, quick breathing and moist hands with some tremor. While they were so engaged both were given a glucose tolerance test. The normals' curve fell more rapidly and farther than before, whereas the patients' curve fell more slowly and not so far as before. It was as if the normals with increased sympathetic activity and motor output had consumed more glucose, whereas the patients had merely decreased their parasympathetic, or vagal-insulin, removal of glucose from the blood.

But the greater fall of the patients' blood sugar might be equally well explained if the patients were more than normally sensitive to insulin secreted in response to the sugar we injected. Our laboratory had already made many insulin tolerance tests in normals to serve as controls for the insulin resistant oneirophrenic group of so-called schizophrenics.[7] In these tests we had used 0.1 units of insulin per kilogram body weight and had taken the samples as in the glucose

---

[5] Alexander and Portis, *op. cit.*; Portis, *op. cit.*; Portis and Zitman, *op. cit.*

[6] As a measure of the Significance of the Difference of means we have employed Student's

$$t = (M_1 - M_2) \div \sqrt{\left(\frac{\Sigma\Delta_1^2 - \Sigma\Delta_2^2}{N_1 + N_2 - 2}\right) \left(\frac{1}{N_1} + \frac{1}{N_2}\right)}$$

[7] G. J. Kronenberg, and W. S. McCulloch, "A Brief Insulin Tolerance Test," *Proc. Soc. Exp. Biol. Med.*, LXIV (1947), 492-496.

tolerance tests. We then ran insulin tolerance tests on all neurotic patients in our wards. For this data we are indebted to J. Mack, E. Laslo Wexler, and G. Kronenberg Herwitz, and to the last alone for all calculations of the statistics.

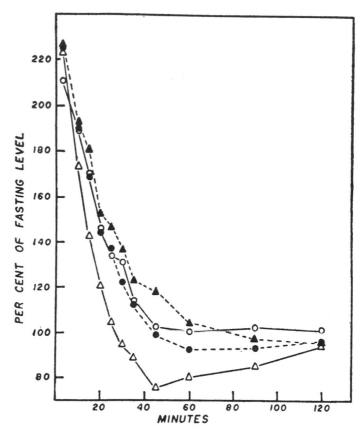

Fig. 1. Per cent of fasting level of blood sugar in glucose tolerance test. ▲ Zesty normal controls not playing game. • Zesty normal controls playing game. △ Vegetative retreat patients not playing game. ○ Vegetative retreat patients playing game.

The table shows that neurotics are statistically more sensitive to insulin than normals principally in that their blood sugar falls more rapidly. It also shows that, on repeating this test with $\frac{1}{80}$ unit of insulin per kilogram, the differences were more significant.

We have subsequently examined the cases of vegetative retreat only to find that their blood sugar falls during insulin tolerance test like that of the normals—not like that of the neurotics. The values show little scatter and their averages are slightly, but not significantly, above those of the normals.

Percentage Fall in Glucose after Injection of Insulin

1/10 U./KG.	15 Minutes		20 Minutes		25 Minutes		30 Minutes	
	Normal	Neu-rotic	Normal	Neu-rotic	Normal	Neu-rotic	Normal	Neu-rotic
Number	28	19	25	19	26	19	26	21
Average	37.6	43.6	48.4	53.5	50.6	55.8	51.7	52.0
S.D.	10.1	5.96	9.49	7.21	8.78	6.27	9.19	8.15
Student's t	2.29		2.24		2.06		0.11	
Level of Significance	2%		2–5%		2.5%		>90%	

1/80 U./KG.								
Number	20	14	18	16	20	16	20	16
Average	33.0	23.2	36.3	29.6	37.6	28.4	29.9	26.8
S.D.	6.97	8.15	7.77	13.2	7.81	10.8	6.83	10.2
Student's t	4.21		1.82		2.93		1.05	
Level of Significance	<1%		5–10%		<1%		20–30%	

This compelled us to seek another explanation of the symptoms of vegetative retreat that might account for the increased rate of fall and the decreased nadir of the blood-sugar-tolerance curve and the production of fat. It would be simplest to suppose that the sugar was converted to fat as suggested by DeWitt Stetten's[8] demonstration that when sugar and heavy water are given simultaneously to animals with plenty of insulin they lay down fats containing the deuterium. The conversion of glucose to fatty acid could conceivably liberate enough oxygen to give a respiratory quotient of 6.0 provided a large enough carbohydrate meal were given with enough insulin. So far as we can discover, the highest respiratory quotient ever recorded was 2.0 in a fattening pig after carbohydrate feeding. With this in mind we have begun to collect on normals and cases of vegetative retreat measures of the oxygen uptake before and during the glucose tolerance test. This series is not great enough to be worth statistical analysis but is clearly important. By means of an ordinary clinical basal metabolic apparatus we have measured the oxygen uptake under standard basal conditions, then given our regular dose of glu-

[8] DeWitt Stetten, Jr. and Marjorie R. Stetten, "The Distribution of Deuterium in a Sample of Deuterio Glucose Excreted by a Diabetic Rabbit, *J. Biol. Chem.*, Vol. CLXV, No. 1 (September, 1946), 147-155.

cose and followed the blood sugar as before. During the decrease of blood sugar at about 15, 30, and 60 minutes after injection we measured the oxygen uptake. In the eight normals so far studied the fluctuations are irregular and small, usually within 5 per cent of the basal rate, that is, within the margin of error of the method. On the other hand, in all five cases of vegetative retreat so studied we have encountered a fall in excess of 10 per cent of the basal rate; that is, they all exceed the error of the method. The average fall exceeded 15 per cent, and the greatest was 29 per cent.

Since we had already verified Alexander and Portis' observation that atropinization brought the blood sugar curve in cases of vegetative retreat to the normal form, we began to try the effect of atropinization upon the change in oxygen uptake induced by injection of glucose. The first case so studied showed an elevation of his nadir by 8 mgm. per cent and accompanying changes in basal metabolic rate as follows:

Minutes	Without atropine	With atropine
20	− 16	0
45	− 20	− 3
60	− 11	+ 3

Summary and conclusion

Interest in movies and games, although it does not alter the average blood sugar level, increases the amplitude of its momentary fluctuations. Want of zest, characteristic of cases of vegetative retreat, leaves the blood sugar level normal, but causes a more rapid and significantly more profound fall on injection of glucose. This cannot be attributed to increased sensitivity to insulin, for, unlike average miscellaneous neurotics, these patients respond only normally to insulin. Because their blood sugar tolerance curves can be rendered normal by atropinization, it is likely that their vago-insulin mechanism is overactive. The resulting increase in insulin should promote the conversion of glucose to fat. This, by liberating oxygen, should decrease oxygen uptake following injection of glucose. This decrease is found to be much greater than the error of the method and to be prevented by atropinization. Presumably this is why they become fat.

The classic neurasthenic symptoms of vegetative retreat, postprandial fatigue, faintness and sweating, occur in these patients after injection of glucose while the blood sugar is falling, even before it has reached the fasting level, or later in cases in which it never goes below that level. Therefore, while these symptoms may be related to uncompensated hyperinsulinism or to the consequent altered metabolism of glucose, they cannot be attributed to hypoglycemia.

The Psychosomatic Approach
in Medical Therapy

◀ 1954 ▶

In discussing this topic it is customary to quote Hippocrates and other great physicians of the remote past to demonstrate that the recognition of emotional factors in physical diseases is as old as medicine itself. If one goes back to the prescientific era, to the medicine man or to medieval concepts, one may even demonstrate that all diseases were thought to be caused by evil spirits and that therapy consisted in procedures by which these *incubi* were exorcised from the body.

This historical position is highly debatable. Just as Aristotle's physics has little in common with modern physics—and Democritus' atom is essentially different from Dalton's atom, so also the psychosomatic approach of today has little or no relation to these older concepts.

Einstein in discussing the atomic theory of Democritus writes: "This idea remains in ancient philosophy nothing more than an ingenious figment of the imagination. Laws of nature relating subsequent events were unknown to the Greeks. Science connecting theory and experiment really began with the work of Galileo." [1] And concerning Aristotle's concepts of physics Einstein maintains that Aristotle's authority was perhaps the chief retarding factor in the development of physics as a science, the beginning of which Einstein places with Galileo as the first one who introduced into human thought the use of scientific reasoning.

In medicine concerning the knowledge of psychological influences upon bodily functions we can also differentiate between a prescientific era and the present one when psychophysiological processes are subjected to methodical observations and experiments. I refer

[1] Albert Einstein and Leopold Infeld, *The Evolution of Physics,* New York: Simon and Schuster, 1938.

345

particularly to our present postulate that both the psychological and the physiological processes must be studied and described precisely with controlled methods of observation. Moreover, also the conceptual tools employed must be clearly defined. This type of approach is of quite recent origin.

Such concepts as "nervous stomach" or "nervous heart" were long popular in medical thought and exemplify the prescientific approach. In making such a diagnosis the physician described precisely his somatic findings, changes in stomach motility and secretion, or in heart rate and rhythm, but neglected to describe precisely the nature of so-called "nervous" factors. He referred to them with such undefined terms as worry, fatigue, excitement or nervous strain in general, concepts which were lacking any concrete content. Even if he assumed on the basis of anatomical and physiological knowledge that the nervous influences are conducted to the end organs via neural and endocrine pathways, his scientific conscience was satisfied by referring to the first link in the psychophysiological chain as "cortical" stimuli. There he stopped because no methods were available to study these cortical processes precisely either physiologically or psychologically.

Every science begins with improving upon the common sense methods of observation and reasoning. The psychosomatic approach in medicine too begins with new methodological and conceptual advancements. One of these is Freud's psychoanalytic method which for the first time made the precise study of psychological causal sequences possible. Another one is Cannon's concept of adaptive bodily responses to emotional states and his first experiments on the influence of fear and rage upon vegetative processes.

Freud began his work with the study of a psychosomatic phenomenon: the hysterical conversion symptom. This contribution, however, soon expanded to the whole field of psychopathology and finally to a theory of human personality. Freud's contribution so far as psychosomatic medicine is concerned is twofold. The more basic of the two is his methodological contribution—the psychoanalytic method which allows the precise motivational reconstruction of psychological sequences by considering both the conscious and unconscious links in causal chains.

The technique of free association and the utilization of the patient's transference manifestations make it possible to observe and to understand precisely in motivational and genetic terms the patient's emotional patterns. This contributed the missing link to the study of psychological processes: it permits the observation and precise understanding not only of the physiological but also of the psychological manifestations. It allows for personality research to acquire that type of a cumulative, collective and controlled knowledge which is the specific mark of science distinguishing it from philosophy.

Freud's other contribution to the study of psychophysiological phenomena was his theory of hysterical conversion symptoms. He explained conversion symptoms which occur in the voluntary muscles and sensory organs as the symbolic expressions of repressed impulses which because of their ego-alien nature cannot be expressed through voluntary behavior. Hysterical symptoms accordingly are symbolic gratifications substituting for full-fledged actions. They are discharge phenomena. The repressed emotion is expressed and discharged through motor innervation or changes in sensory perception. At the same time the symptom also expresses the defenses against the repressed impulses. A paralysis of an arm expresses the ego-alien hostile or sexual desire as well as the repudiation of it. Conversion symptoms express a definite psychological contact which can be reconstructed—sometimes even made conscious—through psychotherapy. Having become conscious it can be modified and thus find adequate ego-syntonic expression through voluntary behavior. Then the symptom disappears.

This theory aroused a great deal of initial controversy but has been largely validated by extensive experience. It is, however, valid only for the explanation of psychogenic symptoms occurring in voluntary muscles and sense organs, organs which have psychological representation and can express ideational content. Various psychoanalytic authors, such as Jelliffe, Groddeck, Simmel, Felix Deutsch, Garma and others attempted to extend this concept to disturbances of the vegetative functions, such as digestion and circulation, functions which are not under voluntary control and mostly have no psychological representation at all. These attempts consisted in arbitrary, sometimes fantastic, interpretations of organic symptoms attributing even to visceral functions specific symbolic meaning. They could neither physiologically nor psychologically be verified by observation.

Cannon's experiments and his concept of adaptive vegetative responses to emotional states led to a different explanation of vegetative, particularly visceral responses to emotional stimuli, an explanation which adequately accounted for both the physiological and psychological processes participating in psychosomatic interaction. Emotional states like rage and fear activate certain physiological processes, which do not express or discharge these emotions, like conversion symptoms do, but prepare the organism for the emergency state which these emotions signalize. Elevation of blood pressure in rage does neither discharge nor express rage, but is an integral part of the rage reaction. It is the result of an adaptive change in the whole vegetative system, a change which prepares the organism for fight or flight, a change from peace to war economy. Unlike in a conversion symptom, rage does not disappear and is replaced by the elevation of blood pressure but as long as the rage persists, the concomitant vegetative changes continue. These are changes which facilitate the organism to meet the emergency by flight or fight reactions. At the same time anabolic-storing functions like digestion are inhibited.

Conversely, in *relaxation* war economy in the vegetative household gives place to a peace economy in which the anabolic processes prevail and the organism has the opportunity to restore its depleted energy supplies.

These basic observations stimulated the psychoanalytic study of patients suffering from various chronic organic conditions. Emotional patterns characteristic for certain diseases have been described as a result of extensive and detailed psychoanalytic observations.

The general dynamic formula is that, whenever certain impulses become repressed or inhibited in their adequate expression in interpersonal relations, a chronic emotional tension state develops, which because of its chronic nature exerts a continued influence upon certain vegetative functions. For example, a chronic state of undischarged resentment through neural and endocrine pathways stimulates the cardiovascular system and thus may lead to a sustained elevation of blood pressure. Although the intermediary physiological mechanisms are still largely unknown, the interaction between the initiating psychological tension state in this case—rage and anxiety on the one hand—and the end organ, the cardiovascular system—on the other, are well established. Similarly a chronic frustration of the wish to receive help and love, which due to neurotic conflict cannot be satisfied in interpersonal relations stimulates the stomach functions which if it persists over a longer period in predisposed individuals may lead to ulcerations in the duodenum. Here, too, the intermediary physiological chain of events is not fully known. That the psychological tension state—a receptive longing for help—activates stomach secretion, is however, well established.

Neither of these conditions, chronic elevation of blood pressure or increased stomach activity, is a conversion symptom. The chronic state of unexpressed hostility is not discharged, relieved or expressed by the concomitant vascular changes; the latter are perpetuated through the specific chronic psychological tension. Similarly, the increased acid secretion of the stomach does not relieve the desire to receive love or help, but is perpetuated by the unrelieved psychological tension. Neither the blood vessels nor the secretory glands of the stomach discharge or express emotions, but they do respond adaptively to specific emotional stimuli. The relation between the psychological stimulus and the organic process activated by the former is not a psychological one; the organic process in itself has no psychological meaning and cannot be interpreted and verbalized in terms of psychology, in contrast with hysterical conversion symptoms which have in themselves a definite ideational content. Elevation of blood pressure is an adaptive vegetative reaction to rage—increased stomach secretion is an adaptive reaction to the receptive emotional attitude to the wish to receive food—help—love.

It should be emphasized, however, that such specific psychophysiological correlations, no matter how well established they may be, do not offer a final etiological explanation of chronic diseases in which emotional factors have been described. The knowledge of such correlations merely accounts for the role of the emotional factor but not for complete etiology. The same emotional conflicts can be observed in persons who do not suffer from any organic symptoms. In order to explain the organic condition other predisposing factors—to which we may refer with the expression of specific organ vulnerability—must be postulated. This vulnerability may be either constitutional —transmitted by genes—or acquired early in life by childrearing practices or by previous diseases involving the organ system in question. The familial nature of many of these chronic diseases is indicative for the constitutional component. Early diseases in the history of some patients involving the organs, which later become affected by emotional tension states, again indicate acquired vulnerability of organ systems.

Only the two types of factors together—organic predisposition and specific emotional tension states—can account for the observations made in patients suffering from those chronic diseases which have been hitherto studied by the psychosomatic approach.

In the remainder of my paper, I shall briefly describe specific psychosomatic patterns, and transference behaviors with their psychotherapeutic implications in the treatment of bronchial asthma, peptic ulcer, ulcerative colitis, thyrotoxicosis, essential hypertension, rheumatoid arthritis, and neurodermatitis.

Peptic ulcer. In peptic ulcer the central dynamic factor is the frustration of oral incorporating urges both receptive and aggressive. These findings made in the Chicago Institute for Psychoanalysis have been corroborated by a number of other authors, such as Kapp, Rosenbaum, Romano[2] and Ruesch.[3] The frustration of oral impulses may be due to internal factors such as guilt about acquisitive tenden-

[2] F. T. Kapp, M. Rosenbaum, and J. Romano, "Psychological Factor in Men With Peptic Ulcers," *Am. J. Psychiat.*, CIII (1947), 700.

[3] Ruesch, Jurgen, *et al.*, *Duodenal Ulcer: A Sociopsychological Study of Naval Enlisted Personnel and Civilians*, Berkeley: Univ. of California Press, 1948.

cies or shame about oral dependent longings or it may be caused by external circumstances. But even those patients whose oral frustration is due to external circumstances display a conflict about their dependency needs.

Those patients who overcompensate for their help-seeking dependent needs in their overt behavior, appear as aggressive independent hardworking men who like responsibility and respond to challenges with an increased striving and activity.

The characteristic transference attitude is, at the beginning of the treatment, a display of self-sufficiency. These patients emphasize that they come to treatment only because their physician explained to them that emotional factors may be involved. Their initial attitude is: "Well, what can I do for *you*, Doctor?" As the treatment progresses and the first defenses against their dependency needs are overcome —which occurs frequently in the third or fourth interview—the patient becomes what George Wilson called the "veritable couch diver." They can scarcely wait until they can throw themselves down on the couch and pour out their worries.

As soon as this dependent type of transference is firmly established, the patients as a rule report a remarkable improvement of their physical symptoms. As soon, however, as in the course of treatment a new wave of resistance develops, the symptoms return.

It is difficult to reduce the therapeutic task into one simple formula because of the great variation in individual features in different patients. In general, however, the therapeutic aim in these patients is to reduce the patients' resistance against accepting help from others, to overcome their shame and guilt about accepting help from others. These patients cannot accept without conflict even the ordinary amount of interdependence which is unavoidable in our civilization. A common example is the businessman who cannot relegate responsibility, who has to pay attention to every detail and carry the whole load of responsibility on his own shoulders.

It is not possible to go into all the details of the psychodynamic events by which this resistance against accepting help can be overcome. The patients' condition improves as soon as they can accept normal give and take relationships and thus become able to satisfy their dependency needs on an ego-syntonic level. Their oral receptive longings constitute a regressive phenomenon. Because they cannot satisfy these needs on the adult level due to an extreme aversion against becoming dependent on others, these longings become repressed and thus frustrated. As a result, a regressive chain of psychodynamic events sets in. The desire for help and love becomes regressively replaced by the wish to be fed which is the first form of receiving help from the mother. This regressively reinforced oral incorporative urge is a chronic stimulus for gastric hyperactivity.

In patients whose oral frustration is due primarily to external circumstances adequate changes in external life conditions affording greater security may greatly improve the physical symptoms.

Recent observations by Engel and Reichsman have substantiated this theoretical concept by direct observation.[4] The patient was a two-year-old girl with a gastric fistula. The latter permitted the continuous measurement of acid secretion. The child's attitude toward her environment could be clearly correlated to the increased and decreased stomach secretions. When the child turned with a receptive positive longing toward the environment the acid secretion rose. Whenever the child withdrew and lapsed into a depressive apathetic state, the acid secretion diminished.

Different forms of colitis. The central dynamic feature in these patients is their tendency to give up easily in the face of obstacles. These patients characteristically develop their bowel disturbance when they lose hope. Even though they may continue their efforts toward achievement, internally they have lost their confidence and have given up all their hopes.

In the past history of these patients we find often that already in early childhood they were exposed to challenges which were beyond their capacity. Ambitious mothers impatient to see their little son become a man is a common finding. The parents of these patients have, as a rule, great expectations toward the child's performance and transplant their own ambitions for achievement into the child. The relative weakness of the patients' ego to achieve the goals which are set higher than their capacity, often leads to disintegrative processes of paranoid coloring. Blaming others for their failures is one of the characteristic manifestations which not infrequently leads to psychotic episodes.

The transference attitude of these patients is as a rule quite the opposite to that of the ulcer patients. While the ulcer patient denies his wish to be helped, the colitis patient is demanding and is apt to shift the blame to the therapist.

Under the continuous stress caused by the discrepancy of the patient's aspirations and his confidence in his ability to realize them, often a disintegrative process in the ego develops which makes the therapeutic task extremely difficult. It has been repeatedly reported that deeper penetration into the patient's conflicts may precipitate

---

[4] George L. Engel and Franz Reichsman, "Affects, Object Relations and Gastric Secretions: The Study of an Infant with a Gastric Fistula," paper presented at the Chicago Psychoanalytic Society meeting, May 25, 1954.

psychotic episodes. A supportive psychotherapeutic approach, on the other hand, may lead to alleviation of the symptoms.

The central therapeutic issue consists in making the patient conscious of the fact that not his actual ability but only his self-confidence is lacking, undermined by previous experiences. This can be achieved by reactivating in the transference those early experiences which laid the ground for the patient's diffidence about himself. On account of the weakness of the ego's integrative capacity, this goal can be achieved only rarely in these patients. The psychophysiological mechanisms are far from being clearly established in these cases. My own view is that we deal here with a regressive psychodynamic process: a regression from meeting the challenges of life on a mature level to a more primitive form of accomplishment on the gastrointestinal level. Defecation is one of the first accomplishments of the child for which he received praise from mother. Increased intestinal activity in the form of evacuation becomes an infantile substitute for coordinated efforts on the adult level.

It is not fully explained how the urge toward evacuation should increase peristaltic activity. It is, however, by no means impossible that the activity of the colon can be stimulated through the ano-colic reflex—innervations ascending from the anal sphincters toward the colon, possibly even to the small bowels. Clinical evidence indicates that the role of psychogenic stimuli may consist merely in favoring an independently existing local organic disease process.

Bronchial asthma. The central conflict in these cases stems from impulses which threaten a person's attachment to mother or a mother substitute. Some mothers react to the first signs of the little son's sexual striving directed toward them with withdrawal or rejection. Sexual strivings thus become an internal danger threatening to alienate mother's affection. Later in life a very common precipitating situation leading to asthma attacks is a pending marriage which these patients are apt to procrastinate. Long periods of engagement have been observed in a number of patients. The son senses the mother's disapproval of his planned marriage and is caught between his love for his bride and the fear of losing mother's love. The girl too may sense mother's unconscious jealousy and is torn between her sexual desires and fear of maternal disapproval.

A further specific feature of these patients is their conflict about crying. Crying is the child's first device for calling mother. In these patients this tendency is inhibited because of fear of maternal repudiation. Asthmatic patients' mothers show consistently an ambivalent attitude—seductive and rejecting at the same time. Later in life the difficulty of calling mother by crying gives place to a difficulty in confiding to an unpredictable mother. These patients show a definite conflict between their wish to confide and the fear of it. Thus, the fear of alienating mother becomes centered on verbal communication which explains the involvement of the respiratory function. Asthmatic attacks can be understood as an inhibition of utilizing the expiratory act for communication, either by crying or confession.

The psychotherapeutic task consists in restoring the patient's ability to confide in people to whom he is attached. In many cases as soon as the patient gains sufficient confidence to confide his secrets— mostly illicit sexual desires—to the therapist, asthmatic attacks disappear. A case to the point has been described by Thomas French and Adelaide Johnson.[5] The disappearance of the symptoms by such briefer approaches, of course, does not mean that the patient's whole disturbed emotional household has been thoroughly restored. This can be achieved only by deeper penetration into the early origins of the emotional conflict situation.

In the transference of these patients an early testing period can be observed. The patient transfers to the therapist the same uncertainty which he had as a child toward the mother and begins by testing the analyst's reactions. He needs reassurance that the analyst's reaction to the patient's hidden desires will be different from that of the mother. Many patients become symptom free as soon as they are able to confide in the therapist.

Essential hypertension. In these cases a continuous struggle against expressing hostile aggressive feelings and the patient's difficulty in asserting himself in any fashion are the central issues. These patients fear losing affection of others and therefore they control the expression of their hostility. Yet as children they were prone to have rage attacks and be aggressive. Sometimes rather suddenly, sometimes gradually, a change in personality occurred. The experience of losing the parents' and other people's affections induced them to control their hostile impulses.

Another related trend is their dogged perseverance in pursuing even insuperable obstacles. Their life history is often that of the beast of burden. They frequently have long standing job records and are staying with the same company for many years. If they are promoted to executive positions they encounter difficulties because of their inability to assert themselves and make others follow orders. Their inclination is to do the job of others instead of insisting on discipline.

The continued control of their own self-assertive and aggressive impulses creates a tension state which through still not fully established

[5] Thomas M. French and Adelaide M. Johnson, "Brief Psychotherapy in Bronchial Asthma," in *Proceedings of the Second Brief Psychotherapy Council, January 1944,* Chicago: Institute for Psychoanalysis, 1944, 14-21.

neural and endocrinological channels contributes to the chronic elevation of blood pressure. The fact that they are prone to carry an
excessive load of work and responsibility even without adequate
recompensation increases their resentment which in turn necessitates
greater and greater control of these hostile feelings. A vicious circle
develops leading to a chronic tension state.

The therapeutic task consists in helping these patients to acquire
a new way of handling their self-assertive and aggressive impulses.
In successful treatment it is not unusual that these patients at the
same time as their blood pressure becomes reduced, show a marked
change in their personality. They become more self-assertive and as
a result they are less easy to handle by those in their environment
who were accustomed to their previous submissiveness. The husband
of one of my patients, a middle-aged woman, whose hypertensive
state had been remedied through psychoanalytic treatment, made the
terse statement to me: "You may have reduced my wife's blood pressure but now she is a much more difficult woman to live with."

Also in their transference attitudes these patients are overcom-
pliant but one can clearly sense underneath a seething rebellious
state. Often intimidating experiences of the past, the retaliatory responses of parents are responsible for the suppression of all manifestations of self-assertion. In such cases, the transference situation supplies
to these patients the needed corrective emotional experiences. As soon
as they begin to feel that the expression of their hostility or self-
assertiveness in the therapeutic situation does not meet with the type
of repressive attitude on the part of the therapist which they had
experienced in relation to their parents, the intimidating influences
of early interpersonal experiences become corrected and they gradually dare to express their feelings more freely.

Neurodermatitis. In these cases we find a complex configuration
between exhibitionism, guilt and masochism, combined with a deep-
seated desire to receive physical expression of love from others. In
the history we find, as a rule, undemonstrative mothers who create
in the child a great hunger for that type of stimulation of the skin
which goes with the physical expression of love on the part of the
mother toward the child.

They want to be stroked, to be cuddled. In general close
physical contact is what is lacking, as their need for it was never
sufficiently satisfied in their early life. They try to get attention
by the means of infantile exhibitionism which is apt to induce
the adults to cuddle the child.

This mode of getting attention becomes complicated by conflicts involved in the Oedipus situation. Their early exhibitionistic
techniques of getting attention and love are aimed at winning the

one parent's affection away from the other parent. This becomes a source of guilt. Following the talion principle, these patients later develop the tendency to exhibit themselves in the negative sense, to put the wrong foot forward and get attention not by physical appeal but by repellant features.

It is impressive to observe how often in the history of these patients we see physical punishments, whipping and beating. The body surface, particularly the skin, becomes highly charged by emotional cathexis. It is the site of exhibitionism in both a positive and negative sense and also the site of pain. The sexual impulses in these patients due to the same historical events become deeply linked with guilt feelings. Pleasure mixed with pain is their solution. They pay with pain for their guilt-laden pleasures.

The disease, as a rule, is precipitated after the patient achieves some form of exhibitionistic victory. The victory arouses guilt and creates a need for suffering precisely on that part of the body which is involved in the exhibitionistic success. By scratching, which is a substitute for masturbation, the patient relieves sexual tension and at the same time inflicts pain upon himself. Some patients vividly describe the pleasure which they derive from scratching. They refer to it as a vicious kind of pleasure. In these scratching orgies they attack their body mercilessly. Scratching they call a pleasureful pain or a painful pleasure.

Also, in the transference manifestations of these patients, the exhibitionistic and masochistic trends prevail. The handling of the transference requires great therapeutic skill and nothing short of the penetrating psychoanalytic approach seems to be of much avail. The early Oedipus involvement has to be revived and resolved in the transference situation.

Arthritis. Like the hypertensive patients, these patients also have great difficulty in handling their aggressive hostile impulses. Unlike the hypertensive patients, however, their solution is a combination of self-control and benevolent tyranny over others.

Most of our knowledge is derived from arthritic women patients. Arthritis is seven times more common in women than in men. When they become mothers, they show compulsive trends and have the inclination to control all the moves of their children and demand their participation in the daily chores of the household. Interestingly, in their own childhood they were exposed to similar maternal influences. The typical mother of the arthritic patient is a restrictive one. In their history we hear consistently the story that as children they were mostly punished by the deprivation of their physical freedom. "Stay put" is the characteristic expression of the mother of the arthritic patient. As young girls in the prepuberty period they react to this physical restriction by becoming tomboys, competing with the boys, fighting with them, climbing trees and fences. In this way they drain the pent-up rebellion against maternal restrictions. Later in life the tomboyish physical expression of rebellion becomes transformed into the tendency to tyrannize others. This they can do without guilt because they exert a helpful type of tyranny. They are strict but take care of the interests of their underlings.

The arthritic condition develops often when this drainage of hostile impulses by helping and ruling at the same time is blocked by some change in their external life situations. Loss of persons whom they dominated before is one common precipitating condition. Arthritic women usually marry submissive men and assume a dominating role in the family. Repeatedly I have seen the precipitation of the disease when the husband made a valiant and successful attempt to stand up against the domination of his wife.

In other cases, an interruption of some kind of physical outlet is the precipitating factor leading to increased tension. The psychophysiological processes through which these emotional factors influence the disease process are largely unknown. There is, however, good indication that increased muscle tonus, that is to say increased simultaneous innervations of both flexors and extensors, may be a factor which unfavorably influences the arthritic process. Most probably this is not a primary etiological factor but increased muscle tonus seems to have a detrimental influence upon the course of the disease. This may, however, explain the capricious nature of the disease characterized by the unpredictable sequences of relapses and remissions.

In their transference these patients, particularly in the beginning, often express latent rebellion by lack of cooperation and a silent spiteful repudiation of the whole therapy, a kind of psychological sitdown strike. This explains why such patients only seldom submit themselves to prolonged psychotherapeutic procedures. This is partially responsible for the fact that our therapeutic experiences are scanty.

To make a general statement concerning the handling of the typical transference attitude of these patients would be premature. In general, we may state that the therapeutic task is somewhat similar to that in the hypertensive patients; at first they have to learn to express their often silent rebellion and then to retrace its origin back to the early mother-child relationship. On account of the capricious nature of the disease characterized by frequent remissions and relapses it is difficult to appreciate the results of psychotherapy. As a whole, our impression is that briefer methods will not prove

effective in these cases and only systematic intensive and prolonged treatment is indicated.

Thyrotoxicosis. The central dynamic issue is a constant struggle
against fear—unadulterated biological fear concerning the physical
integrity of the body and even more specifically, fear of death.
What is characteristic, however, is the way these patients handle
their fear. They try to master it by denying it and by coping with
the dangerous situations by relying only on themselves. In their history we find regularly frequent exposures to death of near relatives
and other traumatic events which constituted a threat to survival.
Equally characteristic is the fact that they mature rapidly. A six-
year-old motherless girl who cooked for the whole family and was
the little mother to her younger siblings is a typical example.

The denial of fear leads to a counterphobic attitude, to the
tendency to seek out actively just those situations which they are
afraid of and repressing the fear of them. The precipitating situation
is often some kind of threat to survival in which the counterphobic
defense breaks down. Thyrotoxicosis following immediately a traumatic event, such as accidents, became known under the term "Shock-
Basedow." In other cases only with careful anamnestic studies can
the threatening event immediately preceding the outbreak of the
disease be discovered.

The psychophysiological explanation of the close correlation between fear and thyroid dysfunction is still not complete. The fact
that these patients have the tendency to early maturation and to
meet dangers in a self-sufficient way may well account for a constant stimulation of thyroid function which after all consists in the
acceleration of growth and metabolism in general. The relation of
thyroid function to anxiety is well established, a relation which goes
both ways. Anxiety activates thyroid function and thyroid hyperactivity manifests itself in increased alertness, vigilance and fearful-
ness.

Psychotherapeutic experiences in thyrotoxicosis are still too
scanty. My and my collaborators' experience consists primarily in
anamnestic studies. The therapeutic task would appear to consist
in helping these patients to admit to themselves their fears and
increase their tolerance for fear. I am not yet in the position to
make a general statement about the ways and means for accomplishing this task.

Summary

The knowledge of specific psychosomatic correlations in different chronic diseases makes a more direct and active therapeutic
approach possible in the comprehensive treatment of the patient. The

general medical management must be coordinated with psycho-therapy. The value of this combined approach has been already demonstrated in the patients suffering from peptic ulcer, colitis, arterial hypertension, bronchial asthma, neurodermatitis and in a few cases of rheumatoid arthritis. The significance of emotional factors in these conditions as well as in thyrotoxicosis, in which psycho-therapeutic experience is still insufficient, can be considered as established.

Psychotherapy of these patients is an integral part of any etiologically oriented therapy. Psychotherapy, however, must be-come coordinated in a rational manner with the somatic handling of the patient. There is no specific technique of psychosomatic therapy. The psychosomatic approach represents a universal principle of medicine which should be applied to every patient because every patient is not only the carrier of a diseased organ but also an individual human being whose emotional reactions are involved in the specific disease process.

The psychosomatic approach consists clearly in a teamwork. During the acute phase of the illness during hospitalization, treat-ment must be of necessity centered around the medical management of the patient. In this phase psychotherapy is mostly limited to creating an adequate interpersonal climate between patient, the physician in charge, nurses and attendants, an emotional climate which changes from case to case. Emotional support combined with show of authority may be helpful in a case of peptic ulcer, while an arthritic patient will do better under a regime of the least pos-sible amount of control. A consistent nonevaluating attitude and willingness to listen to everything the patient may want to confide is again essential during the hospital treatment of asthma patients. Recently, I had opportunity to observe a severe asthma patient whose symptoms have been greatly reduced under the influence of a nurse who became the patient's confidante.

When the acute symptoms are under medical control, the focus of attention should shift to systematic psychotherapy, which aims at a modification of those chronic emotional conflicts which through neural and endocrine pathways influence the disease process.

In all the chronic diseases discussed above the somatic manage-ment alone seldom can bring about permanent cure. If the emotional stress resulting from unresolved conflicts persists, its chronic influence will unavoidably result in relapses. The somatic treatment of the damaged or vulnerable organs alone is only half of the therapeutic task. The chronic emotional stimuli resulting from conflicts which af-fect the diseased organ system must also be eliminated or reduced to insure a permanent cure.

Psychosomatic Study of a Case of Asthma

◄ 1955 ►

History

The patient was a seventy-six-year-old white widow who, in September, 1950, experienced her first episode of illness. Following a rather hard day's work of cleaning a dirty garage, she experienced some dizziness during the middle of the night accompanied by inability to use her legs. She was helped to bed by her youngest son, aged thirty-eight, who was living with her at the time, and recovered completely by morning. In January, 1951, she experienced her first respiratory difficulty following some light work around the house. Following this she experienced a progressive course of respiratory difficulties, with asthmatic attacks, until her present admission to the hospital. She had been admitted to hospitals on several occasions in a severe asthmatic condition. She had been receiving ACTH, adrenalin, and aminophylline, and presented a rather precarious asthmatic condition.

The patient stated that she has never spent a sick day in her life before the present illness, and there was no evidence of any allergic condition either during her childhood or in her immediate family. She was a healthy and vigorous woman, who up to two years before drove her own car and did all her own housework. Three months before, in addition to her asthma, she exhibited a skin reaction which was thought to be either a drug reaction or a neurodermatitis. Removal of all drugs did not result in any clearing of the condition.

Medical examination

On admission to the hospital, the patient was in an acute status asthmaticus. She was sitting up gasping for breath, with loud expiratory wheezes audible throughout the entire chest. The blood pressure

Written in collaboration with Harold Visotsky, M.D.

was 135/65; the pulse was 80; the temperature was 100° F. There was an erythematous lichenified dermatitis over hands, arms, shoulders and upper chest and neck up to the scalp in the back. The pupils reacted to light and accommodation and the fundi were normal. Examination of the chest revealed a widened anteroposterior diameter with rapid, forceful inspirations and retractions of the costal margins on inspiration. The lungs were hyperresonant throughout. There were very loud rasping, expiratory rales and rhonchi with prolongation of the expiratory phase. Examination of the heart revealed the apex to be 2cm. to the left of the midclavicular line. There were no murmurs or thrills; P_2 was louder than A_2; the rhythm was regular. The abdomen was essentially normal. There was a pitting edema of the ankles. Pedal pulses were palpable bilaterally. There was no clubbing or cyanosis of the fingers. The deep tendon reflexes were normal.

Laboratory data

The urine was essentially normal. Initial hemogram revealed a hematocrit of 47 per cent; hemoglobin 13.4 Gm.; white blood count 17,000 with 88 per cent neutrophils, 10 per cent lymphocytes and 2 per cent monocytes; sedimentation rate 26 mm./hr.

The blood chemistry was as follows: nonprotein nitrogen 43 mg./100 cc.; chlorides 108 mEq.; CO_2 combining power 34 vol. %; potassium 3.7 mEq.; sodium 150 mEq.

X-ray of the chest revealed an elongated, tortuous, dilated aorta with predominance of the left ventricle; there was minimal honeycombing of the lung markings of the basilar segments attributable to bronchiectasis; there was minimal emphysema. Sterile sputum culture on admission was essentially normal.

Life history

Patient attributed her asthmatic condition to the shock of her husband's death in December, 1949. When asked which was the saddest day in her life, she promptly stated that the death of her husband was the saddest day in her life. Her husband had been a cardiac patient for several years and died rather suddenly within a period of four hours. They had had a very happy and close marital life. When asked which was the happiest day in her life, she could not name any specific date because she has had "so many happy days."

FAMILY

The patient was the oldest of eight siblings. Her father was a fireman who worked 24 hours straight with six hours off. He was a good, kind man, but not an adequate father because the patient saw him so rarely. The mother was quite a changeable person, sometimes strict, at other times kind and permissive, who had to play the roles of both mother and father. The patient quit school at age fourteen in order to work and help her mother in running the house. She met her husband when she was eighteen and went with him for two years. She explained to the interviewer that she delayed her marriage so long because she felt it unfair to leave her mother with all the work around the house. Moreover, the mother discouraged the marriage at this time, although she was quite fond of the fiancé.

MARRIAGE

Finally the patient married, but they lived in the immediate vicinity of her mother's home—six blocks away. In the next six years the patient moved twice, each time closer to the mother's home. Ten years after the patient's marriage, her mother died and the patient moved to a house she and her husband bought, the home in which the patient has now lived for 40 years. The emphasis she put on her love for this home—being attached to it and not ever wanting to leave it—was impressive. She stated repetitiously that her life with her husband had been completely satisfactory. They had four children—three boys and one girl. In addition, she reared several boys as foster children.

DEATH OF HUSBAND

Following her husband's death in 1949, she felt depressed, neglected, and extremely sad. The day following her husband's funeral, her youngest son promised at the grave of his father that he would never leave her. The two older sons and the daughter were already married at this time. In January, 1950, the patient learned that this son was going steadily with a girl. When she asked him about it, he replied, "She is not my type; I will never marry this kind of a girl." Nevertheless, in December, 1951, the son married this girl. Patient likes the girl, but she did not mix much with the family. During the interview it became quite obvious that patient was quite concerned about the son's marriage and must have been quite suspicious that he only wanted to humor her in his previous denial of the relationship. She was quite certain that the present illness began during the period in which she was deeply disturbed about the son's involvement with the girl.

The son lived for two months in her home and later moved to a home of his own in the suburbs. At this period the patient suffered her most severe attack. For nine months after her son's departure the patient lived alone in her home. It appears to us most significant that during this period her children urged her to leave her home and move in with them or "go to a place like Arizona for her asthma." She felt she could never leave her home. Nine months after her son's departure, her daughter, a divorcée, moved in with her nine-year-old son, and has lived with the patient ever since. The patient emphasized that since her husband's death she has had no confidante other than a sister who has troubles of her own. She could not treat her daughter as a confidante because they did not "very often see eye to eye."

Dreams

While in the hospital the patient had a dream the theme of which has recurred many times. She dreamed she was in her own home, yet she could not account for the other people who were around. Obviously, she referred to visitors, patients, and personnel in the hospital. She completely confused in her dream the hospital with her home. The presence of these strangers disturbed and frightened her in that she thought they were taking over her home. This dream had a hallucinatory vividity.

During a session with the interviewer, she told him a dream in which she saw some men playing cards in her home. When she objected to strangers playing cards in her home the men threw her out, saying "We have taken over." At the end of the interview, the patient reached into a cabinet and gave the interviewer a deck of playing cards. She explained that this was an advertisement which her youngest son received from his company. She was completely unaware of any relation between this and the dream.

Discussion

We have presented this case because this patient for 72 years had no asthmatic symptoms or any serious physical illness and developed asthma quite suddenly at this late phase of her life. This is quite a rare observation and instructive because we were able to establish rather precisely those emotional factors which precipitated her first asthmatic attack. The precipitating emotional factor was clearly the impending danger of leaving the home in which she had lived for 40 years. This woman, because of fortunate circumstances, had never been separated from those persons upon whom she depended and toward whom she had a deep emotional attachment. Until her marriage she lived with her mother and even after marriage she did not leave her mother but lived in the immediate vicinity, having daily contact with her. She married a man who was a perfect mother substitute for her, completely reliable, a man on whom she could depend in every respect.

Even after the death of this man, however, her symptoms did not yet appear. She continued to live with her youngest unmarried son. We do not believe that the son became a substitute for mother and husband. It is common with older people that they become more and more attached to their home which serves as the greatest source for their security.

In some other asthma cases, even among young people, such a deep attachment to the home has been observed. One of the authors treated an asthmatic patient who would become so attached to every hotel room, even after only five or ten days' stay, that every departure was felt as a trauma. His eyes filled with tears every time he was packing his things before giving up the room. Repeatedly he developed asthmatic attacks when ready to leave even temporary domiciles.

The significance of the home for our patient is clearly shown in her hallucinatory dream in which she confused the hospital room with her own home and in the dream in which she saw cardplaying men in the home, who threw her out. During the period when she developed her first attack, the possible separation from her home, the last substitute for maternal security, constantly preyed on her mind. When the son began his relation with the girl, the family repeatedly discussed the advisability of the patient giving up her home after the son's marriage. They maintained there was no sense in her keeping the large home and living alone. Leaving her home was the greatest threat to this woman's security, which was based primarily on her dependency on mother or mother substitutes: at first mother, then husband, then finally the home.

It is not possible on the basis of our material to decide conclusively whether the son also entered into this series of mother substitutes. It appears that it was not so much the son's impending marriage but losing the home, which would be the consequence of the son's marriage, that was the threatening factor which precipitated her attack.

The history of this woman has shown that her previous life circumstances apparently saved her from separation from mother and mother substitutes for 72 years. The first time she had to face the threat of separation she reacted to it with asthma. This observation confirms the finding described in previous publications that a central emotional factor in asthma attacks consists in the threat of separation from a mother substitute.[1]

While emphasizing the nature of the psychological trauma, we do not imply that without an organic predisposition to asthma she would have developed this condition. This underlying predisposing factor became activated when the patient met a specific emotional stress situation which is consistently found as a precipitating factor in asthma attacks.

[1] T. M. French, F. Alexander, *et. al.*, *Psychogenic Factors in Bronchial Asthma*, Washington, D. C.: National Research Council, 1941.

Experimental Studies
of Emotional Stress:
I. Hyperthyroidism

◄ 1961 ►

Objectives of the project

In the last three decades a continuous flow of publications has been devoted to psychiatric, psychosomatic, and psychological observations of patients suffering from chronic diseases, mostly of unknown etiology. Most of these reports were clinical and descriptive and dealt primarily with the biographical reconstruction of emotional conflicts as they evolved in the course of life and were revived by events immediately preceding the onset of the physical symptoms. The hypothesis underlying such psychoetiological studies is that emotional stress evokes physiological responses that have a cumulative effect and may produce chronic, organic, reversible, or irreversible dysfunction. In general, there is no consensus that organic predisposition (constitutional or acquired organ vulnerability) alone is responsible for the choice of disease, or that, in addition, the specific nature of the emotional stress determines the nature of the ensuing organic syndrome (the problem of emotional specificity).

The basic problem, the effect of situations of emotional stress upon the organism, can be approached not only by biographical clinical studies, but more directly by experiment. It is, of course, not possible to study in the laboratory the cumulative effect of emotional stress stimuli that occur over a lifetime, but it is possible to investigate the physiological effects of a well defined, isolated emotional stress situation.

Various methods have been used for the experimental study of

Written in Collaboration with Glenn W. Flagg, M.D., Susan Foster, Ph.D., Theodore Clemens, Ph.D., and William Blahd, M.D.

such emotional stress. One approach[1] was to study the immediate physiological effects of stress interviews. Several authors utilized realistic, recurring stress experiences such as stress situations during military training[2] or physiological changes in students before examinations.[3] Others[4] reproduced lifelike situations in the laboratory by arousing anger or fear in the subjects. By taking advantage of surgical opportunities, observations on stomach activity under the influence of various emotions were made.[5] Finally, hypnotic suggestion was used for the experimental alteration of physiological functions.[6]

The experimental stress chosen for this study was a highly dramatic moving picture. The advantage of this choice consists primarily in the fact that the dramatic film recaptures a real-life situation more realistically than most other experimental techniques. Many experimental conditions oversimplify the conflicts and therefore appear artificial and do not involve the subject emotionally to the extent that real-life experiences do. The emotional involvement in viewing a dramatic film, on the other hand, approaches the intensity experienced in real life, and in spite of the complexity of the emotional stress situation, the same stimulus can be repeated as often as necessary.

The study presented here is part of a larger research program in which the emotional components of different chronic diseases are to be investigated. Thyrotoxicosis was selected for this initial presentation for three reasons:

1. In thyrotoxicosis the precipitating role of emotional stress has been established by previous clinical studies.[7]

[1] M. Doniger, E. D. Wittkower, et al., "Psychophysiological Studies in Thyroid Function, Psychos. Med., XVIII (1956), 310; G. F. Mahl and R. Karpe, "Emotions and Hydrochloric Acid Secretion during Psychoanalytic Hours," Psychos. Med., XI (1949), 2.

[2] R. Grinker, Anxiety and Stress, New York: McGraw-Hill, 1955.

[3] Doniger, Wittkower, et al., op. cit.

[4] D. H. Funkenstein, S. H. King, and M. Drolette, "The Direction of Anger during a Laboratory Stress-Inducing Situation," Psychos. Med., XVI (1954), 404.

[5] G. L. Engel, F. Reichman, and H. L. Segal, "A Study of an Infant with a Gastric Fistula: I. Behavior and the Rate of Total Hydrochloric Acid Secretion," Psychos. Med., XVIII (1956), 374; S. Wolf and H. G. Wolff, "An Experimental Study of Changes in Gastric Function in Response to Varying Life Experiences," Rev. Gastroenterol., XIV (1947), 419.

[6] R. Heilig and H. Hoff, "Beitrage zur Hypnotischen Beeinflussung der Magen Function," Med. Klin., XXI (1925), 162.

[7] W. T. Brown and E. A. Gildea, "Hyperthyroidism and Personality," Am. J. Psychiat., LICIV (1937), 59: A. Conrad, "The Psychiatric Study of Hyperthyroid Patients," J. Nerv. and Ment. Dis., LXXIX (1934), 505; R. Crawford, "Graves Disease; An Emotional Disorder," Kings College Hosp. Rep., 1897, p. 345: G. Ham, F. Alexander, and H. T. Carmichael, "A Psychosomatic Theory of Thyrotoxicosis," Psychos. Med., XIII (1951), 18: N. D. C. Lewis, "Psychoanalytic

2. Clinical studies have indicated that the typical stress in this disease is a well defined and experimentally reproducible emotion, namely, fear concerning biological survival.[8]

3. Changes in thyroid function can be studied by methods that do not affect the patient while he is viewing the dramatic moving picture.

This preliminary study is presented primarily to demonstrate a method for the correlational investigation of physiological and psychological effects of a specific emotional stress imposed on patients with thyrotoxicosis by means of a dramatic film.

Method

SUBJECTS

A total of 19 subjects was studied: seven were acute hyperthyroids, seven were treated hyperthyroids, and five were controls.

The acute hyperthyroid subjects were selected on the basis of a thorough medical and social history. The diagnosis of hyperthyroidism was established by physical examination and pertinent laboratory tests. Patients less than eighteen and more than fifty years of age were excluded.

The following laboratory values were considered prerequisites for inclusion of a subject in the study as an acute hyperthyroid: (1) a 24-hour radioiodine (I^{131}) uptake above 50 per cent; (2) a plasma protein-bound iodine (PBI) level of 9 μg. or above; and (3) elevated BMR and decreased serum cholesterol, if the results of these tests were available.

Treated hyperthyroid subjects were selected on the basis of reliable medical histories consistent with the above criteria for the establishment of the diagnosis of acute hyperthyroidism. All treated patients were in the euthyroid range at the time of the experiment.

Control subjects had normal thyroid function and no other known chronic disease. The control and experimental subjects were matched in terms of age and sex. Although the subjects were not matched for intelligence, we have some data pertaining to this variable.

GENERAL PROCEDURE

There were three main phases of the study: (1) the previewing diagnostic procedures; (2) the experimental stress situation (viewing of the film); and (3) the postviewing procedure.

Previewing diagnostic procedures. Following initial screening, the subjects were given a calculated tracer dose of radioactive iodine

Study of Hyperthyroidism," *Psychoanal. Rev.*, X (1923), 140; T. Lids, "Emotional Factors in the Etiology of Hyperthyroidism," *Psychos. Med.*, XI (1949), 2.

[8] Ham, Alexander, and Carmichael, *op. cit.*

24 hours before the showing of the film. Experimentation with different dosage-time intervals indicated that the 24-hour period resulted in the most satisfactory blood radioactivity levels.

In the early stages of the study the next step in the procedure was a psychiatric interview during which anamnestic and clinical data were obtained, particularly information relating to the subject's defensive patterns. Midway through the study these interviews were conducted only following the viewing.[9]

Psychological testing with the use of various projective techniques was also conducted before viewing of the film, at least one or two days before the film was shown.

Immediately upon the subject's arrival on the experimental day, a blood sample was drawn. Analysis of the blood samples for PBI as a reflection of thyroid hormone levels was carried out by two methods; the standard chemical PBI determination (run in duplicate) and the PBI[131] determination.[10]

Viewing procedure. Subjects were taken into the film-viewing room, and the electrodes for psychophysiological measurement were attached. The subjects were asked not to smoke or chew gum. They were seated in comfortable chairs with head rests improvised from dental equipment, and the function of each electrode was briefly explained. They were instructed not to converse with each other during the film and to avoid movements.

Continuous neck counts of the radioactivity in the thyroid gland during viewing of the film were made. The counter was a "pancake"-type Geiger tube[11] that was positioned centrally over the thyroid. Its position was marked with red ink so that it could be accurately repositioned for hourly postviewing 1-min. counts. Respiration, skin resistance, finger-pulse volume, and heart rate were also measured continuously. The neck counts, as well as all autonomic measures, were recorded on a polygraph. Further details of autonomic measures are reported elsewhere.[12] The subjects reported that they were comfort-

---

[9] In the initial phase of the study, subjects were seen from two to five times by the psychiatrist, who attempted, on the basis of his clinical evaluation of the patient's character structure, to make predictions of the subject's physiological and psychological reactions to the experimental procedure. It became evident, however, that the subjects seemed to use the interviews as a cathartic release and thus lessened the degree of their emotional involvement in the experiment.

[10] S. B. Barker and M. J. Humphrey, "Clinical Determination of Protein-Bound Iodine in Plasma," *J. Clin. Endocrinol.*, X (1950), 1136; R. A. Newburger *et al.*, "Uptake and Blood Level of Radioactive Iodine in Hyperthyroidism," *New England J. Med.*, CCLIII (1955), 127.

[11] Anton Counter Tube 1001 H.

[12] M. A. Wenger, B. T. Engel, and T. L. Clemens, "Studies of Autonomic Response Patterns: Rationale and Methods," *Behav. Sci.*, II (1957), 216.

able with the equipment attached. The fact that two patients went to sleep while wearing the equipment bears out the fact that they were not bothered by it, and many subjects spontaneously reported that they forgot about it completely. Special consideration was given to comfort as well as to the position of the patient's head in the head rest, to offset movement artifacts that might affect the neck counter. Such automatic acts as deep inspiration, expiration, and swallowing did not cause a disturbance in the counter of any great proportion, and instantaneous changes due to movement were clearly recognizable as such on the polygraph records.

The behavior of the subject throughout the entire experimental procedure was systematically observed from behind a one-way mirror. The observer had full view of the subject and a reflected image of the film action. Observations were dictated into a tape recorder. The sound track, as well as a running script describing 168 scenes, enabled us to establish the time relations between film events and behavioral and physiological responses.

Two 16-mm. sound films were shown to the subjects. The first was a 20-minute travelogue depicting pastoral life on a sheep ranch in Australia. This was used to obtain a physiological base line under a presumed state of tranquility.

The stressor film with a specifically chosen plot was a French movie with English dialogue called "Wages of Fear." It ran 100 minutes. Briefly, the plot is as follows.

Four men who are desperate political refugees find themselves trapped in a South American town with no way to leave because of poverty. The hero of the story is a young Frenchman. His companion is an older man who appears quite brave and reassures the young hero. There are two other principal characters, another young man and a slightly older Italian who knows he is dying from lung disease but tries to act unconcerned. An oil company needs two trucks loaded with nitroglycerine driven 300 miles into the mountains to a well fire and offers $2000 per driver. The four volunteers start the journey and overcome many obstacles against seemingly hopeless odds. The older man, who acts so bravely initially, very quickly becomes panicky and has to be forcibly controlled by the younger man. One truck explodes, killing two of the characters, and later it is necessary for the young hero to run over his friend's leg, who dies from the injury. The young hero finally arrives safely and collects his and his dead friend's money.

The details of the perilous journey, as well as their intra- and interpersonal conflicts, are dramatically and vividly portrayed. Previous studies in which 30 subjects were exposed to this and three other films confirmed our impression that the predominant theme of the "specific" plot in the experimental film was seen as the struggle against fear—specifically, fear of death. (Comparison of "predominant themes" with each of the three other movies yielded χ^2 values of 17.08, 20.431, and 17.459; $p = .01$ for $\chi^2 = 6.635$.)

Postviewing procedures. Directly after the end of the film, the second blood sample was drawn for chemical PBI and PBI[131] tests. Then each subject was taken to a private room, given lunch, and allowed to rest for 45 minutes.

A third blood sample was drawn after the rest period, and the Geiger tube was then repositioned over the thyroid and a 1-minute neck count was taken.

A postviewing psychological battery was then administered. This consisted of three previously selected Rorschach cards, four TAT cards, and a specially constructed word association test.

Then the subjects were asked for a spontaneous account of the movie plot. No attempt was made to stimulate recall or to elicit material.

The psychiatric interview was the last part of the procedure. Its function was to assess the reactions of the subjects to the experimental situation. All interviews were recorded and transcribed for later processing.

Results

PHYSIOLOGICAL RESULTS

The first table shows that a significant rise in PBI[131] levels occurred in all acute hyperthyroid subjects during the film and for the 2 hours afterward. In the treated hyperthyroid groups the highest PBI[131] readings were obtained immediately following the film, after which the levels fell sharply. The immediate postviewing level for the control group was well below the initial baseline, whereas the highest level was at the end of the first postviewing hour.

Neck counting. The results of continuous neck counting during the showing of the film and a series of interrupted 1-minute counts taken at 1-, 2-, 3-, 4-, and 24-hour intervals following the viewing of the film indicate some alteration in thyroid function. There appears to be a decrease in neck-counting rates concomitant with melodramatic incidents in the film, as well as a gradual fall in total counting rate until the climax of the film. Subsequently, there appears to be a "recovery" in the counting-rate level. Such decreases in thyroidal radioactivity would indicate the discharge of labeled hormone into the circulation.

Chemical PBI levels in the acute hyperthyroid group reached a maximum during the first postviewing hour (second table). The levels fell, however, during the second hour, approaching previewing levels. In treated hyperthyroid patients PBI levels were highest immediately after the film and then decreased to previewing levels. The PBI levels in control subjects rose above previewing levels but were unchanged at the end of the first post viewing hour. They rose slightly, however, during the second postviewing hour.

PBI[131] Values Obtained at Intervals After the Film

Subjects	Immed. postviewing*	1 hr. later	2 hr. later
Acute			
N = 7	97.88†	110.76	148.60
Treated			
N = 7	38.88	12.77	0.94
Control			
N = 5	− 65.03	33.80	5.50

* Total time for travelogue and stressor film, 2 hr.
† Values are expressed as mean per cent increase over premovie base line.

Chemical PBI Values (μg.) Obtained at Intervals After the Film

Subjects	Immed. postviewing*	1 hr. later	2 hr. later
Acute			
N = 7	1.70†	2.15	1.05
Treated			
N = 7	1.10	0.00	− .05
Control			
N = 5	1.25	1.25	1.55

* Total time for travelogue and stressor film, 2 hr.
† Values are expressed as mean increase, in micrograms, over premovie base line.

Twenty-four-hour postviewing PBI[131] values were usually highest in hyperthyroid subjects, both treated and untreated. The 24-hour chemical PBI levels, on the other hand, were usually equal to or below the initial level in all subjects.

Autonomic nervous system. The predominant finding involved the galvanic skin response (GSR). All six untreated hyperthyroid patients either had a progressive decrease in GSR throughout the measurement period or showed little or no change from their initial resting levels. As contrasted to this pattern, six of the seven controls and the three treated hyperthyroid patients showed progressive increases in resistance beyond the initial resting levels, suggesting adaptation to the film during its showing in the latter two groups. It is interesting to note that the only exception was a nonhyperthyroid subject who had had a goiter removed in 1929 and had a long history of alcoholism with periods of agitation.

By using the "sign test," [13] we found that 15 of 16 "correct" identifications (in terms of the hypothesis that untreated hyperthyroid patients would not show progressive increases in GSR, whereas controls and treated patients would) are significant well beyond the .001 level of confidence.

The respiration and heart rates were at a higher base line level in untreated subjects, as would be expected on the basis of increased metabolic rate. The heart showed greater reactivity in the acute hyperthyroid subjects, in spite of the increased base line.

The finger-pulse-volume differential. The results for the three groups are not clear in this small sample. Fifteen of the 16 subjects (patients and controls) showed periods of marked vasoconstriction during the film. These reactions appeared to be related to the amount of involvement in the film and to its specific content.

Acute hyperthyroid patients were difficult to measure on the plethysmogram because of their continuous hand tremor, which produced movement artifacts. Although they were initially dilated beyond the degree seen in normal subjects, when they become involved in the film and towards the latter ½-⅓ of the movie, they showed severe vasoconstriction and increased tremor, and the plethysmogram became somewhat obscured.

In an over-all view of the differences in automatic patterns between the two groups, it was found that higher metabolic rates were reflected in the untreated hyperthyroid patients by faster respiration and heart rates, but that their *initial* GSR's were *higher* than those of controls and treated patients.

PSYCHOLOGICAL RESULTS

The primary aim of the psychological testing was to measure the impact of the movie on the subjects' defense mechanisms and to correlate variations with the observed physiological and behavioral changes.

A comparison of pre- and postmovie Rorschach results revealed changes in the number of responses on the second testing for almost all subjects. For the control group these changes were indiscriminate with regard to the card on which they occurred and the direction of change (increases or decreases in responses). For the hyperthyroid group, however, these changes were predominantly on the card initially selected as the least-liked card and were almost exclusively increments. The hyperthyroid's increased production on the subjectively

[13] H. M. Walker and J. Lev, *Statistical Inference*, New York: Holt, 1953.

least-pleasant card may have been a delayed or repeated attempt to master an anxiety-producing situation.

Other data seem to support this hypothesis. There was a marked tendency for the hyperthyroid subjects to introduce, often arbitrarily, content from the film into the postmovie Rorschach responses.[14] This inclination was frequently associated with behavior and verbalizations during and after the movie suggesting that they had been little moved by it. None of the control subjects ever introduced film material into the postmovie Rorschach.

Introduction of film material was associated with an appreciable diminution in percept-quality level (i.e., the $F + \%$ on the Rorschach), suggesting some temporary impairment in ego functioning. Two acute hyperthyroid subjects were tested for a third time several days after the film viewing, and their records at that time more closely approximated the initial than the postviewing Rorschach.

In addition to evaluating the impact of the film on the subjects' defenses, the projective tests were used to delineate empirically the characterological differences between the hyperthyroid and the control subjects. The most promising criterion found in the preliminary analysis of these records was the number of responses that were related to, if not equated with, the counterphobic attitude. The control subjects displayed a wide variety of defense patterns on the projective materials, but the hyperthyroids used a counterphobic defense system predominantly.[15]

Grouping all the hyperthyroid subjects, there was 4.05 counterphobic responses per individual compared with 1.5 responses per individual in the control group. However, eight of the 16 hyperthyroid subjects in our sample were from the Los Angeles County General Hospital and differed markedly in intelligence and socioeconomic background from the other hyperthyroid subjects and the control subjects. Considering only the eight hyperthyroid subjects of average and above average intelligence, the hyperthyroids gave 7.2 counterphobic responses per individual, almost five times as many as the control group.

The marked difference in the responses of the hyperthyroid subjects of lower intelligence seemed to be related to their limited com-

---

[14] Examples of this are seeing "oil" on Card I (oil plays a prominent role in the film) or seeing the faces of various characters in the film on different cards.

[15] According to Schafer, the counterphobic defense may appear in any of the following forms in the test situation: "Exaggerated criticality and querulousness; scornful amusement in the form of supposedly weird, frightening or otherwise distressing test stimuli and response content; unyielding determination to persist at problem solving . . . despite all discouraging difficulty encountered and encouragement by the tester to give up" (R. Schafer, *Psychoanalytic Interpretation in Rorschach Testing*, New York: Grune & Stratton, 1954, p. 18).

munication and verbalization. Subjects in this group were the only ones to reject cards, and they produced an average of 1.5 responses per card, compared to 4.4 responses per card for the "brighter" hyperthyroid subjects. The counterphobic attitude, as measured by our test, apparently required a certain minimal amount of verbal fluency. Since many counterphobic responses were spontaneous comments, rather than formal responses to cards (e.g., "Boy, this is really exciting"), it did not seem theoretically feasible to establish a criterion for weighing counterphobic responses per Rorschach response. It is hoped that matching subjects for intelligence will eliminate this difficulty in the future.

It seems reasonable to assume that weakening or disintegration of counterphobic defenses would disclose the underlying phobias. In view of the fairly frequent association of acute hyperthyroidism with a schizophrenic-like psychosis,[16] one might expect a decrement in counterphobic responses and an increment in phobic ones in the records of some *acute* hyperthyroid subjects. In order to compensate for this defensive shift, the sums of phobic and counterphobic responses of the control and "bright" hyperthyroid groups were compared. These sums differentiated these two groups without overlapping. As a further test of this reasoning, the ratio of counterphobic to phobic responses of the hyperthyroid subjects who were acute or just beginning treatment were compared with the same ratio of responses of the hyperthyroids who had received treatment a number of years ago. Although the latter groups contained too few subjects for more than suggestive results, they gave a ratio twice as large as that of the acute subjects.

It was unexpectedly found that the experimental subjects differed from the control subjects in the cards that they selected as best and least liked. The distinguishing factor in these differences seemed to be the presence or absence of coloring. Of the ten Rorschach cards, three are completely colored, two are partially colored, and five are achromatic. For purposes of comparison the cards were assigned arbitrary values: 1.0 for a completely colored or achromatic card, and 0.5 for the partially colored cards. The expected ratio of preference based on chance alone would be four colored to six achromatic cards. Grouping the subjects into hyperthyroids and controls, it was found that the control subjects preferred the colored cards in the ratio of

---

16 D. Brockman and R. Whitman, "Post-Thyroidectomy Psychoses," *J. Nerv. and Ment. Dis.*, CXVI (1952), 340; G. Huber, "Psychosen bei späterworbenem Hyperthyroidismus und Hypoparathyroidismus (Psychoses in Acquired Hyperthyroidism and Hypoparathyroidism), *Nervenarzt*, XXVII (1956), 440: W. Reiss, *et al.*, "Thyroid Activity in Mental Patients: Evaluation by Radioactive Tracer Methods," *Brit. Med. J.*, 4716 (1951), 1181.

4.5:5.5, a ratio closely approximating chance expectations. The hyperthyroid subjects, however, preferred the colored cards in a ratio of 8:2, thus markedly reversing the expected ratio. A χ^2 test revealed that this preference for colored cards was different from the expected ratio beyond the .01 level of significance ($\chi^2 = 10$; $p = .01$; for $\chi^2 = 6.635$, $N = 1$) and from the control group beyond the 0.1 level of significance ($\chi^2 = 8.38$). Considering the card liked least, the expected ratio of colored to achromatic is 4:6. The controls chose in a ratio of 3.9:6.1, whereas the hyperthyroids chose in a ratio of 1.4:8.6. In this case the difference between the hyperthyroids and the expected ratio ($\chi^2 = 3.39$, $p = .10$ for $\chi^2 = 2.70$; $p = .05$ for $\chi^2 = 3.841$) and the control group ($\chi^2 = 2.38$) are not statistically significant, but the former approaches the .05 level.

A possible explanation for the statistically significant differences between the subjects in their color vs. achromatic card preferences without separating the "bright" and "dull" hyperthyroid subjects may be found in the more structured nature of the response elicited. Each subject was asked for only one choice. Differences in productivity and tendencies toward verbalization between different subjects were thus arbitrarily controlled. Since these qualities are associated with higher intelligence, it seems that intellectual dullness may have obscured the counterphobic attitude, insofar as the other projective methods elicited it.

The word association test used in this study was developed concurrently with the running of subjects. Frequent changes of component words and their serial order precludes any systematic analysis of the results thus far obtained. It can be said, however that certain words, particularly those relating to the previously seen movie and those connoting threat and obligation, elicit responses in which the hyperthyroid subjects differ from the control subjects. For example to the word "dread" *each* hyperthyroid subject displayed a disturbance in reaction time or memory; only one of ten control subjects displayed such a disturbance. To the "threat" words generally the hyperthyroids responded with attempts, often primitive, to deny; for example, to the word "explosion" the reply "nonexplosion" was given. In addition, some of the "threat" words seemed to differentiate the acute from the treated hyperthyroids. The responses of the former tended to vacillate between a lack of defense and a primitive denial, whereas the treated hyperthyroids gave better integrated counterphobic responses. An example of this can be seen in a sampling of the responses to the word "danger." From the acute patients: "worried—afraid"; "protection—nondanger"; "protection"; "damage—afraid." From the treated hyperthyroids: "detective"; "lookout"; "exciting"; "I don't ever think of any one particular word for danger to be honest"—after urging: "an abyss, it means, a nothingness, maybe."

It would thus seem that projective tests can be used to distinguish hyperthyroid from nonhyperthyroid individuals on the basis of the counterphobic attitude. Acute hyperthyroid individuals display a lower ratio of counterphobic to phobic responses than treated hyperthyroids, a finding probably related to the clinically described defensive decompensation frequent in acute hyperthyroidism. Finally, the hyperthyroid subjects are more affected by the test film than the controls and display a continuing effort to cope with it as an anxiety-provoking stimulus.

PSYCHIATRIC INTERVIEWS

As stated above, the purpose of the postviewing interviews was to assess the subjects' reactions to the whole experimental procedure, but specifically to study those emotional reactions which seemed directly related to the content of the stress movie. The interviewer was interested in the subjects' opinions and feelings about the story of the movie as a whole because this usually gave some information as to their individual social and political biases. However, most revealing psychodynamically for each individual were his reactions to the four main characters and to certain specific scenes in the movie action. Certain positive and negative identifications as well as omissions and distortions of the plot, along with internal contradictions of the subject's report within a particular interview gave clues as to areas of intrapsychic and interpersonal conflict and revealed the major defenses utilized in dealing with the conflicts.

Many times the movie served as a stimulus for the patient to reveal important anamnestic material.

It was our experience that subjects generally were somewhat reluctant to admit their emotional involvement in the movie. Although true of all categories of subjects, it was most characteristic of those well defended hyperthyroid patients whose counterphobic defenses were still operating relatively efficiently. These individuals had a tendency to make the movie a farce, and typical comments were "It didn't affect me at all," "It was foolish," "I didn't notice it," "A lot of things happened that tickled me," "The hero always gets through," "No involvement," "Amusing," and "It was exciting but I don't know why people were so nervous."

The decompensated hyperthyroid patients, however, frankly admitted that they were overwhelmed by fear, did not like the movie, and wished to leave, or some said it reminded them of their own lives. The treated hyperthyroid patients, as a group, attempted to master the movie situation by intellectualization, e.g., concentrating on technical details of the film or obsessively ruminating about the moral aspects of the major traumatic events. This was especially true of the treated sophisticated subjects. Less sophisticated patients, both treated and untreated, used frank avoidance reactions of closing their eyes or turning their head from the screen (Fig. 1). The control subjects, men especially, were somewhat reserved about admitting fear or the inclination to weep. However, they usually admitted frankly that they were involved, that they felt tense and afraid for the men as well as pathos for them, and that they would not care to have been in a similar situation.

Towards the character who shows bravado in the beginning of the story and who later breaks down, the hyperthyroid patients took an angry, depreciating attitude after initially identifying with him in contrast to the normal subjects, who felt pity or pathos for him and tried to justify his behavior.

Discussion

The results indicate that the hyperthyroids could be experimentally differentiated from the normal controls on the basis of their physiological and psychological reactions to the movie. Furthermore, the acute and treated hyperthyroids could be differentiated from each other by many response measures.

In terms of the autonomic measurements, the treated hyperthyroids resembled the normal controls more than they did the acute hyperthyroids. However, in terms of thyroid measures, the treated and untreated hyperthyroids were alike in that their highest PBI[131] values were the 24-hour levels whereas for the controls these were the lowest. In all subjects the 24-hour chemical PBI tended to be the lowest. It appears that the PBI[131] level is a more sensitive index of thyroid hormone turnover than the chemical PBI level.

Psychologically, the treated hyperthyroids displayed a stable, rigid counterphobic defense. Superficially, at least, they relished being placed in the experimental setting. They minimized discomforts that both the normal controls and acute patients complained about. They seemed to view the procedure as an adventure and spoke of it in terms of being "exciting" and "fun" to a degree that was somewhat inappropriate. Many of them volunteered to participate in any further research projects. The primary characteristic of the treated hyperthyroids, then, was their tendency to attack or actively master situations in which they were afraid. There were many gradations in their ability to do so, and some would "rework" a situation repeatedly before they mastered it; others seemed able to do it immediately.

The acute hyperthyroids were a more heterogeneous group than either the treated or control group. Their autonomic records showed generally an initially higher state of defense with less anxiety (high GSR values), but under the stress of the movie they showed progressive lack of adaption (decompensation with lower GSR values). The treated patients and controls showed the opposite pattern. This general state of psychophysiological decompensation was also reflected in the marked rise in PBI[131] levels, which was dramatic and more prolonged in the acute patients than in treated patients and controls. The chemical PBI reflected the phenomenon in a similar but not so clear manner. Neck-count changes were more rapid and of much greater magnitude in the acute patients.

In accord with these findings, the treated hyperthyroids resorted to primitive, verbal denial of fear, or vacillated between an attempt to deny and/or a pronounced reaction formation. On the word association test, for example, the treated hyperthyroids gave consistently counterphobic responses to the "threat" words, but the acute patients more often responded with a weak denial.

The psychological patterns of the controls were varied; no single type of defense predominated. As indicated in the section on results, the counterphobic attitude was one of a great many defenses employed, but in terms of prevalence it ranked quite low.

It was hypothesized that hyperthyroid subjects have a characteristic manner of dealing with fear stimuli. Specifically, the effect of the fear stimulus on the hyperthyroid subject would be inversely related to the intactness of his capacity to use counterphobic denial and/or mastery as a major defensive technique. Further, increased thyroid secretion, autonomic responses consistent with the physiological manifestations of fear, and decompensation of ego function would occur concomitantly.

Summary

On the basis of this study, we believe that we have succeeded in developing a methodology and instruments sensitive enough to establish reliable correlations between a standardized psychological stimulus (movie), the experimental subjects' psychological defenses, and responses in the autonomic nervous system and in thyroid function of treated and untreated thyrotoxic patients and controls.

◄ *Four* ►

Sociology, Politics, Esthetics, Criminology

The Don Quixote
of America

◄ 1937 ►

Intensive study of criminal personalities with the modern technique of dynamic psychology has revealed that apart from rational motives such as the desire for economic gain there are other more powerful emotional factors which drive individuals into criminal careers. An excessive thirst for prestige, the wish to appear a daring, independent, "tough man," has been found frequently as such an emotional factor, contributing to criminality among young delinquents. The deeper study of such delinquents has revealed the rather unexpected fact that such an extensive craving to appear aggressive and tough is common among people who deep down in the unconscious layers of their personality have an intense longing for dependence, who crave to be loved by others, to receive help and support. Often these "tough guys" in the core of their personality are emotionally immature and insecure. The external shell of bravado is often only a thin cover, a mask by which they try to hide this soft core from others as well as from themselves.

This "soft on the inside, tough on the outside" type of delinquent seems to be more common in the American scene than elsewhere. The reason for this is probably found in the cultural history of this country. The ideal of the successful, resourceful, brave, self-made man who owes everything to himself and nothing to anybody else is the traditional ideal of the pioneer and frontier days. It is obvious that these virtues, the universal value of which is by no means questioned, were extremely important in the frontier days and overshadowed any other human assets in the conquest of a vast continent and the rapid development of a new center of civilization.

In an almost miraculously short period however the conditions of the frontier have vanished. With the help of a highly developed machine civilization the country has progressed to the status of an organ-

381

ized and standardized industrial structure. The great majority of those young men who are still raised according to the ideals of individual initiative, endurance, self-reliance and courage represented by their pioneer forefathers, when grown up become exposed to a changed world in which the possibilities for initiative, bravado and individual-istic accomplishments are extremely restricted. What awaits most of them is to become an employee in a big industrial plant or some other superorganization which gives them opportunity for anything but the realization of those pioneer virtues which they have learned to admire. Instead of initiative there is mechanical, standardized per-formance. Instead of individualistic enterprising spirit and adventure what is required is rigid subordination to a trade union. Moreover in an overorganized industrial civilization in which unemployment becomes a periodically returning condition, the laws of numbers and no longer personal efficiency determine success or failure in obtaining employ-ment or security. The old ideals are still alive but to live up to these ideals becomes day by day more and more difficult.

The maturing young man finds himself in an insoluble impasse. His self-respect depends upon the degree to which he can live up to the ideals of success based on initiative, personal accomplishment and courage. The objective possibilities for this are, however, less and less. One way out of this dilemma is criminality. Driven by the inner neces-sity to become successful, and successful through individualistic, cou-rageous and preferably adventurous accomplishment, many young men take recourse to this caricature of individualism and adventure, to crime. It is easy to understand that the most vulnerable individuals will be those who through heredity but more frequently through early experiences develop a strong dependent attitude, great sensitiveness, the wish to lean on others, to receive from others and be loved by others. Such personalities, in order to retain their self-respect and the approval of the group, will have a doubly strong tendency to compen-sate for this inner insecurity with the display of an overaggressive atti-tude.

Briefly, one important factor in the spread of criminality in Amer-ica consists in the discrepancy between traditional ideals and the changing social conditions. An overorganized civilization requires, apart from individualistic virtues, also a sense for coordination and order. The "land of the free and the home of the brave" is more and more in dire need of becoming also a land of order.

Seen from this point of view modern crime appears as a new form of Don Quixotism. As Don Quixote in his delusions imitated the vir-tues of his predecessors and pursued the ideals and the life of an er-rant knight and thus became an insane criminal, our delinquent youth in pursuing the pioneer ideals of the tough men of the Wild West,

Daniel Boone and Buffalo Bill, for lack of redskins attack their peaceful fellow citizens. The only difference is that Don Quixote used a helmet and a spear and our "public enemies" much more destructive weapons: the automobile and the automatic.

The most direct road to crime prevention therefore leads through education: the development of new group ideals which correspond to present social structure, new group ideals not to replace the old ones but to complement them. To the ideal of independence and enterprising spirit the sense for order and coordination should be added.

Psychoanalysis and
Social Disorganization

◄ 1937 ►

The relation of the psychology of the individual to social phenomena

Social life is lived by biologically independent individuals. Since the constituent parts of what is called society or a group are individual human beings, the logical postulate is inevitable that the nature of social organization is dependent upon the nature of its constituent units— upon human nature. Consequently knowledge of the social processes must depend upon knowledge of the individual. The interrelationship of the individuals, what we call their social life, is based upon psychological processes such as communication of thought; consequently the knowledge of these interrelationships is dependent upon psychological knowledge. In spite of this close relationship between them, sociology and psychology have developed to an amazing degree independently of each other since the time when they emancipated themselves from their common matrix, philosophy. Sociology deals with phenomena considered specifically social, pertaining to the interrelationships of individuals in organized groups; psychology deals with what might be called the private inner processes of the individual—with his sense perceptions, intellectual faculties, memory, and recently also with his love life, sorrows, hopes, and fears. The relative absence of psychology from social science and the seeming disregard of specific sociological facts in the psychology of the individual (in the following we might concentrate ourselves on its most developed form, psychoanalysis) can be explained by a tacit inclusion of certain psychological principles in sociological studies and the tacit recognition of sociological concepts in psychoanalysis and psychiatry. Such a basic sociological concept, namely, that individuals live in groups in order to facilitate the satisfaction of their fundamental biological needs by cooperation and division of labor or in order to defend themselves more effectively against a common external enemy means

384

the recognition of a fundamental psychological fact, the drive for self-preservation. Similarly, the study of family presupposes a sexual instinct, and the theory of supply and demand implies subjective needs and desires.

In psychoanalysis, again, we operate constantly with sociological concepts. The theory of personality formation tacitly assumes the existence of certain historically determined cultural ideals and requirements (tradition) which through parental influence are transmitted from generation to generation. The incorporation within the personality of these traditional normative principles is what we call "conscience" or "superego."

In the first rough approach sociology could deal with psychological factors and psychology with sociological factors as invariable constants. The instinct of self-preservation, and the sexual instinct, are to a high degree similar in all human beings and can be considered as relatively unchanged during the history of civilization, and therefore could be dealt with in sociology as constant factors. The extreme variety of group phenomena as laid down in history is not due to changes in the nature of self- or race-preserving forces (biological forces) but to changes in the social (economico-political) interrelationships of the individuals to one another, and to changes in group attitudes that have developed from social relationships.

Similarly, the psychoanalyst could roughly consider the general cultural patterns as constant factors to which all his patients are similarly exposed because he had to deal with individuals belonging largely to the same Western civilization.

Obviously only the very first and roughest approach could justify the assumption of the constancy of psychological factors in social research or of the constancy of cultural patterns in psychology. With the development of both sciences the need for a more explicit recognition of those factors which hitherto have been dealt with as constant is obviously growing. Hence the need for more explicit recognition of cultural factors in psychoanalysis and the equally strong demand among sociologists for a more precise knowledge of those psychological processes which are the substratum of all sociological phenomena.

Examples of this mutual need of each field for a more precise knowledge of the other field are extremely numerous, and I shall refer to only one example in each field.[1]

[1] The necessity of integrating psychological knowledge of the individual with sociological concepts is comprehensively stated in Ernest W. Burgess, "The Cultural Approach to the Study of Personality," *Mental Hygiene*, XVI, No. 2 (April, 1930), 307-325. This article also contains a careful review of the literature in this field up to 1930.

The study of the careers of certain types of neurotic criminals has shown for instance that their criminal actions are motivated by irrational and emotional factors identical with those which in other cases do not lead to criminal behavior but to neurosis or psychosis. Resentment against the authority (father), envy, sense of inferiority, need for prestige, sense of guilt and fear, play just as important a role in certain criminal careers as they do in some neuroses or psychoses. The comparative study of criminal careers together with statistical and sociological studies leads to the assumption that the different social situations of the individuals suffering from the same emotional conflict is of great significance in determining whether neurosis or criminal behavior will result.[2] If an individual suffering from ill-digested infantile hostilities and resentments against the members of the family has reason, because of his social handicaps, to replace his original hostilities with an aggressive antisocial behavior, he will be more likely to develop into a criminal than into a neurotic. This explains why the overwhelming majority of criminals come from social groups that are underprivileged economically and also in other respects. On the other hand, the early experiences of a child might be of such a nature that in any social situation he will develop into a criminal; not all criminals come from slum districts. It is obvious, therefore, that the specific social position of an individual determines his behavior only to a certain degree. So far as one is contented with averages one might say that the likelihood of a criminal career is greater in the economically underprivileged strata of the population. If we want, however, to understand the personality development of one particular individual, the knowledge of his social position will not be sufficient. Certain emotional experiences of his childhood, which may occur in any social group, may result in a personality for whom aggressive antisocial behavior is an inner necessity independent of social position.

The sociologist who is interested in group behavior—that is to say, in behavior which is common to most of the members of a group—will have to explain these common features in behavior from common factors which all group members share, such as their social position. At the same time he may neglect certain individual differences between the group members. But just these individual differences might be important for a clinician who has to deal with the criminal son of a old patrician family or with a very conventionally behaved compulsion neurotic coming from a slum district where 75 per cent of the youngsters are delinquent and not neurotic.

Thus we begin to realize the importance of differentiating between

[2] Franz Alexander and William Healy, *Roots of Crime*, New York: Knopf, 1935; Clifford Shaw, *Delinquency Areas*, Chicago: University of Chicago Press, 1923.

the task of the sociologist and that of the psychologist in order to avoid confusion. The psychoanalyst who tries to explain crime in general from such a universal phenomenon as the Oedipus complex without paying attention to the specific social situation of the majority of those individuals who become criminal makes an error similar to that of the sociologist who, studying one particular criminal career instead of investigating the specific family situation, contents himself with speaking of the influence of general cultural patterns, which may be typical for a certain group but are absent in just the particular family in which this criminal individual in question has happened to grow up. The delinquent may come from a social group in which most families have a puritanical philosophy, whereas the patient's own family may have an attitude atypical for this group—for example, one of freethinking and atheism. As a rule, the psychoanalyst is interested in individual cases, the sociologist in group phenomena, and therefore the psychoanalyst must pay attention to all individual features of the environment, the sociologist mainly to the features common for all members of a group.[3] But whenever the psychoanalyst is called upon to deal not with problems of individual therapy but with the problem of the frequency of a certain type of neurosis or delinquency in a given community, then he also must recognize the common features in the environmental influences which are characteristic for the community. In other words, he must recognize them as historically determined and traditionally transmitted attitudes: cultural patterns.

We turn now to an example which illustrates the necessity for sociology to formulate more precisely the psychological motivations of human behavior beyond generalizations such as that human beings are driven by hunger and sex. The theory of historical materialism, for example, tries to explain the individual's ideological orientation, for instance his political attitude, primarily from his economic situation. More precisely, individuals who belong to the ruling classes will necessarily have a conservative attitude opposing social changes whereas the underprivileged classes, so far as they are class conscious, will necessarily have a revolutionary ideology. This political theory is founded on the tacit acceptance of a now antiquated rationalistic psychology, which recognizes only those motivations which are based on rational insight. It assumes that human beings act rationally according to their interest, mainly according to their economic interest, provided they know their interests. (Note the emphasis on class consciousness!)

[3] This methodological principle has been clearly developed by Erich Fromm in his *Die Entwicklung des Christusdogmas*, Vienna: Int. Psychoanal. Press, 1931, pp. 4-8.

This theory in spite of certain scientific merits cannot account for this historically so important fact that revolutionary leaders often come from the upper classes, due to some deep hatred of authority that has originated from their emotional experiences during childhood and not from their social situation. I quote this example because it cannot be discarded with the argument that for sociology only the average attitudes and not the exceptions are important. Revolutionary leaders are not unimportant exceptions but highly important facts of great historical consequence. The economic factors may be important in determining current ideologies and political attitudes but they are by no means the only, and in certain cases not even the most important, determining factors. Nor can the materialistic social theory explain why masses may blindly follow leaders who promise them security and may even endorse policies of their leader that are contrary to their ultimate economic interest. Without the knowledge of the passive dependent love of the son for the father, which is duplicated in the relation of follower to leader, this phenomenon, so common and historically so important, cannot be explained. This passive love and admiration of the leader can be, under certain social conditions, so strong as to overwhelm rational insight which would command a different political attitude. Freud correctly considers this emotional attachment of the group members to the leader as the most fundamental sociological phenomenon, the basis of every group formation.[4]

A sociology which considers human beings as rational automatons who always choose the most reasonable behavior in order to satisfy their hunger is a false construction and explains the obvious error in most social theories. Human psychology cannot be dealt with so summarily as is typical of most sociological thought. Especially the so-called irrational factors, certain emotional reactions which do not follow the rules of intellectual thinking, cannot be disregarded in the study of group phenomena. The types of emotional reactions are extremely variable and are determined by a complex variety of factors —such as the fundamental dynamic organization of human personality transmitted through heredity, the external influences of family life, later educational influences, and the social situation of the individual. Among the external influences one can again differentiate between so-called cultural patterns (ideological influences characteristic for a group) and the more accidental factors, such as the temperament of the parents, the presence or absence of one or more siblings, the emotional relationship between the parents, and many other highly individual factors, which vary from family to family. The sociologist is interested mainly in group phenomena common to most members of

[4] Sigmund Freud, *Group Psychology and the Analysis of the Ego*, New York: Liveright, 1940.

a group and can mostly disregard accidental factors; but what he cannot disregard are those underlying psychological mechanisms which determine every individual's reaction to the social situation.

The increasing tendency in psychoanalysis to define sociologically certain types of external influences upon the individual which are common in his group and which are determined by tradition and social situation, and the increasing tendency in sociology to understand the psychological mechanisms underlying group behavior, are healthy signs of progress in both fields. It is not astonishing, however, that the first encounter of sociology with psychology shows certain anomalies which are due to lack of conceptual clarity regarding the mutual relationship of the two disciplines. In the following these anomalies will be discussed.

"Psychoanalyzing society"

It is not out of courtesy that in my critical discussion I first turn to those psychoanalysts who try to psychoanalyze society. The greatest danger, I think, and the greatest confusion consists at present in the unsound application of psychoanalytical knowledge to social phenomena and not in the intrusion of the sociologist into the domain of psychiatry. The reason for this is that clinical psychoanalysis has a highly developed and standardized method to serve as a sound nucleus. Even those psychoanalysts who in their theoretical discussions dilute their precise knowledge of environmental influences and, instead of referring to specific and often quite unique family situations, make use of such general terms as "cultural patterns," in their daily treatments are forced to adhere to the exact study of the individual features of the patient's environment and development, and are forced to recognize all those sociologically more or less irrelevant accidental factors which are of primary importance in the understanding and cure of neurotics and psychotics. Sociology, however, still lacks highly developed and standardized methods and is much more exposed to methodological errors by the assumption of a "psychiatric point of view."

Most of the errors of this category ("psychoanalyzing society") come from not an explicit but rather a tacit assumption of a group psyche, or collective mind.[5] War, for instance, is explained as the combined expression of the sadism and the need for punishment of a nation.

Some authors try to avoid the difficulty of assuming a mystical superindividual group psyche by the attempt to explain historical events from the individual psychology of the leaders. The individual

[5] R. LaForgue, *Libido, Angst, und Zivilisation*, Vienna: Int. Psychoanal. Verlag, 1932.

attitude of the leader is considered alone instead of the extremely divergent and often contradictory attitudes of different groups within the same social unit. Thus, for example, the World War (I) is treated as the private affair of the leaders. Glover writes, speaking of the World War:

Nevertheless, they [the people] obviously had some glimmering of a profound psychological truth. They realised that a world war is simply an extension of a family affair; that the Kaiser and Sir Edward Grey and Poincaré are merely Tom, Dick and Harry on the village green, or little Tommy, young Master Dick and brother Harry in the back garden, or three unbaptized turkey cocks swelling their wattles in the nursery.[6]

Of course if the World War is equated with the individual fight of three or four children in a nursery, then, and then alone, it can be explained on the basis of individual psychology and all the sociological facts of war neglected. The methodological error of such an approach is obvious. The error consists not in considering society a higher form of organization of individuals, each of them governed by psychological principles, but in the naive identification of the psychological processes within one individual with group phenomena, which are the complex end results of the behavior of many different individuals organized in a group.[7]

In unorganized, accidental groups, such as lynching mobs, one may speak correctly of an outburst of emotions of rage, the abandonment of repressions, regression to more primitive uncontrolled forms of behavior, etc. Such a mob can be considered in its activity as a more or less homogeneous group in every member of which the same type of psychological processes take place. A modern war, however, obviously can no longer be described on the same basis. In a modern war, those who declare the war and those who actually engage in war activities are different persons. If one wishes to describe an organized war as an outburst of sadistic impulses and a regression to a primitive level, one must ask in whom does this sadistic outburst and regression take place? In those in the war office who, after long rational calculations comparable to a chess game, decide for war, or the soldiers, the great majority of whom participate in war activities under coercion, with great resistance, and do not seek or find any instinctual gratification in it? It is quite obvious that the

[6] Edward Glover, *War, Sadism and Pacifism,* London: Allen & Unwin, 1933.

[7] The spurious nature of the attempts to explain group phenomena on the basis of analogies with individual behavior has been demonstrated by different authors; also by psychoanalysts, as Erich Fromm, *op. cit.*; and Otto Fenichel, "Psychoanalyse der Politik," *Psa. Bewegung,* IV (1932), 255-268.

declaration of a modern organized war is the end effect of complicated logical operations on the part of leaders who believe that they best serve their nation's or particular group's interests or prestige through this measure.[8] So far as aggression and sadism play a role here, obviously they have only a secondary importance. The war is decided upon beforehand by the leaders; then follows war propaganda which is intended to imbue the prospective soldiers with the right spirit. Mob action is the direct expression of mob spirit. In war, mob spirit is consciously created for a political plan upon which the government has decided after long deliberation. That in this decision emotional factors may play a certain role is of secondary importance. If, for example, a dictator in order to avoid inner trouble quite consciously prepares a war, such a phenomenon must be considered rather as a rational act based on insight (no matter whether false or not) than one which serves the satisfaction of personal sadistic impulses. The understanding of the causes of an organized war must consistently be based on a knowledge of the social situation of the country, in which the economic structure obviously is of decisive importance. To explain it on the basis of an outbreak of sadism or need for punishment is utterly naive and inadequate. Repressed sadism and need for punishment are omnipresent in the human race; nevertheless wars develop only at certain historical moments. The situation of the whole social unit has to be considered and not the ubiquitous general psychological structure of the component individuals. Destructive behavior is one characteristic of the human race, but only in certain historic economic and cultural situations will this destructiveness be expressed in the form of war. Furthermore, it must be again emphasized that in an organized society war is possible without the majority of the participants expressing in it their own instinctual needs. Even in individual psychology it would be entirely false to explain every case of individual murder as aimed to relieve a certain amount of accumulated hostility. Often it is committed mainly from intellectual motives, for the purpose of gain. Even much less is it admissable to explain every war, especially an organized, long-prepared war, as serving for the gratification of the sadism of the masses, because those that initiate and those that carry out the war are different individuals. This simple example shows the futility of attempts like that of Glover to approach the problem of war on the basis of analogy with individual psychology.

It would be similarly false to explain such a group phenomenon as fascism by comparing it with an individual psychosis, such as mega-

[8] Robert Waelder recognized this fact in his "Aetiologie und Verlauf der Massenpsychosen," *Imago*, XXI (1935).

lomania or persecutory paranoia or a combination of both, even though certain similarities can be observed.[9] An etiological explanation must be based on historical considerations approximately of the following nature:

Fascism has developed in the so-called "dynamic" countries in which there is economic stress, lack of raw materials, and need of new territory and economic expansion. Fascistic ideology can be considered as an emergency measure in moments of revolutionary tension. To a downtrodden and desperate population dictators promise a great, glorious, and prosperous future that is supposedly hindered by external enemies alone, and thus create an aggressive spirit, inner solidarity, and a heroic willingness to endure deprivations necessary for final victory. Leaders, if they set their minds to remedy economic stress by imperialistic expansion, are able to create a fascistic war spirit goal consciously and in a relatively short time. This they can do by the help of modern technique, press, and radio. They imbue the population with a spirit suitable for the accomplishment of imperialistic political aims.

This is an entirely different and more realistic explanation of fascism than the paranoic theory. It is based on the historical politico-economic position of a country. It is true that some aspects of this spirit of self-aggrandizement and aggressiveness and also certain persecutory ideas in fascism might be compared with certain psychopathological phenomena in a psychosis, but, even descriptively seen, they are not fully identical. In the fascistic spirit, which is a group phenomenon, we see, for example, the acceptance of self-restriction, heroism, and solidarity mostly lacking in the individual psychosis. It is also true that the situation of the individual who develops megalomania and persecutory ideas and an aggressive attitude can in many respects be compared with the historical situation of a group in which fascism develops. Certain individuals who feel thwarted will tend to cure their feelings of failure by self-aggrandizement in fantasy. Such individuals will also feel resentment against others, will tend to justify their hostility by attributing their resentment to other people, will be inclined to feel persecuted and attack their supposed enemies. No question that in each individual who assumes the fascistic ideology a similar mechanism takes place. Their leader methodically increases their feeling of being thwarted, appeals to their narcissism in the form of creating a national narcissism, and steers their hostilites toward real or imagined external enemies. But this comparison of fascism with paranoia is not a causal explanation. It is a descriptive one. The etiological question is: Why does such

[9] See Bain, "Sociology and Psychoanalysis," *Am. Soc. Rev.*, I, No. 2 (1936), 203-216.

a group phenomenon take place in a certain moment of historical development? This cannot be explained with the help of individual psychology alone, but we must take into account the historical and social position of the group as a whole. The sociological analysis must go even farther than that. One cannot speak of fascism as the paranoia of a nation because the fascistic ideology is accepted in varying degrees by different individuals within the same nation. It will find more fertile soil in certain strata of the population according to their social position. The etiological or dynamic explanation of such group phenomena, therefore, must always be a historical one, cultural, political, and economic history corresponding to the individual life history in psychoanalysis.

Examples of attempts on the part of psychoanalysts to understand social phenomena on the basis of considering the social unit as one magnified individual are extremely numerous. The foregoing examples, however, will suffice here to illustrate this type of methodological error.

This error is the same which, after the introduction of physicochemical principles, has hindered and still to a certain degree retards the development of biology. Not that the principles of physicochemistry should not be utilized in biology. Precisely to physicochemical knowledge it owes its recent developments. But paradoxically the same physicochemical orientation, the source of greatest progress in the attempt to reduce biology to the chemistry of the nonliving substances, is responsible for impeding the understanding of the specific laws of the life process. Biology has to develop its own specific principles which, although they are not independent of physicochemical principles, still do not consist in the simple application of those relationships between molecules which have been studied in nonliving systems. Every partial process within a living cell—such as oxidation, diffusion, reduction, etc.—follows the known physicochemical laws, but life consists in a specific coordination of all these partial processes. The problem of life lies precisely in the specific nature of this coordination of physicochemical processes and just the specificity of this configuration must be understood in order to understand "life." [10] Similarly, social life consists in a specific coordination of individual types of behavior. Therefore, sociology cannot be reduced entirely to individual psychology but has to develop its own principles to which the principles of individual psychology are subordinated. The configuration and interrelationship of various

[10] It is encouraging that this methodological postulate is explicity acknowledged by Sir Frederick Gowland Hopkins in his address to the Harvard Tercentenary Conference of Arts and Sciences on "The Influence of Chemical Thought on Biology," Science, LXXXIV, No. 2177 (September, 1936), 255-260.

types of individual behavior are those specific phenomena which must be studied. The more organized and differentiated the group is, the greater will be the error in applying the principles of individual psychology without paying attention to the heterogeneous nature of the social system. The behavior of an accidentally formed group, such as a mob, can be explained still on the basis of individual psychological principles; a group in which the population is divided into employers, employees, soldiers, tillers of the soil, manufacturers, merchants, political leaders, etc., each with different sociological functions and economic interests, can no longer be considered as a homogeneous psychological unit. Historical phenomena are the end result of the varied behavior of all these individuals who are divided into different political, professional, and social groups. They are no longer comparable with the behavior of one individual. Group actions, like war, are the result of this complicated interaction of forces.

The "sociological orientation" in psychoanalysis

Recently a new form of criticism against the standard psychoanalytic concepts has been repeatedly expressed by both sociologists and psychoanalysts.[11] According to these critics, psychoanalysts, in studying the etiology of neuroses and psychoses, do not pay sufficient attention to those environmental influences which are represented by specific cultural patterns. This reproach is the more challenging because since its beginning psychoanalysis has been concerned precisely with this problem: the influence of environment, especially of the family, upon the formation of character and mental illness. The main contribution of psychoanalysis to this problem consists not only in pointing out the importance of environmental influences in general but in supplying a method by which these influences can be studied in a specific and precise fashion.

Much confusion is brought into this field by the lack of precise definition of what is meant by the expression, "environmental influences."

For the sociologist this expression means mainly certain traditionally transmitted cultural patterns that determine the individual's behavior in almost every manifestation of his life. It determines not only the social attitude in a broader sense but also an individual's eating habits, his excremental habits, the way he raises his children, and the way he treats his wife, economically and even sexually.

For the psychoanalyst this expression means something even more specific. The human material with which the psychoanalyst

[11] I refer especially to Dollard, who devotes a whole book to this question. (John Dollard, Criteria for the Life History, New Haven: Yale Univ. Press, 1935.)

deals is extremely variable. He sees a diversity of mental disturbances: hysterias, compulsion neuroses, neurotic criminals, paranoid individuals, etc. With the help of his psychological microscope he sees an extreme variety of mental maladjustments and personalities. He observes that frequently these quite different types of individuals come not only from the same social group but even from the same family. He cannot be satisfied with speaking of such general influences as are represented by cultural patterns. He must look for more specific factors which vary from family to family, and which have a different significance even within one family for the different children. For example, the environment of an only child is entirely different from that of another child who is a member of a large family, although both may belong to the same social group. The environment of the oldest child is different from that of the youngest and from that of the middle child. Of course we speak here of a subjective or psychological environment. For the anthropologist or sociologist whose interest is focused on culture as a whole system, these differences are not so interesting. He studies the civilization of some part of Africa and compares it with one in central Australia. For the psychoanalyst, the object of study is the individual with his specific emotional problems.

This minute study of individual life histories shows us that the most important factors in personality formation are the early experiences of childhood. The nature of these emotional experiences is determined not only by general factors, such as cultural patterns, but also by extremely individual factors characteristic of each specific family in which the child is brought up. What we learn is that just these individual features are of primary importance—for example, whether the father is temperamental and violent or weak and repressed; whether the mother is overindulgent, overprotective, or neglectful; whether she is sexually frigid toward her husband and consequently overaffectionate toward her children. Such personalities we find in every civilization—not only among Frenchmen, Germans, and Americans but also among people belonging to so-called primitive civilizations. An eminent anthropologist, Linton,[12] emphasizes the interesting fact that he found the same type of personalities as we encounter in our Western civilization in very divergent cultural milieus.

I have, however, no doubt that if we were able to compare the psychological structure of a large number of individuals belonging to different cultural milieus, we would discover certain types of neurotic conflicts more frequently in one culture than in another. But I have just as little doubt that probably in all cultures we can

[12] Ralph Linton, *The Study of Man*, New York: Appleton, 1936.

find almost the whole range of all possible conflict situations, certain types of conflicts prevailing in some, and others in other cultures. One will be able to define the specific influence of certain cultures only after the technique of analysis has been applied to a large number of individuals belonging to different civilizations.

The attempt to substitute such generalizations as "cultural patterns" for the specific details of the environmental influences upon the individual actually found in each individual case is not permissible. "Cultural patterns" is a generalization of certain types of behavior which are typical in certain groups. But we know that the individual differences can be enormous within the same civilization. In our Western civilization, for example, certain children may be trained by nursing habits that are typical only in some of the so-called primitive civilizations. This may contribute to the development of a personality type which in our civilization would be infrequent and yet would be the most common type in another civilization. In the clinical psychoanalytic approach the main aim is to understand each individual in terms of his own life history. The sociologist is interested in the cultural system as a whole, the clinical psychoanalyst in specific individuals.

The neglect of this difference between psychoanalyst and sociologist in regard to the object of investigation becomes a source of confusion when it is demanded that the psychoanalyst should define the environmental influences upon the patient in the terms of such generalizations as cultural patterns. Horney[13] in a recent article feels a certain necessity to modify Freud's view of the relation between culture and neurosis. She describes lucidly the vicious circle created by the well-known conflict between competitive tendencies and the wish for dependence and love. Competitive tendencies create fears in the individual which increase his feeling of insecurity and thus his wish to be reassured by love. This passive attitude creates a feeling of inferiority and envy and thus drives him again into competitive aggressiveness which again creates fear and need for reassurance. Horney finds this common mechanism a typical example of the cultural influence of a double moral standard. The ideals of a competitive civilization are in conflict with social and religious virtues of modesty and a social minded, unselfish attitude, which are in our times held in equally high esteem as are success and personal achievement. For the clinician the emphasis on competitive civilization means very little, because this conflict might be very pronounced in one case and negligible in another according to the specific family environment of the individual. It might be a very frequent or even

[13] Karen Horney, "Culture and Neurosis," *Am. Soc. Rev.*, I, No. 2 (April, 1936), 221-230.

constant conflict situation, because individuals have to compete to a high degree in our present civilization. But what should be emphasized is that acknowledging the frequency of this mechanism does not contribute anything to a better understanding of an individual case, does not increase therapeutic efficiency. Just the opposite is true: if the psychoanalyst begins to think in sociological terms like "competitive civilization" in treating his patients he will likely be satisfied with such generalizations and neglect the study of the specific competitive situations as they actually occur in the playroom, in each case somewhat differently, depending upon specific factors, such as the physical and mental characteristics of the patient's brothers and sisters and the parents' personal attitudes. The discovery of the frequency of the "competition versus wish to be loved" mechanism in its relation to our competitive civilization, however, could be a contribution to sociology if the concept of a "competitive civilization" were more precisely defined in terms of sociology. In clinical psychoanalysis, however, the understanding of each individual must be based on the understanding of his specific experiences and not on knowledge of averages as represented by cultural patterns.

The correct application of psychoanalysis

In the foregoing we have tried to evaluate critically two kinds of methodologically incorrect attempts to integrate the principles of the psychology of the individual with knowledge of social structure and development.

The question is, then: What is the correct methodological relationship between the psychology of the individual and group phenomena? We must differentiate the contribution of sociologists to psychoanalysis from the contribution of the psychoanalysts to sociology. It is evident by now that both the psychologist and the sociologist deal with the same sphere of phenomena, the psychologist focusing his interest on the understanding of individual fates, the sociologist on the complex end result of the interactions between individuals in organized groups. A simple analogy would be the difference between two physicists, the one an imaginary superphysicist studying the individual course of every molecule of a gas, the other studying the behavior of the whole system. It is obvious that for the first physicist, who is interested in the fate of each individual molecule, the knowledge of the temperature and the pressure of the whole system is of little value. He must know the kinetic energy of each specific molecule at every moment, each collision of the molecules with other molecules and with the wall of the container. The pressure of the whole gas system is the sum total of all the collisions of all molecules with the wall of the container. The second physicist, who is interested in the behavior of the system as a whole, can disregard the behavior of each individual molecule and be satisfied with quantities (such as gas pressure) representing averages. Similarly the clinician, who wants to understand individual cases, cannot use sociological concepts such as cultural patterns, etc., because these are too general for his aims. It is entirely irrelevant for the clinician whether or not the atmosphere of one family is typical or extremely atypical, in fact unique, because the clinician is interested in one particular patient and it is not his concern whether his case is frequent or infrequent, whether the patient is a typical victim of a certain civilization or the accidental victim of an unusual mother and an unusual father. And yet the psychoanalyst investigates phenomena of the same scope as the sociologist merely in a more microscopic and individual way. Therefore the psychoanalyst, as a therapist of individual cases, cannot make use of sociological concepts. If he wants to make etiological generalizations, however, to determine, for example, the role of certain group attitudes in the causation of certain types of neuroses, then he must pay attention to features of sociological nature common in certain groups or periods.

The situation is the opposite to that in individual therapy when the principles of individual psychology are applied to group phenomena. Here, as Fromm[14] has pointed out, just the common features among the individuals are of importance. The very definition of group behavior is based upon the similarity in the behavior of more or less different individuals. The similarity in their behavior is due to certain circumstances which the individuals belonging to the same group share with one another in spite of their individual differences. They might be very different personalities but they have certain common features as employers or employees, as executives, physicians, or tillers of the soil. Their behavior, to a certain degree at least, will be determined by these common facts which express specific social functions. The study of group life is concerned mainly with phenomena which are determined by the common and not by the individual features of the group members.

A good example of the correct applications of psychoanalytic principles to group phenomena is Erich Fromm's study of the changes in the Christian dogma during the first centuries of Christianity. After describing the main emotional sources of religious phenomena, he demonstrates that so long as Christianity was the creed of the persecuted pariahs its dogmas corresponded to the emotional needs of the downtrodden group. The belief that a man could become God

14 Fromm, *op. cit.*

afforded encouragement for the hope that "even the last can become first." Fromm also points out the importance of the antagonistic feelings toward the father authority which contributed to the belief in the possibility of the son taking the place of the father: man becoming God. Later, when Christianity became officially accepted and became also the religion of the rulers, it no longer expressed solely the emotional needs of the oppressed classes. Accordingly the dogma changed: God was always God—and man never can become a God. The dogma was now influenced by the conservative attitude of the higher social strata. Furthermore, salvation was promised only for the future life. This helped to appease the discontent on earth and make the poor man acquiesce in his fate without active revolt against it.

We see that Fromm tries to explain the change in the content of religious ideas by reference to the difference in the social situation of those who actively participated in the formulation of the dogma. I do not feel competent to pass a judgment upon the correctness of the historical details of his explanation. Fromm's methodological procedure, however, is unquestionably correct. The emotional needs of different strata of the population vary according to their social situation; therefore one cannot describe in general terms the psychology of religious beliefs without considering the social condition of the believers. The religious needs of the rulers are different from those of the dispossessed.

I have tried above to sketch a similar analysis of a political theory, that of fascism. In this case also it is of little service to compare it with certain individual attitudes, such as megalomania or paranoia. The question is why in a certain period of history, in a certain national unit, a particular type of ideology is inaugurated by the leaders and accepted by great masses. The sociologically and historically important problem is to discover those factors which explain why at a given time a certain psychological attitude develops and becomes widespread among the population, and this can only be explained by the common and not by the individual features of the members of the group, in reaction to their momentary social situation.

What psychoanalysis offers to sociology is the knowledge of a great variety of psychological mechanisms, but what it cannot offer is the etiological explanation as to precisely which psychological mechanism and which emotional attitudes, of all possible ones, will develop at a certain historical moment in a certain group. Such an etiological explanation must be a historical and sociological one, it must be based on the investigation of the actual status and history of the country as a whole, and of the social position of the groups that participate in a group activity and that accept or reject an ideology.

Psychoanalysis and the social problem

The contributions of psychoanalysis which have been discussed in the foregoing have been of altogether theoretical nature. Psychoanalysis, so far as it is a therapy, however, has practical aims—the psychoanalyst attempts not only to understand but also to influence psychological processes. Can this therapeutic function of psychoanalysis contribute to the solution of social problems?

It is obvious that curing neuroses might be of great importance if it could be carried out on a large scale. The cure of a neurotic individual consists in helping him to bring his conflicting subjective needs in harmony with one another and with socially accepted group standards.

Recently more and more psychotherapists have come to feel the increasing difficulties of individual adjustment in a period in which the ideological content of the cultured milieu is rapidly changing. It almost seems as if the majority of individuals would fail in this process of adjustment and become more or less neurotic. The group ideals are themselves rapidly changing and the individual is exposed to different and often conflicting ideals and standards. If this were true, one should consider it appropriate to attempt to change the environment rather than the individual. So long as neurosis was a relatively rare phenomenon the appropriate approach to the problem of mental health was the therapy of those exceptional individuals who failed. If only those individuals develop a neurosis who have been exposed to especially unfortunate influences in their early emotional development, or who have a weak constitution, individual therapy is obviously the logical course. However, as soon as neurosis becomes a general phenomenon it is consistent to speak of society as the patient. L. K. Frank in a brief study[15] gives expression to this opinion in a clear, convincing fashion. He sees the most universal cause of present mental disorder, criminality, and corruption in the lack of generally accepted group values and ideals. Our shifting civilization does not offer to the individual a positive guide, definite status, role, and purpose in life, and therefore the individual fails. Frank's practical conclusion drawn from these premises is an attempt to develop new group ideals which would make adjustment for the individual easier.

The difficulty in applying this advice consists in determining what

[15] L. K. Frank, "Society as the Patient," *Am. J. Soc.* November, 1936, 335-345.

kind of group ideals should be developed. We have seen that group ideals are determined by the social and economic structure of society, by the cultural problems which a social unit has to face.

In the days of the American pioneer, unyielding individualism, adventurous spirit, personal initiative, courage, and success were the most appropriate ideals for the economic conquest of a new continent. This same pioneer ideology is no longer in accordance with a highly organized and standardized industrial civilization which has passed the phase of economic expansion. In such a society the majority of people can no longer live up to the ideals of personal initiative and success won by courage and enterprising spirit. On the contrary this new social structure requires an extreme subordination to powerful industrial units in which the place of the individual is rigidly prescribed and to a high degree restricted. The study of criminal careers has shown that, under the pressure of the highly individualistic traditions of the pioneer times, in the pursuit of prestige and success many are driven toward crime as the only remaining way for the display of bravado, toughness, and adventurous spirit. The relatively rapid transition from economic expansion to economic overorganization did not leave time for the development of a new appropriate ideology. Tradition lags behind the hard facts of social development.

The opposite change from intellectual servitude during the rigidly organized feudal system to the spiritual freedom of expanding mercantilism can be observed during the Renaissance. The Renaissance individual—in many respects similar to the American pioneer—was also the bearer of an expanding and changing civilization. A new rising class of merchants, craftsmen, and intellectuals who did not find their place in the rigidly stratified feudal system and whose activities, the exchange of goods and traveling, required personal intiative, reliance on one's self—this new class required revision of the feudal ideals of intellectual servitude, strict coordination, and obedience.

Changes in group standards correspond to changes in the fundamental social structure and cannot be arbitrarily and *ad hoc* invented. In spite of modern technical facilities to influence public opinion by propaganda, only such ideals will spread and be accepted which correspond to the emotional needs of the people, as they are determined through their social position.

It is quite probable that the increasing spread of neurosis and crime is a universal concomitant of rapid changes in social structure, of the incongruence between new subjective needs and antiquated group ideals which have not adjusted themselves as yet to new social situations. In the past this readjustment of social attitudes took place automatically, though always belatedly. The refined intuition of intellectual leaders—these seismographs of social changes—have always been of importance in giving verbal expression to the need of revising antiquated traditions to which the majority of people adhere on account of their mental inertia, on account of their inability to adjust themselves to new social necessities. The tempting question arises, could not science, the knowledge of man's biological and emotional needs together with an intellectual grasp of social structure, proceed methodically to facilitate and smooth out this perpetual process of readjusting group attitudes and standards to the changes of social structure? The fundaments for such a social psychology are no doubt in our possession. Psychoanalysis can supply the knowledge of psychological mechanisms, of emotional processes by which people react to their social situations, and sociology should supply the adequate analysis of the social structure to which the human psyche is exposed.

The psychoanalytic therapist has an unparalleled opportunity to observe the tension between social structure and ideologies as they are reflected in the mind of each individual patient. These tensions always correspond to certain universal emotional mechanisms. In observing the specific difficulties of adjustment in a great variety of different types of individuals growing up in different social situations, he is also able to recognize certain universal emotional difficulties inherent in social life which are not determined by one special social structure but by life in groups in general.

Every form of social life, independent of the different forms of economic and political organization, requires the acceptance on the part of the individual of certain restrictions of his original nonsocial tendencies. The main problem of social life consists in the control of aggressive destructive impulses which belong to the fundamental characteristics of all animal life. Collective life, the sense of which is mutual cooperation through division of labor, is only possible if the constituent parts of society cease to destroy one another. The development of restrictive forces, which we call "conscience" or "superego," within human beings is therefore the condition of social life because it is the function of the conscience to protect the individuals of the same group from being destroyed by one another. Social order is by no means enforced by external laws only—that is to say, by fear of punishment alone—but in his early years there also develops in the individual himself a restrictive force, which in the course of development becomes more or less independent of external reinforcements, such as admonitions and threats of punishment.

The basic principles of the superego formation that take place in early childhood belong to the best established concepts of psychoanalysis. At birth the child is not adjusted to the requirements of collective life in the least; he is not an antisocial but a nonsocial being, because the social aspect is quite outside of the scope of his merely vegetative existence. Everything which interferes with the immediate satisfaction of his wishes provokes in him violent reactions, which fortunately he cannot realize otherwise than by crying and harmless, disorganized muscular contractions. This truth was anticipated by Diderot in his statement that the very small child would be the most destructive criminal if only he had the physical power to carry out his aggressions. But he is merely a little helpless being, biologically and psychologically entirely absorbed in the process of growth, in the satisfaction of his needs, fully governed by the simple principles of securing pleasure and avoiding pain without consideration for anybody else except himself. Only gradually the child learns to accept certain rules of behavior. At first it is fear of retaliation, of punishment that forces him to renounce certain gratifications and the expression of his hostile impulses. Gradually this fear from without changes into a fear of something within himself. A part of his personality—and it is most important to emphasize that it is only one portion of his personality—gradually assumes the attitude of the adults, and this portion of the personality begins now to demand from the child the same type of behavior that the adults demand. Instead of getting punished and risking loss of the love of the adults whose support the child so direly needs, he begins to forbid himself those things which his parents condemn.

The further study of this complex process of internalization of external rules has shown that fear of retaliation alone cannot bring about a reliable form of self-control. The positive attachment of the child to his parents is indispensable for a thorough assimilation of this inner advocate of the social demands. Education that is based only on intimidation will necessarily result in a pathological superego formation. If the child renounces its nonsocial tendencies only on account of fear, he will assume the same fearful and hateful attitude toward the incorporated image of the parents, against his own superego. The superego will remain a foreign body in the personality, toward which the child will employ the same tricks and compromises as he did against his severe preceptors. Education based only on punishment and intimidation leads to a peculiar caricature of morality. The child learns that a certain amount of punishment is considered as an atonement for a forbidden act. Now he will assume the same technique in dealing with his own conscience—he will inflict on himself punishment which allays his sense of guilt, makes him quit with his own conscience. He treats his own conscience like some foreign agency. He has learned that with a certain amount of punishment he can pay for his misdeeds and therefore he will voluntarily endure sufferings or even provoke punishments in order to get rid of his guilty conscience. The danger which lies in such an attitude is obvious. Suffering becomes not only atonement but provides an emotional justification for discarding the restrictions required by the conscience. Today we know that this peculiar way of dealing with one's own conscience is one of the fundamental mechanisms of mental disturbances known as neuroses and psychoses.[16] Only if the social portion of the personality, the superego, becomes deeply assimilated as an organic portion of the personality, its second nature, can we speak of real social adjustment. Only if the social self becomes one with the rest of the personality can this paradoxical intrapsychic abuse of suffering and punishment which undermines the influence of the conscience be avoided. And we know today that such a deep organic assimilation of the social requirements by the personality takes place solely if the child learns not only to fear but also to love those who demand from him the first restrictions and modifications of his original instincts. In other words, education cannot rely entirely upon fear but must be based also upon love. Education which is based on punishment alone and relies only on fear does not deserve the name education, it is nothing but drill.

It is obvious that such an internal advocate of the social requirements within the individual is indispensable for the maintenance of any social order, although the nature of the social demands which become internally accepted may differ in different cultural milieus. The vital interests of a society, which differ according to its economic and social structure, determine the content of both the external code of laws and the internal code of the superego. Yet, without some forms of self-regulative or self-restrictive force within the individual himself, social order could only be maintained by assigning to every citizen a policeman to keep him in harmony with accepted social behavior.

We must admit at once that in our present civilization the superego can accomplish this function only to a very limited degree. Its main accomplishment is that, instead of totally destroying one another, human beings are contented with mutual exploitation, and one dares say that through their respective superegos they are protected only from the most blatant forms of mutual destruction, and even from this only to a limited degree. Freud, who is not too optimistic regarding the social capacities of human nature, believes that on account of the universality of destructive impulses a social system can only develop if the constituent members of the society

[16] Franz Alexander, *Psychoanalysis of the Total Personality*, New York: Nerv. and Ment. Dis. Pub. Co., 1930.

succeed in diverting their destructive impulses from one another against some common enemy. According to him, destructiveness belongs to the fundamentals of human nature. A group of individuals can only live together in an organized unit if they turn their aggressions outward to some external enemy outside of the limits of the organized group.[17]

Be it as it may, it is unquestionable that the range of those individuals toward whom the aggressive impulses are restricted by intrapsychic forces is relatively small. The social group which today is included in the range of the superego's protective function scarcely goes beyond the limits of the family. Patricide and fratricide, indeed, are infrequent phenomena—much less murder in general. Under certain circumstances, as in defensive war, the killing of members of another nation is compatible with the conscience, and necessarily so, as long as national groups exist who take recourse to aggressive wars to enforce their interests. Thus, we may say that at the present stage of development the superego guarantees a relatively high degree of family solidarity, a somewhat lower degree of class solidarity, an even lower degree of solidarity between different classes, and a very low degree of solidarity between people belonging to different national units. This explains the seemingly insurmountable difficulties in the way of establishing a league of nations. It is obvious that the difficulty of creating solidarity between individuals and groups increases with the divergence of individual interests. In this connection one must remember that the child can develop a conscience—that is to say, can internally accept the restricting rules imposed upon him—only because he learns that through accepting these restrictions eventually he gains equivalent recompensations. In other words, he feels that the parents love him and are concerned in his welfare. Without this conviction it would be impossible for the child to accept internally the imposed restrictions and renunciations. If he felt that the parents were his enemies, he might yield temporarily to their threats and punishments but never could accept frankly and assimilate deeply their rules as his second nature.

Exactly the same is true for group behavior. Only such members of a group will feel solidarity with the rest of the group who feel that the group, no matter whether the leader of the group cr certain institutions, takes care of their interests. One can hardly expect real solidarity from those members of a social group who do not receive any recompensation for socially required restrictions. The greater the restrictions that are required from an individual living in a social group, and the lesser his recompensation, the lesser will be his inner

[17] S. Freud, *Civilization and Its Discontents*, New York: Hillary House, 1953.

solidarity with the group itself. The satisfaction of the primary biological needs being the foundation of every social unit, unsatisfied economic needs of masses will decrease the inner consistency of any social unit. Under the pressure of economic need, destructive impulses of the members will be necessarily directed against one another, and the only way of avoiding inner disruption will remain war, which diverts outward against an outside enemy the inner hostilities that threaten to disrupt the group. This is instinctively felt by the leaders of impoverished nations and explains their need for aggressive foreign policies when they feel threatened by internal disintegration. An iron hand both in inner and external affairs is their only hope. Social stability based on fear and intimidation, however, is just as unstable as a neurotic personality in which the superego has remained a foreign body and a dreaded portion of the total personality. A society in which social conduct is based on intimidation and fear is a volcanic, highly explosive structure in which the most valuable energies must be spent for the control of the disruptive aggressions of the individuals against one another.

With this view of the dynamic structure of society in mind we now turn to our final question: Can psychoanalysis contribute to the social problem by increasing the social conscience in the individual? Obviously sound education is the only possible course.

We have understood that certain external social conditions are indispensable for the individual to identify himself with the group. No society can by education succeed in developing a social attitude in those of its members to whom it cannot offer at least some minimum amount of security of existence. Of course, no social organization is known in which social restrictions and recompensations are equally distributed, but equality of distribution is not a primary requirement because it is highly debatable if such an equality is possible or even desirable. A certain amount of security, however, is indispensable—the conviction of each individual that the community is concerned in his welfare. This feeling of security corresponds to the child's feeling that the parents are interested in his welfare and are not his enemies. We understood that without this feeling in the child the conscience (the inner representative of the parents) necessarily must remain only a fear-inspiring foreign body within the personality. Identification with the parents in a positive sense is only possible under the condition that between the child and parents a positive attachment exists. Similarly only if the individuals of a group have this feeling of security and confidence toward the community and its institutions can social conscience develop. The best proof of this we see in present times. Governments even under the greatest economic stress can induce their subjects to greater and greater self-restrictions if they are able to convince them that the leader takes a paternal interest in their welfare. I do not want to imply by this statement that dicators who have this suggestive influence upon their subjects necessarily live up to expectations and deserve this confidence. The conclusion is, however, obvious: A social conscience can only develop if in the members of the group such a confidence prevails. Of course, as Lincoln stated it, there is a limit to people's gullibility, and therefore the education to social conscience has long-term potentialities only in a community in which this confidence of people is justified and is not based on demagogic promises. If people discover that they have been betrayed by their leaders after they have made all efforts to endure restrictions for the sake of common interests, they will unavoidably be thrown back by this disappointment to a most antisocial attitude.

In this connection I should like to mention that the weak point of existing democracies consists precisely in that they fail to give the citizens this feeling of security, although they cannot be accused of ever pretending or promising to give such security, as the totalitarian states do. But social security should not be the exclusive privilege of the totalitarian states either communistic or fascistic, since it is not in contradiction with democratic principles at all. Democracies would be much better safeguarded against fascistic and communistic experiments if they would assume responsibility at least for a *minimum security* of their citizens—a minimum security that is independent of efficiency. And not more than a minimum amount of security is offered by even the most utopian of totalitarian states.

I am not concerned here, however, with the question of what it the desirable social organization or how to achieve it. Scientists can as yet do little about improving social organization and, as I believe, not only because they are not asked but also because they can offer so little. What concerns us here is what education can contribute to increase the inner solidarity of the members of a group with one another and thus increase the hope of a peaceful evolutionary development. We can investigate this question only by assuming that this education takes place in a society in which the individuals have the feeling that their vital interests are at least approximately protected. This assumption must be made because under extremely unfavorable external circumstances education to a social conscience has no chances whatsoever. Therefore it must be emphasized that what the psychologist and the educator can contribute to this problem may be only of theoretical value at present and will have a practical significance only when the social structure approximates the minimum requirements of security of all members.

Psychoanalytic practice shows us that the early experiences of childhood in most cases create such emotional tensions that most individuals in their later social life are likely to develop greater resentments and aggressions than are warranted by their actual life situations. If this is true it means that, due to the pathogenic emotional experiences of childhood, people's attitude is less social than it could be under the existing social order. We have learned how the individual conscience develops through the identification of the child with the parents under both the pressure of fear and the influence of love. While the infantile conscience or superego is the product of the child's identification with his parents, social conscience means identification with the leader and through him with the other members of the group; in more advanced societies the identification is not so much with a living being but with group institutions and ideals which are shared by all members of the group. Thus, what we call social conscience is nothing but the extension of the sphere of the superego's influence over a larger group of individuals. The principles of its development are the same as the principles of development of the child's first social attitude in the family. The infantile superego is the point around which all later social attitudes crystallize and thus it is the pattern of all later social behavior. A group of individuals with neurotic superego will never be capable of social adjustment even under the best external economic circumstances. If the conscience remains a foreign body in the personality because it has not been assimilated during childhood development, this will have a pathological influence on the adult's social relationships. A variety of neurotic mechanisms well known from psychoanalytic practice are at the disposal of the individual to escape from the influence of his conscience. One of the most universal mechanisms as seen in neuroses and psychoses has been discussed before: the utilization of self-afflicted punishment and suffering to appease conscience and to cling to nonsocial infantile gratifications expressed by neurotic and psychotic symptoms. While this abuse of self-punishment and self-afflicted suffering has its main significance in the etiology of neuroses and psychoses, another mechanism, the projection of guilt and of one's own hostile aggressions onto others, is of paramount social importance. In order to justify internally one's own hostile aggressions, there is the tendency to attribute these aggressions to others: It is not that *I* hate *him*, it is not that *I* want to attack *him*, but *he* hates *me* and *he* wants to harm *me*. This projection necessarily leads to fear and mistrust of others and eventually to hate and supposedly self-protective aggressions. If two such individuals have to deal with each other, each of them will expect to be attacked by the other because each one discovers the shadow of his own hostility in the other one. In its pathological exaggeration this psychological attitude is known as paranoia, a severe form of mental disturbance. Yet a certain amount of paranoid attitude is almost a universal feature of our present age. It expresses itself in a general attitude of mistrust and fear of others. Ferenczi, one of the most ingenious followers of Freud, expressed this to me once by saying that the essence of his life experience as a physician is the tragedy of people's wanting so much to love one another and not being able to do so. They cannot love one another because—justly or not—they fear and mistrust in one another the shadow of their own projected hostile impulses. It is unquestionable that civilized men fear one another—if this is possible—more than necessary. During their childhood development they are forced to control their hostile aggressions. In order to do so, they develop a part in their own personality, a conscience which condemns their aggressions. In order to keep inner peace with their conscience, they must justify their own hostile feelings. This they can only do if they are able to persuade themselves that others wish to attack and destroy them. If they can believe this, then they can justify their own aggressions as necessary self-defense. The universality of this attitude is due to the coexistence in early childhood of a severe conscience with strong hostilities with which the child's ego cannot deal. Both of these forces, the conscience and the hostile feelings, must find their outlet. One way is to give vent to aggressions under the pretense of self-defense, which serves as an excuse toward one's conscience.

What is true for the interrelationships of individuals is also true for the interrelationships of antagonistic groups in which each of the members have acquired in early childhood this tendency to project, to attribute to others their own aggressions. This necessarily will increase antagonisms and make them keener than is objectively warranted.

This emotional mechanism has something oppressing in its inescapable inner consistency. It is a vicious circle in which each psychological link follows the other with the rigid consistency of the logic of emotions. The emotional syllogism is about as follows: Not I am guilty for wanting to attack him, but he wants to attack me—because he wants to attack me, I must mistrust him and be fearful of him. After such a mistrustful and fearful attitude is established under the influence of the unendurable apprehension and expectation of an attack every move of the opponent, even though a most harmless one, will be interpreted as an attack and will serve as a corroboration of the correctness of one's own apprehensions. The answer will be a supposedly defensive attack of desperate viciousness. One believes that one acts in self-defense and that therefore the destructive powers have no more restraint.

This mental attitude is the unavoidable consequence of the faulty developments of early years—of a conscience which did not become assimilated with the rest of the personality but remained a foreign body toward which the invididual has to justify his own hostile aggressions. And these aggressions became so strong and uncontrollable because the first instinctual restrictions were imposed upon the child through punishment and intimidations, and not by winning the child through love and by giving him the feeling that his renunciations are worth while because through them he wins his parents' love and respect. Only if the child can identify himself with the parents on the basis of affection will the process of social adjustment not lead to the accumulation of uncontrollable hostilities.

We understand now that excessive hostile feelings and the presence of a severe conscience together must necessarily lead to such phenomena as the paranoid form of projection or to other neurotic mechanisms of lesser social importance. Of course I do not want to deny the real basis of hostilities among individuals under the conditions of present civilization. What I want to emphasize is that the experiences of early childhood frequently lead to the accentuation of these hostilities by irrational and unjustified fear and mistrust which develops from the necessity of attributing one's aggressions to others in order to appease one's own conscience. No one who knows this fundamental psychodynamic process can fail to recognize this paranoid feature of our social life which manifests itself in the interrelationship of individuals, conflicting social groups, and of nations. The objectively existing divergence of particular interests between individuals, groups, and nations makes it difficult enough, if not hopeless, to arrive at friendly solutions by mutual compromises. The heritage of the emotional experiences of childhood in most individuals increases these difficulties to a degree which cannot be overestimated. Under the double load of real and imaginary fears, individuals, social groups, and nations prepare at first impregnable lines of defense to separate themselves from one another and then more and more deadly weapons to exterminate one another. The first move of the opponent which might be interpreted as aggression must necessarily release all the destructive forces which have become so intense during the anguish of fearful expectations.

It is obvious that the psychological side of this problem can only be solved by introducing on a large scale sound principles for the guidance of the emotional development of the child.

This educational aspect, however, is only one side of the problem. We live in a period in which the future depends on the outcome of a most exciting race. The question is whether the increasing social tension will lead more rapidly to an eruption than sound educational methods will be able to combat those psychological factors which alienate groups farther from one another than their objective situations require. If society will not at the same time succeed in integrating the opposing interest of groups inherent in their objective social situation, the chances of the psychological approach to win this race are extremely low. Needless to say, the peaceful solution of the objective problem—namely, the integration of economic interests—has itself an important psychological implication; it depends upon the willingness of the conflicting groups to compromise, and therefore depends upon social conscience.

Science augmented in an unprecedented fashion the possibility of securing the existence of large masses, but also improved the tools of destruction. With the help of these weapons, exploitation and social injustice can be stressed to an extreme degree. The destructive forces of men, if unleashed, will have today an opportunity for such brutal expression as they never have had before. The educational necessities of the moment are therefore imperative. Only the strengthening of social conscience can guarantee the constructive use of scientific knowledge which without this social restraint must necessarily be utilized for destruction. The contribution of psychoanalysis to this problem does not consist in an actual participation in the educational procedure but in the formulation of those principles upon which the practice of rearing children should be based. The realization of those principles lies in the hands of those to whom the actual upbringing of children is entrusted.

Psychiatric Contributions
to Crime Prevention
◀ 1940 ▶

Crime is one of those problems the scientific study of which offers particular difficulty. This is not primarily due to the complexity of the problem itself but to the investigator's attitude toward crime. Scientific study requires an objective unemotional attitude. Under influence of emotions the intellect becomes clouded and cannot follow its own laws. It is much easier to adopt such an unemotional attitude in physics or in chemistry than in those fields which deal with human nature or social phenomena. Moreover, crime is a problem of great practical and immediate importance. Our interest—and with justification—is not so much to understand this particular type of human behavior but to rid society of this evil. Long theoretical discussions about crime are apt to make us impatient. Hearing complicated theoretical discourses about crime, we feel "Well, that is all well and good but what I want to know is what is the safest and quickest way to protect the law-abiding portion of society from the offenders against the law." Unfortunately this impatience is not a very helpful attitude. If we want to change something in the world we must undertand the nature of the very phenomenon which we want to control. If we want to cure society of crime we must understand its nature. And in order to achieve this, we must study crime with the same detached, objective and scientific attitude as we do the phenomena belonging to the field of physics, chemistry or medicine.

Present attitude of society toward a scientific study of crime

I cannot stress this point emphatically enough. I am convinced that our failure in controlling crime is primarily due to our inability to study it in a calm intellectual way because it necessarily arouses in everyone horror, condemnation and the wish to retaliate.

Our first natural reaction is to protect ourselves and society from

412

the offender against the law. Law and order give us a feeling of security. Its maintenance is not a theoretical issue, but probably one of the strongest desires. The criminal not only endangers our personal safety but undermines our confidence in society's ability to maintain law and order in general. The most natural reaction is fear and a revengeful, retaliatory spirit toward the criminal who endangers one of our most important values, order and security. This explains why the policy of a firm hand and a retaliatory spirit in handling criminals find understanding and approval.

Intimidation by punishment and, if necessary, incarceration for life or even capital punishment, may seem the shortest and safest devices. And this explains also that when a psychiatrist or a sociologist undertakes a painstaking study of criminal personalities and social conditions it is usually considered an esoteric, anemic procedure. One goes even so far as to say that the psychiatric study of a criminal personality is a kind of coddling of the criminal; why waste so much time and give so much attention to these worthless individuals?

Danger of being "too practical" in dealing with offenders

It may appear that I am attacking straw puppets, that this attitude is antiquated and today the public and the authorities have an openminded attitude toward the scientific study of crime. Yet my personal experience in the last ten years in this field has taught me the opposite. Of course we live in an enlightened era and if somebody has such a peculiar hobby as to waste his time studying the personality of a few bad boys, why not permit him to do so? But the majority of those who deal practically with crime, e.g., legislators, judges, wardens, officers—not to speak of the general public—secretly still look upon the psychiatrist or psychologist who studies the human side of the problem of crime, with a benevolent but supercilious if not a contemptuous attitude, with the feeling that they alone know how to handle these boys. I do not question that practically they know much better than the psychiatrists how to handle these boys. Yet nothing is more dangerous than to assume a too practical or a so-called "commonsense" attitude if we want really to master any natural phenomenon. According to "common sense" the earth is still a big flat dish, the sun moves around the earth, the earth is the center of the universe, and man the crown of creation. For common sense it is utterly unintelligible that it is possible to hear a speech of Mussolini delivered in Rome while you are sitting in your apartment. "Common sense" cannot explain electric waves and for "common sense" it sounds incredible that every man is a potential criminal at his birth and might become one if not subjected to proper education and training.

Need for continuous concentration upon the psychological and
social aspects of crime

If the last statement be true, then the problem of criminality immediately assumes an entirely different aspect. The extermination of crime by catching and imprisoning a few clumsy criminals who cannot get away with it then seems similar to an attempt to empty the ocean with a drinking glass. We recognize that the way to crime prevention leads through the study of human nature and of methods by which the originally nonsocial human nature can be made to accept social order.

I must admit that we are only at the very beginning of our understanding of that highly complex interaction which leads to criminal behavior. In practical life we cannot wait until science can answer the most urgent problems. We have to take action and deal with these problems even though imperfectly. Our penal system certainly is not based on scientific principles, but at present even if we had all freedom to do so we would be unable to provide a scientifically founded penal system. Increasing knowledge of the psychological and social aspects of criminality can therefore be translated only gradually into practice by minor but continuous improvements of our present institutions and procedure. We will have to continue to concentrate upon improving our methods of crime dectection, improving the constructive aspects of our jails, improving the parole system, etc. We must realize, however, that by all these measures the evil of crime cannot be radically combatted. We must progress to the roots of crime and this can come only from an unemotional objective study of the mind and of social life. I wish to call attention to a few fundamental psychological facts the clear recognition of which will necessarily indicate certain reforms of our present methods of dealing with criminal personalities.

Child at birth is nonsocial and completely absorbed in satisfying his personal needs

At birth the child is not adjusted to the requirements of collective life in the least; he is not an antisocial, but a nonsocial being, because the social aspect is quite outside of the scope of his mere vegetative existence. Everything which interferes with the immediate satisfaction of his wishes provokes in him violent reactions which fortunately he cannot release otherwise than by crying and harmless, disorganized muscular contractions. This truth was anticipated by Diderot in his statement that the very small child would be the most destructive criminal if only he had the physical power to carry out his aggressions. But he is merely a little helpless being, biologically and psychologically entirely absorbed in the process of growth, in the satisfaction of his needs, fully governed by the simple principles of securing pleasure and avoiding pain without consideration for anybody else except himself.

Only gradually the child learns to accept certain rules of behavior. At first it is fear of retaliation, of punishment, that forces him to renounce certain gratifications and the expression of his hostile impulses. Gradually this fear from without changes into a fear of something within himself—a part of his personality gradually assumes the attitude of the adults, and this portion of the personality begins now to demand from the child the same type of behavior that the adults demand. Instead of getting punished and risking the love of the adults whose support the child so direly needs, he begins to forbid himself those things which his parents condemn. This internalized code of socially accepted rules we call the conscience.

Child atones for sense of guilt by self-inflicted punishment

The further study of this complex process of internalization of external rules has shown that fear of retaliation alone cannot bring about a reliable form of self-control. The positive attachment of the child to his parents is indispensable for a thorough assimilation of this inner advocate of the social demands. Education that is based only on intimidation will necessarily result in a pathological form of conscience. If the child renounces his nonsocial tendencies only on account of fear, he will assume the same fearful and hateful attitude toward the incorporated image of the parents, against his own conscience. The conscience will remain a foreign body in the personality, toward which the child will employ the same tricks and compromises as he did against his severe preceptors. Education based only on punishment and intimidation leads to a peculiar caricature of morality. The child learns that a certain amount of punishment is considered as an atonement for a forbidden act. Now he will assume the same technique in dealing with his own conscience. He treats his own conscience like some foreign agency. He has learned that with a certain amount of punishment he can pay for his misdeeds and therefore he will voluntarily endure sufferings or even provoke punishments in order to get rid of his guilty conscience. The danger which lies in such an attitude is obvious. Suffering becomes not only atonement but provides an emotional justification for discarding the restrictions requested by the conscience. This explains the paradoxical fact that punishment often has not a deterrent effect on the delinquent but just the opposite. His conscience is relieved by the punishment, he feels that he has amply paid for his misdeeds and if the punishment was severe he feels even that he is now justified in feeling inimical to society.

Only if the social portion of the personality becomes deeply assimilated as an organic portion of the personality, its second nature, can we speak of real social adjustment. Only if the social self becomes one with the rest of the personality can this paradoxical intrapsychic abuse of suffering and punishment which undermines the influence of the conscience be avoided. And we know today that such a deep organic assimilation of the social requirements by the personality takes place solely if the child learns not only to fear but also to love those who demand from him the first restrictions and modifications of his original instincts. In other words education cannot rely entirely upon fear but must be based also upon love. Education which is based on punishment alone and depends only on fear does not deserve the word education; it is nothing but drill.

Punishment often a contributing factor to criminal behavior

The description of what I called pathological conscience, based on a neurotic abuse of suffering by which punishment is used for absolution as justification for further crime, makes one think of our present-day penal system. This primitive neurotic concept of justice and some of the ideas underlying our present penal system are unpleasantly similar. Society takes an analogous attitude toward the criminal as does the neurotic conscience toward one's own nonsocial tendencies. Also, society assumes the principle that through punishment the criminal pays for his misdeeds. This can best be seen in the proportioning of punishment according to the severity of the crime. A smaller crime can be atoned for by a smaller amount of punishment—a bigger crime by a bigger amount of punishment. Of course this emotional attitude, which to be sure is deeply rooted and almost universal, cannot stand the test of logical scrutiny.

It is obvious that the suffering imposed upon a person by punishment, no matter how severe, does not represent an exchange value for a criminally extinguished life or misappropriated property. By suffering the criminal does not make good for the damage done. This is so obvious that since the second part of the last century most criminologists—the first of them was Friederich List—discarded the idea that the aim of punishment is retaliation and put all emphasis upon the deterring effect of punishment. This concept is based on the psychological principle that the suffering involved in punishment deters an individual from repeating such acts again which caused him suffering in the past. We saw, however, how the neurotic person abuses suffering so that in the end it has not a deterrent but a stimulating effect for the commitment of new crimes. By receiving punishment he gains absolution from his own conscience. The more severe the punishment, the more he will feel that society has put itself into the wrong and he does not owe anything to society and need not respect its laws. The internal policemen we called conscience is eliminated by severe punishment. There remains only the fear of the external policeman who enforces the law. That explains why hard punishment creates tougher and tougher criminals. All internal inhibitions are eliminated through hard and continued punishment, even those remnants of a conscience which every human being possesses. If such an individual refrains from lawless behavior he will do it only out of fear of severe punishment. But many of these individuals have not much to lose; having a criminal record they are severely handicapped, feel desperate, and are inclined to take risks again.

Here we arrive at a seemingly unsolvable dilemma. We see that punishment has a double effect; its intimidating influence is amply counterbalanced with its demoralizing influence. In other words there are about as many offenders whom punishment will drive toward even more brazen criminality as individuals who through punishment will be deterred from it. This fact is demonstrated by the startlingly high rate of recidivism. This dilemma therefore seems unsolvable apparently because punishment—incarceration in particular—is the only weapon which we have in our fight against crime. And now this weapon turns out to be ineffective and in many cases even a contributing factor to criminal behavior.

Yet there is a solution, a solution which many progressive men in the field of modern criminology are beginning to recognize with increasing clarity. We saw that punishment in its primitive form as retaliation is based on a primitive emotional reaction, that of revenge, which has no constructive aspect whatsoever. We saw, furthermore, that we may discard its retaliation aspect and retain punishment merely as an intimidating factor to curb the violation of law. It turned out, however, that even this deterring effect is only partially successful because punishment has also a stimulating influence upon criminal behavior. It increases the fear of the external police but decreases the inhibiting influence of the internal controlling factor of human personality, that of conscience.

But is there no other way of treating the criminal besides taking revenge on him or intimidating him?

At the present day all the primitive forms of punishment—with the exception of capital punishment—as beating, public exposure, etc., have been abandoned in favor of incarceration. That seems to be in contradiction to the statement that in the development of our penal ideology the revenge aspect of punishment has been more and more abandoned in favor of its intimidating effect. Incarceration obviously is not the best measure whether for revenge or intimidation. It is well known that both whipping and public exposure have upon most individuals a greater deterrent affect that has imprisonment in a more or less humane penal institution.

I was surprised to find during my psychoanalytic studies of inmates in a prison in Boston how often the criminal, without consciously admitting it, dreads the day of freedom which means for him renewed unemployment and insecurity. One of my criminal patients, whom I analyzed in the prison, the day before his release wistfully exclaimed, "Farewell, good old shadow soup," referring to the thin soup served daily for breakfast.

It is obvious that incarceration must contain still another penal principle distinct from both retaliation or intimidation. If we still believed in retaliation and intimidation as the prime factors in dealing with criminals, our present trend to improve prison conditions would be fully inconsistent. This trend could then be rightly defamed as stupid sentimentalism. Yet there is a principle in incarceration different from both retaliation or intimidation which justifies the trend to make the treatment of prisoners more and more humane.

What is the justification for improving conditions in our prisons?

Incarceration, at least for a while, rids society of the criminal. Life imprisonment does it permanently. From this point of view incarceration would seem to be an indication of our helplessness in the fight against criminality. We take recourse to this most expensive way of handling criminals because we realize that retaliation has no constructive value whatsoever and also that the deterring effect of punishment is of questionable value. It seems that tacitly we even recognize that nothing is obtained by increasing the suffering of imprisonment, because by maltreatment we only make the inmates more depraved after their release. And for those who remain in prisons for life or for the major part of their life, the increase of suffering in prison is entirely pointless.

At first, incarceration appears as a kind of social surgery. We get rid of the diseased portion of society by the radical procedure of elimination. Yet this simile does not hold. In surgery we do not care any more for the portion which we have extirpated; we simply throw it away. Unlike in surgery, for the social members which we have cut off from society by incarceration, we pay high taxes to keep them in costly prisons. Through constantly improving the hygienic conditions in the prisons we even rapidly increase these costs. Are we doing all this for merely sentimental reasons? It is obvious that by improving our prisons we are detracting from both the retaliatory and the intimidating effects of imprisonment. What is then the justification for improving prison conditions?

The answer to this question contains the solution of the dilemma which appears so utterly insolvable. The answer is that the primary value of incarceration—a value which at present is far from being fully utilized—is neither revenge nor intimidation or merely temporary segregation of dangerous individuals, but rather those constructive possibilities which incarceration offers. The answer is that we are beginning to recognize the only constructive factor which our present penal system offers; we are in the process of discovering the possibility of rehabilitation, during the period of incarceration. It is clear that the only justification for all expenses involved in the improvement of prison conditions is that by incarceration we hope not only surgically to eliminate a portion of the population like a diseased organ, but we try to save at least a part of them for society.

The argument is irrefutable, and yet if we investigate our prisons as they actually are, we must confess that we are far from having drawn practical conclusions from this insight. Our prisons are far from being primarily educational or therapeutic institutions. Their intimidating and retaliatory aspects are still in the fore. Of course institutions cannot change as fast as scientific insight progresses. We have to reckon with the inertia present in every social development.

I see one of the most important contributions of psychiatry to the prevention of crime in transforming our prisons into institutions in which the offender aganst the law has the opportunity for reform and rehabilitation. Psychiatry in the last forty years has developed systematic procedures by which personality traits can be methodically influenced and changed. The application of these methods to the rehabilitation of the criminal personality is perhaps one of the socially most important functions of psychiatry.

Psychotherapeutic measures should be available to all types of offenders

I may add a few words about the question of how far our present penal procedure, without far-reaching and utopian reforms, can afford opportunity for the realization of certain therapeutic possibilities leading to the rehabilitation of the prison inmates. It is obvious that the period of imprisonment affords excellent opportunities for certain therapeutic measures. Almost all our prisons maintain psychiatric service as a part of their general medical service. Without far-reaching reforms this existing psychiatric service could be intensified and modified, thus making it more effective. This can be accomplished because the management of the criminal during imprisonment is a behavior problem and as such coincides with the psychotherapeutic problems of psychiatry which are the same—behavior problems. The treatment of the prisoner during imprisonment is aimed toward bringing about certain personality changes in him. For example, the occupation of the prisoners and their instruction much resemble the occupational therapy of modern psychiatric hospitals.

This intimate relationship between penal procedures and psychiatry is evinced also by historical facts. The treatment of the mentally disturbed only very recently has differentiated itself from treatment of criminals, having consisted also in confinement (not long ago in chains) if necessary, solitary confinement and other procedures of a punishment type. Between modern prisons and modern psychiatric hospitals similarities are still present to a certain degree. This similarity goes in both ways. The mental hospitals still retain some of their past prison-like character, while at the same time modern prisons are gradually assuming hospital-like features.

How can we achieve adequate psychiatric service in our penal systems?

In spite of the fact that the problems of the management of the criminal during imprisonment are problems overlapping upon the field of psychiatry, psychotherapeutic measures on a large scale would require extremely profound reforms of penal institutions, reforms which would be tantamount to a transformation of the present penal institutions into behavior clinics. As a first step we must be satisfied by introducing a change in our attitude toward the treatment of prisoners. At present the psychotherapeutic needs of the inmates can be best served by the management of the inmates' life during imprisonment in a manner that is conducive to increasing the chances of their rehabilitation.

From the point of view of rehabilitation the attitude of the prison officials, or what one could call the spirit or the atmosphere of the prison, perhaps is of greater importance than anything else. The introduction of such a constructive psychotherapeutic view in the place of the retaliatory attitude is the greatest contribution which the psychiatrist can make at present to the management of prisons.

Therefore, the most constructive use of the psychiatrist in the prison system would consist in advising and informing the prison officials concerning every incident which involves personality difficulties of the prisoners. Apart from giving advice concerning occasional accidents, the function of the psychiatrist should include giving systematic instruction to guards in the main facts of human behavior. Present experience show that the guards' attitudes toward the emotionally unbalanced prisoners are far from being satisfactory or favorable for reconstructive changes in personality during the time of imprisonment.

Since guards at present are given systematic instruction in practically less important fields such as target practice, an elementary course in human behavior easily could be included in the present system.

How can we achieve adequate psychiatric service in our penal institutions?

As has been mentioned before, it would be premature, under the present conditions, to think of individual treatment on a large scale, although unquestionably many prison inmates would profit from individual psychotherapy, especially psychoanalysis.

In order to achieve such an extention of psychiatric service in our present penal system first a clear demonstration of the efficiency of psychotherapy in the rehabilitation of criminals would be important. Consequently the next step should be the establishment of experimental psychotherapeutic units in selected prisons. Such a plan seems to me timely and practically possible, because imprisonment is explicitly considered as a measure to influence the personality of the prisoners in a constructive way leading to their rehabilitation. The occupation and teaching of prisoners in different crafts is based on the clear recognition of this rehabilitating purpose of imprisonment. Those prisoners whose criminal behavior is a symptom of a major or minor mental disturbance, constitute an even more explicit psychotherapeutic problem. Isolated experiences, for example my work in collaboration with Dr. William Healy,[1] have shown the possibility of reforming criminal behavior through psychotherapeutic measures. In experimental units in which such systematic psychotherapeutic work would be carried out on selected cases, the practical significance of psychotherapy for the rehabilitation of criminals could be well demonstrated. It is needless to emphasize that a positive result would be of tremendous practical significance. The period of imprisonment could be used for accomplishing changes in personalities which would decrease the probability of recidivism. Apart from its economic importance, this would be the first really effective step in the problem of crime prevention. This way the excellent opportunity which prisons offer for such an experimental study would be utilized without especially great financial expenditures or any radical reforms.

Prevention rather than therapy is the utimate goal

I am fully aware that these measures do not nearly exhaust the psychiatric-therapeutic aspects of criminality. The major issue lies in the field of crime prevention. The individual criminal is the product of a complicated interplay of hereditary factors, personality features acquired during the early period of life, and general cultural influ-

[1] Franz Alexander and William Healy, *Roots of Crime*, New York: Knopf, 1935.

ences. Almost all of these factors are beyond our control. The attempt to reform the final product of all these influences—the adolescent or adult criminal—does not promise a radical effect upon the crime situation. There is no question that with the continuous improvements of the psychiatric service many individuals could be helped in the direction of rehabilitation, but the core of the problem itself cannot be approached by any therapeutic measures. As in the field of medicine, prevention is the ultimate goal, and not therapy. The study of individuals during the therapeutic procedure constitutes, however, the road which will lead to the knowledge upon which future preventative measures can be based. In the whole field of medicine, prevention requires a much more precise knowledge than therapy. A diseased organ can be eliminated by surgery even if the pathological processes leading to the final disease are not known. To keep the pathological process from developing requires a thorough knowledge of the whole natural history of the disease. In the field of criminology this can only be acquired through an integration of biological, psychological, and sociological knowledge. The study of individual criminal careers, eliciting step by step how these individuals became offenders against the law, is the only way to achieve such knowledge.

Psychiatric contributions to problems of criminology

In conclusion, psychiatry has two great contributions to make toward the problems of criminology. First, it could be utilized effectively for the rehabilitation of the already criminal individual by introducing into penal institutions the modern methods of reforming human personality. This is the therapeutic contribution of psychiatry. Its second, more important contribution lies, however, in the study of those psychopathological processes which lead to criminal behavior. Such a knowledge alone could serve as a scientific basis for crime prevention on a large scale. The period of incarceration in penal institutions offers a unique opportunity for psychiatry to accomplish both these objectives. These goals, however, can only be approached if the treatment of the criminals will be purified from all the emotional remnants of the past. Both the public and those who deal professionally with criminals must be freed from those age-old emotional reactions toward the criminal which interfere with an intelligent, scientifically founded penal procedure. We must finally understand that punishment as retaliation is not conducive to ridding society of crime; that punishment as intimidation by infliction of suffering is of questionable value; and that rehabilitation of the criminal, no matter how difficult it may seem, is the most economical and the only effective method. Above all, we must realize that one cannot apply successfully all three penological principles at the same time—retaliation, intimidation, and reconstruction—as it is done at present in our institutions. We cannot at the same time take revenge on the criminal, intimidate him, and try to reform him, because these different principles require different attitudes which are mutually exclusive because they interfere with each other. One cannot make the prisoner hate his authorities, fear them, and at the same time expect the prisoner to trust them and accept from them advice and guidance.

We must clearly make up our minds what penal principle we want to accept, and then we must treat the criminals accordingly from the time they are detected and arrested by the police until they are released from the prison. On the basis of psychiatric diagnosis, we will have to classify the prisoners into two large groups: those who seem to us unimprovable and resistant to any psychotherapeutic approach, and a more promising improvable group. Toward the latter we have to assume not a retaliatory but a purely therapeutic attitude. The unimprovable group must remain segregated from the rest of society so long as they appear as potential dangers.

Psychiatry, however, will have no chance to contribute anything of real consequence to crime prevention so long as we have not freed our fundamental attitude toward the problem of criminality from those more primitive emotional reactions which have pervaded our whole penal system in the past.

Educative Influence of Personality
Factors in the Environment

◄ 1942 ►

The development of scientific thought follows the dialectic principle. The complexity of natural phenomena permits the observer to select and emphasize one set of factors, to neglect others. No field offers greater opportunity for one-sided analysis than personality research, particularly the genetic problem of personality development. What we term "personality" is the total expression of the integrated activity of a complex biological system which is subject to the laws of heredity and at the same time is molded by postnatal experiences. The deep-going influences exerted on personality formation by the emotional attitudes of the parents, such as ambition invested into the child, maternal rejection, and overprotection, have been well demonstrated by psychiatric and particularly psychoanalytic experience. Partially these influences are highly specific—different in each case, dependent on the particular features of the family in which the child spends its first years, as well as on accidental occurrences. Partially, however, they are uniform—typical for the society of which the famly is a part.

Any of these factors may legitimately become the focus of interest: the biological influences, particularly the role of heredity; the highly specific features of the immediate environment; or, finally, those more general influences which are characteristic of a particular culture. Yet one-sided emphasis on any of these factors necessarily leads to false conclusions. This symposium, which attempts a broad approach from all points of view, therefore appears to me to be of great significance—the more so because at present the field of personality research offers a somewhat confusing picture of shifting fashions and predilections.

Critique of the hereditary point of view

In the second half of the past century the hereditary factor alone was considered. Typical of this view in anthropology was the Lombroso school; in philosophy, Nietzsche, Chamberlain, and Gobineau; and in history, Carlyle. While Lombroso considered the criminal a victim of heredity, Nietzsche saw the future of humanity in the breeding of a super race of supermen, who by reason of their hereditary qualities would be destined to rule over the inferior slave races. Carlyle believed that history is shaped by superior individuals, who are not so much the products as the creators of the age in which they live.

Psychiatry too was completely dominated by the hereditary point of view. Mental diseases, whenever they could not be retraced to infectious origin, such as the postsyphilitic conditions, were explained on a hereditary basis. Genetic etiological studies were limited either to histopathological search after morphological tissue changes or to statistical studies of hereditary traits. Brain research and statistics ruled over psychiatry with an amazing neglect of the personality of the patients and of the environmental influences.

In the course of the last forty years the interest in environmental factors, particularly under the influence of Freud's principles, has gradually permeated psychiatry, although hereditary considerations still prevail. One of the most common diagnostic labels is still that of the "constitutional psychopath," comprising all those cases in which a behavior disturbance appears early in childhood and, stubbornly resisting all therapeutic efforts, persists throughout life. It is much easier for the physician to blame the great idol of inalterable heredity than to admit the ineffectiveness of his own therapeutic measures.

However, at the turn of the century the pendulum in scientific thought began definitely to swing to the opposite direction. The most favorable soil for this reversal was the scientific scene in the United States, particularly the field of the social sciences.

In Europe the hereditary point of view was determined, if not solely, yet to a high degree, by cultural conditions. The aristocratic structure of society, in spite of the French Revolution and the Industrial Revolution which gradually invaded the whole continent, survived to some degree even in economic life and much more powerfully in traditional ideology. The Industrial Revolution did not transform the class system into a society of great class mobility. The individual's fate remained largely determined by birth. Heredity as a social factor loomed large, and accordingly it also retained its distinguished position in scientific thought. The division of the comparatively small and overpopulated continent into small national and linguistic groups had a further powerful influence on theoretical thought.

These racial and linguistic differences remained of primary importance in the shaping of Europe's destiny at a time in which changing technological conditions required the creation of greater political and economic units. This ideology—that there is an unbridgeable gap between racial groups—remained untouched even in the face of the fact that actually the personalities of the Western and even the Central Europeans became more and more similar. In international conventions an Italian physiologist, newspaperman, or executive could not help but recognize that he had more features in common with a German, French, or English scientist, journalist, or industrialist than with a peasant or laborer of his own country. Anyone who wished could have recognized that the peoples of the different countries in Europe were stratified more according to their occupation, educational level, and social status than according to race. Yet the all-pervading ideology that national states are distinguished by racial heredity was the only accepted view that had a dynamic influence on the fate of Europe. The history of Europe since the Industrial Revolution affords one of the most striking examples of the discrepancy between basic social conditions and traditional ideology—a discrepancy which kept the Old World in a permanent turmoil. On closer analysis this nationalistic ideology is seen to be the political equivalent of the theoretical view which maintains that heredity is the sole determinant of personality. It is indeed striking that the untouchable nature of this dogma was accepted, so far as Europe is concerned, even by a great American, Woodrow Wilson. A Europe divided into small and large national states according to racial determinants belongs to a past economic structure and does not fit into our technical civilization. This outmoded state of affairs was kept alive exclusively by the inertia of tradition.

It is most remarkable that another, even more antiquated expression of the hereditary ideology, the institution of hereditary monarchy, was dethroned only after the last World War, after it had ruled over Europe for centuries. It was most emphatically restated by the Congress of Vienna, after which it remained the ruling political philosophy for another hundred years during the emergence of the great national states, nationalism finally reaching Germany and Italy. These national states, indeed, could no longer be considered the permanent property of hereditary monarchs, and yet the system was retained until the First World War. The political philosophies of hereditary monarchy and of national states are merely different gradations of the same all-pervading hereditary ideology. Its scientific expression is the hereditary explanation of personality and mental disease—a theory which is obviously not the cause but the result of the political conditions in Europe.

All these historical side lights may appear to be a detour in the approach to the topic of my presentation. I feel, however, that without a full appreciation of these cultural determinants of scientific thought, the shifting fashions in the field of personality research remain unintelligible. We render lip service today to the cultural determinants of scientific ideas, but, when it comes to applying this principle to our own field, we prefer to remain blind and consider our own point of view as the absolute and the only possible truth.

Critique of the environmental point of view

To understand the extremes to which certain environmental views of personality development go, we must consider their cultural sources with the same unbiased scrutiny which has made us recognize how deeply rooted the hereditary concept was in the traditions of European civilization. Just as the European cultural and political traditions favored the stress on the hereditary factor, so was the American scene ripe for the recognition of the environmental factors. American science readily assimilated the environmental concepts of Freud because it was already oriented in the same direction in the sociological views represented by Sumner and particularly by Boas and his followers. Here the emphasis was on the determining influence exerted on personality by cultural factors, with a consequent underevaluation of heredity.

The most radical blow to heredity is contained in the tenet of the Declaration of Independence that "all men are created equal." It is obvious that this view represented a revolt against the class system of the mother country. Its scientific expression is the belief that man's fate is determined after his birth and not before. How could any other theory survive in a culture in which the supreme ideal is the man who achieves everything by his own efforts and who owes everything to himself? We are all born equal, all of us have the same opportunities, and the race of life starts without any birthrights—from scratch. Birth signifies the shot of the pistol when the contest of life begins. The vast new and undeveloped North American continent was indeed a monumental racing ground for everyone who wanted to participate. Origin did not count; social status was left behind; what determined success was personal achievement. The corresponding attitude was: "Let us forget the more or less insignificant individual differences, at least not emphasize their importance." A race in which cripples and able-bodied men participate is no longer fair play. The ideology of free opportunity given to men, all born equal, does not "jibe" with too much consideration for heredity. The most extreme scientific expression of this view is the concept that man at birth is a *tabula rasa* and that all his later personality traits are molded by external circumstances.

These circumstances may be more or less favorable, but at least the unjustness of inequality is not so great as if heredity were determining everything. Life conditions, unlike heredity, are changeable; and, even though society does not give everyone exactly the same chances, one can improve conditions and can strive to approach an ideal system. Indeed, the American culture, by its political democracy and particularly by its extension of education, opened up opportunities to everyone more equally than had ever been done before.

The environmental theory found an even stronger ally than political theory which, after all, always contains many wishful elements. This ally was sound, well-founded, everyday observation. Here was a civilization in which people belonging to all the different races of Europe were, in a brief period, transferred into a new and different type of personality. The second generation immigrant, under favorable conditions, lost all distinguishable racial or national characteristics and assumed features common to the inhabitants of this country. As so often happens, scientific thought here only lagged behind everyday observation, which in this case indeed could not easily be disregarded. No wonder that heredity became dethroned as the all-important factor and gave way to cultural environment. Thus the pendulum of thought development reached the other extreme.

The study of the influence of the intimate personal environment, as distinguished from the broader cultural environment, is likely to restore the equilibrium between these two extreme swings in opposite directions and to lead to a more seasoned evaluation of the determinants of personality formation.

The importance of early environmental influences

Early environmental influences, both those which are uniformly characteristic for the culture in which the child grows up and also those specific influences which vary from family to family according to the personalities of the parents, act through the family milieu. Following the development of a child as it actually takes place, step by step, we find that the decisive factors are the emotional relationships between the child and other members of the family. In later years the child is exposed to the cultural milieu outside his family. There is little doubt that these later influences, so far as the basic personality structure is concerned, are less deep-going and their effects more reversible than are those earlier influences which the child receives in contact with his parents and siblings. We know that these more superficial character traits are changeable because we can readily observe how adolescents and even some mature persons adjust themselves, often remarkably well, to a new cultural milieu and assume many traits characteristic of their new habitat. Just as people may learn a new language at a relatively advanced age, they can also learn new customs and even a new outlook toward goals and ideals. What remains more unchangeable is the groundwork of the personality, something to which Hippocrates referred in his theory of temperaments. Whether or not a person will become timid or outgoing, cautious or enterprising, self-confident and optimistic or self-critical and pessimistic, aggressive or submissive, dependent or independent, generous or withholding, orderly or careless—all these personality features which make a person a well-defined individual, different from others—depends on the influence of the intimate personal environment on a hereditary substratum.

All these different personality types, although possibly in different statistical distributions, we find in all cultural environments. There is good evidence that they are formed in the early years of growth, when the main problem confronting the child is not yet to adjust to a cultural milieu but primarily to adjust to the rapidly changing phases of his biological growth, which, in contrast to the external, we may call by the expression of Claude Bernard, the "inner environment." [1] Later we shall return to this fundamental aspect of personality development. Before we proceed, however, it will be necessary to clarify certain current dogmatic and one-sided exaggerations concerning cultural influences—exaggerations which come from a lack of precise distinction between specific influences of the human evironment, as represented by the human material of the family, and broader cultural factors. This lack of precision is due primarily to the specific nature of the observational material which served to support these extreme views: I mean the study of the static primitive civilizations. For the sake of brevity I shall refer to this error as "the ethnological bias."

The most recent emphasis on the cultural factors in personality development in general and in the causation of psychoneurosis in particular comes from a group of critics of Freud, to whom occasional reference is made as "Neo-Freudians," represented by authors such as Horney, Kardiner, Fromm, and others. That sometimes I also seem to be included in this group comes from the fact that I, too, recognize the need for re-evaluation of cultural factors in personality development and share the views of this group concerning certain gaps in traditional psychoanalytic formulations.

The essence of the argument runs about as follows: Freud, although the greatest psychologist of all time, under the influence of the nineteenth century's scientific tradition, was too biologically oriented. He postulated a too elaborate, biologically predetermined instinctual structure which, in its main features, unfolds in a more

[1] Claude Bernard, *An Introduction to the Study of Experimental Medicine*, trans. Henry Copley Greene, New York: Macmillan, 1927, p. 118.

or less autochthonous manner, like a flower. He recognized, possibly even overemphasized, the importance of those early experiences which arise in family life, but he overlooked the fact that the parental attitudes themselves are strictly determined by cultural factors. This neglect is the basis of a significant error. Those psychological factors which he discovered as all-important, such as the Oedipus complex, the castration complex, the masculinity trend of women, the repression of sexual and aggressive trends, are not necessarily universal but are of prime importance only in our present culture and may even be lacking in other cultures. Freud, not noticing the cultural determination of family attitudes, assumed that all these psychological factors are biologically determined; he overlooked their local nature. In this respect Freud's attitude was somewhat like the geocentric theory in cosmology, which maintains that the earth is the center of the universe. Also, Freud declared the personality structure of the European and American of the nineteenth century to be the universal human nature, not noticing that what he dealt with was nothing but a specific edition of human nature— if there is such a thing—an alternative among unlimited possibilities.

This is not the place to evaluate in detail the merits of this criticism, but there can be no doubt that much of this contention is valid. However, as so often is the case, the critic, in his dialectic fervor, runs into errors which are precisely the opposite of those which he attacks. Most of the basic psychodynamic constellations, such as the Oedipus complex and the castration fear, have a more fundamental foundation than these critics of Freud want to admit; they have sources which are based on certain biological factors overreaching specific cultural variables. The emotions involved in the Oedipus constellation are the most direct expression of the biological helplessness of the human infant. It is the expression of the possessiveness which the little child feels toward the main source of his security and pleasure, the mother. In this respect it is a parallel manifestation of sibling rivalry. The significance of certain premature, genitally tinged, sexual interest of the little son in his mother is, according to my experience, overrated. Among the sources of this interest, it is difficult to distinguish between infantile forms of pleasure sensations involved in all phases of the nursing procedure and some early appearance of rudimentary genital desires. The jealousy aspect of the Oedipus complex is certainly universal and is based on the prolonged dependence of the human infant on its mother's care. Even among animals similar phenomena can be readily observed; even the puppy, attached to a single person from whom it receives food and care, will show hostility and aggressiveness against any supposed competitor. It is, then, of secondary importance and is dependent on cultural conditions whether hostility is directed against the father or against some other member of the family— the maternal uncle, for instance, who in certain cultures happens to be the head of the family and, as such, the main disciplinarian and obstacle to the child's sole possession of the mother. It is, of course, true that, according to accepted standards of education, this attitude may be strengthened or weakened in different cultures. Where the child in encouraged toward independence, the attachment to the mother may be of shorter duration; where the mother as a rule has a rejecting attitude toward the child, as in the Marquesan culture, the hostility and fear of the mother may overshadow the attachment, which the child may soon transfer to less prohibitive members of the family. In all these cases the essence of the Oedipus complex remains the same, namely, the possessive attachment to a person upon whom the child depends for his gratifications and security, with jealousy and hostility against competitors. The distribution of attachment and hostility among the different members of the family may vary according to traditional customs and parental attitudes. Critics of Freud correctly question the universality of the specific form of this emotional constellation, which Freud called the Oedipus complex. They correctly point out its cultural variations, but they err when they do not recognize its biological origin in the prolonged postnatal dependence of the human infant upon parental care, not necessarily maternal exclusively.

The same argument applies to another fundamental psychological factor known as the "castration complex." There is no question that parental attitudes toward the early genital activities of the child vary according to cultural conditions. Children who exercise early sexual freedom probably have less anxiety in connection with their genital pleasure sensations than do children of our Western civilization. On the other hand, Stärcke[2] and I [3] succeeded in demonstrating the early biological precursors of the castration fear. We showed that it is based on the repeated experience of the emotional sequence—pleasure followed by pain and frustration. The castration threat, customary in the sexually repressed Victorian era, only reinforces the universal emotional attitude: to expect pain and evil after pleasure and gratification. This is expressed in so universal a human attitude as the expectation of misfortune at the peak of good luck. "Knocking on wood" and the fear of envious gods when fortune is too

[2] August Stärcke, "The Castration Complex," *Int. J. Psycho-Anal.*, II (June, 1921), 179-201.

[3] "Concerning the Genesis of the Castration Complex," in this volume.

generous are symbolic of the deeply rooted experience of the continuous sequence of pain and pleasure during the biological process of life.

We come to the conclusion that cultural constellations can reinforce and bring into the foreground certain emotional mechanisms but cannot introduce any fundamental dynamic principles into human nature.

The new and deserved emphasis on the cultural factors of personality development should not make us overlook the fact that the first and fundamental task which the child's ego must accomplish is the continuous adjustment to those biological changes which follow one another in rapid succession during the process of maturation in the first years of life. Though these changes may be influenced by external conditions, in their main features they are universal for the human species. From an endoparasite and after birth an ectoparasite, dependent for its basic biological needs on the mother organism, the child develops into a biologically independent being. This change involves the mastery of diversified functions of body control and of intelligence, and there is a marked emotional resistance in the child against this process of maturation. Psychiatric observations offer the most convincing evidence for the strong resistance which the ego puts up against accepting the gradually increasing independence which biological maturation brings. Psychopathological phenomena reveal a regressive urge to return to earlier, more dependent phases of life. This regressive urge is mobilized whenever external conditions become difficult beyond the organism's capacity to cope with them. Cultural factors as they appear in the methods of child rearing and in parental attitudes undoubtedly have a great influence on the child's readiness to accept the process of maturation. But also the individual attitudes of the parents have an equally powerful influence. There are overprotective and rejecting mothers in every culture, although either type may be the rule in one and the exception in another civilization. In our own culture there is a tremendous variability of parental attitudes, as I shall try to demonstrate in the following paragraphs.

The importance of specific character traits of parents

This leads us back to the error into which the so-called "Neo-Freudians" fall when they underestimate the specific influence of the parental personalities and overstress the cultural factor—an error to which I have referred as the ethnological bias.[4] We saw that the

[4] This underestimation of the significance of the highly specific parental personalities appears only in theoretical formulations. I assume that seasoned and realistic clinicians like Horney continue, in dealing with patients, to pay the same

denial of the biological foundation of the fundamental dynamics of personality was the outcome of the dialectic overemphasis on the environmental factor. The lack of emphasis that the so-called "Neo-Freudians" place on the specific personal influences results from the particular nature of the ethnological source material which is used to demonstrate the cultural determination of personality. The primitive civilizations which serve as material are, in comparison with our Western civilization, characterized by their static nature and their highly rigid organization. These societies undoubtedly offer most valuable material for psychosociological studies. However, they are, in comparison with our world, well-nigh petrified, unchanged for considerable periods, and consequently are not suitable for the study of social dynamics as these manifest themselves in historical development. Their history, as compared with that of the Western world, is relatively uneventful, does not contain deep-going changes of the social structure, and, above all, is almost completely unknown. The static nature of these cultures manifests itself in a stable structure which precisely defines the individual's social place, functions, and attitudes with a rigidity unknown in the dynamic societies of the Greek-Roman type or the European and American civilizations. The role of tradition in these static societies is incomparably greater than in our culture. It is not my aim to decide here whether the rigidity of social organization is the result of lack of historical change or vice versa. Probably it is a reciprocal causal relationship. In any case, we deal in primitive societies with a type of sociological material which in many fundamental features—quantitatively, at least —is so different from our dynamic society, with its ever changing history, that conclusions drawn from the one type of society and applied to the other are necessarily fallacious. It is almost as if one should try to develop the principles of zoology from botany.

The dynamic nature of our culture manifests itself primarily in the fact of social change. In the nineteenth century this change assumed almost astronomic proportions. This change best reflects itself in the literature of the period, one of the most favored topics of which was the clash of ideological attitudes between two succeeding generations. The ideological clash between fathers and sons is something which cannot be overlooked, and it does not allow explanation of personality attitudes by tradition alone. What was right and valid a generation ago is outmoded today. In our age customary attitudes rapidly lose their dynamic power and are replaced with new trends in a fast adaptation to an ever changing world.

---

attention as before to these personality factors, which cannot be well defined in terms of culture.

Another factor contributing to the dynamic nature of our society consists in its extremely complex structure, based on a far-reaching division of labor, that is to say, on the differentiation of social functions. This differentiation leads to a diversified stratification of the population; it is futile to speak of any homogeneous attitudes. Almost every generalization is likely to be fallacious. Even such basic attitudes as those toward property, discipline, and sexuality vary tremendously according to social stratification. One often speaks of the repressive attitude toward sexuality characteristic of the Victorian era. Even this attitude, however, was found mainly among the bourgeois and was absent to a high degree among peasants or in the proletariat. With some neglect of individual differences, one might justifiably speak of the personality structure of a Zuñi Indian. It is more difficult to speak of the typical character of the Swiss, although these mountaineers represent possibly the most uniform nation of the Western world. It is even more difficult to speak of a typical Italian cultural attitude without first defining whether one means the attitude of the Italian peasant, laborer, manufacturer, or artisan. It would be quite impossible for any cultural psychologist at present to try to define a personality type which one could call the North American.

The heterogeneity of ideological trends in present-day America is its most outstanding feature. Certain traditional attitudes of the frontier, of course, still prevail, such as the ideal of the self-made man—self-reliant, enterprising, with a sense of freedom in economic activities and his supreme ideal that of success. But even these trends are mingled with new ones, with a certain longing for order and security, with a new evaluation of purely scientific and artistic accomplishment in contrast to merely technical and practical achievements. And all the old and new attitudes are blended in varying proportions in different groups—different in the East, in the Middle West, and in the South; different among farmers and industrial wage-earners; different among intellectuals, "white-collar" workers, and executives. From psychoanalytic case histories in our culture we learn that every attempt simply to deduce attitudes or a basic personality structure from social determinants is futile. Even in a single group, individual differences are more impressive than conformities, the exception more frequent than the rule. In every other family we see a dissenter, a peculiar type. The crosscurrents of cultural fertilization offer a kaleidoscopic picture. In a solid middle western family of farmers, through three generations there appears a freethinker and radical who becomes a school teacher; the son of an immigrant labor leader becomes a staunch Republican; the son of an orthodox rabbi, a frivolous columnist of a New York periodical. Orientation toward goals in life, sex, property, and children appear in a chaotic confusion and defy every attempt at generalization. Under the microscope of psychoanalytic case studies the reason becomes evident: it is the highly individual determination of personality development by the reaction of the child's inherited constitution to the immense range of individualities as represented by the different personalities of the parents in their relationships to each other and to their children. All this, of course, does not mean that the cultural structure has no influence on personality formation. It means that the cultural structure in our dynamic civilization is complex and changing and accordingly offers an infinite selection to individuals of how they will be influenced by the culture. From the great variety of cultural trends in a changing civilization in which the past, the present, and the future are woven into an intricate pattern, the child's ego selects what it needs. This selection is determined by those emotional needs which develop in early family life under the influence of the particular personalities of the parents. A few brief examples may illustrate this thesis.

A number of my patients have belonged to a similar, rather well-defined cultural background. The patients were second generation Americans, members of immigrant families, and belonged to a racial minority group. The father's role in the family was of determining significance. His success in adapting himself to his new environment had a great influence on the son's development. In most of these cases the father became a more or less depreciated figure. He struggled for his existence, could not speak good English, was a mediocre provider, and sometimes even the target of ridicule of the son's contemporaries. The mother's attitude was likewise typical. She set all her hopes in the son, particularly in her oldest. The husband could no longer fulfill her ambitions. His position in the family was definitely on the decline. The mother's attitude was to sacrifice everything for the son's sake. The son would make up for everything; he would become a real American in a free country in which all possibilities were open for him. Thus the father became dethroned at home, and the whole life of the family revolved around the eldest son. From the meager earnings of the father a disproportionate amount was spent for the education of the son. The father's own little hobbies and customs, brought over from the old country, his weekly card game or some other inexpensive entertainments, were looked on jealously as unnecessary expenditures. His slow ways, particularly if he had some intellectual interests, were considered laziness. The family's future was bound up in the son. Everything must be sacrificed for his sake. This description, with minor variations, shows a typical culturally determined family situation, recurring in thousands and thousands of instances. In the few cases I have had the opportunity to study, I have observed a variety of outcomes, dependent on the specific human characters involved.

One common outcome is that the son, usurping father's place in mother's affections as well as in many material respects, develops tremendous ambition. He wants to justify all the hopes and sacrifices of the mother and thus appease his guilty conscience toward the father. There is only one way to accomplish this end. He must become successful, whatever the cost. In the hierarchy of values, success becomes supreme, overshadowing everything else, and failure becomes equivalent to sin (the greatest sin consists in a senseless and unjustified human sacrifice: the father). Consequently all other vices, such as insincerity in human relationships, unfairness in competition, disloyalty, disregard for everyone else, appear comparatively as nothing; and there emerges the formidable phenomenon of the ruthless careerits, obsessed by the single idea of self-promotion, a caricature of the self-made man, a threat to Western civilization, the principles of which he reduces to an absurdity. I am impressed by the precision with which a new author, Budd Schulberg, in his novel *What Makes Sammy Run?* has grasped this type, a victim of cultural conditions, and how well he portrayed the hero, Sammy Glick, the "frantic marathoner" of life, "sprinting out of his mother's womb, turning life into a race in which the only rules are fight for the rail, and elbow on the turn, and the only finish-line is death."

Much depends, however, on the father's character and attitude. If he accepts the situation graciously and shares the mother's ambitious attitude toward the son, the guilt reaction is likely to become stronger than in cases in which the father responds with aggression or a spiteful neglect of his family. In the latter case the son may feel justified in his attitude. It is more difficult to accept sacrifice from a magnanimous, self-offering father than from an aggressive, rejecting parent. I have seen both constellations. In one case the father was not very effective, but he was an amiable man who fully accepted the mother's attitude toward the son. The outcome for the son, who became socially successful, was a neurosis which manifested itself in severe depressions and anxiety states mixed with a driving ambition. He tried always to discredit the father as much as possible. This deprecatory attitude was then transferred to all authority; a suspicious personality developed, inclined to find fault with everyone, unable to acknowledge real values or generous trends in anyone else. In the other case the father withdrew and neglected his family, obviously resenting the mother's exclusive concern with her son. This son developed a morbid self-confidence, formidable ambition, but comparatively little guilt. The only thing which caused him real concern was his unpopularity, which was the natural reaction of the environment to his personality. Those who did not dislike him feared him because of his uncanny driving power. In this case all the aggressions remained directed toward the environment, whereas in the former case they were turned back against the self. The good father thus proved to be a greater load than was the neglectful parent. The first patient, of course, became a more socialized individual, since he was unable to free himself from the influence of his conscience.

In another case the guilt reaction was so severe that its alleviation required paranoid projections. This patient, in order to justify his ruthlessness, had to see in everyone an aggressor. This view made him feel that his war against the world was waged in self-defense.

In yet another case of similar background, the mother's attitude was not only ambition for the son but also overprotection. Here the father was a better provider and gave no cause for depreciation. The son developed a tremendous lack of confidence, nurtured by his mother's overprotectiveness and by the feeling that he would never be able to accomplish what was expected of him. The father, a self-made man, appeared to him like a giant. He tried to drive himself forward and developed the compulsive urge to face dangerous situations. Gradually, however, all this effort became so much of a strain for him that he withdrew toward a more contemplative, artistic outlook, with a tendency to accept a dependent but secure position. On the whole the outcome in this case was a more continental type of personality which, in another environment, would have received more appreciation.

In one case, as a reaction to the same family situation, a real productive urge developed in the son, the wish to create something of lasting value. In this family the father was himself a productive type who did not lose his social status and did not give up his creative ambitions after his immigration. In this case also the mother's exaggerated ambition was transferred to the boy and created a neurotic conflict between a thirst for external success and real productive tendencies.

These few sketchy examples may illustrate the overwhelming significance in personality development of the specific character traits of the parents and their relations to each other and to their children. Cultural environment accounts only for certain similarities in persons of the same cultural group. For the tremendous individual differences among human beings living in the same group, constitution and the specific human influences are responsible.

The task of the psychiatrist and the educator

The primary concern of the psychiatrist, as well as of the educator, is the human being as an individual, with all his peculiarities and specific makeup. Both deal with personalities and must understand their development in the most specific terms and not in generalities. Psychiatrists and educators cannot be satisfied with recognizing in their patients or pupils the exponents of cultural configurations; they must understand each on his own merits in terms of his own highly individual life history.

The admonition of the so-called "Neo-Freudians" that psychiatrists are not yet sufficiently aware of the cultural determinants in personality development is valid in a sense, but the implication that this cultural point of view will increase their therapeutic acumen is unfounded. For the social planner or reformer, this cultural point of view is of primary importance. The therapist will have to continue to deal with his patients, and the educator with his pupils, as individual cases whose personalities must be understood as the result of specific factors, different in each case. The significance of the cultural point of view lies in another field, which undoubtedly is more significant than individual therapy: in the preventive or mental hygiene aspects of psychiatry and education. Recognizing the influence of cultural factors to which everyone is equally exposed may contribute to the prevention of certain personality disturbances by social reform.

On the other hand, the introduction of the study of case histories is the most important methodological contribution of psychiatry to the social sciences. Social life is lived by individuals. In each person the prevailing social trends necessarily reflect themselves. The recognition of certain common features in individual case histories is thus one valuable method of establishing the ideological trends in a given society. This method will also contribute to the understanding of the dynamics of social change, which is foreboded in the emotional tensions of individuals—emotional tensions which are the result of the discrepancies between traditional attitudes and a changing social structure. Traditional attitudes represent adjustment to earlier, abandoned phases of historical development. It is my conviction that rapid social change is, as a rule, accompanied by a spread of neurosis which results from these discrepancies. In such historical periods neurosis becomes the rule and the normal individual the exception.

In our dynamic civilization, however, recognition of the specific influences of the personal environment, as distinct from the more general cultural factors, will remain an indispensable point of view. The most characteristic feature of our cultural life lies in its great emphasis on the individual. Its complex structure, its highly differentiated distribution of social functions, would be impossible without variegated human material. Through the psychological influence of individualities upon one another, new differences are created and thus is provided that highly diversified human material which is the secret of our rapidly changing world.

From a distant point of view the present cultural period, beginning with the Renaissance, might appear in the history of the human race as somewhat similar to a period of mutation in biological evolution. The breeding of highly differentiated human material is the most characteristic manifestation of this period of social change, in which the traditional influences give place to rapid and enforced adjustments. The accent is on the individual. This period, thought of as beginning with the Renaissance, produced the most individualistic type of art and literature, as represented by the great reproducers of personality: the Italian painters of the fifteenth and sixteenth centuries; Rembrandt and Shakespeare in the seventeenth century; and the great novelists of the past century, such as Stendhal, Balzac, and Dostoevsky. In the past hundred years this period of rapid transformation has assumed the almost explosive qualities of biological mutation. The latest fruit of this development is the scientific mastery of the human personality, the psychological study of the human being, not only as the exponent of a biological specimen or of a social group, but as an individual person, molded by the specific personality influences of his early emotional environment.

A World Without
Psychic Frustration

◄ 1944 ►

The editor's request to write about a world without frustration is an embarrassing one for a psychiatrist, because one of the most outstanding phenomena with which he deals in his daily practice is frustration. When he turns from mental sufferers to what is supposed to be the normal man, frustration as a central phenomenon still glares into his eyes as a universal experience. To him, a world from which frustration is banished appears a fantastic utopia. He knows that the Garden of Eden, the Golden Age—whether projected into the past or, as the millennium, into the future—is a wishful fantasy. Frustration as a psychological experience is such a fundamental aspect of life that he is inclined to question the desirability of a world without it. He would even doubt whether life, as a biological phenomenon, would be possible in a universe where frustration has been fully eliminated.

The emotional experience which we call frustration is an essential part of life. It appears in the consciousness as a state of unfulfillment, discomfort, lack of satisfaction. It stimulates the organism to new attempts at gratifying the need or desire which has been thwarted, to try out new methods and make new experiments. It is theoretically conceivable to eliminate all frustrations from the life of a person by controlling the conditions upon which the gratification of all subjective needs and drives depends—a spoiled child comes nearest to this theoretical assumption; but the most common argument against spoiling a child is that later, when the child grows up, he will be unprepared to face the unavoidable frustrations of life. Under actual conditions everyone—even a spoiled child—is exposed intermittently to frustrations which prompt the organism to undertake groping efforts at their elimination.

As soon as a correct behavior pattern is found suitable for the elimination of a certain type of frustration, it is repeated whenever the

440

same frustrating condition arises. As a result of repetitions, the behavior pattern becomes automatic and is carried out with a minimum expenditure of energy. In this way the organism gradually learns to master a great number of frustrating situations, particularly those which occur frequently during everyday life. Since there are always new situations which the organism has not yet encountered and to which, therefore, it is not adjusted, frustration is an ever recurring experience. Situations with which the organism is unable to cope because of their suddenness or unfamiliarity are called "traumata." When exposed to a trauma, the organism makes unsuccessful attempts to get rid of the excessive excitation caused either by an impact of external violent stimuli or by an excess of frustration caused by unsatisfied needs.

The phenomenology of psychic frustration covers a great variety of experiences: Unsuccessful attempts at the satisfaction of hunger or thirst and the avoidance of exposure to cold; the more complex emotional states, such as thwarted longing for love, futile seeking of recognition or self-expression, all forms of unavailing ambition to achievement; the inability to satisfy a desire for revenge, competition or the domination of others—all belong to the same category and may create the sensation of frustration. Thus frustration is shown to be an ever present part of the emotional life. In fact, a wish is a wish only as long as it is unfulfilled.

Biology also seems to justify the thesis that struggle against frustrating conditions is an essential part of life. A great part of the anatomical and physiological equipment of the organism serves to master obstacles which interfere with the satisfaction of basic needs. Biologists define life as "a state of dynamic equilibrium," which means that the life process consists of expenditure of energy which the organism must replace from the environment if life is to be continued; the expenditure and replacement of energy must be in permanent equilibrium to preserve the continuity of life. The process of life itself creates permanent needs for replacement of energy and substance expended. Since this replacement of energy must be obtained from an environment which virtually always contains obstacles, temporary, recurring frustrations are unavoidable.

Theoretically, however, a life without frustration would appear possible when there have been removed from the environment all those obstacles which have to be overcome for the gratification of those needs which the life process, in constantly using up energy, itself creates.

These obstacles can be divided into two categories—physical obstacles and human obstacles, the latter a result of the competition among men for the resources of life. As to the physical obstacles, we may grant the possibility that further technical advancement and the exploitation of all sources of energy, including the almost unlimited intra-atomic sources, could eventually lead to conditions in which all the basic needs of the human race would be satisfied smoothly, with a minimum of effort. As to the human obstacles also, we may assume that progress in the field of the social sciences and education may gradually lead to a world from which the competition of man against man for the gratification of the basic needs will be eliminated and re-placed by mutual aid and cooperation. It is certain that, in such a planned world, the size of the global population would have to be con-trolled, since the existing resources necessary for the maintenance of life, although vast, are not infinite on this planet.

Unquestionably, our present technical civilization has brought the fantasy of Aladdin's lamp nearer than ever to its realization. A large portion of our population visualizes the future as a world in which physical comfort is the supreme value; it is inclined to consider as progress everything which brings us nearer to its ideal of a push-button civilization, a mechanical "*Schlaraffenland*," in which all our wants and needs will be satisfied, with a minimum expenditure of energy, by the help of clever mechanical devices calculated to satisfy all our needs—shelter, hygienic food, and swift, safe, comfortable lo-comotion. The scientific counterpart of this popular outlook is the ma-terialistic economic theory which considers the problems of social life solved when all the basic needs of man are satisfied with as little effort as possible. True, if the strivings of the human race consisted in noth-ing else but the satisfaction of these basic biological needs, such a me-chanical pushbutton civilization, ruled by equalitarian justice, would mean the end of development, and a static world order would ensue.

It belongs to one of those dialectical contradictions of history that this great emphasis upon the economic bases of social life has become so paramount in our era—an era in which the technical mastery of the resources of life has reached unparalleled perfection. Economic inse-curity, in this era, has become the central theme which animates the masses, influences the internal and external politics of nations, and finds expression in materialistic political theories.

There were periods in our Western civilization, before the great technical advancement took place, in which the maintenance of life was a routine matter; the economic and social functions of everyone were well defined, and the satisfaction of these needs better insured; economic security was taken more for granted than in our industrial era. There are also contemporary, so-called "primitive" societies of sim-ilar structure. In such a society man can emancipate himself from the relentless concern and anxiety for the morrow and turn his energies toward the less material aspects of life. Then the creative functions of the mind become activated in the forms of folk art and in those customs and rituals of everyday life which elevate human existence above mere vegetation.

It is not a mere coincidence that there has been scarcely any period of human history in which popular art—creative expression of the masses—has been at a lower ebb than in our contemporary industrial cities. A mathematically conceived standard of living has taken the place of such unscientific concepts as human happiness. Technical advancement has obviously achieved the opposite of its goal; although it raised the standard of living, it at the same time introduced a far greater amount of that sense of insecurity which drags man down to exclusive concern with the basic needs of existence and absorbs all his energies. The creative aspects of life, of necessity, must recede into the background because they are the expressions of that surplus energy which is liberated from the struggle to maintain vegetative existence. The most grotesque feature of this picture is that the possession of those technical facilities, which should make the vegetative foundations of life easier, has become an all-absorbing goal in itself; for the majority of the population, the essence of life consists in a yearly turning-in of gadgets of lower quality for those of higher quality. The possession of an automobile is no longer subordinated to the purpose of locomotion but becomes a cherished goal in itself. The tourist, rushing blindly from place to place and bringing home nothing but the memory of daily accomplishment measured in miles, bears out the validity of this contention.

All this is not intended as a jeremiad against our technical civilization. I wish only to point out that paradoxical feature of our culture—that the machine, because of our failure to use it in a socially reasonable fashion, instead of minimizing the basic problems of vegetative existence, has increased the sense of insecurity and brought concern for the basic needs into the foreground.

The scientific counterpart of this emotional orientation is the growing emphasis upon the adaptive aspects of life—on the gratification of needs with minimum expenditure of energy, on security and stability—and a neglect of all other aspects of life, such as creativeness, wish for adventure, longing for the challenge of obstacles, all of which are manifestations of surplus energy. This all-pervading sense of insecurity explains the high premium currently set on organization and stability; it explains also the fear of initiative, of chance and frustration.

However, elimination of frustration from human experience can be neither a realistic nor a desirable goal. In fact, frustration and gratification belong together; gratification without some antecedent frustration is hardly conceivable. This principle is instinctively known to every woman who keeps her suitor in suspense; to every mother who playfully teases her baby by now showing, now hiding, the desired object; and to every author who piques his reader's curiosity by withholding the clue to the crime, by making him participate in all the harassing vicissitudes of the hero.

In folklore and fable the most common motif is a frustrating situation. In order to deserve the princess, the hero has to conquer the villain, the seven-headed hydra, the sorcerer, the tyrant; or he must first accomplish some great creative task. This shows only too clearly that, when man is following freely the course of his imagination, frustrating obstacles to be conquered belong to the steady repertoire of desires. Even Aladdin's lamp allows him the gratification of only three wishes and not a continuous indulgence of all his momentary desires. Such a super Aladdin's lamp, indeed, would not appeal to our imagination; life under such conditions would become utter boredom.

It seems, then, that only the poltroon would dream of an existence from which frustration is fully eliminated and in which all wishes are satisfied without expenditure of effort. In fact, one would be inclined to disgnose this type of fantasy in the case of an individual as a sign of infantilism and regression and, in the case of a nation, as a sign of decadence.

That life and struggle are inseparable is the thesis of the Hungarian dramatist Emmerich Madach in his *Tragedy of Man*. Lucifer exposes to Adam the future of the human race—the tyranny of the Egyptian pharaohs, the collapse of the Roman Empire, the Dark Ages, the French Revolution, Fourier's phalanster state leading up to a new Ice Age in which there will be too many Eskimos and too few sea lions. Discouraged, Adam challenges God: "What is the sense of life if it always leads to frustration?" The drama ends with God's voice to Adam: "Man, struggle and trust."

The intuition of the poet here anticipated scientific insight. Frustration *with* hope is a constructive factor of life; *without* hope, it is destructive. Continuous frustrating conditions which do not allow any hope for their mastery lead to defeatism and neurotic failure. Not the elimination of frustration, but the elimination of *hopeless* frustration alone, must be the aim of the social reformer.

There seems to be little doubt that in organic development—both phylogenetic and ontogenetic—frustration is one of the great driving factors. Whenever conditions which the organism has learned to master in the past change, frustration sets in and lasts until the organism learns to master the new situation. Frustration is the sign of a failure in mastery and in the motivation for achieving new mastery.

Where there is change, there is also frustration. Every living or-

ganism grows; and the process of growth is nothing but a series of modifications in the structure and size of the organism. Every new phase
of the growth process involves frustrations requiring new adjustments.
Not only the structure of the organism is altered but also the external
conditions. Stable conditions are not an attribute of the physical universe as we know it. Because of organic growth and changing external conditions, frustration is an integral part of life.

The opposite of frustration is adaptation. Whenever an organism
is adapted to its external and internal environment, frustration is temporarily absent. However, every adaptation is only temporary, because the organism as well as the environment is constantly changing.
Adaptation saves expenditure of energy because adapted behavior
tends to become automatic and to require a minimum expenditure
of energy.

One of the most fundamental but neglected facts of biology and
psychology is that the surplus energy saved by adaptive behavior is
expended in growth and play by the young organism, and in reproduction by the mature organism. Eros is the god of both play and love.
In play activities the young organism exercises those faculties which
later will be utilized for survival. Reproduction on the biological level,
social productivity on the social level, are manifestations of surplus
in the mature organism.

Both in play and in creation, expenditure of surplus energy becomes an aim in itself. In play, obstacles are sought by the organism
for the sole purpose of overcoming them, thus giving opportunity for
the victorious feeling of mastery. In all creative activities, the organism sets a goal outside its own self—a goal which is not subordinated
to anything but is an aim in itself.

The propensity of the living organism to utilize surplus energy in
a creative way makes those arguments pointless which warn us that
universal social security would terminate human progress. It is true
that if our technical mastery of nature were utilized in a socially reasonable manner, it would increase the general security and reduce the
expenditure of energy necessary for the maintenance of life. However, there is no need to fear that this would lead to lack of initiative
and thus to social stagnation. On the contrary—the energy saved by a
socially just utilization of the machine would be used for creative purposes and thus for new progress.

One thing must not be forgotten, however. While biological propagation is an inherited drive, social productivity has to be learned. In
a society in which the machine and its comforts are aims in themselves there is no hope for real productivity, and the surplus energies
saved by the machine will, through lack of constructive goals, be used

for mutual destruction. The raising of the standard of living cannot remain an aim in itself but must be subordinated to the creative use of surplus energies.

If this industrial civilization is to survive, the sound economic understructure of society must be considered merely a means to an end. It is not further technical discoveries but education in the creative use of the energies which have been saved by technological knowledge that is the pressing need of the coming era.

Mental Hygiene in
the Atomic Age

◄ 1946 ►

The central psychological difficulty of our industrial era consists essentially in the need for rapid adjustments to ever changing conditions. In times of slow social change—as for example the eight hundred years of feudal era in Europe—individual adjustments are supported by tradition as represented by attitudes in the family and in institutions like school and church. The life of everyone is rigidly determined by these traditions. A glance at the contours of history in the past one hundred and fifty years presents us with a sharp contrast to this picture. With the Industrial Revolution a fundamentally new era of civilization started, characterized by change and mobility. It is, however, erroneous to limit the extent of Industrial Revolution to the last decades of the eighteenth and the early part of the nineteenth centuries. Since those days we have never ceased to live in the era of industrial revolution, if we define the latter as sudden social changes resulting from rapid advancements of technology.

We have no methods to measure precisely the speed of social change, but it is certain that the rate of this already rapid change has been greatly accelerated in our present days. Our habits and views and our knowledge of yesterday are out of date today, and it seems that the demand for adjusting ourselves to an ever changing world exceeds our adaptability.

The birth of this nation coincided with the beginning of the Industrial Revolution. The American pioneer could turn to technology in his heroic task of conquering a vast, unexplored country. Just as the Spanish Civil War was a rehearsal for modern warfare, the conquest of the American continent was a grand rehearsal for modern technology—at first steam, then electricity, and eventually the combustion engine and electronic devices. The utilization of atomic energies will be the next step. The hero of this development was at first the settler

447

in his steady movement toward the West, later the businessman, the mechanic, and the practical inventor, then the entrepreneur and, finally, in our days of mass production, the organizer, the industrial executive. It is quite natural that the worship of industrial production and distribution of manufactured goods throughout the whole industrialized world became the ideological backbone of our times. A part of this cultural climate is the competitive spirit which has played such an important role in stimulating production and business in general. Accomplishment became the measure of public esteem, and accomplishment meant for the majority production and distribution of economic goods. And this production has gradually become an end in itself, overreaching its social usefulness.

Most people engrossed in their feverish race for achievement are truly terrified at the idea of leisure or inactivity. When the businessman successfully reaches his goal and can stop expanding his business, he does not dare to do so, lest his life become completely empty and senseless. Most of us behave as the tourist who takes a trip but concentrates only on driving his car. The places he includes in his itinerary are only illusory goals. When he arrives at one place, he scarcely notices it; he arrives in the evening, goes to his hotel, sleeps and eats, and starts out early the next morning in order to make the scheduled number of miles to the next stopping place. I can best illustrate the psychology behind this driving for its own sake with a clinical condition which can appropriately be called "retirement neurosis." I see an amazingly large number of these people. Such a patient is, as a rule, a successful businessman between the ages of fifty-five and seventy. For some reason he has to withdraw from active participation in business. His reaction is severe depression; life has ceased to have any meaning for him. From the time he started work as a boy his life has been concentrated on one single goal: financial success. Business has become a passion with him—an all-absorbing mad race. To a psychiatrist's remark that now, when he has to quit business, there might be something worthwhile left for him to do in life, the usual reply is that he has worked all his life, having had little time for other activities, and that if he can't work now, he'd prefer not to live.

One may raise the objection that these are exceptional cases, that for the majority life consists in a continuous effort to raise their standards of living. The embarrassment people feel if confronted with the question of what to do with their leisure time, however, is universal, a typical feature of our times. It is not so conspicuous in those who are struggling for their existence, but it becomes immediately manifest as soon as the necessity for struggle or the opportunity for the improvement of material standards disappears. We tell ourselves that we are striving for a state of affairs in which the material benefits of our technical advancements will be available to every member of society. Since we have not yet arrived at such a universal state of prosperity, we can evade the embarrassing question: What will then be the content of life for people who have learned only how to struggle for such high material standards but are not prepared to use their prosperity for the enrichment of their lives? We look with complacency on our great material achievements and overlook the fact that, while we were achieving these things, we forgot the elementary art of living. We look condescendingly on the peasants of the feudal era because of their primitive material standards, and we overlook their superior capacity of creative expression in folk art, music, dance, handicraft, and folklore, the absence of which makes the life of our industrial masses so drab and colorless. I do not want to be misunderstood. I am not praising the bliss of feudal culture in contrast to industrial civilization. My point is that, while we were busy improving the material foundations of life, we became so engrossed in this endeavor, so fascinated by the possibilities which the machine offers, that we forgot the ultimate aim of all these improvements: a higher cultivation of our specifically human faculties. Eating, sleeping, and propagation are common to men and animals. Division of labor, the exchange of socially useful services, can even be observed in an insect society. But writing poems and novels, building cathedrals, producing plays and operas, discovering the laws of nature and inventing methods of healing, enjoying a landscape, educating and developing the powers of the mind, are specifically human faculties.

There is good evidence that these human faculties developed as a result of man's invention of the tool. The differentiation of the hand as a separate specific organ, relieved of the function of locomotion, together with a highly developed cortex in the brain, the site of the highest intellectual functions, made the discovery of the tool possible. From then on, the use of tools opened the road to an easier life and freed human energies for those higher functions which I have designated as "specifically human."

And now we are witnessing a curious turn in human development: the tool, originally developed to enable us to raise our heads and turn away, at least occasionally, from the struggle for existence, has become our master. For its sake, we are giving up the use of our higher faculties, our higher interests, and are devoting ourselves to improving the machine without ever enjoying its real benefits. We have been so preoccupied with the job of building a home through all these years that we have forgotten that we built it to live in. The industrial production of goods has become almost a form of idol worship with us. We are so absorbed in producing for the sake of production that we forget that the material goods were meant to make us

free from the chores of material existence so that we might do something else. As a last result of this nonsensical development, we are
faced with the ghastly prospect of using the tool to destroy each other
together with all that we call civilization. Man invented the tool to
make life easier for himself: he ends up using it to debase himself to a
button-pushing automaton whose last act will be to push the button
that will exterminate him.

Nothing illustrates more clearly that we consider production not
a means to an end, but an end in itself, than our customary approach
to the most disturbing symptom of our times: unemployment. With
the continuous improvements of mass production with its labor-saving
devices, industrial and agricultural goods can be produced with less
and less human labor. The fundamental function of the tool is saving of
human energy and it is only natural that with the continued improvement of self-regulating tools the need for human labor diminishes. In
itself this should not be a disturbing fact—since man invented the tool
for this very purpose, to secure the necessities of existence with
less effort. Human energies thus saved could turn to other purposes.
And, indeed, science with its steady advancement is creating new
industries and with it new industrial jobs. The experience of the past
decades, however, has been that the speed at which the need for
human labor has been reduced by technology is much greater than
the speed at which new jobs in new industries are created. The conventional remedy for this is sought in expanding the market by creating
prosperity through higher wages. It is obvious, however, that, even in
the most fair social system, this extension of the internal market has
its natural limitations. As soon as this limit is reached the only hope of
averting unemployment lies in imperialistic or competitive acquisition
of foreign markets. Undoubtedly, with the rapid trend toward in-
dustrialization all over the world, this possibility for expansion of production will soon be exhausted. Moreover, as we well know, the desperate competitive struggle for foreign markets has been one of the
traditional causes of war.

The inherent logic of all this is inescapable. The machine was
invented to save human effort and it does and will accomplish its
function unfailingly. It is true that labor thus saved can be directed
into new fields of production but gradually more and more will be accomplished by robotlike machines, mechanisms like those we have
witnessed during war in the form of self-regulating torpedoes and
aerial missiles. All economic devices notwithstanding, such as better
and wider distribution of products, we still have to face the unavoidable consequence: the replacement of more and more human labor by
the machine. The conclusion is inevitable: that human effort which becomes replaced gradually by mechanical devices must find other so-

cially useful outlets that do not consist in the production or distribution of agricultural and industrial goods.

In a complex society there are other socially useful occupations open to people. All those complex services which men render to men, not to increase their material welfare but to increase knowledge, improve health, and make life more enjoyable and richer for each other are examples of such occupations. And yet we are so used to thinking of jobs primarily as work in agriculture, in a factory or store, that we cannot imagine any other significant activity for the masses. We are caught at present in a most dangerous form of cultural lag, a fixation of attitudes belonging to an earlier phase of our national history. During the days of pioneering, of unlimited economic expansion, this passion for producing material goods was most appropriate. But the one-sided preoccupation with the material prerequisites of civilization in the midst of a settled and sophisticated society is now out of place. A wild and blind passion for producing things of which there is plenty can become a most dangerous passion, as we all should know from not too remote occurrences in our economic life when we enjoyed a few years of pseudoprosperity. And it is equally dangerous to try to adjust the economy of a country to this excessive passion for production by artificial economic measures. Artificial employment by government projects, with the slogan, "If private business cannot supply jobs, the government has to do it," is obviously not the answer. The question is not who should give employment but what type of employment it should be. If there is natural need for labor, it is a secondary question whether the government or private industry employs it. And if there is no need for labor, the artificial creation of jobs is economically harmful. Business cannot afford it and government can do it only at the cost of the taxpayers, thus impairing the economy of the nation through increased taxation.

Such suggestions as supporting small business at the expense of big business also miss the real point we have to deal with. If the material goods we need can be produced better and more cheaply by big business, it is nonsensical to support small business artificially. This is the same thing as creating jobs which are not needed. It is putting the cart before the horse. We do not want more business for business' sake, more production for production's sake, but as a means of fulfilling human needs. If these needs can be met with fewer jobs, it is illogical to do it artificially with more jobs.

All this boils down to the fact that unemployment is just as much a psychological and an ideological issue as an economic one. This is the reason why I venture into its discussion. Our ideas as to what should be considered an economically productive occupation are warped by our one-sided preoccupation with production of material goods. In a time of industrial abundance we are still living emotionally according to the tastes and attitudes developed in times of scarcity and primitive struggle against nature. Some may object to my expression of industrial abundance as particularly inappropriate at the present moment. However, I am talking of an economic trend in our time. I am not overlooking the fact that the basic needs today are universally not met, as the suffering and starvation of people in war-torn countries have amply testified. Production *is* needed now in a great measure, production of all kinds of material goods, and distribution of those goods must be improved if we want to relieve the need of millions of people all over the world who are at present crying for help. This, however, obviously is a transitory situation, the immediate result of the war. If we project ourselves into what is called the coming Atomic Age, an age of further technical perfection, we have to visualize an era of industrial abundance. The psychological problems of this coming era, which, considering our industrial potentialities, should not be far away, are the concern of my discussion.

Social life consists in the mutual gratification of human needs by division of functions. It makes no difference what those needs are: whether food, or shoes, or lounging chairs, or poems. As soon as the needs of the body are satisfied, the satisfaction of our so-called higher needs must become our concern. Why should we consider the production of lounging chairs more basic than poems, when one can exist equally well without either of them? And yet the production of lounging chairs is considered productive, increasing the national wealth, while poetry, from the point of view of economics, is quite negligible and has nothing to do with increasing the national wealth except possibly through the paper on which it is printed. Yet if more people were interested in buying poetry than in buying lounging chairs, it would become a much more important item in the national economy than the chairs.

The answer to this problem lies then in ideological changes—in a different scale of values appropriate to the phase of our social development. A country which has succeeded in such an unparalleled manner in laying down the material foundations of civilized life, is ripe for taking the next logical step in its development—the building of a high spiritual culture upon the material foundations. Productive energies can no longer concentrate exclusively on continuing to build the foundations because to a large extent they are already laid down. We shall have systematically to develop needs for less tangible goods which cannot be produced by machines. This can be done through education of the masses with a greater emphasis on the liberal arts and on the merits of aesthetic appreciation and creative expression. Moreover, human energies can more and more turn toward such channels as teaching, healing, and all those human services which make for the enjoyment of life. Human energies liberated by advancing technology must be used either constructively or destructively. The choice is ours. If greater attention is not paid to cultural and moral values, it will lead to our destruction—either moral or physical.

Neither national nor international problems can be solved from a merely economic point of view. We must free ourselves radically from the one-sided overvaluation of the production of material goods, the heritage of the early phases of the Industrial Era. This part of our life we must begin to take almost for granted. The strange thing is that if we apply these same principles to the human organism, we find them as self-evident. We readily admit that the vegetative functions of the body—digestion, breathing, evacuation—are not the aim of life but only the means to live; that our so-called higher interests, our hopes and ambitions, self-expression, human interactions, are what we live for. But when it is said that the same thing is true for society —that industry and commerce, because of organization and further development of machines, will become automatic functions and cease to be the center of our attention—we balk as if the very foundations of our civilization were attacked.

Finally, we must realize that we are misusing our technical knowledge not only if we wage war, but also if we do not use the energies freed by technology for constructive purposes on a higher scale in our national life. We will have to educate our youth not only for production and distribution of goods but also for the higher expression of cultural life, for science, and art, and all those services which make for the art of living. The slogan of the Century of the Common Man needs a new interpretation. Once, it is true, this country's role in history was to open to the common man of all lands the possibility of having a free and prosperous life. But with the years this role has changed. Now it is to enable the common man to be the uncommon man. Advancing technology brings not only advantages but obligations. We who have the highest material standard of living in the world must now give heed to our moral standards and to our culture in general, so that the leisure we have ensured may be used constructively to the higher development of the potentialities of man.

The aim of psychiatry is to help the individual who has failed to adjust himself to the conditions of his life. Mental hygiene attempts to accomplish the same on a large social scale. Like psychiatry, it must begin with the diagnosis of trouble, finding those emotional difficulties of adjustment to which the majority of the people are exposed. In the above diagnosis my conclusion is that we are the victims of a cultural lag inasmuch as we still live emotionally in the past and have not caught up with the new conditions brought about by science and its technical achievements. Following the inertia of habit, instead of making use of labor-saving devices of industry for turning our creative capacities to other fields which lie outside the production of material goods, we are apt to follow traditional patterns and as a result more people will want to earn their living from industrial production than will be needed. This incongruity between ideology and economy will, with the further improvement of automatic tools, steadily increase in the future. The result will be that periodic unemployment will remain with us as a constant source of insecurity and a constant threat to self-esteem, arousing the feeling of having lost one's social usefulness. This insecurity and the frustration of having no opportunity to make use of one's productive capacities are the main source of emotional maladjustment in our times, taking the place of sexual repression which dominated the scene during the Victorian era.

Another manifestation of this cultural lag is our addiction to competition, which makes a race track of our social scene. We live in a world of plenty, at least potentially we do, and yet emotionally we still follow the jungle pattern, "kill or be killed." We continue at home as well as abroad in the belief that it is necessary to prey upon each other. If we do not have to struggle and compete, life becomes empty for us and this feeling is a common cause of emotional maladjustment. We see then that no social group can escape the mentally unsettling consequences of the prevailing discrepancy between emotional orientation and social structure. The effect of this discrepancy upon the struggling masses is insecurity, loss of self-esteem, and frustration; its effect upon those who do not indulge any longer in the race for success is a feeling that life is empty and has lost its meaning. Indeed, machine civilization with all its magnificent material achievements has created a gap in our emotional household by liberating energies which we have not yet learned how to use in a constructive manner. To fill this gap with developing the higher creative faculties of man is the great future task of our era.

I have limited my remarks to defining the nature and source of the most common emotional problems of our times. Making such a diagnosis is one function of mental hygiene. The remedy lies obviously in an emotional reorientation, restoring the disturbed relation between psychological attitudes and social structure. To accomplish this, lies not primarily in the field of psychiatry or mental hygiene. It is the function of the social institutions to which the shaping of the personality and social attitudes are traditionally entrusted—first of all the family, then the church and the school.

On the Psychodynamics of Regressive Phenomena in Panic States

◄ 1955 ►

Before undertaking the discussion of my special topic, a brief review of our present knowledge of anxiety and fear may be appropriate. According to our present views, anxiety and fear are signals of impending danger. *Anxiety* signals an internal danger, the threatening tension of repressed impulses seeking expression which in the past have resulted in painful experiences. They, therefore, become repressed and anxiety is a sign that the repression is challenged by the pressure of the repressed impulses. *Fear*, a subjective experience similar to anxiety, is the response to external danger which is recognized as such by the organism. Since Cannon's work, the physiological function of fear is well known: it introduces adaptive changes in the vegetative processes which are needed in meeting the danger by fight or flight reactions. These adaptive changes consist in stimulation of cortical brain activity, of cardiac and pulmonary functions, of metabolism, particularly of carbohydrate metabolism, and in suitable changes in the distribution of blood, in a relative emptying of the splanchnic reservoir in favor of the muscle system and vital organs needed in effort.

We may define a panic state as a condition in which fear, due to its intensity, fails both in its psychological and physiological function as an alarm signal; it no longer mobilizes the physiological and the psychological resources of the organism for fight or flight but has a *paralyzing* or *disorganizing* effect. Paralyzing fear is a common occurrence, and probably everyone has experienced it at least once in his life. Swift action, coordinated goal-directed activity becomes impossible, and the organism submits to its inevitable fate. Whether or not the vegetative preparation for action in panic remains the same as in normal fear reaction has not yet been sufficiently investigated by experimental methods. There is good clinical evidence, however, that in

455

panic not only voluntary behavior but also the internal vegetative processes are out of gear. Involuntary bowel movement in panic, for example, would indicate increased parasympathetic response instead of sympathetic preponderance which inhibits bowel functions and is normal in emergency. In general neurotic somatic reactions in stress can be roughly divided into two groups: 1) Reactions in which there is a chronic state of organic preparedness for concentrated action, which itself is inhibited. Thus chronically increased heart activity, chronic elevation of blood pressure, or mobilization of carbohydrates from their depots, may ensue, without being followed by appropriate neuromuscular action. 2) A retreat from action accompanied by changes which are physiologically useless or harmful in emergency. Examples are increased stomach and bowel activity as in ulcer or colitis, blocking of respiration as in asthma, or disturbance of carbohydrate metabolism as in hypoglycemia. I call these reactions vegetative retreat because the organism reacts to the need for increased effort paradoxically, with physiological changes which are characteristic for relaxation and sleep, conditions in which the organism withdraws its interest from the external world and engages in anabolic upbuilding of its depleted resources. Szasz refers to these withdrawal phenomena with the expression "regressive innervations," because in these conditions the adult organism reacts to situations which require coordinated voluntary activity with vegetative innervations characteristic of the infant. The small child incapable of adequately dealing with many external situations responds to emotional stress with increased gastrointestinal activity.

It is not possible to enter here into a further discussion of our theory of vegetative retreat and regressive innervations. The important fact is that to outward-directed fear, the oganism may react either with adequate preparation to cope with the emergency, but it may react with paradoxical and morbid responses: with vegetative retreat and paralysis or disorganization of adequate voluntary action. The question of whether or not vegetative retreat and paralysis of action appear always together in the same person can be answered by evidence obtained from experimental studies. The methods developed by Liddell, Gantt, Masserman, and others for the study of experimental neuroses in animals possibly could be applied in such studies. Mahl's experiments in which he studied the stomach secretion of frightened dogs indicate that the stomach reacts paradoxically to paralyzing fear: instead of a normal decrease of stomach activity indicating sympathetic action, he found increased stomach secretion resulting from parasympathetic dominance.

We may summarize all this by saying that according to existing experimental and clinical evidence, fear, when it surpasses a certain intensity, instead of stimulating the organism's defensive measures may have a paralyzing effect upon adequate voluntary behavior and at the same time have a disturbing effect upon vegetative preparedness. The manifestations of the deterioration of outward-directed behavior are well known; they may consist in uncoordinated, futile, motor discharge such as yelling, running in circles, etc., or the response may be complete paralysis of motion and passive submittance to the impending danger. The internal vegetative responses are also inadequate and not only do not supply the physiological energy necessary for concentrated effort, but often are such as to interfere with adequate motor behavior.

After having considered the psychosomatic basis of panic reactions, we may now turn our attention to its psychodynamic analysis. First of all we must consider the influence of anxiety upon external fear. Anxiety and fear may reinforce each other, a fact that has been clearly recognized by Shakespeare: "Thus conscience does make cowards of us all." In other words, the fear of conscience increases the fear of external danger; in psychoanalytic terminology, the ego has to cope with two threats at the same time; with that of the superego and with the actual external emergency. Fear and anxiety may, however, mutually inhibit each other. This we do not know from common sense but only from psychoanalytic experience.

I observed a striking example of how anxiety may decrease fear of external danger in the case of a German infantry officer suffering from a severe compulsion neurosis. He had the compulsion to examine the contents of his pockets from time to time to convince himself that everything—his purse, his keys, his comb, and other small objects—were still in his possession. Hurrying on the street to an appointment, this compulsion would overtake him. He would stop and repeatedly go through his pockets because after each examination he was in doubt whether everything was still there. Not yielding to the compulsion would cause unbearable anxiety. During the war as an officer in the infantry, he was in combat several times, leading his troops to attack. Not infrequently this compulsion would overtake him during infantry attack. Under fire, when everyone was running for shelter, he would stop and go through his ritual, searching his pockets and thus exposing himself to the machine guns. His anxiety that he might have lost something of the contents of his pockets was obviously greater than the fear of being shot. The conclusion is inevitable: his castration fear which was disguised as fear of losing an object from his pocket was more intensive than the realistic fear of death, and overshadowed it to the extent that he preferred to expose himself to dying rather than endure the uncertainty caused by his castration fear. His courage was, of course, a pseudocourage: really, he was merely more influenced by anxiety than by fear.

Our knowledge of quantities involved in psychological processes is not sufficiently advanced to explain fully why in certain individuals neurotic anxiety increases the fear of external danger and thus makes a coward of a person, whereas in other neurotics anxiety apparently decreases the realistic fear of danger and makes a person if not a hero, a foolhardy daredevil. It is reasonable to assume, however, that the more intense the neurotic anxiety is, the more likely will it overshadow the effect of realistic external threats. The intensity of neurotic anxiety increases with the degree to which the internal representations of the parental images remain isolated, ill-integrated parts of the mental apparatus. Such an ill-integrated harsh superego is really an equivalent of an external danger since it lies strictly outside the scope of the ego as a foreign body. It retains the child's concept of the magic power of the parents, and the ego may consequently have a greater awe for the internalized parental image than for external reality. This explains why a neurotic person dominated by internalized anxiety becomes more or less impervious to external reality. Such a person will respond to external danger more acutely only when the external and internal threats, according to their content, are synergistic. If he had entertained intensive guilt feelings toward his father, he will be more intimidated by authorities in his everyday life. But if, for example, the castration fear in a person is directed against men, he may be a coward toward men but be less afraid of women. Or a person, in overcompensating his latent homosexuality, may appear reckless in his dealings with women because his fear of homosexuality is greater than the realistic fear of rash heterosexual involvements. Counterphobic reactions are other examples of anxiety making a person seek external danger.

All this can be formulated by saying that persons with intensive neurotic anxiety may selectively react to external danger with increased boldness or at least imperviousness, or with panic, depending upon the nature of the internal conflict situation and the external danger. A man suffering from height phobia may be paralyzed facing a precipice, but be calm entangled in a violent mob. A person phobic toward crowds may show exactly the opposite reaction. Because he feels more secure in solitude than in crowds, such a person may be an excellent mountain climber but react with panic even to a peaceful gathering.

The Shakespearian thesis, in the light of psychoanalytic knowledge, requires an important qualification. Guilty conscience may make a coward of a person in a certain specific situation and reckless in another one. The answer is that whenever a person is exposed to a kind of external danger situation to which he is specifically sensitized by neurotic anxiety, he is likely to go into a state of panic. In general, we may say that specific guilt feelings either reinforce external fear and precipitate panic states or they may act as a neutralizing agent.

All these considerations may serve as a preparation for dealing with the more complex problem of panic reactions in crowds.

It is well known that panic reactions in groups are highly influenced by leadership or by the lack of it. A leaderless group is more apt to react with disorganized panic reactions than one which is under the guidance of a trusted leader. Obviously in situations of danger everyone is apt to regress to a psychic organization in which dependence on external parental help outweighs the internalized dependence on superego patterns or on the ego's own resources. The superego formation is after all the result of an adaptive change within the organism enabling it to a more independent existence. The more labile the internalization of this dependence is, the greater is the need for actual leadership. In other words, the smaller the confidence is in oneself, the greater is the need to depend on a leader. Self-confidence develops gradually as the child learns to take care of his needs successfully and replaces by identification parental guidance with self-government.

If confronted by an overwhelming situation of both unusual and dangerous character, the task of meeting it may exceed the functional capacity of even a well-developed adult ego. Since regression is a universal trend in all organisms, in overwhelming situations, regression toward a help-seeking attitude is a common response. When adequate external help is not forthcoming, a panic reaction may ensue either in the form of paralysis or disorganized motor activity. Because the individual is not capable of appraising the emergency situation, the urge to act cannot take an organized, goal-directed form and spends itself in disorganized discharge. This may take the form of desperately attempting to achieve some intermediary goal, for example, in a fire to reach an inapproachable door by attacking the next person ahead, or consists in a completely aimless uncoordinated motor activity. The regressive deterioration of behavior is further enhanced by the kind of mental contagion which has been described by LeBon and Freud in unorganized groups. The regressive behavior is reinforced by mutual identification of the members with each other. Since the regressive trend is ubiquitous, the regressive behavior of one person may serve as a seduction for the next one. This is true for panic states as well as for mob violence.

Panic reactions which develop in average persons in overwhelming danger situations can be averted by offering the ego at least some of the help which it actually needs but cannot supply itself. The identification with a self-confident leader may counteract the identification with the helpless members of the group. First of all, confidence must be restored that there is a way out and the leader knows it. Even when he cannot give such help, the leader should act with reassurance because his attitude may diminish panic reactions and thus increase the chances of a favorable outcome. Because the greatest hazard in all unusual situations lies in unpreparedness, the primary function of leadership is to anticipate dangerous situations and work out an adequate blue print of meeting them, a plan which is based on division of labor. Every member of the group must have in such a prepared plan a well-defined function. Acting according to the plan, much of the pressure for activity can be discharged in some useful way, which may or may not lead to a successful outcome. The chances of success, however, are greatly increased if instead of chaotic activity of the members, each one blindly follows a prescribed useful function. This type of preplanned organized group response can be well compared with the functions of a rigid superego which completely relieves the ego from individual judgment. Since we are dealing now with overwhelming situations which the individual alone with his best judgment is not prepared to handle, such a regressive measure, in which the leader takes over the function of the real or introjected parent, is well justified. Such a transitory authoritarian regime in danger represents a partial regression, a compromise by which a complete disaster, resulting in chaotic disorganization of behavior, might be averted.

Personal leadership to some degree can be replaced by such a well prepared, detailed and categorically formulated plan of concerted action which unequivocally prescribes each person's function in the event of danger. This aim is more or less successfully approached by the various brochures prepared by civilian defense authorities. Since, however, the expected reactions under any circumstance will have a regressive character, the presence of a leader supplying immediate personal reassurance emanating from a parent figure greatly increases the chances of preventing panic. Moreover, a prepared plan is of use only if the danger situation has been more or less correctly anticipated. If not, only the reassurance supplied by the presence of acutal leaders on the scene can be of value.

We postulated that in completely novel and overwhelming situations, regression to disorganized behavior is universal. Everyone being susceptible to panic, the question arises: what makes a person suitable for leadership? First of all, his ego should have a greater capacity to withstand the trend to regress immediately toward seeking outside help and if the latter is not forthcoming, to panic. In other words, his first impulse should be to rely on his own resources. He must have a flexible, adaptable ego in which the automatic superego reactions are to a higher degree than average replaced by flexible ego reactions. A further qualification of greatest importance is preparedness. The prospective leader, in order to be in a position to take over in danger, must have all the actual and available knowledge about the nature of the anticipated danger. This is to say, that he must be a specialist in dealing with emergency situations. His technical knowledge makes it possible for him, if his ego otherwise is intact, to rely on self-help. He will be less likely to give up in peril than the unprepared person who is taken unaware by an emergency. The example of a secure leader may check the chain reaction of regressive behavior which otherwise would develop through mutual identification of the group members with each other.

Adventure and Security
in a Changing World

◄ 1957 ►

Man's behavior is governed by two opposing trends, the one toward stability and security, and the other toward adventure, exploration of the unknown and creation. The trend toward security is the manifestation of a basic biological principle, that of self-preservation. It is expressed in the striving to secure the basic necessities for survival. The expansive or progressive trend toward new ventures into the unknown is the manifestation of an equally basic biological principle, that of growth and propagation.

It would be futile to argue which of these two trends is more fundamental. Together they constitute life. It can be said, however, that growth and procreation are the manifestations of that surplus energy which remains over and above what is needed for survival. The organism grows when it takes in from the environment more than it expends. Life being a dynamic equilibrium, energy is expended for extracting from the environment the amount of energy which is needed to maintain the life process itself. Whatever is left over is retained in the form of growth. Growth, however, has its limitations; every organism, as we know, stops growing when maturity is reached. From then on, the surplus of intake can be expended in the form of producing a new organism. Biological procreation, however, is not the only form of creativity. In his social activities man manifests many other creative functions which are above and beyond the utilitarian functions of maintaining his existence. Art, literature, the scientific exploration of the environment, are other examples of sublimated manifestations of the procreative urge. The lust for adventure, the urge to meet the challenge of obstacles, not for survival but merely for its own sake, are equally pure manifestations of the surplus energy which is not needed for survival.

In literature, where man allows free flow to his imagination, both

462

trends can be observed. The longing for serenity and peaceful enjoyment of security is best expressed in the bucolic type of poetry and also in the utopias which dream of a stable, secure social order in which everybody lives happily, free from fear and want. Another type of literary fantasy seeks gratification from adventure, the overcoming of obstacles, the clearest example of which is the epic of Odysseus, or the prince of the fables who has to conquer the nine-headed Hydra before he can gain the hand of the princess. The security motive in such fables has a very subordinate role. It is the happy ending and not much more can be said about it than "they lived happily ever after."

Obviously the security motive offers less variety to the imagination, whereas adventure with all its unpredictable vicissitudes, risks, and uncertainties is an inexhaustible source of appeal. The security motive is expressed in the story of the Garden of Eden and the Golden Age but even the story of the Garden of Eden begins really with the expulsion. About life in the Garden, very little more is said than that it was secure and serene.

Both motives, the quest for security and the lust for venture, have always been present in the social aspirations of man, but they do not always appear in equal distribution. In certain historical periods the need for security dominates the scene; other periods are characterized by the vigorous expression of the experimental spirit of man. Whenever man has to expend all his energy for mere subsistence, not much interest is left for experimentation with the unknown and for creation. When one is exposed to the danger of starvation, of deprivation of the basic necessities of life, it is natural that the first concern will be for security. In general, we may say that fear and danger favor the trend toward security. Also, too much freedom and responsibility stimulate a longing for security. On the other hand, when man is overprotected and at the same time restricted in the free expression of his creative forces, the longing for freedom and adventure increases.

Under the feudal system the majority of the people gave up freedom for security. All individual self-expression was sacrificed for the sake of being protected by the feudal lord. Also in many of the so-called primitive cultures which are characterized by lack of visible social change, the security motive prevails. In Western civilization at the dawn of the modern era, the free expression of man's creativeness and the bold trend toward exploration of the earth, physical nature, the universe, and the animal and human body, appeared in an unprecedented fashion. This Renaissance movement started in the cities of northern Italy where a rapidly increasing population of merchants and artisans gradually superimposed their venturesome spirit on a solidified understructure of feudal society. They introduced adventure and individual self-expression as new powerful factors in economic and cultural life. The American democracy, particularly during the pioneer era, represents the most extreme realization of a rapidly changing free society which can trace its spiritual origin to the Renaissance.

With the recent gradual consolidation of American society, there are definite signs of a slow reversal of this trend. Possibly the Great Depression of the thirties can be considered as the dividing line. There can be little doubt that a growing longing for security and the willingness to give up freedom of expression and venture characterize the last twenty years.

Public opinion polls in 1948, collected from representative samples of American youth show, for example, that when asked what types of jobs they would pick, half of the young men preferred a job which would pay quite a low income but which they were certain of keeping, to jobs where there was a good income with the chance of losing the job. And only 17 per cent were willing to take the risk of depending upon their own personal ability to make a great success and in which everything would be lost if they failed to make the grade.

In the 1949 classes of various colleges, students were questioned by *Fortune* magazine concerning their attitudes toward their future career. It was found that only 2 per cent had the intention of going into business for themselves. There was a definite preference to work for large companies because they offered greater, prolonged security and appeared more "depression-proof." Administrative jobs and personnel work were most desired. To speak of the "vanishing entrepreneur" is certainly a justified conclusion of this poll.

This unsigned article in *Fortune* quotes Elliot Cohen's description of today's young intellectual.

Culturally he feels himself the survivor of a long series of routs and massacres. Insecurity is his portion, and doom and death are to him familiar neighbors. . . . There is very little in him of that lust for life and experience, of the joy of living for its own sake, of a sense of wide horizons, or worlds to conquer, or much of that early curiosity that drove his older brother expansively over the realms of knowledge.[1]

Unfortunately, public opinion polls are not available for the pre-Depression era. There can be no doubt, however, that there is a growing trend in the orientation of American youth toward stability, security and organization rather than toward new ventures and enterprises, a trend which prevailed in earlier phases of the history of this country.

[1] *Fortune,* June 1949, p. 170.

This observation raises several problems: first of all, how to explain this reversal in trend; and second, how to evaluate it from the point of view of the future. Certainly such changes in attitude are reactions to changes in social structure and conditions. There can be little doubt that the expanding economy of the United States gave opportunity for individual initiative in an unparalleled fashion. Equipped with the technological achievements of the Industrial Revolution, the immigrants from the Old World could successfully realize their adventurous aspirations with a good chance of coming out well at the end. They took risks, but the chance for success was in their favor. Moreover, the original ideological pattern was set by a group of enterprising settlers who could not find their place in their home countries. They represented a natural selection from that part of the population which was prone to take chances, due to both their social position and personality. They were protestors against tyranny and suppression and had little to lose.

Since this pioneer era, the socioeconomic scene of the United States has changed considerably. The fact that only 2 per cent of the 1949 college graduates thought of going into business for themselves could be well considered the result of a fairly realistic appraisal of present conditions. The mortality rate of small new business enterprises is notoriously greater than it was in the earlier phases of American history, which were characterized by a rapidly expanding economy.

Economic consolidation, however, and control by big business corporations of many branches of economic activity alone cannot be made responsible for this shift in attitude. One cannot dismiss the intimidating effect of two world wars and the Great Depression of 1930. Equally important was the rapid dissolution of the ideological moorings of the nineteenth century, the leitmotif of which was the optimistic faith in progress. This ideological gap was not filled by a new philosophy of life. The resulting ideological confusion reached its peak after the end of the Second World War. The increasing tension between the political and economic philosophies of the West and East, the constant threat of a third world war, created a feeling of temporariness, a state of transition. Under these conditions, with the ever-changing international scene, under the constant threat of the cold war turning into a real one, long-term planning became impossible, not only for the inexperienced youth, but even for the most mature part of the population. Therefore, no effective spiritual leadership has arisen in the Western world.

The whole cultural climate was pervaded by one great longing, a longing for some order in the chaos, the wish for security, both material and spiritual. The emotional atmosphere was approaching that which made the disorganized masses of the collapsing Roman Empire susceptible to both strong spiritual leadership and religious dogma on the one hand, and for protection by strong men of action, the feudal lords, on the other.

The modern edition of the same situation is the longing for a powerful government. There is no doubt that in addition to these emotional needs there is a realistic objective need in our complex, interdependent industrial economy for greater central coordination of the highly differentiated and specialized economic activities. Can we consider the changes in attitude of youth merely as reasonable reactions to the changing socioeconomic scene? It is obvious that in the present highly interdependent society, the individual cannot rely to the same degree as before on his own resources and ability to provide for himself and his family. More and more, the individual becomes the victim of the impersonal, statistical laws of supply and demand, the ratio of which is rapidly changing with increasing mass production. New technological inventions open up new territories, while overproduction in other fields restricts opportunities so rapidly that no single individual can any longer have a clear perspective of the total ever-changing economic and social scene. Certain regulatory measures on the part of a central government, to be obtained through organization and administration of the achievements of the past, become imperative. The focal interest is then no longer in new ventures, in the expression of individual creativeness, but in social security.

It would appear, then, that this increased preoccupation with security and organization instead of with creative enterprise is an unavoidable reaction to current social developments.

The emotional responses in mass reactions, however, have the tendency to overreach their optimal intensity. Under the influence of intensive emotion, judgment becomes impaired. Attention is focused on only one single aspect of the situation which obscures a correct appraisal of the total situation. This can be best observed in panic. Fear is a most useful biological reaction to danger. It alerts the organism to muster all its resources to meet the emergency. Excessive fear, however, no longer has a stimulating but a paralyzing effect, as best can be seen in a group overtaken by panic. In a fire, everybody tries to reach the nearest exits. The whole attention is narrowed down to a desperate effort to escape through the nearest opening, without consideration for the total situation. Here fear becomes not an asset for the organism but a destructive force.

Emotional responses, particularly in groups, have the quality of becoming overreactive. Everyone knows the behavior of a booming stock market when under the influence of a contagious optimistic rush stocks are bought for prices beyond their actual economic value. The spirit of the boom feeds on itself. Without taking this emotional overreaction into account, the erratic fluctuations of the market cannot be explained. Similarly, in market collapse, securities are thrown away beyond any reasonable economic justification.

The rational nucleus of such mass response is distorted by emotional overreactions and the resulting behavior is not in harmony with the underlying objective conditions: it overshoots its mark. We ask now whether the present preoccupation with security in our chaotic times may not have an element of a similar emotional overreaction? Is this emphasis on security proportionate to the real situation? Is it true that the greater security, the better it is for the general welfare? The correct evaluation of any situation requires sober detached reasoning. A most common fallacy is the belief that more of something which is good is better. The concept of an optimal measure, the principle of the golden mean, does not belong to the repertoire of the average person.

Let me illustrate this with a newly described principle of historical development. The British historian, Toynbee, has proposed the thesis that civilizations come to birth in environments that are unusually difficult and not unusually easy. The difficulties may be geographical, climatic, or may consist in inimical human environment such as outside enemies. Toynbee asks whether this observation can be expressed in a social law: the greater the challenge, the greater its stimulating effect upon the development of a civilization. On the basis of extensive historical evidence he has demonstrated that this is not the case, that there is an optimal amount of challenge. If the difficulties to be conquered are too great, beyond the capacity of the social group, high-grade progressing civilizations will not develop. All that men under such conditions may achieve is some kind of a touch-and-go type of adaptation to a difficult environment which absorbs all energies for maintaining the status quo. The result is a static so-called primitive culture.

The challenge of obstacles has a beneficial effect because it stimulates the phychological resources of man beyond a measure which is needed for mere survival. Under the momentum of the stimulus not only the existing difficulties are overcome, but new creative acts are performed. If the difficulties are so great that the adaptive powers are fully exhausted by merely meeting the challenges, a static type of adaptation will take place.

The problem of challenge is closely related to the problem we are concerned with: the problem of security. Every challenge creates insecurity. Insecurity is the awareness of danger; it is a state of permanent but not necessarily intensive fear. Fear, as we saw before, is the biological stimulus for mobilizing the organism's resources which are required in emergency situations. Complete and permanent security, if such a state could be achieved, would probably lead to a greater relaxation than is compatible with life, and to eventual deterioration.

Biology seems to justify fully the thesis that struggle against frustrating conditions is essential. A great part of the anatomic and physiologic equipment of the organism is designed to master obstacles which oppose the satisfaction of basic needs. The process of life consumes energy which has to be constantly replaced from an environment which nearly always contains obstacles. Overcoming these obstacles is consequently a fundamental aspect of life itself. Whenever a species succeeds in reaching such a perfect adaptation to a fairly stable environment that it can secure all necessities of life by smooth, effortless and merely automatic performances, the result is a static condition, an organism which has no need for further development. *Homo sapiens* is obviously the result of fortunate phylogenetic circumstances which have not arrested his development by highly specific and stable adaptations to a stable environment.

If we turn our attention now to life in society, the problem becomes complicated by the fact that civilized man through his creative faculties produces an ever changing environment which requires newer and newer adaptations. Civilization consists in man-made changes in environment. In fact, in civilization, man creates his own difficulties by his restless creative drive. This is particularly true for progressing civilizations or, if one prefers the expression, changing civilizations. Static societies characterized by very slow change represent highly specific adaptations. In such societies, the external challenges are barely met and do not produce that momentum which drives to further creative acts resulting in new conditions which in turn require new adaptations.

Since the end of the Middle Ages, our Western society has been characterized by rapid change, the speed of which is in steady acceleration. One should compare the extent of the changes which occurred during the seventeenth and eighteenth centuries with those which took place during the Industrial Revolution of the nineteenth century. And the rapidity of social and economic changes in the first half of the twentieth century far exceeds even those of the last century.

Since changing conditions require newer and newer adaptations, a certain amount of uncertainty characterizes dynamic society. As Toynbee expresses it, living in such civilizations is equivalent to living dangerously. The important quantitative factor responsible for dynamic, progressing civilizations is that the response to challenges exceeds what is needed for mere adaptation. This excess of response is the source of new creative activity which again requires new adaptive changes. How long this feedback mechanism can go on is unknown because of our lack of precise quantitative knowledge of the laws of sociodynamics.

The reversal in the attitude of present-day youth from lust for adventure to craving for security could be interpreted as the sign of the fact that the acceleration of change has increased the difficulties of adaptation to a point which produces a paralyzing amount of insecurity. Such excessive insecurity is no longer an invigorating stimulus but is a retarding factor. In other words, the mere adaptation to steadily changing conditions may become so difficult that it absorbs all the concern of the individual. More concretely, our present challenge consists in adapting ourselves to our unprecedented degree of mastery over nature. Our rapidly advancing technology made close neighbors of all the nations of the earth before they had time to learn how to cooperate with each other. Technology gave, into the hands of mistrusting nations, weapons of a destructiveness hitherto unknown. Many observers of the contemporary social scene have come to the conclusion that we are at the end of the road, that we shall not be able to use our technological advancements for creative and peaceful purposes. An excessive part of our national income is spent for armament.

We know that an individual who faces a situation which he cannot master is likely to react with a disorganized discharge of rage and not with behavior appropriate for overcoming the difficulty. Will humanity, baffled by the rapid changes brought about by science, respond with such a disorganized destructive mass reaction? Looking upon the changing psychological climate of our youth, we cannot avoid asking the question: are the present difficulties of adaptation to new conditions in our mechanized era so excessive that all human energies will have to be spent to bring order into the chaos? If this is the case, organization and consolidation of what we have achieved in the past will be the main problem of the immediate future and the era of progression, venture, exploration of the unknown, is over. Has our dynamic, creative civilization come to its natural end? Have we become tired of the vicissitudes and strains of a rapidly changing world? Certainly the clamor of our youth for security at the expense of new creative experimentation would confirm this impression.

The answer, however, may not be quite so simple as this. There are various alternatives. Possibly we will have to pass through a temporary period of consolidation and will have to learn to organize our past achievements without destroying individual creativeness. This problem of organization is the challenge which our society has to meet at this particular phase of development. If we succeed in solving this problem of organization without destroying initiative, this would mean only an unavoidable, necessary slowing down of social and economic development, but not a complete standstill. The other, more sinister alternative is that we will succumb to the extreme challenge of our new technological and social environment, which we ourselves have created.

If we accept Toynbee's hypothesis, it appears as if we were entering a typical phase of social development through which all dynamic civilizations have passed, a phase which Toynbee considers the beginning of decline, eventually leading to disintegration. He calls this phase the era of the "universal state" which is nothing but what was formerly called the centralized, powerful government. In this phase, difficulties are met by uniform and automatic patterns which are enforced by the all-powerful state. The fluid dynamic society at this stage is entering a phase of stabilization which eventually will lead to disintegration, because the internal disharmonies that unavoidably occur from time to time in every complex society can no longer be corrected by flexible measures. Such flexible measures require local autonomy because the corrective measures must be adjusted to the particular local conditions. This is the essence of free democracy. Uniform measures emanating from central governments must be enforced because they do not apply precisely to every local situation. Toynbee emphasizes that because of the need for enforcements, the leaders in responsible positions become rulers instead of leaders and inevitably lose the trust and admiration of the masses. The drastic introduction of uniform patterns creates mistrust, hate and envy. Thus the delicate internal equilibrium of the fluid social organism becomes disturbed. It appears that no civilization after it has reached a certain size and complexity, has succeeded in solving this special problem of coordinating highly differentiated social functions harmoniously, without destroying creativeness.

Another cause of decline Toynbee attributes to external factors consisting of the threat from inimical neighboring civilizations. He gives an interesting example which repeatedly occurred in the past history of advanced civilizations after they reached the phase of the universal state. The lack of creative innovations results in adherence to outmoded weapons, while the adversaries through new discoveries obtain military supremacy. Seen from this perspective, our chances in the present tension between the West and East appear in a favorable light. Even though Western civilization may show the first signs of solidification, the East which is challenging our system has more nearly approached the sterile phase of the universal state. Because of our relatively greater fluidity, our chances for survival are considerably greater.

In summary, the principal cause of the detrimental solidification of a fluid society appears to consist in the growing sense of insecurity of the members of the group. This results in an excessive preoccupation with the problem of security at the expense of individual expression and creativeness. The growing sense of insecurity itself has a rational objective nucleus; it is the outcome of the increasing difficulty of adjusting to the rapid social changes caused by an expansive period of creative innovations. This reasonable—we may even say, objectively justified—insecurity is enhanced by the momentum of an emotional overreaction which is typical for all mass reactions.

We saw that if the challenge is of optimal severity—not too difficult, but not too easy—this emotional overreaction has a beneficial effect; it stimulates progress by eliciting greater response than is necessary for meeting the challenge successfully. This excess of response mobilizes creative aspirations which allow for further progress. This type of overreaction appears as optimistic enthusiasm which does not recognize the existence of insurmountable obstacles. This was the spirit of the America of unlimited possibilities which attracted courageous men from all nations. On the other hand, when the challenge is greater than can be handled by the group, the resulting fear and insecurity may not have such stimulating effect. Even though the result may not necessarily be paralyzing panic, yet people's main concern will become security, nothing but security, which they no longer try to obtain by their own efforts, but from the central government. The same is also true, however, when the challenge only *appears* greater than can be handled.

What is most important in all these considerations is that emotional mass responses are never precisely commensurate with the objective situation. One may react to challenge with a confident spirit, in which case the chances are that it will not only be met, but that the momentum of the stimulation will give rise to creative activity. If one is intimidated or confused, one may react to the same challenge with an undue amount of insecurity and diffidence, and the instinctive reaction will be narrowed down to a desperate effort to save what one can.

The crucial question is: are the present preoccupation of youth with mere security and the lack of courage to take even the necessary, unavoidable risks of life—are these overreactions that are so common in all mass movements? The answer to these questions is of paramount significance. It will decide how we should evaluate the present ebb in the experimental, forward-looking spirit. Is it a sign of the beginning of decline, or is it only a temporary overreaction of an intimidated youth traumatized by a succession of catastrophic world events? If the latter is the case, wise leadership may find a way to restore that courage to our youth which was so characteristic of his ancestors.

All this does not mean that social security in itself is a destructive goal. Whenever we deal with the complex problems of social interaction, all statements which do not include quantitative considerations are likely to be erroneous. An organism enjoying the sense of security does not necessarily degenerate into torpor. A sense of security arises whenever the organism succeeds in adapting itself to its environment in a successful manner, when it can procure the necessities of life in a more or less routinized and effortless manner. Under favorable conditions, this may have a desirable effect: all the energy which is liberated by these effortless, automatic adaptations, can be utilized for creative purposes. Reproduction on the biological level and productivity on the social level are the manifestations of such a surplus in the organism. In creative activity, expenditure of surplus energy becomes an aim in itself and is not subordinated to the goal of self-preservation. It is energy which is at the disposal of the organism, to be utilized for something other than mere self-preservation. In all creative activities the organism sets a goal outside its own realm, a goal which is not subordinated to anything; it is an aim in itself. Such activity for its own sake is the essence of every creation.

The creative propensity of organisms makes those arguments pointless which warn us that universal social security would terminate human progress. While a certain amount of insecurity seems to be necessary to stimulate not only the self-preservative but also the creative impulses, a reasonable amount of security is not incompatible with creativeness and progress—indeed it is required.

One thing must be particularly considered in this connection. Biological propagation is the result of an inherited instinct, while social productivity has to be learned. In a society in which the gadget and the comforts it affords become aims in themselves, there is no real hope for true creativeness. The surplus energies saved by the machine will then be dissipated in sterile competition for the mere sake of competition and will eventually be used for mutual detriment. If our highly mechanized civilization is to survive, the economic and material understructure of society must be considered merely as a basis upon which higher sublimated forms of creative interests can be built. The creative, and not destructive use of those energies which have been saved by advanced technological knowledge is the pressing need of our era. Without such creative channels, the excessive craving for stability and security can only lead at first to stagnation and then to decline.

Introduction to
Group Psychology and the Analysis of the Ego
by Sigmund Freud

◄ 1960 ►

For over thirty years, Freud refrained from building a comprehensive system from his arduously collected observations made during the treatment of his patients. Thus, he was an outstanding representative of the Hippocratic tradition of bedside medicine: his conclusions came from innumerable detailed observations made on individual patients. He was the first among modern psychologists to interest himself in man as an individual person—not in general terms, but in Mr. Smith as a unique case whose emotional problems must be understood on the basis of his own specific life history. Freud used the empirical inductive method to its full in a field in which hitherto speculation and deductive reasoning had reigned for centuries.

Freud repeatedly protested against being considered a philosopher. He conceived psychoanalysis as a scientific discipline: the first methodical study of the human personality, previously the exclusive domain of creative writers. In all his writings, he meticulously distinguished between observation and speculation; even in his speculative writings he started out from what he considered basic, incontestable facts.

Only at the end of the last century when all psychologists still held university chairs of philosophy, did psychology begin to emancipate itself from philosophy. Earlier time physics, chemistry and biology had ceased to be called Natural Philosophy, and the social sciences escaped the designation of Social Philosophy. Freud, a medical psychologist, felt the need to state his position emphatically: he considered himself first of all a scientist who builds his theoretical concepts on detailed studies of individual persons.

473

Group Psychology and the Analysis of the Ego belongs to that group of Freud's systematic writings in which this modern Hippocrates of medical psychology makes an attempt to integrate his observations and more or less fragmented concepts into a comprehensive view of the human mind. The first book in this group, *Beyond the Pleasure Principle* (1920), appeared a year before *Group Psychology* and was followed two years later by *The Ego and the Id* (1922)—the culmination of his system-building efforts.

While *Beyond the Pleasure Principle* is an attempt to revise and systematize his earlier concepts about instincts, *Group Psychology* and *The Ego and the Id* concern themselves with the structure of the personality—of the ego. They were preceded by a more fragmented attempt, his article on "narcissism." In these three books, Freud, the physician, is no longer concerned with mental pathology, but uses all that he learned from the painstaking study of mentally disturbed patients for drawing an admittedly rough draft of the construction and functioning of the normal mind. In *Group Psychology* much of what he formulated three years later in *The Ego and the Id* appears in a more rudimentary form. It conveys the atmosphere of the workroom. Freud takes up many subjects only to leave them unfinished as brilliant but provisional formulations; these include the origin of social justice as a reaction against siblings' rivalry, the problem of identification, the similarities between being in love and hypnosis. He also returns to his widely criticized theory of the primal horde of brothers ruled by a tyrannical, powerful father, which he considered as the beginning of human society—a concept first advanced by Charles Darwin. After the rebellious sons killed the chief, the horde changed into a fraternal society—a community of brothers. The deep-seated longing of the brothers for a powerful leader, however, reasserted itself and led to totemism and later to religious systems—the totem and the deity being the reincarnation of the murdered father. Freud is thoroughly impressed by the indestructibility of the profound emotional need of humanity for strong leadership, which is the cornerstone of all his sociological speculations. It reveals his dim view about the viability of democracies—a view which could be supported by the fact that the human race succeeded in establishing free democratic social systems only for two short periods during its known history: once in Athens and then again in modern Western civilization. In between these two rare occurrences, humanity always lived under the dictatorship of feudal or centralized rulers. Biologists may also adduce the evidence that living organisms consisting of individual cells, have always—with rare exceptions, such as sponges—a "head end" which coordinates and rules over the activities of the constituent parts.

The concept of the superego—the internalized precipitate of parental guidance which Freud elaborated a few years later in *The Ego and the Id*—is closely related to this basic orientation. The superego is foreshadowed by the less clearly defined, vaguer concept of the ego ideal, used synonymously with "conscience." Freud's superego definitely has the characteristics of an absolute, primarily punitive ruler as it actually reveals itself in such psychopathological conditions as the depressions and obsessional-compulsive neuroses. In mature persons, however, it can be no longer sharply differentiated from the ego, which governs by principles more like those prevailing in democratic societies: judgment, flexibility and compromise.

In *Group Psychology* Freud gives full recognition to Le Bon's deservedly famous work, *Psychologie Des Foules* (1895). Le Bon's main thesis is that, as a part of a group, man regresses to a primitive mental state. Isolated he may be a cultivated individual; in the group he is capable of acting as a barbarian, is prone to violence, loses his critical faculties, becomes emotional and may lose all his moral standards and inhibitions. His critical, intellectual ability and control yield to emotionalism, suggestibility and inconsistency. He becomes unpredictable, inconsistent, similar to primitive man or to a child. In groups the individual features of a person, his superstructure, disappears, yielding to the homogeneous common substratum which is preserved as an ancestral heritage in man's unconscious. At the same time new features appear: as a member of a larger group, man feels more powerful while his individual responsibility diminishes since he shares it with all other members of the group.

Freud agrees with this description of Le Bon, but explains the regressive features of mob psychology by his own formulation concerning the nature of human conscience. The essence of conscience is "social anxiety," the fear of public opinion. In following the herd, social anxiety necessarily disappears in the members of the group. As Le Bon, Freud also calls the primitive attitudes which appear in the members of a group "unconscious" trends; but Freud points out that Le Bon's "unconscious" is not identical with his. For Le Bon, these deeply buried features of the mind constitute the archaic heritage of man. Le Bon is not aware of that part of the unconscious mind which, because it is unacceptable to the conscience, is *repressed*. The power behind repression is the conscience. The dynamic concept of repression was not known to Le Bon. In the group, the voice of the individual conscience is silenced. Hence, all that has been repressed, all that violates the standards of the conscience, can now uninhibitedly appear in behavior.

Freud also follows Le Bon in comparing the behavior of the members of the group to that of persons in the state of hypnosis. Freud, however, raises the question: Who is the hypnotizer? Le Bon pays little attention to the leader of the group. For Freud, the leader is the key figure in group psychology. It is he who subjects the members to his hypnotic spell.

Neither Le Bon nor McDougall—another author who influenced Freud in his group-psychological speculations—penetrated to the essence of the problem: What are the forces which hold groups together? What are the psychological factors which make a group a group, rather than a number of individuals gathered in a bunch? No matter how brilliant Le Bon's observations are, they remain brilliant descriptions which, however, fail to explain the central features of group behavior: heightened suggestibility, ebbing of intellectual-critical faculties, and the "mental contagion" by which group members mutually enhance their common emotions. "Mental contagion," which Le Bon uses for explanation, is but an analogy, a figure of speech which, itself requires further explanation.

Freud contends that the key figure in every organized or loosely organized, randomly assembled group is the leader. The group member's relationship to the leader explains also the relations of the members to each other. The leader becomes the individual member's common ego ideal and takes over all the critical faculties, just as the hypnotized individual abandons his self-determination for the sake of the hypnotizer. This common bond which ties every member of the group to the leader also determines their interrelationship. By their common attachment to the leader, they can identify themselves with each other.

To explain the nature of the group member's attachment to the leader, Freud borrows his most fundamental concept, that of *libido*, precisely "aim inhibited libido" or desexualized libido. This is the cohesive, unifying force which binds individual units into higher entities, higher organizations. While the members are bound by libidinous ties to their leader, the leader's psychology sharply differs from that of the members. He has no emotional attachments to anybody but himself and it is precisely this narcissistic quality which makes him a leader. "He loves no one but himself, or other people insofar as they can serve his needs." He is "of masterly nature," "self-confident" and "independent." He represents all those qualities which the group members themselves cannot attain. Thus be becomes their ego ideal.

By introducing the concept of libido which ties the members of the group to the leader, Freud can dispense with Trotter's "herd instinct" as the force responsible for group cohesion. Freud's explanation is unquestionably more elegant since he operates with a concept which was successful in explaining the mutual relationships between the members of what is undoubtedly the most elementary social group—the family. The mutual attachments between the members of the family reveal themselves as libidinous ties, and do not require the invention of a special new kind of instinct. The same principle can be thus applied to account for bonds within the family as well as for those operative in the larger extension of the family: in social groups.

The contemporary reader will miss in Freud's theory a more precise definition of the emotional ties of the group members to the leader. He will find the concept of libido too general. From the vantage point of modern psychoanalytical theory, this emotional relationship can be more precisely described as a return to the infant's dependent attitude toward his parents. There are plenty of references in Freud's text to the dependent nature of this tie, but he does not make full use of its significance. The regressive nature of group behavior finds satisfactory explanation if one stresses the childlike dependence of the members upon their leader. Under the spell of the leader, the group members renounce the internalized parental image (their own conscience) and relegate its role to the leader. They regress to a phase in their development in which they were blindly following the voice and guidance of their parents. During the process of emotional maturation, the child gradually adopts the standards and values of the parents by *identifying* himself with them. Through this process of identification, he becomes more independent. He no longer needs parental guidance after he firmly internalizes their guiding principles into his own personality. He now carries the parental standards inside of himself and no longer needs the actual parents for guidance. Becoming the member of a group, he relegates to the leader the functions of the parents and thus the whole process of emotional maturation is reversed. Under the spell of a strong leader, the group member becomes a dependent child. Apparently most persons retain sufficient residues of childhood's dependency needs and insecurity to be susceptible to such emotional regression. The blissful security of the Garden of Eden remains an ever powerful motif in history. Man seems prone to exchange readily the insecurity and struggle of freedom for the security promised by strong leaders. The image of the welfare state is a modern manifestation of the same regressive trend.

The dependence on the leader resolves the apparent contradiction that a group which may become ferocious and destructive is also capable of self-sacrifice and devotion. The outcome obviously depends upon the nature and ideals of the leader who can influence his followers in either direction.

Further, the phenomenon of panic can be more clearly understood by stressing the dependent quality of the members' attachment to their leader. Exposed to a danger, the need for dependence increases; but if faith in the leader is shaken, the members of the group become overwhelmed by paralyzing anxiety. They have given up self-government and replaced it by obedience and faith in the leader. When the leader fails, they are left without any guidance— internal or external: they become like helpless children deserted by their parents.

In war and national emergencies even democratic societies are apt to sacrifice some of their jealously guarded freedoms and confer greater control on their government.

Freud's group psychology has all the earmarks of a pioneering venture. He made only the first tentative steps toward understanding the principles of social organization. Most of his psychological descriptions are applicable only to the phenomena of mob psychology. He was clearly aware of this and tried to apply the same basic principles to the understanding of the emotional structure of firmly organized groups. Selecting the Catholic Church and the Army as examples, he had to account for a contradiction: conscience develops under the influence of parental leadership, yet leadership may be the source of asocial behavior as seen in loosely organized groups. In other words, living in a social group makes man moral and yet, becoming the member of a group led by a strong leader, man may lose his morality. What then are the conditions under which the conscience, itself the precipitate of social standards, may dwindle away through group influences? Freud clearly recognized that the superego itself originates in social organization inasmuch as the values transmitted by the parents to the child are precisely those which prevail in society.

The Church and the Army were obviously unfortunate choices to formulate the general principles of group dynamics. Freud selected two organizations in which central authority is paramount. The members of both of these organizations retain much of that abject dependence on and obedience to leadership which is characteristic of the child. The central figure is a fatherlike image, and the soldier as well as the flock retain much of childhood's dependency. In this one respect a random group under the spell of a strong leader resembles a structured group organized around a strong authority.

This is not the case in free, democratic societies which consist of more independent, self-governing individuals. Here the attitude toward leadership is quite different. Citizens may trust their leaders, yet they are critically watching them. They elect their leaders and retain the right to vote them out if they do not fulfill their expectations. And the leaders, to a high degree, depend upon their electors. In such societies, the members and the leader are interdependent. Their relation is not as asymmetric as in autocratic systems.

One may justly conclude that Freud's theory of the group was strongly influenced by the social milieu in which he grew up. This may be the reason that he so clearly recognized the role of the leader; yet the very same factors may have induced him to overrate this role. Le Bon and McDougall were oblivious of the significance of the leader. Freud on the other hand was inclined to generalize its role for all forms of social organization. It is true that he occasionally—mostly in parenthesis—refers to the fact that in some societies the leader may be represented not by a human being but by an abstract ideal. He does not, however, elaborate the structure of societies which are held together more by common abstract principles and ideals—such as freedom, individual responsibility and self-government—rather than by a strong leader. Certainly the influence of abstract ideals upon human beings can scarcely be compared with hypnosis. The exalted figure of a leader may, indeed, exert a hypnotic spell upon his followers. But the guiding principles of free societies, the stress on the individual's critical faculty and self-responsibility are contradictory to that blind obedience to authority which is the essence of hypnosis.

Authoritarian organizations, like the Church and the Army, are not suited to throw light upon the regressive phenomena which Le Bon and Freud considered as characteristic of mob psychology. Authoritarian societies, like loosely organized groups which come under the influence of a leader, are based on regressive principles, on childish uncritical obedience. However, only the psychological phenomena which take place in a mob aroused by a leader can truly be called regressive because the persons who constitute the mob otherwise belong to a society in which their individual consciences are effective. Outside of the mob they have higher standards, individual responsibility and critical judgment. The members of hierarchical organizations on the other hand, like the Church and the Army, do not regress but are always dependent on their leaders.

The mentality of free societies can not be explained either by mob psychology or by the spirit prevailing in authoritarian societies.

In spite of the shortcomings of this pioneering venture into the psychodynamics of society, Freud's contribution is of fundamental nature. Some contemporary psychoanalytic authors—often called neo-Freudians—Sullivan, Horney, Thompson, Fromm, to mention only a few—came into the habit of attributing to Freud a lack of awareness of cultural factors in the shaping of human personality. They favorably compare Sullivan's "dynamic cultural point of view" with Freud's "mechanistic biological orientation" (Clara Thompson). The thoughtful reader of this volume can easily convince himself of the fallaciousness of this judgment.

Freud was fully aware of the fact that the development of human personality can be understood only if one considers the influences of the prevailing social standards and values to which it is subjected. This is clearly borne out by his terse statement in this book, that "we must conclude that the psychology of the group is the oldest human psychology." Freud considered conscience (ego ideal and later super-ego) as the precipitate of parental influences which transmit to the child the standards and values of the society in which he matures. Social scientists and psychologists who like to consider themselves distinguished by their cultural orientation, in contrast to Freud's antiquated "nineteenth century biological orientation," actually did not add any new principle to this basic insight. It is true that Freud did not undertake comparative studies on personality development in different cultures. Such studies had to wait until psychoanalytic thought had deeply penetrated into the social sciences and particularly into social anthropology. However, the basic psychological principles by which society exerts its molding influence upon personality development had been laid down by Freud.

◄ *Five* ►

Philosophy, Literature, Methodology, and History of Psychoanalysis

Psychoanalysis
and Medicine

◄ 1931 ►

For about thirty years psychoanalysis, a theoretical concept of the personality, a precise and elaborately described method of psychologic research and a therapy of mental disturbances, has been living a peculiar, isolated existence on the borderline of medicine and of the natural sciences. This borderline existence is not due entirely to the unreceptive attitude of medicine toward psychoanalysis, for psychoanalysis itself has also been undecided as to where it belongs. Many psychoanalysts, in fact, question whether psychoanalysis should not be considered a distinctive discipline, related to medicine but essentially independent of it, just as archeology, though related to history, is nevertheless itself a self-sufficient science, or as paleontology is related to geology but is different in its methods and purpose. Even those psychoanalysts who, like myself, are convinced that, so far as psychoanalysis is a therapy, it belongs to medicine, cannot overlook the fact that its subject matter, methods and language are so different from those of medicine that its assimilation by medicine is especially difficult. Indeed, a clear decision as to the citizenship of this young empiric discipline in the realm of science is theoretically as well as practically a highly complicated and unsolved problem. Medicine aims within certain limits to understand life as a physicochemical process. Psychoanalysis deals with psychologic facts and tries to influence psychologic processes by psychologic methods. Consequently, by definition, psychoanalysis should be excluded from medicine.

Mental processes, however, belong to the characteristic manifestations of biologic systems and, as is generally known, influence such physiologic phenomena as weeping, blushing, or the secretion of the gastric juice. Furthermore, a number of diseases manifest themselves in the mental level as psychoses and psychoneuroses. Even after the

This paper was read before the Harvey Society, January 5, 1931, in New York.

cell physiology of the brain has been highly developed it is not probable that physiologic or pharmacologic methods will be used to influence people's minds, for example, to persuade someone or to explain a mathematical thesis. In influencing pathologic mental processes, psychologic methods are used that are essentially similar to persuasion and to explanation. Probably the best method of influencing disturbances of psychologic nature will always be through psychologic means.

Nevertheless, to preserve the homogeneity of medicine, one might exclude psychologic methods even though their scientific and therapeutic value were acknowledged and regard psychology, pathopsychology and their practical application, psychotherapy, as disciplines related to but still lying outside of medicine.

One must realize, however, that it is artificial to separate mental diseases from physical diseases, mental processes from physical processes. There is a permanent interrelation between them in reality. And in therapy one cannot always easily decide in which cases a psychologic and in which cases a physiologic approach is indicated. One cannot divide the individual into a body and a personality; the individual is a psychobiologic entity.

Development of psychoanalysis

Psychoanalysis started within medicine as a therapeutic attempt to influence hysterical symptoms by psychologic means. Under the influence of Charcot's studies on hysteria and its relation to hypnotic phenomena, Freud and Breuer developed the method of cathartic hypnosis. They observed that patients in hypnosis could remember certain forgotten events in their past lives which had an intimate relation to their symptoms. This recollection in hypnosis was accompanied by outbursts of emotion and was usually followed by the disappearance of the symptoms.[1] Freud soon gave up the method of cathartic hypnosis and replaced it by the technique of free association. This technique supplied a more complete picture of the historical background of the symptoms and, apart from its therapeutic value, has yielded a deeper insight into human personality than was ever possible before. This method is responsible for the fact that psychoanalysis, two decades after it started as a modest therapeutic attempt to influence hysterical phenomena, developed a consistent theory of the personality.

The fundamental concept of the theory of the unconscious has deeply influenced all modern thinking. The discovery of the general dynamic effect of unconscious mental processes on overt behavior, which shows the limitations of the rational and conscious parts of the

[1] This process of emotional abreaction in hypnosis Freud and Breuer called "catharsis" and their method "cathartic hypnosis."

personality, has become so fundamental for the mental attitude of the educated man of the twentieth century that without it one cannot understand many of the products and manifestations of modern mental activities. It is not an exaggeration to compare the change in the attitude of man toward external reality that has resulted from this insight with the change that the system of Copernicus provoked four hundred years ago. The theory of the unconscious involves a new and sensible break in the anthropocentric attitude toward the external world. The system of Copernicus destroyed this anthropocentricity in the spatial cosmological sense, but man soon regained his anthropocentric attitude in a psychologic sense. That becomes especially clear if the doctrines of the rational philosophers of the seventeenth and eighteenth centuries, who put all their faith and hopes in the omnipotence of the cogitant intellect, are recalled. Instead of the earth the human mind became now the center of the universe. This started with the teaching of Descartes that nothing is certain except one's own thoughts, and this doctrine led in a cogent direct line to Kant's consistent anthropocentric thesis: The external world as we see it is dependent on the mind and its categories, which themselves are absolute and belong to the unchangeable structure of the mind. Psychoanalysis as a genetic theory now dethroned these new despots and monarachs of philosophic thinking, the Kantian categories, and considered them as products of adjustment to the physical environment. The infant's mental processes are subject neither to the logical nor to the moral categories of Kant, and, what is even more important, in every one's even in the adult's, unconscious personality there are mental processes which are not subject to the laws of logic. These processes, manifest for example in dreams, do not know the law of causality, only that of temporal sequence, and do not know such axioms as that the same thing cannot be at the same time in two different places. Briefly, rational thinking as well as moral feelings and prescriptions are products of adjustment of the organism to its environment, but they do not determine entirely our thinking and behavior, and a dynamically powerful portion of mental life is neither rational, that is, adjusted to the external world, nor moral, that is, adjusted to the demands of the community. The rationally adjusted part of the personality in everybody is in steady conflict with the unadjusted layers. The means of eliminating the disturbing influence of unadjusted tendencies is a dynamic act called repression, by which the unadjusted mental forces are excluded from consciousness and become unconscious. Thus, human personality can be divided in two portions, the adjusted ego and the original and impersonal id, which is not yet synthetized into a harmonious unity and contains the different conflicting instinctual tendencies. In psychopathologic personalities this conflict between the infantile and the adult portions of the personality is quantitatively greater but qualitatively the same as in normal individuals. Thus mental disturbances, such as psychoneuroses and psychoses, can be understood as the more intensive and more overt manifestations of the unadjusted unconscious parts of the personality.

All these concepts are today not only generally accepted but have already become emotionally assimilated and, like the theory of evolution or the cosmological doctrine of the planetary systems, are now an integral part of modern thinking. The emotional consequence of this modified perspective is that man now feels himself more definitely to be only a small part of the universe. Because his belief in the absoluteness of his rational thinking has been broken, even this last claim to a special position in the world has lost its foundation. Rational thinking can no longer be regarded as its own self-sufficient cause, unapproachable by further scientific research, but as a product of adjustment to the world, and it is not only not absolute but is as relative as that birds fly and fishes swim. Our logical thinking is just as little the only possible form of thinking as flying is the only possible form of locomotion.

The scientific consequence of this new perspective is that psychology becomes relevant to the biologic sciences. Thinking is one of the functions of the biologic system, one means of orientation to the external world. The mental apparatus can be understood in the same way as the circulatory system, which in all its details is adjusted to the hydrodynamic problems which it has to solve. Similarly, the functions of the mental apparatus can be understood as adjustments to the problem of orientation to the environment. No teleologic philosophy is involved in this concept.

Thus definitely separated from philosophy, psychoanalytic psychology becomes a mechanical or, better, a dynamic science and describes the functions of the mental apparatus in terms of mechanisms or dynamisms. It studies in detail the development of the mind in all its phases during the difficult process of adjustment, which can be understood as a process that changes the unorganized, unsystematic, diffused manifestations of the infant's mind into the complicated system of the adult ego. It describes pathologic mental phenomena as due to the incomplete overcoming of early unadjusted periods and to a large extent it can even determine which phase of the development was unsuccessfully passed through, or, in other words, to which phases of the early development certain types of mentally disturbed individuals remain fixated.

This genetic and dynamic approach to the understanding of mental disturbances can be considered a decisive step in psychopathology. The psychodynamic approach makes possible the intelligent and systematic influencing of pathologic mental processes, that is to say, a causally oriented psychotherapy.

Psychotic and neurotic symptoms could be understood on the basis of the conflict just described between the infantile remainders and the adult part of the personality. The chief difference between the neurosis and a psychosis is the extent to which the repressed unadjusted mental content breaks through into consciousness after overcoming the resistance of the repressive forces. This breaking through of the repressed contents is much more complete in the different forms of psychosis. In the end phases of schizophrenia, for example, one has the impression that the ego has given up all resistance and is dominated entirely by hallucinatory mental processes. In a psychosis even the very first adjustment of the ego breaks down; that is, the capacity of subordinating satisfactions of imagination to the evidences of sense perceptions. The consequence is a loss of orientation to the world. Of course, all the later achievements of development, such as aesthetic and moral restrictions and inhibitions, also disappear in the psychosis. Psychosis thus can be considered as a flight from reality and from the adult form of existence back to childhood, to a happier time, in which fantasy prevails unhampered by actuality.

In the different forms of psychoneurosis the conflict between the two poles of the personality, between the conscious ego and the primitive id, is more manifest, since neither of them has a decisive victory. If the end phases of a psychosis be compared with a silent battlefield after all the soldiers on the one side have been killed, a psychoneurosis is a battle still in progress. Psychoneurotic symptoms are partly manifestations of repressed tendencies and are partly reactions of the ego against these tendencies.

In psychoneuroses the conscious ego has still the upper hand, although it does not succeed entirely in repressing the unconscious tendencies. The important fact which shows the partial control of the ego is that this unconscious mental content can appear in consciousness only in distorted forms. These distortions are the compromises between the two antagonistic forces in the mental apparatus; that is to say, they are a compromise between repressed and repressing forces. In these distorted forms the unconscious content can appear in consciousness without hurting the conscious personality.

Psychoneurosis and psychosis can be considered as different stages of the same mental process; that is, of the breaking through of the unconscious repressed, primitive part of personality. In a psychosis this process goes much further, for the difference between the conscious and the unconscious parts disappears and the unconscious dominates the whole personality, whereas in a neurosis the principal achievement of the later ego-development, namely, the acceptance of reality, remains more or less intact, and the unconscious tendencies penetrate the ego only in isolated symptoms, which play the role of foreign bodies embedded in normal tissue.

Apart from these results concerning the field of psychopathology, a certain type of dynamic manifestations of repressed mental forces has a special significance of internal medicine; the so-called hysterical dysfunctions and organ neuroses, in which unconscious psychic tendencies produce physical symptoms. The investigation of this field requires an intimate cooperation of internal medicine and psychoanalysis, and its greater part must be left to the future.

All these findings of psychoanalysis in the field of mental pathology have become integral parts of modern medical thinking, just as the fundamental concepts of the unconscious and of repression have penetrated contemporary thought. The theory of fixation to infantile attitudes and the increased tendency to regress to these early patterns of thinking and feeling as seen in psychoneurotics and psychotics belong today to the basic concepts of psychiatry. But also psychic mechanism such as rationalization and projection, which have been understood as means of solving the conflict between conscious ego and unacceptable wishes and tendencies, are so generally accepted and employed in psychiatry, indeed also in general thought or conversation, that the young student of medicine often does not even know their origination from the psychodynamic system of Sigmund Freud.

In addition to the explanation of these seemingly so senseless mental processes of the psychoneurotic and the insane, psychoanalysis has become the psychology of all kinds of irrational manifestations of the mind, such as errors of everyday life, free fantasying and especially the dream. It demonstrates that the apparent irrationality of all these phenomena is inherent in the fact that as a result of the individual's development our adjusted rational thinking has grown away from the more primitive types of thinking which is especially clearly represented in our dream life. But if we relearn the primitive language of the mental life of our childhood, we are able to understand the psychologic meaning of our dreams.

Resistance to psychoanalysis

In the following we shall concentrate our interest on those fundamental results of the psychoanalytic psychology which have become or are becoming significant for medicine. Indeed, these results by no means explain the resistance to them, especially not the resistance in the medical world. On the contrary, just this kind of approach to the problems of mental life brings psychology nearer to the biologic sciences and severs its traditional connection with philosophy.

As a matter of fact, the resistance to psychoanalysis is a complex phenomenon and has changed its nature during the thirty years since psychoanalysis began to disturb the habits of thinking and feeling of the scientific world and the general public. The first, chiefly emotionally tinged resistance, was entirely due to certain special results of the new empirical and microscopically detailed study of mental life. The discovery of infantile sexuality especially and of some infantile and asocial, consequently repressed, mental tendencies present in everybody's unconscious provoked a general rejection. These first manifestations of resistance have been so often and so well described that I feel no need to repeat them, especially as in the meantime these first reactions have lost their actuality. The world, in the last thirty years, has changed a great deal in its emotional and intellectual attitude, and in this change psychoanalysis has had its decent share. This first heroic period of psychoanalysis, in which it had to fight chiefly against emotional prejudices, is practically over. The Oedipus complex has found its acceptance in the two most conservative places—in the Oxford dictionary and in *Punch*. Psychoanalysts who still think that they have to awaken humanity from its indolent sleep are tilting against windmills.

The resistance has shifted gradually into the intellectual field. This intellectual form of resistance is based on inveterate habits of thinking and methods of investigation. It is no longer directed against the general or philosophic consequences of psychoanalysis which have become generally assimilated by modern thinking. And, indeed, the resistance has disappeared in all fields except in the birthplace of psychoanalysis; that is, in the field of medical research and therapy. Psychoanalysis needs no longer to endeavor to be accepted as a theory of personality but must seek to be accepted as a part of medicine, in spite of the fact that it is due to this new dynamic point of view that psychiatry has overcome its merely descriptive stage and has become an explanatory science.

Let us turn our attention now to this more serious intellectual form of resistance which is at work at present and makes it so difficult for the medical world to orient itself finally toward psychoanalysis.

I have referred already to the gist of this resistance. Psychoanalysis deals with psychic phenomena and this brings quite a new element into medicine. It introduces a subject matter which cannot be expressed in terms of time and space and threatens to disturb the homogeneity of medicine, which would prefer to deal exclusively with physicochemical facts and to employ chiefly experimental methods. The subject matter as well as the nature of psychoanalysis is apt to arouse the general distrust of the natural scientist against psychologic facts and methods. Thus the paradoxical situation arises that also psychiatry, an acknowledged part of medicine, necessarily shares the fate of psychoanalysis in losing the respect of the rest of the medical world, since—especially here in America—it has assimilated so much from psychoanalysis.

The homogeneity of a science, the uniformity of the methods employed, are no doubt respectable postulates, but there are more important principles in scientific research. There *are* mental phenomena and they *are* interrelated with other biologic phenomena, and science cannot close its eyes to phenomena only because it cannot master them with the usual and tested methods. The subject matter is primary— and not the method. The method must be adjusted to the nature of the subject matter. Still it is a common tendency of the mind, a kind of inertia of thinking, to force methods that have proved successful in one field on a new but different field, instead of seeking for new and especially adjusted methods which the new field of phenomena requires. Had psychoanalysis been an experimental science, no resistance to it would have been offered by medicine. It would in this case probably have been accepted by medicine, but it would have had to abandon the investigation of the problems of personality. On the other hand, it is undeniable that distrust of psychologic method was well founded. Although psychology since the middle of the last century claims to be a nonphilosophic discipline, up to Freud's appearance it could not produce results of an empirical nature adequate to dissipate the distrust against it. There has been no prospect that psychology will ever be able to disavow the pessimistic statement of Moebius of the "hopelessness of every psychology."

Indeed, to understand the personality of another individual requires methods in many respects basically different from those employed in the natural sciences. Every empirical science consists in the refinement and systematic development of the methods of observation which one uses in everyday life. In every science we can use only the senses we actually possess, although we can increase their exactness and eliminate to some degree their defects. Psychoanalysis, in contrast to earlier psychologic methods, has simply refined and systematized the everyday methods used to understand other persons' mental situations. This common-sense understanding is, however, a rather complex faculty. Its chief tool is a kind of identification with the other person, that is, a putting of oneself in the other person's mental situation. If you observe the movements of another, the expression of his face, the tone of his voice, and if you listen also to what he says, you get an idea of what is going on in his mind. This understanding is derived from the fact that the object of observation is a similar being to the observer—both are human personalities. This similarity between observer and the object of observation is quite essential and is existent only in the field of psychology. If you observe physical phenomena, such as the behavior of two spheres which move on a table, you are entirely limited to what you see and are absolutely unable to foretell what will happen in the next moment unless you have learned the nature of such rolling spheres through previous experiences. If you observe another person, then you also see external manifestations of his behavior, but at the same time you also know from your own introspective experience: what you feel when you use the same means of presentation, the same facial expression, words, movements, as the observed person does. You understand the other person's motives because you know your own reaction in a similar situation. In psychologic observation the overt behavior of the observed object is supported by direct or introspective knowledge of one's own person.

The importance of this coexistence of objective and introspective observation in psychology cannot be stressed enough, not only because it is the basic difference between physical and psychologic disciplines but also because this peculiarity is the only advantage of the psychologic observation over the physical examination, which, on the other hand, has a great number of advantages, the greatest of which is the possibility of experimentation. All psychologic methods which failed to recognize and exploit this one advantage of psychologic examination must necessarily remain of limited value in the investigation of human personality. I mention only experimental psychology and behaviorism. Both these methods imitated the methods of experimental science and therefore either simply omitted to use and to develop the common-sense faculty of understanding other persons' mental processes or, as in the case of behaviorism, specifically refused to use this faculty. The prescientific man indeed extended the use of psychologic interpretation even into the inanimate world and saw the wrath of God behind thunder and his punishment behind lightning. Behaviorism makes exactly the opposite error and refused to analyze the psychic background even in the behavior of living beings. Animism put personality into inanimate nature, but behaviorism wishes to rob even human beings of their personality. It is an almost tragicomical sight to observe how behaviorism stubbornly deprives itself of one source of knowledge and restricts itself to the observation of the so-called overt behavior. But are not words also objective facts, and when you hear words how can you prevent them from conveying to you a knowledge of the other person's psychic processes?

I admit that this common-sense understanding of other individuals' mental situations is an unreliable method. But is not the task of every science to improve on natural faculties of observation? Is not the common-sense optical observation also unreliable? Was it not necessary to support it by scales and magnifying pointers of physical instruments or by microscope?

Sources of error in psychologic observation

I think it is time now to describe more concretely what I mean by the natural faculty of understanding the mental situations of another person.

You see a common soldier attack an officer. Suppose you ask him why he did it. He tells you how his superior treated him unjustly for a long time and continually humiliated him until finally he lost control of himself. Then you understand his situation because everybody in his life has experienced similar feelings. When you say, then, that the soldier attacked his superior because the latter treated him unjustly and that finally the soldier's embitterment became stronger than his fear of punishment, you have a causal theory of his behavior which contains even a quantitative judgment of a certain degree of probability. So much understanding can be attained by means of the common-sense everyday psychology, which, as you see, is a common and natural faculty comparable to our visual and acoustic faculties except that it is much more complex. This faculty of psychologic understanding employs the various forms of sense perceptions and in addition the introspective knowledge of one's own emotions which one uses to understand another person by means of identification. This faculty, which is possessed in varying degrees by every one, is the basis of the psychoanalytic approach, just as the optic and acoustic perceptions are the basis of physical experimentation. But science begins with the refinement and development of these everyday methods and faculties. That the common-sense method in psychology is rather unreliable is evident. There are several sources of error. The first and most important one is that—referring again to our simple example—the common soldier who tells you the story has no reason for telling you all of his motives in attacking his superior. He will give you a story which puts him in a good light. You may, if you are expert in human nature, which in Germany they call a good *menschenkenner*, guess his real motives and you can discount his distortions, but you have no evidence as to whether you are right or not.

A second source of error is that even if the soldier wanted to tell you the true mental situation in which he acted he is unable to do so because he himself does not know all of his motives. He deceives not only you but also himself, and with his story he tries to put himself in a good light not only in your eyes but also in his own eyes. In mentioning this second source of error, however, I am referring to one of the basic findings of psychoanalysis, that is, the fact of repression, which is a dynamic tendency to keep out of consciousness desires and motives which would disturb the harmony of the conscious ego and disturb the good opinion which we like to have of our own selves.

A third source of error is that the soldier may be so different from you in his psychologic make-up that you cannot understand his motives. The possibility of identification is contingent on similarity between observer and observed. This similarity, of course, is always present to some degree, since both observer and observed are human beings. Nevertheless, differences of sex, race, nationality, social class, and so forth, diminish this similarity and bring into play a new source of error. Men understand each other better than they do women, and women understand each other better than they do men. We understand people of Western civilization better than we do Orientals. The greater the difference between two minds, the greater the difficulty in understanding.

The difficulties of adults in understanding either young children or savages or psychotics and neurotics have the same reason; namely, that their mental processes are different from the mental processes of normal adults and belong to a more primitive level of mental development.

Finally, a fourth source of error is that the observer himself has, as it were, psychologic blind spots based on his own repressions. He has motives which he himself excludes from his own consciousness and does not want to admit to himself. He will not, therefore, be able to detect these in other persons. Again, one requirement of psychologic understanding, the introspective knowledge of one's own state of mind, is often lacking in common-sense observation because in certain situations this introspective knowledge is blocked by repressions of one's own motives. The dynamic importance of one's own repressions as an obstacle in understanding mental phenomena in other persons can be appreciated only if we realize that the uniformity and harmony of our conscious ego are guaranteed to us through repressions. To become an adult it is necessary to forget the infantile way of thinking. The attraction of this infantile form of mental life is great since it is subject in a much higher degree to the pleasure principle than the adult mentality, which has to adjust itself to reality. It is characteristic of infantile mental life that it does not take into consideration the facts of reality which resist the subjective wishes and needs. The recognition of a strange and by no means always benign external reality is the problem which the child has to solve in his later development. The most important means of overcoming the infantile form of thinking and the infantile wishes and tendencies is repression through which the ego puts away the disturbing remnants of his infantile existence. Through repression these infantile remnants become unconscious and form the unconscious part of the personality. The special difficulty in understanding children, savages and the insane is thus based not only on the differences between their mentality and ours but also on a mental force within ourselves which prevents us from understanding them —I mean repression. To be a normal adult one must forget, or in other words, overcome the primitive part of one's personality, and therefore one cannot understand either the primitive mental processes of others or one's own dreams which are manifestations of an infantile personality. Science, in the investigation of mental pathology, has to overcome the subjective difficulty which is inherent in the fact of man's own repressions.

I admit that the enumeration of the many sources of error which have been classified under these four categories is likely to raise in every one a deep skepticism as to the possibility of any scientific psychology. Some of these sources of error seem simply unsurpassable.

This great variety of difficulties sufficiently explains why psychology for such a long time failed to find a method capable of eliminating or diminishing all these types of errors. Therefore, psychology was not a science but the privilege of a few geniuses, the great *menschenkenner*—I mean the great authors—novelists and dramatists. Only such great *menschenkenner* were able to overcome, at least to some degree, most of these difficulties in understanding other persons' real motives in spite of the human tendency to deceive others as well as ourselves, and in spite of differences of age, race and sex. Such geniuses are able to do all this because the fourth of the sources of error, namely, their own repressions, are less developed than in others. The smaller amount of one's own repressions is just the peculiarity which makes some people better *menschenkenner* than others. Knowing their own personality better, they are more able to understand others.

Elimination of the sources of error

Certain methodological discoveries have made it possible for psychology to become a science of personality. That every scientific development follows methodological inventions and innovations is well known. Anatomy began with the introduction of the method of dissection, histology with the microscope, bacteriology with methods of growing cultures. Psychology, as an empirical science of personality, begins with the discovery of the method of free association by Freud.

I do not maintain that all four sources of error are entirely eliminated by the method of free association, but they are reduced to such a considerable degree that the requirements of an objective science are met. The patient is requested to report everything that goes on in him during the analytic session; that is, he is asked to verbalize everything that occurs to him in the original sequence and form without any modification or omission. He is asked to assume a passive attitude toward his own trains of thought; in other words, to eliminate all conscious control over his mental processes to which he is to yield and merely to report. This simple procedure seems at first to be a rather trivial device and it is not so easy to appreciate its research value. But please remember that the methods of percussion and auscultation seem also rather unpretentious and trivial, and it is only the interpretation of the observed small acoustic deviations that make them so important for medicine.

The first source of error, namely, the lack of interest of the object of the investigation in giving a full account of his mental situation, is in this method eliminated by the therapeutic situation. Only a suffering and sick person who hopes to be freed from his symptoms by following the physician's prescriptions will be willing to cooperate and to give such an intimate insight into his personality as is required by the method of free association. When one yields to one's spontaneous trains of thought, ideas soon crop up which one usually would reject and drop and shove away from the focus of attention. While one yields to this uncontrolled manner of thinking, an unknown part of the personality becomes gradually more manifest. In eliminating or at least diminishing the conscious control, all kinds of disagreeable and irrational mental contents appear which controlled thinking would interrupt and block before they should come to full clarity. In the therapeutic situation the patient gradually learns to overcome the reluctance one usually has to giving up the conventional façade which people habitually turn toward one another, and step by step learns to become entirely frank and to display himself mentally nude, and even to give up the façade which he uses toward himself. I might therefore venture to say that the therapeutic situation is the only situation that is suitable for an efficient psychologic investigation, as only this situation guarantees the willingness of the observed object to show himself as he really is.

The only other situation which meets his requirement is the didactic analysis in which a student of analysis subjects himself to the procedure in order to learn the technique of analysis. In this case not the hope of being freed from a disease but the wish to learn the method by studying oneself is the motive that guarantees his frankness and willingness to give insight into his inner processes. Without this cooperation between the object of observation and the observer, psychology is impossible. In physics, the willingness of lifeless objects to be studied is not necessary, but in psychology the analyst is absolutely dependent on this willingness.

The second source of error, namely, that the observed individual on account of his repressions is unable to give a full report of his own mental situation, also has been solved by means of the analytic technique which serves to eliminate conscious control of the mental processes. The uncontrolled trains of thought are in a much higher degree subject to the repressed mental forces than is one's everyday thinking. Such trains of association are no longer determined primarily by conscious processes; therefore they take a much more irrational character, similar to the day dreaming to which men give themselves in leisure hours or before falling asleep. Patient and long observation of these uncontrolled free associations has led to the development of a technique of interpretation which allows the psychoanalyst to reconstruct the unconscious tendencies that determine the sequence and content of these spontaneous trains of thought. In this way he is able to obtain a deeper insight into the make-up of the personality and to understand motives and emotional connections which are normally covered up by the controlling and selective functions of the conscious ego and of which the observed person himself consequently was not previously conscious. Thus, the second source of error, the inability of the patient to give a full account of the motives of his mental processes, is eliminated.

The third source of error was a subjective one in the observer himself; namely, his difference from the observed object. In some cases identification is almost impossible, as for example often in the case of mentally sick persons who revert to primitive infantile forms of mental activity. The long duration of the psychoanalytic observation, daily over a period of months, is the only means by which this difficulty can be overcome. If you travel in a foreign country you are at first quite unable to understand the mentality of the inhabitants even though you may understand their language. Their facial expressions and their reaction patterns are unfamiliar. But in time you learn their reactions without being able to tell how and why, and you gradually become able to orient yourself psychologically in this foreign country. The same thing happens in the course of a long psychoanalysis. Even a peculiar neurotic personality becomes familiar through prolonged and patient observation.

Finally, the fourth source of error due to the blind spots of the observer caused by his own repressions must also be eliminated if psychoanalysis claims to be regarded as a reliable means of investigation. The means of overcoming this difficulty is the preparation of the observer by his own analysis through which he overcomes his own repressions, learns to understand the unconscious part of his own personality, and in this way becomes able to understand manifestations in others to which he was blind before. I feel that I must explain this difficulty in a more concrete way by referring again to the example of the soldier who attacked his superior. Assume that the observer is a person of a basically tyrannical nature who, however, will not admit his tyrannical propensities even to himself and tries to rationalize his own aggressive and domineering tendencies by self-deceptive formulations.

Such a person, observing the scene between the soldier and his superior, will be inclined to overlook the superior's brutality or tyranny and will tend to blame the soldier for the officer's aggressions. He will have great difficulty in understanding the point of view of the common soldier and in recognizing his embitterment, and will tend to see in him a rebel and thus justify the attitude of the tyrannical officer, with whom he can more easily identify himself. For he wants to keep his own tyrannical tendencies hidden from himself and nevertheless, at the same time, to give vent to them. He will therefore be blind to similar tendencies in others, for the recognition of such tendencies in others involves the danger of being forced to admit similar motives in himself.

The didactic analysis of the observer serves to overcome this subjective source of error. It increases the knowledge of the observer's own personality and so enables the analyst to allow for the disturbing influence of his own character trends. The International Psychoanalytical Association has therefore for many years made it obligatory for every psychoanalyst, before undertaking the analysis of others, to undergo a psychoanalysis himself. Just as astronomical observation must discount the subjective error which is called the "personal equation," so psychoanalytic observation is impossible without knowing the peculiarities of one's own personality which may obviate an objective psychologic observation.

There are, therefore, four sources of error inherent in everyday common-sense psychologic observation which systematic psychoanalytic technique eliminates by four devices: The unwillingness of the object to disclose himself to the observer is eliminated by the therapeutic situation; the inability of the object to give a full account of his mental state is eliminated by the method of free association; the difference between observer and observed object by the long and systematically repeated observation; and the blind spots of the observer by the didactic analysis. By the employment of these four devices, psychoanalysis has succeeded in refining the common faculty of understanding other persons' mental processes and in developing it into a scientific method which can be learned by almost any serious student and which can be controlled objectively.

The efficiency of this method has been best proved by the fact that the understanding of other individuals' mental processes has been extended to cases in which the common-sense understanding and even the genius of the great authors has entirely failed. I mean the cases of psychosis and psychoneurosis. The seemingly unintelligible irrational and senseless behavior of the insane, the strangeness and irrationality of the psychoneurotic symptoms can be psychologically explained and can be translated into intelligible language.

Psychoanalysis as a therapeutic method

The importance of the therapeutic situation which, except for the didactic analysis, is the only suitable condition for detailed psychologic research, is responsible for a unique feature of this new discipline. I mean the coincidence of therapy and research. In psychoanalysis the research takes place during the treatment, or, in other words, the ends of the treatment and research coincide.

After Freud had learned that neurotic symptoms are dynamic manifestations of repressed mental tendencies which the patient excludes from his consciousness and which return into consciousness in a disguised form, in the form of unintelligible symptoms, he realized that the way to free the patient from his symptoms was to make conscious the underlying repressed tendencies. In this way psychoanalysis extends the field of activity of the conscious ego over such portions of the personality as are unconscious before the treatment. The patient, especially as a result of the emotional experiences of the analyses, becomes more conscious of himself and becomes able to control a greater part of his mental forces than he could before. He becomes able to master also those forces which were bound up in the neurotic symptoms and to use them for normal activities. This is the way of his healing. And so the aim of therapy and research is the same, a more complete knowledge of the personality. This is indeed a unique fact in the field of medicine. In all other forms of medical treatment the patient plays a passive role. It is not only not necessary to initiate the patient into the details and mechanisms of his disease, but it would be in most cases disadvantageous to do so. In the case of psychoanalysis, however, the patient's knowledge of the repressed mental contents responsible for the symptom formation evinced itself as *the* therapeutic agent. This lucky coincidence of a method of therapy with the method of scientific research is responsible for the unique fact in medicine that therapy is not only one approach to scientific knowledge but the very source of it.

The psychoanalytic technique which I have lauded as the great methodological invention which made of the research of personality a science, and of psychotherapy an etiologic treatment, may appear too simple and trivial to be hailed as responsible for the development of a new science. Some may object: What is the great new thing which psychoanalysis does? It takes suitable objects of investigation who are willing to give an insight into their personalities and gives them the simple technical instructions to give up conscious control of their trains of association. I agree that the method is really simple. The secret of its efficiency is that it is adjusted exactly to the nature of the subject matter of the investigation. The whole development of scientific medicine in the modern age is also due to the simple device, instead of speculating about the human body, to look at it, to dissect it and to investigate all the details of its construction. The psychoanalyst listens in the same way as the anatomist looks. And this analogy goes really deeper than it may seem. The preanatomic medicine consisted also in vague generalizations and speculative concepts similar to those of pre-Freudian psychology. Psychologists spoke about emotions, about will, ideas, perceptions and apperceptions, but they were not interested in the actual and detailed mental content. The introduction of dissection was not a smooth and easy process. It encountered all the emotional prejudices of the contemporary mind just as the dissection of the personality has aroused all the emotional prejudices of our day. If one reads the writings of some critics of Freud in Germany and replaces the word "personality" or "mind" with the word "body," one has the same arguments that were set forth against the dissection of the body in the sixteenth and seventeenth centuries. Psychoanalysis is a sacrilege, it degrades the mind, it drags down into the mud our highest mental possessions. Do you not recognize in these sentences the style of the critics of dissection of the body? Anatomy and physiology no doubt brought about a great disillusion: scientists did not find any place for the spirit. And psychoanalysis also brought about a disillusion. The dissection of the mind reduces the whole complexity of the personality with all of our highest strivings and intimate vibrations to a system of dynamic forces which under sober scientific aspect lose all connotations such as good and evil, high and low, beautiful and hideous. All these evaluations eliminated from the field of science naturally retain their significance in practical life.

I would give a false impression if I stressed only the simplicity of the psychoanalytic method. It is simple only in its general principles; that is, in the principle that one has to listen to what the patient says. The scientific evaluation of the material that is obtained is, however, by no means simple. An elaborate technique of interpretation based on long and painstaking comparisons makes the learning of this method just as difficult as the learning of the use of the microscope. It requires long experience and training of the complex faculty of understanding the mental situations in others. Training in the method of interpretation itself can be compared with the learning of a new language. Dreaming and all the manifestations of the unconscious mind speak a different language from that of the conscious mind. It is a kind of language in pictures and its relation to conscious thinking is similar to the relation of ancient picture writing to modern writing with letters.

Conclusion

I see the significance of psychoanalysis in its relation to medicine in the following two accomplishments: 1) With the help of a technique specifically adapted to the nature of psychic phenomena it developed a consistent and empirically founded theory of the personality suitable to serve as a basis for the understanding and treatment of mental disturbances. 2) It gave a concrete content to the philosophic postulate which considers living beings as psychobiologic entities by investigating in detail the interrelation of physiologic and psychologic processes. The greater part of these investigations must, however, be left to the future to be accomplished.

A Note on Falstaff

◄ 1933 ►

In the study of human nature there is one method which certainly cannot lead to reliable results. This is to ask people about their own personality. Nevertheless, many serious psychologists and sociologists still have a naive confidence in this method, and practice it by sending out questionnaires to thousands of individuals. The sociologist who uses this method in order to establish the presence of certain psychological traits in masses of people, does not know the most elementary characteristic of human nature, which is that people do not know themselves. We might hope that people's actions are more characteristic of them than their opinion of themselves. Actions are indeed more valuable than words, and questionnaires on behavior would yield more interesting results if one could rely on the correctness of the answers. On the other hand, the observation of overt behavior does not disclose real predilections because to a great extent people behave not as they really like to, but as they are supposed to.

Theoretically, the only way to learn about human nature might be to put people on the analytical couch for a year or so and collect reliable data; but unfortunately the whole of humanity cannot be put on the analytical couch and the limitations of the application of this method are well known. There is, however, one situation in which people manifest their innermost feelings more reliably than by words or actions and this is when they attend a play in the theatre or when they read a book. If we could register what people feel at different times during a theatrical performance or while reading a book, we could learn much about their most intimate characteristics. The reader of a book or the spectator of a drama cannot be made responsible for what he feels. If he feels sympathy for the treacherous husband who is caught, it is not he who is unfaithful to his wife. When he enjoys Charlie Chaplin's sticking a needle into a fat lady, not he is the naughty boy; and when he is apprehensive about the hero who becomes involved in a dangerous situation, not he is cowardly. He is not responsible for what is going on on the stage and can enjoy himself innocuously and submit to different trends of his personality without exposing himself to any criticism. Not even his own ego can criticize him, because he did not write the play and, what is even more important, nobody is able to give a full account to himself of what he enjoys in attending a play; why he laughs, why he weeps in the theatre. The underlying psychological processes are to a high degree unconscious.

It seems therefore that, if we could establish people's reactions to different products of art and literature, we would have a method of carrying out mass experiments that would yield data of general value about human nature. Problems could be formulated as follows: Why do people like to see Charlie Chaplin? What explains the great influence of Shakespeare's *Hamlet?* Why do people like to read about Baron Munchausen's lies? What is so fascinating in the tragicomical history of the insane Don Quixote? It is unfortunate only that the list of popular literary characters to which people react universally, because their different emotional needs are gratified by them, could be extended almost indefinitely and that in the face of this long list our hope of ever being able to reconstruct a complete picture of the universal features of human nature by this method dwindles away.

One of the most popular characters of literature is Sir John Falstaff, the cowardly and boasting fat drunkard, who is one of the mainstays of Shakespeare's *Henry IV.* Falstaff's popularity in Elizabethan times is conclusively proved by the fact that before the folio edition, *Henry IV* reached five editions, and it is worth noting that whereas in the first part of *Henry IV* the Falstaff scenes and the scenes in the King's court are evenly distributed, in the second part, which was probably written a year later, the Falstaff scenes are more numerous and outweigh by far the scenes in the court. Falstaff was so appealing a character that Queen Elizabeth ordered Shakespeare to write another play around him, and in pursuance with the Queen's command Shakespeare wrote *The Merry Wives of Windsor.* Probably all historians of literature, however, would agree with Bernard Alexander's opinion, in one of his studies on Shakespeare, that the Falstaff of *The Merry Wives* bears only a slight resemblance to the original Falstaff of *Henry IV.*[1] We may, therefore, disregard for our purposes the Falstaff of *The Merry Wives* and deal exclusively with the hero of the first and second parts of *Henry IV.*

What is the specific appeal of this mass of fat, this cowardly, boasting and loquacious knight, this drunkard and gourmand, who is not even especially witty? *Henry IV* has not one, but two heroes.

[1] Bernard Alexander, *Shakespeare,* Budapest: Franklin Company, 1920.

The impression made by Falstaff can only be understood in connection with his boon companion, the Prince. Prince Hal travels with Falstaff's notorious gang, whose main business in life is drinking and engaging in madcap adventures. They are not real bandits—for that they are too cowardly—but occasionally, when in need of money for their drinking bouts, they are not above holding up merchants on the road. In one of the Falstaff scenes Prince Hal himself participates in a holdup. Indeed the Prince starts out under bad auspices; he is a chronic ne'er-do-well at a time when England requires a strong heir. The feudal barons are in open rebellion against King Henry who usurped the throne with the help of the peers, and are now accusing him of breaking his promise and abusing his power. The historical calling of Prince Henry is to further his father's efforts to reduce the feudal power of the barons and unify England under a strong monarch. At the end, the Prince fulfills his historic task. Under Henry V, the particularistic feudal structure of England was converted into a centralized monarchy and England's international importance begins with his regime. In the Battle of Agincourt Henry conquered France and became one of the most powerful kings of England.

Shakespeare uses this section of English history for a well known dramatic motif. The bad boy, after he had thoroughly destroyed hopes in his future, turns out against all expectations to be good. The popularity of this motif is easily understood. Everyone has experienced moments when in his struggle to approximate his ideals he has made the solemn decision to start a new life, and the hope is never quite lost, and is assuredly reborn when the hero on the stage actually succeeds where we have failed. Prince Henry undoubtedly succeeds in destroying the unfavorable expectations regarding him. In a spectacular duel he kills the famous Henry Percy, called Hotspur, the ideal of all masculine virtues, the chivalrous and heroic leader of the conspiring lords, who was always held up to him as an example of bravery to follow. Hotspur was the most bitter of the king's enemies, stubbornly determined to avenge the alleged mistreatment of his best friend, Mortimer. Prince Hal has at the end of the play to his unquestionable credit the rescue of his father's throne.

In the same battle Falstaff also participates, though unwillingly. At the moment when Henry is fighting with Hotspur, Falstaff meets on the battlefield the famous warrior Archibald, the Earl of Douglass, but the cowardly drunkard goes down at once and escapes by simulating death. Henry finds his body and believing him dead bids him a melancholy farewell; but when Henry leaves, Falstaff rises from the ground, hale and hearty. Falstaff symbolizes a portion of human nature which cannot be destroyed easily, and, strangely enough, no one of the spectators would like to see him dead. We can even forgive

him that childish trick of his when he takes Hotspur's corpse on his
back and later pretends that it was he who killed him. However, before he dares to touch the dead body, to make sure, he stabs the
corpse and swears at it. The symbolic depth of this episode has a
strong dramatic effect. The principle represented by Falstaff is incompatible with the principle personified by Hotspur. The childish, irresponsible hedonism of Falstaff has no greater enemy than the self-
sacrificing masculine heroism of Hotspur who leaves his beautiful
young wife to fight for his ideals and for the honor of his friend.

How is it then that our sympathy is still with Falstaff? The plot of
the entire drama concerns the metamorphosis of Prince Henry from a
hopeless ne'er-do-well into a hero, but Shakespeare makes us feel
throughout that this change from the irresponsible and harmless enjoyment of life to the assumption of responsibilities and duties is by no
means an unambiguous gain. His description of the intrigues of the
court, the partisanship between the peers, the methods by which the
affairs of state are settled does not put the court in a very attractive
light. One may reasonably doubt whether Falstaff's adventures and
drinking bouts are not relatively harmless in comparison with the
high politics of his country. What is the highway robbery of Falstaff's
gang in comparison with the cynical treachery of John Lancaster, the
second son of the King, who in the name of the King promises all the
rebels full amnesty if they will send their army home. Believing in
the King's promise, they actually dismiss their troops and are captured
and executed by Lancaster. There is hardly a Babbitt in the audience
who would not at this point begin to doubt the value of respectability.
Why should the lords of the court be considered better than the naive
and infantile fat boy, Sir John? No doubt they believe in their code of
ethics, and are convinced that they are acting for higher purposes
when murdering each other, but it is difficult to respect their thin
rationalizations. Falstaff indeed has no respect for the policies and accepted code of ethics of the lords; witness his contemptuous remarks
about honor:

Can honour set-to a leg? no! or an arm? no! or take away the grief of a
wound? no. Honour hath no skill in surgery, then? no. What is honour?
a word. What is in that word honour? What is that honour? air. A trim
reckoning!—Who hath it? he that died o' Wednesday. Does he feel it? no.
Doth he hear it? no. Is it insensible, then? yea, to the dead. But will it not
live with the living? no. Why? detraction will not suffer it:—therefore I'll
none of it! honour is a mere scutcheon: and so ends my catechism.

The double structure of the drama permanently forces us to look
alternately at two different aspects of life which are in steady contradiction to each other. Our social self admires the heroism of Hotspur,

and it also identifies itself with the patriotic endeavors of the King, but the next moment another part of our personality is only too ready to accept Falstaff's philosophy of life, with its hedonism and its disrespect for the absoluteness of social values. Prince Hal stands between these two philosophies of life. His social self gradually gains the upper hand, but even at the end of the drama, after he has proved on the battle-field that he will wear the crown to his own and England's honor, he expresses his inner conflict more clearly than ever before.

King Henry IV, lying in his last death struggle, the crown beside him on a pillow, falls asleep as Prince Henry enters. Henry puts on the crown and declaims:

> Why doth the crown lie there upon his pillow,
> Being so troublesome a bedfellow?
> O polished perturbation! golden care!
> That keep'st the ports of slumber open wide
> To many a watchful night—sleep with it now!
> Yet not so sound and half so deeply sweet
> As he whose brow with homely biggin bound
> Snores out the watch of night!

The King, awaking and learning that his heir has taken away the crown, accuses his son of being greedy for power and of hardly being able to wait for his death, but the Prince explains:

> Coming to look on you, thinking you dead,—
> And dead almost, my liege, to think you were,—
> I spake unto the crown as having sense,
> And thus upbraided it: The care on thee depending
> Hath fed upon the body of my father;
> Therefore thou, best of gold, art worst of gold.

We may indeed believe that the Prince is telling the truth. We saw the other side of his personality, in his reckless enjoyment of life with Falstaff. He changed chiefly from a sense of duty and he cannot but consider his rank and position as an undesirable burden. He became a hero and he will become a great king under the pressure of his social self, but his deepest urges are not gratified by this change. The monologue with the crown in his hands demonstrates this with the utmost clarity. Falstaff is the representative of the nonsocial portions of his personality. The Prince seems even after his change not to trust himself entirely; he is uncertain that he will be able to resist temptation and maintain the adjustment he has achieved with such difficulty. Why would he otherwise banish Falstaff and his gang under the threat of death penalty ten miles from his body?

The banishment of Falstaff to ten miles from the king's body in order to eliminate temptation is nothing else than a dramatic presentation of what in psychoanalysis we call repression

Falstaff's effect on an audience is comprehensible now. He represents the deep infantile layers of the personality, the simple innocent wish to live and enjoy life. He has no taste for abstract values like honor or duty and no ambition. Man is only partially social. One part of his personality remains individualistic and resents the restrictions of social life and just these restrictions, especially if they go further than one can tolerate them, mobilize all the destructive instincts of man's nature such as discontent, ill spirit and a negative attitude toward the environment. This is the explanation of the popular belief that people who like to eat and drink well—that is to say, who treat the animal in themselves with consideration—are more amiable and less malicious. The opposite is true of the ascetic self-restricting characters often found among political fanatics and exponents of social doctrines for which they sacrifice their lives. Like Robespierre, the fanatic schoolmaster, under the guise of fighting for humanitarian ideals they can take revenge for all their self-imposed restrictions in destroying their opponents en masse. It is seldom difficult to recognize under the thin surface of their rationalizations, their real motives: hatred and revenge. Hotspur unquestionably belongs to this category of fanatic haters. The King offers him full consideration of all his complaints but what he seeks essentially is a fight. The conditions which he proposes to the King are unacceptable, and even his friends call him drunk with fury. He scarcely can await the battle: "Let the hours be short 'til fields and blows and groans applaud our sport."

Hotspur is the exponent of destruction, but destruction which serves not entirely selfish but also collective, that is, caste, interests. Falstaff is the personification of the wholly self-centered pleasure-seeking principle. Although he represents the opposite of destruction, the principle of life, libido, it is the most primitive manifestation of libido, the primary self-centered, narcissistic libido of the child which he stands for.

Prince Henry in the process of maturing must overcome both of these principles. When he kills Hotspur on the battlefield, he overcomes symbolically his own destructive tendency. In killing Hotspur, the arch-enemy of his father, he overcomes his own aggressions against his parent. But he must overcome also the Falstaff in himself if he is to become a fully balanced adult. In the history of the metamorphosis of Prince Henry, Shakespeare dramatically describes the characteristic course of the development of the male. There are two difficult emotional problems which must be solved by everyone in the course of his development; the first is the fixation to the early pregenital forms of instinctual life which expresses itself in oral receptiveness and narcissistic self-adoration. This old fellow, Sir John Falstaff, is a masterful dramatization of such an early emotional attitude. The second difficulty to be overcome is the hatred and jealousy directed against the father. Hotspur, the rebel who strives against the life of the King, is the personification of these patricidal tendencies. In the play, these inner processes find an externalized dramatic expression. After Prince Henry has overcome these two inner—in the drama, external—enemies he becomes an ideal king.

Bernard Alexander in his essay in which he attempts to reconstruct Shakespeare's development on the basis of his dramas and the few known historical facts about him comes to the conclusion that Prince Henry is the one figure among all the heroes of his plays through which the dramatist tried most directly to give expression to his own personality. But he considers Falstaff as the other pole of Shakespeare's personality:

Near the peak of his productivity he wrote *Henry IV* and *As You Like It*. It was when his gaiety began to turn to seriousness, as if he were saying farewell to the merry period of his life. I have read and seen *Henry IV* numerous times, and have often tried to discover what is so bewitching in Prince Hal, why he is so familiar to us, why we understand and love him so much. I cannot get rid of the thought that Shakespeare wrote much of himself into this figure, probably unconsciously, because he had confidence in the incognito provided by appearing in the trappings of a king. Every time I saw Prince Hal I said to myself, "This is Shakespeare more than any other figure." Of course I am not thinking of his life story but of the basic trends of his character. Henry is a superior man who dares to give himself away to life, to lend himself to entertainment and even to bad company because he is certain that he can always take himself back. Nobody really knows him, least of all his father. But we know him and we trust in him. Why is he not ashamed to travel with a Falstaff? One must not speak contemptuously of Falstaff. In his own type he, too, is a superior man, not merely the old *"miles gloriosus"* (of the latter there is only a particle in him), but a much more universal figure: the personification of the self-forgetting enjoyment of life, entertainment, gaiety, the other pole of man's nature, the witty unique hero of unrestrained orgies. The Prince understands Falstaff better than anyone else, because there is something Falstaffian in himself. But in the Prince the Falstaffian element is only an episode which he has to overcome; it belongs to the treasury of his personality, to which nothing human should be alien.[2]

At the beginning of *Henry V* we learn of the death of Falstaff. With a wistful smile we think of him. With the drainage of swamp lands much romanticism fades away, and this is the fate of this kind of romanticism.

---

[2] Alexander, *op. cit.*, pp. 393-394. (All quotations translated by the author of the article.)

The humor of Falstaff is episodic, not of a permanent nature; the gaiety of a night, a great laughter after which our soul as well as our face is sore. The king is dead! Long live the king! Falstaff is dead and the reign of the intellect has taken its place. . . . But it would not be quite correct to say that in Shakespeare there is a Falstaff and a Prince because in him the Falstaffian element is more an experience than a constituent part.[3]

Who does not sometimes regard Falstaff with envy and longing? Who has nothing of Falstaff in himself? Who would not at times desire to live like him, to sun oneself, to let oneself go, to discharge one's surplus energies, cast off the chains of the world, and forget one's profession, one's worries and life-work. We wake up soon enough and find that this is so difficult to effect. And here Falstaff comes to our assistance. There is no better mentor for this purpose. . . .[4]

In reconstructing Shakespeare's character Bernard Alexander writes:

It is certain that he could greatly amuse himself. The data of the "Mermaid Tavern" are reliable. This was the inn of the literati, the hangout of authors and actors, where they had their drinking orgies. It is just as impossible to invent Falstaff as to create him on the basis of mere external observation. Falstaff lived in Shakespeare as Shakespeare lives in Falstaff. Though Falstaff becomes an independent personality, he is the projection of what existed in Shakespeare as a quickly passing eruption of accumulated tensions. Still possibly Shakespeare was more similar to Prince Henry. There was a great buoyancy in Shakespeare but also a great seriousness.[5]

It is interesting that the pre-Freudian student of literature was inclined to look upon Falstaffian elements more as eruptions of temporary tension than permanent integral parts of the personality. Following our analysis, we are inclined to say that in Prince Henry, Shakespeare gave, if not the expression of his actual self, then the most idealized expression of his own personality or in other words the most successful solution of his inner problems. His father complex found in *Hamlet* a neurotic solution. Hamlet cannot decide to kill his mother's lover due to his unconscious father hatred. In the crown scene of *Henry IV* the Prince's self-coronation is no longer a simple Oedipal act, but a real sacrifice. The inheritance of the father position is not the satisfaction of a wish—rather a duty which the Prince will fulfill indeed honestly but which does not command his enthusiasm. There is sincerity in his calling the crown "an evil gold."

But *Henry IV* is not only a dramatic solution of Shakespeare's Oedipus problem; apart from that, it is even more an attempt at solving his Falstaffian problem. This seems, however, to be more diffi-

[3] *Ibid.*, p. 161.
[4] *Ibid.*, p. 197.
[5] *Ibid.*, p. 409.

cult. The King banishes Falstaff, but Shakespeare in the epilogue of the drama promises the audience a revival of this part of his self which he apparently cannot renounce so easily:

One word more, I beseech you. If you be not too much cloyed with fat meat, our humble author will continue the story, with Sir John in it, and make you merry with fair Katherine of France: where, for anything I know, Falstaff shall die of a sweat, unless already he be killed with your hard opinions.

According to tradition it was the Queen who ordered Shakespeare to write a new play with Falstaff as the chief character; probably also the public expressed this wish with the applause which it gave to this immortal figure, but it seems that Shakespeare even without all these external stimuli was determined to revive Falstaff. Indeed it seems to be more difficult than anything to renounce the Falstaffian side of human nature. Is it posible at all? It represents the deepest source of the individual's personality, the principle of eros in its most primary manifestation as narcissism.

The indestructible narcissism of Falstaff which cannot be shaken by anything is the strongest factor in its effect upon us. This self-satisfaction is not disturbing and provocative because there is no sophistication in it, and we feel that Falstaff does not seriously believe in all his pretended merits. He is childish and sincere; there is no psychological situation, no matter how degrading it may be for Falstaff, from which he cannot extricate himself, from which he cannot escape with unimpaired self-appreciation. After the highway robbery the Prince and one of the members of Falstaff's gang disguise themselves and attack Falstaff and the rest of the gang, and take away their money. Falstaff leaves the money behind and runs for his life. But when the Prince upbraids him for his cowardly behavior and pretended bravado, Falstaff has a ready response:

By the Lord, I knew ye as well as he that made ye. Why hear ye, my master, was it for me to kill the heir apparent? Should I turn upon the true prince?

This primitive mode of lying and the indiscriminate use of any method to save his face, this mentality of a three- or four-year-old child in the body of the fat old man, this unperturbed confidence in his own perfection, has something extremely refreshing in it. Naturally at the same time Falstaff knows that all his false courage, virtues and perfections are fantastic, but his force lies just in the fact that fantasy can take the place of reality. Charlie Chaplin's effect in this respect is very similar to that of Falstaff. Good luck helps Charlie Chaplin over all kinds of external difficulties. The child in us applauds, the child who knows only one principle and that is to live, and does not want to recognize any external obstacle. Since the child actually cannot overcome any external interferences, it takes refuge in fantastic, megalomaniac self-deception. The combination of this childish attitude with the tacit awareness of its fantastic nature is the secret of the never failing appeal of these figures. The naive narcissism of the child, in an adult, is distasteful. But if insight is combined with the childish self-complacence, and indulgence in it assumes the character of play, our forgiveness is immediately secured, and our enjoyment is free from interference on the part of the higher critical strata of our ego.

This superior understanding and forgiving attitude toward one's self is, as Freud has shown, fundamental to the phenomenon which we call humor. But Falstaff's self-satisfaction is somewhat more frank and infantile than the superior self-forgiving attitude in ordinary humor. It is coarser than what is commonly called humor, and we do not take offense at it only because of the contrast between Falstaff's attitude and the destructive heroism of Percy and the hypocrisies of the court. If Falstaff were the main figure of the drama, we could not enjoy this drastic kind of humor so freely, and, in fact, in *The Merry Wives of Windsor*, where Falstaff is the leading figure, his effect is far less artistic.

The narcissistic nucleus of the human personality which Falstaff represents is so indestructible that Shakespeare gave Falstaff three forms of revival. Falstaff lying on the battlefield, rises, safe and sound, as soon as his friend disappears. Falstaff is banished at the end of the drama, but Shakespeare revives him in the epilogue; he is mentioned again in *Henry V*, and though he definitely dies in this play, all is not over; he is resuscitated in *The Merry Wives of Windsor*.

Introduction to
What Man Has Made of Man
by Mortimer J. Adler

◄ 1937 ►

It is unusual to write an introduction to a book of an author whose conclusions, approach to his problems and whole outlook are diametrically opposite to those of the author of the introduction. Why did I then accept Mr. Adler's suggestion to write an introduction to his book and why did Mr. Adler ask me to do so, are both questions which require an explanation. The circumstances under which these four lectures originated will elucidate this paradox.

Engaged in psychoanalytic teaching and clinical studies for a long period of time, I gradually came to the conviction that in this field as in others where students are using a highly standardized technical procedure and are mainly absorbed in minute observation of facts—briefly in all preeminently empirical fields—the students are apt to lose perspective toward their own work. This conviction goes back to those early days that I spent as a research worker in physiology in an experimental laboratory. There, I became first acquainted with the characteristic mentality of modern scientific research. There I learned the mores and virtues of modern research and first recognized the danger which confronts the scientific worker of the present day. This danger is not restricted to scientific laboratories; it is a general problem of the present age. Man, the inventor of the machine, has become the slave of the machine, and the scientist, in developing highly refined methods of investigation, has become not the master but the slave of his laboratory equipment. An extreme amount of specialization of interest and mechanization of activity has taken place and a scotoma for essentials has developed; a naive belief in the magic omnipotence of specific technical procedures leads to a routine, often sterile submersion in details without interest in or understanding of larger connections.

It is no exaggeration to say that in many scientific centers not the interest in certain fundamental problems but the fortuitous possession of some new apparatus directs the research work: a new laboratory technique is introduced which spreads like a fad to all laboratories; then everywhere problems are selected which can be approached by this new technique or apparatus. Scientific interest in the fundamentals is lost, research is dictated more or less at random by the technical facilities at the worker's disposal.

This attitude necessarily must lead to that caricature of scientific ethics which regards suspiciously everything that entails reasoning and not merely observation and is contemptuous about theories, not to say hypotheses that are not as yet proven. There is a naive adoration of "pure facts" which are collected without any leading ideas.

Psychoanalysis is a highly empirical field in which the student is exposed to an extremely variety of observations and—in a certain sense—unique facts, as every patient presents a unique combination of common elements. Today the psychoanalytic clinician is undergoing a healthy reaction against the present abundance of theory and generalizations. He is in the process of accepting the mentality of the natural scientist and is assuming all the virtues and weaknesses of our era of laboratory research. Like his other clinical colleagues also he uses a highly standardized and refined technique but pays a high price for his technical skill: he is gradually losing perspective and correct judgment regarding the validity and limitations of his technique and of his scientific work in general.

To expose the students and the members of the staff of the Psychoanalytic Institute of Chicago to a lecture course dealing with epistemology and methodology seemed to me therefore highly indicated. I hoped that such a course would make them more conscious of and critical toward the methods, achievements and significance of their own field. Although one could not anticipate full agreement with all of Mr. Adler's conclusions, it was to be expected that the discussion of problems of psychological methodology by an expert such as Mr. Adler would be a real challenge and a healthy stimulus for all of us, which would stop us for a moment in our daily work and induce us to give ourselves an account of what we are really doing.

This experiment was successful in one respect. Although Mr. Adler was not able to convince his audience of the validity of any of his major statements, he aroused interest in this type of reflection, so direly needed in any group of specialists.

During the discussions that followed each of his lectures Mr. Adler has realized the basic disagreement of his audience with his theses and was therefore hesitant to publish his lectures without giving me an opportunity to state these fundamental controversies in the form of an introduction to his book.

During these discussions it became evident that our disagreement represents two diametrically opposite points of view, and illustrates the unsurmountable gap between what could be called a scientific *Weltanschauung* and the dogmatic attitude of a thirteenth-century scholastic. As Mr. Adler himself very correctly put it, his lectures represent something which might have been the attitude of a contemporary pupil of Thomas Aquinas, or perhaps of Thomas himself if he could come to life again and be confronted with the new discoveries of Sigmund Freud. If for nothing else, then as such an anachronism, Mr. Adler's lectures may have the interest and value of a curiosity. It became obvious that according to Mr. Adler since the times of Aristotle and his belated scholastic pupil, Thomas Aquinas, man really did not contribute anything much of value to the inventory of his knowledge about the surrounding world and himself. Such radical new accomplishments as the recognition of the fact of biological evolution, the technical achievements of physics, chemistry, and medicine, the better understanding of mental diseases, which have resulted in an ever growing capacity of modern psychiatry to cure psychopathological processes, are of no great importance for him. This contempt for "practical" accomplishments explains why he considers the futile speculations and meditations about human nature of ancient and medieval philosophers like Aristotle and Thomas Aquinas to be superior to our detailed and precise knowledge of normal and pathological mental processes which enable us to influence these processes in a desired direction and thus cure mental ailments. Mr. Adler does not evaluate scientific concepts according to the degree to which they increase our ability to control and influence natural phenomena but according to their ability to be fitted into some preconceived rigid and abstract logical construction. The gap between these two attitudes cannot be bridged. In the following I shall state the main points of our controversy.

1. Mr. Adler defines philosophy as a body of logical conclusions drawn from common-sense observations, and science as a body of conclusions drawn from specific observations obtained by specific investigative methods. I agree with Mr. Adler's definition of science but not with his definition of philosophy. Mr. Adler reduces philosophy to reasoning about inadequate common-sense observations, science representing at the same time reasoning about more adequate observations obtained by refined and improved methods of investigation. And yet, in order to save the medieval hegemony of philosophy, with a peculiar twist of reasoning Mr. Adler tries *to subordinate science—*

that is to say conclusions drawn from improved observations—to philosophy, which according to his own definition consists of conclusions from inadequate observations. If Adler's definition of philosophy is correct, philosophy should be discarded in the proportion to which scientific knowledge progresses by the use of steadily improving special techniques of investigation. With this definition, Adler himself speaks the death sentence of philosophy. However I am much more inclined to accept the view of those philosophers (a view which was most convincingly expressed by Bernard Alexander) who consider philosophic reflection as the manifestation of a deep and universal need in human beings to orient themselves toward the universe with which they are confronted. Science must necessarily leave this deep need for orientation to a high degree unfulfilled because due to its nature its answers are disconnected and restricted to isolated portions of reality, namely to those fields that have already been scientifically explored, and also because scientific answers are necessarily incomplete due to the high claims regarding validity which science sets to itself. In view of this incomplete nature of science, only two attitudes remain for a human being in handling his desire to orient himself in the world in which he lives:

a. A kind of agnosticism, contenting himself with the answers which science can offer at any given time, abandoning the wish for an integrated concept of the universe.

b. An attempt to integrate the isolated and disconnected answers of science into a *Weltbild*. This is philosophy. Such a philosophical picture of the world however must be consistent with what is known by science. It tries to integrate the results of scientific investigations into the best possible synthesis of current knowledge. Therefore philosophy never can disprove science, on the contrary it must always be ready to be corrected by new scientific discoveries. In this sense philosophy never can become superfluous as long as human beings continue to ponder over the world in which they live.

2. One of Mr. Adler's fundamental convictions is that the act of reasoning itself cannot be studied scientifically; that in this regard it has an exceptional position among all psychological processes. Since the reasoning faculties have been subjected successfully both to psychological and physiological investigation, this statement does not need further discussion. Freud's studies of rational thinking, his understanding of it as motor innervations with small quantities of energy on a trial and error basis, his comparative studies of rational thinking in contrast to thinking in dreams, his classical study of denial, and finally his demonstration of the influence of emotional factors upon rational thought have shown that the reasoning process can be psychologically analyzed and genetically understood as the result of a

process of adjustment of the biological individual to its environment. Furthermore the first promising steps have been made by the method of brain operation to establish the relation of rational processes such as the faculty for abstraction, to brain functions.

3. Perhaps the greatest gap between Adler's concepts and the viewpoint assumed by psychoanalysts consists in his insistence upon the nonanimal nature of human beings, in his contention that there is no evolutionary continuity between men and brutes. Adler belongs to that rapidly diminishing, in fact today almost extinct species of thinkers who still try desperately to disregard the solid facts of evolution. The type of argument which is used can be best characterized by quoting the distinguished American thinker, James Harvey Robinson.

Having myself given much time to the comings and goings of beliefs in the past, I see how great a part mere ignorance and confusion always play in blocking the ready acceptance of new knowledge. . . . It is true the biologists have, many of them, given up what *they* call "Darwinism"; they have surrendered Spencer's notion of the hereditary transmission of acquired characters, and they even use the word "evolution" timidly and with many reservations. *But this does not mean that they have any doubts that mankind is a species of animal, sprung in some mysterious and as yet unexplained manner from extinct wild creatures of the forests and plains.* This they simply take for granted; for, unlike the public at large, they distinguish carefully between the varied and impressive evidence which appears to confirm man's animalhood and the several theories which have been advanced from time to time by Lamarck, Darwin, Spencer, Haeckel, and others, to account for the process by which organic life, including man, has developed. The first confusion of which we must relieve ourselves is that between the *facts*, on the one hand, revealed by geology, biology and comparative anatomy, and, on the other hand, the *conjectures* suggested to explain the history of life. As time has gone on the facts which compel anyone acquainted with them to accept man's essentially animal nature have become more abundant and unmistakable, while many of the older theories of evolution have, as a result of further study and increasing knowledge, shown themselves to a great extent untenable. Much light has been cast of late on the history of life, but in some respects it seems more mysterious than ever before.[1]

Adler, like some theologists, in order to refute the unassailable fact of evolution, takes advantage of recent controversies regarding those detailed mechanisms by which man has developed into his present form from more primitive beings.

His methodological discussion about the discontinuity of the different realms of knowledge, his insistence upon insurmountable gaps between the inanimate world, animals and man, are based on a re-

[1] James Harvey Robinson, *The Human Comedy*, New York: Harper, 1937, pp. 23-24.

fusal to draw the correct conclusion from the factual evidence which we possess regarding the relationships between these different sections of the universe. Even though scientists are not able to reduce the processes of life to physics and chemistry there is no doubt that the process of life consists in a specific combination of exactly the same processes as are known in the physics and chemistry of nonliving substances. The specificity of life consists *in the specificity of the combination* of those partial processes which constitute life and which are identical with the chemical processes of nonliving substances. It is true that the specific principles of this coordination are not known as yet. Nevertheless it is quite possible that some time in the future when we shall possess the knowledge of the characteristic combination of physicochemical processes in the living cell we shall be able to create living substance from nonliving substance. It is needless to say that the difference between the higher animals and man is far less incisive than that between animals and inanimate nature. The psychoanalyst considers the difference between man and animals as definitely of quantitative nature because he can observe that the newborn infant shows no human but merely animal characteristics. The difference between men and animals, which is one of Adler's fundamental theses, comes gradually about during the individual's development from an ovum to an adult.

4. Adler's efforts to demonstrate that the Freudian concepts of personality have been anticipated if not more completely elaborated by Aristotle are based upon entirely formalistic and verbal comparisons. Aristotle's theory of personality has the same relation to the Freudian as Democritus' concept of the atom bears to the scientific concepts of Dalton or as Edward von Hartmann's "unconscious" has to the Freudian concept of the unconscious. The similarity is based mainly on the use of the same word. Democritus' "atom" was the result of deductive speculation and did not contribute to a better knowledge of matter, whereas Dalton's atomic concept was concluded from specific observations regarding certain permanent quantitative relationships in chemical compounds and has led to the body of knowledge represented by modern chemistry. Similarly Aristotle's speculations about human nature did not enable any contemporary physician to understand better the nature of paranoia or hysterical blindness, whereas Freud's concepts were derived from painstaking minute observations made by the help of a refined technique of psychological inquiry and have made possible a better understanding and methodical influencing of psychological processes.

5. Mr. Adler's statement that the Aristotelian concepts about personality in a certain respect were more complete than Freud's is obviously true. But this completeness is anything but an asset as com-

pared with the incompleteness of the Freudian concepts. The Freudian concepts are necessarily incomplete; they are, like every scientific concept, in a continuous process of change and improvement because, being of a scientific nature, they must remain in accordance with new observational material whereas the systematic philosophic concepts of Aristotle are "eternal," since they had to be only consistent in themselves, had to fit not observations but vague generalizations and an abstract system of thought.

6. The gap between the scholastic attitude of Adler and the scientific views of Freud becomes widest when Adler takes a stand regarding the psychoanalytic concepts of moral phenomena. Adler evaluates the Aristotelian concepts of morals as superior because they are absolute whereas the Freudian concepts are relative. Freudians consider moral concepts to be the results of parental influences, the nature of which are determined by the structure of the civilization in which the parents live. Aristotle has an anthropomorphic concept and declares the moral ideas of the Greek Peninsula to be absolute values. Freud's concept of morality compares to the Aristotelian as the concept of present cosmology is related to the Aristotelian concept of the earth as the center of the universe. The facts of modern anthropology and ethnology fully corroborate the Freudian view and disprove the Aristotelian, showing that the concepts of good and bad radically differ in different cultural settings depending upon the political, economic and cultural history and situation of a group.

If there is such a thing as turning back the clock of history and science, here we see a classical example of it. Scholasticism, a sterile form of deductive thinking, developed as a harmless outlet for the reasoning powers of man in a period of intellectual servitude when man could not observe the world around himself lest any observation come in contradiction with prevailing dogmas. He had to content himself with flawless deductions from incorrect premises. Free observation of facts was forbidden; rigid acceptance of preconceived ideas was the highest requisite of these medieval centuries. What else remained for the human mind to do but indulge in playful deductive meditations starting from the accepted and prescribed dogmas as premises? Our present freedom of inquiry is nothing but the continuation of that great period of the liberation of the mind which started in the Renaissance, with Galileo, Giordano Bruno, and Bacon. It took centuries before this freedom of investigation was fully achieved. At first the realm of the celestial bodies, the stars, then the human body, was claimed as a legitimate subject for scientific study. The last step in this process of emancipation of the human mind was the accomplishment of Sigmund Freud, the objective unbiased study of the human personality, including its reasoning and moral powers.

In spite of these fundamental disagreements, I am very much indebted to Mr. Adler for his courage in presenting his scholastic philosophy to a group which was so thoroughly biased by what is a scientific credo. The consistency of his presentation, the astuteness and skill of his logical deductions, aroused in us the same admiration as those of some medieval scholasticists. The internal consistency of his lectures representing literally a medieval viewpoint, through the effect of contrast, afforded unprecedented opportunity for his audience to understand better the nature of psychoanalytic methods and the position which this science takes in the present realm of knowledge.

A Tentative Analysis of the Variables in Personality Development

◄ 1938 ►

Commonly in our everyday thinking we assume that different cultures produce different types of personalities. We speak for example of the Western type of mind, contrasting it with the Oriental mentality. With the exception of the extreme representatives of the racial theory who try to explain all such differences by racial constitution, most people believe in the importance of the formative influence of cultural milieu upon personality. However, the scientific analysis of the relative significance of the different factors, constitutional and environmental, which contribute to personality formation, still belongs to the future.

The psychoanalytic study of individual cases has impressed us with the influence of emotional experiences of childhood upon the development of those psychological qualities, the sum of which we call personality. If one wished to summarize very briefly the main contribution of psychoanalysis one could say that it has demonstrated the molding influence of the child's early emotional relationships to the members of his family upon his character and his mental disturbances. It is important to emphasize that the variety of these emotional influences in early family life is not great. They represent the variations of a few fundamental and universal emotional patterns. As perhaps the most powerful emotional trend, the dependence of the child on the mother stands out, his exclusive possessiveness toward the mother with the resultant jealousies, hostilities and fears toward siblings and adults in the environment. Besides this powerful motif of dependence, we see to a large degree conflicting with it, more progressive tendencies centering around primitive forms of sexual desires and curiosity with all kinds of identifications with the adults. Can we expect, from these few basic emotional trends and object relationships, to explain the large variety of individual differences as we observe them in our pa-

519

tients and fellow men? The studies of these emotional relationships within the family conducted by the technique of psychoanalysis were so fertile, they made us temporarily oblivious of the original constitutional differences between the newborn children which unquestionably are responsible at least to some extent for the differences between people. We have no reason to doubt that different human races and individuals in their hereditary equipment may differ from each other as much as an Arabian race horse differs from a Mecklenburger, or a retriever dog from a St. Bernard or a dachshund. (We see among these animals such highly specific qualities transmitted through heredity as a keen hunting instinct, not to speak of such more general characteristics as docility, intelligence, faithfulness, a dependent or an independent nature.) Of course we see individual differences, exceptions, among these animals, yet it is more probable that we will succeed in training a setter rather than a Doberman pinscher into a good bird dog. We are accustomed to speak of racial characteristics also among men. Freud for example refers to the anal erotic trends of the Swiss. One speaks about the temperamentality of the Latin races, about the business ability of the Jew and the Greek, and one refers to the Scotchman as the incarnation of thrift. The animal breeder has little doubt that the character trends of the different dog races is primarily a hereditary quality, although he knows that these trends can be further developed through training, but also may be suppressed, spoiled and distorted. Are we justified, however, to consider those psychological qualities which characterize the Swiss, the Italian, the Scotch or the Swede as racial and attribute them to heredity? In the case of man in contrast to animals, the cultural factor transmitted through tradition in the form of customs, ideologies and institutions, must be given special consideration. Do we find among the Swiss thrifty, cleanly and orderly people because they inherit these traits from their Swiss ancestors, or are these characteristics due to the specific cultural conditions and traditions of that country? Without any meticulous scientific investigation one would be inclined to attribute to the cultural factors a powerful influence. We see common and characteristic personality traits among people belonging to the same cultural group independent of race. We can rightly speak of the characteristics of the peasant as contrasted with the mercantile class of metropolitan areas, regardless of their race. Surprisingly many personality traits we will find in common in the Russian kulak, the Hungarian and French peasant and even in the American farmer. This country is a great living example of the strength of the cultural factor, showing the rapid Americanization of the second and third generation from which only those descendants of immigrants are exempt who live in rather secluded racial groups which have retained much of their original customs and ideologies.

All these statements, I admit, are based on everyday impressions; they are not scientifically controlled observations, yet there is little doubt as to their general validity.

We have differentiated three categories of factors affecting personality, all interrelated yet distinct: 1) *hereditary* factors, 2) early highly individual *emotional experiences in the family situation* which are not typical for a race or a culture but only for one specific family and finally, 3) those *cultural influences* to which all members of a particular social group are equally exposed.

However, no theoretical argument, no common sense, no vague uncontrolled everyday experience can answer the question which concerns us today, namely, of the quantitative significance of these three factors in relation to each other. This is the question to which I refer with the expression: "the depth of the cultural influence" upon personality formation. Are the psychological differences between men primarily due to the different distributions of the genes in their parental cells, to their early specific emotional experiences in relation to the members of the family, or to the fact that they are exposed to different cultural and group influences? It is obvious that the cultural factors alone cannot explain the great variety of individual personalities which come from the same group. These influences can only be made responsible for certain character trends which are common to all members of the group. For the finer individual differences between people, constitution and the early and highly specific family influences together must be held responsible.

Obviously the scientific analysis of this problem will lead us to different categories of personality trends. We shall have to differentiate between characteristics which are common for all members of the same cultural group, for example for all peasants, for all members of a military class; then between characteristics which are common to all individuals of similar heredity, for example, for all Finns, no matter whether they are peasants or university professors, and finer characteristics which are highly individual and distinguish one member of the same cultural or racial group from another. It is justifiable to refer to some of these personality traits as deeper, less changeable and more fundamental, to others as more superficial and flexible. We will not hesitate to consider the characteristics transmitted by heredity as the most fundamental and the least changeable ones, but we will not be able to estimate readily whether the individual structure of a family or the general characteristics of a culture will have a deeper influence. Since culturally determined customs have an influence even upon the early nursing experience of a child it would be erroneous to consider them as more superficial than the influence of a specific neurotic marital constellation prevailing in a family. Such considerations illustrate the complexity of the problem and the difficulty of isolating cultural influences upon personality formation from the highly specific individual experiences represented by particular family constellations.

Ultimately what we call personality is a resultant of all these three categories of factors: heredity, specific family constellations and cultural influences characteristic for a group. We cannot think offhand of any rigid scientific method by which the relative significance of these factors could be determined. Not even the experiment of rearing two identical twins in two different cultures and comparing the resulting products would be conclusive. In this experiment we would keep the hereditary factor constant and vary the cultural factor, but the third factor, the specific structure of the family in which these twins are reared, could not be exactly duplicated. And even if the experiment were carried on outside of a family in an artificial environment it still would be almost impossible to make identical in both cases the emotional influences upon the child of the persons who are in contact with him. Some academic psychologists or sociologists might consider such an experiment as fairly conclusive, but no psychoanalyst would, since he knows too well the tremendous influence upon the child's development of those adult individualities who deal with the child.

Thus we must turn from the experimental method to less exact and simple methods. Obviously the statistical method offers itself as a second choice. The frequency of certain types of neuroses, certain types of criminality and certain types of normal personalities in different cultural groups could indicate the differential influence of culture on personality. Should we find, for example, that compulsion neurosis is more frequent among merchants, industrialists and intellectuals than among peasants, more frequent in England and Germany than in Italy and France, or more frequent in the nineteenth century than in the fifteenth century in Europe, and that hysteria is more common among Catholic peasants than any other cultural group or more common during the middle ages than the twentieth century, important conclusions could be drawn as to the influence of different civilizations on mental development. Such comparative studies could be carried on in a cross section of our present civilization, in studying the frequency of certain neuroses and personality types among different cultural groups, as well as comparing the frequency of certain attitudes and neuroses in different historical periods.

A third method, possibly the most promising one, consists in the comparison of careful psychoanalytic case histories of individuals belonging to different civilizations. The great advantage of this method over all others is, that only such clinical studies can give us a sufficiently detailed and reliable view of the actual structure of a human personality as it develops under certain cultural and specific family influences.

The weakness of the psychoanalytic approach is that it necessarily must remain restricted to a small number of cases. Therefore a combination of the statistical method with psychoanalytic case studies is the most promising. After certain statistical frequencies of different personality types of neuroses in different cultural groups have been established, psychoanalysis might be used for a more detailed study of representative cases in each group to evaluate the nature of the statistically found correlation.

For example, it has been statistically established that American Negroes supply a high percentage of malignant cases of essential hypertension. In comparison, among African Negroes, this condition is not so common. This statistical correlation alone does not permit the assumption that essential hypertension is a reaction of the organism to the cultural conditions in western civilization. This is indicated, however, by the psychoanalytic study of cases suffering from essential hypertension showing the effect upon the blood pressure of aggressive hostile impulses which the patient can neither repress deeply nor express freely. The life in our particular type of civilization is especially conducive to the development of such an emotional state. The competitive structure of our culture stimulates in most people antagonistic aggressive feelings against each other and, at the same time it requires a great amount of control of the free expression of hostile impulses. We must compete with each other and yet outwardly remain the best friends. I am inclined to believe that in certain predisposed individuals this permanent conflict situation may lead to a constant stimulation of the vasomotor apparatus since it is well known that rage is followed by an elevation of the blood pressure. In the course of years this chronic state of controlled hostile attitudes with its continuous influence upon the vasomotor apparatus constitutes a functional overtaxation of the circulatory system and may lead finally to morphological changes in the blood vessels and produce the clinical picture that is known as essential hypertension. This would be an example of how cultural conditions may contribute toward certain emotional conflict situations which may lead even to organic disturbances. Since most people are exposed to these cultural influences additional predisposing factors must be assumed. These may be constitutional factors or specific emotional experiences in childhood or their combination.

I submit these remarks mainly to emphasize the complexity of this problem and tentatively to isolate the variables in the process which we call personality development. Man as a personality is at the same time the object of the biologist, psychiatrist, psychologist and sociologist. Each one is inclined to overestimate the influence of those factors which belong to his own territory. The hereditary factor must be studied with biological methods, the particular emotional experiences in postnatal development by the technique of psychoanalysis, whereas the study of group influences requires historical and sociological methods. The question is not whether personality is the product of either heredity or culture, or of all the intricate accidentalities of the emotional interrelationships between the child, his parents and siblings; the problem consists in the isolation of the influence of all these factors and in establishing their correlations with each other.

Psychoanalysis
Comes of Age
◄ 1938 ►

In two respects this year is a significant one. In recent years due to the adversities in European political and social events, the development of psychoanalysis has shifted its center from Europe to this country. The culmination of this development was reached recently in the dissolution of the Viennese group, the oldest and one of the largest and most active centers of psychoanalysis. Words cannot express the shock of these events upon all of those who devote themselves to the practice and furthering of psychoanalysis. Although the European developments came neither suddenly nor unexpectedly, yet it is almost impossible to realize that the founder of psychoanalysis, in the eighty-second year of his life, has had to leave his residence in Berggasse 19 to accept the hospitality of a foreign country. If individuals have a deep influence on the development of human thought and on the course of human fate, Sigmund Freud is certainly an example. Freud and the Viennese psychoanalytic group are forced to leave Vienna; psychoanalysis however has its home in the whole world. It has become an integral part of modern thought and, as a therapy, an integral part of modern medicine.

A few years ago the breaking up of this great European center of psychoanalytic teaching and research would have been an even greater catastrophe. In the past several years, however, strong centers of psychoanalysis have sprung up in this country upon the foundations that were laid down by the pioneer work of Abraham Brill. The rapid development of psychoanalysis in America was due in part to the disintegration of the Berlin Psychoanalytic Institute and to the permanent threat to which the Viennese group has been exposed for years. A number of experienced European analysts have come to

This paper was the Presidential Address to the American Psychoanalytic Association, 1938.

525

this country and are now contributing to the activities of the American groups.

Psychoanalysis in America has developed in a direction which in certain respects differs from what was characteristic of its European development. Here in a brief period, the relationship of psychoanalysis to psychiatry and to the rest of medicine has changed rapidly. Psychoanalysis, instead of remaining an isolated discipline, with a specific object, method, and way of thinking which were shunned by all the other sciences, has become more and more a part of medicine in so far as it is a therapy, and a part of social science in so far as it deals with human interrelationships. At the same time psychoanalysis has assumed a more scientific character, and the emphasis on its contributions to a *Weltanschauung* has retreated correspondingly into the background. The interest in the theoretical superstructure of psychoanalysis had gradually given place to an emphasis upon the observational foundations of our field. The need for detailed and reliable records of analytical material to facilitate the rechecking of the findings by other observers and also to make possible a careful comparative microscopic study of this recorded material, has been clearly recognized. The fundamental principles discovered by Freud: the existence of the dynamic unconscious, infantile sexuality, and such dynamic concepts as regression, fixation, substitution—have stood the test of further empirical scrutiny sufficiently and investigators have settled down to a more precise study of these phenomena. Meanwhile the world at large has become accustomed to fundamental conceptions of personality which at the time of their discovery by Freud seemed so revolutionary. The emotional resistance of the early post-Victorian period against psychoanalysis has given place to a scientific scrutiny which unfortunately is often confused by psychoanalysts with the former uncritical "resistance." In those earlier days when skepticism was expressed about the fundamental discoveries of psychoanalysis, about the existence and the dynamic influence of unconscious processes, about the Oedipus complex, or the manifestations of infantile sexuality, the monotonous answer was, "You have a resistance against psychoanalysis and should be psychoanalyzed." One must admit that in the overwhelming majority of cases this answer was correct. It is most unfortunate however, that the request for a rigid scientific verification of psychoanalytic findings, the demand for experimental proofs, and questioning of certain theoretical deductions is often confused with earlier forms of emotional resistance. The number of men in different fields of science who thoroughly understand the fundamental principles of psychoanalysis and who at the same time feel the need for more precise and even quantitative tests of psychodynamic formulations is growing steadily. Such a critical attitude is fundamentally different from the former uncritical prejudice which was definitely destructive because it rejected scientific evidence. The newer critical appraisal is the manifestation of a scientific spirit which every true scientist should assume toward the theoretical structure of his own field. This attitude aims on the basis of evidence to establish truth and not to deny it. This type of criticism stimulates more precise work whereas the emotional bias tried to discourage research in the delicate field of the human personality.

I do not want to imply that today there are no signs of preconceived objections to psychoanalysis. The repeated attempts to divert psychiatric research from the psychological field and to substitute premature physiological speculations for well-established psychological causal connections are well-known manifestations of such a resistance. A similar retreat from psychological insight is the substitution of certain sociological generalities, as for example, "competitive civilization" to account for individual motivations actually springing from the rivalry among siblings. Although psychoanalysis must ultimately be integrated with physiology and with sociology, and must constantly try to correlate psychological facts with physiological and sociological phenomena, psychoanalysis nonetheless remains essentially a psychological method which tries to understand human behavior in terms of psychology. The need for a further integration of psychology with physiology and sociology does not justify the evasion of psychological issues by physiological or sociological assumptions. In spite of these aberrations the growing biological and sociological orientation of psychoanalysis is a most healthy development and is a necessary consequence of the fact that man is at once a biological organism, an individual personality, and a member of an organized social group. Every one-sided approach to the understanding of man which does not take into consideration all of these three aspects remains incomplete and gives rise to a distorted picture. It is only natural that increasing knowledge of the human being both from the physiological and psychological point of view must lead to a more integrated view of personality and its disturbances. This increasing knowledge of psychosomatic relationships (which does not imply that there are two disparate entities in man—soma and psyche—but that there are somatic and psychological aspects of man closely coordinated with each other) reflects itself in the increasing medical orientation of psychoanalysis as a therapy. A psychoanalytic therapist who is not a physician is eventually becoming unacceptable to us. On the other hand, understanding of a personality in relationship to group life, to cultural traditions and ideologies, is becoming equally a necessity.

This sociological orientation in psychoanalysis has strong support in the traditional sociological trend in American psychiatry which has developed a new profession, the psychiatric social worker.

From this perspective we can better understand the changes in psychoanalytic ideology of recent years. All of these changes are manifestations of the coming of age of psychoanalysis. All fundamental and new scientific discoveries require an emotional adjustment to the new knowledge. Before such an adjustment is accomplished the new knowledge appears to be a new *Weltanschauung* challenging the old. Only gradually did the emotional reaction to Copernicus' new cosmology (to which Giordano Bruno gave such a magnificent expression in the form of a new *Weltanschauung*) subside and become replaced by a more precise mathematical study of the celestial bodies; similarly Darwinism gradually gave place to experimental genetics. In the same way the heroic period of psychoanalysis, in which it was said to "disturb the sleep of humanity," belongs to the past. The cultural mission of psychoanalysis to force man to face his own nature objectively has been accomplished. It can now leave the arena of public interest where these philosophical issues regarding human nature are fought out and retire to the peaceful and unemotional realm of scientific research.

Yet much of the traditional attitude of psychoanalysts still bears the earmarks of our romantic and heroic past. One still encounters especially among older analysts the stubborn martyr attitude of the fanatic, the insistence upon the specific nature of the psychoanalyst as distinct from all other scientists, an antagonistic attitude toward medicine which is a historical remnant of the initial feud between Freud and the Viennese medical group. In fact these antiquated ideological attitudes in psychoanalysis can best be understood in the terms of Freud's earliest descriptions of a neurotic symptom. Like the neurotic symptoms these attitudes also once had a meaning and were natural reactions to previous situations. Although at present they are out of place and have little or no relation to the current situation, they still persist as souvenirs of the emotional struggles of the past. It is most important that psychoanalysts adjust their emotional attitudes to the changes which time has wrought in their own environment. They should lose the defensive attitude of a minority group, the militant soldiers of a *Weltanschauung* attacked by and therefore antagonistic to the world. Rather than disseminators of a gospel they must become self-critical scientists. For psychoanalysis as a whole, this leads to the simple but unavoidable conclusion that the sooner psychoanalysis as a "movement" disappears, the better. Psychoanalysis today has no more reason to represent a movement than has scientific genetics or ophthalmology. It is to be hoped that the expression, "psychoanalytic movement," will soon sound to us as strange as would "ophthalmological movement." In so far as psychoanalysis consists of the study of the functioning of the mind, it is a part of and a method in general psychology; in so far as it is a therapy it is an integral part of the larger body of medicine.

For all of these developments the American soil proves to be much more suitable than was the European. Not only geographically but psychologically as well we are far from the emotional attitudes which led to the feud between psychoanalysis and medicine. The issues in the early development of psychoanalysis which created these traditional attitudes continued to exist in Europe but have had much less significance in this country; moreover the development of psychoanalysis in America took place after the older emotional controversies had subsided and the fundamental discoveries of psychoanalysis had become a common possession of clinical psychiatry. Finally the tolerant and critical intellectual atmosphere in this country, its political and social traditions, are most conducive to the development of every investigative science. The upswing of psychoanalytic research is only one manifestation of the intensive general scientific life in America which is rapidly taking the lead in this field as well as in others.

However it would be unworthy of any scientist to look back with derision on earlier phases of knowledge. The pioneering period in psychoanalysis, one in which a genius had to militate alone against the prejudices of the whole world, was the really creative and the most productive period. When we try to emancipate ourselves from those emotional attitudes which were necessary and natural reactions in those earlier days but are out of place and quixotic today, we should not overlook the fact that our present scientific contributions consist mainly of more precise reformulations, careful applications and critical reevaluations of fundamental principles discovered by Freud in that romantic period upon which some of us might be tempted to look back with a patronizing smile.

As in social and political history, so with developments in other fields of knowledge and thought: one follows the general dynamic principles of thesis, antithesis, and synthesis. Social development is most sound and constructive however when any period is not the polar antithesis of the preceding one. Evolutionary development, because it does not destroy but takes into account the valuable contributions of the past, is superior to revolutionary development. The best example is England, which probably to a large degree owed its world supremacy in the last century to the fact that the transition from a feudal to an industrial civilization took place not by violent and destructive civil war but by a more smooth evolutionary process. When antithesis follows thesis as an uncompromising reaction formation it usually means not an improvement on the defects of the previous period but only an exchange of the old defects for new antithetical defects. This should be a warning to us that any present reaction against the early romantic phases of our history should not become a similar neurotic reaction formation. Let us not allow our more critical attitude toward the theoretical superstructure of analysis, our demand for more precise, more quantitative knowledge, for more exact experimental evidence—let us not allow these to deteriorate into a one-sided emphasis upon sterile, thoughtless description as a contrast to theory, or into phobic aversion against thinking, misjudging and defaming every deduction as speculation. In our fervor to improve the status of our knowledge let us not under the slogan of "observation versus theory" declare a general war against past accomplishments. In the field of teaching let us not allow the great progress made by replacing the disorganized, primitive form of apprenticeship with well-organized and uniform training in psychoanalytic institutes to deteriorate into routine, bureaucratic, spiritless mass production of practitioners. Our institutes should be small but high grade universities of psychoanalysis in which candidates receive instruction both in practical clinical and in theoretical subjects with a well-balanced biological and sociological orientation, and not merely professional schools with a one-sided emphasis on practical technical instruction, professional schools where—as a cynical observer once said—students learn only how to hold on to their analytic patients.

The city of Chicago is a most appropriate place for the utterance of such a warning because there, Mr. Hutchins, President of the University of Chicago, has for years been engaged in a struggle to save the universities from deteriorating into mere professional schools, to preserve them for their original purpose as places where students receive a broad scientific and cultural orientation rather than restricted routinized professional training.

No other professional man is more in need of a general cultural background and a well-balanced biological and sociological orientation than a psychoanalyst. Our instruction must remain free from a rigid inflexible spirit of routine that insists formally upon a prescribed curriculum and upon a one-sided technical training. Psychoanalysis is a young discipline in a state of flux and transformation. Our institutes accordingly must remain correspondingly flexible, open to innovations, and must abstain from a prematurely rigid, standardized and bureaucratic overorganization. We psychoanalysts are obliged by our knowledge of what distinguishes neurotic from healthy development to avoid the pitfalls of overcompensation or in less technical terms, the dangers of extremes. In emancipating ourselves from the romantic and militant attitude of the past, we should not try to replace the intense urge for a synthetic theoretical grasp of the problems of the personality by the opposite extreme of sterile dissection and an aversion to assumptions and theories without which no science can progress. And in teaching we should not try to overcompensate for the former too personal and disorganized teaching with overorganized and overstandardized mass production.

Nobody knows better than we students of the development of personality that the past cannot be destroyed but should serve as a foundation upon which to build.

Values and Science

◄ 1950 ►

While I am in full agreement with Professor George R. Geiger's position that the problem of "values" is both a legitimate and possible subject of scientific inquiry, the discussion of this topic appears to me as much outmoded as a controversy over whether machines heavier than air can rise up against the force of gravity and fly. Both of these questions are settled by the actual demonstration of their feasibility. That section of human behavior which pertains to values (evaluation, preference, choice) has been and is being successfully investigated by scientific methods of observation and reasoning. The dichotomy between "facts and values" is a pseudodistinction and the problem of whether values belong to a realm which is beyond the reach of scientific methods is a pseudo-problem. This being my position, little remains for me to add to Dr. Geiger's scholarly treatise—little more than to refer the reader to the pertinent literature.

First, in order to delineate the problem, the meaning of the expression, "value" and "evaluation," should be defined. We may well agree upon Professor Geiger's proposition that "values are outcomes of human choice." Taste in the narrower and broader sense is the simplest example—ethical value systems the most complex. Every choice referred to by adjectives—good or bad, beautiful or ugly, useful or useless, worthwhile or unworthy—belongs to the phenomenology of values. The fallacious belief that such value judgment cannot be studied scientifically can be explained partly from such cultural-historical reasons as mentioned by Professor Geiger, partly from the fact that these predilections are perceived as compelling forces which do not require further explanation or justification. Preferring blondes or sweets is not the result of reasoning, and "beautiful" is a judgment which is immediate and does not need the explanation of an aesthetician. The same is true for moral values such as good or bad. One may try to explain post factum why an act is felt good or bad, but no explanations are needed to make such decisions. In fact, when a logical

532

deduction is needed for a choice, we do not deal with the same type of phenomenon as, for example, a move in playing chess. The latter type of choice easily lends itself to scientific explanations by deductive reasoning. The immediate subjective nature of value judgments is one of the reasons why they have been considered as being beyond rational analysis. According to the traditional postulate of philosophy, ethical and aesthetic values have their own immanent laws which are inaccessible to the accepted method of science. The first part of this statement is valid: namely, that the phenomena of aesthetic beauty and morality have their own immanent laws, but the second part of the statement, that these laws are beyond the realm of science, is but the reflection of the state of our ignorance which prevailed at the time when this dogma was postulated. It is noteworthy that in the field of the more prosaic physical appetites, such as sexual or gustatory appeal, the dogma of their inscrutability has never been postulated. Although the laws governing such predilections are not known, it is generally assumed that the nature of the person or of the organism determines in some unknown manner what sexual partner or food will appeal. (For example: "Les extremes se touchent.") Those who defend the dichotomy between "values and facts" obviously must consider aesthetic and moral values as essentially different from the more primitive value judgments in the field of gustatory or sexual taste. The self-contradictory nature of this is easily demonstrated by the irrefutable argument that moral and aesthetic judgments take place in the human organism and therefore must follow the same basic principles which govern all other phenomena of life.

As stated above, however, all this logical quibbling is unnecessary and outdated today, since the phenomena of moral choice and aesthetic appeal, as well as of gustatory and sexual preferences, have been studied with considerable success by the methods of biology, psychology and social anthropology. The following are only a few references to the most important studies made in this field.

1. *Gustatory values.* It has been demonstrated by Richter and others that in animals the choice of food is largely determined by the organism's physiological needs. Rats who were deprived experimentally of certain ingredients in their food chose those foodstuffs which contained the needed ingredients.[1]

2. *Sexual appeal.* Psychoanalytic studies have shown that sexual attractions (extreme cases of fetishism, for example) are largely determined by previous experiences (fixation). Furthermore, it is well

[1] C. P. Richter, L. E. Holt, Jr., and B. Barelare, Jr., "Nutritional Requirements for Normal Growth and Reproduction in Rats Studied by the Self-Selection Method," *Am. J. Physiol.*, CXXII (1938), 734; C. P. Richter, "Biology of Drives," *Psychos. Med.*, III (1941), 103.

established that sexual tastes are governed to a large extent by such phenomena as incest taboo and incestuous fixation. Incest taboo may account for the sexual appeal of persons whose physical or mental attitudes are different from the male or female member of the family, and, conversely, fixations on the family members of the opposite sex will favor the choice of partners who resemble them. These are only some of the determining factors; accidental experiences of early life also contribute to determining sexual appeal in later life.[2]

3. *Aesthetic values.* In this almost virgin field of inquiry, the most fundamental studies are those of Freud on wit and humor. He accounted for the witty effect by a specific combination of form and content which allows gratification for repressed emotions. The pleasurable effect expressed in laughter is derived from the saving of energy which is liberated by lifting repressions.[3] Kris applied the same principle to explain the effect of caricatures.[4] Assuming that the tragic effect in drama and epos belongs to the same category of phenomena (aesthetic effect), Rank and Sachs explained this in terms of dynamic psychology. In addition to the effect of form (rhyme, meter, economy of style) the reader, through identification with the suffering hero, can gratify his forbidden longings.[5] The author of this article attempted to apply the same principles (pleasure derived from saving psychological energy by the combined effect of form and content) to all varieties of aesthetic appeal.[6] Without claiming that the psychodynamics of aesthetic appeal is fully explored in all its details, these studies sufficiently demonstrate the accessibility of aesthetic appeal to exploration by the methods of psychology.

4. *Moral Systems of Value.* The "functionalist school" of social anthropology explains various social institutions, habits and value sys-

[2] S. Freud, "Three Contributions to the Theory of Sex," in *Basic Writings*, New York: Modern Library, 1938; S. Freud, "Contributions to the Psychology of Love, The Most Prevalent Form of Degradation in Erotic Life," in *Collected Papers*, New York: Basic Books, 1959, Vol. IV, 203-216; Franz Alexander, *The Psychoanalysis of the Total Personality*, New York: Nerv. and Ment. Dis. Pub. Co., 1935, 132-138.

[3] S. Freud, "Wit and Its Relation to the Unconscious," in *Basic Writings*, New York: Modern Library, 1938.

[4] Ernst Kris, "The Psychology of Caricature," *Int. J. Psycho-Anal.*, XVII (1936), 285.

[5] Otto Rank and Hanns Sachs, "The Significance of Psychoanalysis for the Mental Sciences," *Psychoanal. Rev.*, II (1915), 297-326, 428-457; III (1916), 69-89, 189-214, 318-335; H. Sachs, *Gemeinsame Tagtraume*, Leipzig: Int. Psychoanal. Verlag, 1924, 1-36.

[6] F. Alexander, "Unconscious Factors in Aesthetic Appeal," in *Deuxieme Congres International d'Esthetique et de Science de l'Art, Paris, 1937*, Paris: Librairie Felix Alcan, 1937, I, 217-220; F. Alexander, "Unconscious Factors in Wit and Aesthetic Appeal," in *Fundamentals of Psychoanalysis*, New York: Norton, 1948.

tems as adaptations of the members of the group to the total social structure in which they live.[7] An example is the explanation of the Japanese emphasis on ancestor worship as an essential feature of the feudal system which persisted in Japan uninterruptedly over many centuries.[8] This specific form of morality is not only the reflection of the feudal ideology in the mind of the individual, but it is also an indispensable guarantee for the survival of the feudal system. Likewise the emphasis upon the self-made man and the depreciation of authority worship in the United States are expressions of the American social structure and American history. The social function of these attitudes in a competitive democratic civilization is obvious.[9]

The explanation of all social institutions and moral systems from their survival value has its limitations, however. First of all, moral value systems change more slowly than the social conditions which originated them. Consequently, many institutions and value systems lose their original function of perpetuating the survival of the social system. They become outmoded, adjusted to past conditions and unfitted to the present (cultural lag).[10] Unless the history of a social group is known, the function of an institution or value system is often not apparent. Since social anthropologists most frequently study so-called primitive cultures which have no written history, the functional theory cannot always be applied successfully to the explanation of social institutions, habits and mores prevailing in such societies.

While these studies in the field of social anthropology have shed light upon the variations of moral value systems, the fundamental moral propensity of human nature is not explained by them.

Man's basic moral propensity can be understood in the light of psychoanalytic theory as the psychological manifestation of the process of biological maturation during which the person's capacity to replace love of himself with love for another gradually increases.[11] I have described this phenomenon as the manifestation of the biological "surplus principle." As long as the organism grows, intake and reten-

[7] Clyde Kluckhohn, "The Limitations of Adaptation and Adjustment as Concepts for Understanding Cultural Behavior," in John Romano (ed.), *Adaptation*, Ithaca: Cornell Univ. Press, 1949, 99-113; Abram Kardiner, *The Individual and His Society*, New York: Columbia Univ. Press, 1946.

[8] Ruth Benedict, *The Chrysanthemum and the Sword*, Boston: Houghton Mifflin, 1946.

[9] Margaret Mead, *And Keep Your Powder Dry*, New York: Morrow, 1942; Geoffrey Gorer, *The American People*, New York: Norton, 1948; F. Alexander, *Our Age of Unreason*, Philadelphia: Lippincott, 1942, 294-312.

[10] W. F. Ogburn, *Social Change with Respect to Culture and Original Nature*, New York: B. W. Huebsch, 1923; Alexander, *Our Age of Unreason*, Philadelphia: Lippincott, 1942, 131-138.

[11] S. Freud, "On Narcissism: An Introduction," in *Collected Papers*, New York: Basic Books, 1959, Vol. IV, 30-59.

tion of matter and energy outweigh their expenditure. Otherwise growth would not be possible. Accordingly, the emotional orientation of the immature organism is primarily self-centered. The process of growth, however, has a natural limit: when a biological unit reaches a certain size, addition of substance and energy becomes impossible because its capacity to organize living matter in one system reaches its limit. Individual growth then stops, and surplus energy is released in the form of propagation. The psychological concomitant of this biological maturation is the replacement of self-love by object love. It manifests itself in generous outwardly directed creative attitudes of the healthy mature person which in ethics is called altruism. Without this capacity for interest in and love for others, no social organization can exist since every form of social organization requires from the individual a certain amount of consideration for others with a simultaneous curtailment of concentration on the promotion of self-interest.[12]

Though moral systems may differ radically in detail, they have one feature in common: they all require a consideration of the interests of other members of the society with greater or less sacrifice of selfish interests. Merely on the basis of "you must," no society could survive. What makes it possible for the moral "must" to become a vital force is the biological and psychological phenomenon of excess energy which is not needed for self-preservation and which can be expended for propagation and neighborly love. Only in this way can a group be successfully preserved.

A social organization in which respect for each other's interests is based alone on coercion, on fear of law or of a tyrannical leader, has never been proved stable. Internal frictions caused by competing interests eventually break up the cohesion of such a system. Social organizations can only be explained by the existence of a cohesive force which Freud called "eros" and which this author describes as the surplus energy of the mature organism—energy not needed for self-preservation and expendable for creative activity and object love. According to this view, altrusim has a biological foundation; it appears in its most undiluted form in the maternal instinct. I assume that this productive and creative faculty is what Kluckhohn had in mind when he postulated in addition to the utilitarian (functional) principle in culture, the existence of another culture forming principle.[13]

Such anthropological and psychodynamic considerations vali-

---

[12] Franz Alexander, *Fundamentals of Psychoanalysis,* New York: Norton, 1948, 41-48, 75-81; and "Emotional Maturity," Ill. Soc. Mental Hygiene, *Mental Health Bull.,* XXVI, No. 5 (November-December, 1948).

[13] Kluckhohn, *op. cit.*

date the contention that moral phenomena can be studied by the methods of science and retraced to universal biological and psychological principles. These phenomena can be explained partially as adaptive mechanisms and partially as the manifestations of biological and psychological maturation, which allows the organism to apply some of its energies not alone to its own growth and survival but also to the preservation and benefit of others.

A Review of Two Decades

◄ 1953 ►

Twenty years is not a long period in the lifetime of an academic institution. Time, however, particularly in the era of Einsteinian physics, is a relative concept. In the field of our young discipline in which organized teaching can look back only thirty years, two decades represent a considerable portion. And teaching is only one aspect of academic institutions. Organized, collective research carried out by a staff of co-workers has an even shorter history in psychoanalysis. Prior to the founding of the Chicago Institute for Psychoanalysis, this type of research existed neither in Europe nor in this country. The twentieth anniversary of organized teaching and research in a psychoanalytic institute may be considered a noteworthy date.

Thirty years ago when I decided to leave the well-established areas of the medical sciences to devote myself to the study of psychoanalysis, quite a few of my medical and nonmedical friends expressed their skepticism, nay, consternation, about this decision. Even those who recognized the historical significance of Freud's discoveries in the evolution of human knowledge doubted that psychoanalysis as a method of treatment was here to stay and that a psychoanalyst would ever become a recognized specialist in the field of medical therapy.

Thirty years ago, for a physician to decide to become a psychoanalyst was, no doubt, a grave matter. That the new knowledge of the unconscious mind would become the foundation of a new profession was still to be determined. There was only a handful of psychoanalysts, practicing in different countries but united in the International Psychoanalytic Association. They were trained by themselves or by each other and they were recognized by no other existing authority in the field of medicine. To make the decision to become a psychoanalyst meant to embark upon a highly insecure career; no psychoanalyst at that time could foresee his future status as a member of a larger group of professionals. He could have been certain of one thing, however: namely, that by becoming a psychoanalyst he placed

538

himself outside the fraternity of medical colleagues and he abandoned all that aura of prestige which surrounded the modern descendants of "medicine men," the graduates of the standard medical schools.

It is true that the national psychoanalytic societies, unified under the aegis of the International Psychoanalytic Association with the leadership of Sigmund Freud, gave the new adept a spiritual haven, a kind of citizenship in a small but devoted group. In the early twenties there was scarcely a cultural center in Europe where the young psychoanalyst, once recognized by his local society, would not have found friendly acceptance by the local psychoanalysts. Among them he felt at home at once, with the sensation that he belonged to the chosen few who were enlightened by Freud's teachings about the nature of man and society. An important part of his outlook was that he and the other analysts were surrounded by a hostile world, by people who, because of their emotional resistances and ignorances, continued to live in their traditional hypercritical self-deception. Whether he was visiting his confreres in Vienna, Zurich, Berlin, Munich, Budapest, Rome, Amsterdam, Paris, or London, the conversation soon turned to the hostility and prejudice which the local analysts met on the part of the medical societies and the universities. Soon a well-told anecdote about a slip of the tongue or an observation about the Oedipal behavior of a little son or daughter, an account of an interesting dream fragment, created the feeling of complete solidarity, the feeling that we all shared the same new knowledge for which the rest of the world rejected us. Such is the psychodynamic soil in which all new spiritual movements thrive. In our minds we had no doubt that psychoanalysis was here to stay, and that it would gradually change the outlook of contemporary men and reform the sciences, including medical therapy, the principal object of which is man.

I cannot forgo this opportunity to confess that it is a great privilege to have had the fortune to spend the early part of one's life as a member of such a courageous pioneering group which was destined to have a deep reforming influence upon our Western civilization. One felt that whatever one's contributions were, one lived for a worthy cause and that the results of one's efforts would continue to live. This feeling is the strongest defense against the fear of personal death and explains why those who are devoted to a cause they believe in show more courage and less concern about their personal fate. They extend the boundaries of their ego by identifying themselves with something outside of themselves.

The great inner gratification derived from being a militant member of a new spiritual movement, be it in religion, art, science, or social reform, explains also the difficulties of reorienting oneself after the cause for which one fought has become accepted and respected.

Every leader of an opposition, when elected to govern, faces the same difficulty. The transition from the heroic phase of a movement into its consolidation represents a particularly difficult emotional situation for the devotee. The whole personality was geared to pursue the truth in spite of a hostile world. Now the world turns to you not to fight, but to ask you to teach and to lead. The gratification of martyrdom is over. Your responsibilities increase tremendously at once and you must seek satisfaction from teaching those who want to learn and from fulfilling the promises which you implicitly made while you were fighting your opponents. This is a critical period of re-evaluation of the new truth which you have professed to own. This is the day of accounting. As long as all that you stated was contradicted, and contradicted mainly because of emotional prejudice and not because of reason, your moral position was comparatively easy. In the fervor of the battle, it was no time to look for precision and validation. In the main, *you* were right and the *world* was wrong. Even at the first rough approach to your subject, there was sufficient evidence for your teachings. You knew positively that not all human motives are conscious, that neurotic symptoms and dreams express something meaningful, that repressed sexual impulses were the main source of neurosis of the Victorian and post-Victorian Westerner, and, above all, that sexuality was there from the beginning of life and its objects in the infant were incestuous. As long as all these facts were denied, your position was easy: you were fighting for the truth. The whole dynamics of the interpersonal field change, however, as soon as all that you have professed is accepted and the world is asking you sincerely and avidly to explain the new truth. They turn to you now: "Please tell us all about it. How does this knew knowledge help us, how can we use it constructively to cure a neurotic or psychotic patient, to improve child rearing, to alleviate social prejudice and international tension, and to prevent war?"

And you are bombarded with more and more embarrassing questions. "Many of my friends were analyzed for years without any results. How can the majority of people afford such long treatment? Why does training in psychoanalysis last so much longer than in any other specialty? Why is it so expensive?" The most pertinent and penetrating questions, however, are asked by our scientific confreres in other fields of knowledge, concerning the precision and validity of our formulations and the nature of our evidence. The time is past when you could retort with the once-valid formula: "You are asking all these questions because of your emotional resistances." Today we must answer these sincere and pertinent questions in good faith, and in order to do so we must search our own souls and evaluate what we know and what we do not know. This is the moment when our field, which was a combination of a nucleus of a new science with a new creed, begins to change into a rigorous science which has to accept universal standards of validation in research and to adopt academic standards of teaching established by tradition in all other fields of knowledge. Since psychoanalysis is not only a body of theoretical knowledge but also a medical specialty, this is the time when it must accept the established principles of medical practice.

Whenever such a transition from leading an opposition to participating in government, from heroic fight to responsible teaching and practice, takes place within a short period of time, there is danger that the pioneers will not be flexible enough for the required emotional reorientation; that they may remain—as we psychoanalysts say —fixated to an attitude which has become outmoded. The result is the tendency to misinterpret the attitude of others, a Don Quixote fight against windmills. Every question is misunderstood as a sign of hostility based on resistance. Valid criticism provokes, instead of reconsideration and re-examination, violent counterattacks. Smug complacency can only partly cover up the inner insecurity which accompanies the new position of responsibility. Instead of progressive improvement of knowledge and practice, the tendency to rest on the laurels of the past appears in the form of dogmatism. Repetition of the common historical pattern of a once progressive movement changing into stagnant doctinairism is imminent.

The questions pertaining to psychoanalysis as a theory and practice must be met. They can be satisfactorily answered only by a self-critical re-evaluation of all that we can offer; else we must evade the answers by ignoring the questions. This re-evaluation necessarily leads to changes and requires improvements in theory and practice. The complacent reiteration of earlier achievements and the routine continuation of former practices result in sterility.

In this country, with the general acceptance of the fundamental discoveries of psychoanalysis and of psychoanalytic treatment based on these discoveries, we have left behind the heroic era of psychoanalysis and have entered a new phase of responsibility. And here is where the story of the Chicago Institute for Psychoanalysis begins.

At the International Congress of Psychiatry in Paris in 1950 one of the keynotes of the meeting was the recognition of the fact that in the United States of America, not in Europe, psychiatry has assimilated Freud's principles and has become what one may call a psychoanalytically oriented psychiatry. I am happy to say that our great master was wrong in his pessimistic prediction in this one regard. He did not consider America a fertile soil for his teachings. He spoke of the danger that here his teachings could be accepted only in a diluted fashion. His genius, however, foresaw even in this erroneous prediction an element of truth. The question before us is: What is dilution? Is what is happening today a change in meaning or is it a penetration of our knowledge into neighboring fields during which process our previous discoveries and formulations appear in a new perspective? The fact that today in this country the majority of psychiatric residents consider their training in psychoanalysis an indispensable part of their preparation, that many departments of psychiatry encourage their residents to undergo training in analytic institutes, that some medical schools undertake full training in psychoanalysis, that the U.S. Public Health Service grants fellowships for training in psychoanalysis and supports teaching and research in psychoanalytic institutes without any strings attached—all this cannot be regarded as "dilution" of psychoanalysis, but as "penetration" into medicine. This means genuine "acceptance."

You may expect that at the celebration of the twentieth anniversary of this Institute, our accomplishments should be reviewed. I feel, however, that it is not my job or that of my collaborators to evaluate our work. That we shall leave to the members of the American Psychoanalytic Association and the representatives of the neighboring fields of education, biology, and the social sciences who have joined us on this occasion. Instead of reporting our work, let me make a few remarks, not about our accomplishments, but regarding our intentions. To estimate what we have achieved is up to others, but as to what we intended to do, we are the best judges. Let me say a few words about the ideals which have animated our work.

The word "ideal" comes from the Greek and its meaning came to its clearest expression in Plato's philosophy. All later so-called idealistic philosophies are reformulations of Plato's conceptions. To Plato, the idea was the essence of all things, a directive principle, never achieved in reality, only approached. The essence of all existence is the realization of the idea. Plato's conception is particularly applicable to human phenomena such as personal destiny and history. It would be difficult for modern biology to explain the evolution of organisms as an approach toward the fulfillment of an idea, although if we omit the teleological implications, progressive adaptation might be described in somewhat similar terms. On the other hand, even such material things as a man-made machine can be described as an attempt to realize an ideal design. Fichte interpreted history as the gradual realization of an abstract idea. For him the supreme idea was the state. For Hegel, history was a continuous pendular movement between ideas, the thesis, the antithesis, which finally coalesced in a synthesis. American historians like to describe the epic of America as the realization of the American dream, a free country for all men.

This reference to dreams is appropriate. The dynamics of dreaming offers possibly the best opportunity to demonstrate the Platonic thesis. The dreamer tries to overcome in his dream all the external and internal obstacles preventing him from the fulfillment of his needs and desires. That it is difficult to reconcile our desires with all of the external interferences, as well as with the obstacles set by our own standards, is best shown by the complexity of our dreams. Why could we not otherwise simply dream of complete fulfillment of all that we want and strive for?

What was the dream of the Chicago Institute? Only the recognition of the underlying ideas which we have tried to realize can explain our history and predict our future. The central idea, around which all the other objectives can be understood as subsidiary parts of something which French calls a goal structure, was conceived twenty years ago when the Institute was founded. It was based on the conviction that psychoanalysis in this country was about to enter a new phase of its development; that it was emerging from a heroic into a responsible period. This new era required first of all a change in our attitude toward the nonpsychoanalytic world, particularly the field of medicine in general and psychiatry in particular. At the same time, it required a change in attitude toward our own knowledge, our methods of teaching and treatment. The attitude toward ourselves is easier to describe. First of all, it was an emphasis on systematic collective research based on recorded clinical material, on the comparative study by different workers of cases belonging to the same category, on the re-evaluation of what we consider as evidence, on the development of methods to check the validity of interpretation, and on the testing of our formulations by the technique of prediction. One example of systematic comparative clinical studies is our work on the psychological factors in gastrointestinal disturbances and other organic conditions. Benedek's correlational studies of the ovarian cycle are an example of testing psychological formulations by physiological methods. French in his studies of dream sequences uses an elaborate technique for checking the validity of interpretations. Study of borderline fields in other sciences has proved particularly suitable for improving methods of validation. In such studies the same phenomenon is approached by two independent techniques and by conceptual tools belonging to different disciplines. This offers opportunity to check the validity of each approach against the other. Our studies of the specific emotional factors active in organic conditions show the use of borderline concepts. For example, a certain psychodynamic configuration is noted consistently in all patients suffering from peptic ulcer. The validity of such a psychological finding can be tested by making a diagnosis on the basis of the psychological findings alone, a diagnosis which can be verified by the methods of roentgenology.

Our emphasis on research as the primary objective of our Institute in itself was a sign of a reorientation. It expressed our deep conviction that psychoanalysis is not a static body of knowledge inherited from Freud, but a developing discipline. This emphasis upon research also expresses our conviction that in our young field new knowledge is paramount and even more important than teaching the little which we know about the human mind.

However, research without teaching is as incomplete as teaching without research. First of all, we need new workers to explore and develop our discipline. And there is also the great practical need for treatment and our responsibility to utilize all that we know at present for relieving human suffering, no matter how incomplete this knowledge may be. Our dream was to build a really advanced school of learning, patterned after the university, with salaried teachers who could devote the major part of their time to teaching. We could approach this ideal only to a limited degree.

A further ideal in teaching was to emphasize from the beginning that instruction should be based on the students' own observations. We thus reversed the traditional sequence of analytic training in which early theoretical indoctrination was followed by the application of theory to the patient. Thus we tried to avoid the danger of producing students who find in their patients only what they are prepared to find as a result of instruction in theory. This is the only sound way to promote the development of a field rather than merely to consolidate it. In such an early stage as that of psychoanalysis at present, rigid indoctrination is equivalent to paralysis.

Our goals in regard to therapy are of too wide scope to be discussed in any detail. We hold to the principle that our method of treatment is far from being advanced enough for consolidation. The greatest contribution of Freud was to develop a method of studying human behavior, thus acquiring a knowledge which gradually can be converted into effective and economic treatment. This requires constant revision of techniques of treatment and steady experimentation. About seven years of our brief existence has been spent primarily on such experimentation in therapy and on a critical evaluation of the therapeutic factors in psychoanalysis.

Underlying all these strivings is the conviction that in the present era of acceptance of psychoanalysis our principal responsibility is to evaluate what we know and what we can offer in good conscience to advance both our theoretical and practical knowledge, to avoid dogmatic consolidation by emphasizing that psychoanalysis is a developing discipline and not a finished product.

Our attitude toward others—the medical community and the neighboring fields—follows logically our attitude toward our own field. In this era in which the medical profession, particularly psychiatrists, want to learn all they can about psychoanalysis, our responsibility is to open up our gates and to give all we can. Instead of working in splendid isolation, we must find ways and means to reunite with the medical community which Freud had to leave for compelling historical reasons. His conceptions and findings were too novel and revolutionary to be accepted by contemporary medicine and he was forced to take the course he chose: to build an organization of his own with his own societies, journals, teaching institutions, and press.

Twenty years ago the founders of this Institute came to the conviction that in this country the time was ripe to begin the liquidation of the academic isolation of psychoanalysis and enter upon a new era of unification with the other sciences of man. The Chicago Institute was founded to create a model which might show the way for the future incorporation of analysis into the traditional places of teaching and lecturing, the universities. The Associated Psychiatric Faculties of Chicago,[1] of which our Institute is a vital component, is the nearest we have come thus far toward the realization of this goal: the coordination of residency training in psychiatry with the psychoanalytic curriculum.

Twenty years' work in this Institute represents the major portion of my professional life. This may explain my need to add on this occasion a few autobiographical remarks. By temperament and predilection I am not a revolutionary. I believe in evolution and synthesis. I know well enough, however, the function of revolution in biology and social development as well as in physical nature. It was not long ago that Schroedinger called attention to the fact that the physical principle of quantum mechanics prevails also in biology, in the phenomenon of mutation. Events in nature—physical or biological—do not always take place in continua but sometimes in distinct jumps. Schroedinger showed why it would be disadvantageous in biology if mutations occurred too frequently. I should like to extend his generalization by calling attention to the fact that in history, too, gradual change by evolution and sudden changes by revolution can be observed side by side. The Platonic approach toward the realization of ideas follows both principles, evolution and revolution.

About thirty years ago when I joined the psychoanalytic frater-

[1] George J. Mohr, "Psychoanalytic Training," in Franz Alexander and Helen Ross (eds.), *Twenty Years of Psychoanalysis*, New York: Norton, 1953.

nity, it was not because its revolutionary nature attracted me. It is true that I partook thoroughly in the gratifications derived from belonging to a group of militant innovators. I enjoyed this role not because of fighting a skeptical world but because it appealed to the most consistent tradition in my personality. I grew up in an academic environment at a time in Europe when the heritage of the nineteenth century's cultural ideology was still powerful; indeed, it was at its peak. I mean the religious adoration of the arts, literature, and the basic sciences. When I read Freud's analysis of religion in his *Future of an Illusion,* it struck me forcefully that in dethroning the formal religions, without noticing it he injected his own nineteenth-century religion of science, which was first formulated by the French encyclopedists of the eighteenth century. My earliest memory is of when I was five years old, playing in my father's library. From the top of the high bookcases the busts of Aristotle, Plato, Spinoza, Kant, Voltaire, and Diderot were looking down on me. Sitting on the floor, I tried to decipher the golden letters on a heavy volume at the bottom of a bookcase. Finally I succeeded and triumphantly exclaimed the word, "Diderot." My father was sitting at his desk engaged in writing a book on Diderot, the greatest rationalist, the most erudite exponent of the religion of reason and science. Psychoanalysis, when I turned to it, did not represent a revolution at all, but the purest tradition, that of rationalism, the unerring pursuit of knowledge, an attempt to understand the irrational components of human behavior on a rational basis. Its revolutionary history—only incidental—is due to the inertia of the human mind which cannot at once assimilate a novel combination of ideas. My loyalty to Freud in his feud with the universities and medical societies did not in the least interfere with my admiration for the temple of science, the university, where my father had taught for fifty years. If I may try to reconstruct the Platonic ideal or, in our analytic language, the psychodynamic formula, which determined my own fate, it consists in relentless striving to reconcile these two loyalties, the one to the truth represented by psychoanalysis and the other to the traditional places of learning. This is the emotional source of a continued effort to lead psychoanalysis back to its original and legitimate place: to the university. I can only thank fate, which brought me to this country which believes in change and development and where the feud between Freud and official science was not so deeply rooted, where the repatriation of psychoanalysis was a realistic possibility.

It is difficult to foresee the course which the development of psychoanalysis will take in the future. There are those who would like the status quo to be preserved, psychoanalysis remaining an autonomous independent field apart from the other sciences of men, with its own teaching organizations and accreditation procedures. Others, like those in the Chicago Institute for Psychoanalysis, consider the isolated development of psychoanalysis a historical incident, the sources of which lie in Europe. We feel that as a method of treatment, psychoanalysis belongs to psychiatry, from which it sprang and with which it should be reunited. We feel that this is basically the only logical trend, that it cannot be checked, although it can be retarded by administrative measures which are dictated by the old fears and mistrusts. Those who want to see psychoanalysis become an integral part of psychiatry differ among themselves only as to the optimal speed with which this unification should take place. We believe that if not *de jure*, then *de facto*, psychoanalysis in the United States, where the majority of psychiatric residents consider training in psychoanalysis as the most important part of their curriculum, has already become an integral part of psychiatry. This course of events is not different from all social processes: legislation lags behind actual social change; legislation actually ratifies, sometimes quite belatedly, a state of affairs which has arisen according to the immanent logic of historical evolution.

We believe that the historical function of our Institute was and still is to liquidate the last remnants of mistrust and tension which in the past separated psychoanalysis from the rest of medicine, from psychiatry, and from the other social sciences. This requires more than effective teaching and demonstration of our methods, conceptual tools, and results. It requires that we abandon those defensive attitudes which developed at a time when psychoanalysis was emotionally rejected both by the public and by the academic world. I daresay that these defensive attitudes today are a greater obstacle than the emotional resistance of nonpsychoanalysts.

One of the most undesirable forms of defense is intolerance of criticism from others and insistence upon uniformity, both in theory and practice. The Institute in true academic tradition will continue to invite criticism from others and encourage differences of opinion among ourselves. Above all, we shall continue in our teaching to make students constantly aware of the preliminary nature of knowledge in our youthful field. In other words, we shall continue to have a greater reverence for what is still unknown in the complex field of human nature, than to be proud of the little we now know.

Impressions from the Fourth International Congress of Psychotherapy

◄ 1959 ►

The central topic of the Fourth International Congress of Psychotherapy, held in Barcelona, September 1-6, 1958, was the impact of existential philosophy on psychotherapy. Existential thought, while little known in this country, has become one of the outstanding cultural trends in contemporary Europe. American thought is characterized by its pragmatic heritage, and epistemologically the instrumental or operational points of view are prevalent in it. Existentialism, on the other hand, can be best characterized as a reaction against the pragmatic and the operational orientation. It returns to the traditional question of philosophy: What is the ultimate meaning of human existence? It puts emphasis not on the *how*, but on the *why, from where, for what,* and *where to.*

The steadily advancing scientific orientation of the last centuries is rejected by the existentialists, not as invalid, but as insufficient to answer the most meaningful questions of human existence. They often refer to the scientific orientation as "methodolatry," the worship of techniques by which, for the sake of exactness, the scientist blinds himself to the essential problems of humanity. It is no overstatement to say that the existentialist has a condescending, if not contemptuous, attitude toward the utilitarian trend characteristic of Anglo-Saxon philosophy, and that he substitutes for utility, as the supreme value, the self-realization of the unique individual personality. Although this is not explicitly stated, adjustment appears to be considered a necessary evil dictated by the laws of biological survival, but certainly not the *summum bonum* of life. It ultimately leads to conformism, which is the polar opposite of the existential credo, for existentialism wants to save the uniqueness of every human personality, the individual from

548

becoming submerged into the "faceless masses." What gives meaning to human existence is to find one's *authentic self*, a concept first introduced by the Danish philosopher, Søren Kierkegaard, the predecessor and patron saint of the existentialists.

The conference, as the preliminary announcements stated, was held under the spiritual aegis of Martin Heidegger, the German philosopher who is claimed to be the real originator of existentialism—and who was a pupil of the famous phenomenologist, Edmund Husserl, whose lectures I attended as a young medical student in Göttingen. During these meetings Heidegger was often compared to Freud, to whom some lip service was rendered by several of the main speakers. In the opinion of most existentialists, Freud made valiant beginnings in the exploration of the human personality, but eventually bogged down in technicalities. His main error was to try to apply the scientific method to the study of man. He became an applied scientist in contrast to Heidegger, who laid down the basic principles for the understanding of personality.

Many of the leading psychiatric representatives of existential thought were present. Ludwig Binswanger, who perhaps is at the top of this new hierarchy, sent a message which was read to the audience. Dr. Meddard Boss, originally a psychoanalyst from Zurich, trained in Berlin, gave one of the important orientation lectures. Other leading existential therapists who came were Dr. Freiherr von Gebsattel from Germany, Dr. Eugène Minkowski from Paris, who appeared in spite of his advanced age, and Dr. Viktor E. Frankl, professor of psychiatry in Vienna, who with his semireligious oratory obtained a veritable ovation. Professor Henri Ey from Salpetrière, Paris, gave the most concrete and lucid clinical presentation demonstrating the existential point of view. From the United States, existential therapy was represented by Dr. Rollo May, the Harvard psychologist, and Dr. Erwin Straus, who, however, did not discuss the central theme but gave a most original and convincing paper on infantile amnesia. Dr. Iago Galdston, from New York, gave a lucid historical review.

Most of the presentations were along orthodox existentialist lines. Here I may interpose an observation which I found most illuminating. This new school of thought—new so far as psychiatry is concerned—shows remarkable similarities to certain aspects of the early psychoanalytic movement. There is the tendency to set up a central authority as the father image of the group, in the person of Martin Heidegger. Then, in hierarchical order, follow the major disciples, reminiscent of those who originally gathered around Freud: Ludwig Binswanger, Karl Jaspers, Boss, Frankl, Gebsattel, and Straus. Jean Paul Sartre is considered a deviationist. Outside of Straus, the major American proponent of existentialism is Rollo May, who, however, seems to be looked upon as not entirely a pure specimen. Another American representative is Dr. H. Kelman from New York.

Rollo May gave a sober paper which lacked the passionate oratory and proselytizing fervor of most of the presentations. A young English existentialist, whose name I did not preserve, bitterly attacked May's dispassionately delivered paper, charging May with a remarkable lack of understanding of the essence of existentialism because he referred to William James' ideas as historically leading up to existential formulations. According to this critique, William James—and, of course, even more, John Dewey—represent the polar opposites of existential tenets, for pragmatism and instrumentalism are exactly those evil influences from which the existentialists are trying to rescue Western civilization. This utilitarian orientation perpetuates and fosters the atomization and fragmentation of human personality, which existential thinkers consider the most potent factor in producing "existential despair" in modern man—his estrangement from nature, from society, and, above all, from his own self. According to the existentialists, modern man has lost his God, his values, and, with these, the meaning of life. Existentialism is a saving response to this dehumanization of man, an attempt to restore to him his human dignity by a new philosophy of the meaning of existence. The vivid and profound realization of existence, of "being"—not in a static sense, but in a dynamic sense, as "becoming"—is the basic requirement for fulfilling one's latent potentialities. This experiencing of one's being is highlighted by the ever present realization of not-being, of death, a possibility which must be faced in every moment of life. This gives the impetus for finding one's authentic self and for self-realization. The so-called adjusted person who is freed from all his anxieties is looked upon as a subspecies. The attempt to free the patient from his normal existential anxiety is a futile and erroneous undertaking. Anxiety, the normal existential anguish, is an integral part of existence. It must be faced and tolerated.

The psychoanalyst exposed to these papers could not help but recognize in them some of the most important newer results of psychoanalytic research. The psychoanalyst refers to contemporary man, who has lost the meaning of life, as the man who has lost his ego identity. The concept of ego identity expresses essentially the same thing for which the existentialist uses the term, *authentic self*. The concept of self-realization is common to both schools of thought. Some existentialists distinguish three aspects of man—body, psyche, and soul; psyche encompasses the total of the personality, and soul corresponds to what the psychoanalyst means by integration on the highest level.

Every person has his own unique integrative pattern, and in

this sense the soul or the authentic self is unique for every person. To save this uniqueness from the leveling and fragmenting influences of industrial mass society is the main concern of the existentialists, as well as the main concern of most psychoanalysts—all those who have not fallen victims of a one-sided adaptational theory.

There were a number of psychoanalysts present at the Congress from France, Italy, Germany, Switzerland, and the United States. I was in charge of the Psychoanalytic Section. The vice-chairman of the Section was Dr. René Diatkin from Paris, a conservative analyst. Dr. Jacques Lacan from Paris, who belongs to the seceded psychoanalytic group, gave a provocative lecture, "La Psychanalyse vrai et la fausse." Although not an existentialist, he was on the whole in sympathy with some existentialist emphases.

The program listed a number of names from the United States. Some of them, such as Karl Menninger and Felix Deutsch, did not appear. Papers were given by May Romm, George Wayne, and myself from Los Angeles; Sandor Rado and Gregory Zilboorg from New York, and Jules Masserman from Chicago. Several Italian psychoanalysts presented papers, the Drs. Nicola Perotti, Emilio Servadio, J. Tolentino, and others. All in all, the psychoanalytic sessions represented a sideline, but two psychoanalysts—Boss and Zilboorg—spoke about the main topic. Boss was one of the official proponents of existential psychiatry, while Zilboorg delivered a politely critical paper warning against the dangers of letting philosophical generalizations take the place of concrete clinical studies. Rado's brilliant paper on adaptational psychotherapy attracted only a few people—probably because of the tabooed word, *adaptation*, in the title.

My presentation of our Los Angeles studies of the Therapeutic Process did not seem to be directly related to the main topic. It was announced as a special presentation, and I was given two hours for the paper and its discussion. My expectation that in the highly philosophical atmosphere of the Congress the presentation of a strongly empirical study would be out of place was not fulfilled, however. In the first place, I was fortunate enough to select the theoretical, even philosophical, presuppositions of our study, which met with considerable interest and provoked a constructive discussion. The lecture was delivered in the same large *aula* where the official papers were given, and it attracted a large audience. The other circumstance which explains the warm reception I received was the emphasis in our research upon the therapist's personality and on the radical departure from the blank-screen concept of the analyst. This orientation is very much akin to the existential analyst's stress upon the fact that in psychotherapy, as in psychoanalysis, two human personalities interect as two distinct, unique individualities. For this the existentialist's term is *encounter*.

This point was highlighted later in May Romm's presentation of the recording of one of her own interviews with one of our present research patients—a most beautiful example of a real encounter of two personalities during a therapeutic interview.

This may be the proper moment to try to formulate my own reactions to the existential movement in psychiatry. First, on the positive side I find that many of the propositions of the existentialists are reactions against the recent stress in psychoanalysis on technical details and routine, rather than the understanding of the patient as a unique personality, who must, in the first place, be accepted on his own terms, and not forced into a theoretical frame of generalizations. In fact, Rollo May, in his recent book on existentialism, came independently to some formulations about flexibility which are identical with my own formulations, published in the last ten years in several articles and books.[1] Another existential criticism, to which I can wholeheartedly subscribe, concerns a sterile and misunderstood form of preoccupation with past history. Of course, nothing is more important than the understanding of the patient's past development. But this should serve in treatment—which is not etiological research—to illumine the patient's present and even his future. The actual present, as it reveals itself in the interview situation, is the main concern, as well as the future, which evolves out of the present constellation and which is influenced by the therapeutic experience. Furthermore, the emphasis on the therapeutic experience as the primary therapeutic factor, giving to the intellectual digestion of this experience only a second place, is one which I share with the existentialists, and at which I arrived independently, not from philosophical deduction, but from actual practice.

The main objection which can be raised against existential writings is that often they attempt to describe psychological realities in terms of philosophical generalities, many of which are taken over from scholastic tradition. This is the case in spite of the contention that the existential approach is based on the most concrete and immediate phenomenological analysis of all the data of self-awareness. Some existentialists, like Boss, for example, frankly admit that their actual therapeutic approach does not differ essentially from the psychoanalytic approach; what they offer is a new philosophical outlook and a more comprehensive interpretation of the interview material, which is not in contradiction to psychoanalytic interpretations, but an addition to them. This outlook puts the separate dynamisms, the conflicts, the manifestations of transference and resistance in the perspective of the

[1] Rollo May, *Existence: A New Dimension in Psychiatry and Psychology;* New York: Basic Books, 1958.

totality of the individual unique personality. This is not different from what analysts call ego analysis. The term *integration* seldom, if ever, appears in existential literature, but actually what the existentialists are struggling with is the highest integrative aspects of self-awareness. Psychoanalysts consider integrative patterns to be unique for each person, and the true aim of the psychoanalytic approach is to find this specific unity of each person. The experiencing of the self as a unique example of all possible combinations is implicit in psychoanalysis. Furthermore, the contention of the existentialists that every mental act, such as perception and memory—not to speak of striving and making decisions—is an active, nay creative, phenomenon, has been stressed by psychoanalysts and by Gestalt psychologists. The old concept of the passive ego driven by the id, the superego, and external reality is yielding to a more dynamic picture of the ego, the main function of which is the exquisitely active, integrative, decision-making act.

Much of the existential contribution consists in restating this fundamental insight in old philosophical terms, which lack the clarity and precision of Gestalt psychological and psychoanalytical conceptualizations. This does not detract from the value of restating all this with a new emphasis, but the claim for novelty cannot be granted to the existentialists. Neither do I see much merit in the new use of old scholastic expressions, such as *potentia* for developmental possibilities, or *experiencing existence* and *being* (*Dasein*) for self-awareness, or reviving such scholastic pseudo-problems as the difference between essence and existence, or replacing with the poetic, visionary, and passionate language of a Kierkegaard or a Nietzsche the more sober but more precise and better-defined expressions with which Freud tried to describe and interpet the same fundamental facts of self-awareness which are the central issue in existentialism. Neither does it yield more profound insight to speak of the struggle of the neurotic to find his authentic self without explicitly acknowledging the fact that the most important factor in the fragmentation of the personality and the loss of ego identity is the fundamental failure of the neurotic ego in its integrative functions, excluding by repression, projection, and other well-described psychodynamic processes all that it cannot harmoniously reconcile within its unity. The role of multiple contradictory identifications is equally overlooked. The concepts of the dynamic unconscious and repression are circumvented by many existential psychiatrists, and it is difficult not to interpret this as an instinctive avoidance of the most basic discoveries of psychoanalysis, without which the inauthentic self of the neurotic remains a mere literary expression, or at best a general idea. The trend toward bombastic pathos in style, the tendency to confuse value judgments with factual observations, the propensity to preach instead of describe and explain are at least partially due to the fascination which the existentialists feel for Kierkegaard's and Nietzsche's highly intuitive but unsystematic—psychologically speaking—prescientific writings.

The most authentic existentialist presentations at the congress clearly displayed this tendency toward prophetic preaching, reminiscent of Biblical Jeremiads. The most enthusiastic reception was awarded the Viennese Frankl's exquisite oratory, delivered in the best German style. It was a veritable sermon, a blend of philosophical, psychological, and crypto-religious orientations. Less attention was paid to such sober and concrete papers as Ey's clinical presentation of the dream of a young woman expressing the rejection of the female role, and his attempt to demonstrate what I would call the ego-psychological implications of this dream. Rollo May's paper was also delivered in a sober, intellectual fashion, putting the existential approach in a historical perspective, and while it was attacked on the basis that it was tainted by American pragmatism, I suspect that the real reason for this rejection was the sobriety of the delivery, reminiscent of that "scientism" which is the *bête noir* of the existentialists.

Yet the existential movement cannot be simply ignored as an inconsequential trend in modern psychiatry. While its total impact has not yet reached American shores, it is one of the most influential currents in European philosophy and psychiatry. Primarily it is not a new contribution to the content of psychiatry or psychotherapy. It is a consistently formulated basic orientation. It is a vocal protest against the prevailing trend toward reducing the human individual to a cog in the social machinery. For such a society the uniqueness of the individual is useless; hence, it prefers to deal with him in his social role, and not as a distinct personality with the specific mission of realizing his unique potentialities. It emphasizes utility and adjustment—the polar opposite of creativity, for to be creative means to produce something which is not yet in existence; adjustment means to accept and to conform with what is already there. The existential revolution is inspired by the despair of the European man who feels threatened with reduction to the level of the faceless masses. It is a desperate cry for preserving the most specifically human aspect of man, his self-awareness as a unique being different from all others. Existentialism is the philosophical expression of this revolt, which manifests itself in all fields of human creativity, and, above all, in modern art and literature. More than in any other cultural era, the modern artist creates his own universe instead of depicting that which is around him; he reassembles the parts of the human body according to his own delight; if he is a cubist, he creates his own space, he changes, he exaggerates, he omits, and he may even completely disregard the world as it presents itself to the senses. In literature the dread of estrangement from the world and from the self—the existential despair—appears most effectively in the writings of Kafka, Rilke, and Camus, and in the nihilistic philosophy of Sartre.

Psychotherapy is a natural medium for absorbing the existentialist outlook. The way was prepared by psychoanalysis, for which every person is a unique problem, who must be understood in his own unique world. Existentialists who emphasize the principle that every patient must be understood in his own specific world, and not in general terms of universal mechanisms and conflicts, should not overlook the fact that the essence of Freud's endeavors as a therapist was precisely this highly individualistic orientation. One should not confuse psychoanalysis as a therapy with Freud's theory, which tries, as every scientific theory does, to formulate general principles which then have to be applied to each human being in the light of his specific features. From this perspective one must welcome the existential emphasis as a counterbalance to the prevailing trend of psychoanalytic practice and teaching—namely, the trend toward losing sight of the gap between theoretical generalizations and the individual patient, whose uniqueness of necessity requires a flexible application of general principles, toward replacing the individual approach to each specific person with rigid technical rules. This trend eventually leads to a deification of technique as an aim in itself, as the essence of psychoanalysis instead of a servant of its goals. And finally, by the challenge which the existential viewpoint places on psychoanalysts to re-examine the basic presuppositions of their own field, it counteracts both the dogmatic and naive acceptance of theoretical improvisations as final answers.

The Barcelona Congress left me strongly with the conviction that the existential movement in itself does not contribute to the actual and operational knowledge of psychoanalysis, but represents a general orientation which, with all its vague and awkward terminology and passionate style, with its relapse to a scholastic type of reasoning, with its confusion between descriptions and value judgments, nevertheless must be considered a profound cultural revolt against the dehumanizing propensities of modern life.

By devoting my attention to the central theme of the Congress, I am in danger of giving an incomplete picture. There were one thousand participants, who listened to or participated in presentations in all fields of psychiatry. There were sections, in addition to that on psychoanalysis, on clinical psychology, group therapy, psychodrama, psychosomatic medicine, psychotherapy and religion, psychopharmacology, hypnosis, forensic psychiatry, psychiatry's relation to cultural anthropology, child psychiatry, and social psychiatry, and a special session on the influence of Oriental psychology on contemporary psychotherapy. I participated in a meeting on psychosomatic medicine which was very ably conducted by Professor Van der Horst of Amsterdam. In this meeting he stated the basic propositions of the theory of specificity of psychological factors in psychosomatic disease, after which the meeting was thrown open to the floor and I was asked to answer all the questions on and criticisms of the specificity concept. This meeting was attended by about two hundred psychiatrists interested in psychosomatics, from a great many different countries.

The Conference was genuinely international, conducted in four languages—Spanish, French, German, and English, with a fairly well functioning translation system. I met visitors from all European countries, one representative from Yugoslavia, several from Israel, and one from Saudi Arabia. The Italian psychoanalysts were practically all present, and many came from France, Germany, and Switzerland. Professor D. Ramon Sarro, a teacher of psychiatry at the University of Barcelona, presided and gave one of the official lectures, on the interpretation of the Oedipus myth by Freud and by Heidegger. His thesis was the superiority of the Heidegger formulation.

The organization, particularly in the first few days, was extremely poor. No lectures started on time, and the speakers and the chairmen of the Sections had to search for their locations, which were often mixed up. The human aspects of the arrangements were, however, most impressive. The Spaniards were most hospitable and genuine in their kindness, very proud of their cultural heritage and personal dignity. For them, among human indignities, hurry is probably the worst. Everyone moves deliberately, observing all the formalities of social intercourse, showing the utmost respect for both the other person and for himself. We were wined and dined publicly and privately and entertained with folk dances, excursions, a special bullfight, and Catalonian art exhibits of the tenth and eleventh centuries. I found the living and working conditions of our Spanish confreres most enviable, whether in a penthouse in a modern apartment building, like Dr. Bofill-Tauler, the president of the Spanish psychoanalytic group, or in a century-old palace, like Professor Sarro, with two huge formal gardens surrounded by high stone walls.

The choice of Spain for an existentialist Congress was most appropriate. Spain is perhaps the country in the Western world which has, until very recently, remained most outside of the general industrial trend. Insistence on the uniqueness of the individual is here still a part of the whole cultural scene. The onslaught of collective industrial civilization finds here the most stubborn resistance, primarily on the psychological level. It is the country from which much of the existential spirit has emanated in the last fifty years. It is the country which has contributed the leading modern painter to the present era. It is the country of Miguel de Unamuno, and of José Ortega y Gassett, one of the most prophetic modern philosophers, and the author of the classic, *The Revolt of the Masses.* The existentialists claim him as one of their chief contemporary representatives. He starts his book by saying:

There is one fact which, whether for good or ill, is of utmost importance in the public life of Europe at the present moment. This fact is the accession of the masses to complete social power. As the masses, by definition, neither should nor can direct their own personal existence, and still less rule society in general, this fact means that actually Europe is suffering from the greatest crisis that can afflict peoples, nations, and civilization. . . . Towns are full of people, houses are full of tenants, hotels full of guests, trains full of travellers, cafes full of customers, parks full of promenaders, consulting-rooms of famous doctors full of patients, theatres full of spectators, and beaches full of bathers. What previously was, in general, no problem, now begins to be an everyday one, namely to find room.

And then he adds:

The mass crushes beneath it everything that is different, everything that is excellent, individual, qualified and select. Anybody who is not like everybody, who does not think like everybody, runs the risk of being eliminated.[2]

I could testify that the beautiful public parks in Madrid as well as in Barcelona are, indeed, crowded and enjoyed by the masses. Are they really as faceless as Nietzsche maintains? I haven't seen two Spaniards who look alike.

[2] José Ortega y Gasset, *The Revolt of the Masses,* New York: Norton, 1932; pp. 11-12, 18.

► *Six* ◄

Teaching of Psychoanalysis, Psychodynamics, Psychosomatics

Training Principles in Psychosomatic Medicine

◄ 1946 ►

The first prerequisite of sound teaching in any field is the clarification of fundamental principles and concepts. The psychosomatic approach, although as old as medicine itself, has developed only very recently from bedside manner and medical art into a method which is based on controlled observations and scientific concepts. It is not surprising, therefore, that there is not yet general agreement even concerning fundamental questions. Limitation of time does not permit discussion of the whole question of psychosomatic teaching, research, and practice; I shall therefore limit myself to the definition of the field and a clarification of some controversial issues. These considerations may serve as a basis for sound teaching in this field.

The term "psychosomatic" is principally used in two ways: 1) referring to a method of approach in research and therapy, a method which can be applied in the whole field of medicine; 2) referring diagnostically to certain conditions which some authors (Haliday) call "psychosomatic affections." The first use of the term, which is entirely methodological, is sound and generally accepted; the second, which is diagnostic, is open to controversy.

In my opinion one should restrict the meaning of "psychosomatics" to the methodological principle. In the present phase of our investigative techniques, certain body functions and their disturbances can best be studied by psychological methods, while other functions can only be approached by physiological methods. In studying the totality of organic processes, both methods must be applied at the same time in order to account for the whole phenomenon. For example, stomach secretion as an isolated process in itself can be studied only by the methods of biochemistry; its nervous control, however, cannot be studied completely by physiological methods alone because the latter cannot adequately account for certain central (emotional) influences

561

without utilizing psychological information. The fact that receptive dependent wishes mobilize stomach secretion cannot be ascertained by physiological methods alone because these wishes cannot be identified by any existing physiological technique. *Theoretically*, emotional influences can be studied also as brain processes; *practically*, however, this will be possible only after physiological techniques have been developed by which different emotions can be identified.

The same considerations hold true for the study of the disturbances of physiological functions. The disturbance of stomach secretion, as is observed in peptic ulcers, might be caused by different factors, both central and local, emotional and dietary. At the present state of our knowledge, there is no method of appraising the quantitative proportions of these various local and central factors in each case. We have good reason to believe that the emotional factor plays a significant role in the majority of cases. Haliday, himself, an ardent advocate of the concept of psychosomatic affection, in one of his recent articles refers to the peptic ulcer of cholorotic girls in which "physical" factors are important. Also in adult males and females, the emotional and nonemotional factors vary in relative significance from case to case. Peptic ulcer is not a nosological entity, but a symptom caused by a multiplicity of etiological factors which vary in different cases. Postoperative stomach ulcers in cases of mid-brain tumor (Cushing) have an etiology different from that observed in chronic cases which develop as a result of emotional tensions. And even in the latter types, faulty dietary habits may be of etiological importance.

The same is true for the etiology of bronchial asthma in which both allergic and emotional factors are present and have a complementary relationship to each other. The important fact is that the typical emotional factors which are found in certain organic diseases are present also in persons who show no organic symptoms. It is obvious, therefore, that emotional factors represent merely a category of factors which, only in combination with certain nonemotional factors, produce organic diseases. Psychosomatic affection, consequently, is an inappropriate concept: it implies the preponderance of emotional factors in certain affections, although the significance of emotional factors varies from case to case, and their relative importance in respect to coexisting nonemotional factors cannot be ascertained by our present investigative methods.

Ours is a very young field and the scattered knowledge that we have does not allow us to accept such an arbitrary diagnostic classification. Evidence is rapidly growing that in almost all chronic diseases emotional factors play an important role. The importance of the emotional factor varies from patient to patient. This might be the case even in certain chronic infectious diseases. If the expression "psychosomatic disease" means the presence of emotional factors of etiological significance, the major part of diseases are psychosomatic. It is much more appropriate, therefore, to limit the concept of psychosomatics to the study of the psychological component in organic diseases and to the therapy which attempts to influence this psychological component. This orientation will put an end to the present-day confusion.

At present, young physicians often express their desire to specialize in psychosomatic medicine. When urged to state concretely what they have in mind, it usually turns out to be a desire to specialize in the treatment of certain vegetative disturbances in which, in recent years, the etiological significance of emotional factors has been established. This obviously would lead to an anomalous specialization within medicine. Patients suffering from peptic ulcer, asthma, essential hypertension, disturbances of metabolism, and other conditions in which emotional factors play a role, will need in the future as in the past both organic and psychological treatment at the same time. The organic treatment requires, as it always has, a thorough knowledge of the existing medical specialties; the psychotherapeutic approach requires a thorough knowledge of psychiatry. Cooperation of psychiatrists with the different medical specialists will remain the only sound approach. While psychiatric teaching will need to become more and more an integral part of the training of every physician, psychotherapy will have to remain a specialty requiring specific and thorough training as does surgery.

Teaching Psychodynamics

◄ 1947 ►

The growing influence of psychiatry upon the theory and practice of medicine has by now developed to a degree which calls for a fundamental reorientation of undergraduate and postgraduate teaching.

In the undergraduate curriculum the teaching of psychiatry has two different functions. The first is that of presenting the fundamental principles of psychodynamics which must be considered as one of the basic sciences occupying a position similar to that of anatomy, physiology, physics, and chemistry. The understanding of the integrated behavior of the total organism requires, in addition to anatomy and physiology, a dynamic knowledge of personality functions. This knowledge should serve as the basis for the appraisal of the personality factors in medical diagnosis, etiology and prognosis, and for that part of therapy which is aimed to influence the personality factors. In the second place, undergraduate teaching gives the student a preliminary knowledge of psychiatric conditions.

My own experience in teaching the fundamentals of psychodynamics has increasingly impressed me with the limited value of theoretical lecture courses. Even when well-digested and clearly presented they remain more or less meaningless for the student if he is not confronted first hand with the empirical sources of the theoretical formulations and generalizations. I came to the conviction that most of the teaching of psychodynamics should be done in a rather unsystematic manner in connection with the demonstration of cases, using each case as a point of departure for abstractions and generalizations. Only a very general orientation course dealing with the basic facts of integrated behavior and emotional expression which can be illustrated by universal everyday experiences should be given before the student undertakes interviewing and presenting cases in clinical demonstrations. This orientation course should also deal with the methods of psychological investigation, and the theory of interviewing, and should be given during the first two years of the curriculum.

564

Clinical demonstrations should follow in the junior year and continue during the senior year. In the senior year a special psychiatric and psychopathological demonstration course on a more advanced level should complete the undergraduate training. All theoretical teaching with the exception of the first orientation course should be done in connection with such case demonstrations. The desirability of a systematic theoretical course in psychopathology and genetic psychology at the end of the curriculum in the senior year is an open question. Even the best course of this type is of limited value and does not add much more to the theoretical instruction which the students have had in connection with case demonstrations. It is quite possible, however, that after a good textbook has been written in this field such a course could be given to advantage.

Regarding postgraduate teaching, I shall restrict myself to a discussion of the psychiatric teaching of internes, medical men in general practice, and medical specialists outside of psychiatry. My experience concerning postgraduate training is based primarily on teaching in the psychoanalytic institutes of Berlin and Chicago and postgraduate teaching in the psychiatric department of the University of Illinois. To present my point of view it will be necessary to say a few words about the development of psychoanalytic training of psychiatrists, because our experiences with this also apply, to a great degree, to the postgraduate training of nonpsychiatrists.

In psychoanalytic institutes in the past there was a tendency to stress the indoctrination of the student with the theoretical concepts of psychoanalysis as a preliminary to his practical training consisting in supervised analyses and case seminars. Recently, there is a consistent trend in our Institute as well as in some other places of psychoanalytic training to emphasize clinical training versus a too rigid theoretical indoctrination. The basic principles of psychodynamics and therapeutic procedure probably should continue to be taught but with greater clarity and economy. We are avoiding, however, the superabundance of theoretical concepts which belong to the different historical phases of psychoanalysis. Our emphasis is more and more on keeping the student in constant touch with observational material, best done by teaching theory in connection with concrete case histories. My belief is that most of the theoretical teaching can be done this way. It is a less systematic form of teaching than was customary in the past, but far more sound and effective, and should be even more constantly applied in the teaching of medical men who do not intend to become psychiatrists.

Before going into further details, I wish to put this present clinical orientation in teaching into historical perspective. Psychoanalysis appeared as a reaction against the purely descriptive psychiatry of the nineteenth century. It is only natural that therapy, so long as the nature of psychiatric conditions was not understood, had to be merely empirical and therefore highly ineffective. At the end of the last century, when in the whole field of medicine the understanding of causes became the trend, psychiatry also began to turn toward a more etiological orientation. Explanation took the place of mere description. Psychoanalysis was the main representative of this trend. The quest for understanding stimulated the development of theoretical systems. The large observational material, unearthed by the development of psychological investigative techniques by Freud, called for a system of theoretical concepts and hypotheses. As in other fields of medicine, there followed a period characterized by a superabundance of abstractions and hypotheses. As is so often the case, these theoretical constructions began to lead their own lives without their relationship to facts being sufficiently reinforced by constant revision. This was true also in psychoanalysis in spite of the fact that Freud himself was a courageous revisionist of his own theories. Among his followers there was a tendency to attribute a finality to his working hypotheses. This was true both as far as theory and therapeutic procedure were concerned. Many of these somewhat crude concepts, such as that of the structural theory of personality were excellent guideposts for an initial orientation, but if taken too literally they blocked more precise understanding of the personality. More or less vague abstractions, such as narcissism or sublimation, after they served their initially useful purpose of general orientation, later interfered with a more detailed study of the great variety of phenomena to which they refer. As a whole, theory and psychodynamic knowledge, which became more and more precise, lost intimate contact with each other.

In teaching, this manifested itself most clearly in the discrepancy of many of our students' ability to understand precisely individual cases, and their inability to formulate this understanding in the framework of psychoanalytic theory. And vice versa, other students who were strongly indoctrinated saw in their patients only the generalizations of the doctrine and failed to understand the individual structure of their patients. Nevertheless, the student of psychoanalysis who will become a psychiatrist must be acquainted with all phases of psychoanalytic theory, preferably more in a critical than in a merely didactic presentation. This is not true to the same degree for the general medical man. What he needs is a solid foundation in the basic principles of psychodynamics and in the methods of the psychiatric interview. He should be able to understand the nature of the personality factors in his cases; that is to say, he must be trained in the psychosomatic approach to the patient. As I stated a year ago at this same meeting, I do not believe that there is a medical specialty such as psychosomatics, nor a group of diseases which can be called psychosomatic affections. I consider psychosomatics a point of view which should be applied in the whole field of medicine in the study and in the therapy of every case. In order to train a medical man in the psychosomatic point of view, one must teach him primarily the principles of psychodynamics and the techniques of studying personality factors. And, above all, he must learn this on the basis of firsthand information from patient material.

Since we have only very recently begun to teach medical men in this new approach it would be premature to introduce rigid regulations and red tape into their teaching. We must feel our way and find the best methods by which we can offer medical men the type of information they need to improve their medical activities in their respective fields. We must give special consideration to the growing group of investigators using the psychosomatic approach. These pioneers, belonging to different branches of medicine, should be offered an individual type of instruction according to their needs and interests. A pediatrician interested in the psychosomatic approach to children will need a type of training in many respects different from a man who is working in the field of metabolic research. It is most important to be aware of the fact that we are teaching a field which is yet in its beginnings, is in constant flux both in regard to its theoretical conceptions and factual knowledge. We should therefore refrain from formulating prematurely a standard curriculum, and retain an experimental spirit and an individual approach.

To summarize my opinion, sound teaching of psychiatry requires a critical evaluation of the state of our field. We have a sound foundation of psychodynamic knowledge; we know a great deal of what can be called the logic of emotions. We have developed an effective method of studying and understanding the motivational dynamics of human behavior. All this can be taught safely to undergraduate medical students as an integral part of their curriculum. We must realize at the same time that our theoretical abstractions superimposed upon this fundamental knowledge require constant critical revision and further improvement regarding conceptual precision and clarity. This is true for every theoretical superstructure in every field. It is particularly true in our young discipline in which theory has been prematurely developed into a consistent system and has tended to become dogmatic and rigid. The same is true for our therapeutic technique. Our teaching of theory and therapy, therefore, must be less didactic and more critical. This critical tenor of psychiatric teaching is particularly important in postgraduate training.

Psychoanalytic Education
for Practice

◄ 1961 ►

My report will not focus on reviewing our present training practices which have been so well summarized by the Lewin-Ross Report,[1] but on discussing desirable improvements in the spirit and the content of our educational system. Suggesting reforms, however, requires critical evaluation of the prevailing procedures. This task is greatly facilitated by the careful and authentic descriptions of Bert Lewin and Helen Ross. They deserve credit both for the completeness and considerable objectivity of their presentation. The great value of such nonevaluative fact-finding reports is that they make further improvements possible. Unfortunately, they also can be used not only for codification of prevailing practices, but for the perpetuation of their defects. I shall try to bring into focus those features of our present educational system which call for reforms.

The weaker a prevailing educational system is, the greater is the danger of abusing a merely descriptive report for codification of its errors.

For many years the psychoanalytic community could be roughly divided into two large groups. They are not opposing each other in basic concepts of psychoanalytic theory. They differ somewhat more in their emphasis on certain aspects of the treatment. But even these differences, although on some questions quite definite, are not fundamental. They overlap and it would not be possible to differentiate the two factions simply on the basis of their divergent orientation towards treatment. The real difference between these two groups consists in the degree of their satisfaction with prevailing standards in training, practice and theory. The one group is markedly more dissatisfied than the other with the state of affairs in our field. Such differences, of

[1] B. D. Lewin and H. Ross, *Psychoanalytic Education in the United States,* New York: Norton, 1960.

568

course, are present in all fields: in politics, in economy, in art, and in the sciences. Usually one refers to the more satisfied group which wants to perpetuate the status quo, as conservative. The dissatisfied ones are called variously as "individualists," "progressives," "radicals," or, to use a phrase of Lewin and Ross, "eccentrics." The epitheton with the most negative connotation is "deviationist," who frequently is no longer tolerated in the fold.

The more advanced a discipline is, that is to say, the better established the validity of its fundamentals is, the more it can indulge in the luxury of tolerating, even welcoming, differences of opinion. In such advanced fields there is no fear lest new propositions will undermine the solid foundations.

There are two situations in which differences of orientation do not exist. The one is rare and exists perhaps only in theory, namely, when the codified knowledge and practices are so perfect that further advancement is neither necessary nor possible. The second condition is a common one: it is characteristic of young disciplines where stringent evidence of theoretical generalizations is lacking, and where practices are based not primarily on well-established precise concepts, but more on tradition, on ingrained habits and on some general, not fully tested, assumptions inherited from earlier days. These are the conditions which breed intolerance against reform and an inclination to defend the prevailing notions not with cogent arguments, not with careful unbiased observation and experiment, but by authoritative assertions. This intolerance for differences of opinion and practices is an unmistakable sign of insecurity. Dogmatic allegiance to prevailing views and partisanship substitute for close reasoning and factual well-controlled evidence. The paradoxical nature of this type of conservatism is evident. Just in fields where a free experimental spirit is needed and where there is a desperate need for improvement, one sees a deadly paralyzing insistence on prevailing standards of teaching and practice.

Psychoanalytic training for practice is precisely such a field. The general principles of psychodynamic theory rest on more solid foundations than their practical application to treatment. This explains why tolerance for new theoretical concepts is somewhat greater among psychoanalysts than is tolerance for changes in treatment procedure. The prevailing theory and the rules of practice are most jealously guarded. Anything which deviates from an illusory model—illusory because it is taught but not actually practiced—is rejected with the time-worn formula: "This may be fine therapy but it is no longer psychoanalysis."

All these emotional investments make the education for practice such a difficult but such an urgent topic for discussion. A rigid organization of education according to traditionally sanctioned standards of necessity perpetuates the prevailing practices: their merits, but also their defects. Lack of strict organization, on the other hand, which gives a far-reaching freedom to carefully selected teachers, seems to be most desirable in a new and complex field pregnant with a large amount of uncertainties. Such a free educational system, however, leads to another kind of difficulty. The question can be justifiably raised: "Why should one assume that in a young and not yet exact discipline the deviant orientation of certain teachers is sounder than the accepted standard?" Just because of the relative inexactness of the field, experience and tradition rate highly. Even if the deviant view were sounder, it is difficult to demonstrate its validity. Accordingly, common-sense wisdom would dictate to rely on a traditional procedure. It can be argued that even with its admitted weaknesses, it is still the best we have. The wisdom of such an empirical position can hardly be questioned. Yet it necessarily slows down progress and perpetuates not only the merits but also the weaknesses of the traditional procedure.

What is then the best policy to preserve the achievements of the past without jeopardizing badly needed improvements? Only a thorough and open-minded evaluation of the prevailing standards can answer this vital question. Such an evaluation will have to center around three points: 1) What are in the present developmental phase of psychoanalysis the advantages and the disadvantages of a highly standardized and uniform training program? How much initiative and latitude for differences should be left to the local institutes? 2) How far should the institutes, but also outside organizations, such as universities and research clinics, be encouraged for a critical evaluation of standard training procedures? Or, to put this question more pointedly: Is it desirable, nay, imperative at the present time for institutes to foster research programs in the therapeutic process which could provide sound guidance for teaching sound practices? And finally, 3) what are those aspects of the currently taught treatment procedure which appear at present even before methodical studies are carried out questionable and require testing, and possibly even radical reforms?

I shall try to take up these three questions in sequence.

1. The American Psychoanalytic Association's attitude to the first question concerning the value of a highly standardized and uniform training program versus greater local autonomy of institutes, is known. It was not long ago when the then prevailing autonomy of local institutes was curtailed and minimal standards of training were introduced and universally enforced, overruling a minority opinion which favored local autonomy. This caused great tension and threatened to disrupt

the unity of the American Psychoanalytic Association. To avoid such a rupture, the minority with gaining only small concessions yielded to the majority view.

The Lewin-Ross Report gives interesting historical data illustrating the growing organization of training, but is strangely silent about this critical phase of psychoanalytic history in the United States.

It is common knowledge that there was and still exists a considerable minority which believes that many of the prevailing regulations of training are unnecessarily rigid, that local autonomy of institutes would have greater advantages than drawbacks. It would stimulate further improvement of our educational system by encouraging a more experimental and self-critical attitude in the institutes. The conservative opinion, on the other hand, proudly points out that the enforcement of minimal standards reduced some defects and laxities of previous days, and made the teachers more conscientious. Particularly —it is argued—the numerical rules prescribing a minimum number of interviews in training analyses, a minimum of supervisory hours and the frequency of interviews in treatment, ensured the thoroughness of the personal analysis of the candidates and the supervision of their clinical work. Indeed, if one considers merely the formal quantifiable aspects of training, the Lewin-Ross Report reads encouragingly. It appears that there prevails now a great order in our educational system.

Unfortunately, the value of these organizational measures cannot be ascertained by figures alone. The question is, how do the numerical rules and uniform standards influence the moral aspects of training? How do they influence the morale of the teachers and of the students? More specifically, the question is whether or not these numerical regulations introduced a greater evil than the individual laxities of the past, when training was less uniformly regulated and centrally controlled. I mean the evil of fostering formalistic perfunctory attitudes both in students and teachers. Does this uniform and standardized system encourage striving for more knowledge? Does it encourage self-criticism? Does it produce more effective practitioners? Can individual conscience and thirst for knowledge be replaced by fulfilling formalized quantifiable requirements which, to a considerable degree, are arbitrary because they are not supported by factual evidence, but by tradition sanctioned by custom? Does such uniformity have a levelizing influence downwards because it does not allow sufficient individualization and imposes upon the gifted candidates standards which may be necessary for the average? In brief, does this standardized system produce better therapists?

Among the many undesirable results of the uniform numerical training rules one striking anomaly came recently to my attention dur-

ing my supervisory activities. In several instances the regulation that
the student must have at least fifty supervisory hours on a case in order
to get credit for it occasioned highly unhealthy therapeutic situations.
These candidates were concerned that the patients might leave the
treatment before the fifty supervisory sessions had been reached, because of certain transference difficulties or other resistances, or in one
instance because the treatment was ready to be terminated. These candidates quite naturally became concerned and tried to hold on to the
patients by any means. Their concern was intuitively perceived by the
patients, who exploited this situation as a powerful weapon—for emotional blackmail—threatening the therapists with leaving treatment if
the latter did not give them more attention and satisfy their unconscious needs. Many other instances could be cited demonstrating the
fact that psychoanalytic treatment does not lend itself to regulation
by arbitrary, rigid, quantitative rules and requires that the therapist
flexibly adjust the treatment procedure to the ever changing exigencies
of the existing dynamic situation. In many instances these types of
numerical regulations are contradictory to the best interests of the patients whose treatments are carried out under supervision. At the same
time, such regulations undermine the candidates' confidence in the
soundness of our educational system.

The cardinal test of therapeutic procedures in the whole field of
medicine is therapeutic result. Everyone knows, however, the difficulties of evaluating therapeutic results. The answer to all these disturbing questions, therefore, will have unfortunately to wait until
systematic controlled studies of the therapeutic process and results
will decide whether the presently taught standardized treatment procedure is really the most effective therapeutic application of our basic
psychodynamic knowledge.

We have, indeed, a great order in our educational system. Did
this great order help to better approach our educational ideals? One is
reminded of an anecdote. A poor man complained to his friend about
his immediate need for a loan. The friend advised him to ask Baron
Rothschild for it. He went to the palace of the famous banker, while
the friend waited outside. The doorman referred the beggar to a
secretary who gave him a slip with instructions to present it on the
second floor in a certain room. On the second floor he received another slip which directed him to the fourth floor, where another secretary gave him a slip which led him back to the doorman. The doorman
opened the gate and kicked him out into the street. The waiting friend
asked with curiosity, "Well, did you receive your loan?" The beggar replied, "No, not that, but you should see the organization!"

I do not propose to give a final evaluation of the merits of our
present system of training for psychoanalytic practice. At present I

can only raise questions and express my doubts about the merits of the premature standardization of the treatment procedure and the enforced indoctrination of our students with it.

Only an open-minded and self-critical evaluation of results, and even more, the critical study of the therapeutic process by experimental variation of the inherent variables can give us further information. The descriptive report of prevailing methods of training by Lewin and Ross must be followed now by critical studies of the therapeutic value of the standardized treatment method which we are teaching to our students with such uniformity and infallible certainty.

2. This brings me to the discussion of my second point. Should, at the present state of affairs, the obligation of the institutes remain merely to teach a standardized procedure, or is it equally—perhaps even more important—that the institutes engage also in research into the theoretical soundness, practical effectiveness and economy of the procedure which we teach?

The study of the therapeutic process which we have undertaken in the Mount Sinai Hospital in Los Angeles,[2] as well as similar studies undertaken by others,[3] in particular, those of Strupp and his collaborators,[4] seem to indicate that our present theoretical conceptions about the therapeutic process are highly schematic and disregard some of its significant aspects. Indeed, the actual transactional processes between patient and physician have been neglected and were not fully accounted for in our prevailing theory of treatment. From the direct observation of the actual happenings between patient and therapist by nonparticipant observers, a more realistic picture evolves. It appears that the neglected aspects of the treatment are of fundamental importance. The full understanding of their significance will necessarily lead to a revision of many of the prevailing rules which we are teaching to our students. In other words, we are teaching something which is highly schematic, and is often quite removed from reality. Such observations even indicate that some antitherapeutic factors are inherent in some aspects of the standard psychoanalytic treatment, factors which are currently considered essential and therapeutic. The preliminary results of these investigations which are based on actual observation of the process are sufficiently impressive to call for their energetic continuation by as many psychoanalytic research workers as at

[2] Franz Alexander, "Unexplored Areas in Psychoanalytic Theory and Treatment," in this volume.

[3] H. Bolgar, "Values in Therapy," in Jules Masserman (ed.) *Science and Psychoanalysis*, Vol. III: *Psychoanalysis and Human Values*, New York: Grune & Stratton, 1960.

[4] Hans H. Strupp, *Psychotherapists in Action*, New York: Grune & Stratton, 1960.

all possible. Indeed, these preliminary studies affirmed my conviction—which I have had for thirty years since the organization of the Chicago Psychoanalytic Institute—that further research in our field is a primary requirement for forging from our basic psychodynamic knowledge an improved therapeutic tool.

Looking back on my own experience from the time when I was a student of the Berlin Psychoanalytic Institute in the early twenties until the present day, I am mostly impressed by the striking fact that this highly complex and delicate procedure underwent so few essential changes since it was developed by the intuitive genius of Freud. At the same time, psychoanalytic theory made considerable advances since the early 1920's when Freud's books on *Beyond the Pleasure Principle* and on *Inhibitions, Symptoms and Anxiety* and *The Ego and the Id* were published.[5] One often refers to this as the development of ego psychology. The advancement consisted primarily in viewing psychological processes no longer in an isolated manner, but as processes which take place in an organized system: the total personality. Indeed, in this respect the publications before and after this change in orientation are strikingly different. In contrast, Freud's technical recommendations in his five classical papers on psychoanalytic treatment published between 1912 and 1915 still serve with small additions as the basic guiding principles of psychoanalytic treatment.[6] Pragmatically stated, a psychoanalyst who was trained in the Berlin Institute in the twenties uses today just about the same procedure which is called classical psychoanalysis. As I mentioned before, such a relatively small amount of change can be explained only two ways: either the original procedure is so perfect that it does not require any major improvement or this stagnation must be due to the general trend of the human mind to adhere to knowledge arduously acquired in the past and abhor relearning. We know this dynamic trend under the name of "fixation." This inertia—the tendency to rest on the laurels of the past —is powerfully supported by what has been so well described by Allan Wheelis as the principle of institutionalization.[7] Even individual persuasions and convictions change slowly. When they become formalized and codified in institutions they become petrified. A thor-

[5] Sigmund Freud, *The Ego and the Id,* New York: Norton, 1960; *Inhibitions, Symptoms and Anxiety,* London: Hogarth, 1936; *Beyond the Pleasure Principle,* New York: Liveright, 1960.

[6] S. Freud, "The Employment of Dream-Interpretation in Psycho-analysis," "The Dynamics of the Transference," "Recommendations to Physicians Practising Psycho-analysis," "Further Recommendations on the Technique of Psycho-analysis, I: Beginning the Treatment; II: Remembering, Repeating, and Working Through; III: Observations on Transference-Love," all in *Collected Papers,* Vol. II, New York: Basic Books, 1959.

[7] Allan Wheelis, *Quest for Identity,* New York: Norton, 1958.

ough historical evaluation of psychoanalysis will find that in our field the conservative trend in treatment methods has been remarkably strong. Advancement in treatment practice did not keep pace with advancing psychodynamic knowledge. The result is that the thoughtful practitioner after graduation sooner or later—sometimes unnoticed by himself—practices under the exigencies of his daily work differently from what he learned in the school. In my experience this discrepancy between actual practice and teaching in the schools is steadily growing. The new emphasis on psychoanalytically oriented psychotherapy, which is being used more and more widely both by experienced and young practitioners, is one of the signs of this discrepancy. Do our institutes give sufficient attention to the growing trend toward psychoanalytically oriented psychotherapy? This trend I consider a most significant development in the field of psychiatry, far outstripping the significance of advancements in psychopharmacology. In contrast to this rather unchanging state of affairs in the field of psychoanalytic treatment, in other fields of medicine revolutionary advancements have taken place. Practices and theories prevailing forty years ago are mostly dated.

It is a worthwhile undertaking to inquire into the causes of this striking discrepancy between the rate of change in medical and psychoanalytic practice. Is the desire for advancement less intensive in our field? Or is our inertia due to unfortunate historical circumstances, such as the need to protect our new field from its uninformed critics and even more from self-appointed charlatans? This need for protection is what motivates primarily the trend toward premature standardization and overorganization. To protect the field from charlatans is important indeed. Yet, the price which we pay by this method of protection appears too high a price. The remedy we use may be more harmful than the disease. By our rigid regulations and enforced conformity of thought and practice, we ligate the life blood of scientific advancement: free inquiry and self-criticism.

3. All this can be stated in more concrete terms when we turn to the last point and try to spell out those aspects of the currently taught treatment procedure where radical changes are indicated and are actually taking place in the daily practice of analytically oriented psychiatrists.

Since Freud gave up hypnotic catharsis and tried to recover repressed memories in the waking state—first by suggestion and later by free association—the emphasis shifted more and more toward giving the patient insight into the origins of his ailment. The dramatic emotional abreactions in cathartic hypnosis were replaced by the intellectual process of gradually gaining insight. It was fortunate, said Freud, that the aims of therapy now coincide with the aims of research. The patient in order to recover, the therapist in order to learn, had to reconstruct the past pathogenic experiences. Free association in a permissive objective atmosphere, was the method to achieve this goal. As soon, however, as the emotional involvements of the patient with his physician had been discovered, the emphasis shifted more and more toward the emotional experiences in transference. Now the avenue toward cure was no longer simply remembering but emotionally reliving on the couch the pathogenic past experiences in relation to the therapist. The two factors, cognitive insight and emotional experience, finally fused into one indivisible unity in the concept of the corrective emotional experience. This concept emphasizes the difference between the original pathogenic and the actual interpersonal involvement between patient and therapist, and considers this difference as the primary therapeutic agent. This therapeutic factor has been in different terms emphasized by Strachey,[8] Sterba,[9] and myself.[10] The original persons in the patient's early life were neither fully objective nor solely interested to help the patient to understand himself. The child and his siblings and parents interacted with each other in the family and all dramatis personae were emotionally involved with each other. The therapist's attitude is uninvolved and this uninvolvement is the key to the corrective value of the treatment. The repetition of old patterns of feelings and behavior in this new setting challenges the ego to find new patterns more appropriate to the new situation. Uninvolvement, however, is a negative concept. Does the difference between the therapist's attitude and the original parental attitudes consist merely in the therapist's uninvolvement? And is the therapist really completely uninvolved? What about his own values, his theoretical orientation and expectations? The question how the therapist as a person influences the course of the therapeutic process is gaining more and more attention. Theoretically, of course, much has been written about this subject. Examples are recent articles by Jerome D. Frank,[11] and by Clara Thompson.[12] Only recently this topic has been subjected to systematic study based on the observation of the

[8] J. Strachey, "The Nature of the Therapeutic Action of Psychoanalysis," *Int. J. Psychoanal.*, XV (1934).

[9] R. Sterba, "The Fate of the Ego in Analytic Therapy," *Int. J. Psychoanal.*, XV (1934).

[10] Franz Alexander, "Analysis of the Therapeutic Factors in Psychoanalytic Treatment," in this volume; "The Quantitative Aspects of Technique," *J. Am. Psychoanal. Assn.*, II, 4 (1954); *Psychoanalysis and Psychotherapy*, New York: Norton, 1956.

[11] Jerome D. Frank, "The Dynamics of the Psychotherapeutic Relationship," *Psychiatry* (1959).

[12] C. Thompson, "The Role of the Analyst's Personality in Therapy," *Am. J. Psychotherapy*, X (1956).

process of sound and film records. I refer particularly to the studies of Strupp and his collaborators,[13] those of Frank,[14] of Leary and Gill,[15] and of Saslow and Matarazzo.[16] In the Mount Sinai Hospital we are also engaged in a study of the therapeutic process, which is focused mainly on the therapist's individual personality.[17]

I should like to point out that the technical consequences of this *difference* between the pathogenic past experiences and the interpersonal events between therapist and patient has not yet been drawn, either in theory or in practice. It is not given sufficient consideration in our teaching. The procedure which we are actually practicing differs essentially from the model we are teaching to our students. According to the latter, the therapist tries to achieve a kind of incognito which cannot be achieved by the very nature of the transactional process, and which if it could be realized would minimize the therapeutic effectiveness of the treatment procedure. This model is still based on the concept that the transference is a one-sided affair and is solely determined by the patient's past experiences. It was assumed that to make the undisturbed transference repetition of the infantile neurosis possible, the therapist must remain in complete incognito. He should try to protect his incognito by not reacting to the patient's material in any other way but by interpreting it. Interpretation means to point out connection with the past pathogenic patterns and their repetition in transference and the patient's actual behavior in life, and to point out the patient's resistance against recognizing these connections. This is the conceptual model on which our treatment rules are founded.

It is remarkable that in spite of the growing popularity of the countertransference phenomenon, the official therapeutic model has not changed. The existence of countertransference—noted by Freud as early as 1910—necessarily invalidates the *blank screen concept*. A blank screen does not react, only reflects. It does not contribute anything to the picture projected upon it. The full recognition of the countertransference phenomenon should introduce the therapist into the therapeutic equation as an individual person with his own idosyn-

---

13 H. Strupp, *op. cit.*

14 J. D. Frank, *op. cit.*

15 T. Leary and M. Gill, "Dimensions and Measures of the Psychotherapeutic Process." My comments are based upon the version of the system presented at the research conference; it has since been revised.

16 G. Saslow and J. D. Matarazzo, "A Technique for Studying Changes in Interview Behavior," in *Progress in Psychotherapy*, Vol. IV, New York: Grune & Stratton, 1958.

17 N. A. Levy, "An Investigation into the Nature of the Therapeutic Process— A Preliminary Report," in Jules Masserman (ed.), *Progress in Psychotherapy*, Vol. V, New York: Grune & Stratton, 1960.

cratic qualities. In order to avoid a more radical reformulation of the theory of treatment, there is a tendency to regard the countertransference merely as an impurity which should be minimized by further personal analysis of the therapist. At present the concept of countertransference is, indeed, but a qualifying footnote in our teaching. Teachers vary in their dealing with the subject. It cannot be overlooked in the supervision of candidates. One of the most common criticisms of a candidate's work is that "he is too much involved with his patient," or that "he identifies himself too much with the patient." The customary conclusion is that the candidate needs further personal analysis until he sufficiently becomes free from his own neurotic residues, and can more fully live up to the ideal of an uninvolved emotionally non-participant objective observer. Undoubtedly, very often an overinvolvement on the part of the therapist actually exists. Yet, the quoted typical remarks imply that the goal should be to approach the image of the therapist as an impersonal, de-emotionalized, pure intellect who does not reveal his own personality in the least. This whole picture becomes, however, confused when one observes in supervisory activity the often extremely beneficial influences of the candidate's particular countertransference reactions. Only recently a young candidate presented to me a case with good therapeutic results. It consisted in a marked improvement in sexual activity and spectacular occupational successes, following a long period of almost complete failures. A distinct personality change was unmistakable. I asked the candidate whether he could account psychodynamically for these remarkable therapeutic achievements. Without hesitation he answered that this patient was his "favorite child." He looked forward to the interviews. He enjoyed the patient's talent, his wit and his whole personality. The patient's history revealed that from his very early childhood he was deprived of paternal guidance and acceptance. His father was consistently absent from home and played practically no role in the family. The patient had to deal alone with a controlling and at the same time very seductive mother. The therapist's countertransference happened to supply just that type of an emotional experience which the patient never had, and which was essential for his recovery. In this atmosphere under the guidance of an understanding, warm, and helpful father surrogate, a belated personality growth became possible, and the patient's fear of and flight from women was halted. He mustered more courage for experimentation and a much belated identification with a father image could take place. With this developmental link missing, the patient's emotional maturation was not possible. This sensitive and intuitive candidate obviously was not troubled by the "bugaboo" of emotional involvement, and permitted his natural inclinations to color the therapeutic climate in the desired direction. In this specific case his countertransference reaction had a desirable effect, and one wonders whether a poker-faced therapist with a studied reserve and detachment could have achieved the same results. Of course, one must hasten to add that countertransference attitudes can as often disturb and obviate the therapeutic process as help it.

I do not feel that I should give further examples to illustrate the outstanding significance of the parameter which we may call the therapist's personality. It is obvious that in preparing our student for practice, this aspect of the treatment process cannot be neglected. On the other hand, what can we teach in this unexplored area? The answer is that the students must recognize the tremendous uncertainties and gaps in our present-day knowledge. Our students are not children who must be protected from facing the crude facts of life. To overrule doubts and uncertainties with dogmatic indoctrination by inadequate concepts and rules of treatment deduced from these inadequate concepts, is certainly not the answer. The teaching of the theory of the treatment must contain at the present stage of knowledge a great many question marks. Instead of generalized sweeping theoretical formulations, the emphasis must be even more today on individualized teaching, using actual case material. The focus of our education should be to teach psychodynamic reasoning. Attention given to the candidate's personality as it enters in his therapeutic activities is already becoming an important part of supervision. Most important is that differences of opinion among teachers in this unsettled area should not be discouraged, but freely incorporated in the teaching of every institute. There are those who still consider countertransference merely as an evil to be eradicated by more and more training analysis. Others believe that better self-knowledge of the candidate may make him able to recognize and control his countertransference reactions. Another opinion that I share with other authors is that countertransference is only one of the manifestations of the therapist's personality. Instead of allowing the individual countertransference attitudes to enter haphazardly into the therapeutic work, the therapist should learn to create planfully a suitable interpersonal climate which will further the patient's ego development and readaptations. This desirable emotional climate can be well deduced from knowing the history of the patient's personality development and should substitute for spontaneous unconsciously determined countertransference reactions.

A similar, equally important question concerns the problem of interruption and termination of the treatment. Here again, certain attitudes became traditional in our field. It is held that the longer an analysis lasts the greater is the hope for recovery. Experience contradicts this generalization: this is the exception and not the rule. Equally unproven is another tenet, that therapy should be as much as possible a continuous process; interruptions are a necessary evil permissible only for such practical considerations as the therapist's illnesses or his need for a vacation. Underlying all these concepts are not well-established facts, but vague unsubstantiated traditional beliefs. Indeed, the therapeutic effects of psychoanalysis are unpredictable. There are strong indications that even after long analysis, important therapeutic results develop after the termination of the treatment. The importance of the critical postanalytic year is widely recognized. Obviously, the treatment released or initiated further personality growth. It appears that the most lasting changes occur not on but after the couch.

Transference cures after brief contact with the therapist are known to practically every psychoanalyst. The usual prediction, however, that they cannot be lasting because early conflicts have not been worked through or even touched upon, often proves to be fallacious. Follow-ups by me and by authors like Jerome Frank often show that what was achieved was not some temporary symptomatic relief, but the beginning of a new ego development which was made possible through profound corrective emotional experiences occurring during the brief contact with the therapist.[18] In the light of psychodynamic theory, such observations can be well explained. In the last two decades I methodically studied this type of phenomenon by using the technique of planful interruptions of treatment. The personality growth which took place during these intervals is truly impressive.[19]

This leads us to the seldom discussed question of overtreatment. Freud remarked early in his psychoanalytic career that many patients reach a phase in which to be treated becomes more important for them than to be cured. The significance of this observation has never been systematically investigated. Our current theory is that the transference neurosis becomes a substitute for the patient's original—we may call it—"life neurosis." It must be pointed out, however, that in this new form the neurosis lost a great deal of its crippling connotation. Every neurosis contains an element of satisfaction in addition to suffering. This gratification nucleus is considerably enhanced in the form of transference neurosis, whereas, its conflictual elements are minimized. This leads to a tendency to prolong the treatment. If this unconscious wish of the patient coincides with the analyst's faith that prolongation of the treatment will bring the patient nearer to the cure of his neurosis, these two factors together become

[18] J. D. Frank, op. cit.

[19] F. Alexander, "The Quantitative Aspects of Technique," op. cit.; Psychoanalysis and Psychotherapy, New York: Norton, 1956.

a powerful, sometimes insuperable force to bring about what Freud called an "interminable analysis." There is a strong indication that our theory of treatment will have to deal with this phenomenon, not merely by recommending that it should be analyzed. The secret of therapeutic success might turn out to be preventing this shift from the wish to be cured to the wish to be treated. It might be necessary to interrupt or even terminate the treatment before this critical point is reached.

Another related and highly controversial problem pertains to the amount of activity of the therapist. There is again a traditional belief that the therapist's role is merely to verbalize preconscious material and to analyze resistances to make possible for the patient to gain insight; otherwise he should follow the spontaneous flow of the patient's material. In my experience there is a definite indication that this laissez-faire attitude, which is excellent for research, is not the most economical procedure in every treatment. In a former publication I called attention to two kinds of regression: the one, a tendency to return to a preconflictual, relatively well-adjusted phase of development, and another form of regression, to return to an unsettled traumatic phase, which is the ego's effort for a belated mastery of something which remained unsettled.[20] This second form is highly therapeutic, whereas the regression of preconflictual, mostly pregenital phases is a regressive evasion of the conflict which interrupted the patient's personality development. It is a most common form of resistance. I consider it crucial to teach the students to differentiate between these two forms of regression and to bring back the patient actively to material which he regressively evades. Reluctance to face the current life situation is one common form of this type of resistance. The therapist's misjudging early pre-conflictual material which the patient uses for a regressive evasion as really deep pathogenic material, may make the difference between an interminable treatment and successful termination.

Another powerful but so-called "nonanalytic" and therefore neglected therapeutic factor which is present to some degree in all psychoanalytic treatment, consists in the patient's positive expectations, in his trust in the healing power of the procedure and in that of the therapist. Recently, French in his most careful studies demonstrated the cardinal significance of hope, which increases the integrative capacity of the ego.[21] In an equally thoughtful paper, Jerome D.

[20] F. Alexander, "Two Forms of Regression and Their Therapeutic Implications," in this volume.

[21] Thomas M. French, *Integration of Behavior* (4 vols.), Chicago: University of Chicago Press, 1952.

Frank convincingly explained the healing function of faith, and re-viewed the literature devoted to this subject.[22] Most significant is his conclusion that transference cures based on this phenomenon may not be necessarily transient, as is erroneously held by many psychoan-alysts. Such successes increase hope for recovery and powerfully aid the integrative powers of the ego, which were damaged during the patient's unsuccessful solitary struggle with his neurosis when he felt he was at the end of his rope. A change from such a state of hopeless-ness to hopeful expectation revitalizes the integrative powers of the ego, which thus restored may sometimes without further outside help bring about recovery, or more precisely stated, a continuation of inter-rupted personality growth.

It must be emphasized, however, that hope and faith in a large majority of patients is in itself not sufficient. The ego cannot always accomplish the integrative task without external help. In the treatment of most cases of chronic neurosis the re-experiencing in the transfer-ence situation of the pathogenic emotional events of the past, as well as the interpretative activities of the therapist, are needed. At present we have no reliable method to predict in which cases and to what degree this arduous procedure is necessary. The psychological proc-esses involved in pure faith healings have not yet been systematically explored. To what degree faith and hope can produce lasting cures by initiating spontaneous personality growth is equally unknown. It can be assumed, however, with a fair amount of certainty, that early inter-ruptions of ego development, deeply ingrained nonadaptive patterns, require penetrating uncovering procedures in which early pathogenic experiences are worked through step by step. The answer to the ques-tion of how much can be left to the ego's native integrative powers cannot be generalized. All in all, it appears that we psychoanalysts in our therapeutic fervor forget the Hippocratic principle—the confidence in the natural healing powers of the organism. Pride in our psycho-dynamic knowledge favors emphasis on our continued indispensability, the belief that the patient must be cured on the couch five times a week over years. This fundamentally un-Hippocratic orientation is what per-vades our whole educational system. Perceptive and open-minded students discover only in their own practice after they left the school that the principle of prolonged uninterrupted interviews scheduled as frequently as possible cannot be generalized as a fundamental re-quirement of psychoanalytic treatment, and often does not promote personality growth and recovery, but hinders it. As long as the stu-dent has no other experiences to compare with the so-called classi-cal procedure, he cannot but accept the principle of continuity and frequency. Indeed, he cannot graduate if he does not accept it. Yet

22 J. D. Frank, *op. cit.*

fortunately the exigencies of practice do not permit always to apply this principle uniformly. This gives opportunity to the student to discover flexibility as the logical and desirable principle. It takes, however, years of experience to discover that equal and often better results are achieved by briefer and less routinized contact with the patient. Is it permissible to withhold such experiences from the students during their training?

There is every indication that there is an optimal balance varying from case to case between the amount of both intellectual and emotional support given by the therapist on the one hand and stimulation of the ego's own integrative efforts on the other. The dogma of uniform frequency and uninterrupted continuity over the whole or the major part of the treatment prevents finding this optimal balance.

Most untherapeutic is the universally practiced and taught advice to tell the patient at the beginning of the treatment that it necessarily will last long, not less than a year or probably much longer. A fundamental tendency of the neurotic ego—but to some degree also of the healthy ego—is to rely on outside help and follow the path of least resistance. The stereotype of the poker-faced silent therapist who insists on daily interviews, no matter what, is ideally calculated to foster this path of least resistance, the regressive evasion of pathogenic conflicts. The most important interpretative activity of the therapist consists in winning the cooperation of the patient's ego to counteract this evasive tendency. The most important ally in this therapeutic endeavor is the innate integrative urge of the ego. We call this "motivation." Integration is the biological function of the ego. To see is the function of the optic apparatus, to hear that of the acoustical equipment, to integrate data of internal and external perception is the ego's natural function. The therapist can help in creating conditions favorable for the ego to perform this function. By his interpretative activities which constitute a kind of cognitive exercise, he can increase the patient's native introspective cognitive faculties. To foster cognitive insight, to reduce paralyzing anxiety, to raise reasonable hope, to allow the ego to make a new attempt in the therapeutic situation to find new solutions for earlier failures in interpersonal involvements, is the therapist's aramentarium.

Nothing is more contradictory to the aim of educating sound practitioners than the habit of shrugging off novel therapeutic suggestions by declaring that they may be fine, but are no longer psychoanalysis. If a therapeutic approach in spite of being declared nonanalytic, nevertheless does promote the analytic goal to increase the patient's integrative faculty, then something must be wrong with psychoanalysis. In fact, nothing is wrong with psychoanalysis, only with its narrow definition.

In view of the complexity of the psychotherapeutic process, the multiplicity of recognized and still not understood therapeutic factors, there is no excuse for declaring one single principle—which may even turn out not to be the most effective one—as supreme by calling it truly psychoanalytic. There is general agreement that the aim of psychoanalysis is to enlarge the ego's integrative and creative capacities. This is, however, an aim and not a technical procedure. How to achieve this goal is another question. It matters little whether it is achieved by interpretation, by emotional experience, by stimulation of the innate integrative urge by giving hope, by temporary support or by correctly timed withdrawal of support by less contact and interruptions. In reality, it is achieved in most cases by a combination of all these factors. What makes the procedure psychoanalytic is not the emphasis on one or another therapeutic factor, but that it is based on psychoanalytic knowledge. What makes it psychoanalytic is that the therapist knows what is going on in the patient and knows what he is doing in terms of existing psychodynamic knowledge.

What is it then in our educational system that requires a change? It is not the details of our system that require revision, but its spirit. The institutes teach well the principles of psychodynamics, psychoanalytic psychopathology, dream theory and practice of dream interpretation, the known facts of personality development. Our educational system requires fundamental improvement in basic orientation suitable for preparing sound practitioners who can use theoretical knowledge for therapeutic purposes, unimpeded by traditional not sufficiently tested rules and regulations. Our present overschematized and rigid prescriptions do not help our students to learn from experience. We do not expose them sufficiently to the great uncertainties inherent in our standard treatment procedures. In spirit our system is painfully un-Hippocratic. We do not give sufficient weight to the natural healing powers of the mental apparatus. We stress what the therapist does and not what is going on in the patient's mind. We stress in our teaching the external formalities of the treatment, the reclining position, its quantifiable aspects, such as frequency, continuity and duration. We still stress the incognito and neglect the fact that in the therapeutic process two individual personalities meet in a complex transactional process. In spite of the evidence which stares in our face we do not give sufficient thought to the cardinal question: how can the inevitable fact that the therapist is a unique person, and is perceived as such by the patient, be turned to therapeutic advantage? We repeat history. We behave as Breuer and not as Freud did. Breuer turned his back to psychoanalysis after he sensed the implications of the patient's emotional involvement. Freud after some initial apprehension turned the transference into the axis of the treatment procedure. We are becoming more and more aware of the significance of the therapist as a person and his involvement in the treatment. We look uneasily upon the countertransference phenomenon and deal with it merely as an impurity, although we know that transference if excessively intensive is also an impurity. Even more reluctant are we to recognize officially in our teaching that the analyst enters into the process as a whole person and not only with his circumscribed countertransference reactions, and that the patient often reacts to him as a real person. We are all intuitively aware of this factor in our treatment, but we are reluctant to incorporate it into the therapeutic model which we are teaching to our students. Indeed, we are better therapists than teachers.

The central core of all these weaknesses of our educational system is that in teaching we are more past- than future-oriented. Not as individuals, but as an organized group of teachers, we do not stress sufficiently to our students that psychoanalysis—particularly its therapeutic application—does not represent a static system of well-substantiated rules of procedure, but that it is a steadily developing field, pregnant with uncertainties, and that it requires steady revision. Our function is to develop students who can think and speak independently, who can learn from their experience, and thus participate in improving our procedure. For this we must avoid indoctrination, that is to say, presenting our existing knowledge as if it were better established than it actually is. *What we can teach to the students without reservation is the science of psychodynamic reasoning demonstrated on live clinical material.*

In his recent writings Rado drew attention to what he called the parentifying spirit of standard psychoanalytic treatment.[23] Contrary to theory, the therapist accepts the parental role which the patient attributes to him, not only temporarily but mostly for the duration of the treatment. The same parentifying attitude slips in also into our educational system, treating grownup students, with psychiatric experience, as school children. Interminable training analyses and a trend toward more and more supervision, encourages this spirit. After the first case, supervision should focus on teaching psychodynamic reasoning, using the actual case material, rather than helping to handle two or three individual cases. The supervisor should not feel that he must always be right, particularly if he has no opportunity to observe directly the student at work and must rely on the highly selected material the student presents to him. Direct observation of the candidate in work and a recording of his interviews are highly desirable procedures.

Just because so much still has to be explored, we must not only tolerate but encourage individual differences, personal initiative of teachers and also of the students, instead of insisting on strict uniformity and conformity. We must return to local autonomy of institutes from a uniformly systematized centrally regulated educational system. In view of the great many existing uncertainties in the theory of treatment, we are far from being ripe for the degree of standardization we adopted some years ago. If we continue with the present educational policies, the best qualified group, the psychoanalysts, will lose leadership in developing Freud's heritage. Then not we but the rapidly growing borderline group of psychoanalytically oriented psychiatrists who are unhampered by rules and the dogmatic censorship of their confreres will accomplish the inevitable reforms necessary for training effective practitioners.

[23] Sandor Rado, "Adaptational Development of Psychoanalytic Therapy" and "Recent Advances in Psychoanalytic Treatment," in *Psychoanalysis of Behavior,* New York: Grune & Stratton, 1956.

Sources and Permissions

I am extremely grateful to the editors and publishers listed below who graciously gave me permission to reprint the various papers in this volume. The papers are listed in alphabetical order:

"About Dreams with Unpleasant Content," *Psychiatric Quarterly*, July 1930.

"Adventure and Security in a Changing World," in Iago Galdston (Ed.), *Medicine in a Changing Society*, New York: International Universities Press, Inc., 1957.

"Analysis of the Therapeutic Factors in Psychoanalytic Treatment," *Psychoanalytic Quarterly*, Vol. 19, 1950.

"Brief Communications: Impressions from the Fourth International Congress of Psychotherapy (Barcelona)," *Psychiatry*, Vol. 22, No. 1, February 1959 (Copyright 1959 by the William Alanson White Psychiatric Foundation, Inc.).

"Buddhistic Training as an Artificial Catatonia," *Psychoanalytic Review*, Vol. XVIII, No. 2, April 1931.

"The Castration Complex in the Formation of Character," *International Journal of Psycho-Analysis*, Vol. IV, Parts 1 and 2, 1923.

"Concerning the Genesis of the Castration Complex," *Psychoanalytic Review*, Vol. XXII, No. 1, January 1935.

"Current Problems in Dynamic Psychotherapy in Its Relationship to Psychoanalysis," *American Journal of Psychiatry*, Vol. 116, No. 4, October 1959.

"Current Views on Psychotherapy," *Psychiatry*, Vol. 16, No. 2, May 1953 (Copyright 1953 by the William Alanson White Psychiatric Foundation, Inc.).

"The Don Quixote of America," *The News-Letter*, Vol. VII, No. 1, 1937.

"Dreams in Pairs or Series," *International Journal of Psycho-Analysis*, Vol. VI, 1925.

"Educative Influence of Personality Factors in the Environment," in Ernest W. Burgess, W. Lloyd Warner, Franz Alexander, and Margaret Mead, *Environment and Education*, Chicago: University of Chicago, No. 54, March 1942.

"Experimental Studies of Emotional Stress" (with others), *Psychosomatic Medicine*, Vol. XXIII, No. 2, March-April 1961.

"Introduction," in Mortimer Adler, *What Man Has Made of Man*, New York: Longmans, Green and Co., 1937.

"Introduction," in Sigmund Freud, *Group Psychology and the Analysis of the Ego*, New York: Bantam Books, 1960.

"The Logic of Emotions and Its Dynamic Background," *International Journal of Psycho-Analysis*, Vol. XVI, Part 4, 1935.

"Mental Hygiene in the Atomic Age," *Mental Hygiene*, Vol. XXX, No. 4, 1946.

"A Metapsychologic Description of the Process of Cure," *International Journal of Psycho-Analysis*, Vol. VI, 1925.

"The Need for Punishment and the Death Instinct," *International Journal of Psycho-Analysis*, Vol. X, 1929.

"The Neurotic Character," *International Journal of Psycho-Analysis*, Vol. XI, 1930.

"A Note on Falstaff," *Psychoanalytic Quarterly*, Vol. II, 1933.

"On the Psychodynamics of Regressive Phenomena in Panic States," in Géza Róheim (Ed.), *Psychoanalysis and the Social Sciences*, Vol. IV, New York: International Universities Press, 1955.

"The Problem of Psychoanalytic Technique," *Psychoanalytic Quarterly*, Vol. IV, 1935.

"Psychiatric Contributions to Crime Prevention," *Federal Probation*, Vol. IV, No. 2, May 1940.

"Psychoanalysis and Medicine," *Journal of the American Medical Association*, Vol. 96, April 25, 1931.

"Psychoanalysis and Psychotherapy," in Jules H. Masserman (Ed.), *Psychoanalysis and Human Values*, New York: Grune & Stratton, Inc., 1960.

"Psychoanalysis and Social Disorganization," *American Journal of Sociology*, Vol. XLII, No. 6, May 1937.

"Psychoanalysis Comes of Age," *Psychoanalytic Quarterly*, Vol. VII, 1938.

"Psychoanalysis in Western Culture," *American Journal of Psychiatry*, Vol. 112, No. 9, March 1956.

"Psychoanalysis Revised," *Psychoanalytic Quarterly*, Vol. IX, 1940.

"Psychoanalytic Education for Practice," in Jules H. Masserman (Ed.), *Psychoanalysis and Human Values*, New York: Grune & Stratton, Inc., Vol. 3, 1961.

"The Psychosomatic Approach in Medical Therapy," *Acta Psychotherapeutica Psychosomatica et Orthopaedagogica*, Vol. 2, 1954.

"Psychosomatic Study of a Case of Asthma" (with Harold Visotsky), in *Psychosomatic Medicine*, Vol. XVII, No. 6, November-December 1955.

"The Relation of Structural and Instinctual Conflicts," *Psychoanalytic Quarterly*, Vol. II, No. 2, April 1933.

"Remarks about the Relation of Inferiority Feelings to Guilt Feelings," *International Journal of Psycho-Analysis*, Vol. XIX, Part I, 1938.

"A Review of Two Decades," in Franz Alexander and Helen Ross (Eds.), *Twenty Years of Psychoanalysis*, New York: W. W. Norton & Co., Inc., 1953.

"Teaching Psychodynamics," *American Journal of Orthopsychiatry*, Vol. XVII, No. 4, October 1947.

"A Tentative Analysis of the Variables in Personality Development," *American Journal of Orthopsychiatry*, Vol. 8, 1938.

"Three Fundamental Dynamic Principles of the Mental Apparatus and of the Behavior of Living Organisms," *Dialectica*, Vol. 5, 1951.

"Training Principles in Psychosomatic Medicine," *American Journal of Orthopsychiatry*, Vol. XVI, No. 3, July 1946.

"Two Forms of Regression and Their Therapeutic Implications," *Psychoanalytic Quarterly*, Vol. XXV, 1956.

"Unexplored Areas in Psychoanalytic Theory and Treatment—Part I," *Behavioral Science*, Vol. 3, No. 4, October 1958.

"Unexplored Areas in Psychoanalytic Theory and Treatment—Part II," *Behavioral Science*, Vol. 3, No. 4, October 1958.

"Values and Science," *Journal of Social Issues*, Vol. 6, 1950.

" 'The Voice of the Intellect is Soft . . . ,' " *Psychoanalytic Review*, Vol. 28, No. 1, January 1941.

"A World without Psychic Frustration," *American Journal of Sociology*, Vol. XLIX, No. 5, March 1944.

"Zest and Carbohydrate Metabolism" (with Warren S. McCulloch and Helen B. Carlson), in *Life Stress and Bodily Disease*, Vol. XXIV of the 1949 Proceedings of the Association for Research in Nervous and Mental Disease (1950).

Index